LLAM

# Criminal Detection and the Psychology of Crime

**The International Library of Criminology, Criminal Justice and Penology**
*Series Editors: Gerald Mars and David Nelken*

### Titles in the Series:

# Criminal Detection and the Psychology of Crime

*Edited by*

# David V. Canter
# and
# Laurence J. Alison

*University of Liverpool*

## Ashgate

### DARTMOUTH

Aldershot • Brookfield USA • Singapore • Sydney

Published by
Dartmouth Publishing Company Limited
Ashgate Publishing Limited
Gower House
Croft Road
Aldershot
Hants GU11 3HR
England

Ashgate Publishing Company
Old Post Road
Brookfield
Vermont 05036
USA

**British Library Cataloguing in Publication Data**
Criminal detection and the psychology of crime. – (The
  international library of criminology, criminal justice and
  penology)
  1. Criminal psychology  2. Criminal investigation
I. Canter, David V.  II. Alison, Laurence J.
364.3

**Library of Congress Cataloging-in-Publication Data**
Canter, David V.
    Criminal detection and the psychology of crime / David V. Canter
and Laurence J. Alison.
        p.  cm. — (The international library of criminology, criminal
justice and penology)
    Includes bibliographical references and index.
    ISBN 1-85521-454-7 (hardbound)
    1. Criminal investigation.  2. Criminal psychology.  3. Criminal
behavior.  I. Alison, Laurence J.  II. Title.  III. Series:
International library of criminology, criminal justice & penology.
HV8073.C335  1997
363.25—dc21
                                                                97-6099
                                                                CIP

ISBN 1 85521 454 7

Printed in Great Britain by Galliard (Printers) Ltd, Great Yarmouth

# Contents

## PART IV   DETECTING DECEPTION

## PART V   EVALUATING TESTIMONY

## PART VI   DELINQUENTS' CHARACTERISTICS

## PART X  INFERRING OFFENDER'S FROM OFFENCE CHARACTERISTICS

# Acknowledgements

The editors and publishers wish to thank the following for permission to use copyright material.

American Psychological Association for the essays: Norman Poythress, Randy K. Otto, Jack Darkes and Laura Starr (1993), 'APA's Expert Panel in the Congressional Review of the USS *Iowa* Incident', *American Psychologist*, **48**, pp. 8–15. Copyright © 1993 by the American Psychological Association. Reprinted with permission; Paul Ekman and Maureen O'Sullivan (1991), 'Who Can Catch a Liar?', *American Psychologist*, **46**, pp. 913–20. Copyright © 1991 by the American Psychological Association. Reprinted with permission; Robert P. Delprino and Charles Bahn (1988), 'National Survey of the Extent and Nature of Psychological Services in Police Departments', *Professional Psychology: Research and Practice*, **19**, pp. 421–5. Copyright © 1988 by the American Psychological Association. Reprinted with permission; Bruce W. Ebert (1987), 'Guide to Conducting a Psychological Autopsy', *Professional Psychology: Research and Practice*, **18**, pp. 52–6. Copyright © 1987 by the American Psychological Association. Reprinted with permission.

American Sociological Association for the essays: F. Ivan Nye and James F. Short, Jr. (1957), 'Scaling Delinquent Behavior', *American Sociological Review*, **22**, pp. 326–31; John Finley Scott (1959), 'Two Dimensions of Delinquent Behavior', *American Sociological Review*, **24**, pp. 240–43.

The British Psychological Society for the essay: Eric Shepherd (1991), 'Ethical Interviewing', in Eric Shepherd (ed.), *Criminological and Legal Psychology*, **18**, pp. 46–56. Copyright © 1991 Police Review Publishing Company.

Cambridge University Press for the essay: 'The Destruction of Bel' (1970), *The New English Bible with the Apocrypha*, 22 verses, Oxford University Press and Cambridge University Press, pp. 206–7. Revised English Bible. Copyright © 1989, Oxford University and Cambridge University Presses.

Chilton Publishing for the essay: Gisli H. Gudjonsson and James A.C. MacKeith (1988), 'Retracted Confessions: Legal, Psychological and Psychiatric Aspects', *Medical Science Law*, **28**, pp. 187–94.

Constable and Company Ltd for the essay: Dermot Walsh (1980), 'Burglars: Characteristics of Offenders', in Dermot Walsh, *Break-Ins: Burglary from Private Houses*, London: Constable, pp. 57–65, 188–9.

Criminal Justice Press for the essay: D. Kim Rossmo (1995), 'Place, Space, and Police Investigations: Hunting Serial Violent Criminals', in John E. Eck and David Weisburd (eds), *Crime and Place*, Monsey NY: Criminal Justice Press, pp. 217–35.

Elsevier Science Limited for the essay: David C. Raskin and Phillip W. Esplin (1991), 'Statement Validity Assessment: Interview Procedures and Content Analysis of Children's Statements of Sexual Abuse', *Behavioral Assessment*, **13**, pp. 265–91. Copyright © 1991 Pergamon Press Ltd. Reprinted with permission by Elsevier Science Limited, Oxford, England.

Elsevier Science B.V. for the essay: Malcolm K. Sparrow (1991), 'The Application of Network Analysis to Criminal Intelligence: An Assessment of the Prospects', *Social Networks*, **13**, pp. 251–74. Copyright © 1991. All rights reserved, with kind permission from Elsevier Science – NL, Sara Burgerhartstraat 25, 1055 KV Amsterdam, The Netherlands.

Harcourt Brace & Company Ltd for the essay: David Canter and Paul Larkin (1993), 'The Environmental Range of Serial Rapists', *Journal of Environmental Psychology*, **13**, pp. 63–9. Copyright © 1993 Academic Press Ltd.

Harcourt Brace & Company (Orlando) for the essay: Bill McCarthy and John Hagan (1995), 'Getting into Street Crime: The Structure and Process of Criminal Embeddedness', *Social Science Research*, **24**, pp. 63–95. Copyright © 1995 Academic Press.

Heldref Publications for the essay: Herbert C. Quay and Lawrence Blumen (1963), 'Dimensions of Delinquent Behavior', *Journal of Social Psychology*, **61**, pp. 273–7. Reprinted with permission of the Helen Dwight Reid Educational Foundation. Published by Heldref Publications, 1319 Eighteenth St. N.W., Washington, D.C. 20036–1802. Copyright © 1963.

Human Sciences Press, Inc. for the essay: David B. Buller and R. Kelly Aune (1987), 'Nonverbal Cues to Deception Among Intimates, Friends, and Strangers', *Journal of Nonverbal Behavior*, **11**, pp. 269–90. Copyright © 1987 Human Sciences Press.

Oxford University Press for the essays: Don C. Gibbons (1975), 'Offender Typologies – Two Decades Later', *British Journal of Criminology*, **15**, pp. 140–56. By permission of Oxford University Press; Michael Clarke (1989), 'Insurance Fraud', *British Journal of Criminology*, **29**, pp. 1–20. By permission of Oxford University Press.

Routledge for the essays: David Canter and Rupert Heritage (1990), 'A Multivariate Model of Sexual Offence Behaviour: Developments in "Offender Profiling".I', *Journal of Forensic Psychiatry*, **1**, pp. 185–212; Steven Greer (1995), 'Towards a Sociological Model of the Police Informant', *British Journal of Sociology*, **46**, pp. 509–27.

Skeptical Inquirer for the essay: Richard Wiseman, Donald West and Roy Stemman (1996), 'Psychic Crime Detectives: A New Test for Measuring Their Successes and Failures', *Skeptical Inquirer*, **20**, pp. 38–40, 58.

SLE Publications Ltd for the essay: David Canter (1992), 'An Evaluation of the "Cusum" Stylistic Analysis of Confessions', *Expert Evidence*, **1**, pp. 93–9.

Social Forces for the essay: Robert J. Bursik, Jr. (1980), 'The Dynamics of Specialization in Juvenile Offenses', *Social Forces*, **58**, pp. 851–64. Reprinted from Social Forces. Copyright © 1980 The University of North Carolina Press.

Springer-Verlag GmbH & Co for the essay: Floyd Feeney (1986), 'Robbers as Decision-Makers', in Derek B. Cornish and Ronald V. Clarke (eds), *The Reasoning Criminal: Rational Choice Perspectives on Offending*, New York: Springer-Verlag, pp. 53–71. Copyright © 1986.

Sweet & Maxwell Limited for the essay: Hans Gross (1962), 'Certain Qualities Essential to an Investigator', in *Criminal Investigation: A Practical Textbook for Magistrates, Police Officers and Lawyers*, London: Sweet and Maxwell Ltd, pp. 15–19.

U.S. Federal Bureau of Investigation for the essay: David J. Icove and M.H. (Jim) Estepp (1987), 'Motive-Based Offender Profiles of Arson and Fire-Related Crimes', *FBI Law Enforcement Bulletin*, **56**, pp. 17–23.

John Wiley & Sons, Inc. for the essay: Theodore H. Blau (1994), 'Psychological Profiling', in Theodore H. Blau, *Psychological Services for Law Enforcement*, New York: John Wiley and Sons, Inc., pp. 261–74. Copyright © 1994 John Wiley & Sons, Inc.; Günter Köhnken (1987), 'Training Police Officers to Detect Deceptive Eyewitness Statements: Does it Work?', *Social Behavior*, **2**, pp. 1–17. Copyright © 1987 John Wiley & Sons, Inc.; David Canter (1995), 'Psychology of Offender Profiling', in Ray Bull and David Carson (eds), *Handbook of Psychology on Legal Contexts*, Chichester: John Wiley and Sons, pp. 343–55. Copyright © 1995 John Wiley & Sons, Inc.

Marvin E. Wolfgang for the essay: Stuart Palmer (1960), 'Psychological Frustration – A Comparison of Murderers and Their Brothers', in Marvin E. Wolfgang (ed.), *Studies in Homicide*, New York: Harper and Row, pp. 134–55. Copyright © 1967 by Marvin E. Wolfgang.

Every effort has been made to trace all the copyright holders, but if any have been inadvertently overlooked the publishers will be pleased to make the necessary arrangement at the first opportunity.

The editors are also grateful to Thandi Milner and Rachel Mintern for their assistance in chasing up the most elusive of documents.

# Series Preface

The International Library of Criminology, Criminal Justice and Penology, represents an important publishing initiative designed to bring together the most significant journal essays in contemporary criminology, criminal justice and penology. The series makes available to researchers, teachers and students an extensive range of essays which are indispensable for obtaining an overview of the latest theories and findings in this fast changing subject.

This series consists of volumes dealing with criminological schools and theories as well as with approaches to particular areas of crime, criminal justice and penology. Each volume is edited by a recognised authority who has selected twenty or so of the best journal articles in the field of their special competence and provided an informative introduction giving a summary of the field and the relevance of the articles chosen. The original pagination is retained for ease of reference.

The difficulties of keeping on top of the steadily growing literature in criminology are complicated by the many disciplines from which its theories and findings are drawn (sociology, law, sociology of law, psychology, psychiatry, philosophy and economics are the most obvious). The development of new specialisms with their own journals (policing, victimology, mediation) as well as the debates between rival schools of thought (feminist criminology, left realism, critical criminology, abolitionism etc.) make necessary overviews that offer syntheses of the state of the art. These problems are addressed by the INTERNATIONAL LIBRARY in making available for research and teaching the key essays from specialist journals.

GERALD MARS
*Professor in Applied Anthropology, University of Bradford*
*School of Management*

DAVID NELKEN
*Distinguished Research Professor, Cardiff Law School,*
*University of Wales, Cardiff*

# Introduction:
## Precursors to Investigative Psychology

The Biblical story of how Daniel showed that the priests of Bel were cheating King Cyrus (reprinted here as Chapter 1) is probably the first recorded detective story, its longevity illustrating just how enduring is the tradition of criminal investigation. Faced with the puzzling and seemingly inexplicable, Daniel showed, through systematic examination, that the apparently magical was mere fraud. We can see how Daniel, already known for strongly criticizing magicians and astrologers, penetrated the deceptive intentions of the Babylonians and drew instead on what we would now recognize as an objective approach. Through such objective strategies he was able to overcome superstition and hypocrisy.

Even in this early account psychological issues fundamental to criminal detection are apparent. Firstly, Daniel had to provide *evidence* for his suspicions in a rigorous and impartial way. No matter how convinced he was that the priests themselves (rather than the Idol) were eating the sacrificial food, he had to demonstrate the facts to a gullible, idolatrous King in a way that would brook no challenge. So the whole process of investigation was shaped, not by the scepticism of science, but by the demands of producing convincing evidence. The role of the detective focused more on collecting demonstrable evidence than on providing a thorough explanation of *why* the fraud was perpetrated.

Although Daniel was objective, he was only partially scientific. For the scientist the prime skills are those associated with theory building and testing. A scientific psychologist in Cyrus's court, for example, would have wanted to interview the priests to get their account of what was going on and may have been interested to know, as a control group, if any of the Jewish priests were up to similar chicanery. For the detective, evidence is paramount. What the court does with it is a separate, although of course relevant, matter. One important implication of this aspect of detective work is that the skills and culture of detection are likely to be different from those of the scientist and worthy of special study. The second aspect that Daniel illustrates, then, is that there is a process of decision making in the daily work of the detective that is complex, demanding and poorly understood.

Daniel also had to be able to set up a specific information collection exercise, directly relevant to the assumed crime *and* he had to be able to interpret the results. Leaving an unobtrusive recording device on the floor of the sealed temple (in his case dirt scattered so that it would reveal clandestine footprints) required careful preparation and the collusion of the King. Detectives since then have not been so fortunate in drawing upon such incontrovertible information. They often have to rely upon the accounts people give of their own actions and the actions of others. This raises many questions, both about the most effective way of collecting such information, as well as more challenging questions about how to evaluate the information that is given.

The third point that the story of Daniel and the priests of Bel illustrates is perhaps the richest psychological vein in detective work – the questions that are raised about the appropriate assumptions and theories of criminal behaviour. Detectives must operate on some theory of the nature of criminals' actions and the inferences that can be drawn from them. Usually these ideas are not derived from direct contact with social science studies of criminals but from personal experience of police officers. Daniel assumed that the regular disappearance of the food was due to some fraudulent activity involving the priests. He had a hypothesis based upon his understanding of priestly behaviour; he may have heard stories about other deceptions perpetrated by priests, or possibly he knew something about the backgrounds of people who ended up as priests to Bel. What Daniel, presumably, did not have available was a general theory about the forms of deception that were typical of different priestly classes. In other words he did not have access to any general psychological principles or models about criminal behaviour that had been empirically supported.

In sum, then, Daniel's uncovering of fraud illustrates the three main strands of criminal detection that are open to psychological study:

1.  police decision making and the associated skills and culture of detection,
2.  interviewing and information assessment, and
3.  the psychology of criminal behaviour.

These three areas of study constitute the emerging discipline recently identified as 'Investigative Psychology' (Canter, 1995).

Of course, detectives throughout time and across the world have been able to do effective work without the backup of such a discipline. Although many of them will still believe that they can continue to be effective without knowing anything about Investigative Psychology, an increasing number are looking to the discipline to turn the ancient craft of investigation into a professional activity that draws upon current psychological theories and findings. The interest in what psychology has to offer criminal investigations goes beyond police activities to include those of many other law enforcement agencies, such as customs and excise, the inland revenue and commercial organizations concerned, for example, with business fraud. Whilst these practical considerations cannot be ignored, there are many other reasons for the development of Investigative Psychology.

The most significant reason for the rapid expansion of this new area of psychology is simply that it is full of fascinating questions – questions whose origins lie in police investigations but whose answers have much broader implications. For instance, if we can understand the social and organizational influences on the processes of dealing with the complexities and ambiguities of trying to solve a crime, we will have understood a lot about decision making under uncertainty. To take a further example from the evaluation of evidence strand, the examination of investigative interviews and the data police have to deal with reveals a lot about how facts are socially constructed and the consequent influence of social transactions on memory. Further, by considering the actions of criminals in the pursuance of a crime we may learn much that is relevant to the rehabilitation and punishment of offenders, not just their apprehension.

The field of Investigative Psychology therefore has its roots in a century of criminology and criminal psychology. In part, it has grown directly out of the contributions of psychologists to legal proceedings that Haward (1981) described so richly under the heading of 'Forensic Psychology'. The difference between what Haward describes and the newer field of 'Investigative Psychology' is one of emphasis rather than rigid demarcation. By focusing on the processes of identifying and apprehending an offender rather than proving the case against him or her in court, a different range of issues are brought to the fore. In part this can be simplified by proposing that forensic psychologists have in the past typically worked for the defence, whereas Investigative Psychologists have usually had their closest contact with the prosecution. However, like all simplifications, this is only partly true.

The new field of Investigative Psychology has emerged very rapidly but it does, nonetheless, have well established roots in a wide range of scholarly activities. Many, perhaps most, of the authors of these earlier writings may not have realized their relevance to criminal investigations, but an appreciation of the mass of earlier studies that are relevant enables us to understand the dawn of this new field and why its growth has been so rapid.

The links between these earlier studies, though, have only become apparent with the recognition that they may all contribute to the practical challenges of the investigation and prosecution of crime. Most of the studies brought together for the present volume were not carried out with any notion of their relevance to the work of detectives, but with hindsight they can be seen as laying the basis for our understanding of criminal activity and its investigation. The present volume therefore brings together publications that lay the groundwork for social science contributions to criminal detection.

## Detection and Detectives

*'Detection is, or ought to be, an exact science, and should be treated in the same cold and unemotional manner'*
– Sir Arthur Conan Doyle
from 'The Sign of Four'

### Demands on Detectives

Detectives' needs for systematic help from psychology and the social sciences can readily be seen from a list that one of them compiled of their job requirements. The almost super-human capabilities that Gross indicated in 1950 (see Chapter 2) exemplify this professional pressure:

indefatigable zeal … self denial and perseverance, swiftness in reading men and a thorough knowledge of human nature … education … an agreeable manner, an iron constitution and encyclopaedic knowledge.

The ability to understand a criminal's behaviour and even his or her mind (a 'swiftness in reading men' as Gross describes it) is then added to these qualities. Clearly then the possibility of training investigators effectively on the job through the handing down of experience becomes an impossible task. Gross's account is in a limited but long tradition of writings that try to pass on the skills involved in investigating crimes. One of the more recent of these is by Swanson *et al.* (1992). Their text perhaps contrasts with Gross's by setting out to show that investigation is not an art 'with unneeded mysticism' but is in large part a science that adheres to 'rigorous methods'. But they reiterate the very wide range of skills that investigators need, whilst not describing these qualities as so exceptional and rare as Gross did 40 years earlier. Without systematization and the identification of central principles, it would take a lifetime to master this knowledge and practice.

But even if all the knowledge that was necessary for investigations was distilled to the point that it could be provided as a digestible training package, there are still further demands placed upon police officers that do not affect laboratory bound scientists. These demands emanate from the legal context in which the police operate and the potential for abuse of the law inherent in giving officers too much freedom.

In Britain the framework within which the police operate has from time to time been codified by Royal Commissions. In a report from one of the earliest such commissions in 1929 (see Chapter 3), issues were identified that are still significant today, even though the law relating to these matters has been modified and the forms of guidance elaborated. The selection of material from the 1929 report therefore highlights how integral to an understanding of the work of detectives is the need to appreciate how police officers must operate within a code of conduct that goes beyond the mere need to establish the facts. As then, detectives today are bound by how they can obtain statements from accused persons, as well as how they use the information obtained during an investigation. There are limits on the admissibility of statements and other forms of evidence and on the use of such strategems as *agents provocateurs*.

## The Nature of Police Organization

The detective has to steer a demanding course between seeking out a range of complex and subtle information whilst not overstepping the bounds of social and legal acceptability. One way in which police forces throughout the world attempt to deal with this challenging balancing act is to operate within a broadly militaristic organizational model. As Franz and Jones show in Chapter 4, this has many weaknesses. For example, the military model reduces the flexibility of police officers to provide all the different types of services required of them. It is very likely, however, that detectives, who after all are typically 'out of uniform', deliberately operate in a less hierarchical and military manner, though the military framework is never totally absent.

The context of detective work within the organization of the police also helps us to understand the often conflicting demands made on police officers. Franz and Jones's study will resonate with anyone who has been associated with police forces, throwing light on the curious paradox of police work. On the one hand there is the enormous discretion enjoyed by the officer in contact with a member of the public. On the other there is the military structure, with its associated communication difficulties, within which each officer operates. This highlights the very broad question of the efficiency of the structure of the police force and related psychological implications in terms of decision making. The hierarchical framework extends communication channels and hinders enquiries. As Franz and Jones note:

> ... there were greater amounts of distrust, particularly of the higher echelons ... low levels of morale ... and lower perceived levels of organisational performance (p. 39).

*Psychological Contributions to Policing*

Detection of criminals is a relatively small aspect of police work and the direct investigation of crime is not a very large feature, contrary to fictional and factual accounts in the mass media. Public order and the preparation of material for court, the apprehension of criminals and a variety of welfare activities, such as dealing with suicides or helping people to deal with the consequences of a theft, are far more common. So, the psychological contribution to police activities needs to be seen as part of a much broader range of contributions than direct involvement in solving crimes, not least because that much wider range of contributions is already well established. In 1988 Delprino and Bahn recognized a twofold increase in the uptake of psychological services by police forces over the previous decade, running a very full gamut from officer selection to post-crisis counselling. Given the current belief that behavioural science has only recently started to contribute to detective work, it is interesting to note that 'offender profiling' was already well established in one in four forces at the time of Delprino and Bahn's second survey (Chapter 5). They appear to take this for granted, not even mentioning it in their commentary. Further, given the nature of their survey it seems unlikely that these 'profiles' were provided by specialists such as the much publicized FBI 'Behavioral Science Unit' agents. Certainly Delprino and Bahn's account accords well with the much fuller and more recent review in Blau's 1994 book. In Chapter 33, Blau also gives examples of psychologists producing 'profiles' at least from the early 1970s, showing that psychologists are a well-established component of US police departments and thus are naturally involved in a variety of aspects of police investigations.

## Information and Informants

*'You see, but you do not observe'*

– Sir Arthur Conan Doyle
from 'The Crooked Man'

*Psychological Autopsies*

The basic information that an investigator has to work with are the details of a crime – where, when and how it occurred and who were the explicit or implicit victims. In many cases the only direct information is that available from the crime scene. This has to be augmented by finding out as much as possible about the people and processes associated with that scene. When there is a death then details of the deceased may be of great significance. In some cases the deceased is, in effect, the prime suspect in that his or her role in the events that led up to the death are in question. The attempt to understand the deceased and his/her activities is thus a strong example of how psychological theories and methods can inform the processes of collecting investigative information and acting on inferences drawn from it.

The attempt to understand the character and activities of a person found dead under suspicious circumstances has been called the 'psychological autopsy'. This is an attempt to form a view of a deceased person and the circumstances surrounding his/her death by means that draw upon psychological modes of examination. Examples of such autopsies being carried out, say for insurance companies or coroners, can be traced back to Haward's work at the end of World War II (Haward, 1981), but they certainly occurred on a reasonably regular basis in the US from the mid 1950s. In Chapter 6, Ebert makes clear that this is still a challenging area of activity that requires exhaustive consideration of many different aspects of the subject's life. The work needs to be informed by clinical experience and a thorough knowledge of the appropriate research literature. Despite such demands, the use of psychological autopsies is a powerful illustration of how concepts and methods from existing areas of psychology can be harnessed to new applications within the investigation of crime, such as those of clinical analyses of mental states and aspects of psychometric assessment.

However, the possibility for abuse of the ideas behind such autopsies, when used by people who do not have the appropriate training or knowledge, is revealed in the important review by Poythress and his colleagues (Chapter 7) of the much criticized FBI analysis of the explosion on USS *Iowa*. Taking the perspective of experienced criminal investigators, with their tendency to see maliciousness in many human actions, the FBI agents formed the view that the explosion was the product of a suicide. Unfortunately they implied that their conclusions were based upon a *bona fide* psychological autopsy. The American Psychological Association set up a special panel to consider these claims and came to the conclusion that the FBI analysis was invalid. Subsequent technical tests revealed further evidence that the cause of the explosion was accidental. Indeed, the FBI contribution here was clearly outside of the bounds of effective professional activity and raised questions about the ethics of drawing apparently authoritative conclusions based on little more than opinion. As later cases in the UK have shown, pseudo-psychological contributions can do more harm than good.

## The Information Collection Process

The psychological autopsy is one example of how, regardless of the way in which information about a crime is obtained and whatever the noise in that information, detectives still need to make sense of it and interpret it in the light of their understanding of the behaviour of the people involved. This is especially true in the case of inferring characteristics of potential suspects. The idea of interpreting criminal actions from the crime scene has been heralded as a new art – popularly known as 'offender profiling'. However, in Chapters 33 and 35 respectively, Blau and Canter show that such inferences have always been possible and probably always been available, even if not labelled and packaged so neatly as movies suggest. In their contribution discussed above, Poythress et al. make clear that the validity of what they call 'reconstructive evaluations' (by which they include both 'profiles' and the FBI use of psychological autopsies) relates in some considerable measure to the effectiveness of the information on which the evaluations are made. Investigative Psychology therefore pays considerable attention to the collection and analysis of investigative intelligence.

The obtaining of information on which to base the detection process often includes transactions with witnesses and suspects, usually in the form of interviews. This gives rise to two broad sets of demands for help from psychologists. The first concerns the evaluation of the information collected through interviews and other means, whilst the second concerns the nature of interviews and how they can be improved. Rather different requirements come from dealing with witnesses as compared with dealing with suspects or informants.

The development of interviewing techniques and strategies is perhaps the greatest contribution that psychology is making to investigations. This has gone largely unnoticed by the media, probably because the whole tenor of psychological influence on interviews is to remove the drama from the situation. This has been greatly enhanced by techniques taken from cognitive psychology, as promulgated by Fisher, Geiselman and others in Chapter 8. A variety of procedures, all related to the exploration of memory processes, has guided their work, in particular the reinstatement of context, the use of free recall to report everything (even seemingly trivial details), the re-ordering of events and the use of recall from different perspectives. Revisions of the cognitive interview have led to improved recall of up to 45 per cent which, as Fisher and Geiselman note, comes with the advantage of no increased error. Interestingly, whilst the process theoretically should be generally applicable, there has been little research on the use of such techniques with suspects.

When it comes to interviewing suspects, the general assumption is that they would not be cooperative enough for the cognitive interview – although this assumption never seems to have been tested. Instead, the focus has been on how police officers approach the interview, encapsulated in Shepherd's notion in Chapter 9 of 'ethical interviewing'. Shepherd tends to focus on ethical principles rather than systematic study, and outlines a set of maxims that he proposes constitute an appropriate 'conversational-management' framework. These include issues of disclosure, sincerity, open mindedness and integrity.

This work contrasts with that of Fisher and Geiselman in terms of their respective psychological backcloths – the former focusing on conversation management and stemming from a social psychological perspective, the latter from an exploration of cognitive psychology relating mainly to multi-modal memory processes. This juxtaposition of psychological approaches to essentially the same problem – i.e. the elicitation of accurate information – may sit rather uncomfortably with the general principle that suspects and witnesses should be interviewed in the same manner so as not to introduce bias. It is also remarkable that although the report of the 1929 Royal Commission (Chapter 3) emphasized the importance of the ethics of police interviews, it has only been in the last few years that psychologists have contributed to these matters.

## Suspects, Witnesses and Informants

The different psychological approaches to interviewing suspects as opposed to witnesses may reflect the differences in the views of officers in their *dealing* with these two groups. It may not be appropriate or indeed warranted, as is often assumed, to treat all witnesses differently from all suspects. The police are likely to have different agendas depending on whom they think they are dealing with. In other words, with a witness, interviewers are usually genuinely interested in soliciting the maximum amount of accurate and relevant information, whilst in the case of suspects the process is seen as one of persuasion towards a confession. However, some suspects are key witnesses and some witnesses may emerge as suspects, so the distinction has to be treated with caution.

The rather ambiguous relationship that police officers can have with people providing information is most apparent in the use of informants. The British police now have an active policy to utilize informants who may often be either witnesses or suspects. However, none of the issues raised in the consideration of interview strategies has been related directly to this shadowy area. Indeed Greer's review in Chapter 10 is one of the few available and it focuses on motivations and reasons for informing rather than interview strategies for effective interactions with informants.

In part, the lack of attention to the detailed handling of informants is, of course, due to the very sensitive nature of the topic. It is probably also a function of informants being a much more integrated part of the investigation. The information they have and the ways in which they may make it available are much more determined by the details of the particular investigation to which they are contributing rather than the more generic provision of information by witnesses or suspects. The study of informants therefore provides an important link between the decision making processes of investigations and an understanding of the sources of crucial information. In the detection process of many investigations, information is deliberately sought out from sources who are themselves often part of a potentially criminal context.

The reasons why people inform are poorly understood but, clearly, any evaluation of the reliability and validity of their information, as well as any determined investigative strategy of how to use them, will benefit from understanding the varieties of informant and the reasons for their actions. Greer's examination provides such a framework. Curiously he sees this as 'sociology', serving to show that phenomena that exist outside of academia are often relevant to several academic disciplines. The classification of informants also illustrates the variety of motivations they may have for providing police with information. This perspective has never been integrated with the more overtly psychological study of the most effective ways to carry out police interviews, yet it does seem likely that the distinctions that Greer draws could have implications for investigative information retrieval beyond the simplistic categories of 'snouts' and 'grasses'.

## The Detection of Deception

It is in the context of the interview of suspects, but also relevant to many other investigative interviews, that the question of deception and its detection frequently occurs. There have been many explorations of the detection of deception and the possibilities of training police officers in the skills involved, but with little success. In Chapter 11, Buller and Aune show that one of the central difficulties in detecting deception is that, although deceivers may have an emotional response to their own acts, they also have ways of controlling and masking relevant cues. Ekman and O'Sullivan's study which follows is particularly interesting in showing just how difficult it is to detect deception. They found no differences between the ability of a sample of students, psychiatrists and law enforcement officers to detect the masking of strong negative emotions. Only the Secret Service performed significantly better, apparently by using a variety of non verbal as well as verbal cues to deception. Needless to say, it would be useful to know what cues they are utilizing.

Ekman (1992) is quite confident that there are cues to deception. He has published widely on this topic as part of his seminal studies on the expression and interpretation of emotions. Under certain conditions, as Horvath et al. point out in Chapter 13, some of these cues may be distinguished, but as Ekman, O'Sullivan, Friesen and Scherer (1991) emphasize, there may be individual differences in what aspects of behavioural deception liars may be better at masking. Thus, work on deception suggests that the majority of individuals – even experienced police officers – are not equipped to distinguish between the truth or falsehood of assertions made by suspects in the interview.

Furthermore, in Chapter 14, Köhnken shows the difficulty of training police officers to improve the detection of deception using cues that have been experimentally demonstrated as correlates of lying. Police officers trained in various procedures are no better able to detect whether statements are true or false than other people, trained or untrained. What is important to note, though, is the consistent finding that people are generally better able to identify truth than to detect deception. However, the confidence in their assessments is optimistically high and very inaccurate. One important practical consequence of this pheno-mena is that it explains why police officers may often be reluctant to accept guidance on interviewing procedures except in so far as it helps to detect deception. They will be confident in their judgements and will get positive reinforcement more often in assuming that someone is telling the truth.

Perhaps this confidence in believing that someone is telling the truth is supported further when the view being expressed significantly advances the investigation. A confession from a suspect is just such. Hence the importance of what amounts to a scientific discovery by Gudjonsson and MacKeith in Chapter 15 that even in conditions that are not overtly coercive, people will falsely confess to a crime. In particular they have examined the conditions that lead people who have made confessions to later retract them. From the clinical context within which the authors operate, they have been able to show that there are certain types of people in certain circumstances who will falsely confess. Yet the complexity of this area of research should not be minimized. It is rare that objective, incontrovertible evidence to support a confession or its retraction exists, so the clinical interpretation is often treated as the criterion rather than the predictor.

*Statement Analysis*

The lack of objective indicators for deception or false confessing has given rise to a search for other procedures external to the person making the statement without resorting to clinical assessments. This is of course relevant in many different circumstances where the validity of a statement is in question. The Statement Validity Analysis that Raskin and Esplin describe in Chapter 16 is a particularly lucid approach to examining the detail of a written statement. This has been applied in particular to statements made by children who are claiming abuse. Stemming from Undeutsch's early work in the 1950s (see Undeutsch 1982), a series of studies have explored the validity of accusations in an attempt to identify what components tend to be associated with true statements. An important restraint on the power of the tech-nique, however, is that a significant part of the assessment relies on the way that the interview itself is carried out – once again drawing our attention to the fact that the investigative processes comprise an interlocking and integrated system. Curiously, no work seems to have been published analysing the statements that Gudjonsson and MacKeith claim to have been falsely made (see above).

Yet, as in many other areas of Investigative Psychology, claims to be able to establish whether a person's utterances are indeed genuine and can in fact be attributed to a particular person, may often be much stronger than is scientifically warranted. One notorious attempt at this intriguing task was the 'Cusum' or 'Qsum' technique. This had quite a following and was even allowed as evidence in court before systematic scientific studies were carried out that totally discredited it. As is shown by Canter in Chapter 17, there is absolutely no validity to this technique. Subsequent studies by other researchers have substantiated Canter's claims (e.g. Hardcastle 1997).

Perhaps because of the ready access to data, especially laboratory derived data, the consideration of interviews and the evaluation of statements are probably the most intensively studied area of Investigative Psychology. However, it may well be that, precisely because of this academic interest, the studies have had more direct relevance to unravelling the processes of memory than to contributing to improved investigations. The main findings from these studies are nevertheless being incorporated into the training of police officers and that will doubtless lead to new perspectives on their utility and new directions for research.

## Crime and Criminals

*'He is the Napoleon of Crime'*

Sir Arthur Conan Doyle
in 'The Final Problem'

### Classifying Offenders

By the late 1940s a lot had been established about the basic characteristics of offenders. Two of Britain's leading developmental psychologists, Burt and Bowlby, had mapped out the predetermining conditions that lead to an unfolding life of crime (see Chapters 18 and 19). The results they reported have not been substantially challenged in subsequent studies. Indeed Burt's most telling point resonates throughout the criminological literature:

> All the conditions enumerated... – hereditary, environmental, physical, and psychological – are positively correlated with delinquency; but no one of them singly to a very high degree (p. 226).

Burt concludes with some passion that crime springs from

> a wide variety, and usually from a multiplicity, of alternative and converging influences (p. 219).

He opts for some innate conditions being relevant, but also gives great weight to social circumstances. Bowlby concurs, but gives much more emphasis to family circumstances and especially separation from parents. It is interesting to note that in studying such a practical problem as juvenile delinquency, both these psychologists provided highly influential theories relevant to understanding many aspects of the human condition.

What has not been appreciated about these studies is how they can give direct guidance to investigations. Hindering their potential contribution has been the assumption that such broad research findings describe the general characteristics of criminals. This, however, is potentially very misleading. As Burt and Bowlby were well aware, many people with the background characteristics of delinquents do not turn to crime. However, in the context of an investigation with a range of suspects, it must be the case that those with certain dys-functional backgrounds have a higher probability of having committed the crime than others. The crucial issue, as important for civil liberties as for effective detection, is to identify reliable and valid background characteristics.

One approach taken by a number of researchers is to attempt a classification so that the characteristics of sub-sets of offenders can be identified. In essence, although usually in a rather unsystematic way, this is what 'offender profilers' attempt to do: identify the class or sub-type of individual that a given crime is typical of and then review its known characteristics. However, for such an exercise to be any more accurate than assigning a person to his or her star sign, it has to be based on validly established classification schemes. A primary concern is the necessary first step of establishing that offenders *do* specialize and to clarify the nature of their specializations. This is not a task for the fainthearted. The whole process of classification involves a variety of conceptual and methodological assumptions which, as Bursik shows in Chapter 20, have often been dealt with in a very confused way. He demonstrates that juveniles involved in crime do not have very specific criminal career trajectories but that, nonetheless, the majority do tend to specialize in property offences. From the investigative point of view, this provides a first clue to the consideration of offender types. Those committing crimes against the person are in the minority and are likely to be somewhat different from those who commit run of the mill property crimes.

, Distinguishing between types of offender draws attention to the need to specify as clearly as possible the nature and, if feasible, the intensity of any criminal's activity. This requires moving away from broad categories such as 'delinquent or not' and the identifying of classes and grouping of crimes. At its methodologically most simple level, it must be empirically demonstrated that a particular set of offences relate to each other in some meaningful way. Possibly the most direct test is to establish if there are scales of offences such that the more serious are committed by people who have also carried out less serious offences but not vice versa. This notion of a 'cumulative' scale, sometimes called a Guttman scale after the person who first developed it, is a very powerful illustration of how simple qualitative components can be combined to produce quantitative measures. Nye and Short's demonstration in Chapter 21 of the possibilities of this scaling process in relation to the crimes of known delinquents is an early but powerful illustration of the potential of this approach.

Curiously, though, until the advent of Investigative Psychology no one seems to have noticed the implications for detectives of such a cumulative scale. Within Nye and Short's sample, for instance, every one of the boys who had stolen something of medium value had also skipped school or driven a car without a licence. Again caution is warranted in that one cannot assume that all boys who skip school are likely to be thieves, but it does mean that if a class of children is being considered for a possible medium value theft, there is a higher probability that those who have skipped school are the culprits. Of course, this inference is only valid if just one scale of delinquency exists. If there are many routes into more serious offending, then it may be possible that the group of boys who have not skipped school contain a larger subset of thieves than those who have.

The possibility of multiple routes further opens up the question of offender typologies and shows that, as elegant as Nye and Short's cumulative scale is, such indicators will never be the whole story. As a consequence, since that early work there have been many attempts at the empirical classification of offenders. In Chapter 22, Scott develops two distinct

Guttman scales relating to personal as opposed to impersonal theft, not very different from Bursik's findings (see above) which were undertaken 20 years later using a much more sophisticated methodology.

Scott was aware that he was trawling through his data looking for scales and made the crucial point that delinquency is 'multidimensional', in effect throwing down the gauntlet to future generations (with their more sophisticated statistics and computers) to explore this complex mathematical space. Factor analysis was the obvious choice and, as Quay and Blumen demonstrate in Chapter 23, soon showed that interpretable factors of criminal history can be established, pointing to the possibility of a classification system. However, a dozen years later Gibbons had '*become increasingly sceptical about the prospects for uncovering a relatively parsimonious set of criminal role-careers*' (Chapter 24). His review attempted to deal with criminals in a wide range of settings, but drew on typologies that were empirical only in that they related to known individuals, not in the stricter sense of their validity being tested by statistical means. The conclusions that he reached are nonetheless important, especially in drawing attention to the greater potential value of classifications specific to particular contexts and aimed at particular purposes. The message for investigative psychologists is to explore typologies that relate directly to criminal activity rather than the broader framework that concerns most criminologists.

A remarkably prescient classification of offence activity was the study published over 20 years ago by Green *et al.* (Chapter 25). They recognized that the problem of demonstrating that a number of burglaries may have been committed by the same person – a classic difficulty in identifying the *modus operandi* (*m.o.*) of an offender – could be open to assistance from multivariate statistical procedures. By using relatively few overt aspects of an offence, such as mode of entry and type of property stolen, they were able to reveal degrees of similarity and difference between crimes. They chose the powerful procedure known as multi-dimensional scaling (MDS) in which crimes are represented as points in space: the more similar crimes are in terms of their *m.o.* the closer they appear. Using only a small sample, Green *et al.* demonstrated that this geographical pattern did put crimes by the same offender closer together, thus opening up the possibility of linking offences. (Ten years later, ignorant of this earlier work, Canter (1995) 're-discovered' this approach, utilizing somewhat different MDS procedures, to help police investigations of serial rapists and a serial murderer.) Green *et al.* were very aware of both the potential and the pitfills of such an approach but, with advances in computing and statistics, this is clearly a direction for research with enormous potential, as Canter and Heritage have shown in Chapter 32.

*Offence Actions, Offender Characteristics*

One important contribution of these MDS based studies is their emphasis on the actions of criminals when they commit crimes. These papers are especially instructive in showing the benefits of considering the details of the various ways in which crimes are committed. Such considerations also throw light on the characteristics of criminals, whether it be the studied decisions of robbers (Chapter 31) or differences in the levels of intimacy of rapists (Chapter 32). It is on the basis of these careful analyses of the details of behaviour that any scientific principles for inferring the characteristics of unknown offenders will be built.

Some offender characteristics can be inferred, in general, from knowledge of the type of crime involved, without the need for very detailed consideration of all aspects of how the crime was committed. In Chapter 26, after summarizing a number of these studies, Walsh shows that a remarkably distinct sub-set of the population carries out most burglaries from private houses. The combination of the sorts of results that Walsh reports with the approach of Green *et al.* in Chapter 25 is what lies at the heart of Investigative Psychology.

Researchers have made various attempts to provide systematic links between offence characteristics and offender characteristics. In some cases they have gone beyond direct observations of offence activity and attempted to use motive based classification schemes. This is a potentially fraught approach because of the slipperiness of the concept of motivation and because of the likely difficulties of reliably assigning cases to a class on the basis of some 'invisible' phenomenon. Despite the dangers, in terms of arson it can be argued that the details of a fire may reliably indicate motivations. In Chapter 27, Icove and Estepp include details of offender profiles to help them determine the 'motives' of typical fire setters; thereby, unfortunately, they reduce the applicability of their results to an investigation, as well as confuse descriptions of people with their 'motives'. However, they do break new ground by showing that their 'motive-based' classes of arson do, in fact, have distinct offender characteristics. This is particularly helpful in examining the distinct varieties of arson.

*Variations Between Offenders*

The question arises as to what the bases for variations between offenders may be. As this is related to the central criminological question of the aetiology of crime in general, similar types of answer are likely to be forthcoming. These will be broadly related to issues of nature and nurture. However, from an investigative point of view, the overt influences of surroundings (in so far as they reflect social contacts, areas of residence and family circumstances, all of which are more open to investigation than personality or physiology) appear to be a particularly fruitful route for consideration. For that reason McCarthy and Hagan's examination in Chapter 28 of how social contact – what they call 'criminal embeddedness' – relates to the type and intensity of criminal activity in a particular sub-group of offenders is of great potential significance. It also draws attention to the inherently social aspects of crime, turning the emphasis away from the antisocial loner as the prime example of a criminal.

The 'profile' of the 'typical' criminal is challenged even further when white collar crime is considered, most notably insurance fraud in which the offender must be well enough established to make insurance seem appropriate. Yet because such crimes do not attract media attention and are also more complex and bureaucratic to unravel, they have seldom been studied. Clarke's classification of insurance fraud in Chapter 29 is thus an important first step in considering how such crimes should be systematically analysed to facilitate investigations.

Clarke's classification is somewhat different from that which Icove and Estepp propose for arson or Green's use of simple *m.o.* to classify burglars, in that it relates directly to the opportunities available rather than to any assumptions about the motives of the offender or the particular details of how the crime was committed. In general, crime that has an obvious material objective – what is often referred to as 'instrumental crime' – can be usefully considered in terms of the particular gains that the criminal is seeking. When the crime involves interpersonal violence, then it is more difficult to establish these instrumental gains; indeed, the nature of the interpersonal transaction may be the key to understanding variations between offenders. These variations may be rather subtle, as Palmer shows in his important comparison of murderers and their brothers in Chapter 30. As a consequence, it may be more difficult to read the nature of the person committing the offence from the crime details.

Palmer's summary of his study of 51 men convicted of murder is an elegant resumé of the life story of many murderers:

> [They] apparently experienced psychological frustrations which were significantly greater in number and intensity than those experienced by their control brothers. ...Battered by physical frustrations, the murderers were beset by psychological frustrations which swelled their reservoirs of aggression to a point where that aggression would, and eventually did, burst its confines violently (p. 375).

The bursting of the reservoirs of aggression of the person who kills someone he knows is, on the face of it, different from the actions of a robber. Certainly, as Feeney shows in Chapter 31, it is possible to model the apparently rational decisions of a robber but, as he also makes clear, there are often non-instrumental reactions that give rise to robbery as well. Examples may include a search for excitement or to impress friends; even issues of frustration reduction can be discerned behind the more overt reasons given. There is thus a need to disentangle the externally identifiable aspects of an offence from those that might be inferred about the 'inner state' of the offender. Indeed, the varieties of gain that offenders seek, material as well as physical, are all aspects that need to be distinguished if classifications are to be of value to the investigative process.

## The Future of Psychological Contributions to Investigations

Earlier studies carried out with the general intention of understanding criminality have thus tended to combine a mixture of objectives, motives, characteristics and actions of offenders. Even Icove and Estepp, whose work was aimed at contributing to arson investigations, drew on both internal inferences and external actions to develop their classifications. These precursors to Investigative Psychology have shown that useful distinctions can be drawn between different types of offenders who can be shown to have characteristic backgrounds. The next stage is therefore clear. Such distinctions need to be tied firmly to the sorts of information available to police investigators, namely crime scene material and victim (or witness) reports of the offender's actions. Canter and Heritage initiated empirical studies of just such data in Chapter 32, showing that, for rape, it is possible to distinguish the patterns of actions of different offences, as Green *et al.* had identified for burglary (Chapter 25). The question that arises is how far this type of research can be taken. Do all forms of crime lend themselves to this type of analysis? Can the characteristics of offenders be narrowed to distinguish between sub-groups of particular crimes: for instance, do people who carry out different types of rape have different features? This is the central question of Investigative Psychology. What inferences can validly be made about an offender from the way in which he commits a crime? This is a more precise form of the populist question as to how 'offender profiles' may be drawn.

The last section brings together current approaches that explore the exciting possibilities for a scientifically based framework for psychological offender profiling. Blau's account in

Chapter 33 is probably the most unbiased view available of the early stages of profiling in the US. As an experienced, professional psychologist who has worked for many years with a variety of police forces in many different contexts, the summary of his conclusions is worth emphasizing:

> All in all, although psychological profiles are probably a potentially useful tool, spotting serial killers and serial rapists from those procedures is currently a difficult and unreliable procedure. ...Particular mental disorders do not correlate highly with specific crimes leading to some question about the point-to-point method of developing a picture of the perpetrator (p. 459).

It is clear from Blau's review that although autobiographies written by FBI special agents about their own practice (Ressler and Shachtman 1992, Douglas and Olshaker 1996) and even a few of the more academic accounts that they published (Hazelwood and Burgess 1987) have all the bravado one might expect of Federal Law enforcement officers, they are lacking any clear statement of the conceptual, theoretical or empirical basis of their judgements. Nonetheless, they have indicated a direction that others are following and beginning to turn into a scientific discipline, as reviewed by Canter in Chapter 35. Using empirical examples, his paper outlines the psychological theories that are relevant to such an endeavour and takes rather further the approach discussed around case studies in the author's recent book (Canter 1995).

The work reviewed by Canter in 'Psychology of Offender Profiling' focuses on individual criminals and their particular activities, but many forms of criminal activity are social and, as McCarthy and Hagan argue in Chapter 28, this social context may be a defining aspect of their criminality. There is thus clearly much to be gained from considering the networks that make up a considerable proportion of criminal activity. In Chapter 34, Sparrow reviews the applications of network analysis and shows how the social psychology of groups, combined with the information technology based analysis of group processes, are enabling investigators to recognize when crimes are occurring as well as to identify some of the features of the perpetrators.

One area in which research has made great strides where computer systems help police directly is in the study of the location of criminals' residences. In Chapter 36, Canter and Larkin describe the basis for an expert system that builds upon the theory of criminals' mental maps and systematically studies 45 rapists in order to derive a direct indication of where the offender might be living from knowledge of where he commits his crimes. They show that very high levels of validity can be produced by their system, although more work needs to be done on reducing the search area. Rossmo takes a more pragmatic approach in Chapter 37, trying to produce the smallest search areas with assumed probabilities. Future work will doubtless see the convergence of these related approaches, as well as increasing attempts to link them to other aspects of offenders' lifestyles.

There have clearly been huge developments in thinking about the possibility of psychological contributions to criminal detection, from the early public concerns with police powers, through the growth of interview processes, and on to the possibilities of offender profiling and expert systems to help the police locate criminals. Out of this has emerged the new field of Investigative Psychology which aims to provide a professional base to the investigation and prosecution of crime.

The studies in the present volume show that such developments can be firmly grounded in a wide ranging academic literature. But they also indicate the many pitfalls that may be encountered on the way to creating this new area of science. Some of these exist because of the gullibility of practitioners who wish to use these services, and some because the 'experts' want to provide simple, ready-made solutions to the complex and often poorly defined problems that practitioners present. Because police officers and others involved in law enforcement may not be able to assess the soundness of advice they are given, invalid and poor information can masquerade as a substantive contribution, as Poythress *et al.* pointed out in Chapter 7. It is therefore appropriate that the final study in this volume should examine the contribution of 'psychic crime detectives'. In revealing the weakness of the claims of these psychics, yet the readiness with which some police officers embrace them, Wiseman and his colleagues provide a present day illustration of the task that Daniel took on when dealing with the priests of Bel.

The inevitability of these developments is perhaps foreshadowed in the writings of crime fiction writers. So in Chapter 39 we give the last word to one of the masters of the genre, Raymond Chandler. He provides a view that perhaps many police officers will share after reading this book.

## References

Blau, T.H. (1994), *Psychological Services for Law Enforcement*, New York: John Wiley.

Canter, D. (1995), *Criminal Shadows*, London: HarperCollins.

Douglas, J. and Olshaker, M. (1996), *Mind Hunter: The FBI Elite Serial Crime Unit*, London: Heinemann.

Ekman, P. (1992), *Telling Lies*, London: Norton.

Ekman, P., O'Sullivan, M., Friesen, W.V. and Scherer, K.R. (1991), Invited Article: 'Face, Voice and Body in Detecting Deception', *Journal of Nonverbal Behavior*, 15 (2).

Hardcastle, R.A. (1977), 'CUSUM: A Credible Method for the Determination of Authorship?', *Science and Justice*, 37 (2), pp. 127–38.

Haward, L. (1981), *Forensic Psychology*, London: Batsford.

Hazelwood, R.R. and Burgess, A. (eds) (1987), *Practical Aspects of Rape Investigations: a Multidisciplinary Approach*, Amsterdam: Elsevier.

Ressler, R.K. and Shachtman, T. (1992), *Whoever Fights Monsters*, London: Simon and Schuster.

Swanson, C.R., Chamelin, N.C. and Territo, L. (1992), *Criminal Investigation*, 5th edn, New York: McGraw-Hill.

Undeutsch, U. (1982), 'Statement Reality Analysis', in Trankell, A. (ed.), *Reconstructing the Past: The Role of Psychologists in Criminal Trials*, Deventer: Kluwer, pp. 27–56.

# [1]
# DANIEL, BEL, AND
# THE SNAKE

### The destruction of Bel

1
2 WHEN KING ASTYAGES was gathered to his fathers he was succeeded on the throne by Cyrus the Persian. Daniel was a confidant of the king, the most honoured of all the King's Friends.

3 Now the Babylonians had an idol called Bel, for which they provided every day twelve bushels of fine flour, forty sheep, and fifty gallons of wine.

4 The king held it to be divine and went daily to worship it, but Daniel

a clove: *literally* mastic.          b clove . . . cleave: *there is a play on words in the Gk.*
c yew: *literally* oak.               d yew . . . hew: *there is a play on words in the Gk.*

206

*The destruction of Bel*     DANIEL, BEL, AND THE SNAKE

worshipped his God. So the king said to him, 'Why do you not worship Bel?' He replied, 'Because I do not believe in man-made idols, but in the 5 living God who created heaven and earth and is sovereign over all mankind.' The king said, 'Do you think that Bel is not a living god? Do you not 6 see how much he eats and drinks each day?' Daniel laughed and said, 'Do 7 not be deceived, your majesty; this Bel of yours is only clay inside and bronze outside, and has never eaten anything.'

Then the king was angry, and summoned the priests of Bel and said to 8 them, 'If you cannot tell me who it is that eats up all these provisions, you shall die; but if you can show that it is Bel that eats them, then Daniel shall 9 die for blasphemy against Bel.' Daniel said to the king, 'Let it be as you command.' (There were seventy priests of Bel, not counting their wives 10 and children.) Then the king went with Daniel into the temple of Bel. The 11 priests said, 'We are now going outside; set out the food yourself, your majesty, and mix the wine; then shut the door and seal it with your signet. When you come back in the morning, if you do not find that Bel has eaten it 12 all, let us be put to death; but if Daniel's charges against us turn out to be false, then he shall die.' They treated the whole affair with contempt, 13 because they had made a hidden entrance under the table, and they regularly went in by it and ate everything up.

So when the priests had gone, the king set out the food for Bel; and 14 Daniel ordered his servants to bring ashes and sift them over the whole temple in the presence of the king alone. Then they left the temple, closed the door, sealed it with the king's signet, and went away. During the night 15 the priests, with their wives and children, came as usual and ate and drank everything. Early in the morning the king came, and Daniel with him. The 16 17 king said, 'Are the seals intact, Daniel?' He answered, 'They are intact, your majesty.' As soon as he opened the door, the king looked at the table 18 and cried aloud, 'Great art thou, O Bel! In thee there is no deceit at all.' But Daniel laughed and held back the king from going in. 'Just look at the 19 floor,' he said, 'and judge whose footprints these are.' The king said, 'I see 20 the footprints of men, women, and children.' In a rage he put the priests 21 under arrest, with their wives and children. Then they showed him the secret doors through which they used to go in and consume what was on the table. So the king put them to death, and handed Bel over to Daniel, 22 who destroyed the idol and its temple.

# Part I
# The Investigation of Crime

# [2]

## Dr. HANS GROSS

### CERTAIN QUALITIES ESSENTIAL TO AN INVESTIGATOR

It goes almost without saying that an Investigator should be endowed with all those qualities which every man should desire to possess—indefatigable zeal and application, self-denial and perseverance, swiftness in reading men and a thorough knowledge of human nature, education and an agreeable manner, an iron constitution, and encyclopaedic knowledge. Still there are some special qualities the importance of which is frequently overlooked, and to which attention may be forcibly directed.

First and above all he must possess an abundant store of energy. He who recognises that he is wanting in energy can but turn to something else, for he will never make a good Investigator. Again he must be energetic not only in special circumstances, as when, for example, he finds himself face to face with a witness or an accused person who is hotheaded, refractory, and aggressive, or when the work takes him away from his office and he proceeds to record a deposition or make an arrest; but energy must always be displayed when he tackles a difficult, complicated or obscure case. It is truly painful to examine a report which shows that he has only fallen to his work with timidity, hesitation, and nervousness, just touching it, so to speak, with the tips of his fingers; but there is satisfaction in observing that a case has been attacked energetically and grasped with animation and vigour. The want of special cleverness and long practice can often be compensated by getting a good grip of the case, but want of energy can be compensated by nothing.

The Investigator must have a high grade of real self-denying power. It is not enough for him to be a clever reckoner, a fine speculator, a careful weigher of facts, and to possess a good business head, he must also be self-denying, unostentatious and perfectly honest, resigning at the outset all thoughts of magnificent public successes. The effective summing-up of the judge, the clever conduct of the case by counsel, all meet with acknowledgment, astonishment and admiration from the public, but such triumphs are not for the Investigator. If the latter be working well, those few people who have had an opportunity of really studying the case as it goes along will discover his unceasing and untiring work from the documents on the record and will form some correct idea of the brain work, power of combination, and extensive knowledge which he has employed. He will be held responsible for the smallest and most pardonable mistake, while his care and his merits are seldom acknowledged. Let him be conscious of having done his duty in the only possible way. Beyond this we can only say, " Virtue is its own reward."

Another quality demanded at any price from the Investigator is absolute accuracy. We do not mean by this that he must set out details in the official records exactly as they have been seen or said, for it goes without saying that this will be done. The quality indicated consists in not being content with mere evidence of third parties or hearsay when it is possible for him to ascertain the truth with his own eyes or by more minute investigation. This is to say no more than that he should be accurate in his work, in the sense of being " exact," as that word is used in its highest scientific sense. Indeed, the high degree of perfection which all sciences have today attained is entirely due to " exact " work; and if we compare a recent scientific work, whatever the subject, with an analogous book written some decades ago, we shall notice a great difference between them arising almost wholly from the fact that the work of today is more exact than that of yesterday. Naturally in all inquiries a certain amount of imagination is necessary; but a comparison between scientists of our time will always be to the advantage of the one whose work is most exact, the brilliant and fruitful ideas of the scientist which astonish the world being often far from sudden and happy inspirations but the outcome of exact research. In close observation of facts, in searching for their remotest causes, in making unwearied comparisons, in instituting disagreeable experiments, in short, in attempting to elucidate a problem, the Investigator will observe it under so many aspects and passing through so many phases that new ideas will spontaneously come to him which, if found to be accurate and skilfully utilised, will certainly give positive results. Since " exactness," or accuracy of work, is of so much importance in all branches of research, this accuracy must also be applied to the work of the Investigator. But what is to be understood by accurate work? It consists in not trusting to others but attending to the business oneself, and even in mistrusting oneself and going through the case again and again. By so proceeding, one will certainly bring about an accurate piece of work. A thousand mistakes of every description would be avoided if people did not base their conclusions upon premises furnished by others, take as established fact what is only possibility, or as a constantly recurring incident what has only been observed once. True it is that in his work the Investigator can see but a trifling portion of the facts nor can he repeat his observations. He is obliged largely to trust to what others tell him and it is just here that the difficulty and insufficiency of his work lie. But this inconvenience can to a certain extent be remedied; on the one hand by, wherever possible, making sure of things for himself instead of accepting what others tell him; and, on the other hand, by trying to give a more exact form to the statements of others, by comparison, experiment and demonstration, for the purpose of testing the veracity of the deponent's observation and obtaining from him something exact, or at least more exact than before. In endeavouring to verify the facts for himself the Investigator must personally examine localities, make measurements and comparisons, and so form his own opinion. If a small matter which can only be established by accurate observation is in question, not data furnished incidentally, but only ascertained facts and investigations specially carried out, must be relied upon.

In an important case the circumstantial evidence had been brought together and conclusions thereby suggested drawn, results which might have been of decisive importance in clearing up the case. At the last moment it came into the head of some outsider to ask if the distance between two points was really two thousand paces. That was one of the grounds of the argument so artistically built up: in fact two witnesses had declared the distance to be two thousand paces. It was decided to visit the ground, and when the distance was found to be only four hundred and fifty paces, the new conclusions rendered necessary contradicted the former ones. This is a typical example among hundreds of similar instances.

It is much more difficult to point out how depositions can be rendered more exact, when they cannot be verified by actual inspection. Let it be granted that the witness is really desirous of speaking the truth and is merely a bad observer. In general, the matter should be elucidated by experiment, by ocular demonstration. Suppose a witness affirms that he was beaten by H for ten minutes. Let him demonstrate how long he believes that he was beaten, and time him by a watch. After a quarter of a minute he may exclaim, " It certainly did not last longer than that."

Again, a witness asserts that he is perfectly certain that he heard a cry coming from below, but trials on the spot prove that he never can guess correctly whether a cry comes from right or left, above or below. Again, a witness says that, though he did not look very closely, H held at least twelve coins in his hand; that he can swear to. " Very well," he is asked, " how many coins have I at present in my hand? " " Also about twelve," he answers. But there are twenty-three. Again, a witness declares, " When once I see a man I always recognise him again." " Did you see the witness who went out as you came in? " you ask him. " Certainly I saw him very well," he answers. " All right, go and pick him out from ten other persons."

A witness estimates an important distance at, let us say, 200 yards: let him be brought out of doors and say how far might be 100, 200, 300, 400 yards; if now these distances be measured, one can easily judge if and with what degree of accuracy the witness can judge distances. As this judging of distances is often necessary, it becomes important to measure beforehand from a convenient window certain visible fixed points and to note the distances for future examinations. For years the author had many occasions for doing so from his office-room window and knew, for instance : to the left corner of the house—65 yards; to the poplar tree—120; to the church spire—210; to the small house—400; to the railway—950. By these distances he has often tested witnesses. If the witness proves fairly accurate in his estimates, his evidence may be considered important for the case under investigation. One can even rectify wrong estimates if, for instance, we find out that the witness is accustomed to estimate always too high or too low, we can correct them by a species of personal equation.

Such checks give the most instructive and remarkable results; whoever practises them will soon be convinced that their importance cannot be exaggerated.

If accuracy of work is necessary in even the most insignificant cases, it becomes in the highest degree important in serious cases where increased working material must be laid out for the future and a base of operations established. Here often the most incomprehensible things happen. While reading the papers connected with grave cases one often remarks that, the base of operations once established, the work has been carried on with the greatest care and accuracy and much sagacity has been expended. But all this has been a dead loss, for in establishing the base of operations an accessory circumstance of seeming insignificance has not been accurately observed or estimated, a false premise has been included, and the whole

## *Certain Qualities essential to an Investigator*      19

of the stately fabric built up so laboriously reposes on a tottering and yielding foundation.

DUTIES OF THE POLICE IN THE INVESTIGATION OF CRIMES AND OFFENCES — OBTAINING OF EVIDENCE (PART I).

*General Duty of the Police in the Collection of Information.*

55. As stated in Chapter I, the primary duty of the Police is the prevention of crimes and offences, but when once a crime or offence has been committed their duty is to detect the offender and bring him to justice. In this task much assistance is derived from a variety of technical methods which have been developed of late years, such as identification by finger-prints, the analysis of stains, the microscopic examination of materials connected with the crime, and the study of records, photographic and otherwise, of all known criminals. These methods may provide positive evidence of the greatest importance and even when the results are of a negative character they are often of value in narrowing the field of enquiry at the outset of the investigation and thus obviating fruitless and unnecessary interrogations. We have not regarded ourselves as required, or indeed competent, to examine these methods in their technical details but obviously they should be developed and improved to the fullest extent.

56. We wish, however, to record certain impressions which we have formed and which have some bearing on the technical equipment of the Force as a whole.

In particular we must mention the depressing and almost penal atmosphere which we have noticed in some Police stations. This criticism applies mainly to some of the older stations which no doubt it has not been found possible to remodel, for reasons of economy. But in our view a Police station should be recognised, primarily, as an office for the conduct of public business, and the cells, whilst a necessary adjunct, should not set the tone to the whole building.

Insufficient use also seems to be made of shorthand-writing and modern office equipment.

We are also impressed with the need for developing Police mobility and with the importance, in this connection, of the Police Box system. This, however, and the other points referred to in this paragraph, are matters of organisation with which we are not empowered to deal.

57. The principal feature of the initial investigation into a crime is usually a widespread search for information, involving enquiries of any and all persons who may have knowledge bearing on the matter. Such enquiries range from a few simple questions addressed to some person in the street to the taking of a formal written statement.

Although it is the duty of the Police to obtain all possible information regarding a crime, they have no power (save in such

23

exceptional cases as offences against the Official Secrets Acts) to compel any person to disclose facts within his knowledge, or even to answer direct questions put to him. The position of a constable collecting information as to the commission of a crime differs from that of a private citizen in two particulars only; that it is his special duty to obtain such information and that, in doing so, he is a " person in authority." The latter point is of importance, as we shall show later, when he approaches a person who may ultimately be accused.

### Police Use of Information Obtained.

58. In the initial stages of an enquiry it is the duty of the Police to seek information from all persons who may have knowledge of facts relevant to the crime, including persons whom they may have some reason to suspect as possible culprits. Indeed, at this early stage the Police may have formed no theory as to who committed the crime. But, from the point of view of subsequent proceedings in Court, there is an essential difference between statements taken from a potential witness and from the person ultimately charged with a crime.

59. Statements made to the Police by the former cannot be given in evidence and the persons making them must appear as witnesses in Court and give evidence themselves. Statements made by potential witnesses thus serve two main purposes; first, as affording clues to the Police for further lines of enquiry, and secondly, as enabling them to determine who are the persons who can testify to the guilt of the person ultimately charged with the crime. The statements made are in effect " proofs " of evidence, indicating the information which a witness is in a position to give if called upon in Court. Occasionally, however, a witness for the prosecution gives evidence in Court which differs materially from that which he has previously given in his proof of evidence. In such cases the prosecuting Counsel, if he has reason to believe that the witness's original story was accurate, can ask permission to treat the witness as " hostile." If this permission is granted he may cross-examine the witness on the basis of his proof of evidence.

On the other hand, statements made by a person who is charged with an offence may be given in evidence by the persons to whom those statements are made, provided that the circumstances in which they were taken do not render them inadmissible.

60. It follows that it is of greater importance to secure an accurate record of a statement made by a person who is later charged with an offence than of a statement made by a witness. But at the outset of an enquiry, unless the issue is of the simplest description, the Police cannot say which of the persons from whom they seek information may later prove to be the culprit

24

or his accomplices. Unwillingness to disclose information may be due to other causes than complicity in the crime which has been committed; as for instance, relationship with the criminal, the social opprobrium attaching to even a remote connection with the offence, or simply unwillingness to be bothered. Readiness to answer questions, on the other hand, may spring either from a genuine wish to help the Police, or from a desire to mislead them. At this early stage the Police must approach everyone in the same manner and they cannot tell whether the answers given to them will ultimately prove to be an admission made by the culprit, a proof of evidence of an essential witness, or one of the countless statements which in any difficult criminal investigation yield only negative results.

### Admissibility of Statements made by Accused Persons.

61. Any statement previously made by an accused person is potentially admissible, at his trial, as evidence against him, but the criteria by which this admissibility is to be determined in any particular case, as expounded in the leading decisions of the Courts, form a complicated part of the law of evidence with which we are not required or competent to deal. The underlying principle appears to have been that any statement made by an accused person is admissible if true, but that any form of threat or inducement prior to its being made introduced so great a risk of unreliability that any statement made under threat or inducement came to be treated as necessarily inadmissible. This principle of law has long been expressed in the maxim, *Nemo tenetur prodere seipsum* (i.e., no one should be compelled to incriminate himself), and has finally given birth to the law as to the admissibility of voluntary confessions. To quote from Stephen's " Digest of the Law of Evidence " (Articles 21 and 22), " a confession is an admission made at any time by a person charged with a crime stating or suggesting the inference that he committed that crime. . . . . . No confession is deemed to be voluntary if it appear to the Judge to have been caused by an inducement, threat, or promise, proceeding from a person in authority."

62. As we have already mentioned, a Policeman for this purpose is a " person in authority " and it is therefore necessary when he approaches the culprit (and it must be remembered that he may not then even suspect him of being the culprit) that he should studiously avoid holding out any threat or inducement which would render the resulting statement inadmissible in evidence. We were authoritatively informed that if a prisoner complained in Court of the manner in which any statement had been taken from him the Judge or magistrate would at once investigate the matter, whether or not the statement had been tendered in evidence by the prosecution. Cases sometimes arise in which the prosecution refrain from

25

tendering in evidence a statement made by an accused person to the Police, on account of some doubt as to its admissibility, or in which the Court decides that some statement should not be admitted in evidence against the accused. But the evidence of Police witnesses, without exception, has been that the practice of the Police is to approach any person who is or may be suspected of a crime in such a way that any statement he may make will not be rendered inadmissible in evidence by reason of the circumstances in which it was taken.

63. The above summary is intended to indicate in outline the general principles which, we understand, underlie the law as to the admissibility of statements. This law is, however, interpreted by the decided cases on the subject and these are apparently of a somewhat conflicting and contradictory character, permitting what may be described as wide " limits of deviation." Within these limits there is room for an extensive range of variation and it rests entirely with the Court, in each particular trial, to decide what evidence may and may not be admitted.

This uncertainty of the law in regard to the admissibility of evidence, and the diverse rulings of different Courts on different cases, are a source of great embarrassment to the Police whose business it is to get evidence which will be admissible against the prisoner at his trial. The Judges' Rules, with which we deal in Chapter VI, were drawn up in order to give them guidance in this difficult matter.

## *" Cautioning."*

64. Although we have heard evidence from a great number of witnesses on this subject, we had obtained no information as to the origin and development of the constable's caution until we were furnished by the Home Office with the Historical Memorandum\*, the Summary of which is reproduced in Appendix 4.

From this Memorandum it appears that the constable's caution owes its origin to the principle expressed in the common law that a prisoner's statement, to be admissible in evidence, must be voluntary. In other words it was introduced to ensure that the prisoner's statement was voluntary and to establish, to the satisfaction of the Court, that the prisoner knew that he was under no obligation to make a statement or to incriminate himself out of his own mouth.

The Judges' Rules, which will be found on pages 70 and 71, set out the occasions on which a constable is at present required to administer a caution.

In this Chapter of our Report we propose to deal only with the cautioning of persons before an arrest is made, but it will be convenient at this stage to make certain general observations on the subject.

---

\* The full text is printed in the Volume of Evidence and other documents submitted to the Commission.

26

65. Many witnesses, speaking from considerable experience, have been sceptical as to the value or effect of a caution, and have expressed the view that it has little if any result upon either the " interests of justice " or the " rights and liberties of the subject." Some authorities go further and would wish it to be dispensed with altogether.*

The majority of witnesses, however, would retain the caution, not only for historic and sentimental reasons, but because they believe that it is a genuine protection to persons who are being questioned by the Police and who, but for it, might run the risk of making statements involuntarily which might incriminate themselves.

After hearing and weighing much evidence on this subject, we have come definitely to the conclusion that the " caution " should be retained, and that its use should be regularised and clearly explained both to the public and the Police.

66. At present there is considerable divergence of opinion as well as practice, as to the form which the caution should take, and as to the circumstances and moment at which it should be administered. In consequence its incidence and effect vary greatly in different hands, and in different parts of the country; a result which is obviously undesirable. Before going further, it may be well to recall the existing practice of the Police as to " cautioning," prior to the moment when an accused person is arrested or charged.

67. Rule (1) of the Judges' Rules states that there is no objection to a Policeman, who is endeavouring to discover the author of a crime, putting questions in respect thereof to any person or persons, whether suspected or not, from whom he thinks that useful information can be obtained.

Rule (2) says that whenever a Policeman has made up his mind to charge a person with a crime, he should first caution such person before asking any questions, or further questions, as the case may be.

---

* A good deal of support for this view may be found, not only amongst those engaged in the suppression of crime, but in the minds of laymen. The detection and punishment of criminals, it is said, is not a game to be played according to a code of technical rules; it is a serious business of the community, working through its agents—the Police. Why then should a person who is supposed to have committed a crime be discouraged from talking freely, or in a way which may incriminate himself and thus serve the ends of justice ?

The legal answer to this question has already been explained in para. 61. But over and above that, is the British sense of "fair play"—even to the criminal—which probably originated, so far as modern procedure is concerned, in the general revulsion of feeling which manifested itself at the beginning of the nineteenth century, or even earlier, against the shocking severity of the criminal laws at that time, and the old memories of judicial torture. Under stress of this sentiment, rules of evidence and procedure which tended to increase the chances of escape of prisoners from conviction were regarded with widespread approval by both lawyers and laymen and have (with much less necessity) persisted until the present day.

27

The combined effect of these two Rules is that a Policeman can question a suspected person without administering a caution, right up to the moment at which he makes up his mind to arrest or charge.

68. We have given much thought and anxious consideration to this point and have finally come to the following conclusions.

First, as regards the moment at which the caution should be administered. This, in our view, should not be capable of being used or varied for tactical reasons, and the Police should be relieved of a responsibility which is peculiarly difficult to exercise with impartiality and which tends to expose them to allegations of unfairness towards suspected persons.

If, as we understand it, the spirit and object of the caution are to bring home to persons who are being questioned that they are under no obligation to make any statement which might incriminate them, it would seem only fair and proper that such warning should be extended to them from the very outset of their interviews with the Police. Otherwise there is always the possibility that they will give themselves away, or create an atmosphere of suspicion from which they cannot subsequently emerge, before any warning has been given them as to the consequences of their garrulity or indiscretion. Such a result may be helpful to the " interests of justice " but is a violation of the whole spirit of " cautioning."

69. We can understand the point of view of those who would do away with the caution altogether and take advantage " in the interests of justice " of any unguarded admissions that a suspect might make, but we find it difficult to appreciate the value or ethics of a caution which is deliberately withheld until the suspect has succeeded in incriminating himself sufficiently to justify his arrest. In this latter case the caution comes too late to constitute any real warning to its recipient, and, if it has any effect at all, it is to hamper from that moment the " interests of justice."

The only logical and effective escape from this dilemma would seem to be the administration of a caution, in simple and easily understood language, at the very outset of any questioning either of a suspect or of any material witness. We have received evidence in support of this conclusion from many responsible and official witnesses, and we are convinced that the procedure suggested, in para. 73 below, is quite as much in the higher interests of the Police Force as of the " rights and liberties of the subject."

70. The precise effect of this procedure would necessarily vary with the circumstances of the case and the temperaments of individuals. The evidence upon this point, and the views laid before us by responsible authorities, show great divergences of opinion, although to some extent no doubt they may be affected

28

by the prestige of the caution as a hallowed shibboleth, the real significance or value of which has seldom been critically analysed.

Generally speaking, however, there is agreement that, on the mind of an experienced criminal, a " caution " has little or no effect—whatever its form or whenever it is administered. The case of a new offender may be somewhat different, and we have been given to understand that men and women are apt to react differently to a caution administered by the Police. Women especially are said to regard it as an unfriendly or discourteous interposition in an interview and to become less communicative in their answers to enquiries. To this extent the caution may be a disadvantage, but, even so, it seems not undesirable that a potential witness—particularly in serious cases—should realise the importance of the occasion and the need of giving none but truthful and well-considered replies to enquiries, seeing that they may have to be repeated in Court and possibly affect the liberty or life of another.

71. On the other hand if the person interrogated is a suspect, who may subsequently turn out to be the actual criminal, the caution would appear to be an almost superfluous warning. In such a case he is conscious of his guilt and can have no illusions as to the seriousness of his position when approached and questioned by a Policeman on the subject of the crime. His mind will be fully on the alert in any case, and the caution will not put him any further on his guard. This would seem to dispose of the objection to administering the caution at the commencement of any enquiries by the Police. If its effect is to afford any real or additional warning to the individual questioned, that would only be in accordance with its original intention and it would seem fair that such effect should be continuous over the whole period of questioning. This procedure, moreover, would relieve the Policeman of the very invidious and almost impossible task of " making up his mind " and determining the moment, accurately and impartially, when the caution should be administered.

72. The crux of the whole matter is the question of *admissibility* of answers or statements elicited from suspects when being examined by the Police. This, as already explained earlier in this Chapter, is primarily a matter for the Courts and there is much variety in the decisions given in recent years. No. (6) of the Judges' Rules is the only one which touches directly on this question, and there appears to be no clear or definite rule as to the effect of a caution upon the admissibility or inadmissibility of evidence obtained as a result of questioning a suspect or prisoner. However this may be, the position would be much simplified by the administering, in all cases, of a preliminary caution, since every statement by the accused which the Police tendered in evidence would, *ipso facto*, have been made after the giving of a caution.

29

It might be contended that only a suspect should be cautioned, and that the Courts could easily determine whether the proper moment had been observed, but it may often be impossible, at the outset, to distinguish who is or is not a suspect. We have therefore recommended that the caution should be given to everyone alike. Moreover, to prescribe that the caution should be administered only to a suspect would entail, in many cases, that the incriminating statement which caused the suspicion would have been made before a caution had been given at all. The Policeman would also remain in the difficult and invidious position envisaged in No. (2) of the Judges' Rules, where he is left to make up his mind as to the moment when he ought to caution. It advances that moment, it is true, but the mental process is as elastic, and capable of tactical abuse, in the one case as the other.

73. Our precise recommendation, therefore, is that, at the outset of any formal questioning, whether of a potential witness or of a suspected person, with regard to any crime or any circumstance connected therewith, a constable should first caution that person in the following words :—

"I am a Police officer I am making inquiries (*into so-and-so*), and I want to know anything you can tell me about it. It is a serious matter, and I must warn you to be careful what you say."

In framing this caution, we have deliberately avoided the use of any technical phrases, and have made use of the simplest possible words which we think will be readily understood by all persons with whom the Police come into contact. This is a point to which we attach great importance.

74. It is of course only intended that this caution should be given at the outset of what may be called *formal* inquiries where statements are being taken for use as evidence at a trial. A Policeman enquiring of a bystander which way a pick-pocket has been seen to run should certainly not be expected to preface his question with a caution. Still less would the caution be necessary in connection with enquiries of an informal character, on miscellaneous subjects, which Police officers have to make in the ordinary course of their day to day contact with the public.

75. In recommending the use of this preliminary caution, in place of the procedure outlined in para. 67, we do not suggest that no other caution should ever be administered between the giving of the one proposed above and the caution on formal charging. In order to be satisfied that a statement made by an accused person is voluntary, the Courts sometimes require that a fresh caution should have been given; as, for example, when a suspect is interrogated for a second time or by another officer. This is a matter which we are content to leave to the discretion of the Police officers concerned, provided that the preliminary caution, specified in para. 73, has already been administered.

30

*Special Warning to Witnesses whose Personal Character is Involved.*

76. We have dealt in the preceding section with the attitude which the Police should adopt in approaching any persons from whom they are seeking information. In this section we shall deal with the special question of a witness whose personal character is involved.

This question came into prominence as a result of the Inquiry into the interrogation by the Police of Miss Savidge, and formed the subject of one of the 15 questions suggested in the Minority Report. For the reasons explained in para. 5, we included this point in the Preliminary Questionnaires which we issued and we have been at pains to secure the fullest expression of views upon it. Shortly after the issue of the Report of the Tribunal to which we have referred the Home Secretary issued to the Metropolitan Police a provisional General Order, providing that special warning should be given to a witness whose own character or reputation was the matter chiefly involved in the case, and whose youth, inexperience or ignorance made some warning desirable, before any effort was made to obtain a statement from that witness.* This Order was issued provisionally and was not circulated by the Home Office to any Force other than the Metropolitan Police. We understand that the

Q. 2612. Order was regarded as experimental only, pending the submission of our Report, and also as subject to review in the light of experience. We assume, therefore, that our opinion is desired as to whether it should be confirmed, and issued as a Home Office circular to other Police forces, or whether it should be

Q. 10. amended or withdrawn. We have also been informed that the provisional Order was in any event intended to be very limited in scope and that it was anticipated that cases in which it would operate would be very rare. This, we understand, has proved to be the case, only one instance of its application having occurred since it was issued.

---

* The Order, dated 1st August, 1928, is as follows:—

SECTION V—PRISONERS—CHARGES—GENERAL INSTRUCTIONS.

*If witness's own character chiefly involved etc.—special directions.*

4a. In any case in which a witness's own character or reputation is the matter chiefly involved in the inquiry, and where the consequences of making a statement may be gravely to his or her prejudice, the matter is to be referred to the Central Office at New Scotland Yard before any steps are taken to obtain a statement. Detailed instructions should then be issued to the officer told off to take the statement, which instructions, while framed to suit the circumstances of the particular case, should be such as to ensure that in any event the person concerned shall be clearly informed, before the statement is taken, of the nature of the statement required, and, where that person's youth, inexperience or ignorance makes it desirable, of the possible consequence involved to him or her in consenting to make it.

31

77. A few witnesses who have given evidence before us have favoured the suggestion of giving a special warning to a witness whose personal character is involved, before any attempt is made to take a statement from him, in order that he may be fully aware of the possible consequences to himself. But the weight of evidence has been strongly opposed to any such warning, or to the issue of any general Instruction on the lines of the provisional Order.

78. We take a "witness whose personal character is involved" to mean, not a person who may be *particeps criminis* but a person who if called upon to give evidence in Court would be bound either to admit disreputable conduct on his own part or at least to lay himself open to the suggestion, in cross-examination, that the facts to which he had deposed reflected discredit upon his character. No doubt the Police often require evidence from persons whose character does not deserve any special consideration and we should imagine that such persons are not usually in need of any special warning. There are, however, others who belong to a different category.

79. We have found the fullest recognition, on the part of the Director of Public Prosecutions and of the Police, of the existence Q. 1128/3a of cases in which a potential witness deserves to be treated with Q. 1340 special consideration in order to avoid the disclosure of some *et seq.* fact that would be damaging to his reputation. In some types of offences, such as blackmail, the Courts are often willing to allow the names of witnesses to be suppressed, since without a promise of non-disclosure it would be difficult to institute proceedings at all. But where it is impracticable to suppress the name of the witness it is necessary to strike a balance between the interests of justice and the interests of the witness concerned. It must not be assumed, however, that the interests of justice always Q. 5978. involve the successful prosecution of some guilty person. The evidence of a witness whose personal character is involved may be as necessary to prevent the conviction of an innocent person as to secure the punishment of an offender.

In practice, the Police cannot know the extent of the em- Q. 3783. barrassment which would be caused to a deponent by being called upon to give evidence, or determine whether, on balance, it would be right to call him as a witness, until after they have taken his statement. Moreover it is their duty to find out not Q. 147. only what a witness knows but what manner of person he is; that is to say, whether his credibility is sufficient to withstand an attack from defending Counsel.

80. The question " whether a witness whose personal character is involved should be given a warning before any statement is taken from him," framed in this form, seems to us to involve a misconception of the true position. The motive underlying this question is, no doubt, the desire to protect a witness from being

32

forced into an embarrassing position without consideration of the consequences to himself. But the witness is not the only person whose interests have to be considered and the time for consideration does not arise until the Police, having obtained his statement, are in a position to balance the interests of the witness on the one hand and the claims of justice on the other. A statement taken from a witness by the Police, being only a proof of evidence, does not of itself involve any disclosure to the public. What is required therefore from the Police is not so much a warning to an inexperienced witness that he may be led into damaging disclosures, as a tactful handling of the matter by the Policeman taking the statement, followed by an impartial survey of all the circumstances of the case by those responsible for instituting proceedings and prosecuting the offence. The point at which a question of discretion arises is when the witness is produced in open Court to give evidence on his statement. The duty to protect the witness, within the terms permitted by the law, rests upon the Judge or magistrate and is not the concern of the Police.

81. We have already recommended that a preliminary caution should be given to all persons, whether suspects or material witnesses, from whom the Police wish to take formal statements and this procedure should go some way to effecting the object of the provisional Order. In the ensuing sections we make further proposals with regard to the procedure for taking statements which are calculated to meet other criticisms of Police procedure, such as were made for instance in the case of Miss Savidge. Our recommendation therefore is that no special warning, apart from the caution at the outset of any questioning, is necessary in the cases of witnesses whose personal character is or may be involved, and we suggest the withdrawal of the provisional Order now in force in the Metropolitan Police District.

*Conditions under which Statements are Taken by the Police from Persons not in Custody.*

82. Criticisms have been made from time to time as to the conditions under which formal statements are taken by the Police and we propose to deal with this matter under the four following heads :—

(i) The place and time at which statements are taken.

(ii) The methods of taking down statements.

(iii) The length of time occupied in the taking of statements.

(iv) Persons present during the taking of statements.

On each of these questions we have taken much evidence. We have been informed, in detail, as to the existing practice of the Police and particular incidents have been brought to our notice with a view to showing the need for the issue of more precise instructions than those at present in force. Various suggestions have also been made to us as to the form which those instructions should take.

83. We deal below with these suggestions, but our general view is that the circumstances in which the Police are called upon to take statements are so various that it would be a mistake to attempt to establish a code of hard and fast rules for their guidance. We think that any public disquiet which may have arisen with regard to some of the questions to which we shall refer has been based on a few isolated instances which are at variance with the generally accepted practice of the Police, and we do not believe that the possibility of an occasional abuse of Police powers can be eliminated by the issue of any regulations. We have therefore endeavoured to set out the broad principles which we think should guide the conduct of the Police in these matters and which should be made the basis of the instructions issued to them. The application of these principles, however, must to a considerable extent be left to the discretion of the individual constables concerned.

(i) *The place and time at which statements are taken.*

84. The main criticism under this head has been directed to the fact that a large proportion of statements are taken at Police stations. The evidence which we have heard from Police witnesses shows that it is the recognised practice, as in our opinion it should be, to consult, so far as possible, the convenience of the person from whom a statement is to be taken, both as regards place and time, but that in the case of many persons with whom the Police have dealings it is difficult to find any place other than the Police station where sufficient privacy can be obtained. We have also been informed that many people prefer to come to the Police station rather than to be visited elsewhere, largely no doubt in order to avoid exciting the curiosity of their neighbours. Also, on occasion, the need for prompt action may make it essential that the Police officer in charge of an important case should see a number of persons in a short space of time and this may only be possible if the persons concerned are asked to forego their own convenience and to attend at the Police station. This probably accounts for the frequency with which statements are taken at Police stations.

At the same time we consider that it should be a general instruction to the Police to avoid, whenever possible, causing embarrassment or injury to the reputation of a witness, such as may be occasioned, for example, by visiting an employee at his place of work, or a child at school.

85. We think that a record should be kept of all visits to Police stations at the invitation of the Police, whether the Uniform Branch or the C.I.D. are concerned. The record should show the times of arrival and departure, and a brief note of the reasons for the visit.

70952

34

(ii) *Methods of taking down statements.*

86. In paras. 58-60 we have explained the use made of statements taken by the Police and the essential difference between a statement taken from an accused person and that taken from a witness. It is obviously of the utmost importance that the Police should be in a position to tender in evidence the clearest and fullest record of any statement made by an accused person, whilst in the case of a witness it will normally suffice to have a brief but accurate record of the facts within his knowledge. But, as we have already indicated, in any important investigation the Police are bound to make widespread enquiries, and it is not until the information so obtained has been collated that it is possible to build up a connected story of the crime and to classify the persons from whom statements have been taken into the separate categories of suspected persons, essential witnesses, or persons whose evidence proves to be irrelevant or immaterial.

87. The differences in intelligence, temperament, and willingness of witnesses have also to be considered. Not many people can tell a connected story without assistance.* They omit essential facts and require to be prompted and guided if they are to retain any sense of sequence; even an hour's discursive conversation may be necessary, so we were told, to extract the answers to one or two simple questions.

88. For these reasons we regard it as impracticable to lay down any precise instructions as to the taking of statements, but we think that the attention of Police officers should be drawn to the following points.

First, we have been shown a number of statements, in narrative form, taken from suspected persons who were subsequently put on their trial, which clearly embody the answers given by the deponent to questions put to him by the Police, although the questions themselves are not recorded. We understand that this is the general practice at the present time.

When the Police take a statement from a suspected person, they usually have knowledge of some facts which have given rise to their suspicions and the purpose of taking the statement is to ascertain whether those suspicions are well founded. The questions put by the Police in such circumstances are an essential part of the interrogation and we therefore recommend that, in all cases in which there is a likelihood of a statement being subsequently tendered in evidence against a deponent, all important questions put to him should be recorded, as well as his replies to them.

89. Secondly, we recommend that any statement of an accused person which is tendered in evidence should, so far as practicable, be communicated to the Court in the language of the accused him-

---

* Actual examples of this inability are given in Appendix 5.

self. In cases where this is not possible throughout the whole statement, the essential passages should be given in the accused's own words. We attach importance to this on account of the danger that a statement may imperceptibly change its meaning in the process of passing through the mind of another person, who expresses in different, though possibly better, language, what he considers to be the true meaning of the deponent, but who has a preconception of the facts in his own mind to which he is perhaps unconsciously aiming to make the narrative conform.

90. The evidence laid before us goes to show that the use of a certain official phraseology has become traditional and is perhaps even encouraged in the Police. We think this is to be deprecated, both on account of the risk inherent in attempting to express another person's meaning in different words, and because the air of sameness thus given to Police evidence tends to create doubts as to its complete accuracy. In this connection, whilst we attach most importance to the statements of accused persons, we would add that in exceptional cases it may be necessary to take the same precautions with regard to statements made by essential witnesses. Q. 1898<br>Q. 6009

91. We therefore recommend that the instructions issued to the Police as to the method of taking down statements should aim at ensuring that, in all cases in which there is a likelihood of the statement being subsequently tendered in evidence against the deponent, both questions and answers should be taken down as nearly as possible in the actual words used, rather than be paraphrased into official Police language.*

---

* In this connection the following extract from an article, published in the *Justice of the Peace*, vol. XCII, p. 792 (8th Dec., 1928) is of some interest :—

"The Police method has its advantages and its disadvantages. It produces a concise and readable narrative that is easily followed by those who will have to read it and consider it as a basis of action. It has the vice of all narrative, the loss of some of the essential truth of the story, because truth is many-sided and complex, not successfully to be run into a mould of rather stilted language. What happens has a counterpart in depositions taken in court. One deposition taker will produce a smooth and, on paper, convincing narrative, yet one impossible to connect with the actual mind and tongue of the witness in the box; another will manage, in reporting the witness's words, to get on to the paper something of the witness's attitude towards the case, a touch of his personality, above all some of these vivid expressions which show up as telling the veritable things seen and heard by the one who is testifying. It is bad enough to lose all tone and facial expression. To add the distorting medium of another's mind and phraseology is to introduce a further source of misunderstanding.

"The leading question is the most insidious enemy of truth. Making a statement and accepting one are not the same thing. How often in court does a witness accept counsel's statement when put to him. Presently he makes another statement, this time of his own, inconsistent with the earlier one, and is genuinely surprised to be told he has just said the opposite. In fact he has not done so; he has only accepted the opposite, either because his mind is naturally not alert enough to notice what he is doing, or because he is tired."

70952

36

(iii) *Length of time occupied in the taking of statements.*

92. Allegations have been made as to the length of time occupied in the taking of statements by the Police, and it has been suggested that the examination of witnesses and suspects has sometimes been deliberately prolonged in order to extract admissions from them. This matter is touched upon in Chapter X, and we will only say, here, that in our view there is a real danger that a person may, through exhaustion, give misleading and unreliable answers at the end of a long interview.

6447.
The suggestions which have been made to us with a view to meeting these allegations commonly involve the setting up of some form of time limit, beyond which interrogations should not be permitted to continue. With the exception of that of the Howard League for Penal Reform, which took as the permissible maximum in any one day the period of five hours (with an interval) which represents a normal Court session, all these suggestions propose some quite arbitrary period of time, bearing no relation to any existing practice.

93. Any proposal for a fixed time limit seems to us to be open to two fatal objections.

In the first place the capacity to make a statement and to answer questions varies according to the sex, temperament, or state of health of the individual, and the subject matter of the enquiry. Unless the limit is placed absurdly low, the time allowed will be too long for some people and unnecessarily short for others.

Secondly, we think that the fixing of a time limit might implant in the Police a belief that, provided the limit was not exceeded, it was not necessary to watch for any signs of fatigue in the deponent. It might even act as a direct incentive to a Police officer to press his questions unduly, when the prescribed period was drawing to an end, in order to secure admissions which seemed to be in sight or to avoid the inconvenience and delay of an adjournment.

94. We therefore regard any proposals for a time limit as inappropriate and dangerous and we think that the length of time occupied in the taking of statements must be left to the discretion of the Police. We recommend, however, that the following general instructions should be issued for their guidance in this matter.

(i) The Police should watch the deponent for signs of fatigue and offer a break (with or without refreshments) at suitable intervals, or even a postponement until the following day.

(ii) If a statement is of sufficient importance to make it desirable that the deponent should sign it, he should not be asked to do so immediately on the conclusion of a lengthy or fatiguing interview. In any case reading over is

37

often a delusive safeguard, particularly if the statement is read out to the deponent by the Police—a procedure which should be confined to cases where the prisoner is illiterate.  Ample time is also necessary, as, even in the case of an educated person, it is only by slowly reading a statement to himself and pondering every line, that he can be sure whether or not it accurately represents what he has said or meant to say.

Moreover, if statements of this kind are to be really " voluntary," and therefore admissible in evidence, the person making them should retain the right either to amend or withdraw them before being called upon to append his signature.  If therefore the Police wish the deponent to sign a statement they should, except when it is of a very brief or simple character, offer him ample time (extending if necessary to the next day) to consider, and if he so desires to amend it, before signing; a copy being meanwhile retained by the Police.

(iii) The times of starting and finishing any statement, and of any breaks, also the time and date of signature, should invariably be recorded as part of the statement itself, and if the latter is signed by the deponent these details should also be initialled by him.

(iv) *Persons present during the taking of statements.*

95. In most cases persons who are to be interviewed by the Police are allowed, if they so desire, to be accompanied by a friend or legal adviser.  There is general agreement that, whenever possible, this is a desirable practice, on the ground that it is bad policy to make unnecessary mysteries and that the greater confidence engendered by the presence of a friend of the deponent is in the best interests of all concerned.

There are, however, certain types of cases in which this practice would be open to grave objection.  For example, the third party present at an interview can be under no effective obligation to maintain secrecy, and in the case of a crime committed by more than one person there would be the risk that any friend attending the interrogation might thereby be enabled to warn confederates or procure the destruction of evidence which the Police were seeking.  There is also a risk of the examination following a course unforeseen by the deponent and leading to disclosures which he would not wish his friend to hear.

96. For these reasons we think it impossible to lay down any rule that friends or legal advisers should be present when statements are being taken by the Police from persons not in custody, but we think that in the many cases where their attendance can be open to no objection the deponent should always be offered the option of having them present.  Some person other than the Police should always be present with any child under 16 from whom a statement is being taken.  The subject of

70952

38

statements by women and children in sexual cases is dealt with in Chapter IX.

97. The presence of a friend or legal adviser often has the advantage of giving confidence to the deponent. There is the further consideration that if no one is present but the Police taking the statement and the deponent, and if any subsequent dispute arises as to the manner in which the statement was taken, it may be difficult to decide which of the two conflicting accounts of what took place should be given credence. We have had legal evidence to the effect that in such cases there would be far less difficulty in ascertaining the truth of what occurred if Counsel for the defence had the opportunity of comparing in cross-examination the accounts of two or more Police officers. In any case we do not think that the Police should be left in the position that there should be no means of testing allegations as to improper pressure, made by a deponent, and we therefore recommend that a second officer should always be present, if possible, when a statement is being taken which may ultimately be tendered in evidence, although, in our view, only one officer should be permitted to ask the questions.

### Unwilling Witnesses.

98. It is the duty of every law-abiding citizen, when appealed to by constituted authority, to give every information in his power. But, as we have shown, there is no power in law to compel persons to answer questions put to them by the Police. Apart from this, although a person can in some circumstances be punished for refusing information, there is (on the principle that you may take a horse to water but be unable to make him drink) no possible means of compelling him to speak. If a witness who has information relevant to a criminal prosecution is unwilling to say what he knows, there is no power whereby he can be compelled to do so until the case is heard in open Court, when he can be called on subpoena or witness summons and required to answer in the witness box any questions which are held by the Court to be proper.

It is, however, a somewhat embarrassing proceeding for prosecuting Counsel to put a witness into the box without knowing what he will say, and the examination-in-chief of such a witness presents special difficulties. In present circumstances either this difficulty must be faced or the case must be conducted without relying on the evidence of the witness.

99. A more serious difficulty presents itself in certain cases in which there is no power to arrest without a warrant, and it is therefore necessary to apply to the magistrate for the issue of such warrant. It sometimes happens that the Police know that a certain person is in possession of evidence as to the commission of a crime, but that he refuses to give any information. As a subpoena cannot be issued until process is obtained, an

*impasse* results and it may become impossible for the Police to prosecute the offender.

We have been informed by the Director of Public Prosecutions that " such an *impasse* occurs far more often than is suspected " Q. 1220. and we have carefully considered whether any practicable means can be devised which would solve this difficulty. As a result of much inquiry, we have come to the conclusion that the only effective solution of this problem would be the grant by statute of powers under which a summons could be issued requiring a person, believed to be in possession of material information, to attend before a magistrate before the issue of process and to be examined on oath, with penalties for neglect to obey the summons or to answer questions put to him.

100. The grant of such powers, which was specifically recommended by the Talbot Committee* in 1924, would undoubtedly meet the difficulty to which we have referred and we are aware that provisions of this nature already exist in Scotland and in Canada, and in this country in the special case of the Explosives Substances Act, 1883.

Any such proposal, however, would involve a serious alteration of the existing law and we believe that there would be political and other difficulties in reconciling the grant of such powers with the spirit of our criminal procedure, despite the fact that stringent powers of the same kind are already given to Customs and Excise officers, and inspectors under various Acts†, who are inquiring into breaches of the law or regulations.

We have given this matter most careful consideration, and whilst we agree that such powers would on occasion prove to be of great value, we have come to the conclusion that, on balance, we should not feel justified in recommending special legislation to deal with witnesses who are unwilling to give information to the Police.

---

* Report of Committee appointed to review the provisions of the Restoration of Order in Ireland Act, 1920, etc. (Cmd. 2278 of 1924).

† e.g. Factory and Workshop Acts, National Health Insurance Acts, Aliens Acts.

40

DUTIES OF THE POLICE IN THE INVESTIGATON OF CRIMES AND
OFFENCES — OBTAINING OF EVIDENCE (PART II).

101. We have dealt at some length in the preceding Chapter
with the taking of statements from persons not in custody, since
this forms an important duty of the Police in the investigation of
crimes and offences and has given rise to many difficult questions.
In this Chapter we propose to refer to certain other matters concerning the duties of the Police in the obtaining of evidence.

### Use of Police in Plain Clothes.

102. The use of plain clothes Police is essential in some circumstances for the investigation and detection of crime and for
certain types of observation work. The extent to which they
should be used is a matter which must be left to the discretion
of superior officers of the Police, but we think that so far as
possible only officers who are actually engaged on detective
work should wear plain clothes.

103. We understand in this connection that it is a common
practice to employ plain clothes officers to work in pairs, for the
purpose of obtaining information as to certain types of offences.
The fact that Policemen are employed in plain clothes exposes
them to greater temptations than when they are in uniform.
For this reason there is an advantage in not using plain clothes
officers singly, but the prolonged partnership of the same two
officers largely nullifies the safeguards which the presence of a
second officer affords. We therefore recommend that a system of
frequent interchange should be adopted, in order that the same
two officers should not work together indefinitely.

We have no further general observations to offer on the employment of Police in plain clothes, but we deal, in the ensuing
sections of this Chapter and in Chapter VII, with their employment on certain special types of duty.

### " Agents Provocateurs."

104. The allegation that the Police are occasionally employed
as *agents provocateurs* arises, in all probability, from the methods
which they are forced to adopt to obtain evidence in certain
types of cases.

This allegation is usually made in somewhat general terms
and it is rare to find any attempt to define the objectionable
features of the practice complained of, although the use of a
foreign phrase for which there is no exact English equivalent
indicates that the practice is regarded as alien to our habits and
traditions. We assume that an *agent provocateur* may be taken
to mean a person who entices another to commit an express

41

breach of the law which he would not otherwise have committed,
and then proceeds or informs against him in respect of such
offence.   As it is the primary duty of a constable to *prevent*
the commission of crimes and offences, any conduct on his part
leading to the commission of offences would be highly repre-
hensible, and we have been at pains to inquire whether the
methods adopted by the Police in the investigation of crimes and
offences afford any foundation for such allegations as have been
made.

105. It is the bounden duty of the Police to enforce the law,
notwithstanding the difficulties that may be encountered in the
obtaining of evidence on which prosecutions can be instituted.
The offences in regard to which such difficulties most frequently
arise are drinking in licensed premises or clubs during prohibited
hours, betting in licensed premises, street betting, offences
against the Shop Hours Acts, and cases of clairvoyants or for-
tune tellers.

The Police cannot expect to obtain evidence from those who
take part in these offences.   It is also unlikely that persons who
are present when these offences are committed, but who did not
participate in them, will, except in rare instances, be willing
to give evidence on which a prosecution can be based.   It is
therefore necessary that the Police should be present at the
time when these offences are committed, without their identity
being known.

106. The issue which at once presents itself is what action,
if any, a Policeman may properly take beyond concealing his
identity and observing what goes on.   We have found two clearly
marked schools of thought on this subject which are reflected
in a division of opinion among the Police themselves.

One school holds that the duty of the Police should Q. 1006,
be strictly confined to observation only and that they Q. 3164/101
should not participate in the offences committed.   It was said
by one responsible supporter of this view that it must be a poor Q. 3851.
case if the Police cannot obtain evidence by observation only,
and that there was a danger that a Policeman who participated
in the offence might unconsciously induce others to participate
who would not otherwise have done so.

# [4]

Journal of Police Science and Administration
Copyright ©1987 by IACP, Inc.

Volume 15, No. 2
Printed in U.S.A.

# Perceptions of Organizational Performance in Suburban Police Departments: A Critique of the Military Model

## Verl Franz and David M. Jones

Verl Franz is a retired assistant professor of sociology, University of Wisconsin, Oshkosh. He received his Ph.D. in sociology from Michigan State University. For many years, Dr. Franz was affiliated with the Division of Governmental Projects of the Industrial Relations Center, University of Chicago. His main area of interest is applied sociology.

David M. Jones is an assistant professor of political science, University of Wisconsin, Oshkosh, WI 54901. He received his Ph.D. in political science from the University of Kansas. Dr. Jones has been published in both the *Justice Professional* and the *American Journal of Criminal Justice*.

A pervasive feature of American police departments in the twentieth century has been their use of the military or quasi-military model of organization. This pattern of organization was adopted in the earlier part of the century because of the need, perceived by the "first generation of reformers," to root out corruption, sever ties with big-city political machines, and wage an effective "war" on the criminality that was thought to infest the cities of the day (Fogelson 1977). While many of the factors that precipitated the felt need for such a means of organization appear to have declined, the model has remained popular with law enforcement agencies. Indeed, one prominent observer of the police has asserted that the model is so pervasive that it has been largely taken for granted by many in the field (Bittner 1980).

However, in the recent past many commentators have criticized this form of organization as being inappropriate for the needs of modern police departments and the educated personnel they are seeking to recruit and retain. For instance, such an organizational model is accused of discouraging upward communication and risk taking by patrol officers, while at the same time encouraging the development of authoritarianism in such officers (Sandler and Mintz 1974). It has also been charged with undermining the morale of front-line personnel (Goldstein 1977), in part because it adds to the demoralizing and dysfunctional uncertainties that face many urban police officers (McNamara 1967).

On this point, Cordner (1978, p. 30) has been especially emphatic. He has written that the dominant organizational approach in police departments has caused many problems:

> Among these are feelings of demoralization and powerlessness in the lower ranks, a conception of top command as arbitrary, a growing cynicism among supervisory and middle-management personnel, and the subsequent development of a we/they attitude toward top management. . . . Ideas are stifled, officers are not confident of the support of top management, and the CYA syndrome takes hold.

The military model has been criticized, too, for deterring the development of a much-desired professionalism in police departments because of the alleged inhibitions it puts on departmental civilianization and restrictions on lateral entry (Staufenburger 1977). It has also been held to be inappropriate for the highly discretionary method of operation inherent in police work (Bittner 1980) as well as for the effective handling of the new breed of better-educated officers (Bopp 1975). Finally, such an "authoritarian" means of organization may, it has been suggested, add to the already stressful life that is the lot of the typical police officer (Smith and Ward 1983).

Thus, in the eyes of a large number of commentators, the military model has been largely discredited. In fact, the author of an influential text on police administration has asserted that it is imperative that police organizations move from their present state toward a more "organic" structure of operations (Roberg 1979).

However, it is very important to note here that these assertions about the deficiencies of the military model appear to lack much supporting systematic empirical data. Though it is *asserted* that the military model encourages, or at least is associated with, poor intra-organizational communications, lack of trust, and a consequent demoralization of police officers, little "hard" data is cited to substantiate these charges. While studies of other organizations have suggested that greater amounts of hierarchy are often associated with decreased communications effectiveness (Katz and Kahn 1978), that better communications seem to encourage higher levels of trust within an organization (Golembieski and McConkie 1975; Gaines 1980), that greater amounts of trust encourage more effective problem solving (Zand 1972), and that more open organizational systems—with their higher degrees of participation—are often associated with higher degrees of employee satisfaction (Marrett, Hage, and Aiken 1975; Evan 1977; Greenberg 1980), the authors are aware of few studies of *police* institutions that would substantiate in a systematic, empirical fashion the allegations put forth by critics of the quasi-military model (for a partial exception, see Harrison 1975).

What this present study will do is to help fill this gap in the literature by providing empirical evidence which suggests that there is, indeed, substance to the critics' charges. That is, we will show that, compared to employees in other urban bureaucracies (none of which have been inflicted with the quasi-military format of organization), police officers in a number of suburbs of Chicago did perceive the existence of many of the pathologies associated with this unique form of organization. The data herein presented comes from a larger study developed when, in 1969, the "Public Service Improvement Inventory" (PSII) was administered by the Division of Governmental Projects of the Industrial Relations Center, then associated with the University of Chicago (an organization that the senior author was associated with at the time of the study), to a number of bureaucracies in four Chicago suburbs. While these data may appear "dated" it is important to note that they were collected prior to the time when the quasi-military model came under attack and when, as a consequence, some police departments sought to modify their organization. In this sense it constitutes a better test of the deficiencies of the tradi-

tional patterns of police organization than would data collected at a later point in time.

## THE PSII AND THE SAMPLE

### The PSII

The questionnaire contains slightly over eighty questions. These can be grouped into twelve categories concerned with various elements of work, employee motivation, and employee morale. The categories include: work organization, work efficiency, administrative effectiveness, leadership practices, communications effectiveness, personnel development, pay and benefits, immediate supervision, work associates, job satisfaction, organization identification, and reactions to the survey itself. All questions could be answered "agree," "neither agree nor disagree," or "disagree." The questionnaire was used as a diagnostic instrument. After the questionnaires were administered, "profiles" of answers were charted for the respective departments. These profiles could then be compared to similar organizations in different communities, different organizations in the same communities, and to norms established from surveys of other organizations. This information was then fed back to management personnel in the different departments in the various cities for their use (*Management Information Service* 1969).

The value of this instrument for our purposes is that it asks a number of questions directly relevant to some of our concerns.[1]

### The Sample

The questionnaire was distributed to a total of 557 city employees, 120 of whom were police officers. The sample included department heads, mid-level managers, and first-line employees in the Chicago suburbs of Glencoe, Lake Forest, Northbrook, and Winnetka, Illinois. Employee organizations surveyed included, in addition to police officers, firefighters, utility workers, and a rather all-inclusive group of "others." This last category included people who worked in the libraries, on the golf course, and in the cemeteries of these communities. Those to whom the questionnaire was administered constituted virtually all of the full-

---

[1]This questionnaire is on record in the Political Science Department, UW Oshkosh. For permission to use it for research contact Professor David Jones, UW Oshkosh, Oshkosh, WI 54901.

time employees of the above-named cities at this point in time.

Since the military model is not a part of the tradition of these other bureaucracies, a comparison of the responses of these workers with those of police officers can shed light on the impact of the military model on certain aspects of law enforcement. This comparison shows that, in many ways, critics who question the military model of police organization seem to have made some valid criticisms.

## THE DATA

One can summarize much of the criticism of the traditional model of police organizations alluded to earlier in the following way: because the model emphasizes decision making and order giving at the top and order receiving and order executing at the bottom, communication problems (especially of the "upward" variety) result. This problem is exacerbated by the "punishment" orientation (McNamara 1967) characteristic of many police departments, a feature which may be inherent in the military model. These factors also combine to decrease the amount of trust between front-line and upper-level management personnel. In part because of these pathologies, morale problems arise. These, in turn, lead to a situation where the organization is, or is perceived to be, operating in a less than optimal fashion. The argument is schematized in figure 1. Does this happen to police organizations in our sample? Put another way, are there problems perceived to be more operative in police than in the other bureaucracies in the study? These elements will be examined in turn.

In order to examine this question the responses of the police officers of these four communities to a number of questions on the PSII will be compared to those of other city workers. The "test"[2] will be used to determine if the percentage of favorable responses between these two groups is statistically significant. A significance level of .05 or less is utilized.[3]

### Communications

A number of questions on the PSII dealt with the nature and effectiveness of communications in various city bureaucracies in the sample. These included:

> Little effort is made to get the opinions and thinking of the people who work here.

> Most of the time it is safe to say what you think around here.

> The city does an excellent job of keeping us informed about matters affecting us.

> We usually hear about important matters first through the grapevine.

---

[2]Significance of the Difference Between Proportions.
[3]Exact probability values are reported.

FIGURE 1

A SCHEMATIC REPRESENTATION OF THE PATHOLOGIES
OF THE "MILITARY MODEL" OF POLICE ORGANIZATIONS

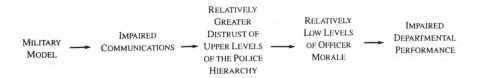

We get all the information we need on city policies and practices.

As the different responses of police compared to other city officials to these questions (found in table 1) indicate, the first charge against the military model appears to be correct. For example, the police in this sample tended to feel that upward communication was not encouraged in their organization. In fact, they felt rather insecure about even trying to communicate with their superiors. Moreover, as their responses to the last three questions in table 1 show, they were also decidedly unhappy with the city-wide nature of "downward" communications in their police departments. On all of these items, the members of the various police departments were, in a statistical sense, significantly less likely to give positive responses than were members of other city bureaucracies. Moreover, in no instance did a majority of the police respondents give a positive answer to these questions. In fact, in a number of cases, about three-fourths of the officers polled responded negatively. In effect, then, for this sample at least, the criticism of the military model appears to hold true as applied to the issue of communications. Communication was not perceived to be as effective in police organizations as in other public bureaucracies.

## Trust

Are these poor communications practices associated with relatively low levels of trust in police organizations, as alleged by some critics? Again, a number of questions on the PSII can be used to answer this. These include:

The decisions management makes are fair to everyone.

I think my performance on the job is judged fairly here.

I sometimes doubt what management tells us is true.

I am confident that my responses will be kept confidential.

As table 2 indicates, here again there is evidence to confirm the criticisms of the military model. For instance, the responses to the first two questions show a lack of trust in the willingness and/or the ability of members of the police hierarchy to treat lower levels fairly. Police officers also showed in their responses to the last two questions that they were less trusting of the veracity of their superiors than were other city employ-

TABLE 1

A COMPARISON OF THE PERCEIVED EFFECTIVENESS OF
ORGANIZATIONAL COMMUNICATIONS, POLICE VS. OTHER CITY WORKERS

|  |  | % Favorable | T | P |
|---|---|---|---|---|
| "Little effort is made to get the opinions and thinking of the people who work here." | Police Others | 25 42 | − 3.41 | .001 |
| "Most of the time it is safe to say what you think around here." | Police Others | 35 50 | − 2.85 | .005 |
| "The city does an excellent job of keeping us informed about matters affecting us." | Police Others | 23 45 | − 4.26 | .000 |
| "We usually hear about important matters first through the grapevine." | Police Others | 11 30 | − 4.24 | .000 |
| "We get all the information we need on city policies and practices." | Police Others | 31 46 | − 2.93 | .004 |

TABLE 2

A COMPARISON OF THE LEVELS OF INTRAORGANIZATIONAL TRUST,
POLICE VS. OTHER CITY WORKERS

|  |  | %<br>Favorable | T | P |
|---|---|---|---|---|
| "The decisions management makes are fair to everyone." | Police<br>Others | 26<br>38 | −2.55 | .001 |
| "I think my performance on the job is judged fairly here." | Police<br>Others | 47<br>66 | −3.84 | .000 |
| "I sometimes doubt what management tells us is true." | Police<br>Others | 41<br>57 | −3.19 | .002 |
| "I am confident that my responses will be kept confidential." | Police<br>Others | 76<br>81 | −1.37 | .167 |

ees. Moreover, the differences in the responses of the two groups in the sample were large. On the first three questions members of the police departments were, to a statistically significant degree, less likely to give a positive answer to the questions asked than were other city employees. Moreover, in none of these three questions was a majority of the police respondents willing to give a positive answer. It is only on the last question in table 2 that a majority was willing to respond affirmatively.[4] Furthermore, in this table, it is only on this question that the differences are not statistically significant. Thus, the police were far less trusting than were members of other occupations. It might also be noted that this response is in line with the observation of McNamara (1967) that his sample of New York City police officers did not trust his assurance that they were not being "marked" by the fact that they were being questioned by him. In sum, the police in our sample appeared to be less trusting of their managerial officials than were members of other urban bureaucracies. Thus, it may well be that the suspicion and cynicism found by so many observers to be part of the patrol officer's "working personality" (Skolnick 1967) may be a response not only to events that take place on the street, but also to conditions that are found in the department.

---

[4]This may be more of a function of the researcher's guarantee of confidentiality than of the attitude expressed about the department.

**Morale**

There is also evidence to suggest that, compared to other city employees, the police in the communities under study had some morale problems. A number of questions relating to morale issues were asked in the survey. Among these were the following:

A few of the people in my department think they run the place.

I seldom feel I am really part of what goes on around here.

Management here is interested in the welfare of its people.

Management fails to take action on our complaints.

There are good opportunities here for those who want to get ahead.

In my opinion, the people who get promotions around here deserve them.

An examination of this table indicates that, again, the critics of the traditional police organization model have made a valid point. That is, in their responses to all of these questions, police officers were less likely than other city employees to display good feelings about their place in their organization. As their responses to the first two questions indicate, police tended to feel that they were not part of their department's decision-making apparatus and, as was alluded

TABLE 3

A COMPARISON OF LEVELS OF MORALE IN THE ORGANIZATION,
POLICE VS. OTHER CITY WORKERS

|  |  | %<br>Favorable | T | P |
|---|---|---|---|---|
| "A few people in my department think they<br>run the place." | Police<br>Others | 34<br>48 | − 2.62 | .009 |
| "I seldom feel I am really part of what goes on<br>around here." | Police<br>Others | 54<br>59 | − .87 | .391 |
| "Management here is interested in the<br>welfare of its people." | Police<br>Others | 39<br>56 | − 3.33 | .001 |
| "Management fails to take action on our<br>complaints." | Police<br>Others | 27<br>43 | − 3.16 | .002 |
| "There are good opportunities here for those<br>who want to get ahead." | Police<br>Others | 30<br>47 | − 3.36 | .001 |
| "In my opinion, the people who get<br>promotions around here deserve them." | Police<br>Others | 27<br>59 | − 6.22 | .000 |

to earlier, this situation does not enhance morale levels in an organization. Moreover, as many of these items indicate, the members of the police bureaucracy were much more likely than others to see management as uncaring and capricious. Finally, their responses indicate that they felt their chances of moving up in the organization were relatively limited, in part because they saw factors other than competence as being operative in this regard.

Moreover, the charge that many of these problems stem from a lack of communications in the quasi-military police organization is strengthened when one looks at responses to questions dealing with the performance of immediate supervisors. These include the following:

My supervisor is often unfair in his dealings with me.

My supervisor ought to be friendlier toward his people.

My supervisor gives us credit for very good work.

My supervisor keeps his promises.

My supervisor tries to get our ideas about things.

My supervisor puts things off; he just lets things slide.

My supervisor has the work in our group well organized.

As table 4 indicates, police department personnel rank their immediate supervisors about the same way as do members of other bureaucracies. That is, both groups gave generally positive evaluations of middle-management personnel. In other words they saw this group of officials as being generally fair, honest, open, and competent. However, unlike other city workers, police became suspicious about the motives and capabilities of those ensconced in higher bureaucratic echelons. Is it possible that this suspicion is related to the poor communication perceived in these quasi-military organizations? Certainly, that is what the model suggests.

**Effectiveness**

Finally, the model derived from the criticisms of the traditional police organizations holds that there will be a reduced level of agency effectiveness because of the above-mentioned pathologies. Is this the case in our sample? To be more exact, were police department

TABLE 4

A COMPARISON OF ATTITUDES TOWARD IMMEDIATE
SUPERVISORS, POLICE VS. OTHER CITY WORKERS

|  |  | %<br>Favorable | T | P |
|---|---|---|---|---|
| "My supervisor is often unfair in his dealings with me." | Police<br>Others | 79<br>70 | 1.84 | .063 |
| "My supervisor ought to be friendlier toward his people." | Police<br>Others | 65<br>58 | 1.32 | .185 |
| "My supervisor gives us credit for very good work." | Police<br>Others | 79<br>71 | 1.84 | .063 |
| "My supervisor keeps his promises." | Police<br>Others | 62<br>65 | − .60 | .557 |
| "My supervisor tries to get our ideas about things." | Police<br>Others | 56<br>59 | − .63 | .536 |
| "My supervisor puts things off; he just lets things slide." | Police<br>Others | 57<br>61 | − .79 | .438 |
| "My supervisor has the work in our group well supervised." | Police<br>Others | 54<br>56 | − .33 | .741 |

personnel more likely than others to see performance problems in their organization?

In this case, too, a number of questions dealing with perceptions of agency performance are found in the PSII. Moreover, these items also indicate that criticisms of the military model appear to be on target. Such questions include the following:

This city fails to operate efficiently.

The quality of work done here is excellent.

So far as I can see, management here makes the right decisions.

The way they run things around here makes it difficult for me to do a good job.

A lot is being done here to improve our methods of getting work done.

There is too much red tape which keeps me from doing my work.

We have up-to-date methods of getting work done here.

In my opinion, too much time is wasted around here.

Our office (internal) procedures and practices help us give good service to our citizens.

Here, too, the results (see table 5) show that the police were relatively less likely to give positive answers to these questions. That is, their responses to a number of them indicated that they were more critical of the efficiency and effectiveness of their organization than were other city workers. Furthermore, they were also more likely to feel that departmental procedures stood in the way of their doing the kind of job they would like to do. Finally, they were relatively doubtful about the willingness and ability of their superiors to correct the problems that they saw in the operations of their organization. Here again, the statistics shown in table 5 indicate for the most part a statistically significant difference in the responses of the two groups. Consequently, the last element of our model appears to be vindicated also.

In summary, our empirical evidence suggests that there is a great deal of validity to the criticisms made by many commentators of the quasi-military model that has for so long permeated thinking about police

TABLE 5

A COMPARISON OF PERCEIVED ORGANIZATIONAL EFFECTIVENESS,
POLICE VS. OTHER CITY WORKERS

| | | %<br>Favorable | T | P |
|---|---|---|---|---|
| "This city fails to operate efficiently." | Police<br>Others | 42<br>57 | −3.07 | .002 |
| "The quality of work done here is excellent." | Police<br>Others | 37<br>54 | −3.16 | .002 |
| "So far as I can see, management here makes the right decisions." | Police<br>Others | 23<br>41 | −3.50 | .001 |
| "The way they run things around here makes it difficult for me to do a good job." | Police<br>Others | 42<br>60 | −3.51 | .001 |
| "A lot is being done here to improve our methods of getting work done." | Police<br>Others | 35<br>51 | −3.03 | .003 |
| "There is too much red tape which keeps me from doing my work." | Police<br>Others | 56<br>73 | −3.72 | .000 |
| "We have up-to-date methods of getting work done here." | Police<br>Others | 31<br>54 | −4.54 | .000 |
| "In my opinion, too much time is wasted around here." | Police<br>Others | 38<br>53 | −2.82 | .005 |
| "Our office (internal) procedures and practices help us give good service to our citizens." | Police<br>Others | 48<br>68 | −3.86 | .000 |

organizations in the United States. That is, officers in these suburban communities perceived, in relation to other city employees, the existence of communications problems in their organization. This, in turn, was associated with relatively low levels of trust in the upper management echelons and relatively low levels of morale. Finally, the police also felt, when compared with other city employees, that the organization of which they were a part functioned rather poorly. In summation the data fits our model of organizational pathology quite well. It should be noted, of course, that since this data was collected there have been many efforts to reorganize police departments along different lines. Consequently, research similar to ours relating to the efficiency of these different organizational forms would definitely contribute to a more extensive test of the quasi-military police organizational model.

## CONCLUSION

We began this paper by indicating that, in the past few years, a number of commentators have written many harsh things about the traditional organization of police departments in the United States. They asserted that such an organizational form hindered effective communications among its members. In part because of these poor intraorganizational communications, distrust was engendered between front-line officers and members of the upper elements of the police hierarchy. These poor communications and lack of trust led to morale problems within the organization. Such problems, in turn, hindered effective organizational performance. We further commented that, while such criticisms are intuitively appealing, they have not always been substantiated by hard evidence.

Fortunately, data from the PSII can be used to examine such allegations. When tested, the model constructed from the works of these critics was substantiated. Police organizations in our sample did have relatively greater communications problems; there were relatively greater amounts of distrust, particularly of higher echelons in police departments; there were relatively low levels of morale associated with these phenomena and there were lower perceived levels of organizational performance associated with all these factors.

In conclusion, the data presented in this paper seriously question the capacity of the quasi-military police organizational model to meet today's needs. However, future research needs to be done, using more extensive and representative samples, before the traditional police organization model can be discarded.

In a period of change and experimentation in public administration it would be prudent for future research to be directed toward testing alternative organizational theories and practices in police administration.

Certainly, the "popular inclination" to overgeneralize and overapply the "business organization model and method" to city, county, state, and federal governmental agencies is equally suspect theoretically, administratively, and empirically. If governmental managerial effectiveness in general (and police effectiveness in particular) is to improve, all alternative administrative models demand careful empirical verification.

## REFERENCES

Bittner, E. 1980. *The functions of the police in modern society.* Cambridge: Oelgeschlager, Gunn, & Hain.

Bopp, W.J. 1975. The traditional approach to police organization. In *Police administration: Selected readings,* edited by W.J. Bopp, pp. 79-82. Boston: Holbrook Press.

Cordner, G.W. 1978. Open and closed models in police organizations: Traditions, dilemmas, and practical consideration. *J. Pol. Sci. & Adm.* 6:22-34.

Evan, W.M. 1977. Hierarchy, alienation, commitment, and organizational effectiveness. *Human Relations* 30:77-54.

Fogelson, R.M. 1977. *Big-city police.* Cambridge: Harvard University Press.

Gaines, J.H. 1980. Upward communications in industry: An experiment. *Human Relations* 33:929-942.

Goldstein, H. 1977. *Policing a free society.* Cambridge: Ballinger Publishing Co.

Golembieski, R.T., and McConkie, M. 1975. The centrality of interpersonal trust in group processes. In *Theories of group processes,* edited by C.L. Cooper, pp. 13-186. New York: John Wiley & Sons.

Greenberg, E.S. 1980. Participation in industrial decision-making and work satisfaction: The case of producer cooperatives. *Soc. Sci. Qtrly.* 60:551-569.

Harrison, F. 1975. Bureaucratization: Perceptions of role performance and organizational effectiveness. *J. Pol. Sci. & Adm.* 3:319-326.

Katz, D., and Kahn, R.L. 1978. *The social psychology of organizations,* 2nd ed. New York: John Wiley and Sons.

*Management Information Service.* 1969. Training methods of the University of Chicago Industrial Relations Center. 1:16.

McNamara, J.H. 1967. Uncertainties in police work: The relevance of police recruits' backgrounds and training. In *The police: Six sociological essays,* edited by D.J. Bordua, pp. 163-252. New York: John Wiley and Sons.

Marret, C.; Hage, J.; and Aileen, M. 1975. Communication and satisfaction in organizations. *Human Relations* 28:612-626.

Roberg, R.R. 1979. *Police management and organizational behavior: A contingency approach.* St. Paul: West Publishing Company.

Sandler, G.; Benner, H.; and Mintz, E. 1974. Police organizations: Their changing internal and external relationships. *J. Pol. Sci. & Adm.* 2:458-463.

Skolnick, J. 1967. *Justice without trial: Law enforcement in a democratic society.* New York: John Wiley and sons.

Smith, B.L., and Ward, R.M. 1983. Stress of military and civilian personnel: A comparative analysis. *Amer. J. Pol.* 3:111-117.

Staufenberger, R.A. 1977. The professionalization of police: Efforts and obstacles. *Pub. Adm. Rev.* 37:678-685.

Zand, D.E. 1972. Trust and managerial problem solving. *Adm. Sci. Qtrly.* 17:229-239.

# [5]

Professional Psychology: Research and Practice
1988, Vol. 19, No. 4, 421–425

# National Survey of the Extent and Nature of Psychological Services in Police Departments

Robert P. Delprino
Old Dominion University

Charles Bahn
John Jay College of Criminal Justice
City University of New York

In this study, through a national survey of municipal and State police departments, we identified the current use, perceived need, and anticipated future use of psychological services by police agencies. Of the 336 police agencies invited to participate in the survey, 232, which included 193 municipal and 39 state police departments, returned completed questionnaires. We make comparisons with a previous study conducted in 1979, which covered much of the same ground but on a smaller scope. A principal finding of our study is the substantial growth in the current use of psychological services in police departments. Areas of projected change in the use of psychological services are presented.

Recent legal and social developments have defined new roles for psychologists working with law enforcement agencies and have substantiated current existing roles. Police organizations must deal with the possibility of being held negligently responsible for the inappropriate actions of employees who had not been adequately trained for the job. Also, a police department may be found negligent for accepting individuals who are not psychologically fit for the position or for jeopardizing the public by retaining police officers who are not functioning adequately. Psychologists can assist by screening and testing applicants to determine their probable future success as police officers, or can apply therapeutic skills to help officers cope with the stressful nature of their job (Stratton, 1980).

To all levels of society, the police are the visible symbol of the legal system and may often be the only element of the criminal justice system with which a major segment of the population ever comes into contact. Changes in societal and organizational expectations of the police have enhanced the role of police officers as providers of social services. Heightened awareness of the potential role of social institutions in determining the general quality of life has led to recognition of the police as a major help-giving resource to the community (Mann, 1980). The majority of the modern police officer's duty time is dedicated to some type of interpersonal service

or maintaining order; a small percentage of duty time involves actual law enforcement or crime investigation (Bard, 1969; Wilson, 1968). In addition to the traditional skills of police work, the officer is expected to be knowledgeable in other areas such as dealing with the mentally ill, rape victims, and family disputes and assessing suicide risk. The police officer has come to be seen as an applied primary prevention professional who requires the knowledge and skills of the behavioral sciences.

The recognition of the stressful nature of police work has also led to psychologists' involvement in police agencies. The police officer functions in a highly supervised situation in which an elaborate set of legal and organizational guidelines limit autonomy. At the same time, the officer on patrol is required to make critical decisions with little opportunity for supervision or consultation with an expert. The modern police officer functions daily as an executive in a wide variety of situations (Reiser, 1974). These situations are rarely well structured and do not neatly conform to a preconceived letter of the law. However in all circumstances, an officer is expected to take appropriate action and operate within accepted legal boundaries. Failure to do so may result in a department reprimand or have more serious consequences such as endangering oneself, a partner, or a member of the public. There is no room for minor mistakes.

The increased involvement of psychologists in police work is indicative of the recognition by both police administrators and psychologists of the expertise needed to deal with the many difficult issues confronting police organizations. The many potential contributions of psychologists to law enforcement have been presented by Brodsky (1972), Reiser (1972) and Loo (1986). These and other recent reports (Chandler, 1986; Fisher, 1986; Gents, 1986; Green, 1986; Swink & Altman, 1986) provide a thorough description of the various uses of psychologists in law enforcement agencies. The majority of the reports are based on personal experience in specific police departments, or are speculations about the potential role of psychologists in police work. They do not, however, present a representative account of psychologists' involvement in police agencies nationally.

ROBERT P. DELPRINO is a doctoral candidate in industrial/organizational psychology at Old Dominion University. He received a master's degree in forensic psychology from the John Jay College of Criminal Justice of the City University of New York in 1986. His areas of interest include police psychology and the application of industrial/organizational psychology to the criminal justice system.

CHARLES BAHN is Professor and Graduate Coordinator in the Department of Psychology at John Jay College of Criminal Justice of the City University of New York. His areas of interest are organizational psychology and its application to police, corrections, probations, and other aspects of the criminal justice system.

CORRESPONDENCE CONCERNING THIS ARTICLE should be addressed to Robert P. Delprino, Department of Psychology, Old Dominion University, Norfolk, Virginia 23508.

In this study, through a national survey, we identified the current use, perceived need, and anticipated future use of psychological services by urban and state police agencies.

The only published study to date in which the researchers attempted to identify the then-current use and perceived needs for psychological services by large urban police agencies nationally was conducted in 1979 (Parisher, Rios, & Reilley, 1979). Those authors, on the basis of the survey results, predicted a minimal future use of psychological services in police departments. They reported that of the 112 departments that responded to the question concerning future use, only 18% indicated plans to enlarge or start psychological services in the next two years; 62% had no such plans, and 21% did not know.

There is a discrepancy between those findings and the general positive trend that is indicated by the literature on this topic. The literature indicates a high level of interest in the use of psychological services by police officers and agencies (Brown, Burkhart, King, & Solomon, 1977; Burkhart, 1980; Somodevilla, 1978). In addition, the use of psychological services is perceived as a needed area of growth (Engle, 1974; Keller, 1978; Loo, 1986; Reiser, 1978; Wagner, 1976). There exists an obvious need for studies in which the current extent and nature of psychological services in police departments is investigated on a broad base.

## Method

### Subjects

The sampling frame consisted of 287 large municipal police agencies and the 49 primary state police agencies. (The state of Hawaii is unique in that it does not have a state police organization.) Municipal agencies included in this study were police departments administered by a municipality that served a population of 100,000 or greater. The source used for city selection was the *Statistical Abstracts of the United States, 1984* (United States Bureau of the Census, 1983). Primary state police agencies consisted of departments that are administered by the state and have general law enforcement authority throughout the state. These agencies were titled Division of Public Safety, Highway Patrol, or State Police. Of the 336 police agencies invited to participate in the survey, 232 (69%) of the departments returned completed questionnaires. The respondents included 193 municipal police departments and 39 state police agencies.

### Procedure

The questionnaire, "Psychological Services in Police Departments Questionnaire," which we developed for this study, consists of 17 items. From a review of the literature on the use of psychological services by police agencies, we compiled a list of the 25 most commonly cited services (see Table 1), and it served as the basis for four questions about the department's current use, perceived need, future use, and providers of psychological services. The remaining questions concerned the agency's plans to enlarge or implement the use of psychological services in the next 2 years, qualifications required of the providers of services, the obstacles and advantages related to the use of these services, and the job title of the individual who completed the questionnaire.

Five judges with experience in the criminal justice system, police work, or test construction were instructed to review the questionnaire for content, clarity, and ease of response. We made minor modifications that included altering item presentation so that less threatening questions, such as number of officers employed and current use of services, preceded questions dealing with future use of and obstacles to the use of psychological services.

Initially the survey instrument was sent to the chiefs of police of the 336 agencies in the sample. A second mailing was sent to nonrespondents 5 weeks after the initial mailing. In the cover letter that accompanied the questionnaire, we instructed that the survey be completed by a member of the psychological service branch of the department or other appropriate personnel. In the survey instrument we requested the job title of the person who completed the questionnaire. Of the 232 respondents to the survey, 224 identified their job titles. The job titles ranged from Sergeant (assigned to the psychological services unit) to the mayor of the city. The more frequent titles included Chief of Police, Police Legal Advisor, Psychologist, Coordinator of Psychological Services, and Personnel Director.

Telephone interviews were conducted with a selection of the municipal and state police agencies who did not respond to either of the two mailings. The purpose of the structured telephone interview was to determine whether the content of responses of the nonrespondent group was similar in its variability to that of the respondents, or whether any consistent bias resulted from these agencies' refusal to participate in the study. The tenor of nonrespondents' experiences and attitudes of psychological services were similar to those of respondents. Agencies indicated that their inability to respond to the initial inquiry was due to changes in administration or the processing of new recruits that were occurring when the questionnaire was received.

## Results

Results are reported by percentage, indicating the variability of responses to each item.

We made an initial inquiry of the specific qualifications of those who provide services in police departments; slightly more than one third (36.92%) of 214 respondents to the question did not specify qualifications of providers of psychological services. For the 135 agencies that indicated specific requirements for providers of psychological services, the preference was toward licensed psychologists with a clinical background. The most frequently cited group of providers of psychological services were consultants. Doctoral-level psychologists, the most frequently used consultants (40.60%), were also identified as the primary providers of each of the 25 psychological services presented in the questionnaire.

More than one half of the departments reported the use of psychological services for the assessment of recruits and to provide personal, family, and job-related stress counseling.

In terms of general use, the range of training functions currently provided by mental health professionals includes training in crisis intervention (41.15% of 226 respondents), hostage negotiations (35.39% of 226), and handling both suicide situations (30.40% of 227) and the mentally ill (36.89% of 225). Other services used by more than a third of responding departments include special examinations for suspended and problem police officers, and curriculum development for training programs.

Table 1
*Police Agencies' Current Use, Perceived Need, and Future Use of Psychological Services*

| Services | Currently used | | Perceived need | | Perceived future use | |
|---|---|---|---|---|---|---|
| | % | $n^a$ | % | $n^a$ | % | $n^b$ |
| Counsel police officers for job-related stress | 53.18 | 220 | 78.51 | 228 | 57.14 | 35 |
| Psychological assessment of police recruits | 52.29 | 218 | 90.39 | 229 | 62.50 | 40 |
| Counsel police officers for personal and family problems | 52.25 | 222 | 71.62 | 229 | 53.33 | 45 |
| Develop curriculum for training programs | 45.33 | 225 | 59.91 | 227 | 34.50 | 58 |
| Counsel police officer's spouse and family members | 41.70 | 223 | 63.60 | 228 | 50.00 | 70 |
| Train police personnel in crisis intervention techniques | 41.15 | 226 | 73.01 | 226 | 57.14 | 35 |
| Special examination for suspended and problem police officers | 38.91 | 221 | 67.11 | 225 | 43.39 | 53 |
| Train police personnel to deal with the mentally ill | 36.89 | 225 | 71.49 | 228 | 59.62 | 52 |
| Assist in crisis intervention | 36.77 | 223 | 46.05 | 228 | 31.51 | 73 |
| Provide workshops/seminars | 36.11 | 180 | 62.35 | 162 | 59.94 | 34 |
| Special problems of police work | 33.18 | 214 | 69.20 | 224 | 66.10 | 59 |
| Alcohol abuse | 25.36 | 209 | 61.99 | 221 | 57.89 | 57 |
| Abnormal behavior | 22.97 | 209 | 61.44 | 223 | 53.57 | 56 |
| Drug abuse | 22.12 | 208 | 59.09 | 220 | 60.00 | 60 |
| Cultural awareness | 18.96 | 211 | 54.75 | 221 | 55.71 | 70 |
| Personal growth | 20.67 | 208 | 60.18 | 221 | 51.90 | 79 |
| Retirement from the job | 9.57 | 209 | 59.15 | 222 | 55.43 | 92 |
| Train police personnel to deal with hostage negotiations | 35.39 | 226 | 61.23 | 227 | 51.16 | 43 |
| Train police personnel in human relations techniques | 35.27 | 224 | 75.98 | 229 | 46.16 | 31 |
| Train police personnel to deal with suicide situations | 30.40 | 227 | 66.67 | 228 | 56.63 | 83 |
| Assist in hostage negotiations | 29.91 | 224 | 44.30 | 228 | 27.78 | 72 |
| Assist in suicide situations | 29.46 | 224 | 42.73 | 227 | 30.12 | 83 |
| Act as liaison with other behavioral scientists or consultants | 26.87 | 227 | 40.09 | 227 | 28.57 | 112 |
| Assist in developing community relations | 25.44 | 228 | 48.25 | 228 | 36.45 | 107 |
| Assist in improving department command and leadership techniques | 24.89 | 225 | 55.56 | 225 | 41.30 | 92 |
| Psychological assessment of civilian employees of police departments | 22.57 | 226 | 48.24 | 228 | 42.06 | 126 |
| Develop psychological profiles for crime investigations | 22.32 | 224 | 37.61 | 226 | 43.21 | 81 |
| Research and programs evaluations | 21.49 | 228 | 42.04 | 226 | 39.09 | 110 |
| Assist in management development | 18.50 | 227 | 46.02 | 226 | 31.90 | 166 |
| Counsel crime victims and their family members | 14.60 | 226 | 50.00 | 226 | 31.29 | 131 |
| Assist in investigations through hypnosis of witness or suspect | 12.44 | 225 | 20.61 | 228 | 21.35 | 89 |
| Evaluations of candidates for promotion | 9.29 | 226 | 77.63 | 228 | 38.99 | 154 |

$^a$ Number of responses to each item.   $^b$ Number of responses from agencies who do not currently use service or plan to expand current use of service.

The only services showing low usage were some innovative areas such as hypnosis (12.44% of 225), retirement counseling (9.57% of 209), promotion evaluation (9.29% of 226), and victim counseling (14.60% of 226).

In most cases the perceived need for a particular service was almost twice as great as the percentage of the departments who indicated using that service. For some, the recognition of need far outweighed its current use; for example, in the area of victim counseling, 14.60% of departments reported current use of such counseling, whereas 50% indicated a need for this service. The most drastic contrast was in the sacrosanct area of promotion evaluation, in which 9.29% (of 226) re-

ported using this service, but 77.63% (of 228) of respondents recognized the need for such evaluations.

Almost all respondents affirmed the need for psychological evaluations of recruits (90.39% of 229), in most cases conforming with a specific legislative requirement. The perceived need for counseling services was also quite high, particularly for job-related stress (78.51% of 228).

The statement of perceived needs represented an idealized future. The statement of current use indicated pragmatic limitations. Questions addressing the likelihood that agencies not currently using a particular service would do so in the future were also presented. To the general question concerning plans to enlarge or implement the use of psychological services in the next 2 years, 36.74% (*n* = 79) of 215 respondents indicated plans to do so. This is an increase over the 18% of the 112 respondents in Parisher et al.'s (1979) study who gave this affirmative response.

When asked to indicate the level of acceptance of psychological services on a 7-point scale (1 = *highly accepted* and 7 = *not accepted*), 82.2% of 225 responses to the question indicated acceptance at 4 and above; 46.66% of respondents indicated a very high acceptance level (1 or 2). Also, more than 70% of respondents indicated that the use of psychological services could be of great help in the prevention of and dealing with problem police officers, improving the quality of police screening, and supervising police officers. Although there appears to be a high acceptance among police organizations of the use of psychological services, the moderate number of departments that indicated plans to expand or implement services may be due to a budgetary problem, which was reported by 64% (of 225) of departments as the greatest obstacle related to the use of psychological services.

## Discussion

In this study we report the current state of psychologists' involvement in police agencies on a national level. The principal finding is that between 1979 and the present, there has been an enormous growth in the use of psychological services in police departments. Parisher et al. (1979) found that only 20% of the police departments surveyed used psychological services. Our results indicate that more than half of all departments surveyed are currently using some type of psychological service.

As in the earlier study (Parisher et al., 1979), we found that assessment of applicants is the primary service used. Parisher et al. (1979) also reported personal counseling as a main duty of police psychologists. Our results also indicate that officer counseling is a commonly used psychological service; job-related stress counseling was reported by 53% of respondents. It is not surprising that police agencies and officers have recognized the usefulness of counseling services in preparing for and dealing with stress experienced as a result of the job, considering that over the last 15 years more than 100 articles, numerous books, and manuals that deal with the police stress problem have been published (Loo, 1986; Reiser & Klyver, 1987).

One area of counseling that seems to have been neglected is counseling for the victims of crimes. Only a small number of police departments reported the current use of this service. There appears to be very little change or prospect of change since the earlier study (Parisher et al., 1979), in spite of the fact that Knudten and Knudten (1981) demonstrated the extent of dissatisfaction with current police dealings with crime victims and suggested possibilities for police counseling with crime victims to alleviate negative effects. In our study, 50% (*n* = 226) of respondents indicated a need for victim counseling. It appears that this service is commonly provided by voluntary organizations, support groups, and self-help programs that are not affiliated with police agencies (Walker, 1987).

One area of projected changes is in the use of psychologists for various training programs. These programs include instruction in dealing with the mentally ill, dealing with alcohol and drug abuse, and cultural awareness. Approximately 60% of those responding to each of these items indicated a need for more effective workshops and seminars in these areas and plan to introduce such services in the near future. Although the police officer has always provided a first aid role in dealing with the mentally ill, family disputes, and victims of crimes, it is only recently that the officer has come to be seen as an applied social scientist. Because an officer may potentially have a great impact on the attitudes of the community toward police, it is essential that officers develop applied behavioral skills to maximize their effectiveness. Also, the officer who acquires an understanding of interpersonal situations that may be encountered while on the job will be better prepared to handle such situations.

There appears to be a substantial growth in the use of psychological services by police agencies. Although earlier researchers speculated about the potential use of psychological services in police agencies, this study has demonstrated an increase in the range of the current uses and a high perceived need for many of the 25 specific psychological services presented in the questionnaire. Some of the psychological services presented have been used for a long enough time that their effectiveness can be measured. Evaluation studies in which researchers use outcomes such as officers' injuries, indices of police officers' mental health, and efficiency of officers' handling of specific situations are needed.

The extent and nature of psychological services in police agencies seem to be influenced by a unique mixture of political, social, technological, and economic forces. The future impact of psychologists on police officers and police organizations will be greatly determined by the goals of the organization. Innovations in policing do not necessarily lead to improvements until they are matched against specific agency objectives (Heaphy, 1978). Therefore, the successful implementation of psychological services in police departments may rest heavily on the police administration. Equally important is the ability of the provider of psychological services to work effectively in the quasi-military, bureaucratic structure of the police organization. If a service that comes from police needs is provided, it is less likely to be perceived as being imposed on the officers and the department and therefore has a greater chance of success. From the results of this study, it appears that once providers of psychological services have had the opportunity to demonstrate their value to the organization, they become an established arm of the police agency.

## References

Bard, M. (1969). Family intervention as a community mental health resource. *Journal of Criminal Law, Criminology and Police Science, 60*, 247–250.

Brodsky, S. (1972). *Psychologists in the criminal justice system.* Chicago: University of Illinois Press.

Brown, S., Burkhart, B., King, G., & Solomon, R. (1977). Roles and expectations for mental health professionals in law enforcement agencies. *American Journal of Community Psychology, 5*, 209–215.

Burkhart, B. (1980). Conceptual issues in the development of police selection procedures. *Professional Psychology, 11*, 121–129.

Chandler, J. (1986). A statewide police psychology program: Guidelines for development. In J. T. Reese & H. A. Goldstein (Eds.), *Psychological services for law enforcement: A compilation of papers submitted to the national symposium of police psychological services, F.B.I. Academy, Quantico, Virginia* (Stock No. 027-0000-01266-3, pp. 225–230). Washington, DC: U.S. Government Printing Office.

Engle, D. (1974). Police training in non-crime related functions. *The Police Chief, 41*(6), 61–65.

Fisher, C. (1986). Some techniques and external programs useful in police psychological services. In J. T. Reese & H. A. Goldstein (Eds.), *Psychological services for law enforcement: A compilation of papers submitted to the national symposium of police psychological services, F.B.I. Academy, Quantico, Virginia* (Stock No. 027-0000-01266-3, pp. 111–114). Washington, DC: U.S. Government Printing Office.

Gents, D. (1986). A system for the delivery of psychological services for police personnel. In J. T. Reese & H. A. Goldstein (Eds.), *Psychological services for law enforcement: A compilation of papers submitted to the national symposium of police psychological services, F.B.I. Academy, Quantico, Virginia* (Stock No. 027-0000-01266-3, pp. 257–258). Washington, DC: U.S. Government Printing Office.

Green, J. (1986). Genesis—Beginning of a psychological services unit. In J. T. Reese & H. A. Goldstein (Eds.), *Psychological services for law enforcement: A compilation of papers submitted to the national symposium of police psychological services, F.B.I. Academy, Quantico, Virginia* (Stock No. 027-0000-01266-3, pp. 283–285). Washington, DC: U.S. Government Printing Office.

Heaphy, J. (1978). The future of police improvement. In A. W. Cohen (Ed.), *The future of policing* (pp. 275–295). Beverly Hills, CA: Sage.

Keller, P. (1978). A psychological view of the police officer paradox. *The Police Chief, 45*(4), 24–25.

Knudten, M., & Knudten, R. (1981). What happens to crime victims and witnesses in the justice system? In B. Galaway & J. Hudson (Eds.), *Perspectives on crime victims* (pp. 52–62). St. Louis: C. V. Mosby.

Loo, R. (1986). Police psychology: The emergence of a new field. *The Police Chief, 53*(2), 26–30.

Mann, P. (1980). Ethical issues for psychologists in police agencies. In J. Monahan (Ed.), *Who is the client? The ethics of psychological intervention in the criminal justice system* (pp. 18–42). Washington, DC: American Psychological Association.

Parisher, D., Rios, B., & Reilley, R. (1979). Psychologists and psychological services in urban police departments. *Professional Psychology, 10*, 6–7.

Reiser, M. (1972). *The police department psychologist.* Springfield, IL: Charles C Thomas.

Reiser, M. (1974). Mental health in police work and training. *The Police Chief, 41*(8), 51–52.

Reiser, M. (1978). The police department psychologist. *Police, 23*, 86–94.

Reiser, M., & Klyver, N. (1987). Consulting with police. In I. B. Weiner & A. K. Hess (Eds.), *Handbook of forensic psychology* (pp. 437–459). New York: Wiley.

Somodevilla, S. A. (1978). The psychologist's role in the police department. *The Police Chief, 45*(4), 21–23.

Stratton, J. (1980). Psychological services for the police. *Journal of Police Science and Administration, 8*(1), 31–39.

Swink, D., & Altman, K. (1986). The use of mental health professionals in the implementation of action training models. In J. T. Reese & H. A. Goldstein (Eds.), *Psychological services for law enforcement: A compilation of papers submitted to the national symposium of police psychological services, F.B.I. Academy, Quantico, Virginia* (Stock No. 027-0000-01266-3, pp. 299–301). Washington, DC: U.S. Government Printing Office.

United States Bureau of the Census. (1983). *Statistical abstract of the United States, 1984* (104th ed.). Washington, DC: U.S. Government Printing Office.

Wagner, M. (1976). Action and reaction: The establishment of counseling services in the Chicago police department. *The Police Chief, 43*(1), 20–23.

Walker, L. (1987). Intervention with victims/survivors. In I. B. Weiner & A. K. Hess (Eds.), *Handbook of forensic psychology* (pp. 630–649). New York: Wiley.

Wilson, J. Q. (1968). *Varieties of police behavior.* Cambridge, MA: Harvard University Press.

Received June 1, 1987
Revision received September 14, 1987
Accepted September 25, 1987 ∎

# Part II
# Psychological Autopsy

# [6]

Professional Psychology: Research and Practice
1987, Vol. 18, No. 1, 52-56

# Guide to Conducting a Psychological Autopsy

Bruce W. Ebert
Beale Air Force Base, California

Much of the writing on the psychological autopsy is reviewed. Several writers opinions about what should be included in a comprehensive behavioral analysis conducted after an individual's death are compiled in an Appendix. Several additional and new areas to be covered in a psychological autopsy are included. The primary emphasis is on the provision of a practical guide for the working professional. Twenty-four separate factors, ranging from reconstruction of events that occurred before the death to the deceased's family death history, are presented. Some legal considerations are examined briefly in order to acquaint the professional with the significant impact that the results can have on family benefits and criminal prosecution.

The psychological autopsy is a process designed to assess a variety of factors including behavior, thoughts, feelings, and relationships of an individual who is deceased. In effect, it is a psychological evaluation conducted without benefit of direct observation but often with greater access to behavioral data about a person than a standard evaluation would provide. This posthumous study of a person is gaining in popularity, probably because of the proven value of using behavioral scientists in a variety of legal settings. The advent of the forensic psychologist, coupled with increased credibility with members of the criminal justice systems, has led to more demands for consultation. The psychological autopsy is a tool that is at the outer edge of professional knowledge and practice in that it requires an application of skills, experience, and training for solving problems with limited help from research. There is a paucity of writing about actual procedures for conducting a psychological autopsy, leaving the psychologist somewhat alone when confronted with the challenge of working on this type of autopsy with police, district attorneys, coroners, or other members of the criminal justice system. The importance of the results cannot be underrated because they can affect such things as insurance payments, homicide prosecution, and national security issues.

The psychological autopsy, which was developed by Shneidman and Farberow (1961) and later described in detail (Litman, Curphey, Shneidman, Farberow, & Tabachnick, 1963), has numerous applications: It has been used to analyze aircraft crashes (Jones, 1977; Yanowitch, Mohler, & Nichols, 1972), in the assessment of staff behavior before a death (Neill, Benensohn, Farber, & Resnik, 1974), and in homicide investigations (Danto, 1979). The technique has been applied to answer complex legal questions (Bendheim, 1979), in the

Bruce W. Ebert, PhD, is a licensed clinical psychologist who is currently on active duty as a captain in the United States Air Force, stationed at Beale Air Force Base as Chief of Psychological Services, and provides services in the area of forensics, hostage response, disasters, testing, prevention, and aerospace psychology. He is also a student of law at the McGeorge School of Law in Sacramento, California.
Correspondence concerning this article should be addressed to Bruce W. Ebert, 3458 Tumblewood Court, Rocklin, California 95677.

assessment of cases with significant political importance (Selkin & Loya, 1979), and as a device of therapeutic value (Sanborn & Sanborn, 1976). Weisman and Kastenbaum (1968) developed a technique to be used primarily in a hospital. More data could be accumulated on an individual in such a setting because of expanded contact with a patient. The interdisciplinary conference was used and included social workers, nurses, psychiatrists, psychologists, chaplains, and occupational therapists. It is important that 50% of the protocols examined by his team contained explicit references to death.

Further elaboration of the technique was provided by Weisman (1974). He referred to the psychological autopsy conducted in a hospital on a previously hospitalized patient as the *Omega version*. Because actual contact with a patient has occurred, information that is both helpful and normally ascertained only by educated speculation is available. Observations of the patient, clinical interviews, and multidisciplinary assessments based on direct contact provide invaluable information that can be used to train providers and understand the dynamics of death. Diller (1979) suggested its use as a method of assessing the sociological and psychological health of a community. The widespread usage of the psychological autopsy, coupled with the importance of the results, has caused some experts to call for the development of a systemic methodology that can serve as a standardized guideline for all who may engage in such a process (Rudestam, 1979). Yet some professionals seem resistant to clearly defining how they conduct a death assessment. Shneidman (1981) wrote that he did not normally have a rigid outline in mind, but then he proposed 16 separate categories deemed important (Shneidman, 1969). Shneidman (1973, 1981) provided the most comprehensive guidelines for conducting the autopsy. In his 16 areas the details of the death were examined along with the deceased's history, life-style, problems, relationships, and personality. A critical factor described by Shneidman (1981) is the rating of lethality. Lethality is divided into four categories: high, medium, low, and absent. The investigator assigns a category on the basis of the role that a previously deceased person played in one's death. The use of the lethality scale is important, directly relating to the purpose of the psychological autopsy.

## Purpose of the Psychological Autopsy

The primary reason why a behavioral scientist is involved in a psychological autopsy is that the mode of death is equivocal. Shneidman (1973, 1977) simplified this into the categories "why," "how," and "what," referring to the reason why a person committed suicide, the actual cause of death with special emphasis on the timing of the death, and determining the mode of death. There are four basic modes of death that Shneidman (1981) referred to, using the acronym NASH: natural, accident, suicide, or homicide. Often the cause of death is quite clear, but the mode is not. For example, suppose a parachutist falls to the ground from an altitude of 5,000 feet and dies presumably as the result of multiple injuries to the head and body. The cause of death is the injuries resulting from the impact, but the mode is unclear. One cannot directly ascertain from the cause of death whether the person fell out of the plane (accident), was pushed (homicide), intentionally jumped with a bad parachute (suicide), or whether death occurred because a heart attack on the way down prevented the person from opening the parachute (natural). A more common example confronting the forensic psychologist is the case of an unattended death involving a gunshot wound. I was involved in a case involving such a scenario in which the cause of death, head injuries from a gunshot, was clear. The most important question, however, involved the mode of death: Did the deceased purposefully pull the trigger (suicide), was he surprised that the gun went off (accident), or did someone else fire the weapon (homicide)? The first purpose of the psychological autopsy is to establish the mode or the reason for the death.

The second purpose of performing a psychological autopsy is to ascertain why a death occurred at a particular time (Shneidman, 1981). To address this question, the investigator must examine important events in the life of the deceased to ascertain any connection between them and that individual's death. Deaths that occur on or near the anniversary of a loved one's death are seen often in clinical practice. One man in his late 60s was in and out of hospitals for a year and was suffering from a terminal illness. One day from his hospital bed he alertly looked at his wife and said, "Is is time?" She replied that it was, and he died instantly thereafter. Assessing the timing of a particular death can be helpful in identifying behavior that can influence a client's decision to die (Neill et al., 1974). In one example Neill et al. described how a psychological autopsy uncovered conflicts between staff members that may have affected critical decisions made in regard to a client, which may have influenced the death at that particular time.

A third purpose of the psychological autopsy is to gain information that may be invaluable in the prediction of suicide as well as assessment of the lethality of the suicidal individual. Shneidman (1973) created three classifications of motivation for a death: intentional, subintentional, and unintentional. Data generated from psychological autopsies can be used to identify common behavioral patterns of each group of intent. Applications to clients who are living can occur in the dynamics of choice in the decision to take one's own life. Trends can be identified, eventually leading to more accurate

identification of high-risk people and groups. For example, Rudestam (1971) studied communication of suicidal intent in Los Angeles and Stockholm with information found in psychological autopsies. Research from this study showed that 62% of suicide victims communicated their intent to at least one person before killing themselves. In one study with a large sample, Curphey (1968) found that 20%–30% of successful suicides were accompanied by a note. This information is invaluable to the investigator as well as to the clinician.

A fourth purpose is for psychotherapeutic value to the survivors. Sanborn and Sanborn (1976) described four cases involving positive therapeutic gain for those close to the decreased. They poignantly reported that "Interviewers . . . encountered survivors who desperately wanted someone to talk to, someone to help clear up misrepresentations and to check distortions with reality" (p. 5). It is probable that in discussing the actions, feelings, relationships, and attitudes of the deceased, the survivor experiences a release of emotion or catharsis, which allows the survivor to come to terms with the loss of a loved one. Shneidman (1981) also suggested that the interviews associated with a psychological autopsy may be therapeutic. He implied that in order for this to happen, the interviewers must "participate in the anguish of the bereaved person" (p. 330).

The psychological autopsy is especially important because the determination of suicide as a mode of death is dependent on the attitude of a coroner (Litman, 1968). Valuable information serving multiple purposes is obtained by the procedure. The data serves to change the process of the coroner or medical examiner from one of guessing to one of educated guessing.

## Structure of the Psychological Autopsy

Although there have been calls for standardized procedures to be used in conducting a psychological autopsy (Rudestam, 1979) and the methodological problems of not doing so have been stated (Selkin & Loya, 1979), a thorough outline of procedures does not exist. Weisman (1967) identified some guidelines for analysis of a death of an individual who was hospitalized. He identified four areas of study that are necessary in studying the life of a deceased: (a) final illness—identify illness and patient's expectations of death; (b) premedical period—explore marital stress, premonitions, references to death; (c) hospital course—relationships with others during hospitalization, crises, and problems; (d) prehospital situation—medical condition and mental status at the time of hospitalization, attitude towards admission.

This is by no means a thorough guideline for assessing a hospital patient who has committed suicide. Neill et al. (1974) offered more areas to assess. Their list included (a) reviewing nurse and physician notes. (b) interviewing friends, staff, and family, (c) documenting events preceding the suicide, (d) uncovering the psychological and social history, and (e) discovering who are aware of the patient's feelings.

Curphey (1968) believed that it is important to review the results of the medical autopsy as well as any toxicological study conducted. He suggested examining the patient's history for psychiatric idiosyncrasies, recent loss, change in habit patterns, and morbid content of thought. Because the best predictor of future suicide and attempts is past attempts, a complete history of such must be retrieved. It is recommended that the investigator visit the scene of death to make observations that would be useful in constructing a picture of the environment as it was before the death. Ungerleider (1971) added analysis of drug use and abuse, educational achievement, and job history to the list. Selkin and Loya (1979) believed that it is important to examine all medical and military records. Shneidman (1981) offered the most comprehensive list, including identification of recent stressors; death history of family; details of death; patterns of response to stress; fantasies, dreams, premonitions, and fears of death; and rating of lethality via his system of high, medium, low, or absent. He also examined the deceased's plans, successes, intent, as well as the overall personality and life-style. Although many writers have suggested various areas or topics to cover in a psychological autopsy, most lists are not comprehensive. I compiled a list of essential areas that should be considered for conducting a psychological autopsy. Many of the aforementioned authors' ideas have been incorporated in order to make this list comprehensive.

The psychological autopsy guide listed in the Appendix was developed as a tool to aid the psychologist in conducting a psychological autopsy. One is not required to review all 26 areas for every investigation. The guide provides a spectrum of factors that can be useful in formulating an opinion about the mode of death. I organized this list after conducting several psychological autopsies and finding many aspects of the deceased's life useful to evaluate. There was a lacuna of guidance for such an examination that if filled would make the search for background easier and more structured. In conducting psychological autopsies with the list, I have found that the picture of the deceased and the report generated from the study are more comprehensive. It is a practical guide as long as the psychologist chooses carefully which segments to use and which to ignore. The guide is presented in the Appendix.

A complete written report should follow investigation by the behavioral scientist with an opinion as to the mode of death, provided that one can be made. The psychologist should not be afraid to study the aforementioned factors and state that the mode remains unclear or unknown. Often discussions and coordination with police, medical examiners, district attorneys, and other law enforcement personnel will lead to a better understanding of what activity occurred to cause the death in question. The best example of a written report was depicted by Blau (1984). In the report the author compared baseline data regarding occupation and risk with the deceased. This novel technique provides a context for evaluation of data. He divided the report into six sections ranging from purpose of the evaluation to conclusions, with special emphasis on a thorough analysis of the stress experienced by the deceased shortly before his or her death. There is no substitute for active coordination because the investigation is truly a team effort in which the psychologist plays an important role. This role is not the only important role because the behavioral scientist does not have all the answers. Keeping this in mind will help one to function better and to be accepted as a person who can make a valuable contribution

by members of the criminal justice system. The results must be carefully compiled because they have impact on many legal issues (Lichter, 1981). Adherence to a methodology and the willingness to secure information from a variety of sources will increase the probability that complete facts will be discovered.

## References

Bendheim, O. L. (1979). The psychiatric autopsy: Its legal application. *Bulletin of the American Academy of Psychiatry and the Law, 7,* 400–410.

Blau, T. H. (1984). *The psychologist as expert witness.* New York: Wiley.

Curphey, T. J. (1968, July). The psychological autopsy: The role of the forensic pathologist in the multidisciplinary approach to death. *Bulletin of Suicidology,* pp. 39–45.

Danto, B. L. (1979). New frontiers in the relationship between suicidology and law enforcement. *Suicide & Life Threatening Behavior, 9,* 195–204.

Diller, J. (1979). The psychological autopsy in equivocal deaths. *Perspectives in Psychiatric Care, 17,* 156–161.

Jones, D. R. (1977). Suicide by aircraft: A case report. *Aviation, Space, and Environmental Medicine, 48,* 454–459.

Lichter, D. H. (1981). Diagnosing the dead: The admissibility of the psychiatric autopsy. *American Criminal Law Review, 18,* 617–635.

Litman, R. E. (1968). Psychological–psychiatric aspects in certifying modes of death. *Journal of Forensic Sciences, 13,* 46–54.

Litman, R. E., Curphey, T. J., Shneidman, E. S., Farberow, N. L., & Tabachnick, N. D. (1963). Investigations of equivocal suicides. *Journal of the American Medical Association, 184,* 924–930.

Neill, K., Benensohn, H. S., Farber, A. N., & Resnik, H. (1974). The psychological autopsy: A technique for investigating a hospital suicide. *Hospital and Community Psychiatry, 25,* 33–36.

Rudestam, K. E. (1971). Stockholm and Los Angeles: A cross-cultural study of the communication of suicidal intent. *Journal of Consulting and Clinical Psychology, 36,* 82–90.

Rudestam, K. E. (1979). Some notes on conducting a psychological autopsy. *Suicide & Life Threatening Behavior, 9,* 141–144.

Sanborn, D. E., III, & Sanborn, C. J. (1976). The psychological autopsy as a therapeutic tool. *Diseases of the Nervous System, 37*(1), 4–8.

Selkin, J., & Loya, F. (1979). Issues in the psychological autopsy of a controversial public figure. *Professional Psychology, 10,* 87–93.

Shneidman, E. S. (1969). Suicide, lethality, and the psychological autopsy. In E. Shneidman & M. Ortega (Eds.), *Aspects of depression* (pp. 225–250). Boston: Little, Brown.

Shneidman, E. S. (1973). *Deaths of man.* New York: Quadrangle Books.

Shneidman, E. S. (1977). The psychological autopsy. In L. A. Gottschalk, F. L. McGuire, E. C. Dinova, H. Birch, & J. F. Heiser (Eds.), *Guide to the investigation and reporting of drug-abuse deaths* (pp. 42–56). Rockville, MD: National Institute of Drug Abuse, U.S. Department of Health, Education, and Welfare.

Shneidman, E. S. (1981). The psychological autopsy. *Suicide & Life Threatening Behavior, 11,* 325–340.

Shneidman, E. S., & Farberow, N. L. (1961). Sample investigations of equivocal deaths. In N. L. Farberow & E. S. Schneidman (Eds.), *The cry for help* (pp. 118–129). New York: McGraw-Hill.

Ungerleider, J. T. (1971). Psychological autopsy: A case commentary. *Bulletin of Suicidology, 8,* 90–91.

Weisman, A. D. (1967, December). The psychological autopsy and the potential suicide. *Bulletin of Suicidology,* pp. 15–24.

Weisman, A. D. (1974). *The realization of death: A guide for the psychological autopsy.* New York: Jason Aronson.

Weisman, A. D., & Kastenbaum, R. (1968). The psychological autopsy: A study of the terminal phase of life. *Community Mental Health Journal* (Monograph No. 4). New York: Behavioral Publications.

Yanowitch, R. E., Mohler, S. R., & Nichols, E. A. (1972). The psychosocial reconstructive inventory: A postdictal instrument in aircraft accident investigation. *Aerospace Medicine, 44,* 675–678.

Appendix
## Psychological Autopsy Guidelines

### 1. Alcohol History

a. Collect family history
b. Research amount ingested regularly
c. Research evidence of binge drinking
d. Research evidence of blackouts (known from friends, family, acquaintances
e. Research evidence of driving under the influence of alcohol
f. Research evidence of alcohol-related offenses
g. Research evidence of family problems (alcohol related)
h. Research evidence of work difficulties connected to alcohol
i. Research evidence of blood level (BAL) g/l at time of death

### 2. Suicide Notes

a. Examine content
b. Examine style
c. Have handwriting expert review writing style

### 3. Writing

a. Review any past writing by the deceased
b. Peruse any diary of the deceased
c. Examine school papers for topics of essays or term papers
d. Read letters to friends, family, co-workers, acquaintances

### 4. Books

a. Examine books of the deceased
  i. Look for books on the occult, life after death, death
  ii. Look for actual books on suicide
b. Assess books checked out of local libraries

### 5. Relationship Assessments

a. Interview people who knew the deceased including:
  i. Close friends
  ii. Close intimate heterosexual or homosexual companions
  iii. Acquaintances
  iv. Mother, father, siblings
  v. Co-workers and supervisors
  vi. Other relatives
  vii. Physicians and/or mental health professionals
  viii. Teachers
b. Construct level of intimacy on the basis of discussions with "close" friends
c. Assess people's reactions to the victim's death
d. Secure a history of marriages and divorces
e. Examine relationship with children
f. Look for anger directed to particular people

### 6. Marital Relationship

a. Note any significant problems that may have made the deceased person depressed
b. Look for history of extramarital relationships
c. Assess the overall quality of the relationship

### 7. Mood

a. Identify mood fluctuations
b. Look for symptoms of depression:
  i. Weight loss
  ii. References to depression
  iii. Problems with memory
  iv. Fatigue
  v. Sleep disturbances
  vi. Withdrawal
  vii. Decreased libido
  viii. Appetite and/or taste changes
  ix. Constipation and diarrhea
c. Look for mood indicators during last few days:
  i. Interview friends and family
  ii. Interview anyone surrounding the deceased

### 8. Psychosocial Stressors (note and chart importance on Holmes & Rahe Scale factors)

a. Recent loss: deaths of people or pets
b. Relationship separations: divorce, breakups of significant relationships
c. Loss of job
d. Legal and financial problems
e. Demotion, promotion, and so on
f. Reaction to stressors
g. Move to a new location

### 9. Presuicidal Behavior

a. Giving away important possessions
b. Paying up insurance policies
c. Payment of debts
d. Arrangements for children and pets
e. Sudden order in deceased's life
f. Change or initial creation of a will

### 10. Language

a. Identify any specific references to suicide (deceased may have stated, "Have a party in remembrance of me," or "You won't have to worry about me anymore")
b. Note any changes in language before suicide
c. Analyze language (tapes, recollections of conversations, writing) for morbid content

## 11. Drugs Used

a. Identify all drugs used by deceased
b. Assess interactional effects of legal and illegal drugs in use

## 12. Medical History

a. Review complete medical history
b. Note any unusual symptoms or diagnoses
c. Note any terminal illnesses or diagnoses

## 13. Reflective Mental Status Exam of Deceased's Condition Before Death

a. Orientation
b. Memory
c. Attention
d. Concentration
e. Mood and affect
f. Hallucinations or delusions
g. Cognition, IQ
h. Language
i. Judgment

## 14. Psychological History

a. Look for previous suicide attempts (type, method)
b. Assess reason for treatment if involved in therapy
c. Research evidence of depression, manic depression (bipolar disorder)
d. Research past psychiatric hospitalizations
e. Examine diagnoses
f. Examine evidence of impulsive behavior
g. Examine any recent or past psychological tests (e.g., was the victim given the Rorschach and was the suicide constellation served via the Exner system?)

## 15. Laboratory Studies

a. Examine ballistics
b. Evaluate powder burns on hands and body

## 16. Coroner's Report

a. Conduct complete drug screen
b. Identify any poisons
c. Read for detailed description of physical functioning/health of deceased at time of death

## 17. Motive Assessment

a. Make a chart divided four ways: Murder, Suicide, Accident, and Natural, recording data to support each as it is uncovered.
b. Report the possible reasons for suicide
c. Report the possible reasons why subject could have been murdered (identify enemies, illicit activities)

## 18. Reconstruction of Events Occurring on the Day Before Deceased's Death

a. Make a step-by-step chart of subject's movements and activities
b. Form a chronological history of the victim that immediately preceded death

## 19. Assess Feelings Regarding Death as Well as Preoccupations and Fantasies

## 20. Military History

a. Look for evidence of difficulty adjusting such as letters of counseling (LOC), letters of reprimand (LOR), Article 15 action (A15), or court-martial proceedings [Note: A15 is a form of nonjudicial punishment for offenses not serious enough to warrant a court-martial and include repeated lateness, driving under the influence of alcohol, sleeping on duty, or negligence on duty. Punishment from an A15 can include reduction in rank, fines, or removal from duty.]
b. Attempt to secure job ratings (airman promotion rating and officer effectiveness rating)
c. Look for decorations or awards
d. Notice whether deceased was in a combat zone at any time
e. Look for evidence of posttraumatic stress disorder in Vietnam veterans
f. Determine the number of assignments and which were at the request of the victim

## 21. Death History of Family

a. Examine history for suicide by other family members
b. List immediate deceased family members and their mode of death

## 22. Family History

a. Identify family members and relationships with deceased
b. Examine the socioeconomic status of family
c. Identify any conflicts that occurred before death of the victim

## 23. Employment History

a. Identify number and types of jobs (high-risk work may indicate the existence of subintention behavior for quite some time)
b. Look for repetitive problems
c. Assess whether any problems existed before death (e.g., co-worker conflict, failure to progress as planned)
d. Note any disciplinary action

## 24. Educational History

a. Assess educational level
b. Identify any problems with teachers or subjects
c. Note special interests or topics (e.g., in particular, look for special interests in death)

## 25. Familiarity With Methods of Deaths

a. Examine belongings for guns, knives (e.g., the deceased may have had five or six loaded weapons around his or her house regularly)
b. Look for lethal drugs
c. Note deceased's interest and knowledge in weapons

## 26. Police Report

a. Critical facts will be obtained by review of the police investigation
b. Pay special attention to ballistics data

Received February 19, 1986 ∎

# [7]

# APA's Expert Panel in the Congressional Review of the USS *Iowa* Incident

Norman Poythress, Randy K. Otto, Jack Darkes, and Laura Starr

*In 1989, an explosion aboard the USS* Iowa *killed 47 sailors. The navy attributed the explosion to the intentional suicidal acts of Gunners Mate Clayton Hartwig, a conclusion supported primarily by an "equivocal death analysis" conducted by the Federal Bureau of Investigation (FBI). The U.S. House of Representatives Armed Services Committee (HASC) was highly critical of the FBI's report and the navy's conclusions, in part because of the peer review provided by 12 psychologists organized by the American Psychological Association (APA). This article (a) reviews the nature of equivocal death analysis and related reconstructive psychological evaluations, (b) describes the nature of APA's consultation and involvement with the HASC, (c) discusses the conclusions reached by the HASC and the influence of the APA panelists, and (d) suggests limitations on the use of equivocal death analysis and related procedures in light of scientific concerns and ethical considerations.*

On April 19, 1989, an explosion occurred in Turret 2 of the USS *Iowa*. Five 94-pound bags of smokeless powder ignited while being loaded into the open breach of a 16-inch gun, resulting in the deaths of 47 U.S. Navy sailors. In an extensive investigation, the navy sought to uncover the causes of the explosion. Initial efforts focused on the possibility of an accidental or unintentional explosion. However, in a statement to the Committee on Armed Services of the U.S. House of Representatives on December 12, 1989, Rear Admiral Richard D. Milligan reported that, after conducting extensive tests, the navy had concluded

that an accident did not cause this explosion. It was not caused by unstable propellant. It was not caused by a direct flame or spark. It was not caused by frictional heating, or by impact and compression. It was not caused by electrostatic discharge. It was not caused by hazards of electromagnetic radiation. It was not caused by the kind of procedural errors or negligent acts crew members might have made. (*Review of Navy Investigation,* 1990, p. 24)

Having ruled out accidental or unintentional causes, the navy's investigation of the USS *Iowa* incident ultimately attributed the explosion to the intentional acts of one sailor, Gunners Mate Clayton Hartwig, who was himself killed in the explosion. This conclusion was reached after the Naval Investigative Service (NIS) conducted interviews with Hartwig's friends, family members, and former shipmates, and had gathered additional archival information (e.g., letters, personal writings, bank account balances) offering clues to his habits, life-style, aspirations, and personality. These data were provided to agents at the National Center for the Analysis of Violent Crime, a division of the Federal Bureau of Investigation (FBI). The reconstructive psychological evaluation (termed an *equivocal death analysis* [EDA] by the FBI) conducted by the FBI resulted in an unequivocal conclusion that Clayton Hartwig had acted alone and intentionally to cause the explosion on the USS *Iowa.* The FBI report was the primary piece of evidence in support of the navy's attribution of responsibility for the incident to Clayton Hartwig.

The navy's investigation of the incident was closely scrutinized by the U.S. House of Representatives Armed Services Committee (HASC). The HASC enlisted the assistance of the American Psychological Association (APA) in reviewing the FBI's report and the navy's conclusions. In this article we (a) review the nature of EDA and related reconstructive psychological evaluations, (b) describe the nature of APA's consultation and involvement with the HASC, (c) discuss the conclusions reached by the HASC and the influence of the APA panelists, and (d) suggest limitations on the use of EDA and related procedures in light of scientific concerns and ethical considerations.

## Reliability and Validity of Equivocal Death Analysis and Related Techniques

The HASC was concerned with the reliability and validity of equivocal death analysis as a clinical-investigative method. This was evident from its vigorous interrogation of the agents who wrote the FBI report (*Review of Navy Investigation,* 1990, pp. 234–268) and its request that APA provide a panel of psychologists to offer independent evaluations of the NIS data and the conclusions drawn by the FBI and the navy.

Except in the FBI's own documents and in the publications of its staff (e.g., Hazelwood, 1984) the term *equivocal death analysis* is virtually unknown in the psychological–behavioral sciences community.[1] Testimony

Norman Poythress, Randy K. Otto, Jack Darkes, and Laura Starr, Department of Law and Mental Health, Florida Mental Health Institute, University of South Florida.

Melissa G. Warren served as action editor for this article.

Correspondence concerning this article should be addressed to Norman Poythress, Department of Law and Mental Health, Florida Mental Health Institute, University of South Florida, 13301 Bruce B. Downs Boulevard, Tampa, FL 33612-3899.

[1] A review of *Psychological Abstracts* failed to reveal any citations to *equivocal death analysis.*

by FBI Agents Richard Ault and Robert Hazelwood before the HASC indicated that EDA is an extension of and conceptually related to criminal profiling (*Review of Navy Investigation,* 1990, p. 234). The FBI behavioral science experts consult in cases in which a police investigation has failed to determine the manner of a death. The EDA does not involve direct data gathering by the FBI agents; rather, they use the evidence developed by the referring agency to generate a psychological analysis of the victim, leading to a conclusion regarding the manner of death. The conclusion is couched in categorical terms (indeterminate, accident, homicide, or suicide (*Review of Navy Investigation,* 1990, p. 236) and is routinely offered with absolute rather than probabilistic certainty (p. 249). The indeterminate finding is rarely an outcome; Agent Hazelwood reported to the committee that he could recall only 3 of 45 cases (7%) in which he was unable to arrive at a conclusive opinion (p. 267).

EDA is conceptually related to two other procedures—criminal personality profiling and psychological autopsy—that have some level of acceptance in behavioral science circles. An important feature of all three procedures is that each involves the imposition by the profiler of a theoretical framework on selected data from a large, complex data set; thus, the training, experience, and theoretical preferences of the profiler may be important determinants of the weights assigned to individual pieces of data and to the manner in which the data are integrated. However, EDA is distinguishable from the other two procedures in important ways.

Criminal personality profiling has been developed primarily by the FBI (Douglas, Ressler, Burgess, & Hartman, 1986; Geberth, 1981; Holmes, 1989; Porter, 1983; Turco, 1990). Its application is thought to be limited to cases in which the crime scene itself indicates psychopathology (e.g., sadistic torture in sexual assaults, postmortem slashings, ritualistic crimes, and rapes; Pinizzotto, 1984). It is distinguished from EDA in that (a) the focus is on a (presumably) living, but unknown, perpetrator; (b) the profilers conduct their own investigation and examination of the crime scene; and (c) the objective is to develop investigative leads based on perpetrator personality traits. Identification of the suspected perpetrator is not considered helpful in criminal personality profiling. "Profiling does *not* provide the specific identity of the offender" (Douglas et al., 1986, p. 402), and "information the profiler does *not* want included in the case materials is that dealing with possible suspects. Such information may subconsciously prejudice the profiler and cause him or her to prepare a profile matching the suspect" (p. 406). In contrast, EDA rests on knowing the identity of the suspected perpetrator and then offering conclusions about likely scenarios based on this information.

Psychological autopsy is more similar to EDA in that the focus is on a deceased person and involves a reconstruction of a personality profile on the basis of interview and archival data (Ebert, 1987). This method has been associated primarily with inquiries into possible or known suicides (e.g., Brent, 1989; Litman, Curphey,

Schneidman, Faberow, & Tabachnick, 1963), although conceptually it may be applied to any postmortem psychological analysis (e.g., Fowler, 1986; Selkin, 1987; Selkin & Loya, 1979). It differs from EDA in that profilers typically examine the death scene (in the case of suspected or known suicide) and conduct their own interviews rather than rely on evidence developed by a police investigation.

There has been some empirical investigation of the use of psychological autopsy by medical examiners in determinations of the manner of death (Jobes, Berman, & Josselson, 1986), although the accuracy of judgments rendered as a result of psychological autopsy has not been systematically studied (Shuman, 1986). However, some proponents of psychological autopsy recognize the need to establish the reliability and validity of medical–legal certifications of suicide (Jobes, Berman, & Josselson, 1987). Preliminary conceptual work to identify operational criteria for the determination of suicide (Rosenberg et al., 1988) and to test empirically the utility of these criteria (Jobes, Casey, Berman, & Wright, 1991) has begun.

There have been no published studies of the reliability or validity of EDA. In contrast to the general concern of the scientific community with issues of reliability and validity, and despite the preliminary efforts to investigate the reliability and validity of psychological autopsy, FBI Agent Ault spoke of these issues with disdain when questioned by members of the House committee about the validity of EDA and the integrity of the data on which EDA is based:

I certainly appreciate that wonderful academic approach to a practical problem. It is typical of what we find when we see people who have not had the experience of investigating either crime scenes, victims, criminals and so forth in active, ongoing investigations. . . . [I]n the field of psychology and psychiatry, there are existing raging arguments about the validity of the very techniques that exist. They won't be resolved in this world. So, to ask us to provide the validity is an exercise in futility. (*Review of Navy Investigation,* 1990, p. 253)

## The Role of Organized Psychology in the Review

The House Armed Services Committee requested that the APA provide assistance by identifying psychological experts to conduct independent evaluations of much of the data provided by the NIS to the FBI, and to comment on the conclusions reached by the FBI and the navy on the basis of that data.[2] The APA identified psychologists with credentials and expertise in diverse areas including adolescence and young adulthood, suicidology, assess-

---

[2] The APA psychologists did not have every item of data that had been provided to the FBI. As noted in the Report of the Investigations Subcommittee "The NIS and FBI did not keep a comprehensive inventory of the documents reviewed for the psychological profile. The subcommittee used as a baseline those documents known to have been retained by the FBI for their significance, as well as the Equivocal Death Analysis, and subcommittee staff interviews of several witnesses" (*U.S.S. IOWA Tragedy,* 1990, p. 43, Footnote 4).

ment of personality and psychopathology, violence and risk assessment, forensic psychology, and peer review. From a larger pool of candidates, 12 panelists were selected "based on the amount of research and experience in their area of expertise as well as their national prominence in their respective fields" (*Review of Navy Investigation,* 1990, p. 285). Two psychiatric experts were appointed by the HASC without input from the APA.

The committee asked the panelists to comment on four basic issues:

1. The validity of the navy's conclusion (How valid is the Navy's conclusion about Hartwig based on the evidence?);
2. The adequacy of the database that was developed by NIS (How valuable are the materials for developing Hartwig's psychological profile? Was the investigation exhaustive?);
3. Hartwig's personality and tendencies (What motives or predispositions for suicide did Hartwig have, if any? And if he was suicidal, what is the likelihood that he'd commit such an act? What other conclusions, if any, would you draw from the material about Clayton Hartwig's psychological profile?); and
4. The validity of posthumous psychological profiles (What are the pitfalls of posthumous determination of suicidal tendencies and behavior?).

The 14 panelists worked independently and served on a pro bono basis. Each prepared a written report for the committee; six panelists (five psychologists, one psychiatrist) testified before the Investigations Subcommittee on December 21, 1989.[3]

## Conclusions of the House Armed Services Committee

In rejecting the conclusion reached by the navy (that Hartwig acted alone and intentionally to cause the USS *Iowa* blast), the committee characterized the navy's effort as "an investigative failure" (*U.S.S. IOWA Tragedy,* 1990). Committee Cochair Les Aspin said "The major problem with the Navy investigation is that it fell into the trap of an excess of certitude. Thin gruel became red meat. Valid theories and hypotheses were converted into hard fact" (HASC, 1990, p. 1). The committee was particularly critical of the FBI's equivocal death analysis. This criticism appeared to be based, in part, on the results of the peer review in which the APA panelists participated. Committee Cochair Nicholas Mavroules commented,

[T]he psychological analysis performed by the FBI for the Navy may be the real villain of this case. The Committee gathered a panel of 14 psychologists and psychiatrists to review the FBI's work. The FBI flunked this peer review. (HASC, 1990, p. 2)

In its final report the Investigations Subcommittee and Defense Policy Panel noted:

Ten of the 14 experts consulted considered the FBI analysis invalid. And even those who believed the analysis to be somewhat credible were critical of procedures, methodology, and the lack

of a statement of the limitations of a retrospective analysis of this nature. (*U.S.S. IOWA Tragedy,* 1990, p. 4)

We conducted a study in which independent raters used an instrument composed of Likert scales that we designed to quantify the judgments and opinions contained in the reports of the 12 psychologists and 2 psychiatrists organized by APA and the HASC (Otto, Poythress, Darkes, & Starr, 1992).[4] Twenty-four clinical psychologists and psychiatrists rated the reports of the 14 panelists and the report read verbatim by Agent Hazelwood at the HASC hearings. Each report was rated (without knowledge of who wrote it) by three subjects.

Our raters' responses indicated that the 14 panelists generally agreed that psychological autopsies designed to determine suicidal tendencies and behavior are of moderate value and utility. However, a cluster analysis of the ratings revealed clear majority and minority positions among the panelists' reports regarding the specific methods used and conclusions reached by the FBI and navy. A majority of the panelists ($n = 11$) were critical of the approach used and conclusions reached by the FBI and navy. A minority of 3 psychologists believed that the navy's report was relatively unbiased and that the conclusions were appropriately stated. All panelists agreed that additional information regarding Hartwig would have been useful. Adopting broad criteria for agreement, there was moderate agreement with respect to Hartwig's adjustment and psychological functioning. Generally, the FBI's impressions of Hartwig were more negative than those developed by the 14 panelists called by the HASC.

After the committee hearings, the investigation into the USS *Iowa* incident was reopened. Media reports indicated that additional tests conducted at Sandia National Laboratories revealed new evidence suggesting an accidental cause for the explosion (Nelson, 1990; "Test Rejects USS Iowa Sabotage," 1992).

## Implications for Reconstructive Evaluations in Practice

The EDA conducted by the FBI led the navy to conclude that Clayton Hartwig was responsible for a disastrous explosion, a conclusion with substantial implications on a number of fronts. At a personal level are the effects on Hartwig's reputation and on those friends and family members whose memories of him were affected by the controversy. The FBI–navy findings could potentially have influenced decisions regarding benefits due Hartwig's family or other beneficiaries (e.g., if his insurance policy paid differentially depending on the cause of death). The navy's findings could also potentially affect future decisions regarding benefits to families of other sailors. The Associated Press reported that 37 families of sailors killed

---

[3] A transcript of the complete testimony and the reports of all 14 panelists are contained in the reports of the Joint Hearings (*Review of Navy Investigation of U.S.S. IOWA Explosion,* 1990. HASC No. 101-41. Washington, DC: U.S. Government Printing Office.)

[4] A report of this study may be obtained from Norman Poythress.

---

10

aboard the USS *Iowa* were suing the navy for wrongful death, alleging negligence on the navy's part ("Families of USS Iowa Victims Sue," 1991). Although it may not have been intended as such, Admiral Milligan's choice of words in reporting the navy's conclusion that the explosion "*was not caused by* the kind of procedural errors or *negligent acts* crew members might have made" (*Review of Navy Investigation,* 1990, p. 24, italics added) can be read as a preemptive strike against subsequent allegations of negligence by navy personnel.

The general conclusions of the review panel raise several questions about the status and utility of reconstructive psychological evaluations. Although most cases involving reconstructed psychological profiles will not receive as much attention as the USS *Iowa* explosion and investigation, their impact remains great. Such investigations may affect decisions about whether to pursue criminal explanations for otherwise unexplained deaths, or the kinds of benefits due to survivors of persons who die under ambiguous or mysterious circumstances. Given the potential unreliability of these procedures, should they be used? If so, for what purposes or in which situations, and what should be the limits or parameters of such procedures? What protections can or should be offered to potential consumers?

## Should Reconstructive Psychological Procedures be Allowed?

Certainly, good arguments can be mustered against using reconstructive psychological procedures such as criminal profiling, psychological autopsy, and EDA. Critics have expressed concerns about the reliability and validity of psychological reconstructions in other contexts, for example, in determining a person's mental state at the time of an offense—arguably a less problematic application than those considered here, given that clinicians gather their own data and have direct access to the subject of the inquiry. Criminal profiling, psychological autopsy, and EDA all require judgments about persons not available for direct assessment; in the case of EDA, the indirect assessment is done by someone other than the investigator–clinician. Furthermore, given less (or at least less desirable) data to work with, the clinician is asked to do more with it. The EDA invites the investigator to go beyond the conventional realm of his or her presumed expertise (the person's mental state) and to reach opinions and conclusions about the legally relevant act itself.

The important differences among these three reconstructive procedures provide grounds for being differentially concerned with their use. As noted earlier, criminal profiling is an attempt to glean clues about the *type* of person most likely to have been involved in particular kinds of cases. At least at the earlier stages of an investigation, such profiling is not used to identify the offender. Reliance on profile analysis may induce law enforcement officers to concentrate their investigative efforts on particular individuals. Thus, this procedure is more likely to pose an increased threat to individual liberty (in terms of investigative intrusions into a person's privacy) than

to inappropriately direct the legal fact finder or usurp the fact finder's role. Although we have not found published, programmatic research on the reliability or validity of criminal profiling (see Pinizzotto & Finkel, 1990, for one such study), its utility in guiding police investigations in particularly heinous cases or cases involving suspected serial murderers may be tolerated, if not justified, in the absence of clear evidence of privacy abuses.

We have greater concerns about the use of psychological autopsy and EDA, although we decline to develop and extend earlier arguments regarding why psychologists should not (or should not in legal contexts be allowed to) engage in such practices. It is clear that these investigations are sought out of necessity to help resolve difficult questions. In the absence of a governmental or professional regulatory agency having the authority (if not the inclination) to limit the use of these procedures, the question of whether they should be allowed is a moot one. The demands of the marketplace and the necessity that some resolution be achieved in certain contexts will provide the impetus for their use. The appropriate considerations, then, deal with limiting their use in ways consistent with the limits of the expertise of the professions involved.

## Scientific Considerations Regarding the Use of Psychological Autopsy and Equivocal Death Analysis

We suggest at least the following three limits on the clinical–legal application of reconstructive psychological procedures.[5] First, the use of these procedures should not be extended at present to nondeath situations. To date, psychological autopsy and related techniques have been used primarily to assess and describe issues related to cause of death. Logically, however, if one accepts wholeheartedly that psychologists, psychiatrists, or other social scientists can accurately reconstruct the mental state, motives, and actions of the deceased from third-party and indirect information, then the door should be open to other applications (e.g., "equivocal burglary analysis" or "equivocal kidnapping analysis"). Such extensions should be resisted at all levels, unless considerably more evidence of high reliability and validity of judgments from these procedures is in hand. There should be less political or other external pressure to resolve such events by psychological autopsy, and most nondeath events will not create the need to resolve issues of distribution of the actor's assets (e.g., insurance, will, etc.). Even with regard to equivocal death situations, however, we would discourage extended or widespread use of EDA. The FBI's record of reaching a "conclusive" opinion in 42 of 45 cases notwithstanding, we urge exceeding caution in deciding to use posthumous psychological investigations; many equivocal or unsolved death cases may simply have to remain unsolved.

---

[5] For a discussion of other uses of psychological autopsy, such as assessing the quality of care provided to a person prior to death or determining risk factors for suicide, see Clark and Horton-Deutsch (1992).

Second, in legal and quasi-legal contexts, persons who conduct reconstructive psychological evaluations should not assert categorical conclusions about the precise mental state or actions suspected of the actor at the time of his or her demise. The conclusions and inferences drawn in psychological reconstructions are, at best, informed speculations or theoretical formulations and should be labeled as such (Bonnie & Slobogin, 1980; Melton, Petrila, Poythress, & Slobogin, 1987). In its report to the navy, the FBI stated unequivocally that Clayton Hartwig was responsible for the explosion on the USS *Iowa* as an act of suicide, and advised the navy of the method used to start the explosion on the basis of social history and third party interview data. The kinds of unequivocal, bottom-line statements offered by the FBI in its EDA report regarding Clayton Hartwig are not defensible within the technical limitations of our science.

Third, clinicians and social scientists should be careful not to mislead consumers about the accuracy of conclusions drawn from psychological reconstructions by offering inadequate proxies for nonexistent validation studies. It is tempting, particularly when defending one's testimony in an adversarial setting, to overstate one's position. Such efforts, however, can be confusing and misleading. The testimony of Commander Thomas Mountz before the House Armed Services Committee is illustrative. Mountz was sensitive to the limits of psychological reconstructions, as indicated by the statement in his report that "Due to the post-dictive nature of this assessment, the results should be regarded as speculative" (*Review of Navy Investigation,* 1990, p. 270). When asked about his confidence level in his findings (that Hartwig was responsible for the explosion), Mountz responded "better than 99%" (p. 277). It is not a problem that a social scientist–clinician may believe, and even be able to illustrate, that one hypothesis or theoretical formulation seems to fit the available data somewhat better than others. On the other hand, such people should also be aware of the failure of confidence to correlate highly with accuracy in other areas of psychological or personal judgment (e.g., the eyewitness identification and clinical judgment literatures) and avoid misleading consumers with what might be construed as statements of overconfidence.

## Ethical Guidelines and Implications Regarding the Use of Psychological Autopsy and Equivocal Death Analysis

It is clear that these types of investigations or assessments are performed out of the necessity to answer difficult and important legal questions that arise in a variety of situations.[6] Given the importance of these questions, it seems that mental health professionals should offer their assistance, if they are able to provide some information that helps the fact finder answer important questions. Mental health professionals, in determining whether and how to undertake such assessments, should take into consideration relevant ethical and professional obligations. The 1990 Ethical Principles of Psychologists (APA, 1990) require psychologists to (a) avoid acting in ways

that violate the civil rights of others (Principle 3); (b) prevent distortion or misuse of their findings (Principles 1 & 8); and (c) identify any reservations that exist regarding the validity or reliability of an assessment technique (Principle 8). The Specialty Guidelines for Forensic Psychologists (Committee on Ethical Guidelines for Forensic Psychologists, 1991) are also relevant to psychologists' involvement in psychological autopsies and related pursuits. The Specialty Guidelines, among other things, require psychologists to (a) document or make available for review all data that form the basis of their opinions; (b) ensure that data gathered by others is gathered in such a way that is professionally acceptable; and (c) note the limitations of making statements about persons who were unavailable for examination (Section VI).

Used together, these guidelines can limit whether psychologists engage in these evaluations and how they present their findings. Ethical guidelines promulgated by related organizations (e.g., American Academy of Psychiatry and Law, 1987/1991) can have a similar effect on those organizations' members.

The Standards for Educational and Psychological Testing, which are published by the American Educational Research Council (AERC), the APA, and the National Council on Measurement in Education (1985) may also be used to protect the consumer of these evaluations. Although these standards primarily apply to traditional measures of behavior, they may also be applied to "the entire range of assessment techniques" (AERC et al., 1985, p. 4). These standards obligate those using assessment techniques to (a) evaluate the validity and reliability -of their techniques (Standard 6.1) and (b) demonstrate the validity of a technique if it is used for a purpose that has not been previously validated (Standard 6.3).

Assuming these standards are applicable to psychological autopsies and similar reconstructive assessments, they require those who engage in such assessments to try to evaluate the reliability and validity of their techniques. In light of this, FBI Special Agent Ault's response to the House committee's questions about validity of EDA, "I certainly appreciate that wonderful academic approach to a practical problem. . . . So, to ask us to provide the validity [of EDA] is an exercise in futility" (*Review of Navy Investigation,* 1990, p. 253) is unacceptable. Similarly, simply citing customer satisfaction or gross evaluation of the general technique also fails to meet the requirements of reliability and validity established by these standards. Thus, Ault's statement that "we have done research on the amount of work we do, and the feedback has been that in probably 80 percent, well above chance, the cases we have were successful" (*Review of Navy Investigation,* 1990, p. 253) should be considered, like statements of subjective confidence, another example of

---

[6] Our review of legal cases indicated that attorneys have used or attempted to use psychological autopsies to assist in testamentary, life insurance, and workers' compensation cases, as well as in criminal defenses and criminal prosecutions.

an inadequate proxy for having validated the procedures that one uses.

Although ethical guidelines and ancillary professional standards could protect consumers and the general public from overstated conclusions based on techniques of limited or unknown reliability, they often do not. Two principal reasons are that professionals who use these techniques disregard the tenets and their colleagues fail to hold them accountable for this, and that some persons who use these techniques are not members of the relevant professional organizations and thus do not feel bound by the relevant professional and ethical principles. More troubling are employment settings in which professionals are not answerable either to governmental regulatory agencies (e.g., licensing boards) or to professional organizations. Compounding this is the potential for these persons to be professionally isolated.[7] Professional isolation may make it difficult to keep abreast of developments in the discipline and may severely limit the opportunity or potential for quality control. In some cases, education of consumers or legal protections appear to be necessary to regulate practice, particularly when these assessments have such serious consequences and are of questionable validity. The APA's response to the House subcommittee's request for assistance in the USS *Iowa* case is one example of how the profession can serve an important public interest function.

## Legal Protections

The law of evidence also has the potential to protect the public from techniques that are of questionable reliability and validity. The law of evidence determines whether mental health professionals may offer courtroom testimony about their conclusions based on psychological autopsies, EDA, or profiling. Although the law varies across jurisdictions, admissibility of psychological autopsies is largely affected by either the *Frye* test (*Frye v. U.S.*, 1910) or the Federal Rules of Evidence and their state equivalents.

The *Frye* test holds: "[the scientific technique] from which the deduction is made must be sufficiently established to have gained general acceptance in the particular field in which it belongs" (*Frye v. U.S.*, 1910, p. 1014). Whether these reconstructive techniques can pass this test is arguable given their lack of development, questionable reliability, and unproven validity. Given the published literature that describes at least the conceptual and theoretical basis for psychological autopsy, a stronger argument for general acceptance can be made for this procedure than for EDA, which is virtually unheard of in the psychological and psychiatric community. Ultimately, of course, this test must be applied by a trial judge.

The admissibility of evidence based on these techniques might also be determined by various sections of the Federal Rules of Evidence, 1990 (or state equivalents of this rule). Rule 401 limits admissible evidence to that which is relevant. Assuming EDA and similar techniques are believed to have some validity, meeting the requirements of Rule 401 should not be difficult. Perhaps a more

challenging hurdle for EDA and related techniques is Rule 403: "Although relevant, evidence may be excluded if its probative value is substantially outweighed by the danger of unfair prejudice, confusion of the issues, or misleading the jury." The law is always concerned about the possibility of the legal decision maker (i.e., judge or jury) being unduly influenced by particular evidence. Testimony or evidence which comes close to the legal decision that must be made (the "ultimate issue"; see Slobogin, 1989, for a discussion) is considered to present such a risk (e.g., Rule 704 bars mental health professionals from offering ultimate issue testimony in insanity cases). Thus, EDA or psychological autopsy might be deemed inadmissible on the grounds that the conclusions are too close to the legal decision to be made and, consequently, may overwhelm or bias the legal decision maker.

The Federal Rules of Evidence (1990) concerned with expert evidence and testimony are also relevant to a discussion of the admissibility of EDA and related procedures. Rule 702 reads

If scientific, technical, or other specialized knowledge will assist the trier of fact to understand the evidence or to determine a fact in issue, a witness qualified as an expert by knowledge, skill, experience, training, or education, may testify thereto in the form of an opinion or otherwise.

Admissibility, according to Rule 702, appears to hinge on the degree to which the technique of psychological autopsy may be considered to constitute scientific or specialized knowledge and to assist the trier of fact in understanding evidence or determining a fact at issue. Again, because psychological autopsy is relatively undeveloped, with little known about its reliability or validity, it may have difficulty passing the first requirement. The second prong appears easier to meet, insofar as mental health professionals might be able to provide the fact finder with information, hypotheses, or theoretical formulations about the individual in question, or actuarial data about populations similar to the individual, that is of some assistance in determining issues in question. Whether psychological autopsy and related techniques pass these requirements, of course, is to be decided by the trial judge.

The courts appear to be struggling with the admissibility of psychological autopsies and related techniques (Dregne, 1982; Harris, 1990). Although psychological autopsies have been admitted by a number of courts (*Brown v. Hartford Life*, 1992; *Campbell v. Young Motor Company*, 1984; *Evans v. Provident Life*, 1990, 1991; *Gaido v. Weiser*, 1988; *Harvey v. Raleigh Police Department*, 1987, 1989; *Jackson v. State*, 1989; *Lockwood v. Rolfe*, 1967; *Mache v. Mache*, 1991; *Rodriguez v. Henkle Drilling*, 1992; *Starkey v. Springfield Life*, 1975), other courts have refused to admit such testimony (*Skulina v. Boehning*, 1988, 1991; *State v. Montijo*, 1989; *Thompson v. Mayes*, 1986).

---

[7] Laudably, some organizations attempt to reduce isolation through the use of outside consultants.

A recent, high-profile Florida case (*Jackson v. State,* 1989) is illustrative of the unusual ways in which psychological autopsies may be used in legal proceedings and demonstrates the reasoning underlying their admission into evidence. Theresa Jackson encouraged her underage daughter, Tina Mancini, to work as a nude dancer, and charged her room and board from her earnings. Tina later committed suicide. The state retained a psychiatrist, who performed a psychological autopsy on Tina. The psychiatrist concluded that "the nature of the relationship, (and) the abusive relationship with the mother, was a substantial contributing cause to Tina Mancini's suicide" (cited in Harris, 1990). The psychiatrist's approach in this case was similar to the EDA in that much of the information he reviewed was collected by third parties. Ms. Jackson was convicted of child abuse and two other related charges; she subsequently appealed, challenging the trial court's decision to admit the psychiatrist's testimony. The appellate court affirmed the trial court's decision to admit the psychiatrist's testimony and compared psychological autopsies to more accepted and well-established forensic pursuits:

we perceive no distinction between the admission of the expert's opinion in this case and, for example, admitting psychiatric opinion evidence to establish a defendant's sanity at the time of committing an offense or to prove the competency of an individual at the time of executing a will. (*Jackson v. State,* 1989, p. 720)

Although the law in this area is still evolving, some courts are willing to accept psychological autopsies and related procedures in a variety of circumstances. This obligates mental health professionals and professional organizations alike to take steps to ensure that consumers are informed and well educated about the nature and limitations of these techniques.

## Conclusion

As long as serious, unexpected, and seemingly unpredictable events occur, interested parties will attempt to discern why they happened in order to identify responsible persons or parties, prevent future occurrences, and attempt to make whole those persons who have suffered. When human behavior is involved, mental health professionals are likely to be approached, on the supposition that we have some expertise in matters of human behavior. Although psychologists and other mental health professionals clearly have expertise in many aspects of human behavior, this expertise has limits. We are obligated to define our expertise carefully and to note our limitations. This is particularly necessary when the stakes are so high and the effect of errors so great, as is the case with EDA, psychological autopsies, and psychological profiling. The repercussions of the USS *Iowa* explosion and investigation demonstrate this very clearly. We should tread slowly and carefully when entering such relatively uncharted waters: To do any less would be a disservice to the public and to our profession.

## REFERENCES

American Academy of Psychiatry and Law. 1991. Ethical guidelines for the practice of forensic psychiatry. In Committee on Psychiatry and Law, Group for the Advancement of Psychiatry, *The mental health professional and the legal system* (pp. 156–161). New York: Brunner/Mazel. (Original work published 1987)

American Educational Research Association, American Psychological Association, and National Council on Measurement in Education. (1985). *Standards for educational and psychological testing.* Washington, DC: American Psychological Association.

American Psychological Association. (1990). Ethical principles of psychologists (Amended June 2, 1989). *American Psychologist, 45,* 390–395.

Bonnie, R., & Slobogin, C. (1980). The role of mental health professionals in the criminal process: The case for informed speculation. *Virginia Law Review, 66,* 427–522.

Brent, D. A. (1989). The psychological autopsy: Methodological issues for the study of adolescent suicide. *Suicide and Life-Threatening Behavior, 19,* 43–57.

Brown v. Hartford Life, 593 So. 2d 1376 (Ct. App. La. 1992).

Campbell v. Young Motor Company, 211 Mont. 68, 684 P.2d 1101 (1984).

Clark, D. C., & Horton-Deutsch, S. L. (1992). Assessment *in absentia:* The value of the psychological autopsy method for studying antecedents of suicides and predicting future suicides. In R. Maris, A. Berman, J. Maltsberger, & R. Yufit (Eds.), *Assessment and prediction of suicide* (pp. 499–519). New York: Guilford Press.

Committee on Ethical Guidelines for Forensic Psychologists. (1991). Specialty guidelines for forensic psychologists. *Law and Human Behavior, 15,* 655–665.

Douglas, J. E., Ressler, R. K., Burgess, A. W., & Hartman, C. R. (1986). Criminal profiling from crime scene analysis. *Behavioral Sciences & the Law, 4,* 401–421.

Dregne, N. (1982). Psychological autopsy: A new tool for criminal defense attorneys? *Arizona Law Review, 24,* 421–439.

Ebert, B. W. (1987). Guide to conducting a psychological autopsy. *Professional Psychology: Research and Practice, 18,* 52–56.

Evans v. Provident Life and Accident Insurance Company, 15 Kan. App. 2d 97, 803 P.2d 1033 (Kan. App. 1990).

Evans v. Provident Life and Accident Insurance Company, 249 Kan. 248, 815 P.2d 550 (1991).

Families of USS Iowa victims sue. (1991, April 18). *St. Petersburg Times,* p. 9.

Federal rules of evidence. (1990). 28 *United States Code Annotated.* St. Paul, MN: West.

Fowler, R. (1986, May). Howard Hughes: A psychological autopsy. *Psychology Today,* pp. 22–33.

Frye v. U.S. 293 F. 1013 (1910).

Gaido v. Weiser, 227 N.J. Super. 175, 545 A.2d 1350 (N.J. Super. 1988).

Geberth, V. J. (1981). Psychological profiling. *Law and Order, 29*(9), 46–52.

Harris, A. A. (1990). The psychological autopsy: A retrospective study of suicide. *Stetson Law Review, 20,* 289–309.

Harvey v. Raleigh Police Department, 96 N.C. App. 540, 384 S.E.2d 549 (N.C. App. 1989).

Harvey v. Raleigh Police Department, 85 N.C. App. 540, 355 S.E.2d 147 (N.C. App. 1987).

Hazelwood, R. (1984). *The behavior-oriented interview of rape victims.* Washington, DC: Federal Bureau of Investigation, Department of Justice.

Holmes, R. M. (1989). *Profiling violent crimes: An investigative tool.* Newbury Park, CA: Sage.

House Armed Services Committee. (1990, March 5). HASC releases U.S.S. IOWA investigation report [news release]. Washington, DC: Author.

Jackson v. State, 553 So.2d 719 (Fla. 4th DCA, 1989).

Jobes, D. A., Berman, A. L., & Josselson, A. R. (1986). The impact of psychological autopsies in medical examiners' determination of manner of death. *Journal of Forensic Sciences, 31,* 177–189.

Jobes, D. A., Berman, A. L., & Josselson, A. R. (1987). Improving the validity and reliability of medical–legal certifications of suicide. *Suicide and Life-Threatening Behavior, 17,* 310–325.

Jobes, D. A., Casey, J. O., Berman, A. L., & Wright, D. G. (1991). Empirical criteria for the determination of suicide manner of death. *Journal of Forensic Sciences, 36,* 244–256.

Litman, R. E., Curphey, T. J., Schneidman, E. S., Faberow, N. L., & Tabachnick, N. D. (1963). Investigations of equivocal suicides. *Journal of the American Medical Association, 184,* 924–930.

Lockwood v. Rolfe, 254 Cal. App. 309, 62 Cal. Rptr. 230 (Cal. Ct. App. 1967).

Mache v. Mache, 218 Ill. App. 3d 1069, 578 N.E.2d 1253 (Ill. App. 1991).

Melton, G., Petrila, J., Poythress, N., & Slobogin, C. (1987). *Psychological evaluations for the courts: A handbook for mental health professionals and lawyers.* New York: Guilford Press.

Nelson, R. (1990). What really happened on the IOWA? *Popular Science,* 1990(12), 84–87 & 120–121.

Otto, R. K., Poythress, N. G., Darkes, J., & Starr, L. (1992, February). *The reliability and validity of psychological autopsies: An analysis of the USS IOWA incident.* Paper presented at the 44th Annual Meeting of the American Academy of Forensic Sciences, New Orleans, LA.

Pinizzotto, A. J. (1984). Forensic psychology: Criminal personality profiling. *Journal of Police Science and Administration, 12*(1), 32–40.

Pinizzotto, A. J., & Finkel, N. J. (1990). Criminal personality profiling: An outcome and process study. *Law and Human Behavior, 14,* 215–233

Porter. B. (1983, April). Mind hunters. *Psychology Today,* pp. 44–52.

*Review of Navy Investigation of U.S.S. IOWA Explosion.* (1990). Joint Hearings before the Investigations Subcommittee and the Defense Policy Panel of the Committee on Armed Services, House of Representatives, 101st Congress, 1st Session (HASC No. 101-41). Washington, DC: U.S. Government Printing Office.

Rodriguez v. Henkle Drilling, 16 Kan. App. 2d 728 (Kan. App. 1992).

Rosenberg, M. L., Davidson, L. E., Smith, J. C., Berman, A. L., Buzbee, H., Gantner, G., Gay, G. A., Moore-Lewis, B., Mills, D. H., Murray, D., O'Carroll, P. W., & Jobes, D. (1988). Operational criteria for the determination of suicide. *Journal of Forensic Sciences, 33,* 1445–1456.

Selkin, J. (1987). *Psychological autopsy in the courtroom.* Denver, CO: Author.

Selkin, J., & Loya, F. (1979). Issues in the psychological autopsy of a controversial public figure. *Professional Psychology, 10,* 87–93.

Shuman, D. (1986). *Psychiatric and psychological evidence.* Colorado Springs, CO: Shepard's/McGraw-Hill.

Skulina v. Boehning, 168 Mich. App. 704, 425 N.W.2d 135 (Mich. App. 1988).

Skulina v. Boehning, 187 Mich. App. 649, 468 N.W.2d 322 (Mich. App. 1991).

Slobogin, C. (1989). The "ultimate issue" issue. *Behavioral Science and the Law, 7,* 259–266.

Starkey Paint Company v. Springfield Life, 24 N.C. App. 507, 211 S.E.2d 498 (N.C. App. 1975).

State v. Montijo, 160 Ariz. 576, 774 P. 2d 1366 (Ariz App. 1989).

Test Rejects USS Iowa Sabotage. (1992, August 29). *Tampa Tribune,* p. 12.

Thompson v. Mayes, 707 S.W. 2d 951 (Ct. App. Texas 1986).

Turco, R. N. (1990). Psychological profiling. *International Journal of Offender Therapy and Comparative Criminology, 34,* 147–154.

*U.S.S. IOWA Tragedy: An Investigative Failure* (1990). Report of the Investigations Subcommittee and the Defense Policy Panel of the Committee on Armed Services, House of Representatives, 101st Congress, 2nd Session.

# Part III
# Investigative Interviewing

# [8]

Journal of Police Science and Administration
Copyright ©1987 by IACP, Inc.

Volume 15, No. 4
Printed in U.S.A.

# Enhancing Enhanced Eyewitness Memory:
# Refining the Cognitive Interview

Ronald P. Fisher, R. Edward Geiselman,

David S. Raymond, Lynn M. Jurkevich, and Monica L. Warhaftig

Ronald P. Fisher is an associate professor of psychology at Florida International University, Miami, FL 33181. He holds a Ph.D. in experimental psychology from Ohio State University and has contributed several articles on memory theory and retrieval processes to scientific and police journals.

R. Edward Geiselman is an associate professor of psychology at the University of California, Los Angeles. He holds a Ph.D. in experimental psychology from Ohio University and has contributed several articles on memory theory and applied psychology to scientific and police journals.

The three junior authors were undergraduate and high school students working as research assistants at Florida International University. They played an integral role in the conduct and analysis of this research.

During the past twenty years, there has been a growing interest among experimental psychologists in the area of eyewitness testimony. The focus of this interest has been to demonstrate the fallibility of eyewitness memory, and to understand it in terms of known principles of psychology. As a result, psychologists have discovered a variety of factors that may detrimentally affect eyewitness recall. These factors include, among others, stereotyping, high arousal, post-event information, cross-racial perception, and, in general, limitations of perception and memory (see Loftus 1979 for a review).

While psychologists have made valuable contributions in making known the limitations of eyewitness testimony, they have contributed very little to assist the beleaguered eyewitness. Recently, however, Geiselman and Fisher have developed a novel interviewing technique (the Cognitive Interview), based on laboratory-tested principles of cognitive psychology, that has been demonstrated to enhance eyewitness recall. Across a variety of studies, the Cognitive Interview has been found to be approximately 20 to 35 percent more effective than the traditional police interview, even when conducted by experienced law enforcement agents (Geiselman et al. 1985; 1987). The Cognitive Interview was equally effective for college students and nonstudents as eyewitnesses; it enhanced eyewitness recall for innocuous as well as highly arousing stimulus events; it is not as sensitive as the standard police interview

to the detrimental effects of leading questions; and, as shown in the present study, it can be learned and applied effectively by novice investigators.

Although the Cognitive Interview elicited better recall than traditional interviewing techniques, eyewitnesses still could not recall many of the details they had initially observed. Therefore, we set out to refine the technique to increase its effectiveness. One limitation of the original Cognitive Interview was that, while it provided for a general set of instructions to be given in the beginning of the interview, little guidance was provided about the remainder of the interview. Specifically, no guidelines were offered about the sequential structure of the interview—the order in which questions are asked.[1] This is noteworthy, as a recent study indicates that a major flaw of current police interviewing techniques is that question order seems to be unsystematic (Fisher, Geiselman, Raymond 1987). Furthermore, it was suggested that inappropriate sequencing of questions could hinder memory retrieval. An important goal of the present study was to refine the Cognitive Interview by developing guidelines about the sequential order of the interview.

[1]We had suggested earlier (Geiselman et al. 1984) that it is preferable to ask open-ended questions first, and then follow up with specific, closed questions; however, this suggestion had not been formally included in the Cognitive Interview.

One source of information about how to refine the Cognitive Interview came from analyzing the interviews tape recorded in earlier laboratory studies. Second, the Metro-Dade Police Department (Miami, Florida) graciously provided us with tape recordings of interviews conducted under field conditions. Following hours of careful examination of these interviews, and having conducted and been subjected to scores of interviews ourselves, it became apparent that there were several specific areas in which the Cognitive Interview could be improved. Examples of some of these suggested improvements include (1) allowing more time between questions, (2) not interrupting the eyewitness in the middle of a narrative response, and (3) not phrasing questions in the negative form. Because of limited publication space, a complete account of the modified techniques cannot be provided. We will be publishing a manual of police interviewing techniques in which we explain in detail all of the suggested techniques. For the present, an outline of some of the major conceptual guidelines of the refined Cognitive Interview follows.

The revised Cognitive Interview builds upon the principles of memory-enhanced interviewing established earlier. Thus, one of the main principles of the revised Cognitive Interview is to mentally reinstate the physical and psychological environment of the original event. To effect the reinstatement principle, eyewitnesses are asked to think about the physical context surrounding the original event (for example, weather, time of day, lighting conditions, and so on). In addition, they are asked to think about their psychological reactions during the original event. Were they surprised, angry, scared? What were they thinking about at the time? The second principle, using many retrieval perspectives, was also incorporated into the revised technique, as before, by instructing eyewitnesses to recall the original event in both a forward and reverse temporal order. In addition, they were asked to recall the event both from their own, personal perspective and also from the perspective of another participant (for example, put yourself in the victim's place and tell me what you think he saw). The two aforementioned principles were common to both the original and the revised Cognitive Interview. Two other basic principles were incorporated into the revised technique: (1) structuring the interview to be compatible with the eyewitness's mental operations and (2) facilitating the eyewitness using focused memory retrieval.

In our analysis of the taped police interviews, we often found that the questions were more compatible with the interviewer's invetigative needs than with the eyewitness's mental operations. For example,

police interviewers are typically required to file an official report containing objective facts about the suspect's appearance. As a result, they ask direct, short-answer questions about these features, usually in a predetermined order. The problem is that the requested information is not necessarily organized in the eyewitness's mind in the same format as prescribed by the police report. By imposing the police report organization on the eyewitness's memory retrieval, recall will likely suffer. Ideally, the structure of the interview should conform to the format of the eyewitness's knowledge. The interviewer's goal is to infer how the relevant knowledge is stored by the eyewitness and to formulate questions that are compatible with the eyewitness's knowledge.

The second major guideline is to facilitate the eyewitness conducting a focused memory retrieval. Memory retrieval, like other mental activities, requires focused attention. Analysis of the taped police interviews revealed, however, that interviewers often engaged in activities that prevented eyewitnesses from searching through memory in a focused manner. Two of the more common activities that prevent focused retrieval are (1) frequent interruptions of the eyewitness's narration and (2) the overuse of direct, short-answer questions. As such, two of the guidelines of the revised Cognitive Interview are to minimize the number of interruptions and to ask fewer short-answer questions.[2] As an alternative, it is suggested that the interviewer structure the interview to elicit more eyewitness-controlled narrations.

As mentioned before, the revised Cognitive Interview also provides guidelines about the sequential structure of the interview. In the typical police interview, the interviewer begins by requesting the eyewitness to provide a narrative account of the event in question. After this standard opening, there is little systematic or uniform about the temporal sequence of police interviews (Fisher et al. 1987). It has been suggested that one sequential principle for effective interviewing is to ask for open-ended responses before detailed, specific questions (Geiselman et al. 1984; Weston and Wells 1970). Unfortunately, because of the frequent interruptions that punctuate the eyewitness's open-ended narration, this principle seems to be generally ignored in practice. Our first suggestion, then, is that interviewers carefully adhere to this general principle. In addition, it is suggested that, following the initial

---

[2]Similar suggestions have been proposed by others, e.g., Flanagan (1981).

open-ended narration, the interviewer return to specific episodes within the general scenario to elicit a more detailed narration. After completing this second line of narrative responses, interviewers are instructed to probe with specific short-answer questions any undescribed facts. When concluding the interview, interviewers should summarize the eyewitness's response. This permits the eyewitness to check for accuracy of the interviewer's notes and also affords an additional opportunity for the eyewitness to monitor memory.

## METHOD

### Design

Since the purpose of the present study was to improve upon the original Cognitive Interview, we compared only the revised version of the Cognitive Interview with the original version. We did not include a standard police interview condition, since we have found in previous studies that it is less effective than the Cognitive Interview. Three memory-performance dependent variables were examined: number of correct statements, incorrect statements, and confabulations. In addition, we examined time per interview, as it covaries with interview condition.

### Interview Conditions

The instructions to conduct the original Cognitive Interview were similar to those provided to the interviewers in previous studies (see Geiselman et al. 1985 for a more detailed description). Briefly, the interviewers were instructed to describe to the eyewitnesses at the beginning of the session four general memory-retrieval techniques:

1. Reinstate the environmental and psychological contexts of the original event.
2. Report everything. Do not edit anything out of your report, even things you may consider trivial.
3. Recall the events in different orders, both forward and backward.
4. Try to recall the incident from different perspectives, both from your own perspective and from that of prominent characters in the scene.

The instructions for the revised Cognitive Interview are much more extensive, and too detailed to describe here completely. As a brief summary, the main points included, in addition to the four general principles

of the original Cognitive Interview, the ideas developed in the introduction: tailoring the interview to be compatible with the eyewitness's mental operations and facilitating the eyewitness using focused retrieval. Several specific instructions were also provided (for example, developing the eyewitness's subjective descriptions into objective facts, using appropriate language and phrasing, noticing eye movements and different speech rates, and so on). Finally, the interviewers were instructed to use the sequential order summarized in the introduction: start with an open-ended narration, follow with a return to specific episodes, and end with a recapitulation.

### Subjects

The subjects (eyewitnesses) were sixteen male and female undergraduate students at Florida International University (FIU), who participated for course credit. The subjects were assigned randomly to one of the two interview conditions, eight per condition.

### Interviewers

There were three interviewers: two high school students and one undergraduate college student at FIU. None had received any formal training in investigative interviewing before the current study. Each interviewer interviewed five or six eyewitnesses, approximately half with the original Cognitive Interview and half with the revised interview.

### Materials and Apparatus

Stimulus Event. The stimuli were two videocassette recordings of the films we had used in previous studies (Geiselman et al. 1985). The original films are used by the Los Angeles Police Department as part of a computerized training process in which police officers are exposed to simulated, life-threatening situations. Each film presents an audiovisual scenario of a violent crime (a bank robbery or a liquor store holdup) and lasts approximately four minutes. The video cassettes were shown on a Panasonic NV-9300A (3/4-inch U-Matic) videocassette recorder and appeared on a 20-inch JVC color monitor. All of the interviews were audio tape recorded on standard cassette recorders.

### Procedure

Each subject participated in two sessions. During the first session, groups of 2-5 subjects went to a small faculty office at FIU and saw one of the two videotaped crime scenes. The subjects were asked to refrain from discussing the events of the crime. Approximately 48 hours later, the subjects went to a different room (small classroom) to be interviewed. The subjects were interviewed individually by one of the three interviewers. The interviewers were not given any information prior to the interview about the crime depicted on the videotape. They were told only that the subject had seen a videotape of a crime two days ago. Each interviewer conducted one or two interviews every day. When two interviews were conducted on a single day, one was an original and the other a revised Cognitive Interview. Approximately half the time the original interview was conducted first and the revised second, and half the time in the opposite order.

Interviewer Training. In the first phase of training, the interviewers were instructed to use the original Cognitive Interview. They listened to sample Cognitive Interviews conducted by the best interviewers in our earlier studies (Geiselman et al. 1985; in press). In addition, they received the same 30-minute training session given to police interviewers in the prior studies. Since the current interviewers were novices, they practiced the original technique by conducting several interviews with friends and relatives. After each of these practice sessions, the interviewers received critical feedback on their performance. This first stage lasted approximately one month.[3]

In the second phase, the research team thoroughly examined tape-recorded field interviews to note effective and poor interviewing techniques. Following this, a master set of positive and negative suggestions was formalized, which the interviewers then studied. The interviewers received two learning sessions on the use of the revised technique and observed a sample interview session. Again, the interviewers practiced using the revised Cognitive Interview by conducting several interviews with friends and relatives, and then received critical feedback on their performance. Finally, the interviewers conducted one last set of refresher interviews with both the original and revised methods until they felt comfortable with both techniques. This second phase lasted approximately ten weeks. After completing both training phases, the experimental interviews were conducted, half with each interview method.

Analysis of Protocols. Each of the tape-recorded interviews was transcribed and scored for accuracy. Only objective, relevant (to the crime) statements

were scored. For example, eyewitness claims that he or she viewed the videotape at 3:30 p.m. (irrelevant) or that the suspect appeared nervous (subjective) were not included in the scoring. Each objective, relevant claim was categorized as either correct, incorrect (for example, suspect had brown hair, but eyewitness reports it was red), or a confabulation (for example, suspect's hair is covered, but eyewitness reports it was red). In the few cases (approximately 5 percent) where the scorer could not decide how to categorize a statement—for example, whether subjective or objective—a committee of three scorers resolved the decision. Some of the scorers may have been more lenient than others. Similarly, some of the interviewers may have been more effective than others. Neither of these effects should alter the results, however, as each interviewer and scorer worked with approximately half original and half revised Cognitive Interviews. Thus, any effects due to interviewer effectiveness or scorer bias would have been evenly distributed across the two interview types.

## RESULTS

As seen in table 1, the revised Cognitive Interview elicits 45 percent more correct information than does the original interview, $F (1, 14) = 7.60$, MSe = 169.37, $p < .02$. By comparison, there are no reliable differences between the two interviews for either number of incorrect statements, $F (1, 14) < 1$, MS3 = 33.99, $p > .20$, or for number of confabulations, $F (1, 14) < 1$, MSe = 2.24, $p > .20$. It may appear as if there are more incorrect responses elicited by the revised (12.00) than by the original (9.38) interview; however, one must keep in mind two factors. First, these differences are not reliable; second, and more important, the rates of incorrect responses (number of incorrect responses/total number of responses) actually favor the revised (.17) over the original (.19) interview (although, again, these differences are not reliable). The overall rate of incorrect responses found in the present study (.18) is consistent with error rates found in previous studies (Geiselman et al. 1985; in press) as is the rate of confabulations (.03). In summary, the revised Cognitive Interview generates considerably more correct information than does the original, without increasing the error or confabulation rates.

Some interviewers were obviously more effective than others. The range of correct responses elicited by the interviewers varied from a low of 37.4 to a high of 55.9. Perhaps the effectiveness of the revised technique is limited only to the best or worst interviewers. In fact, all three interviewers were

---

[3]A long time was required to train the interviewers, as they were full-time students.

TABLE 1

PERFORMANCE MEASURES FOR REVISED AND
ORIGINAL COGNITIVE INTERVIEWS

| Measure | Interview | |
|---|---|---|
| | Revised | Original |
| Number correct | 57.50 | 39.56 |
| Number incorrect | 12.00 | 9.38 |
| Number confabulated | 1.75 | 1.38 |
| Question time (min.) | 38.50 | 29.25 |
| Number correct (adjusted for time covariate) | 54.20 | 42.80 |

more successful when using the revised than with the original interview. The poorest interviewer elicited 25 percent more correct statements with the revised than with the original interview, the intermediate interviewer 45 percent more, and the best interviewer 74 percent more. One might be tempted to conclude that effectiveness of the revised technique is correlated with interviewer skill; however, at the present time, we caution against such an interpretation because of the paucity of data. There were only three interviewers, each of whom interviewed only five or six people. Nevertheless, we did find that each of the interviewers was more successful with the revised than with the original interview.

It can be noted from table 1 that it takes approximately nine minutes longer to conduct the revised interview than the original interview. While this difference was not reliable, $F (1, 14) = 2.34$, MSe $= 146.39$ p $> .10$, perhaps the extra time to conduct the revised interview accounts for its greater effectiveness. To examine this possibility, we reanalyzed the data with questioning time as a covariate. As can be seen from the adjusted scores in table 1, the revised interview still elicits more information than does the original, although the effect is attenuated somewhat, $F (1, 13) = 4.43$, MSe $= 100.59$, p $< .06$.

The preceding analyses examined all of the crime-relevant statements, irrespective of their importance. Perhaps the revised interview simply elicits more trivial statements, information with no investigative value. If this were true, the revised technique would not have any greater practical import. To examine this possibility, we rescored the data for only the facts with the greatest investigative value (for example, suspect description). Twenty critical facts were isolated for the liquor store holdup and 25 for the

bank robbery.[4] These are the same critical facts used in an earlier study of the original Cognitive Interview (Geiselman et al. 1985). When the data are scored for these critical facts only, the same trends are obtained as before: 49 percent more correct information is elicited from the revised (12.45) than the original (8.33) Cognitive Interview, $F (1, 14) = 7.07$, MSe $= 9.64$, p $< .02$. (There is no reliable difference between the two conditions for number of errors on these critical facts, $F = 1.39$, MSe $= 1.61$, p $> .20$.)

## DISCUSSION

In the present study, the revised interview elicited 45 percent more correct information than did the original Cognitive Interview, which has been shown earlier to be about 30 percent more effective than the standard police interview. The additional information gathered with the revised technique has investigative value, and it does not come at the expense of increased error. Given that extensive and accurate eyewitness information is the goal of police investigation, the Cognitive Interview is potentially a major advance over traditional techniques. In relation to other memory-enhancing techniques used by police, specifically hypnosis, the revised Cognitive Interview has the advantage of being more effective—the revised interview is more effective than the original Cognitive Interview, which was as effective as hypnosis (Geiselman et al. 1985). In addition, the revised Cognitive Interview is more reliable, easier to learn, and easier to implement. Furthermore, at least for the present, the Cognitive Interview has none of the legal constraints that beset hypnosis interviewing. In fact, it has already been suggested as a viable alternative to hypnosis for forensic interviewing (Orne 1985).

One potential problem of the revised Cognitive Interview is that it makes extensive cognitive demands on the interviewer. There are increased memory demands imposed by the attempt to minimize interruptions—the interviewer must store his current comment or question until a later time, when it is more appropriate. He must listen more attentively, in order to infer correctly the eyewitness's organization of knowledge. He must be more flexible in order to make on-line decisions to restructure the interview, thereby abandoning any preestablished sequence of questioning. In return for this expenditure of cognitive effort, however, is the expectation of significantly more eyewitness information, which ultimately is the goal of investigative interviewing.

---

[4]There were two suspects in the liquor store holdup and three suspects in the bank robbery.

One possible criticism of the present study is that the original Cognitive Interview condition was not comparable to the Cognitive Interview that was conducted in prior studies (Geiselman et al. 1985; in press). In the present study the interviewers were students with no prior experience in investigative interviewing, whereas in the prior studies the interviewers were practicing law enforcement agents with hundreds of hours of experience conducting investigative interviews. Thus, perhaps the "improvement" found with the revised technique is not over the true Cognitive Interview, but simply over some impoverished form. If so, the revised technique may not be a true advance over the original. In order to examine this possibility, we compared the effectiveness of the current interviewers using the original Cognitive Interview with the experienced detectives using the (original) Cognitive Interview in two earlier studies.[5] In fact, the two sets of scores are very similar: the number of correct facts elicited was approximately the same for the present study and the earlier studies (39.56 and 45.24, respectively) as was the number of incorrect facts (9.38 and 8.24) and the number of confabulations (1.38 and 1.26). Even the time to conduct the interviews was equivalent for the two studies (29.25 and 30.11 min.) It is always dangerous to compare the scores across two sets of studies, since the experimental conditions are never identical. In this case, however, any methodological differences between the current and earlier studies should favor performance in the earlier studies. In the earlier studies, the medium used to present the crime scene was the original film used by the LAPD, whereas in the present study, the medium was a *copy* of a *videocassette recording* of the original film. Furthermore, in the earlier studies, the film was shown on a large, 9-foot x 9-foot screen, with 4-track nonoptical sound, whereas in the present study, the video cassette was shown on a 20-inch television monitor with conventional speakers. Thus, the visual resolution and auditory clarity were far greater in the earlier studies than in the present study. Nevertheless, despite this potential advantage, eyewitness recall was no better in the earlier studies than in the present study using the original Cognitive Interview. We are confident, therefore, that the original Cognitive Interviews of the present study were as well conducted as the Cognitive Interviews of the earlier studies and, therefore, that the superiority of the revised Cognitive Interview is a valid finding.

Given that the event to be recalled was so much clearer in the original studies than in the present study, and given that the original interviews were conducted by experienced detectives whereas the current interviews were conducted by novice students, the superiority of the revised Cognitive Interview over the standard police interview is even more impressive. In the two earlier studies, the standard police interview elicited an average of 29.3 correct statements, whereas in the present study the revised Cognitive Interview elicited 57.5 correct statements, an increase of almost two-fold (96 percent). Part of this difference may be due to different scoring criteria used in the two studies or to the inclusion of all facts, trivial and important, in the scoring. When the scores are analyzed only for a common set of investigatively important information—the 20 (or 25) critical facts—the results still favor the revised Cognitive Interview. On the average, the standard police interview elicited 9.2 critical facts,[6] whereas the revised Cognitive Interview elicited 12.45 facts, a difference of 35 percent.

We reported earlier (Fisher et al. 1987) that, perhaps because of the lack of formal training in eyewitness interviewing, police investigators approach their task from a common-sense perspective. Our research in developing the Cognitive Interview suggests that interviews could be conducted more effectively if investigators made use of currently available scientific knowledge about memory retrieval. In light of our findings, showing consistent enhancement with the Cognitive Interview, we strongly recommend that investigative interviewers receive formalized training on scientific principles of memory retrieval, especially as applied to the interviewing of eyewitnesses.

## ACKNOWLEDGEMENTS

The present research was supported by a grant from the National Institute of Justice (USDJ-85-IJ-CX-0053).

We appreciate the assistance of the Metro-Dade Police Department (Miami, Florida) in providing tape-recorded field interviews.

## REFERENCES

Fisher, R.P.; Geiselman, R.E.; and Raymond, D.S. 1987. Critical analysis of police interview techniques. *J. Pol. Sci. & Adm.* 15(3):177-185.

Flanagan, E.J. 1981. Interviewing and interrogation techniques. In *Criminal and civil investigation handbook*, edited by J. Grau, pp.4/3-4/23. New York: McGraw-Hill.

Geiselman, R.E.; Fisher, R.P.; Firstenberg, I.; Hutton, L.A.; Sullivan, S.; Avetissian, I.; and Prosk, A. 1984. Enhancement of eyewitness memory: An empirical evaluation of the cognitive interview. *J. Pol. Sci. & Adm.* 12:74-80.

---

[5]These data reflect only the scores from the bank robbery and liquor store holdup films.

[6]Only the scores from Geiselman et al. (1985) are included.

Geiselman, R.E.; Fisher, R.P.; MacKinnon, D.P.; and Holland, H.L. 1985. Eyewitness memory enhancement in the police interview: Cognitive retrieval mnemonics versus hypnosis. *J. Appl. Psych.* 70:401-412.

———. In press. Enhancement of eyewitness memory with the cognitive interview. *Amer. J. Psych.*

Loftus, E.F. 1979. *Eyewitness testimony.* Cambridge, MA: Harvard University Press.

Orne, M.T. 1985. *State* v. *DeNicola* (Pennsylvania).

Weston, P.B., and Wells, K.M. 1970. *Criminal investigation.* Englewood Cliffs, NJ: Prentice-Hall.

# [9]

# Ethical interviewing*

## Eric Shepherd

Any conversation is a task of joint orientation. In what they say and the way they say it, participants send two types of information concerning the way in which they have chosen to define reality i.e. the way they each see the world and the way in which they wish the other to see the world (Shepherd, 1982). They communicate object information - facts of the matter as they see them and wish to see them handled in the encounter. Simultaneously they communicate relationship information, their definition of the type of relationship that they each perceive to be the case, or would like to be the case, between them (Watzlawick et al., 1967). Conversational roles are assumed, assigned, accepted and rejected in everyday encounters, a process of negotiation with each participant seeking to influence the other's perception of the relationship (Nierenberg, 1986).

There are many ways of describing relationships. One way is to describe a relationship in terms of the *direction* and *degree of directiveness* over the conversational exchange. A relationship can be either *up-down* (characterized by dominant/submissive or superior/subordinate talk) or *across* (with participants talking as equals) (Bateson, 1972).

*Up-down* relationships are very pervasive in everyday life, and in working life in particular. People have come to accept that the one in the *up* position is notionally in charge - the one with power, particularly expert power, referential power and coercive power. In these circumstances the one in the *up* position has even greater capacity to impose his or her definition of reality on the situation. When the other goes along with this definition, the outcomes will be real even though the shared definition of reality may be wholly unreal, even madness, to any detached observer. In the clinical world such relationships are called a "folie à deux".

Being in the *up* position is particularly of advantage to police officers, especially as part of their personal *anxiety reduction programme*. It implies a tight, inflexible rein on content and conduct. It has disadvantages. Tightness and inflexibility constrain the investigative potential of their police-public and police-police encounters. It limits commitment, disclosure and feedback on both sides.

*Across* relationships are much less common. They imply a more tentative definition of reality in terms of information content and more flexible management of the encounter. They also have the disadvantage that the other person might seek to exploit the situation and to turn it into an *up-down* relationship.

In signalling how tight will be their rein on the reality-defining process, police officers send another powerful message: to the person opposite, to observers, and to those who learn at second hand about police officers' conversational performances. How a police officer behaves in a *given* case is taken to be illustrative of his or her moral perspective on *all* investigative encounters: the "right" way to think and to deal with people in order to do the job.

## Morality, ethics and conversation

Morality has to do with a particular outlook on the world, a set of values about the way the world ought to be in respect of rationality (appropriate forms of logical relationship) and sociality (appropriate forms of social relationship - Wilson, 1972). Many people are not conscious of having a particular moral perspective or set of values. Despite this, an examination of history and across cultures suggests that two central moral concepts are respect for the person and the obligation to tell the truth (Downie and Telfer, 1969; Peters, 1966).

* *Policing*, 7, 42-60. © 1991 Police Review Publishing Company. Reproduced by permission.

The two concepts are interdependent. Observing both protects integrity - from the Latin *integer* the whole - and the society of which the person is taken to be representative. It is therefore no accident that the corner-stone of law is respect for the person and the application of law rests upon telling the truth (Kant, 1964). The observance of both distinguishes a free from a totalitarian society. In the former police officers behave lawfully, in the latter expediently.

The everyday process of living poses people as individuals with the task of translating their implicit, cloudy moral perspective into action. This is the essence of *ethics* - deliberate thought into action deemed to be "right" - moral, justifiable and defensible. The central concept of ethics is *obligation* - what *ought* to be thought and done (Kinget, 1975). Ethical action presupposes freedom of choice to act one way rather than another. Which of the possible courses of action to take depends upon the individual's interpretation of conduct which is ethical. The evidence for this choice is conversation.

## Ethical conversations and unethical interviews

Ethical conversation implies communicating respect for the person. This involves signalling to the person opposite that he or she like the speaker is also human and has the same rights: the right to be treated with dignity and the right to make free choices - to decide whether or not to engage in the exchange, and to evaluate and to respond to the content and the conduct of the exchange.

To be ethical in a conversation presumes an *including* relationship founded on *empathy* - a commitment to thinking and acting from a *two-sided, self and other* perspective - talking *across* - as one human being to another (Shepherd, 1982). Buber (1958) called this an *I-Your* relationship. It contrasts with an *I-It* relationship in which the speaker adopts an *excluding*, one-sided self-centred perspective, conversing in asymmetrical terms to the person opposite as though he or she were an object to be manipulated. Ethical conversations - *I-You* conversations - are fostered and maintained by observing six ethical principles and managing the conversation ethically.

### The six principles of ethical conversation

*Principle 1 (The prior investigation principle)*

I must be sufficiently aware of the breadth and depth of knowledge necessary to substantiate my assertions and arguments.

Implies: I must be able to cope with you questioning my knowledge (content and quality).

In sum: I must know what I'm talking about: "bullshitting" is unethical.

*Principle 2 (The sincerity principle)*

I must select information and arguments fairly and present them fairly in the way I make assertions (statements, questions, observations and comments).

Implies: You are able to make fair judgements and choices as to the validity of my information.

In sum: I must tell the truth, must not bluff, evade, confuse or use pretence.

*Principle 3 (The disclosure principle)*

I must be open and tell the truth about where my knowledge comes from.

Implies: You are able to make fair judgements as to the reliability of my sources and the existence of biases and prejudices.

In sum: I must be prepared to disclose my sources.

*Principle 4 (The open-mindedness principle)*

I must be non-judgemental in my approach to information gathering and processing prior to and during the conversation.

Implies: The other person should be protected from my personal biases and prejudices.

In sum: I must not have a closed mind.

*Principle 5 (The tolerance principle)*

I must be able to acknowledge (though not have to accept) rejection of my information, arguments and sources.

Implies: Tolerating your dissent from my view.

In sum: I must cope with rebuttal and resistance.

*Principle 6 (The integrity principle)*

In attempting to influence you to accept my information I must maintain integrity.

Implies: The desire to change your thinking and responses does not remove the obligation to protect your dignity and continued freedom of choice.

In sum: I must not allow my personal goals to blind me to my moral obligations.

### Ethical conversation management

An ethical conversationalist converses with two-sided logic, with self and other in mind, evidencing verbally and non-verbally a commitment to co-operative talk by: using appropriate conversational style; consciously orientating the other person as to the reason for the conversation (to avoid the "guessing game" and to signal no "hidden agenda"); to work at making the exchange mutual by sharing the talking turn and talking time, balancing assertions (questions, statements, observations and comments) with responsive listening; striving not to talk disruptively (overtalking, interrupting, minimally responding and rapidly changing the topic); and not bringing the exchange to an ill-considered or inconsiderate close.

Unethical conversation is the converse of all of these behaviours - a conversation grounded upon non-observance of the key principles of ethical conversation. If, and when, we encounter such people we can only hope that we recognize them, sooner rather than later, to be conversing unethically and to minimize the degree of insult to our dignity and our ability to judge the world aright. However, much more injurious are those exchanges when an individual ignores ethical principles and practices when seeking to talk with us to achieve a purpose - interviewing us unethically. They can seriously damage our faith in ourselves, the "system" and human nature itself.

### Unethical interviewing

Unethical interviewers subscribe to another morality: one founded on valuing expediency. The logic for handling information and social relationships is framed upon self-interest. The investigative, and therefore interviewing, purpose is distorted. The most endemic and enduring distortion of all is without doubt "getting a cough", despite Lord Devlin's (1979) observation that confession is not the short cut to justice. Such goals are achieved by the blundering or the malevolent (Mirfield, 1985) distorting reality prior to and during the interview.

### Distorting reality prior to the interview

Expedient investigation implies a narrow definition of the range of required information, and arbitrariness in the processes of collection, collation, integration and evaluation. The self-interest goal ensures that the officer's definition of the situation remains unrevised in the light of emergent information. Negative information - that which does not "fit" - is coped with by being selectively screened out - ignored, forgotten, deleted or disposed of. The product of such information gathering and processing is a knowledge base of dubious status, in terms of validity (quality of content) and reliability (quality of source). Of course this does not matter to an interviewer who is already committed to a path of "premature closure" and confirmation, rather than disconfirmation, of prior perceptions.

Shortcomings in preparation lend momentum to an investigative process which is in effect a self-fulfilling prophecy in the making. Meetings with third parties (e.g. a solicitor or appropriate adult) are to be avoided. Their role and performance as moral monitors, as it were, could prejudice the officer's definition of reality. If moral monitors cannot be excluded then "briefings" by the police officer are likely to be characterized by attempts to side-step the necessity to observe the six principles of ethical conversation in the attempt to prolong the currency of his or her distorted, and distorting, definition of reality (Irving and McKenzie, 1988).

*Distorting reality within the interview*

The relationship, the investigative process and emergent information in the interview are managed in a contrived manner to fit in with the unethical interviewer's frame of reference. It is a frame of reference in which thought and action are directed at eliciting and recognizing responses which confirm a preconception of facts of the matter, the situation, and the interviewee. Findings from as diverse endeavours as government-commissioned inquiries and psychological research point to the pervasiveness of the contribution of this confirmation bias, to the distortion of reality in the interviewing context.

An unethical interviewer, in common with all interviewers, has a notional advantage. The typical interview relationship in everyday life is *up-down*, but is particularly expected and assumed to be so in the policing context. Interviewees in general are *down* by virtue of possessing less ability to influence the conduct, the course and the content of the finding out process. Unethical interviewers take this "fact of life" further and seek to establish an *I-It* relationship with the interviewee.

*Up-down* relationships and their refinement, *I-It* relationships, increase an unethical interviewer's potential to manage the conversation in a manner which distorts information and creates conditions leading to the acceptance of this information. Unethical interviewers dominate the talking time and the talking turn, since monologue aids the foregrounding of their "one-sided" logic. Such logic is also aided by leading, closed confirmatory, option, marathon and multiple questions, filled pauses and open-closed sequences. It is extended by listening behaviour consistent with being a non-attender, an assumer or a word-picker (Shepherd, 1986).

In varying degrees and in varying combinations unethical interviewers lie, falsify, evade, bluff and confuse. Wittingly or unwittingly the interviewee's vulnerability is increased. Crucial are the interviewee's disposition towards compliance and suggestibility. Compounding factors are desire to please, age, intellect, personality, psychological state of mind (apprehension, anxiety, fear, and depression), and level of arousal (elevated by the physical, perceptual, social and psychological isolation of being in custody). Failure to detect these processes is necessarily unethical. Particularly unethical, however, is interviewer preference to interpret signs of arousal as "lie signs" and to ignore the possibility of emergent compliance and suggestibility.

Unethical interviewers interfere with the interviewee's ability to make accurate judgements. Their unprincipled approach to the content and conduct of the interview creates a distorted definition of reality in terms of information, information handling and the relationship between the interviewee, the interviewer and the outside world. The outcome is an interviewee who can be forced to make choices he or she would not normally make and denied the opportunity to make choices he or she would normally make.

The result is an account of facts of the matter which ranges from the partially to the wholly inaccurate. Those who engineer the conversational circumstances to create such accounts are *not* monsters. To attribute their attitude and conduct to incompetence or a character failing would be to miss the point utterly.

Social psychology has drawn our attention to the fact that people tend to be biased in the way in which they explain behaviour (Forgas, 1985). They are disposed to attribute an individual's behaviour to his or her "personality" rather than the circumstances surrounding or confronting the individual. This tendency is even greater when it is behaviour to which we take exception, which makes us feel uncomfortable and which arouses negative emotions (Ross, 1977). It is therefore necessary to reflect upon those aspects of police officers' working lives which lead them to believe that to think and act unethically is the "right" way to do their job.

## The origins of unethical interviewing

To paraphrase Cribben (1981), the most bothersome management problem is ethical behaviour. High sounding platitudes abound. Clear ideas are notable by their absence. Absolutists rigidly insist that everything is either right or wrong. Relativists say it all depends, contending that life consists of variables, not constants. Sceptics doubt that a workable ethical code can be formulated, let alone one acceptable to the majority of individuals in the organization. Cynics snigger at "lofty" proposals expounded by those at the top, while those who claim to be realists snort that ethics is a luxury.

Organizational realities create the conditions for cynicism and distorted definitions of what is "real" when it comes to ethics. Unethical interviewing is born of individual attempts to resolve moral contradictions and to conform to organizational "realities" - organizational "oughts" of acceptable performance - of what constitutes "getting it right" in terms of a "good" job and the "right" way to handle social relationships (Shepherd, 1988).

It is worth pondering the links in the chain of logic which connects the Chief Officer's force goals with the unprincipled goals of an unethical interviewer. Clearly, top-landing statements of purpose and mission statements have to be translated into actual performance which must be amenable to monitoring and evaluation. This is an enduring problem for the police service. The "service" it delivers does not readily lend itself to being assessed in terms of quality of effort. Understandably there is a pressure from outside the police service - its constitutional masters and the media - to show that it is "doing something" - whether it be in response to a rise in crime or the investigation of a "high profile" crime. One impactful method of demonstrating that something is being done is to measure performance, statistically, in terms of amount of effort and, more importantly, the tangible results of this effort. The pressures are great to think and act in terms of "results".

At the level of the working group - the next link in the chain of "results" logic - the counting emerges as "league tables" which enable comparison between one working group and another. Groups comprise individuals - managers, supervisors and those they manage and supervise. In a counting culture the individual officer, irrespective of rank, role or seniority, must come to terms with being assessed in terms of quantity - arrests, counters, "results", "coughs" (admissions), TICs (admitted offences taken into consideration), and "clear ups".

The making of a career is wrapped around acceptance by those around you. Competence based on counting leads to notions of prowess, power and potential to progress - the essential ingredients of status. Those with such status are the moral models of "right" thinking and "right" behaviour in the group. What they say and do creates the "ethos" (Graeff, 1989). Uncomfortable it may be, but we have to recognize that a culture which thinks, measures and rewards, according to quantity to demonstrate that something is being done, will always be at risk of distorting and devaluing social relationships - within the organization and at the point of contact with the public.

## Distorting and devaluing social relationships

### Depersonalizing talk: the use of I-It language

When communicating with each other contact professionals characteristically use the language of objective categories - "object" language - to refer to those with whom they deal in problematic circumstances. Thus in the professions associated with health and illness an individual will be treated as a person and as an instance of a problem e.g. "Joan Smith is in Bed 3 on the left; she is the "case" of oat-cell carcinoma". The use of "object" language here is appropriate: talking about Joan does not press the professional to lose respect for her as a person.

The police service is perhaps noteworthy for its inappropriate use of "object" language. Take for example the use of the word "body" to refer to an arrested person. To a police officer pursing results this "body" counts. Thinking about the human being shrouded in the body in such peculiar distancing terms is but a rice paper's width away from thinking and acting towards that person in *I-It* terms (Shepherd, 1982).

Such depersonalizing thought and action in social relationships is not reserved for police-public encounters. Police officers talk and handle each other in depersonalizing ways. Who in the police service has not sat on the receiving end of a "monologue" staff appraisal - particularly one delivered by someone who does not know the appraisee, who does not know about the appraisee, and who sees this as yet another in a series of sessions to be got out of the way. Yet further evidence of that fact of organizational life: *Management style equals management conversation* (Kite and Shepherd, 1989).

The Preliminary Report on Stress in the Police Service (Manolias, 1983) indicted police management style, i.e. police managers management of conversations with the managed. Management conversation is a major source of stress. "There's more stress inside the nick than outside on the streets" said that much quoted anonymous constable in the Report.

Management conversations create management systems. Despite the increasing efforts being expended on developing human resource management systems it is still a source of cynicism and stress for individual officers that their lives, and careers, are decided arbitrarily - that they are pawns to be moved around like objects in time and space. Before working with the police service the author had never heard of that peculiar phenomenon, the "obligatory false promise" - that deluding police management device used to motivate the person opposite.

*Categorizing and valuing purposeful encounters: "interviewing" vs "interrogation"*

Categorical thinking about types of police-public encounter is widespread. Unfortunately these definitions are constraining to say the least. In the counting culture, "coughs" count. Probationers quickly learn that interviews with suspects are more important than interviews with witnesses, and those special witnesses called victims. The "system" requires, and therefore places greater attention to, admissions. Every eye is turned to the interview with the suspect. This counts. Proof of the primacy of this type of interview is to be found on interviewing courses when officers are asked to generate a "practical" of their own. Almost invariably it is an interview with a suspect.

Despite the vital forensic value of information gained from victims and witnesses, in order to yield information of sufficient breadth and depth to interview the suspect, scant attention is given to achieving high standards here. The implications for the police service, and the public it serves, are literally disastrous (Shepherd and Kite, 1988).

The notion is that interviews can be categorized according to the type of interviewee and the potential for the interviewee to present the officer with difficulties. From this perspective "interviews" are conducted with non-problematic interviewees - victims and witnesses; "interrogations" are purposeful conversations with those problematic people called suspects. However, the appropriateness of this perspective breaks down when the interviewee acts out of stereotype - when victims and witnesses choose not to go along with the interviewer's management of the conversation and information prior to and within the interview. According to this perspective victims and witnesses co-operate and do not dissent (Shepherd, 1986). This raises the spectre of the resistant interviewee and the necessity to cope with that type of person.

Police officers dread resistance such as silence, "no comment", non-cooperation, hostility or lying. Resistance is in effect the product of two dimensions - *willingness to talk* (motivation) and *ability to tell* (capacity) (Shepherd, 1986; 1987). Police officers tend to define resistance, unidimensionally, where unwillingness arises from guilt or having something to hide. Resistance thus defined gives rise to another way of categorizing the finding out process.

"Interviewing", a very fuzzy notion, is that form of conversation required when little, transient or no resistance is anticipated or encountered. The key assumption in respect of interviewing is that since everyone has to do it, anyone can do it. Interviewing, according to this perspective, is a low-status skill.

Not so "interrogation". Although definitions are again hazy, the term implies a set of behaviour patterns - or *strategies* - enacted by the officer to overcome increasing, sustained or total interviewee resistance to the officer's management of information and the conversation (Walkely, 1987). Selection of strategy is heavily based upon an evaluation of the interviewee's "personality" (Irving, 1980). (It only struck the author recently that the person being interrogated is still termed an *interviewee* - not an *interrogatee*.)

The ability to evaluate "personality" - so crucial to strategy selection - is assumed, in all senses of that word. This is rather unfortunate given that psychological research has consistently shown that people are particularly poor judges of personality. Professionals differ from the person in the street only in their efforts and capacity to convince lay people (and fellow professionals) that they are good at it (Shepherd and Kite, 1988). Such convenient misperceptions of prowess in judging human nature add weight to the belief that "interrogation" is hard to do. Like interviewing, it is picked up by watching practitioners, characteristically within the world of the CID work, employing particular behaviour patterns to overcome resistance exhibited in the main by suspects.

In the community at large, the word interrogation evokes negative images of someone being "hard", unpleasant, remorseless, or unkind with another person: a bright anglepoise lamp shining into the eyes of the questioned with the questioner seated opposite in the dark; degrading and undermining the interviewee's dignity; disorientating the interviewee by such means as hooding and "white noise"; "softening up" the interviewee by psychological stress, physical exhaustion and physical torture. Some will strike the link with a process called "brainwashing".

In the police service, however, "interrogation" is perceived to be a high-status skill consistent with the necessity to "be on top" in a relationship. It gives rise to further misperceptions concerning alternative forms of relationship. *Either-or* thinking prevails: if you're not "on top" you must be "below"; the opposite of being "hard" - of "giving it" to them - is being "soft", associated with giving in. Interestingly, this mirrors beliefs widely held and endorsed daily about appropriate social relationships between police officers (Graeff, 1989).

*Appropriate social relationships and the problem of assertion*

The police service is hierarchical. *Up-down* thinking and action are seen as defining properties of a "disciplined" service, chain of command, career progression and capacity to resort to rank to require an officer junior to you to follow your instructions, to do as he or she is told. This presents a few problems. Officers very quickly grasp what constitutes *dominant* behaviour - patterns of talking and acting which contrast with *submissive* behaviour. They have problems comprehending and implementing a behaviour pattern which is neither dominant nor submissive: *assertive* behaviour (Shepherd, 1988; Stubbs, 1985).

Assertion is all about letting the person opposite know (irrespective of his or her status, position or power to coerce) that you also have rights to be treated as a person and to hold and express a view. It is feedback to another that there is a necessity to bear in mind and act according to the basic tenets of morality - respect for persons characterized by empathetic, considerate and considered two-sided communication and conduct.

It is difficult to foster and develop appropriate assertion skills and practice in hierarchical organizations. In the case of the police service, the outcome is that police officers in general experience extreme problems acting with appropriate assertion and coping with those who assert themselves in purposeful encounters e.g. solicitors and, of course, resistant interviewees. The problem of understanding, coping with and implementing assertion exemplifies the necessity to examine fundamentally the issue of social relationships within the service. This pervasive inability of officers to assert themselves appropriately lies at the heart of the problem of stress in the police service.

There are, however, additional sources of stress which make it difficult for the non-assertive to cope with distorting notions of getting it right in terms of the job and conversing with people.

## Additional sources of stress

### Internal pressures

Like other human beings police officers have psychological needs. Of particular relevance when exercising choice as to how to think and act in purposeful encounters are self-concept creating and sustaining needs arising from their interactions with those they work with: affiliation, acceptance, affection, control, inclusion, approval and worth.

Being a cross-sample of the population, personality or character shortcomings and developmental difficulties necessarily are to be found in the police service and have their effect upon the individual officer's commitment and ability to communicate ethically. Emotion - both state and trait - will have its effect, compounding problems of frustration, particularly that created by that phenomenon in hierarchical organizations: the *passive-aggressive link* - a kick from one above results in a kick given to the one below.

### Absence of coping skills

Training to date has failed the majority of officers. it has not equipped officers to cope with the demands to investigate professionally, to process information and to prepare professionally, to manage conversations professionally - all essential to ethical interviewing, which puts to the test an officer's ability to negotiate appropriately, i.e. to influence with integrity the other person's perceptions of the relationship.

### Absence of ethical moral models

The power of social and group influence is well known. It can, and does, lead men and women to act in ways which they know (or once knew) to be wrong even though endorsed as right in the eyes of the group. It takes a strong person indeed to dissent - particularly if he or she lacks assertion skills. No one likes to speak out when the risks are that the group (and even the organization) does not want to be reminded that what it is doing is wrong.

Without moral models who reject definitions of doing the job founded on expediency, "results" and self-interest, who think and act in *I-You* terms, who reject stereotypic notions of police interviewing, and who encourage assertion, an officer will continue to cope with the dilemma by going along with the "ethos".

How can the service develop an alternative ethos?

## Creating the right ethos for ethical interviewing

The unethical interview is the ostensibly logical outcome of a commitment to measure and evaluate "doing the job" based on "results". Perhaps the time has come to face up to the fact that the police service should, like many other organizations, think and act in terms of quality. Interviewing is but one part, albeit a very public insight, into the quality of police investigative performance.

Many interviews fail before they ever begin because of inadequate pre-interview investigation, planning and preparation, compounded by inability to manage time. There is a rush to get it wrong. It would be unfair to put this down solely to the individual. Too many times line supervisors and managers exhort officers to "get in there and empty him out". Absence of assertion skills is likely to lead the officer to start interviewing at a wholly unacceptable information disadvantage. The drift towards unethical interviewing has started before entering the interview room - any resistance from an interviewee who dissents, particularly one who detects the officer does not really know - in terms of breadth and depth is likely to confront the officer with an impossible, and inappropriate, dilemma: dominate or submit ("I am ending this interview. The time is ...") The rush to interview - to "empty out" interviewees or to empty out the cell-block for the satisfaction of managers of the reviewing process - is the rush to get it wrong.

This thinking actually prevents the service providing a professional investigative, including investigative interviewing, service. The organization - from top to bottom - must commit itself to quality of investigation. Rather than attributing incompetence, contrariness and other, ulterior, motives to the CPS for "bouncing" files and "failing" to progress prosecutions, the police service should reflect upon whether something absolutely vital is being communicated here. The service has got to develop as an organization which gets it right, professionally, in terms of individual and group investigative competence. Investigation does mean systematic examination of information in terms of fine-grain detail - in pursuit of what the Romans aptly saw at the heart of investigation - the footprint (vestigium).

Quality service through quality investigation implies ability to cope, and come to terms, with negative information. It just will not do to say that it is "human nature" to filter out subconsciously that which does not fit. Police officers get paid to ensure that they consciously combat such "facts of life" by appropriate organization and working practices. This applies to the whole spectrum of police investigation, not just dramatic cases. The conscious alternative to this - ignoring, suppressing or losing counter-information - will in the long term erode public trust in every context of police investigation and communication.

There needs to be a commitment to *quality* of service - professional investigation - for the survival of the service. The numbers game breeds low quality. Implementing quality could well mean fewer "clear-ups" in the short term, but more investigations which lead to a greater likelihood of appropriate outcome. The morale of the service (and the Crown Prosecution Service) would progressively increase. Commitment to quality would in the middle term lead to a greater degree of success in crime prevention, detection and conviction of guilty criminals. Increasing morale would be a natural concomitant of increasing professionalism and pride in what we do and how we do it. Such *esprit de corps* arising from a commitment to quality requires conscious and explicit commitment to other aspects of organizational development.

### Getting rid of the distorted notions and practices of "appropriate" social relations

*Esprit de corps* will only truly emerge if the service - as a whole, in its working groups and between individuals across the rank, role and seniority spectrum - works hard at instituting genuine *I-You* conversations. This will present some difficulty and discomfort. Difficulty since, although *I-It* conversations are inherently corrosive to the organization, the working group and the individual, they are rather good at getting things done in the way the one in the *up* position wants without having to cope with the complication of considering the view of the person in the *down* position. The price of consultation is the potential of having more reality defining information - especially negative information, "ifs" and "buts" - and *up-down* managers are apprehensive of their ability to cope with this.

Discomfort since *I-You* conversations require the abandonment of *up-down* notions of relationship and challenge our capacity to cope with talking *across* to people, who have the right to dissent. The need here is to reframe this negative into a positive. Firstly dissent does *not* mean abandoning decision making to the dissenter nor does it mean leadership by committee: so managers and supervisors need not panic. It does mean accepting that assertion - appropriate assertion by all police officers talking across to each other - is not only a *right* it is an *obligation* since it is an essential ingredient of the organizational commitment to investigate facts of the matter fully, irrespective of the findings.

This is not preaching revolution. In fact the organization has said, at least in part, that it is committed to this. Is not the training of the incoming and upcoming generations of probationer police officers an attempt to create a culture of "reflective practitioners" (Schon, 1983)? Are not the formal and informal ("on the job") training systems purportedly telling them the same thing - that they have to frame problems, investigate, act and communicate reflectively? Ethically? Are they not telling them to think and act with accountability in mind - starting with the basic unit of account the person opposite: whether victim, witness, suspect, or fellow police officer - irrespective of rank, role, sex, origin, and past and present behaviour, including that which signals attitudes which may be singularly unethical.

The service needs to dispense with much of its counterproductive terminological baggage. It needs to embark on some mental spring cleaning. Goodbye *interviewing vs interrogation!* Hello *investigative interviewing!* Farewell *strategies* to cope with narrowly defined resistance! Welcome *ethical interviewing* based on legality, morality and psychology.

## The implementation and implications of a commitment to ethical interviewing

Top management must commit the organization to total quality. Top management must translate this into a commitment to implementing change through a combination of interview development training and organizational development.

### Interview development training

A career span perspective on interviewing training is essential (Shepherd, 1988). Training to interview is not something that can be done on a once and for all basis. Since interviewing constitutes the conversational core of policing, career development implies an explicit programme of training aimed at ensuring the officer is ready, willing and able to fulfil the range of purposeful conversation - police-public, police-police, one-to-one, one-to-many, one-with-many - in which they will be expected to think and act ethically, two-sided, with empathy. The Bishop of Oxford observed that all ethics is training in empathy (Harries, 1990). It is a training that extends across a lifetime for all people but one which the police service as an organization must explicitly require *and* enable across an officer's working life.

This may raise a few eyebrows since it implies a major commitment in resource of all kinds to plan and deliver a personal programme of development aimed at the individual officer. An analogy is appropriate here. Since the Working Party report following the Waldorf incident, the service has to come to terms with the necessity to train officers continuously to fulfil the high-risk role of carrying a firearm. But language is also a loaded weapon. Unethical interviewing by a police officer is akin to using that loaded gun, blunderingly and malevolently, to coerce the person opposite to submit to the officer's view of the world. Language will always be a loaded weapon. The only difference between the firearms and interviewing context is that in the latter *every* officer is armed.

It is also necessary to spell out the necessity to face up to what is really involved in a commitment to train in a skill (Shepherd and Kite, 1989). For too long the service has deluded itself that consciousness raising (large numbers of officers, exposed to information, short period of time, one classroom, talking about it) is skills training. Unless every officer has a chance to put concept into practice, to experiment and to develop competence and confidence in the reflective practitioner role - to disclose, discuss, and to give and receive feedback - upon actual personal performance then we cannot claim he or she is trained.

### Organizational development: fostering and maintaining appropriate moral models

A commitment to providing a quality service, to changing perspectives on social relationships, to fostering a vocabulary of interviewing which is founded upon shared meanings of what is, should and must be the case, to training aimed at the individual officer across the career span, will count for nothing if the organization does not develop an infrastructure of appropriate moral models.

All the statements of purpose or mission statements, all the resource in the world devoted to ethical interviewing development, will founder unless the organization fosters and maintains the right kind of moral model. There is nothing new in this. It is the dilemma of current approaches to train the very new members in probationer training and their peers and seniors in professional development programmes. It all counts for nothing if practice - for real - does not marry up with declared policy and promises.

Two, quite well worn but nonetheless useful dicta are apposite here. "There are no bad followers only bad leaders" and "Leaders lead by example". It is immoral to blame those who follow and model themselves on inappropriate exemplars. It is down to the organization to ensure that the appropriate behaviour *is* exhibited by leaders who are grounded in, trained in, and committed to ethical interviewing. Current inappropriate models can be helped to change but it is difficult. It is an uphill task to tell those with rank that although it has its privileges these do not include undermining the spirit of the organization (Humble, 1973), distorting reality, sending double messages, and failing to act on the knowledge that officers are doing things in conversations with the public and other officers which are morally wrong in order to get the job done, badly.

*The necessity to monitor and to evaluate*

Change is a precarious process - for organizations and individuals within organizations, for management and the managed. A commitment to think and act in terms of quality, to engage in quality training, to endorse moral models who are quality leaders implies continuous monitoring and evaluation at the level of the individual and the group. In effect monitoring and evaluation is the commitment of the organization to engage in meta-reflection. The organization is the practitioner reflecting upon its processes and products, assessing the change in quality of life arising from quality of service and quality of social relationships, within the organization.

## A conclusion

The public tends to forget, but nonetheless understands and will agree with the service that officers are busy people, hard pressed, pressured by limited resources and pressing demands, often reflective of primitive emotions rather than considered reflection. The public, however, entrusts the police service - from top landing to the "front line" - to keep its head and to observe society's moral guidelines to respect the person, to tell the truth and to converse accordingly. Doing the job in response to a call to cope with a rise in crime or to catch the perpetrators of an outrageous crime can never be taken to be a licence to act with expediency when dealing with information or with people.

## References

BATESON, G. (1972) **Steps to an Ecology of Mind**. New York: Ballantine

BUBER, M. (1958) **I and Thou**. Translated by R. Smith. New York: Scribner's

CRIBBEN, J. (1981) **Leadership**. New York: AMACOM

DOWNIE, R., and TELFER, E. (1969) **Respect for the Person**. London: Allen & Unwin

FORGAS, J. (1985) **Interpersonal Behaviour**. Oxford: Pergamon

GRAEFF, R. (1989) **Talking Blues**. London: Collins Harvill

HARRIES, R. (1990) **Ten to Eight**. BBC Radio 4

IRVING, B. (1980) **Police Interrogation: A case study of current practice**. London: HMSO

IRVING, B., and MCKENZIE, I. (1988) **Regulating Custodial Interviews**. London: Police Foundation

KANT, I. (1964) **Fundamental Principles of the Metaphysics of Morals**. Translated by H. Paton. New York: Harper and Row

KINGET, G. (1975) **On Being Human**. New York: Harcourt, Brace Jovanovich

KITE, F., and SHEPHERD, E. (1989) The way we talk. **Police Review, 870**

MANOLIAS, M. (1983) **Stress in the Police Service**. London: HMSO

MIRFIELD, P. (1985) **Confessions**. London: Sweet and Maxwell

NIERENBERG, G. (1986) **The Complete Negotiator**. London: Souvenir

PETERS, R. (1966) **Ethics and Education**. London: Allen & Unwin

ROSS, L. (1977) The intuitive psychologist and his shortcomings: Distortions in the attribution process. In L. Berkowitz (Ed), **Advances in Experimental Social Psychology, Volume 10**. New York: Academic

SCHON, D. (1983) **The Reflective Practitioner**. New York: Basic

SHEPHERD, E. (1986) Interviewing development: facing up to reality. **Police Journal, 59**, 35-44

SHEPHERD, E. (1987) **Telling Experiences: Conversations with child victims.** Paper presented to The British Psychological Society Conference, University of Sussex

SHEPHERD, D. (1988) Developing interviewing skills. In P. Southgate (Ed), **New Directions in Police Training.** London: HMSO

SHEPHERD, E., and KITE, F. (1988) Training to interview. **Policing, 4,** 264-280

SHEPHERD, E., and KITE, F. (1989) Teach 'em to talk. **Policing, 5,** 33-47

STUBBS, D. (1985) **How to Use Assertiveness at Work.** Aldershot: Gower

WALKELY, J. (1987) **Police Interrogation.** London: Police Review Publishing

WATZLAWICK, P., BEAVIN, J., and JACKSON, D. (1967) **Pragmatics of Human Communication.** New York: Norton

WILSON, J. (1972) **Ideals.** Guildford: Lutterworth

# [10]

Steven Greer

# Towards a sociological model of the police informant

ABSTRACT

Despite the extensive legal, psychological, historical, and police studies literatures on a range of issues raised by police informants there is, as yet, no adequate sociological model. Proposing a particularly wide framework of inquiry, this article both suggests how such a model might be constructed and considers some of the related public policy implications.

## A. INTRODUCTION

Police informants come in many forms, the information they supply can be used by crime control systems in a variety of ways, and together these variables open up a range of opportunities and dilemmas, particularly for law enforcement professing commitment to due process and the rule of law. There are two main difficulties. The first concerns the extent to which informants genuinely assist in the prevention, detection and punishment of crime, and how this contribution can be measured. It should be stressed that this is not the same issue as the extent to which the police consider certain types helpful in their investigations. The second problem concerns the establishment of effective mechanisms of democratic and legal accountability especially since reliance upon certain kinds of inform- ant appears to require much secrecy and great faith in police discretion. Political or administrative accountability involves the establishment of effective, thorough, systematic, and regular reviews by the legislature into internal police supervision of the use of certain types of informant by officers on the ground, while legal account- ability involves finding answers to three questions in particular: (1) when, if ever, is it appropriate to permit the police to refuse to disclose to a court that an informant has been used in a criminal prosecution or that his or her identity should be kept secret? (2) how can the reliability of the information which informants supply be assessed, particularly

510                                                        *Steven Greer*

when it takes the form of testimony in criminal trials ? (3) when, if ever, can police use of *agents provocateurs* be justified?

Virtually all the legal, sociological/police studies, and historical literatures are concerned with police *informers* rather than *informants*, and there is, as yet, no adequate general sociological model (Skolnick 1975; Marx 1974 and 1988; Wool 1985–86; Oscapella 1980; Navasky 1982; Schliefman 1988: Dorn *et al.* 1992). While the term *informer* has certain cloak and dagger connotations, police *informants* include everyone who provides the police with information about any matter whatsoever, however useful or useless this may be for crime prevention and detection. It follows that many participants in the criminal justice process more familiar in other guises, for example the eye witness, the suspect who confesses, the accused who turns Queen's evidence, and even victims of crime, can be regarded as 'police informants'. It may be thought that to recast these familiar figures in this manner obscures rather than clarifies universally acknowledged roles, and it would certainly be a mistake to suggest, for example, that the victim's role as informant is more important than his or her role as victim. But this is not what is intended. The purpose of this article is to consider the implications of an expanded conception of the police informant both for social science and public policy.

The few attempts which have been made to understand the police informer (as opposed to the informant) have tended to distinguish different types by reference to motivation, criminal background, level of secrecy, and frequency of information-flow. While it cannot be denied that these are all important factors they can best be considered within a broader structural framework where the key to classification lies in two main variables: the relationship between informants and the people upon whom they inform, and their relationship with the policing agencies to whom they supply this information. Apart from the 'confession informant', considered more fully at the end of this study, two distinctions emerge when the first variable is applied. These are between, on the one hand, Outsiders and Insiders and, on the other, between Single Event Informants and Multiple Event Informants. Together these yield a fourfold typology: the Outside Single Event Informant (the casual observer), the Outside Multiple Event Informant (the snoop), the Inside Single Event Informant (the one-off accomplice witness), and the Inside Multiple Event Informant (the informer, *agent provocateur* and supergrass). Victims of crime can also be inside or outside informants depending upon whether or not they were present when the offence in question was committed. More research is needed to determine if their information is likely to be systematically distorted, and if so whether such defects are offence or offender related or derive from the manner in which victims are processed by the criminal justice and other official systems. Whether an informant is on the 'inside' or the 'outside' of an activity, and

*Towards a sociological model of the police informant* 511

whether they have knowledge of just one or a whole series of incidents, will critically affect the kind of information which they can supply and its accuracy, detail, and the correct identification of suspects. The events reported by insiders and outsiders may be either criminal or political or a hybrid of the two but this distinction assumes greatest significance within the Inside Multiple Event Informant category where the relationship between informant and policing agencies critically determines whether the informant remains a pure informer, or becomes an *agent provocateur* or supergrass.

## B. OUTSIDERS

As the name suggests outsiders are not directly involved in the activities they report to the police but merely observe them from the 'outside'. Recent research reveals the centrality of such informants to routine modern police work in Britain with some 80–90 per cent of offences reputedly brought to the attention of the police by victims, by-standers or other members of the public (Runciman Report 1993: 10).

### 1. The Casual Observer

The typical casual observer will be a member of the public who, on an isolated occasion and usually by chance, happens to observe a crime or any activity which they think should be brought to the attention of the police. Their information, which may either be volunteered or elicited during the course of a police investigation, may prove crucial in the detection and prosecution of crime or it may be of no significance whatsoever. Although it may also be systematically unreliable this is unlikely to be due to deliberate distortion by the witness him or herself. Psychological studies have sought to identify systematic sources of unreliability in the evidence of casual observers, e.g. poor quality of light at the scene, the distance between the observer and the event, the duration of the observation, the observer's contemporaneous awareness of what precisely was being observed, and the distorting effect of leading questions by investigators afterwards (Loftus and Wells 1984; Farrington *et al.* 1979; Clifford 1978 and 1979). In the UK juries are permitted to convict on the evidence of such witnesses without corroborative or supporting evidence, but judges must caution them about its possible defects (*R v Turnbull* [1976] 3 All ER 549).

### 2. The Snoop

As the name suggests, this kind of informant supplies the police with information about a number of incidents which will usually follow a pattern, e.g. drug dealing or vice. Some snoops are merely nosey parkers who like to tell tales on their neighbours while others, whose occupations put them in a position to observe other people without drawing undue attention to themselves – e.g. shop keepers, bar and hotel staff, janitors, street sweepers, post office delivery workers and taxi drivers – can provide a kind of informal police surveillance service (Skolnick 1975).

Snoops' motives may be varied. Some may act out of a sense of civic responsibility, while others may seek revenge for having been victimized by their targets in, for example, a protection racket which may or may not be connected with the activities they report to the police. Petty criminal snoops will themselves be actively involved in petty criminal activity, usually divorced from the behaviour they observe, and their prime motive for informing will generally be to ingratiate themselves with the police in the hope that their own criminality will be overlooked.

Since it may be given under the explicit or implicit threat of prosecution, information supplied by snoops, particularly petty criminal snoops, may be systematically unreliable, and there are also considerable opportunities for police corruption, i.e. not only connivance at the snoop's own criminality but sharing in its profits. The police will generally be strongly opposed to the disclosure of the identity of a particularly valued snoop, especially as a trial witness, unless the squandering of the source of information which this would entail is deemed cost-effective, while the courts have attempted to strike a balance between permitting non-disclosure to protect vital police sources and compelling disclosure when the defence of the accused demands it (Tapper 1990: 473–4). The common law treats snoops as eye witnesses unless the court takes the view that their evidence is given from improper motives in which case the judge may warn the jury of the dangers inherent in accepting their evidence (_R v Beck_ [1982] 1 WLR 461).

C. INSIDERS

### 1. The One Off Accomplice Witness

The accomplice witness who testifies on a one off basis for the prosecution against his alleged associates may emerge with respect to any offence which involves more than one offender, in any part of the jurisdiction, and under the influence of one or more of a variety of motives including genuine contrition, the hope of striking a bargain with the prosecuting authorities in the selection of charges and/or the courts in passing sentence, revenge against fellow accomplices, or a configuration of all three. However, the decision to cooperate with the

*Towards a sociological model of the police informant* 513

police is generally only taken after arrest and may be influenced by police suggestions. Since the accomplice witness is an offender who is likely to become a defendant and then a witness in the trial of others, there will generally be no problem from the police point of view in the disclosure of identity nor any opportunity for their participation in surveillance, much less as *agents provocateurs*, and little risk of police corruption. The transformation from suspect to Crown witness is thus amenable to an unusually high degree of public disclosure and legal accountability, although informal understandings regarding charge and sentence may be reached 'off stage' (Sanders and Young 1994: ch 7). Hitherto judges in the UK were obliged to warn juries about the dangers of convicting on the evidence of an uncorroborated accomplice testifying for the prosecution. However, s. 32 of the Criminal Justice and Public Order Act 1994 has made such warnings discretionary.

## 2. Informers and Agents Provocateurs

Inside Multiple Event Informants, the classic police informers, are notorious under a host of nicknames in the English language alone, for example, tout, rat, singer, finger, mule mouth, squealer, fink, snout, mut (apparently short for 'mutter'), snitch, stool pigeon, stoolie, and nark (probably derived from the French 'narquois', mocking or derisive). They have also been vilified in novels by, for example O'Flaherty (1925) and Seymour (1985), and despised by diverse cultures (Navasky 1982). The modern police informer will typically be closely involved in criminal organizations or political/ social associations which the police find suspicious. It should be observed, however, that these informants are likely to be merely cogs, albeit vital ones, in a complex intelligence-gathering system in which a variety of other methods, such as technological surveillance, are also likely to be employed. The pure informer merely supplies information to the police about the activities of any given political or criminal group and may do so with varying regularity. Some, generally described as police spies or agents, discharge what amounts to a professional informing role and may be either undercover police officers or private citizens, although in certain contexts the distinction may be difficult to draw. In Northern Ireland the British army distinguishes between

an *agent*: . . . one who is authorized or instructed to obtain or to assist in obtaining information for intelligence or counter-intelligence purposes' and 'an *informant*: . . . any individual who gives information. The term is generally used to describe a casual or undirected source as distinct from an *informer*, who is normally connected with criminal activities, can be directed, and receives payment for his services. (Dillon 1991: 309)

Informer information can be put to various uses by policing agencies; from merely keeping tabs on the activities of suspects, to the preparation of cases for court and even, in certain circumstances, selective assassination.

While also merely supplying information the *agent provocateur* will, by definition, also seek to encourage the activities of criminal or political organizations, whether or not authorized to do so by police handlers. Strangely, and in spite of strong evidence that their information is likely to be the most unreliable of all types of police informant, an *agent provocateur* or spy was not regarded by the common law as an accomplice with the result that the danger warning was not mandatory (Tapper 1990: 232). However, a warning could, and may still, be issued at the trial judge's discretion.

*(i) In criminal organizations*    Several studies have discussed the role of the informer in particular kinds of crime, e.g. official corruption (Grabosky 1991), conspiracy and related offences (Haglund 1990), narcotics, liquor law violations, larceny, vice, illegal gambling and prostitution (Lawler 1986; Manning and Redlinger 1977), auto theft and organized crime (Parker 1986), illegal gambling, prostitution, and pornography (Parliamentary Joint Committee on the National Crime Authority 1988), and insider dealing (Greer 1995: ch 10). Although the classic empirical study of the modern criminal informer was conducted in the USA by Skolnick in the 1960s (Skolnick 1975), more recent work suggests that little has changed in the processes described (Marx 1988; Dorn *et al.* 1992). Skolnick found that informers are particularly useful to the police in identifying those responsible for victimless offences with the police themselves typically playing the roles of complainant and witness. Policing which is heavily reliant upon informers, e.g. narcotics, tends to be highly proactive, providing the police with a challenging, high status, game-like job, and symbolizes efficient professionalism and thorough detective work (Baldwin and Kinsey 1982: 64–74). Attempts by the police to cultivate a relationship with the addict and build dependence upon particular police handlers hinge upon the bolstering of the informer's low sense of self-esteem, and the vital reinforcement of the undertaking that under no circumstances will his or her identity be disclosed to the underworld.

An informer's primary interest tends to be lenient treatment by the criminal justice system rather than financial reward (Harney and Cross 1960; Goodman and Will 1985). Skolnick also claims that the allegation that the police grant informers a licence to commit crime tends to be untrue although myths to this effect are often cultivated by informers themselves in order to ingratiate themselves with their quarry. However, officers in one police department, e.g. narcotics, tend to turn a blind eye to offences committed by their own informers which fall within the jurisdiction of another police department, e.g. burglary (Baldwin and Kinsey 1982: 72). Since secrecy is the key ingredient in the management of the informer system police records may even fail to record that an informer has been used in cases where, Skolnick claims, it is difficult to believe that this has not been the case. Even though informers are almost invariably used in crimes of vice, only 9 per cent of 508 narcotics cases on the files of the Westville police from December 1961 to March 1963 mentioned that an informer had been involved in the investigation.

Marx's study indicates that there have been two further important changes in the broader context since the mid-1970s. First, the technology available for covert policing in the USA has increased dramatically. Secondly, the scope of undercover police operations, including those in which informers are involved, has been greatly extended with these methods now increasingly being used by law enforcement agencies which never had recourse to them before, e.g. the Immigration and Naturalization Service and the Internal Revenue Service, and in respect of offences never before a target of this kind of policing, e.g. relatively unorganized street crime, burglary, and white-collar crime. A tendency has also developed for covert operations to be targeted upon individuals or groups to see what offences they may be committing, rather than upon offences to see who is committing them (Marx 1988).

*(ii) In political movements*  In spite of the rich historical literature on informers in various political movements, little systematic attempt has been made to study the phenomenon sociologically. In some ways this is surprising because, as the case-studies show, undercover agents can seriously affect the life of a movement by providing a means through which its activities are successfully repressed or contained. However, they can also, ironically, prolong a group's lifespan and even channel it in directions which are more dangerous to the status quo. As with the study of other brands of police informant, social scientists can find access to data difficult due to the inherent secrecy of the political informer's world. Researchers sympathetic to the groups under analysis may also be reluctant to admit that some of the movement's potency may have derived from planted agents rather than genuine devotees, while some observers may attribute participants' accounts of infiltration to paranoia and an exaggerated sense of their own importance. The source of much social research, the printed word, may also not give much indication of the informer's occult role.

In the nineteenth century police penetration of subversive organizations was widespread in Europe, especially in the Austro-Hungarian empire during the Metternich period, in the France of Louis Philippe and Napoleon III, and in Prussia under Friedrich Wilhelm IV (Schliefman 1988). Schliefman's study shows that those who informed on the Russian Socialist Revolutionary Party (hereafter referred to as SR) in the early twentieth century fell into three broad categories: informers – non-party members who passed information to the police which they had picked up casually; secret agents or *agents provocateurs* – party members who reported regularly to the police and were paid for their information; and external agents, filers or *shpiki* – low-ranking police officers whose sole task was to tail suspects, known only by a code-name, and to monitor where they went and whom they met (Schliefman 1988). Although some were volunteers, many secret agents were recruited after arrest and confession and, in order to dispel suspicion were released by way of a staged 'escape'. Schliefman concludes that, although the number of secret agents operating in the SR party was smaller than the party itself believed, they eventually became the lynch-pin of political police work hastening the party's organizational and ethical breakdown, deepening rifts within the leadership, and bringing grass roots discontent to the surface. However, in spite of this, police preconceptions exaggerated the SR's importance and the inefficiency of the police organizational structure resulted in poor intelligence coordination which prevented its full potential from being realized.

Navasky (1982) and Marx (1974) offer some particularly valuable insights into the role of informers in modern non-violent political movements in the USA. In his study of informers in the McCarthy anti-communist witch-hunts of the 1950s, Navasky distinguishes four types according to motivation: the informer as patriot – who informed out of hostility to the group in question; the espionage informer – a police officer or other official who penetrated a given movement; the conspiracy informer – a member of the movement who regularly supplied official agencies with information; and the liberal informer – the non-political individual who liked to be helpful to the authorities when the opportunity arose. Navasky also identifies numerous other kinds according to a variety of other variables: the reluctant, enthusiastic, informed and philosophical, truth-telling, combative, denigrating, noisey, comic, husband-and-wife, volunteer, informer-by-dispensation, and resister-informer. The dubious information supplied by informers was not only instrumental in ruining numerous careers, particularly in the glamorous Hollywood film industry, but also assisted in the conviction of many suspected subversives in the late 1940s and early 1950s. The trial of eleven leaders of the Communist Party in New York in 1949, for example, 'wrote the script for a series of similar trials across the country' featuring a 'parade of FBI informants and ex-Communists many of them professional informers' (Navasky 1982: 4). Navasky concludes that apart from the shattered lives of those denounced as communists or fellow-travellers,

> the informer's particular contribution was to pollute the public well, to poison social life in general, to destroy the very possibility of a community; for the informer operates on the principle of betrayal and the community survives on the principle of trust. (p 347)

In his study of informers in the radical US political and social movements of the 1960s Marx lists five principal motives – patriotism/ ideological opposition to the group in question; coercion from the police (principally the threat of arrest and prosecution followed by the prospect of offers of immunity from prosecution, leniency in the selection of charges, release from police custody or help with various official problems, e.g. those concerning naturalization); inducement; activist disaffection (e.g. a transformation in beliefs, personal vendettas, leadership contests, attempts to change the direction of the organization, and rivalry with other groups at the same end of the political spectrum); and the desire to become a double agent. While the line between the coercion and the inducement categories is blurred the distinction is none the less important, the latter referring to those informers who were motivated purely by the prospect of financial gain. The desire to become a double agent can also be complex. Marx found that some double agents deliberately gave the authorities false information and acted as the movement's spy deep in officialdom, others were opportunistic and cooperated with, or misled, either side as it suited their own interests, while others were ambivalent about their true allegiances and shifted their loyalties back and forth. The double agent can, therefore, present problems both for the police and the movement to which they belong.

Marx discovered that, in two-thirds of the 34 cases he examined, informers went beyond passive information gathering to active provocation and that certain kinds of agent may become *agents provocateurs* by 'going native', a particular risk with movements based upon distinct ethnic or socio-economic characteristics which the informer must share if he or she is to infiltrate effectively. The political *agent provocateur* may encourage both further legal and illegal activities but his or her classic function is to push political groups which have been acting legally into committing crimes in order to provide the police with a justification for making arrests and initiating prosecutions. The police may have other motives for using political *agents provocateurs*, e.g. to encourage divisions within a given group between those who favour and those who are opposed to illegality, or to damage the group's public image. Even with strong institutional supervision, however, bureaucratic pressures can militate against the careful and thorough assessment of the reliability of the information which a political informer or *agent provocateur* supplies. The efficiency of police checks on reliability is also likely to decrease the more the information confirms preconceptions of the nature of the group under surveillance.

Marx argues that since most of the information gathered by political informers never featured in court cases, the political informer in the USA in the 1960s may have merely enabled the police to take action 'consistent with their own sense of justice and morality, independent of the substantive and procedural requirements of the law' (Marx 1974: 436). Although police corruption, in the sense of bribery and profiteering, is not particularly likely in this context, there is a risk that distorted police perspectives will, in their turn, have a distorting impact upon the politics of the society in question, arguably a corruption of a potentially more serious kind. Civil libertarians have suggested various restrictions upon the deployment of undercover political agents, including making their use in a preventative capacity a violation of the First and Fourth amendments to the US Constitution; subjecting the use of informers to the same restrictions the authorities now face with respect to wire-tapping and search and seize operations; and the establishment of a domestic intelligence advisory council to monitor intelligence activities. As far as social science is concerned, the researcher interested in social movements would be well advised to be alert to the possible distorting effects that a police interloper may be exerting (Marx 1974: 439).

## 3. Supergrasses

The term 'supergrass' was first coined by journalists in the early 1970s – from the slang 'grass' for informer – to refer to members of the London underworld who were prepared to break the traditional code of silence and offer their testimony to the prosecution. While they can fulfill the functions of both pure informer and *agent provocateur* the supergrass's unique contribution is to allow the carefully cultivated results of sophisticated police intelligence-gathering systems to be presented in court for the purpose of convicting large numbers of suspected terrorists or organized criminals, typically in mass trials. For this reason they can have no role in legal political organizations. The four key factors conducive to the construction of supergrass systems are: the construction of mature informer and intelligence-gathering systems, the perceived failure of other methods to deal with a particularly serious problem of crime or political violence, a crisis of allegiance on the part of at least some members of the target organizations, and the attractiveness of the officially sanctioned rewards on offer – typically immunity from prosecution, reduced prison sentences, and new lives and new identities elsewhere (Greer 1995).

The dangers associated with accomplice evidence, discussed above, are particularly acute with respect to supergrasses. Each has been involved in serious, and mostly violent crime and will, therefore, be regarded by the legal system as of unusually bad character even compared with other possible accomplice witnesses. The pressure to tell a story sufficiently appealing to attract the various rewards on offer is also likely to be more intense than with most other accomplices turning State's evidence. There is, in addition, ample time and opportunity during the many months spent in police protective custody for false evidence to be rehearsed in preparation for a convincing courtroom performance. The risk of unreliability is greatly increased by the complexity of the issues which any case is likely to raise, even assuming incorrigible bona fides on the part of all concerned. As already noted, psychological studies illustrate how accuracy of recollection can be seriously, and unintentionally, distorted by the lapse of time between the event and the recording of statements and by intervening suggestions as to what, and who, the original event may have involved (Clifford 1979; Loftus and Wells 1984).

Employing the services of supergrasses is a high-risk strategy for the police and other agencies in the prosecution process since, if it succeeds, the punishment of tens, if not hundreds, of suspects is assured. But if it fails, a valuable source of intelligence plus considerable resources will have been squandered, exposing the police and criminal justice system to considerable public criticism. It follows that the decision to promote supergrass trials in any jurisdiction is likely to be taken at a high political level with resources made available in advance for its successful administration.

The police are the key agency in any supergrass process, since they will be most instrumental in deciding whom to recruit and whom to prosecute. Supergrass systems are based upon proactive policing and the deployment of what, in the context of criminal informers, Skolnick (1975) calls 'aggressive intelligence', with the management of the supergrasses themselves likely to be high-status police work. It is also clear that, like Skolnick's informers, what motivates supergrasses most is self-interest, particularly the prospect of leniency in, or the avoidance of, punishment. The rewards available are, characteristically, the most generous any criminal justice system is prepared to offer informants and can include immunity from prosecution, lenient prison sentences and comparative luxury while serving them, money, and new lives with fresh identities away from the original sphere of operations.

Supergrass systems create some risk of police profiteering, but only in relation to organized acquisitive crime. But the possibility of corruption of the rule of law is an inherent danger because without proper and effective supervision by legislature and courts, supergrass processes enable the police to by-pass more mundane and painstaking investigative methods effectively enabling them to determine who deserves punishment for which offence. Such systems also create the further risk that informer and supergrass-based policing may be extended into other areas of police work because of the amount of time and effort it can save.

*(i) In criminal organizations* Supergrass systems directed against organized crime appeared in England and the USA in the 1970s and in Italy in the 1980s. In spite of broad similarities each system has had its own unique characteristics with particularly significant differences having emerged in relation to institutionalization and formal inter-agency co-ordination. Both the US and English systems were successfully institutionalized, although co-ordination between relevant official agencies has been different in each jurisdiction, with more formal arrangements in the former than in the latter. The lack of effective inter-agency coordination in the Italian anti-mafia process has been a key factor inhibiting its successful institutionalization.

The English supergrass system was constructed in direct response to a dramatic rise in the incidence of serious organized crime, particularly bank robberies in the London area in the early 1970s and an official perception that existing methods of dealing with it were ineffective (Criminal Law Revision Committee 1972; Zander 1974; Seymour 1982; Goodman & Will 1985; Slipper 1981; O'Mahoney with Wooding 1978). It declined in the 1980s, however, for three main reasons. First, in order to facilitate the move from armed robbery to illegal drugs, professional criminals formed more close-knit organizations which were less open to penetration by informers. Secondly, the penalties for betrayal became much more severe – death or serious injury. Thirdly, juries became more distrustful of supergrass evidence (Campbell 1994).

The origins of the US Witness Protection (or Witness Security) Program lie in the US Task Force on Organized Crime which, in 1967, identified inadequate protection for vulnerable witnesses as a major law enforcement shortcoming in this context. From the decision of the Supreme Court in *Roviaro* v *United States* in 1957 (353 U.S. 53) both state and federal courts have upheld the principle that an informer's identity must be disclosed where it is relevant and helpful to the guilt or innocence of the accused, but not where it merely goes to the issue of probable cause in respect of an arrest or the issuing of a search warrant (Schlichter 1971). The Witness Protection Program, established by Title V of the Organized Crime Control Act 1970, authorized the Attorney General to provide short-term or permanent protection plus new identities, credit cards, indefinite subsistence payments, plus fictitious work histories, military service records and school reports, to vulnerable witnesses involved in organized crime trials – the majority of whom are criminals themselves – and to their families.

*Towards a sociological model of the police informant*                    521

In 1984 the Witness Protection Program was overhauled by Congress to offer the public greater protection against recidivism by protected witnesses (Levin 1985). Title V of the 1970 Act was repealed and a new statutory foundation was provided by the Witness Security Reform Act 1984. The WPP was extended to include 'organized criminal activity or other serious offence' (Pub.L. No. 98–473, § 1208, 98 Stat. 2153) and the admission criteria were also more fully specified. Most of those involved in the WPP cooperate in return for one of three rewards: immunity from prosecution, a lenient sentence, or early release from prison. By law all inducements, including express or implicit promises of leniency must be disclosed to lawyers defending those implicated by a protected witness's testimony (*Giglio* v *United States*, 405 U.S. 150 (1972); *People* v *Westmoreland*, 58 CA3d 32 (1976); *United States* v *Oxman et al.*, 3d Cir. No. 83–1531, August 1, 1984; CNPDS 1987; 232). Requests for immunity from prosecution are reviewed by senior prosecutors but final approval needs to be obtained from the US Assistant Attorney General and the general rule is that immunity is to be given only as a last resort (CNPDS 1987: 159–160). It is also possible for accomplice witnesses to be offered 'post-conviction use-immunity', i.e. immunity from prosecution *after* they have given their testimony (CNPDS 1987: 255–259; *People* v *Stewart*, 1 CA3d 339 (1965); *People* v *Watson*, 89 CA3d 376 (1979); *People* v *Campbell*, 137 CA3d 867 (1982)) while those convicted can also be placed on probation on condition that they cooperate with the prosecution (*United States* v *Worcester*, 190 F. Supp. 548 (D. Mass. 1961)). Cooperative accomplices can also be convicted with sentence deferred until after they have testified in the trial of others (CNPDS 1987: 172; *United States* v *Dailey*, 759 F.2d 192 (1st Cir.) 1985).

An anti-mafia offensive in Italy, in which the evidence of *pentiti* (repentants) was of central importance, began with the arrest of the most celebrated supergrass of modern times, Tommaso Buscetta, in the USA in 1984 (Greer 1995: ch 10). However, as a result of political inerta stemming from collusion between the mafia and elements within the Italian political establishment, a formal witness protection scheme was not established until 1991, the success of which remains to be seen (Falcone with Padovani 1992: xvi and 46) Buscetta's information, plus other evidence including that of fellow *pentito* and US protected witness Salvatore Contorno, led to the first Italian mafia supergrass trial involving 475 defendants held in the specially constructed 'bunker' courtroom inside Palermo's ancient Ucciardone prison. On 16 December 1987, twenty two months after it had begun, the trial's 350th session ended with 338 convictions. These 'maxi-proceedings' were followed by a string of others involving both major and minor supergrasses. However, in February 1989, 80 allegedly prominent mafiosi were acquitted in Palermo's third bunker trial when the testimonies of the *pentiti* involved were rejected, and, on 22

February 1992, 40 defendants in the first bunker trial were set free under a new law prohibiting detention for longer than 12 months between conviction and appeal. In 1992 the mafia war in Italy entered a further deadly phase with the murders, in May and July respectively, of Italy's two most experienced anti-mafia investigating magistrates, Giovanni Falcone and Paolo Borsilino, amidst suspicions of security service involvement. In June that year legislation was passed which, amongst other things formalized the contribution of *pentiti* with guarantees of reduced sentences and protection. Some 700 alleged mafiosi were swiftly arrested and in the spring of 1993 Buscetta re-emerged from hiding confirming suspicions that, when in power, former Italian premier and senior statesman, Guilio Andreotti, had protected the clans from successful prosecution.

*(ii) In violent political movements*  In the 1980s counter-terrorist supergrass systems appeared in Northern Ireland and Italy. While the law in France and Spain was also changed in the 1980s to encourage members of violent political organizations to cooperate with the authorities in the arrest and prosecution of their confederates, this did not result in mass trials on informer evidence. Experiments with supergrass evidence also occurred in Germany in the mid-1970s but it was not until the 1990s that a supergrass process enabled the rump of the left-wing Red Army Faction to be successfully prosecuted. The supergrass processes in Italy and Germany have been regulated by temporary legislation and have been used to devastating effect particularly against both armed left and right. The Northern Irish process, on the other hand, uniquely failed to be successfully institutionalized, the result of an unusual judicial responsiveness to an effective public campaign against the lack of adherence to due process safeguards at its inception (Greer 1995).

The emergence of the supergrass system in Northern Ireland in the early 1980s stemmed from the maturing of the intelligence system throughout the 1970s, the difficulties which the police faced in obtaining confessions from key terrorist suspects following restrictions on police interrogation methods implemented in the wake of the Bennett report in 1979, and a crisis of allegiance amongst certain paramilitary activists especially the 'second-time rounders' who, by the early 1980s, had already served one period of imprisonment and, having been arrested again, could not face another. It began hesitantly with two comparatively modest trials in 1981, experienced a brief ascendancy in 1983 when three major trials resulted in the conviction of 56 of the 64 defendants, then experienced a prolonged decline and ultimate collapse as the courts reversed their original decisions that uncorroborated convictions could be justified. The only convictions to survive the appeal hearings, which ended in 1986, were those sustained almost entirely by confessions (Greer 1995).

*Towards a sociological model of the police informant*        523

The construction of a *pentiti* process against the armed left in Italy began with the re-organization of the intelligence-gathering system in the mid-1970s (Seaton-Watson 1988), followed by the enactment of a series of temporary laws designed to encourage terrorists to collaborate with the authorities (Vercher 1992). By the early 1980s the frequency of terrorist incidents has declined, *pentiti* had decimated the armed right (Seaton-Watson 1988), hundreds of left wing suspects had been arrested, and whole armed leftist organizations had been dismantled (Mosconi and Pisapia 1981). However, no attempt was made in Italy to protect the political *pentiti* in the manner of the Witness Protection Program of the USA, or even the less formal arrangements found in the supergrass system in Northern Ireland (Hallenstein 1984).

Although the trial, in May 1975 in Germany, of the four founding members of the Red Army Faction (or Baader-Meinhof gang), Andreas Baader, Ulrike Meinhof, Jan Karl Raspe and Gudrun Ensslin, hinged upon the testimony of Gerhard Müller – who had turned states evidence – it was not until the mid-1980s that a number of trials of leading neo-Nazi activists took place in which accomplice evidence was of some importance. In June 1989 a new temporary scheme which lapsed in 1992 was introduced by the legislature (*Nr. 26 Tag der Ausgabe: Bonn, 15 Juni 1989*) which enabled several former RAF activists, who had enjoyed the protection of the secret police in the former East Germany, to turn *staatzeuge* (state witness) in return for greatly reduced prison sentences.

D. THE CONFESSION INFORMANT

The term 'confession informant' is reserved here for those suspects who, unlike all the others considered so far, inform only against themselves. Although there are now substantial psychological and legal literatures on how and why confessions are made in police custody, the issues discussed have rarely, if ever, been considered part of the debate about police informants. Yet the process by which suspects confess is highly relevant to the informant debate for two reasons. In the first place confessions are prized by the police for their information content, for their potential use as evidence against those who have made them, and because they signify the point in police interrogations where the suspect has been 'broken' and where negotiation of charge and plea can begin in earnest. Secondly, the dynamics of the interrogation itself, together with certain psychological and sociological characteristics of the suspect, can be potent sources of distortion in this kind of information (McConville 1993).

The problem with confessions as a source of police information can be simply stated. True confessions voluntarily offered provide a cast-iron legal basis for conviction. But confessions which may appear to be true and apparently elicited without improper pressure may be made by entirely innocent parties. The genuinely guilty may retract true confessions falsely claiming they were improperly obtained, while the innocent may offer no objection to what are in fact false confessions. The Runciman report notes these difficulties and refers to the substantial body of psychological research which has allowed four types of false confession to be distinguished: what may be called 'fantasy confessions' made by people suffering from severe mental problems which prevent them from distinguishing fact from reality; what may be termed 'diversionary confessions' made in the attempt to protect someone else from interrogation and prosecution; 'coerced-complaint confessions' made by those who desperately want to escape the stress created by police interviews; and 'coerced-internalized confessions' made by the highly suggestible who, though entirely innocent and sometimes even physically incapable of having done what is alleged, none the less accept police accusations. (Runciman Report 1993: 57; Gudjonsson 1992). The task for the criminal justice system is to devise adequate procedures to enable true confessions to be distinguished from false, and those obtained under undue pressure from those offered without it. There are broadly three, not necessarily mutually exclusive, methods of attempting to achieve these objectives: attempting to control the circumstances in which confessions are made, typically police custody, in order to reduce the risk of unreliability; establishing appropriate tests for the admissibility of this kind of evidence at trial linked to the manner in which the confession was obtained or to the strength of other prosecution evidence; and seeking to regulate reliance by courts upon confessions which pass the admissibility test by, for example, discouraging or even prohibiting, conviction on this basis alone. The majority of the Royal Commission on Criminal Justice recommended that confessions unsupported by other evidence should be capable of being put to the jury subject to judicial warnings about unreliability (Runciman Report 1993: 54).

E. CONCLUSION

In spite of extensive literatures ranging across several disciplines the problems posed by the police informant are still imperfectly understood. While the sources of systematic distortion in the information provided by the casual observer are generally well appreciated and recognized by the legal system, this is not so obviously true of that provided by crime victims or snoops. The problem of the confession as a source of information for the police has been hotly debated and the proper approach which the criminal justice system should take

*Towards a sociological model of the police informant* 525

remains controversial. Although vital, the distinction between the accomplice witness and the supergrass has not always been fully accepted and while the justification for a mandatory accomplice evidence warning may be difficult to justify for all accomplices who testify for the Crown, the evidence of supergrasses clearly requires it. The failure of the legal system to treat the evidence of *agents provocateurs* as inherently unreliable and requiring a danger warning is also difficult to defend as is the use of police informants in legal political movements. Finally, the strong emphasis upon Congressional scrutiny in the US Witness Protection Program is, in this respect at least, a model worth following, and suggests that informer and supergrass systems in the UK should be much more closely monitored by parliament, perhaps through standing Informer Commissions.

It would be naive to think that modern democratic policing could dispense with the services of informants, but their role, and the effectiveness of existing and potential channels of public accountability, ought to be kept constantly under review in order to guard against the various problems identified above. The principal task for social scientists and policy analysts in this domain is to attempt to discover in more detail the role played in police investigations by information from various sources – informants, objects, documents, audio and video recording – together with the sources of systematic distortion and other problems to which it may give rise, and to suggest how the mechanisms of public accountability could be improved.

(Date accepted: January 1995)

*Steven Greer*
*Department of Law*
*University of Bristol*

BIBLIOGRAPHY

**Baldwin, R. and R. Kinsey** 1982 *Police Powers and Politics*, London: Quartet Books.
**Bennett Report** 1979 *Report of the Committee of Inquiry into Police Interrogation Procedures in Northern Ireland*, Cmnd. 7497, London: HMSO.
**Campbell, D.** 1994 *The Underworld*, London: BBC Books.
**Clifford, B.** 1978 *The Psychology of Person Identification*, London: Routledge and Kegan Paul.
**Clifford, B.** 1979 'Eye Witness Testimony: The Bridging of a Credibility Gap' in Farrington *et al.* (1979).
**CNPDS** 1987 *Convenzione per una recera su normative ed esperienza di maxiprocessi e sulla* utilizzabilita e gestibilita probatoria dei c.d.testimoni della testimoni della corona e della relative tutela. *Confronto con l' esperienza Italiane. Rapporto finale*, 2 Allegati, II, Milan: Centro Nazionale di Prevenzione e Difesa Sociale.
**Criminal Law Revision Committee** 1972 *Eleventh Report, Evidence General*, Cmnd 4991, London: HMSO.
**Dillon, M.** 1991 *The Dirty War*, London: Arrow Books.
**Dorn, N., Murji, K. and South, N.** 1992 *Traffickers: Drug Markets and Law Enforcement*, London: Routledge.
**Falcone, G. with Padovani, M.** 1992 *Men of Honour: The Truth About the Mafia*, London: Warner Books.

**Farrington, D., Hawkins, K. and Lloyd-Bostock, S.** 1979 *Psychology, Law and Legal Processes*, London: Macmillan Press.

**Goodman, J. and Will, I.** 1985 *Underworld*, London: Harrap.

**Grabosky, P.N.** 1991 'Prosecutors, Informants and the Integrity of the Criminal Justice System', Unpublished Report, Australian Institute of Criminology.

**Greer, S.** 1995 *Supergrasses: A Study in Anti-terrorist Law Enforcement in Northern Ireland*, Oxford: Clarendon Press.

**Gudjonsson, G.H.** 1992 *The Psychology of Interrogations, Confessions and Testimony*, Chichester: Wiley.

**Haglund, E.** 1990 'Impeaching the Underworld Informant', *Southern California Law Review* 63: 1407–47.

**Hallenstein, D.** 1984 'Walking Corpses', *The Sunday Times Colour Supplement* 4 September.

**Harney, M.L. and Cross, J.C.** 1960 *The Informer in Law Enforcement*, Springfield, Illinois, USA: Charles Thomas.

**Lawler, L.E.** 1986 'Police Informer Privilege: A Study for the Law Reform Commission of Canada', *Criminal Law Quarterly* 28: 91–128.

**Levin, J.M.** 1985 'Organized Crime and Insulated Violence: Federal Liability for Illegal Conduct in the Witness Protection Program', *Journal of Criminal Law and Criminology* 76: 208–50.

**Loftus, E. and Wells, G.** (eds) 1984 *Eyewitness Testimony: Psychological Perspectives*, Cambridge: Cambridge University Press.

**Manning, P.K. and Redlinger, L.J.** 1977 'Invitational Edges of Corruption: Some Consequences of Narcotic Law Enforcement' in P. Rock (ed.) *Drugs and Politics*, London: Transaction Books.

**Marx, G.T.** 1974 'Thoughts on a Neglected Category of Social Movement Participant: The *Agent Provocateur* and the Informant', *American Journal of Sociology* 80: 402–40.

**Marx, G.T.** 1988 *Undercover: Police Surveillance in America*, Berkeley: University of California Press.

**McConville, M.** 1993 *Corroboration and Confessions. The Impact of a Rule Requiring That No Conviction Can Be Sustained on the Basis of Confession Evidence Alone*, London: Royal Commission on Criminal Justice Research Study No. 13, HMSO.

**Mosconi, G. and Pisapia, G.** 1981 'The Stereotype of the Repentant Terrorist: His Nature and Functions', *European Group for the Study of Deviance and Social Control, Working Papers in Criminology* 3: 188–207.

**Navasky, V.** 1982 *Naming Names*, London: Calder.

**O'Flaherty, L.** 1925 *The Informer*, London: Jonathan Cape.

**O'Mahoney, M. with Wooding, D.** 1978 *King Squealer: The True Story of Maurice O'Mahoney*, London: W. H. Allen.

**Oscapella, E.** 1980 'A Study of Informers in England', *Criminal Law Review* 136–46.

**Parker, R.** 1986 Confidential Informants and the Truth Finding Function, *Cooley Law Review* 4: 565–73.

**Parliamentary Joint Committee on the National Crime Authority** 1988 *Witness Protection*, Canberra: Australian Government Publishing.

**Runciman Report** 1993 *Report of Royal Commission on Criminal Justice*, Cm.2263, London: HMSO.

**Sanders, A. and Young, R.** 1994 *Criminal Justice*, London: Butterworths.

**Schliefman, N.** 1988 *Undercover Agents in the Russian Revolutionary Movement: The SR Party, 1902–14*, London: Macmillan.

**Schlichter, J.** 1971 'The Outwardly Sufficient Search Warrant Affidavit: What If It's False?', *University of California Los Angeles Law Review* 96: 96–147.

**Seaton-Watson, C.** 1988 'Terrorism in Italy', in J. Lodge (ed) *The Threat of Terrorism*, Brighton: Wheatsheaf Books.

**Seymour, D.** 1982 'What good have supergrasses done for anyone but themselves?', *Legal Action Group Bulletin*, Dec. 7–9.

**Seymour, G.** 1985 *Field of Blood*, London: Collins.

**Skolnick, J. H.** 1975 *Justice Without Trial: Law Enforcement in Democratic Society* (2nd ed), New York: John Wiley and Sons.

**Slipper, J.** 1981 *Slipper of the Yard*, London: Sidgwick and Jackson.

**Tapper, C.** 1990 *Cross on Evidence* 7th edn, London: Butterworths.

**Vercher, A.** 1992 *Terrorism in Europe: An International Comparative Legal Analysis*, Oxford: Clarendon Press.

**Wool, G.J.** 1985–86 'Police Informants

*Towards a sociological model of the police informant* 527

in Canada: The Law and the Reality', *Saskatchewan Law Review* 50: 249–70.

**Zander, M.** 1974 'Are Too Many Professional Criminals Avoiding Conviction? – A Study in Britain's Two Busiest Courts', *Modern Law Review* 37: 28–61.

# Part IV
## Detecting Deception

# [11]

# NONVERBAL CUES TO DECEPTION AMONG INTIMATES, FRIENDS, AND STRANGERS

David B. Buller
R. Kelly Aune

ABSTRACT: Buller and Burgoon (in press) propose that deceivers attempt to encode strategically nonverbal cues which indicate nonimmediacy and project a positive image. At the same time, deceivers leak arousal and negative affect via their nonverbal display. This experiment tested these predictions, while examining the influence of relational history on deception cues and the stability of deception cues within deceptive conversations. The nonverbal behavior of 130 strangers, friends, and intimates was measured. Results indicated that deceivers signalled nonimmediacy, arousal, and negative affect, but they did not appear to project a positive image. Deception cues were mediated by relational history and showed considerable temporal variation. Strangers leaked more arousal and negative affect than friends and intimates. Further, deceivers, particularly deceiving friends and intimates, seemed to monitor and control their nonverbal behavior during deception by suppressing arousal and negative affect cues and moderating nonimmediate behavior.

Research into behavioral cues to deception has linked several types of behavior with deceptive intent. Recent meta-analyses and summaries provide some of the best evidence on the cues related to deception (DePaulo, Stone, and Lassiter, 1985a; Kraut, 1980; Zuckerman, DePaulo, & Rosenthal, 1981; Zuckerman & Driver, 1985). Zuckerman and Driver report that 58% of the behaviors examined in two or more of the studies they meta-analyzed reliably distinguish truthtellers from liars. Further, a number of additional experiments not included in the meta-analyses provide evidence of recurrent patterns in deceivers' behavior.

Buller and Burgoon (in press) argue that the behaviors which distinguish truthtellers from liars can be characterized as either strategic or

David B. Buller is an assistant professor of Communication at the University of Arizona. R. Kelly Aune is an assistant professor of Speech Communication at the University of Hawaii. Address all correspondence to Dr. David B. Buller, Dept. of Communication, University of Arizona, Tucson, AZ 85721.

270

JOURNAL OF NONVERBAL BEHAVIOR

nonstrategic. According to Buller and Burgoon, strategic nonverbal behaviors are encoded to reduce the deceiver's responsibility for the deceptive statement and to avoid the negative consequences of detection. Buller and Burgoon identify four classes of strategic nonverbal behaviors: (a)uncertainty and vagueness, (b) nonimmediacy, reticence, and withdrawal, (c) disassociation, and (d) image-protecting behavior.

In contrast, some nonverbal behaviors inadvertently leak the deceiver's deceptive intent. Buller and Burgoon's notion of nonstrategic leakage behaviors incorporates a substantial portion of Ekman and Friesen's (1969) leakage hypothesis and Zuckerman et al.'s (1981) four-factor theory of deception behavior. Nonstrategic cues leak information about arousal and nervousness and negative emotional reactions which often occur when the communicator deceives. Another cognitive change which often results in nonstrategic deception cues is an increased cognitive effort directed at controlling the strategic behaviors and masking the cues of anxiety and negative affect. As Zuckerman et al. argue, this increased effort can produce mixed or inconsistent messages which create an incompetent presentation.

From Buller and Burgoon's (in press) review, nonverbal cues appear to play the most significant role in two classes of strategic behavior—nonimmediacy, reticence, and withdrawal behaviors and image-protecting behaviors—and in two classes of nonstrategic leakage—arousal and nervousness cues and negative affect cues. In contrast, uncertainty and vagueness, disassociation, and incompetent communication performances are comprised largely of verbal cues and therefore were not investigated in this experiment.

## Nonimmediacy, Reticence, and Withdrawal

Nonverbally, deceivers appear to indicate nonimmediacy, reticence, and withdrawal through the use of shorter replies, more pauses, and longer response latencies (Baskett & Freedle, 1974; deTurck & Miller, 1985; Feldman, Devin-Sheehan, & Allen, 1978; Goldstein, 1923; Knapp, Hart, & Dennis, 1974; Krauss, Geller, & Olson, 1976; Kraut, 1978; Mehrabian, 1971; Motley, 1974). Similarly, Mehrabian (1972) and Knapp et al. (1974) report that liars decrease the frequency and duration of glances, decrease forward body lean, and increase distance. The overriding result of these studies is that deceivers become more withdrawn and inaccessible to their conversational partners, perhaps in an effort to hinder surveillance and probing by a suspicious partner. Zuckerman, DeFrank, Hall, Larrance, and Rosenthal (1979) found that deceptive answers do in fact create impres-

DAVID B. BULLER, R. KELLY AUNE

sions of less personal involvement. In the verbal domain, Kuiken (1981) reported that deceivers use more nonimmediate language when they fabricate a reply, and the Zuckerman and Driver (1985) meta-analysis supports the use of verbal nonimmediacy by liars.

This conclusion, however, has not always been supported. Studies have showed that some liars increased, some decreased, and some alternated between increasing and decreasing their reaction time (English, 1926; Marston, 1920) and one study (Matarazzo, Wiens, Jackson, & Manaugh, 1970) found the topic influenced whether liars gave shorter or longer answers and had shorter or longer response latencies. Further, some experiments failed to find gaze differences between liars and truthtellers (Matarazzo et al., 1970; McClintock & Hunt, 1975) or found increased eye contact from liars (Riggio & Friedman, 1983). DePaulo et al. (1985a) have claimed that liars do not avert their eyes any more than truthtellers do. However, the weight of the findings appears to support the following hypothesis:

> H1: Deceivers will display more nonverbal behaviors indicative of nonimmediacy, reticence, and withdrawal than truthtellers.

## Image-Protection

The notion of image-protecting behavior was first suggested by DePaulo et al. (1985a). These authors speculate that a major objective of deceivers is to protect their image. Deceivers do so by displaying innocuous conversational behaviors such as nodding, smiling, and refraining from interruptions. Presumably, such behaviors deflect attention away from the deceiver by maintaining a positive demeanor. In fact, evidence of a more pleasant demeanor by deceivers is mixed. A few experiments have found that liars do encode more smiling, nodding, and pleasant faces, particularly if they are not anxious (e.g., Ekman, Friesen & Scherer, 1976; Mehrabian, 1971, 1972); however, more studies find the opposite pattern or no differences in these behaviors (e.g., Bennett, 1978; Ekman & Friesen, 1974; Feldman et al., 1978; Hocking & Leathers, 1980; Kraut, 1978; Mehrabian, 1972; Zuckerman et al., 1981). Finally, the meta-analyses generally conclude that smiling decreases when a communicator deceives. While these results do not make it clear what deceivers do to protect their image, it is an appealing hypothesis that deserves further investigation:

> H2: Deceivers will display more nonverbal behaviors designed to protect their image (i.e., project a positive demeanor) than truthtellers.

272

JOURNAL OF NONVERBAL BEHAVIOR

### Arousal and Nervousness

That deception induces arousal is one of the more consistently cited propositions in the deception literature. It is a major component in Ekman and Friesen's (1969) leakage hypothesis and Zuckerman et al.'s (1981) four-factor theory about behaviors emitted during deception. These researchers propose that arousal is "leaked" by the actions of deceivers. This leakage, however, is moderated by the extent to which actors can monitor and exercise control over particular communication channels, resulting in a leakage hierarchy among the channels of nonverbal communication. Deceivers are least likely to display arousal cues in the face and most likely to display them in the body and voice (DePaulo et al., 1985a; DePaulo, Zuckerman, & Rosenthal, 1980; Ekman & Friesen, 1969, 1974; Zuckerman & Driver, 1985).

The research on arousal-linked deception cues generally supports the leakage hierarchy. The meta-analyses, as well as experiments not included in them (Berrien & Huntington, 1943; Clark, 1975; Ekman et al., 1976; Ekman, Friesen, O'Sullivan & Scherer, 1980; Hocking & Leathers, 1980; Knapp et al., 1974; McClintock & Hunt, 1975; Mehrabian, 1971; O'Hair, Cody, & McLaughlin, 1981; Riggio & Friedman, 1983; Streeter, Krauss, Geller, Olson, & Apple, 1977), have found that liars engage in more blinking, pupil dilation or instability, self- and object-manipulations, higher pitch, vocal nervousness, more speech errors and hesitations, more word repetitions, and less gesturing. Research has been mixed on whether liars engage in more or less postural shifting; random leg, foot, and head movement; gestural activity; and other bodily indicators of nervousness (cf. Ekman & Friesen, 1974; Ekman et al., 1976; Knapp et al., 1974; Hocking & Leathers, 1980; Mehrabian, 1972). It may be that liars attempt to suppress bodily activity to mask their anxiety. Alternatively, the lesser gestural animation and bodily movement together may be indicative of less involvement and commitment to what one is saying. Either way, the net result is often stiff, restrained trunk and limb positions indicative of tension.

> H3: Deceivers will display more nonverbal behaviors indicative of arousal and nervousness than truthtellers.

### Negative Affect

Ekman and Friesen (1969) and Zuckerman et al. (1981) also believe that deception is an unpleasant experience for most communicators. Consequently, one of the clues to deception that may be leaked is negative

DAVID B. BULLER, R. KELLY AUNE

affect. As already noted, some experiments report that deceivers smile less and display fewer positive head nods. Thus, deceivers may be revealing a state of negative affect by failing to give positive feedback to their conversational partners. The reduction in gaze reported in some studies (e.g., Knapp et al., 1974) may be a further indication of liars experiencing unpleasant emotional states, which they attempt to mask by closing off the visual channel. In sum, while only a few studies have focused directly on negative affect, the data tend to support such displays as one by-product of deception:

> H4: Deceivers will display more nonverbal behaviors indicative of negative affect than truthtellers.

It is apparent from the foregoing discussion that some nonverbal cues, particularly smiling and head nodding, can serve multiple functions in a deceptive conversation. For instance, smiling and head nodding may decrease when deceivers experience negative affect; however, smiling and head nodding may increase as deceivers attempt to present a positive image. Also, smiling may function as an immediacy cue, although Buller and Burgoon (in press) did not include it in their nonimmediacy classification. As an immediacy cue, smiling may decrease during deception. The multi-functional nature of some of the nonverbal cues makes predictions about specific cues, difficult. Therefore, general hypotheses about the display of nonimmediacy, image-protecting, arousal, and negative affect cues were formulated in this study.

*Moderating Factors*

Although there appears to be some consensus in this research, several important issues remain unexplored that could modify the conclusions on the nonverbal cues to deception. One issue is whether the cues identified in previous research—research which has examined almost exclusively deception among strangers—are generalizable to deceiving relational partners such as friends and intimates. Three factors may alter the nature of deception when communicators deceive friends and intimates: (1) deceivers' belief that relational partners can detect deceit better than strangers due to their greater familiarity with the communicators (Buller, 1987; McCornack & Parks, 1985), (2) deceivers' increased concern about the negative consequences if deceit is detected by the relational partners (Buller, 1987; Ekman, 1985), and (3) deceivers' prior experience deceiving the relational partners.

274

JOURNAL OF NONVERBAL BEHAVIOR

The first two factors potentially could increase the number of cues displayed by communicators when deceiving relational partners. In particular, the presence of a relationship may increase communicators' motivation to lie successfully which, in turn, would increase some of their strategic behaviors such as nonimmediacy and image-protecting behavior. In their meta-analyses, Zuckerman et al. (1981) and Zuckerman and Driver (1985) showed that under high motivation more changes in nonverbal behavior were evident in deceivers than under low motivation. Some behaviors, such as vocal pitch and hand shrugs increased as motivation increased, whereas other behaviors such as blinking, facial expressions, head movements, adaptors, postural shifts, response length, and speech rate decreased. Further, deceivers' anxiety about and negative reactions to lying may be higher when attempting to deceive relational partners, resulting in more arousal and negative affect leakage.

DePaulo and her colleagues (DePaulo et al., 1980; DePaulo, Stone & Lassiter, 1985b) have speculated that while motivation increases deceivers' attempts to control their behavioral displays, their success at controlling cues will be determined by the amenability of particular channels to control. This argument along with the leakage hierarchy suggests that if relational partners are more motivated to deceive successfully, they will more successfully control facial cues than body and vocal cues. DePaulo, however, notes that control over one's behaviors decreases as emotional reactions to deception increase. This suggests that, as relationships become more intimate, control over leakage will become more difficult as the detection apprehension (fear of detection as defined by DePaulo et al., 1985b) increases. Thus, one might conclude that friends would be most successful at masking cues which leak arousal and negative affect, particularly in the face, whereas strangers and intimates would exhibit more of these cues.

Finally, a communicator may have prior experience deceiving a relational partner and this prior experience could affect a communicator's behavior in much the same way that planning and rehearsal has been shown to affect lies prepared for strangers. O'Hair et al. (1981) and Zuckerman and Driver (1985) found that deceivers given time to rehearse their lies have more dilated pupils, engage in more postural shifts, increase long body adaptors, respond more quickly, give shorter answers, speak faster, display more affirmative head nods, exhibit briefer laughter or smiling, and use somewhat fewer gestures than deceivers who give spontaneous lies. Thus, planning and rehearsal may allow communicators to conceal some deception cues such as reducing response latency and providing more

275

DAVID B. BULLER, R. KELLY AUNE

affirmative responses, but it can also backfire as can high motivation. Thus, an additional objective of the present experiment was to examine whether the presence of a relationship with the target affects a communicator's nonverbal behavior during deception.

A second issue related to the generalizability of the conclusions about nonverbal cues to deception concerns the display of these cues in actual deceptive interactions. This concern stems from the lack of interactive designs in many of the previous experiments. Only a few experiments have permitted deceivers to interact with the targets of their deceit (cf., Toris & DePaulo, 1985). Instead, many experiments have communicators (1) encode deception in isolation while being videotaped or filmed or (2) encode deception while interacting with a receiver who is restricted to follow a predetermined script. Further, in the analyses of interactive designs, very little attention has been paid to the consistency with which deceivers display nonverbal cues over the duration of the conversation. There are reasons to believe that an interaction can influence the display of nonverbal behaviors. First, communicators may expend more effort to control their nonverbal displays when interacting with a receiver who can probe their statements, set traps, and compare an answer to a previous statement. That is, they may be more motivated in interactive designs. In addition, the mere possibility that a receiver can respond to the communicator's messages may increase the communicator's arousal over that experienced when presenting to a camera, in a public speaking setting, or in other situations where the receiver's ability to detect deception is restricted.

There is also some reason to speculate that changes in a communicator's nonverbal behavior during deception will vary as the conversation progresses. First, to maintain a deception throughout a conversation may require many small individual lies. While the initial few lies may be anticipated by the communicator, it is likely that several lies must be created on the spur-of-the-moment, in response to statements by the receiver. Thus, communicators may have less ability to control their behaviors and mask nonstrategic leakage, because they must expend greater cognitive effort creating spontaneous lies. Second, interaction might affect deception cues to the extent that communicators receive information about the success of their deception and the receivers' suspicions. If communicators perceive that suspicion is low, they may reduce their efforts to mask nonstrategic leakage and to encode strategic behaviors indicative of nonimmediacy and image-protection. On the other hand, heightened suspicion may increase arousal and negative affect cues, as well as increase strategic cues such

276

JOURNAL OF NONVERBAL BEHAVIOR

nonimmediacy and image protection. Consequently, a final objective of this experiment was to see if a communicator's nonverbal behavior during deception varies over time in the conversation.

## Method

### Participants

One hundred eighty-three undergraduate students from a large southwestern university participated in this study. Forty-eight targets were recruited from upper division communication courses and required to bring to the experiment a person with whom they had an intimate relationship ($N = 47$) and a person with whom they had a friendship ($N = 42$). No gender requirement was specified in the request for the intimate and friend. Thus, the intimate designation refers to relationship development not sexual intimacy, though some intimates were sexual partners with the targets. Strangers ($N = 46$) were recruited from a lower division communication course and had not met the targets prior to the experimental sessions.

There were more female than male participants in the study (Table 1). Therefore, the most common sex composition was female-female, and the least common was male-male. Examining relationship level, there were more cross-sex intimate dyads than same-sex intimate dyads, with male-male intimate dyads being rare; however, a chi-square analysis showed that this variation by relationship level was not significant, $\chi^2(6, N = 130) = 8.53$, $p > .05$. Each gender composition was split equally between the truth and deception conditions, $\chi^2(3, N = 130) = 0.80$, $p > .05$. The potential confounding of relationship level and sex composition is noteworthy; however, it is not clear from past research how this might affect deceivers' behaviors. In the only study examining sex composition, DePaulo et al. (1985b) argued that deceivers are more motivated to deceive successfully in cross-

## TABLE 1

### Sex Composition of Experimental Dyads

|  | Male Source | | Female Source | |
|---|---|---|---|---|
|  | Male Target | Female Target | Male Target | Female Target |
| Total | 17 | 38 | 23 | 52 |
| Stranger | 7 | 8 | 6 | 19 |
| Friend | 7 | 11 | 6 | 18 |
| Intimate | 3 | 19 | 11 | 15 |
| Truth | 8 | 17 | 11 | 28 |
| Deception | 9 | 21 | 12 | 24 |

DAVID B. BULLER, R. KELLY AUNE

sex *stranger* dyads, because the opportunity for a more intimate future interaction motivates the deceiver to make a favorable impression on the opposite-sex target. Whether this motivation generalizes to cross-sex intimate dyads is not established. However, deceivers may be less concerned with creating a positive impression on a cross-sex intimate than on a cross-sex stranger, because the continuation of the intimate relationship does not depend on making a good impression on the intimate in the experimental interactions. Thus, an overabundance of cross-sex stranger dyads would raise greater concern than the disproportionate number of cross-sex intimate dyads in this experiment.

## Target Pretest

A pretest assessed the target's evaluations of the relationships with the intimate and friend, using the Wheeless and Grotz (1975) trust scale and Fisher's (Fisher, 1981; Narus, 1981) relationship scale. In addition, three items selected from Wheeless and Grotz' (1976) self-disclosure scale measured the degree of self-disclosure by the partner and by the target. The target also completed the trust scale for strangers in general. Analyses reported elsewhere confirmed that targets had a more intimate relationship with the intimate than the friend and that intimates were trusted most and strangers least (Buller, 1987).

## Source Pretest and Posttest

The source pretest consisted of three personality measures. (1) Crowne and Marlowe's (1964) Social Desirability scale, (2) Snyder's (1974) Self-Monitoring scale, and (3) Christie and Geis' (1970) Machiavellianism IV scale. Responses to these personality scales were used as topics for the experimental interactions, since DePaulo et al. (1985b) assert that many lies between relational partners are identity-relevant, encoded to influence how partners perceive personality traits, intentions, abilities, attitudes, values, behaviors, and social characteristics. These topics may be more salient to and more likely to be detected by relational partners than the objective, factual topics employed in many deception experiments (Comadena, 1982; DePaulo et al., 1985a; Miller et al., 1981; Miller & Burgoon, 1982).

## Procedure

The target brought the intimate and friend to the experimental session where they were joined by a stranger. The experimenter explained that the study examined how people in different relationships communicate. After consenting to be videotaped, the stranger, friend, and intimate were taken to separate rooms where they completed the source pretest. The target was seated at a table in the corner of the interaction lab and completed the target pretest. When the target finished the pretest, the experimenter gave her/him a blank copy of the three personality scales. The experimenter told the target that in the subsequent interactions the target would be interviewing each source about his/her responses to the scale. The target was to begin by asking for the answer to the first question on the scale and then to discuss the source's reasons for the answer. The target was then to move to the second question, asking for the answer and discussing the reasons for the answer. The target was to continue with this format until the experimenter returned after

278

JOURNAL OF NONVERBAL BEHAVIOR

five minutes to stop the interview. The target was told to take as long as he/she wanted to discuss an answer and not to become concerned if all the questions on the scale were not discussed. The target was given a minute to look over the statements on the scale to be used in the first interaction.

Meanwhile, an experimental assistant gave similar instructions to the first source. For truthful sources, the last instruction was to be honest in their answers and their reasons for their answers. For deceptive sources, the final instruction was to lie about all their answers (e.g., say "false" when actually responded "true" on the scale item and say "true" when actually responded "false") and to provide false reasons for their answers. After this final instruction the source was immediately escorted by the assistant to the interaction lab to avoid any opportunity for planning the deceit.

When the source arrived, he/she was seated in a chair facing the target. The chairs were placed approximately 3.5 feet apart. The experimenter briefly repeated the interview instructions, reminded the interactants that they would have five minutes to discuss the source's responses, signalled an experimental assistant to begin the videotape recorder, and left the room.

During the interaction, an experimental assistant, seated behind a two-way mirror, recorded the responses the source reported he/she had given to each statement on the personality scales. The experimenter returned to the interaction lab at the end of five minute period and stopped the interaction. The experimental assistant immediately returned the source to the pretest room and administered the source posttest and a debriefing protocol. The second and third interactions followed that same procedure as the first interaction.

The order of relationships and personality tests in the three experimental interactions was counterbalanced to protect against order effects. The deception manipulation was varied such that at least one source deceived the target and at least one told the truth. Thus, for half of the targets, two sources deceived while for the other half, two sources told the truth. In the 14 cases where only two sources appeared at the experimental session, one deceived and the other told the truth. This procedure produced an equal number of deceptive and truthful interactions.

The target was debriefed following the third interaction. While a few targets had suspected that the experiment had some purpose other than simply observing how people communicate within different relationships, no targets deduced that deception was being examined.

## Behavioral Coding

Fourteen undergraduate students enrolled in a nonverbal communication class were trained to code the nonverbal behaviors emitted by the sources (deceivers and truthtellers) in the 130 experimental interactions. The coders were trained in coding procedures by the experimenter. This training consisted of describing the coding procedures, providing definitions and examples of the behaviors to be measured, and checking the measurements made during the first six interactions for mistakes. Coders worked individually and were assigned to code a subset of nonverbal behaviors (e.g., eye behavior and kinesic behavior). Each coder measured the assigned behaviors of sources in approximately half the groups.

Each interaction was divided into five one-minute periods. During each period, coders made two types of behavioral assessments. For some behaviors, cod-

DAVID B. BULLER, R. KELLY AUNE

ers counted the number of behaviors emitted during each one minute period. For other behaviors, coders provided Likert-type ratings of the behaviors at the end of each one-minute period. Five sets of nonverbal behaviors were measured (see Table 2). These nonverbal behaviors were subjected to principal axis factor analysis. Three small factors emerged with eigenvalues greater than one and primary loadings exceeding .50. Factor one, *gestural animation*, was comprised of illus-

## TABLE 2

### Interrater Reliabilities

| Behavior | Type of Measure | Interrater Reliability |
|---|---|---|
| BODY MOVEMENTS: | | |
| 1. Forward Lean | Count | .28 |
| 2. Postural Shifts | Count | .80 |
| 3. Leg and Foot Movement | Count | .57 |
| 4. Chair Twisting | Rating (1 = Infrequent, 7 = Very Frequent) | .70 |
| 5. Body Angle | Rating (0 = 0 degrees, 1 = 45 degrees, 2 = 90 degrees, 3 = 90 + degrees to partner) | .65 |
| 6. Immediacy | Rating (1 = Nonimmediate, 7 = Immediate) | .81 |
| | | |
| KINESIC BEHAVIOR (Friesen, Ekman, & Wallbott, 1979) | | |
| 1. Illustrators | Count | .86 |
| 2. General Animation | Rating (1 = Not Animated, 7 = Very Animated) | .68 |
| 3. Short Face and Head Adaptors | Count | .88 |
| 4. Long Face and Head Adaptors | Count | .66 |
| 5. Short Body Adaptors | Count | .32 |
| 6. Long Body Adaptors | Count | .46 |
| 7. Short Object Adaptors | Count | .25 |
| 8. Long Object Adaptors | Count | .70 |
| | | |
| FACE AND HEAD BEHAVIOR: | | |
| 1. Facial Pleasantness | Rating (1 = Unpleasant, 7 = Pleasant) | .77 |
| 2. General Happiness | Rating (1 = Unhappy, 7 = Happy | .81 |
| 3. Smiling | Count | .87 |
| 4. Head Nodding | Count | .77 |
| 5. Head Shaking | Count | .57 |

280

JOURNAL OF NONVERBAL BEHAVIOR

## TABLE 2 (cont.)

| Behavior | Type of Measure | Interrater Reliability |
|---|---|---|
| EYE BEHAVIOR | | |
| 1. Gazing | Count | .84 |
| 2. Gaze Avoidance | Count | .62 |
| VOCAL BEHAVIOR (Burgoon, 1978) | | |
| 1. Fluency | Rating (1 = Disfluent, 7 = Fluent) | .38 |
| 2. Pleasantness | Rating (1 = Unpleasant, 7 = Pleasant) | .34 |
| 3. Pitch Variety | Rating (1 = Monotone, 7 = Varied) | .34 |
| 4. Rate | Rating (1 = Slow, 7 = Fast) | .18 |
| 5. Volume | Rating (1 = Soft, 7 = Loud) | .63 |
| 6. Clarity | Rating (1 = Not Clear, 7 = Clear) | .79 |
| 7. Pitch Level | Rating (1 = Low, 7 = High) | .75 |

trator frequency and general animation rating (alpha reliability $r = .89$; interrater reliability $r = .81$). Factor two, *vocal activity*, included ratings of vocal clarity, loudness, pitch variety, pleasantness, rate, and fluency (alpha reliability $r = .86$; interrater reliability $r = .70$). Factor three, *general pleasantness*, contained ratings of facial pleasantness and general happiness, and frequency of smiling (alpha reliability $r = .82$; interrater reliability $r = .89$). Factor totals were created by summing the items within each factor. When combining counts and ratings in the general animation and pleasantness factors, individual items were first converted to z-scores.

To check the interrater reliability, all coders rated the first group of three interactions and two other groups of three interactions chosen at random from the set of 48 groups. Ebel's intraclass correlation was calculated as a measure of interrater reliability (Table 2). Most interrater reliability coefficients were high. The backward lean and shrug emblem measures and the vocal intensity rating were dropped from the analysis, because they had very low interrater reliability.

### Statistical Analysis

A series of three (relational history) X 2 (deception condition) X 5 (time period) MANOVAs were used to test hypotheses one through four. In all analyses, the time period factor was treated as a within-subjects factor and for both this factor and the relational history factor, polynomial contrasts were performed to test for linear and nonlinear trends.

In these analyses, three comparisons were of primary interest. First, the nonverbal behaviors of truthtellers and deceivers were compared. It was expected that deceivers would display more nonimmediacy, image-protection, arousal, and

281

DAVID B. BULLER, R. KELLY AUNE

negative affect than truthtellers. Second, the nonverbal behaviors of truthtelling and deceiving intimates, friends, and strangers were compared by examining the relationship development by deception condition interactions. Third, the nonverbal behaviors of truthtellers and deceivers were compared across five one-minute intervals in the recorded conversations. This comparison was tested by the interaction between deception condition and time period and by the three-way interaction between relationship development, deception condition, and time period. These two interactions provide information on the occurrence and stability of behavior changes induced by deception.

## Results

### Manipulation Check

To check the deception manipulation, a posttest asked the sources whether they told the truth or lied during the interactions and the percentage of truth contained in the source's communication. All 66 sources in the deception condition reported that they lied to the target, and all 64 sources in the truth condition reported that they had told the truth. In addition, deceptive sources communicated very little truthful information ($M = 14.8\%$), while truthful sources communicated almost entirely true information ($M = 91.8\%$). The answers given by the source to the targets during the conversations also were compared to the sources' actual answers on the personality scales. Forty-one of the deceiving sources gave false answers to all the questions ($M = 12.45$ questions/interview), and the 25 deceptive sources who did not provide all false answers averaged only 1.46 true answers/interview. Similarly, 41 of the truthful sources gave true answer to all questions ($M = 11.24$ questions/interview) and the 23 truthful sources who did not provide entirely true answers averaged only 1.90 false answers/interview. Taken together, these data indicate that the deception manipulation was successful.

### Nonimmediacy, Reticence, and Withdrawal

Hypothesis one predicted that deceivers would exhibit more behaviors indicative of nonimmediacy, reticence, and withdrawal than truthtellers. Seven behaviors that potentially communicate nonimmediacy were included as dependent variables in the MANOVA: forward lean, body angle, mutual gaze, one-sided look by target, one-sided look by source, no gaze by either conversant, and immediacy rating.

282

JOURNAL OF NONVERBAL BEHAVIOR

Contrary to hypothesis one, the MANOVA did not produce a significant main effect for deception condition, $\Lambda = .94$, $F(7,108) = .91$, $p > .05$), but deception condition interacted significantly with relational history and time period. There was a significant linear interaction between relational history and deception condition, $\Lambda = .85$, $F(7,108) = 2.71$, $p = .01$ and a significant three-way interactions for the quadratic contrast on relational history, $\Lambda = .96$, $F(7,450) = 2.96$, $p = .005$. Univariate analyses revealed that the linear relational history by deception condition interaction was significant for forward lean, $F(1,114) = 4.96$, $p = .03$, and for the frequency of one-sided looks by the target, a measure of the source's gaze avoidance, $F(1,114) = 7.02$, $p = .009$. The three-way interaction was significant for no gaze, $F(1,114) = 3.94$, $p = .049$, and for one-sided looks by the source, $F(1,114) = 4.79$, $p = .03$.

As predicted by hypothesis one, strangers signalled more nonimmediacy when deceiving by encoding fewer forward leans $(M = .65)$ than when telling the truth $(M = 1.90)$. Conversely, intimates, and to a lesser degree friends, signalled more nonimmediacy by avoiding the targets' gaze when deceiving. One-sided gazes by the target were more frequent with deceiving intimates $(M = 17.65)$ and friends $(M = 17.10)$ than with truthful intimates $(M = 14.40)$ and friends $(M = 16.20)$. Intimates also displayed more frequent periods of no gaze when deceiving $(M = 3.75)$ than when telling the truth $(M = 3.53)$.

The interactions with time period showed that deceptive friends and intimates became more immediate as the conversations progressed, suggesting that they actively managed their display of immediacy cues. Specifically, deceptive friends $(Ms = 3.37, 4.10, 4.10, 3.58, 3.79$ respectively by period) decreased their rate of no gaze in periods 4 and 5 and deceptive intimates $(Ms = 3.95, 3.64, 3.50, 3.32, 4.36)$ decreased their rate of no gaze from periods 1 to 4. Truthful friends and intimates, in contrast, increased their incidence of no gaze. Similarly, deceptive friends $(Ms = 1.95, 3.00, 2.74, 2.16, 2.37)$ and deceptive intimates $(Ms = 2.36, 2.86, 2.54, 2.91, 3.04)$ increased one-sided gazing after beginning the conversations with less one-sided gazing than truthful friends and intimates. Deceptive intimates continued to maintain a higher rate of gazing while deceptive friends moderated their one-sided gazing as the conversations progressed. In contrast, deceptive strangers became less immediate late in the conversations, by reducing their one-sided gazing $(Ms = 2.70, 2.50, 2.65, 2.40, 2.45)$, while truthful strangers displayed more gazing over time. Period did not interact significantly with deception condition, $\Lambda = .94$, $F(28,1624) = .97$, $p > .05$.

283

DAVID B. BULLER, R. KELLY AUNE

## Image-Protecting Behavior

Hypothesis two predicted that deceivers would engage in more image-protecting behavior by maintaining a positive demeanor. To test this hypothesis the sources' head nodding, head shaking, and general pleasantness were entered into a MANOVA. The MANOVA failed to support hypothesis two. There were no significant effects on this set of behaviors for the following factors: (1) deception condition, $\Lambda = .99$, $F(3,109) = .47$, $p > .05$; (2) relational history by deception condition, $\Lambda = .97$, $F(6,109) = .50$, $p > .05$; (3) deception condition by time period, $\Lambda = .97$, $F(12,1170) = 1.16$, $p > .05$; and (4) relational history by deception condition by time period, $\Lambda = .96$, $F(24,1282) = .70$, $p > .05$.

## Arousal and Nervousness

Hypothesis three predicted that deceivers would leak arousal and nervousness by displaying more arousal cues than truthtellers. The leakage hierarchy proposes that arousal cues are displayed more in the body and voice than in the face. Therefore, hypothesis three was tested by analyzing nine body behaviors (six types of adaptors, chair twisting, postural shifts, and gestural animation) and the vocal activity factor.

The MANOVA produced a significant main effect for deception condition, $\Lambda = .83$, $F(10,95) = 1.97$, $p = .046$ and a significant interaction between relational history and deception condition, $\Lambda = .73$, $F(20,190) = 1.66$, $p = .04$. However, this main effect and the two-way interaction was overridden by a significant three-way interaction between relational history, deception condition, and time period, linear contrast on relational history $\Lambda = .93$ $F(10,407) = 3.23$, $p = .001$, quadratic contrast on relational history $\Lambda = .96$, $F(10,407) = 1.86$, $p = .049$. Inspection of the univariate analyses showed that the three-way interaction was significant for brief head and face adaptors (linear relational history by condition by quadratic period $F(1,104) = 4.56$, $p = .03$), brief body adaptors (quadratic relational history by condition by quartic period $F(1,104) = 6.57$, $p = .01$), long body adaptors (linear relational history by condition by quadratic period $F(1,104) = 4.75$, $p = .03$), chair twisting (linear relational history by condition by linear period $F(1,104) = 4.20$, $p = .04$), general animation (linear relational history by condition by quartic period $F(1,104) = 4.53$, $p = .04$), and vocal activity (linear relational history by condition by linear period $F(1,104) = 11.16$, $p = .001$).

Contrary to hypothesis three, arousal cues were *less* apparent in deceivers than in truthtellers. The only cue which consistently signalled

284

JOURNAL OF NONVERBAL BEHAVIOR

more arousal in deceivers was chair twisting (strangers: deception $M$ = 2.45, truth $M$ = 2.28; friends $Ms$ = 3.12 and 2.04, respectively; intimates $M$ = 2.68 and 2.38). Beyond this cue, deceptive strangers showed more arousal in their display of brief face and head adaptors (deception $M$ = .39, truth $M$ = .24) and deceptive intimates showed more arousal in their display of vocal activity (deception $M$ = 26.71, truth $M$ = 26.06).

The results imply that deceivers monitored and controlled nonverbal arousal cues. Not only were arousal cues less apparent in deceivers, but the time period effects showed evidence of behavior control. For instance, the display of brief face and head adaptors by deceivers was more stable (and lower) than by truthtellers, particularly among friends (truth $Ms$ = .81, .71, .57, .95, 1.00; deception $Ms$ = .35, .41, .24, .12, .35, by period) and intimates (truth $Ms$ = .60, .80, 1.10, .80, .40; deception $Ms$ = .44, .27, .11, .39, .33). Deceptive initimates reduced brief body adaptors ($Ms$ = .39, .39, .67, .56, .39) and long body adaptors ($Ms$ = .56, .50, .50, .28, .39) at the end of the conversations, and initimates had decreased chair twisting ($Ms$ = 2.76, 2.77, 2.68, 2.38, 2.58) by the end of the conversations. Finally, there was a substantial reduction in general animation by deceivers from periods 1 to 2; however, only intimates were able to maintain this reduction: strangers $Ms$ = .26, −.11, .03, .10, .19; friends $Ms$ = −.53, −.68, −.56, −.29, −.63; intimates $Ms$ = −.38, −.72, −.68, −.76, −.71. By periods 4 and 5, deceptive strangers and friends had returned to their initial level of animation. The interaction between deception condition and time period was not significant in the MANOVA on arousal cues, $\Lambda$ = .94, $F(40,1545)$ = .68, $p > .05$.

## Negative Affect

Hypothesis four predicted that deceivers would leak negative affect when lying. To test this hypothesis, a MANOVA was performed on the factor assessing general pleasantness and the single item measuring vocal pleasantness. The main effect for deception condition was not significant, $\Lambda$ = .97, $F(2,108)$ = 1.56, $p > .05$. There was, however, a significant linear relational history by deception condition interaction, $\Lambda$ = .94, $F(2,108)$ = 3.56, $p$ = .03, and a significant relational history by deception condition by time period interaction, linear relational history contrast $\Lambda$ = .99, $F(2, 435)$ = 3.09, $p$ = .047, quadratic relational history contrast $\Lambda$ = .98, $F(2, 435)$ = 3.86, $p$ = .02). As would be expected from the leakage hierarchy which proposes that leakage is greater in vocal than in facial channels, univariate analyses revealed that both the two-way interaction, $F(1,109)$

DAVID B. BULLER, R. KELLY AUNE

$= 7.14$, $p = .009$, and the three-way interaction, $F(1,109) = 4.96$, $p = .03$, were significant only for vocal pleasantness. Consistent with hypothesis four, strangers were less vocally pleasant when deceiving (deception $M = 4.15$, truth $M = 5.31$). On the other hand, friends and intimates did not express less vocal pleasantness when deceiving (friends: deception $M = 4.85$, truth $M = 4.56$; intimates: deception $M = 4.66$, truth $M = 4.60$). The time effect was evident in a tendency by strangers and friends, regardless of deception condition, to express greater vocal pleasantness as the conversations progressed. The deception condition by time period interaction was not significant, $\Lambda = .99$, $F(8,870) = .64$, $p > .05$.

## Discussion

The findings supported the hypothesized increase in nonimmediacy and negative affect cues during deception. However, the predicted increase in arousal cues was only weakly supported and deceivers did not engage in image-protecting behaviors. Deceivers communicated nonimmediacy through a lack of forward lean and increased gaze avoidance. The possibility also exists that some deceivers exhibited nonimmediacy by gazing at the target only when the target was not gazing at them. This behavior may have been an attempt to monitor the targets' responses to the deceptive source without engaging in eye contact. Conversely, one-sided gazing could be unsuccessful attempts by deceivers to make eye contact and increase immediacy with the target.

In this experiment, negative affect was leaked by deceiving strangers via their vocal cues, rather than via the facial cues assessed by the general pleasantness measure. Not only does this result support the proposition that deceivers experience negative affect during deception, it also conforms with predictions made from the leakage hierarchy. Namely, the voice has a lower sending capacity than the face and therefore is more likely to leak negative affect (Buller & Burgoon, in press; DePaulo et al., 1985a; Ekman & Friesen, 1969; Zuckerman et al., 1981; Zuckerman & Driver, 1985).

The hypothesized increase in arousal cues due to deception was only evident in the frequency of chair twisting by all sources. Deception did increase the number of brief head and face adaptors by strangers and vocal activity by intimates; however, the more dominant trend was a general decrease in arousal cues by deceivers, resulting in a more rigid, inhibited nonverbal display. Deceivers exhibited fewer adaptors, were less animated, and encoded less vocal activity.

286

JOURNAL OF NONVERBAL BEHAVIOR

The results did not support the prediction that deceivers would strategically encode a positive demeanor. Deceivers did not increase their rate of head nodding, head shaking, and general pleasantness. It may be premature to dismiss the appealing notion that deceivers attempt to project a positive image to their targets, given the paucity of research on this dimension. Further, in this study friends were slightly more positive vocally, perhaps indicating that deceivers create a positive image via positive vocal cues as well as positive facial cues.

More important than the foregoing effects of deception was the variation in nonverbal deception cues across relationship type and time. All of the main effects of deception on the nonverbal cues were overridden by interactions with relational history. Reviewing these interactions, it appears that strangers displayed more nonverbal cues to deception than either friends or intimates. Specifically, strangers were most nonimmediate, displayed more arousal cues in the body (chair twisting, face and head adaptors, and general animation), and expressed greater negative affect vocally when deceiving. In contrast, friends and intimates were more immediate, indicated less arousal (only displaying chair twisting and vocal activity), and did not leak negative affect when deceiving.

Earlier, three factors were identified that might alter the deception cues emitted by strangers, friends, and intimates: (1) belief that intimates and friends are better able to detect deceit, (2) increased concern for negative consequences of detection by friends and intimates, and (3) prior experience deceiving friends and intimates. All three of these factors suggested that friends and intimates might attempt to monitor and control their nonverbal presentation more than strangers, although the concern for negative consequences might produce a curvilinear trend with friends being most controlled.

The interaction between relational history and deception condition on arousal and negative affect cues implies that relational partners did attempt to monitor and control their arousal and negative affect cues more than strangers. There are, however, two qualifications to this conclusion. First, strangers seemed to monitor and control some of their arousal cues, but they were not as successful as relational partners in masking as many arousal cues. Second, friends and intimates were not able to mask successfully all deception cues. Chair twisting was not controlled well by friends or intimates. Intimates did reduce their frequency of chair twisting late in the deceptive conversations, but they leaked arousal by displaying greater vocal activity throughout the conversations. This last finding may indicate that a compensation effect occurs which deceivers attempt to mask deception cues. That is, when a deceiver controls one set of cues, arousal and negative affect are leaked by other cues.

287

DAVID B. BULLER, R. KELLY AUNE

The three-way interactions with time also provide evidence that deceivers monitored and controlled their nonverbal display. First, some of the deceivers' behaviors were very stable throughout the conversations, whereas the same behaviors by truthtellers varied considerably in the conversations, suggesting that deceivers were controlling these behaviors more than truthtellers. This was true of brief face and head adaptors and to a lesser extent of general animation. Second, deceivers appeared to suppress some arousal cues which were evident at the outset of the conversations. Specifically, intimates suppressed chair twisting near the end of the conversations and all deceivers reduced their general animation from period 1 to period 2. Similarly, strangers, while being less vocally pleasant in general, became more vocally pleasant as the conversations progressed. There was also evidence that deceivers, particularly deceptive relational partners, monitored their immediacy behaviors. All deceivers displayed some nonimmediacy; however, friends and intimates increased their immediacy as the conversations progressed. It may be that friends and intimates must exercise care when appearing nonimmediate, reticent, and withdrawn. Buller and Burgoon argue that nonimmediacy serves to distance the deceiver from the deceptive conversation and reduce suspiciousness, because reticent and withdrawn deceivers provide less information to the target. However, the presence of a relationship with the target may dictate that deceivers maintain at least a moderate level of conversational involvement or they run the risk of violating the relational partners' expectations, triggering the suspicion they are trying to avoid. Friends and intimates may have monitored their immediacy cues and adjusted their immediacy as the conversations progressed.

The relational history and time effects have important implications for research on deception. The overriding effect of relational history in this experiment means that results from deception experiments on strangers should be generalized cautiously to deceiving relational partners. As the experiment shows, one cannot assume that relational partners will behave like strangers when deceiving. Further analysis of the effect of relational history on deception and the factors which underlie this effect is needed before the relational dynamics of deception are clear.

The pervasive time effects in this experiment call for more concern over temporal variation in deception cues. Investigators who merely obtain measures of nonverbal behavior over the entire deceptive interaction run the risk of ignoring theoretically important changes. In this experiment, most deception cues fluctuated over time. Very few changes occurred at the outset of the conversations and were maintained through all five minutes. Instead, several initial changes dissipated as the conversations progressed, other changes arose only after several minutes of communication

288

JOURNAL OF NONVERBAL BEHAVIOR

had transpired, and still other changes were manifested in the middle of the conversation but ceased before the conversation ended. Further temporal analysis is needed to understand the dynamic nature of deceptive communication and the factors that contribute to temporal fluctuations in deceivers' behaviors.

In conclusion, the experiment supported the prediction that deceivers display nonverbal behaviors signalling nonimmediacy, negative affect, and arousal; however, relational history moderated deceivers' nonverbal display. Deceiving friends and intimates may monitor and control deception cues more than deceiving strangers. Temporal variation also was evident in many deception cues, providing further evidence that deceivers at all relational levels monitored and controlled their nonverbal behavior. This study has added additional complexity to the deception picture. The data challenge deception researchers to move beyond studies which examine merely strangers and measurements which record only the total amount of behavior change exhibited by deceivers during a conversation.

## References

Baskett, G., & Freedle, R. O. (1974). Aspects of language pragmatics and the social perception of lying. *Journal of Psycholinguistic Research, 3,* 112–131.

Bennett, R. (1978, April). Micromoments. *Human Behavior,* 34–35.

Berrien, F. K., & Huntington, G. H. (1943). An exploratory study of pupillary responses during deception. *Journal of Experimental Psychology, 32,* 443–449.

Buller, D. B. (1987). *Deception among intimates, friends, and strangers: Attributional biases due to relationship development.* Paper presented to the annual meeting of the Speech Communication Association, Boston.

Buller, D. B., & Burgoon, J. K. (in press). Deception. In J. A. Daly and J. M. Wiemann, *Communicating strategically: Strategies in interpersonal communication.* Hillsdale, NJ: Erlbaum.

Burgoon, J. K. (1978). Attributes of the newscaster's voice as predictors of his credibility. *Journalism Quarterly, 55,* 276–281.

Burgoon, J. K., Buller, D. B., & Woodall, W. G. (in press). *Introduction to nonverbal communication.* New York: Harper & Row.

Burgoon, J. K., & Hale, J. L. (1987). Validation and measurement of the fundamental themes of relational communication. *Communication Monographs, 54,* 19–41.

Christie, R., & Geis, F. L. (1970). *Studies in machiavellianism.* New York: Academic Press.

Clark, W. R. (1975). *A comparison of pupillary response, heart rate, and GSR during deception.* Paper presented at the annual meeting of the Midwestern Psychological Association, Chicago.

Comadena, M. E. (1982). Accuracy in detecting deception: Intimate and friendship relationships. In M. Burgoon (Ed.), *Communication yearbook 6* (pp. 446–472). Beverly Hills, CA: Sage.

Crowne, D., & Marlowe, D. (1964). *The approval motive: Studies in evaluative dependence.* New York: Wiley.

DePaulo, B. M., Stone, J. I., & Lassiter, G. D. (1985a). Deceiving and detecting deceit. In B. R. Schlenker (Ed.), *The self and social life* (pp. 323–370). New York: McGraw-Hill.

DePaulo, B. M., Stone, J. I., & Lassiter, G. D. (1985b). Telling ingratiating lies: Effects of target sex and target attractiveness on verbal and nonverbal deceptive success. *Journal of Personality and Social Psychology, 48*, 1191–1203.

DePaulo, B. M., Zuckerman, M., & Rosenthal, R. (1980). Detecting deception: Modality effects. In L. Wheeler (Ed.), *Review of personality and social psychology* (pp. 125–162). Beverly Hills, CA: Sage.

deTurck, M. A., & Miller, G. R. (1985). Deception and arousal: Isolating the behavioral correlates of deception. *Human Communication Research, 12*, 181–202.

Ekman, P. (1985). *Telling lies: Clues to deceit in the marketplace, politics, and marriage.* New York: Norton.

Ekman, P., & Friesen, W. V. (1969). Nonverbal leakage and clues to deception. *Psychiatry, 32*, 88–105.

Ekman, P., & Friesen, W. V. (1974). Detecting deception from the body or face. *Journal of Personality and Social Psychology, 29*, 288–298.

Ekman, P., Friesen, W. V., O'Sullivan, M., & Scherer, K. (1980). Relative importance of face, body and speech in judgments of personality and affect. *Journal of Personality and Social Psychology, 38*, 270–277.

Ekman, P., Friesen, W. V., & Scherer, K. (1976). Body movement and voice pitch in deceptive interaction. *Semiotica, 16*, 23–27.

English, H. B. (1926). Reaction-time symptoms of deception. *American Journal of Psychology, 37*, 428–429.

Feldman, R. S., Devin-Sheehan, L., & Allen, V. L. (1978). Nonverbal cues as indicators of verbal dissembling. *American Educational Research Journal, 15*, 217–231.

Fisher, J. L. (1981). Transitions in relationship style from adolescence to young adulthood. *Journal of Youth and Adolescence, 10*, 11–23.

Fisher, J. L., & Narus, L. R. (1981). Sex roles and intimacy in same sex and other sex relationships. *Psychology of Women Quarterly, 5*, 444–455.

Friesen, W. V., Ekman, P., & Wallbott, H. (1979). Measuring hand gestures. *Journal of Nonverbal Behavior, 4*, 97–112.

Goldstein, E. R. (1923). Reaction times and the consciousness of deception. *American Journal of Psychology, 34*, 562–581.

Hocking, J. E., & Leathers, D. G. (1980). Nonverbal indicators of deception: A new theoretical perspective. *Communication Monographs, 47*, 119–131.

Knapp, M. L., Hart, R. P., & Dennis, H. S. (1974). An exploration of deception as a communication construct. *Human Communication Research, 1*, 15–29.

Krauss, R. M., Geller, V., & Olson, C. (1976). *Modalities and cues in the detection of deception.* Paper presented at the annual meeting of the American Psychological Association, Washington, DC.

Kraut, R. (1978). Verbal and nonverbal cues in the perception of lying. *Journal of Personality and Social Psychology, 36*, 380–391.

Kraut, R. (1980). Humans as lie detectors: Some second thoughts. *Journal of Communication, 30*, 209–216.

Kuiken, D. (1981). Nonimmediate language style and inconsistency between private and expressed evaluations. *Journal of Experimental Social Psychology, 17*, 183–196.

Marston, W. M. (1920). Reaction-time symptoms of deception. *Journal of Experimental Psychology, 3*, 72–87.

Matarazzo, J. D., Wiens, A. N., Jackson, R. H., & Manaugh, T. S. (1970). Interviewee speech behavior under conditions of endogenously-present and exogenously-induced motivational states. *Journal of Clinical Psychology, 26*, 141–148.

McClintock, C. C., & Hunt, R. G. (1975). Nonverbal indicators of affect and deception in an interview setting. *Journal of Applied Social Psychology, 5*, 54–67.

McCornack, S. A., & Parks, M. R. (1985). Deception detection and relationship development: The other side of trust. In M. L. McLaughlin (Ed.), *Communication yearbook 9* (pp. 377–389). Beverly Hills: Sage.

290

JOURNAL OF NONVERBAL BEHAVIOR

Mehrabian, A. (1971). Nonverbal betrayal of feeling. *Journal of Experimental Research in Personality, 5*, 64–73.

Mehrabian, A. (1972). *Nonverbal communication.* Chicago: Aldine.

Miller, G. R., Bauchner, J. E., Hocking, J. E., Fontes, N. E., Kaminski, E. P., & Brandt, D. R. (1981). ". . . and nothing but the truth": How well can observers detect deceptive testimony? In B. D. Sales (Ed.), *Perspectives in law and psychology. Volume III: The jury, judicial and trial process.* New York: Plenum.

Miller, G. R., & Burgoon, J. K. (1982). Factors affecting witness credibility. In N. L. Kerr & R. M. Bray (Eds.), *The psychology of the courtroom* (pp. 169–194). New York: Academic Press.

Motley, M. T. (1974). Acoustic correlates of lies. *Western Speech, 38,* 81–87.

O'Hair, H. D., Cody, M. J., & McLaughlin, M. L. (1981). Prepared lies, spontaneous lies, Machiavellianism, and nonverbal communication. *Human Communication Research, 7,* 325–339.

Riggio, R. E., & Friedman, H. S. (1983). Individual differences and cues to deception. *Journal of Personality and Social Psychology, 45,* 899–915.

Snyder, M. (1974). Self-monitoring of expressive behavior. *Journal of Personality and Social Psychology, 30,* 526–537.

Streeter, L. A., Krauss, R. M., Geller, V., Olson, C., & Apple, W. (1977). Pitch changes during attempted deception. *Journal of Personality and Social Psychology, 35,* 345–350.

Wheeless, L. R., & Grotz, J. (1975). *Self-disclosure and trust: Conceptualization, measurement, and inter-relationships.* Paper presented at the annual meeting of the International Communication Association, Chicago.

Zuckerman, M., DeFrank, R. S., Hall, J. A., Larrance, D. T., & Rosenthal, R. (1979). Facial and vocal cues of deception and honesty. *Journal of Experimental Social Psychology, 15,* 378–396.

Zuckerman, M., DePaulo, B. M., & Rosenthal, R. (1981). Verbal and nonverbal communication of deception. In L. Berkowitz (Ed.), *Advances in experimental social psychology* (Vol. 14, pp. 1–59). New York: Academic Press.

Zuckerman, M., & Driver, R. E. (1985). Telling lies: Verbal and nonverbal correlates of deception. In A. W. Siegman & S. Feldstein (Eds.), *Multichannel integrations of nonverbal behavior* (pp. 129–148). Hillsdale, NJ: Erlbaum.

# [12]

# Who Can Catch a Liar?

Paul Ekman        *University of California, San Francisco*
Maureen O'Sullivan        *University of San Francisco*

*The ability to detect lying was evaluated in 509 people including law-enforcement personnel, such as members of the U.S. Secret Service, Central Intelligence Agency, Federal Bureau of Investigation, National Security Agency, Drug Enforcement Agency, California police and judges, as well as psychiatrists, college students, and working adults. A videotape showed 10 people who were either lying or telling the truth in describing their feelings. Only the Secret Service performed better than chance, and they were significantly more accurate than all of the other groups. When occupational group was disregarded, it was found that those who were accurate apparently used different behavioral clues and had different skills than those who were inaccurate.*

Lies occur in many arenas of life, including the home, school, and workplace, as well as such special contexts as in police interrogations and courtroom testimony. In low-stake lies, the liar suffers no more than embarrassment if caught, but in a high-stake lie, the consequences for success or failure may be enormous for both the liar and the liar's target. Examples of such high-stake lies include those between heads of state during crises, spousal lies about infidelity, the betrayal of secrets through espionage, and the range of lies involved in perpetrating various crimes.

Lies fail for many reasons. The lie may be exposed by facts that contradict the lie or by a third party who betrays the liar's confidence. Sometimes, such outside information is not available or is ambiguous. Then the lie succeeds or fails solely, or primarily, on the basis of the liar's behavior, which the legal profession terms *demeanor* (see Ekman, 1985, for a discussion of different forms of lying, the role of stakes in the detection of deceit, and why lies fail or succeed).

Two types of errors may occur when truthfulness based on demeanor is judged: In a false negative, a liar is incorrectly judged to be truthful; in a false positive, a truthful person is incorrectly judged to be lying. In a high-stake lie, either type of mistake can have serious consequences. In dealing with such situations it would be important—for the clinician, the jurist, the businessman, the counterintelligence agent, and so on—to know how much confidence should be placed in judgments based on demeanor, by layman or expert, about whether someone is lying or telling the truth.

The answer from 20 years of research is "not much." In every study reported, people have not been very accurate in judging when someone is lying. In the usual study, observers are given video or audiotapes and are asked to judge whether each of a number of people is lying or telling the truth. Average accuracy in detecting deceit has rarely been above 60% (with chance being 50%), and some groups have done worse than chance (see reviews by DePaulo, Stone, & Lassiter, 1985; Kraut, 1980; Zuckerman, DePaulo, & Rosenthal, 1981). Most of these studies examined college students, who may not have had any special reason to learn how to tell when someone is lying. Perhaps professional lie catchers, those whose work requires them to detect lying, would be more accurate.

Surprisingly, three studies of professional lie catchers did not find this to be so. Kraut and Poe (1980) found that customs officials were no more accurate than college students in detecting deceit in mock customs examinations. DePaulo and Pfeifer (1986) found no difference between federal law enforcement officers, regardless of experience, and college students. Kohnken (1987) found police officers did no better than chance when they judged videotapes of college students who had lied or been truthful in an experiment.

It is difficult to draw any conclusions from these three studies of professional lie catchers because in none of them was there any evidence that the observers were exposed to behavior that differed when the people who were judged lied or were truthful. DePaulo and Pfeifer's (1986) study is the only exception, as they used materials that had earlier been shown to be significantly different in observer-rated deceptiveness (DePaulo, Lanier, & Davis, 1983). However, the differences were small, and the data were not analyzed in a way that would indicate how many liars could actually be differentiated on the basis of their observable behavior. Perhaps accuracy has been meager and no advantage found for professional lie catchers because there just was not much information in the videotapes that would allow very good discrimination when people lied.

Ours is the first study to use behavioral samples drawn from a set of videotaped interviews that prior behavioral measurement showed differed when subjects lied or told the truth. Facial muscular movements measured with the Facial Action Coding System (Ekman & Friesen, 1976, 1978) included more masking smiles when the subjects lied and more enjoyment smiles when they told

Paul Ekman's work is supported by Research Scientist Award MH 06092 from the National Institute of Mental Health.

Correspondence concerning this article should be addressed to Paul Ekman, Human Interaction Laboratory, University of California, 401 Parnassus Avenue, San Francisco, CA 94143.

the truth about their feelings (Ekman, Friesen, & O'Sullivan, 1988). Vocal measurement also distinguished the lying and truthful interviews. There was an increase in fundamental pitch when the subjects lied. When both the vocal measure and the two facial measures were combined, it was possible to classify 86% of the subjects correctly as either lying or being truthful (Ekman, O'Sullivan, Friesen, & Scherer, 1991). Because there were known behavioral differences between the honest and deceptive samples, our study could focus on the question of how well observers can detect deception.

We took advantage of opportunities to test a number of different groups in the criminal justice and intelligence communities to determine whether those who have a specialized interest, and presumably more experience, in detecting deceit would do better than the usual college student observer. We made no hypotheses about the relative proficiency of the professional lie-catcher groups, although we hoped that at least one of them might do better than chance.

In addition to analyzing average accuracy on a group-by-group basis, as is usually done in studies of deception detection, we also planned to examine accuracy on an individual basis. The mean accuracy of a group of observers might be only at chance, but individual observers might reach either very high or very low levels of accuracy. Of course, it is also possible that all observers might perform at or close to chance, but that cannot be known from the usual method of examining only mean accuracy.

Because most of our observers were professional lie catchers, we were interested in their thoughts and opinions about lie catching in general, and in their own lie-catching ability, in particular. DePaulo and Pfeifer (1986) reported that confidence in one's ability to detect lying was unrelated to actual accuracy, although the federal law enforcement officers they studied were more confident than were college students about their ability to detect deception. They also reported that amount of experience in law enforcement was not correlated with accuracy. Kohnken (1987) also found no relationship between confidence in one's ability to detect lying and actual accuracy. Unlike DePaulo and Pfeifer, however, he found a significant negative correlation between experience and accuracy when age was partialed out. We sought to replicate these findings, and so we asked our professional lie catchers about their confidence in their ability to detect deception before and after taking our test, as well as the amount of time they had been in their present job.

We also asked our professional lie catchers to describe the behavioral clues they relied on in making their judgments. We had two reasons for being interested in this matter. First, we wanted to test our hypothesis that those who make accurate judgments, regardless of their occupational group, would describe different behavioral clues than those who make inaccurate judgments. On the basis of our prior analyses of observers' judgments of these videotapes when they were exposed to either the verbal, nonverbal, or combined verbal and nonverbal behaviors

(O'Sullivan, Ekman, Friesen, & Scherer, 1991), and our findings that there were clues to deceit in the nonverbal but not in most of the verbal behaviors we measured (Ekman & Friesen, 1976; Ekman et al., 1988; Ekman et al., 1991). Hypothesis 1 predicted that accurate observers would report using nonverbal clues more than would the inaccurate observers.

Our second reason for asking the observers to describe the behavioral clues they relied on in making their judgments was to have data that would be relevant to resolving the question of whether any individual differences in accuracy we obtained were due to chance. If those who were highly accurate gave different reasons for their judgments than those who were inaccurate, it would argue against the possibility that individual differences in accuracy were simply chance variations.

In one of our groups, we were also able to test how well subjects could recognize microexpressions, facial expressions that last no more than 1/25 of a second. On the basis of Ekman and Friesen's (1969) proposal that microexpressions are an important source of behavioral clues to deceit, Hypothesis 2 predicted a positive correlation between accuracy in detecting deceit and accuracy in recognizing microexpressions of emotion.

## Method

### Observers

Following the publication of his book *Telling Lies*, Ekman (1985) was asked by a variety of groups that had a professional interest in lying to conduct a workshop on behavioral clues to deceit. At the start of each such workshop, the participants were given a test of their ability to detect deception, which provided the data for this study. None of the observers had read Ekman's book prior to being tested. The following groups were tested:

1. U.S. Secret Service. All members of the Forensic Services Division of the Secret Service who were available in Washington, DC, when the workshop on lying was given were tested.

2. Federal polygraphers. All participants in a Federal Inter-Agency Polygraph Seminar organized by the Central Intelligence Agency (CIA) held in the Federal Bureau of Investigation (FBI) Academy at Quantico, Virginia, were tested. This included 10 CIA, 10 FBI, 5 National Security Agency (NSA), 21 Army, Air Force, or Marine personnel, and 14 polygraphers employed by other federal agencies.

3. Judges. All of the participants in three courses on fact finding offered in the midcareer college for municipal and superior court judges organized by the California Center for Judicial Education and Research, and judges taking a similar course in Oregon, were tested.

4. Police. Those attending the annual meeting of the California Robbery Investigators Association, which included city, county, state, and federal law enforcement officers who specialize in dealing with robbery were tested.

5. Psychiatrists. Texas psychiatrists attending an annual professional meeting, as well as psychiatrists at-

tending staff training sessions in Texas and San Francisco, were tested.

6. Special interest group. People who enrolled for a day-long University of California Extension course on deceit were tested. This group included businessmen, lawyers, accountants, police officers, housewives, social workers, psychologists, and nurses.

7. Students. For comparison with prior studies, we also used a sample of undergraduate psychology students at the University of San Francisco.

Table 1 shows that these groups differed in age and in sex.

### Detecting Deception Measure

The detecting deception measure consisted of 10 one-minute samples taken from 10 videotaped interviews, preceded by a practice item. The videotapes showed a black-and-white, head-on view of the full face and body of each subject.

The observers were told that they would see 10 college-age women, about one half of whom would be lying to an interviewer as she answered questions about how she felt about a film she was watching. Each subject would describe positive feelings she would claim to be feeling as she watched what she said were nature films. Some subjects were actually watching such films and would honestly be describing their feelings. Other subjects would really be watching a terribly gruesome film that was very upsetting to them, and they would be lying when they claimed to be having positive feelings about a nature film. The observers were told that all of the subjects were highly motivated to succeed and believed that success in their deception was relevant to their chosen career. After seeing each interview, the observers were allowed 30 seconds to record their choice as to whether the subject was honest or deceptive (more information about the deception scenario is provided in Ekman & Friesen, 1974).

The 10 subjects who were shown to the observers were selected from a group of 31 subjects who had participated in a study of deceit. Behavioral measurements (described earlier) on all 31 subjects had found that both facial and vocal measures differentiated the honest from the deceptive interviews. Most of those findings had not

been published when the test was given (Ekman et al., 1988, 1991).

Prior to seeing the videotape, all of the observers except the college students and the special interest group responded to the following questions: "How good do you think you are in being able to tell if another person is lying? Check one of the following: very poor, poor, average, good, very good." "What evidence or clues do you use in deciding that another person is lying or telling the truth?" (Three lines were given for the observers' handwritten responses.)

The videotape was then shown. After seeing each of the 10 persons, the observers recorded their judgment by circling either the word *honest* or the word *deceptive*. Following the second and the eighth videotape samples, the observers were also asked to indicate briefly their reasons for deciding that the interview was honest or deceptive. These two items were selected because pilot data indicated that they differed markedly in difficulty level, although the subjects in both items were lying. The handwritten responses were categorized using a coding system developed in previous research (O'Sullivan & Morrison, 1985) for categorizing observers' descriptions of their reasons for believing that subjects were lying or telling the truth. This system classified responses into 20 categories with interrater agreements ranging from 87% to 94%.

After judging all 10 people, the observers were asked the following questions: "How well do you think you did in telling who was lying?—very poorly, poorly, average, well, very well." "If your job required it, could you lie and conceal a strong emotional reaction?—yes, probably, maybe, probably not, no." Additional questions were asked in some of the groups prior to seeing the videotape. These questions, as well as another experimental test that was given to the special interest group, will be described next.

## Results

### Which Group Is Most Accurate?

The observers had judged whether each of the 10 persons they saw was lying or telling the truth. The observers' accuracy scores could range from 0 to 10 correct. Because

---

**Table 1**
*Total Sample Size, Sex, Age, and Job Experience in Observer Groups*

| Observer group | N | Women (%) | Age (in years) M | Age (in years) SD | Job experience (in years) M | Job experience (in years) SD |
|---|---|---|---|---|---|---|
| Secret Service | 34 | 3 | 34.79 | 5.96 | 9.12 | 6.69 |
| Federal polygraphers | 60 | 8 | 39.42 | 6.76 | 6.54 | 6.19 |
| Robbery investigators | 126 | 2 | 39.21 | 8.26 | 14.77 | 7.15 |
| Judges | 110 | 11 | 52.64 | 9.37 | 11.50 | 7.77 |
| Psychiatrists | 67 | 3 | 54.24 | 10.28 | 23.63 | 10.28 |
| Special interest | 73 | 53 | 43.33 | 13.44 | 10.76 | 9.89 |
| College students | 39 | 64 | 19.90 | 1.74 | — | — |

---

exactly one half of the 10 persons they judged were lying, the observer would obtain only a chance total accuracy score if an observer were to judge everyone to be lying or to be telling the truth.

A one-way analysis of variance (ANOVA) on the total accuracy scores for the seven groups was computed. There was a significant between-groups effect, $F(6) = 2.07$, $p < .05$. A Duncan procedure showed that the Secret Service differed from each of the other six groups at the .05 level and none of the other groups were significantly different from one another; Table 2 gives these means and standard deviations.

Another way to consider these data are in terms of the numbers of individuals in each group who scored very high or very low. Table 3 shows three levels of accuracy scores for observers in the seven groups. The first column includes scores from 0 to 30%; these observers can be termed *inaccurate*. The middle column for scores from 40% to 60% includes the mean accuracy levels reported in prior research on either college students or specialized occupational groups, and is close to or at chance. The last column (70% to 100%) represents higher accuracy than has been reported before. None of the Secret Service observers performed below chance (i.e., at or below 30%), and 53% of them scored at or above 70% accuracy. Their superior performance is more markedly shown by considering just those who achieved accuracy scores of 80% or more. Nearly one third (29%) of the Secret Service sample reached this very high level of accuracy. The next closest was the psychiatrist group, in which only 12% reached this high level of accuracy in detecting deception. We also computed binomial tests for each group separately, to ascertain whether any of the groups' accuracy was significantly different from chance (defined as 50%). Only the Secret Service group had a better than chance distribution ($p < .03$).

### What Variables Are Related to Accuracy in Detection Deception?

*Demographic characteristics.* Although there were few women in the Secret Service, federal polygrapher, and police groups, sex differences in lie-detection accuracy were examined in the remaining groups. There was no significant correlation between accuracy in detecting deception and sex in the judge, psychiatrist, special interest, or student groups, or across all of these groups combined.

Correlations were also computed across all groups, between age, years of job experience (this measure was not relevant to the college sample), and accuracy in detecting deception. None of these correlations approached significance. This was not so, however, when these correlations were computed separately in each occupational group. Age was negatively correlated with accuracy for both the Secret Service ($r = -.347$, $p < .03$) and the federal polygraphers ($r = -.343$, $p < .005$). The scatterplots for these correlations suggested that the relationship with age was strongest at the 80% or better accuracy level. In both the Secret Service and federal polygrapher groups, all of the observers who scored 80% or higher in lie-detection accuracy were less than 40 years old.

Years of job experience were also negatively correlated with accuracy in the Secret Service group ($r = -.376$, $p < .02$), but this correlation was not significant for the federal polygraphers ($r = -.102$, $p < .23$). Age and experience were very strongly correlated in the Secret Service group ($r = .88$, $p < .000$), so that when the influence of age was removed from the correlation between accuracy and experience, and the influence of experience was removed from the correlation between accuracy and age, the partial correlations were not significant. Age and experience were less strong correlated among the federal polygraphers ($r = .35$, $p < .005$). When accuracy was correlated with age, removing the influence of experience, the partial correlation was still statistically significant ($r_{(12.3)} = -.330$, $p < .05$). The correlation between experience and accuracy, controlling for age, was nonsignificant.

*Confidence in their ability to detect deception.* All groups except the special interest and college students were asked twice to estimate their ability to tell when other people are lying. Before seeing the videotape they were asked about their general ability to detect lies. After the videotape, they were asked specifically how they thought they had done on that measure. When computed, disregarding occupational group, neither observers' general predictions about their ability to tell when other people are lying ($r = .03$, $p < .282$) or their more specific

### Table 3
*Percentage of Observers In Each Group Achieving Different Lie-Detection Accuracy Levels*

| Observer group | 0–30 | 40–60 | 70–100 |
|---|---|---|---|
| Secret Service | 0 | 47 | 53 |
| Federal polygraphers | 5 | 73 | 22 |
| Robbery investigators | 8 | 66 | 26 |
| Judges | 9 | 57 | 34 |
| Psychiatrists | 5 | 63 | 32 |
| Special interest | 10 | 59 | 31 |
| College students | 15 | 59 | 26 |

*Note.* Each column heading denotes percentage correct.

### Table 2
*Deception Accuracy Means and Standard Deviations in Observer Groups*

| Observer group | M | SD |
|---|---|---|
| Secret Service | 64.12 | 14.80 |
| Federal polygraphers | 55.67 | 13.32 |
| Robbery investigators | 55.79 | 14.93 |
| Judges | 56.73 | 14.72 |
| Psychiatrists | 57.61 | 14.57 |
| Special interest | 55.34 | 15.82 |
| College students | 52.82 | 17.31 |

postdiction of how well they had done in detecting deceit in the videotape they had just viewed ($r = .02$, $p < .358$) were significantly correlated with their actual accuracy. When the correlations were computed separately for each group, there were two exceptions. The federal polygraphers' initial ratings of their general ability to tell when someone is lying was correlated with their actual accuracy ($r = .217$, $p = .05$.), and the Secret Service ratings of how well they had done after viewing the videotape was negatively correlated with actual accuracy ($r = -.31$, $p < .035$). This negative correlation can be attributed to five subjects who rated their ability very high, although their accuracy scores were among the lowest. Examination of the group-by-group scatterplots showed that the failure to find a correlation between prediction and performance in the other groups was not due to outliers or other idiosyncrasies in the distribution of the responses.

Table 4 reports the means and standard deviations of the pre- and posttest ratings of confidence in ability to detect deception. A one-way ANOVA showed that the average ratings of the five groups were significantly different before they saw the videotape, $F(4, 351) = 16.66$, $p < .000$. A Duncan post hoc procedure found that the psychiatrists rated their ability to detect lies in general significantly lower than did all of the other groups and the judges rated themselves lower than did the other law-enforcement groups. A one-way ANOVA of the ratings made after viewing the videotape about how well the observers thought they had done in detecting deceit, was also significant, $F(4, 356) = 7.54$, $p < .000$. The Duncan test showed that the psychiatrists and judges were not different from each other, but that the ratings of both groups were significantly lower than those of Secret Service, police, or federal polygraphers.

The special interest group had been asked a similar question (i.e., "I am very good at telling when another person is lying"), using a nine-point rather than a five-point scale. Special interest observers who rated themselves as good lie detectors scored high in detecting deception in the videotape ($r = .322$, $p = .007$).

*Willingness to lie.* Observers in three of the occupational groups (Secret Service, federal polygraphers, and psychiatrists) had been asked how well they could conceal an emotional reaction if their job required it. Responses

to this question were not significantly correlated with accuracy, either within each of the three groups or across all groups. A one-way ANOVA across the three groups was, however, significant, $F(2, 142) = 7.05$, $p < .0012$. Duncan's post hoc procedure showed that the psychiatrists were significantly different ($M = 2.85$) than federal polygraphers ($M = 2.16$) in their belief that they were able to conceal an emotion if their job required it.

*Other self-ratings.* To determine whether clinical orientation might be related to accuracy, one of the samples in the psychiatric group had been asked whether they worked from a psychodynamic or a behavioral perspective. To determine whether psychiatrists who had courtroom experience might be better in detecting deception, we also asked whether they did forensic work. Neither of these variables was significantly correlated with lie-detection accuracy in the psychiatrist group.

*Recognizing microexpressions.* A measure of the ability to recognize emotional facial expressions presented at very brief exposures (1/25 s) was given only to the special interest group. It consisted of 30 black-and-white slides of facial expressions of six prototypic emotions (happiness, sadness, fear, anger, surprise, and disgust), preceded by three practice slides. The 30 items were scored to yield a total accuracy score. The correlation between accurately recognizing the emotions displayed in this test and accuracy in judging which subjects were lying was significant ($r = .270$, $p = .02$), supporting Hypothesis 2.

### Observers' Descriptions of Behavioral Clues to Deceit

The observers in all of the groups, except for special interest and students, gave open-ended descriptions of behavioral clues they used in judging whether someone was lying on three occasions: prior to seeing the videotape, after judging the second person shown on the videotape, and after judging the eighth person shown on the videotape. The handwritten answers varied in the amount of detail given and in the number of verbal and behavioral clues mentioned. To test Hypothesis 1, a simple three-way classification was performed: all responses that referred only to *speech* clues (e.g., "answers too slowly," "evasive," "talks too much," "contradicts herself"), responses that referred only to *nonverbal behaviors* (e.g., "voice strained," "avoids eye contact," "phony smile," "body language"), or responses that mentioned both speech and nonverbal behaviors. Across both items and all observer groups, 37% of observers reported using speech clues alone, 29% reported nonverbal clues alone, and 25% reported using both verbal and nonverbal clues. The coder performing the classification did not know the occupational group nor the accuracy scores.

Chi-square analyses showed that there were no significant differences among the five occupational groups in the types of clues mentioned prior to their viewing the videotape. Disregarding occupational group, those whose accuracy scores were 80% or more were compared with those whose accuracy scores were 30% or less. Again,

**Table 4**
*Confidence in Lie-Detection Ability Before and After the Deception Detection Measure (DDM)*

| Observer group | Before DDM | | After DDM | |
|---|---|---|---|---|
| | M | SD | M | SD |
| Secret Service | 3.76 | 0.61 | 3.26 | 0.57 |
| Federal polygraphers | 3.56 | 0.57 | 3.14 | 0.61 |
| Robbery investigators | 3.53 | 0.58 | 3.26 | 0.81 |
| Judges | 3.34 | 0.59 | 2.77 | 0.74 |
| Psychiatrists | 2.86 | 0.75 | 2.86 | 0.75 |

there was no difference in the types of deception clues listed prior to seeing the videotape.

The observers had also been asked to describe the behavioral clues they had relied on immediately after making their judgments of 2 of the 10 subjects. The second person they saw had been expected to be difficult to judge accurately, and indeed only 44% of the observers accurately identified her as deceptive. Also as expected, the eighth person they judged was easy to detect; 84% accurately identified her as deceptive. In support of Hypothesis 1, Table 5 shows that for both of these items, more of the accurate observers described using nonverbal or nonverbal plus speech clues to arrive at their correct choice than did the inaccurate observers, who listed speech clues alone as the basis for making their judgment.

## Discussion

### Why Did We Find Differences in Accuracy When Others Did Not?

Our results directly contradict those reported by Kraut and Poe (1980), DePaulo and Pfeifer (1986), and Kohnken (1987), all of whom found that occupational groups with a special interest in deception did no better than chance or no better than college students did in detecting deceit. Three reasons may explain why we found differences in accuracy among occupational groups and between the occupational groups interested in deceit and college students, whereas they did not. First, they did not examine the Secret Service, and we did. If we had not examined this group, our results would have replicated theirs. Second, we performed a subject-by-subject analysis, which revealed that there were both highly accurate and inaccurate observers. There may have been significant numbers of such observers in their samples, but they did not report examining their data to determine that. Third, we used samples of honest and deceptive behavior that we knew through prior behavioral measurement did differ. Previous investigators did not establish that their samples of honest and deceptive behavior actually differed, or if

**Table 5**
*Percentage of Accurate and Inaccurate Observers Describing Each Type of Behavioral Clue to Deceit*

| Judgments | Speech only | Nonverbal only | Nonverbal plus speech |
|---|---|---|---|
| Subject 2 | | | |
| Accurate observers | 22 | 54 | 22 |
| Inaccurate observers | 52 | 28 | 20 |
| $\chi^2$ (2) = 45.5, $p$ < .001 | | | |
| Subject 8 | | | |
| Accurate observers | 43 | 27 | 30 |
| Inaccurate observers | 67 | 24 | 9 |
| $\chi^2$ (2) = 10.96, $p$ < .01 | | | |

they did, that they permitted accurate classification of most of the subjects, and so their observers might not have had much of a chance to detect deception.

### Did We Actually Measure the Ability To Detect Deceit?

Although our lie-detection measure contained different behaviors in honest and deceptive samples, some critics might argue that we measured the ability to distinguish positive from negative emotion rather than the ability to detect deception. Such an argument would point out that in the deception samples the subjects were experiencing negative affect from two sources: the negative emotions aroused by the gruesome films they were watching, and negative affect aroused by the need to conceal their feelings, including but not limited to the fear of being caught.

Measurements of the behaviors shown in the videotapes suggest that they do *not* differ in affect valence. There were *no* negative emotional facial expressions in the deceptive interviews, except for those masked by a smile. Also, the generally poor performance by most of our observers—as compared with the very high levels of accuracy obtained when observers are shown samples in which positive and negative affect is elicited without any deliberate attempt to deceive (Ekman, Friesen, & Ellsworth, 1972)—suggests that this was not simply a test of positive versus negative affect discrimination.

Granting that we measured the ability to detect deception, questions can be raised about whether the deception shown in the test is relevant to the interests and experience of the observers who were tested. Clearly, none of the observers were familiar with the particular deception scenario they encountered on our detecting deception measure. Nor do they typically have to make judgments based on one-minute samples of unfamiliar people shown on videotape. Nevertheless, the results showed that this measure did discriminate among observers in predicted ways (Hypotheses 1 and 2). For some of our professional lie catchers (Secret Service, psychiatrists, and police), observing people in an interview format in order to evaluate them is not too dissimilar from their everyday work. The professional experience of federal polygraphers and judges, however, occurs in far more ritualized surroundings—either the stylized administration of the polygraph or the mannered choreography of the courtroom.

This question, about the relevance of this or any other type of deception to the interests and experience of any particular group of observers, raises a theoretical issue about whether behavioral clues to deceit are situation specific or generalizable across situations, regardless of the type of deceit that occurs. Ekman's (1985) analysis of why lies fail, suggests that the behavioral clues to deceit that are generated by emotions are likely to generalize across situations. Not every deceit, of course, involves concealing emotions, but even those that do not may still generate emotion-based behavioral clues to deceit if the liar has strong emotional reactions about engaging in the lie, such as being fearful of being caught, guilty about lying, or excited by the challenge. When lies do not involve strong emotional reactions, more cognitively based clues, which are more specific to the lie being told, may be more useful. This reasoning is consistent with the findings of DePaulo and her colleagues (DePaulo, Kirkendol, Tang, & O'Brien, 1988) that there are more behavioral clues to deceit when the liar is more motivated to succeed in the lie. We are currently doing research that examines the generality versus situation specificity of behavioral clues to deceit.

It is also important to note the special nature of the deception scenario we showed in this study, one that is not directly relevant to *any* of the occupational groups we studied. Frank and Ekman (1991) have begun to test different occupational groups, using two other deception scenarios: lying about the theft of money and lying about one's opinion. Although their study is not complete, preliminary findings replicate some results reported here, such as the negative correlation between accuracy and age and the lack of correlation between confidence and accuracy. Their work directly addresses the question of whether people who are accurate in detecting one type of lie are also accurate when judging a different type of lie.

### Why Are Some People More Accurate in Detecting Deceit?

Across our total sample, we found no relationship between accuracy in detecting deception and age, sex, or job experience. Within two groups, the Secret Service and federal polygraphers, age was negatively correlated with accuracy, with the most highly accurate observers (accuracy 80% or greater) all being under 40 years of age. Although Kohnken (1987) found a positive relationship between accuracy and age for his truth detection task, when he partialed experience out of the relationship between age and accuracy it became significantly negative for his overall task. We found a sizable correlation between experience and accuracy only for the Secret Service. Experience and age were very highly correlated in this group. When age was partialed out of the experience–accuracy relationship, it dropped to insignificance. Kohnken's sample was both younger and more homogeneous than any of our professional groups. Within a younger group, experience may contribute to lie-detection accuracy up to a point of diminishing and even negative returns. More experienced professionals typically are less involved in face-to-face interrogation and more involved with administrative duties, which may result in a decline in their skill in detection deception.

Like our colleagues (DePaulo & Pfeifer, 1986; Kohnken, 1987), we found that observers' confidence in their overall lie-detection ability bore little relationship to their measured accuracy. Ratings of overall lie-detection ability were not significantly related to detection accuracy for either the total sample or any of the separate occupational groups. Most observers' ratings of how well they thought they did, even after they viewed the videotape, were unrelated to actual accuracy.

Our findings suggest that accurate lie catchers used different information than did the inaccurate ones. They listed different and more varied behaviors, emphasizing nonverbal more than verbal ones, and also mentioned using both verbal and nonverbal, rather than relying on verbal behavior alone. This is consistent with the findings from Knapp's (1989) study of what clues military interrogators report they rely on, namely, "subtle cues and nonverbals." Interestingly, our accurate and inaccurate observers did *not* describe different behavioral clues when answering general questions about how they make their decisions before they saw the videotape; they differed only when they described the basis of their decision about a specific person they had just seen.

Also, our finding that accuracy in identifying microexpressions was correlated with accuracy suggests that in addition to informational differences, accurate observers may possess superior skills in spotting and decoding emotional information displayed on the face. One way to test this explanation would be to provide information to observers based on behavioral measurements and train them in recognizing microexpressions. Prior attempts to train observers to detect deceit have yielded contradictory results. Zuckerman, Koestner, and Alton (1984) found benefits only in judging the person on whom training was given; Kohnken (1987) reported no benefits of training, but Zuckerman, Koestner, and Colella (1985) reported benefits of training beyond just the person on whom training was given. However, the training in these studies was simply to tell the observers the correct answers, not to provide information about specific behavioral clues nor to train specific perceptual skills.

### Why Is the Secret Service Better Than Other Occupational Groups?

There are a number of possible explanations. Many of the members of this group had done protection work, guarding important government officials from potential attack. Such work may force reliance on nonverbal cues (e.g., scanning crowds), and that experience may result in greater attention to nonverbal behavior in our test. Also, there may be a difference in the focus of their interrogations. The members of the Forensic Services Division of the Secret Service whom we tested spend part of their time interrogating people who threaten to harm government officials. Secret Service officials told us that most of these people are telling the truth when they claim that their threat was braggadocio, not serious. It is only the rare individual who is lying in his or her denial and actually intends to carry out such a threat. Members of the criminal justice community told an opposite story; they believe that everyone lies to them. Thus, the Secret Service deals with a much lower base rate of lying and may be more focused on signs of deceit, whereas the criminal justice groups, with a higher base rate of lying, may focus more on obtaining evidence, not detecting lies. There is no way to test such speculations, although experimental studies could try to manipulate these variables.

In discussing our findings with members of the other occupational groups, they suggested other explanations for their poor performance. The polygraphers claim to focus on the polygraph exam itself, the preparation of the questions to be asked, and the reading of the charts. Many of them specifically disavow attending to nonverbal behaviors, which in our test were the measurably discernible source of clues to deceit. Judges told us that they usually are seated in a position that prevents them from seeing the faces of those who testify, and are often focused on taking notes rather than attending to the nuances of behavior. They tend to pay most attention to the words the witnesses say, rather than to their behavior. Many psychiatrists claim not to be interested in lying, saying that patients will eventually reveal the truth to them. This is not so for those who do forensic work, and thus it was surprising that we found no difference between them and psychiatrists who do not do forensic work.

## Conclusion

Our study demonstrated that some lie catchers (viz., the Secret Service) can catch liars, that more accurate lie catchers report using nonverbal as well as verbal clues to deceit, that they are better able to interpret subtle facial expressions, and that in some occupational groups, accurate lie catchers are younger rather than older. Accurate lie catchers cannot be identified by either sex or their confidence in their lie-catching ability. Some caution about these findings must be maintained, however, because they are based on judgments of only one kind of deception, the concealment of strong negative emotions.

We are developing a psychometrically sound test of the ability to detect deceit that includes a number of forms of deception, which could be used to identify those individuals who are very good and very poor at this task. In different aspects of the criminal justice process, in certain business settings, and in some clinical situations, it may be useful to have such information.

### REFERENCES

DePaulo, B. M., Kirkendol, S. E., Tang, J., & O'Brien, T. (1988). The motivational impairment effect in the communication of deception: Replications and extensions. *Journal of Nonverbal Behavior, 12,* 177–202.

DePaulo, B. M., Lanier, K., & Davis, T. (1983). Detecting the deceit of the motivated liar. *Journal of Personality and Social Psychology, 45,* 1096–1103.

DePaulo, B. M., & Pfeifer, R. L. (1986). On-the-job experience and skill at detecting deception. *Journal of Applied Social Psychology, 16,* 249–267.

DePaulo, B. M., Stone, J. I., & Lassiter, G. D. (1985). Deceiving and detecting deceit. In B. R. Schlenker (Ed.), *The self and social life* (pp. 323–370). New York: McGraw-Hill.

Ekman, P. (1985). *Telling lies: Clues to deceit in the marketplace, marriage, and politics.* New York: Norton. (Paperback ed., Berkeley Books, New York, 1986)

Ekman, P., & Friesen, W. V. (1969). Nonverbal leakage and clues to deception. *Psychiatry, 32,* 88–105.

Ekman, P., & Friesen, W. V. (1974). Detecting deception from body or face. *Journal of Personality and Social Psychology, 29,* 288–298.

Ekman, P., & Friesen, W. V. (1976). Measuring facial movement. *Environmental Psychology and Nonverbal Behavior, 1*(1), 56–75.

Ekman, P., & Friesen, W. V. (1978). *Facial Action Coding System: A technique for the measurement of facial movement.* Palo Alto, CA: Consulting Psychologists Press.

Ekman, P., Friesen, W. V., & Ellsworth, P. (1972). *Emotion in the human face: Guidelines for research and an integration of findings.* New York: Pergamon Press.

Ekman, P., Friesen, W. V., & O'Sullivan, M. (1988). Smiles when lying. *Journal of Personality and Social Psychology, 54,* 414–420.

Ekman, P., O'Sullivan, M., Friesen, W. V., & Scherer, K. R. (1991). *Face, voice and body in detecting deceit.* Manuscript submitted for publication.

Frank, M., & Ekman, P. (1991). [Success in detecting deception across situations]. Unpublished raw data.

Kohnken, G. (1987). Training police officers to detect deceptive eyewitness statements: Does it work? *Social Behaviour, 2,* 1–17.

Knapp, B. G. (1989). *Characteristics of successful military intelligence interrogators* (USAICS Tech. Rep. No. 89-01). Fort Huachuca, AR: U.S. Army.

Kraut, R. E. (1980). Humans as lie detectors: Some second thoughts. *Journal of Communication, 30,* 209–216.

Kraut, R. E., & Poe, D. (1980). On the line: The deception judgments of customs inspectors and laymen. *Journal of Personality and Social Psychology, 39,* 784–798.

O'Sullivan, M., Ekman, P., Friesen, W. V., & Scherer, K. R. (1991). *Judging honest and deceptive behavior.* Manuscript submitted for publication.

O'Sullivan, M., & Morrison, S. (1985, April). *How can I tell you're lying? Let me count the ways.* Paper presented at the meeting of the Western Psychological Association, Burlingame, CA.

Zuckerman, M., DePaulo, B. M., & Rosenthal, R. (1981). Verbal and nonverbal communication of deception. In L. Berkowitz (Ed.), *Advances in experimental social psychology* (Vol. 14, pp. 1–59). San Diego, CA: Academic Press.

Zuckerman, M., Koestner, R., & Alton, A. O. (1984). Learning to detect deception. *Journal of Personality and Social Psychology, 46,* 519–528.

Zuckerman, M., Koestner, R., & Colella, M. J. (1985). Learning to detect deception from three communication channels. *Journal of Nonverbal Behavior, 9,* 188–194.

# [13]

*Frank Horvath,*[1] *Ph.D.; Brian Jayne,*[2] *M.S.D.D.; and*
*Joseph Buckley,*[2] *M.S.D.D.*

## Differentiation of Truthful and Deceptive Criminal Suspects in Behavior Analysis Interviews

**REFERENCE:** Horvath, F., Jayne, B., and Buckley, J., "Differentiation of Truthful and Deceptive Criminal Suspects in Behavior Analysis Interviews," *Journal of Forensic Sciences*, JFSCA, Vol. 39, No. 3, May 1994, pp. 793–807

**ABSTRACT:** The Behavior Analysis Interview© (BAI) is a commonly used procedure designed to assist investigators in distinguishing between suspects who are concealing their involvement in a criminal event (deceptive) from those who are not (truthful). During a BAI a protocol of questions is asked and suspects' verbal responses and accompanying nonverbal behaviors and attitudinal characteristics are assessed. Based on this assessment the likelihood of involvement in the criminal event is determined.

The purpose of this study was to determine the effectiveness with which trained evaluators were able to distinguish between truthful and deceptive suspects undergoing BAIs. Sixty videotaped interviews, 30 of truthful and 30 of deceptive suspects, were observed by four evaluators, each of whom independently scored suspect's behaviors and attitudes and judged the suspect's truthfulness. The results showed that, excluding inconclusive decisions, evaluators' average accuracy on truthful suspects was 91% and on deceptive suspects, 80%. Suspects' status did not affect confidence of evaluators' decisions but confidence was greater when correct as opposed to incorrect calls were made. Deceptive suspects manifested "theoretically" predicted behaviors and attitudes of "deceptiveness" to a significantly greater degree than did truthful suspects. The BAI appears to be useful for investigative purposes in order to differentiate between suspects who are concealing involvement in a criminal offense from those who are not.

**KEYWORDS:** criminalistics, behavior, suspects, interviews

In spite of the popular, and sometimes even professional perception to the contrary, it is relatively uncommon to find that criminal investigations are resolved solely because of systematic sleuthing and scientific successes [1–5]. In fact, physical evidence and scientific analyses become most useful once a suspect is identified, although they can, of course, be helpful in circumscribing investigative efforts. Nevertheless, it is interpersonal communication that most typically leads to the identification of an offender. Simply put, detectives "solve" cases by talking with victims, witnesses and suspects and, in many instances, by interviewing and interrogating criminal suspects. In performing these

Received for publication 19 July 1993; revised manuscript received 22 Oct. 1993; accepted for publication 23 Oct. 1993.

[1]Professor, School of Criminal Justice, Michigan State University, East Lansing, MI.

[2]Director of Research and Development and President, respectively, J. E. Reid and Associates, Chicago, IL.

Presented at American Academy of Forensic Sciences, February 1993, Boston, MA.

©J. Reid and Associates, copyright.

**794**   JOURNAL OF FORENSIC SCIENCES

communication tasks detectives are almost always confronted with an age old dilemma: how to distinguish between those who are telling the truth and those who are not [6,7]. How they make such distinctions and the degree to which they are successful at it is likely to depend on a number of personal and professional qualifications and the extent to which there are observable differences between those who tell the truth and those who lie.

Although interrogation and interviewing serve different goals and are related but separate procedures, the questioning of criminal suspects, whether to gain information (interview) or to elicit an admission against interest (interrogation) are essential practices in which successful detectives spend a large portion of their time [2,3,5]. Perhaps, in recognition of this, field practitioners in recent years have developed methodologies of questioning suspects that are said to improve the ability to distinguish between those who are concealing involvement in a criminal offense ("deceptive") from those who are not ("truthful"). These methods rest on the assumption that there are observable behavioral differences between deceptive and truthful persons. These differences may lie in verbal, nonverbal, paralinguistic and attitudinal dimensions, many of which are widely discussed in the popular literature [8,9] but not strongly substantiated by rather extensive scientific investigation [10–19].

There is a great deal of disagreement in the scientific literature about the usefulness of specific behaviors as indicators of deception, although there is agreement that at least for some measures, observers can detect lies (or liars), or at least certain statements of "liars," at rates slightly exceeding chance levels [12,17,20]. It is frequently mentioned, however, that one of the serious shortcomings in the available research is that almost all of it has been carried out in laboratory environments [21]. In such circumstances it is difficult, if not impossible, to replicate the emotionality, the motivation and the psychological orientation that would be expected in real-life circumstances. When one's reputation, employment, or the possibility of arrest and prosecution are at stake, behavioral indicators of deception may differ in degree, if not in kind, from those that are observed in artificially constructed laboratory settings.

Although the research that is not laboratory based is sparse there are four reports that shed light on behavioral differences between truthful and deceptive persons in real-life settings. In the first of these Reid and Arther [22] showed that when undergoing polygraph testing, liars tended to exhibit certain mannerisms such as, poor eye contact, nervousness, etc., not generally displayed by truth-tellers. In addition, liars more often expressed reservations about the situational context and were more likely to complain about the procedure than were truth-tellers. These observations were supported by Horvath [6] who tabulated verbal and nonverbal behaviors of a sample of 100 suspects who had undergone polygraph examinations; the behaviors of the deceptive suspects were generally significantly different from those of truthful suspects. Unfortunately, in both of these studies there was a reliance on information collected impressionistically and, while these data are certainly suggestive of behavioral differences between truthful and lying suspects, there is reason to be cautious in generalizing from them.

A third field study was reported by Barland [23] as part of a larger project to determine the validity of polygraph examinations. Barland scored a small sampling of suspects' behavior and found that 87% of his behavior-based assessments correctly predicted test outcomes on guilty (deceptive) suspects whereas only 50% of the assessments on innocent (truthful) suspects were predictive of the polygraph outcomes. Barland also reported, however, as some field polygraph examiners contend, that his assessment of suspects' behavior provided an important reality check on the polygraphic data.

The fourth and most recent field study by Horvath and Jayne [24] investigated the relative contribution of different sources of behavioral data derived from structured interviews of persons suspected of theft. Four trained evaluators made judgments of 14 confession-verified deceptive and six confession-verified truthful suspects' behavioral responses to a set of standard interview questions. These judgments were made under four different conditions. In three of these conditions the evaluators' judgments were based on an assessment of the interviewer's questions, and the suspects' responses to them, when each of the question/response segments was considered independent of the others and out of the context in which they originally occurred. In one of these conditions, judgments were made solely by review of a written transcript of the question/ response segments; in another an audio recording was reviewed; and, finally, in another condition an audiovisual recording of the question/response segment was evaluated. In most of these evaluations the accuracy of the decisions made by the evaluators exceeded chance levels but was not exceptionally high. However, when evaluators made judgments in a fourth condition, by reviewing question/response segments in the context in which they actually occurred, the accuracy of the decisions was in excess of 90% on both truthful and deceptive suspects.

These results suggest that structured interviews may produce findings quite different from those typically reported in the laboratory [21]. However, the Horvath and Jayne [24] study used only a small sample and all of the interviews that were assessed had been verified by a confession of the guilty person in each investigation. Consequently, the suspects may not have been a representative group. That is, as is true with other field research involving detection of deception, suspects in confession-verified cases may differ from the population encountered in most real-life circumstances [25]. In addition, this study, as well as all of the other field research, relied on behavioral assessments of suspects involved in polygraph-testing circumstances. Since most police questioning of suspects is not carried out in that context, the research may not generalize to nonpolygraph settings.

From this brief review, it can be seen that while the available literature provides only sketchy support for a correlation between behavioral cues and deception, the direction and nature of the information suggests that in real-life circumstances the value of behavioral assessments may differ from that commonly reported in laboratory-based studies. This conclusion is reinforced by the development and widespread application in recent years of "behavior analysis interviewing," a method of discriminating between "truthful" and "deceptive" suspects based on observations of their behavior while undergoing a structured interview. This technique, the "Behavior Analysis Interview" (BAI) was originated by J. E. Reid and Associates [26]. The BAI was empirically developed from experiences in interviewing and interrogation and although it was initially carried out in the context of polygraph testing, it is now performed independent of that context and does not involve instrumental (that is, physiological) measurements.

Generally, investigators who have been trained in the BAI technique have reported quite favorable results. Moreover, there is an increasing number of field personnel who seek out such training. These observations indicate that sound research on the effectiveness of the BAI would be of practical as well as scientific value. This paper reports the results of a project designed to investigate—as a part of a larger study—the accuracy of classifications made on the basis of the BAI in real-life circumstances.

## The Behavior Analysis Interview

In this study, all suspects whose behaviors were assessed freely chose to practice deception or to tell the truth, knowing that there were likely serious consequences for failing to avoid detection or for giving false indicators of deception. Because these suspects were questioned during BAIs is necessary that the general nature and format of these interviews is understood. Therefore, a brief description of the BAI follows.

The BAI consists of a 30 to 45 minute non-accusatory, structured forensic interview designed to elicit verbal and nonverbal behaviors and attitudinal characteristics of the

**796**   JOURNAL OF FORENSIC SCIENCES

suspect being questioned. During the initial period of the BAI the interviewer (investigator) seeks background information from the suspect and attempts to establish "normative" behavioral patterns such as "eye contact," response latency and nervousness. Questions asked after behavioral norms are established are either those that attempt to assess the suspect's opportunity, motivation and propensity for involvement in the issue at hand ("investigative" questions) or, are those used to elicit differential verbal and nonverbal behaviors and attitudinal characteristics from truthful and deceptive persons. Questions used for the latter purpose are known as behavior-provoking questions.

These questions have been developed empirically and models useful for interpreting the content and the accompanying verbal and nonverbal behaviors of suspects' responses to them can be found in the literature [6,26,27]. However, since there has been little information reported about truthful and deceptive suspects' attitudinal and related differences during the asking of such questions, a brief overview is given here.

During the asking of behavior-provoking questions, deceptive suspects reveal an attitude toward the investigation in which they are involved, and the interview about it, that differs from that manifested by truthful suspects. Deceptive suspects, for example, are said to be less likely to offer helpful investigative information to an interviewer. They do not exhibit an appropriate level of concern about being a "suspect" and often lack spontaneity and sincerity in their responses. They speak in a guarded way and appear to edit their verbal responses. On the other hand, truthful suspects are helpful to the interviewer and show an expectancy to be exonerated. They often exhibit resentment toward the "guilty" person and their responses to the interviewer's questions are spontaneous and sincere.

The evaluation of a suspect's attitude may involve consideration of a number of behavioral cues, including postural changes. A more open, forward-leaning and comfortable posture, for example, is indicative of "truthfulness" and a positive attitude, whereas a rigid, frozen and defensive posture is commonly associated with "deception."

Aside from the report of Horvath and Jayne [24] there has not been any systematic research on the effectiveness of the BAI in discriminating between truthful (innocent) and deceptive (guilty) persons. Since, the BAI is now rather widely used in the investigation of criminal offenses, such an assessment is reported here.

## Method

### Data Collection

This study required the analysis of behaviors drawn from real-life settings but, because it was not possible to do such analysis contemporaneous with the occurrence of the behaviors, it was necessary to collect audiovisual (AV) documents from interviews of persons being questioned about involvement in criminal activity. This was done by videotape recording BAIs conducted by trained and experienced staff members of John E. Reid and Associates. The selection of the sample of these AV documents and the procedures used in subjecting them to analysis are described in this section.

### Sample Selection Criteria

In order to select a sample of AV documents as free from selection bias as possible, a procedure was established to obtain a sample of AV documents prospectively. It was desired, however, that the sample meet certain criteria for selection. These were: (1) that each BAI involve an investigation of a loss or suspected theft of a specific amount of money or property. BAIs that investigated an on-going loss or general inventory shortage or an offense not involving theft were excluded from consideration; (2) that the gender, race, type of verification (that is, either confession or other corroboration of ground truth) and verification status (that is, truthfulness or deception) were as evenly matched as possible in the final sample; (3) that BAIs conducted by those who were assigned to serve as evaluators in the study were excluded from consideration; and, (4) that "ground truth," that is, the actual truthfulness or deception of the suspect, could reasonably be established.

Between November 1, 1989 and November 15, 1991 110 BAIs carried out on the premises of J. Reid and Associates were made available for AV-taping. This group included all BAIs carried out during that period except for those that had to be excluded because a suspect declined to be video-taped, equipment was not available, or the issue did not involve theft. Of these 110 BAIs, 23 (21%) had to be excluded either because the interviewer was scheduled to participate in this study or the interview itself concerned multiple thefts that may have been unrelated.

Thus, 87 videotape documents, each an AV recording of one person undergoing a BAI, were ultimately available for use in the study. These 87 documents represented BAIs carried out in 56 independent theft investigations which interviewers employed by J. Reid and Associates were hired to investigate. Five different interviewers administered these BAIs, each specifically trained in behavior analysis techniques. The experience of these interviewers in administering BAIs averaged ten years with a range of from 8 to 14 years.

### Establishment of Ground Truth

Of the 87 suspects' whose interviews were video taped the "guilt" (deception) or "innocence" (truthfulness) of 34 of them was established by a corroborated confession of the guilty suspect in each of the investigations in which these persons had been involved. In two other instances, the suspects' innocence was established by solid information that showed that the theft under investigation did not actually occur. Hence, the ground truth status of 36 suspects was confirmed by either a confession or, in two instances, by other documented circumstances that verified truthfulness. For simplicity, unless otherwise specified, all of these are referred to as "confession-verified" cases in the remainder of this paper. The remaining 51 suspects were not involved in either confession-verified cases or in cases in which there was other reasonably certain independent verification. For that reason, "ground truth" was established in these cases by means of systematic factual analysis as described by Jayne [28].

To carry out factual analysis it was necessary to process the information pertaining to each of the different investigations as the audiovisual tapes in each were collected. To do this case facts were extracted from each case file as well as from information provided by the suspect(s) during the interviews. These data were summarized in a narrative statement that was then given to two evaluators who independently completed a "factual analysis data sheet" on each suspect.

Factual analysis required the two evaluators, neither of whom was otherwise involved in the study, to assign individual probabilities of "guilt" or "innocence" in each of five separate areas for each suspect. These were: biographical; opportunity/access; personal activities; motivation/propensity; and, evidence.

From the two evaluators' results in each of the areas of evaluation an overall probability of guilt or innocence for each suspect was calculated by one of the researchers (BJ). The evaluators who completed factual analysis did not know whether their assessments, individually or collectively, would include or exclude a suspect from the study group.

All 87 suspects were subjected to factual analysis. Of the 36 suspects whose ground truth was established by confession or other evidence, only one produced a final score

**798** JOURNAL OF FORENSIC SCIENCES

from both evaluators which was greater than 90% and that was also inconsistent with ground truth. That is, when there was agreement by both evaluators at levels of 90% or higher all but one of the confession-verified suspects were correctly classified. Therefore, requiring at least a 90% confidence level from both evaluators for the inclusion of non-confession-verified suspects appeared to provide a satisfactory criterion when ground truth could not otherwise be established.

From the group of 87 video taped BAIs, 60 were included in the sample. These included all 34 suspects (13 truthful and 21 deceptive) whose interview results had been verified by a confession. Two other truthful suspects were included because information was developed that independently established their truthfulness. The remaining 24 suspects in the sample (15 truthful, 9 deceptive) were included because: (1) factual analysis by two independent evaluators indicated at least a 90% probability of truthfulness or deception; and, (2) they most closely balanced the sample in terms of "truthfulness" (status), race and gender. In this way, 60 video tapes of field BAIs were assembled for use in the study.

Table 1 shows the number of suspects in the sample categorized by gender, race, and type of verification. It can be determined from those data that 57% of the suspects were female; 43% were male. Fifty-five percent of the suspects were white and 45% were non-white. Sixty percent of the sample had been verified by confession, 40% by factual analysis.

*Differences Between Sample Subjects*

The mean age of all suspects in the sample was 28 years ($s = 8.22$). White suspects had a mean age of 27.1 years ($s = 8.5$) while the mean age of non-white suspects was 28.0 years ($s = 7.9$). Females had a mean age of 29.7 years ($s = 8.8$); the mean age of males was 24.7 years ($s = 6.3$). An analysis of variance (Anova) in which there were three factors (Status—truthful/deceptive; Race—white/non-white; Gender—male/female) with age as a dependent variable indicated that there were no statistically significant differences in the mean age of the sample for Race or Gender. However, the mean age of those who were deceptive ($M = 24.4$) was significantly [$F(1,52) = 5.8$, $P < .01$] lower than that of suspects who were truthful ($M = 30.6$). The mean age of suspects who were confession-verified was 26.4 years ($s = 6.8$); for suspects whose status was established through factual analysis the mean age was 29.2 years ($s = 9.8$). A t-test showed that this difference was not statistically significant [$t(59) = -1.3$, $P = .21$]. Chi-square tests revealed no significant relationship between the method of establishing ground truth (con-

TABLE 1—*Distribution of sample suspects by method of verification, race and gender.*

| Race/Gender | Verification Type | | | |
| --- | --- | --- | --- | --- |
| | Confession | | Fact Analysis | |
| | ($n = 36$) | | ($n = 24$) | |
| | Truthful | Deceptive | Truthful | Deceptive |
| Non-White/ | | | | |
| Female | 4 | 5 | 5 | 3 |
| Male | 2 | 4 | 1 | 3 |
| White/ | | | | |
| Female | 4 | 6 | 7 | 0 |
| Male | 5 | 6 | 2 | 3 |
| Totals | 15 | 21 | 15 | 9 |

fession/factual analysis) and either Race [$\chi^2(1)$ = .40, $P$ > .05] or Gender [$\chi^2(1)$ = .55, $P$ > .05].

As shown in Table 1, the sample included males and females and white and non-white suspects. Because it was not possible to balance the sample such that these characteristics were equally distributed and, since the interest here focused on differences between truthful and deceptive suspects, these variables were not considered in statistical analysis.

### Preparation of Audio-Visual Documents

Each of the 60 AV tapes contained the complete BAI (30 to 45 minutes) of one of the 60 suspects included in the sample. Each of these BAIs originally included three types of questions asked by the interviewer: background ("normative") questions, which established the suspect's age, marital status, employment position, salary and related items; "investigative" questions that gave the suspect an opportunity to provide information about the investigation at hand; and finally, "behavior-provoking" questions, asked to elicit behavior to differentiate between truthful and deceptive suspects [6,26].

From each of the 60 video-taped interviews, the 15 behavior-provoking questions that are the most commonly asked during theft investigations were extracted and dubbed onto a single tape for each suspect. The interviewer's asking of each question as well as the suspect's response (and accompanying behavior) were included in each dubbed segment. However, even though it is customary in real-life BAIs for interviewers to ask "follow-up" questions when a suspect's initial response to a behavior provoking question is ambiguous, such follow-up questions were excluded in order to maintain greater consistency between each of the 60 video documents. Moreover, in each of the dubbed video documents that were prepared, the order of the behavior-provoking questions was identical for all suspects even though in actual field conditions the order may vary somewhat. Finally, it is important to note that in real-life circumstances, an interviewer may consider it inappropriate to ask certain questions because of the investigation at hand; for that reason, the number of behavior-provoking questions was not identical for each suspect.

In addition to the 15 behavior-provoking questions, a 90-second block of each suspect's behavior during the asking of "normative" questions was also extracted. The normative behavior segment for each suspect was dubbed onto a video tape for each of the 60 suspects. In this way a single videotape document was prepared for each suspect; the normative behavior was presented first in sequence on this tape; that segment was followed by the behavior-provoking questions that were available for each suspect presented, as specified previously, in the same order on each tape.

The behavior-provoking questions extracted for use in this study in the order in which they were presented on each of the 60 video tapes were as follows [see: 6,26,27]:

1) *Purpose*:
What is your understanding for the purpose of this interview today?
2) *You*:
(Name) If you stole (this money) you should tell me that now. Did you steal that money?
3) *Knowledge*
Do you know who stole (this money)?
4) *Suspicion*
Who do you suspect may have stolen (this money)?
5) *Vouch*
Is there anyone you can vouch for, who you do not think was involved in (this theft of money)?

800   JOURNAL OF FORENSIC SCIENCES

6) *Opportunity*

Who would have had the best opportunity to (steal this money) if they wanted to?

7) *Think Stolen*

Do you think this (money) was actually stolen?

8) *Feel*

How do you feel about being interviewed regarding this (theft)?

9) *Results*

How do you think the investigation will come out on you?

10) *Think*

Have you ever thought about (stealing money)?

11) *Punishment*

What do you think should happen to the person who stole (this money)?

12) *Second Chance*

Do you think the person who (stole this money) should be given a second chance?

13) *Why Not*

Tell me why you wouldn't (steal this money)?

14) *Motive*

Why do you think someone did (steal this money)?

15) *Tell Loved One*

Have you told your (mother/spouse/family) about coming in for the interview today?

### Evaluation of Videotape Documents

Four persons, trained and experienced in "Behavior Analysis Interviewing," viewed each of the 60 videotape documents over the course of a number of monitored reviewing sessions. In these sessions the evaluators independently blind-scored several dimensions of suspects' behavior and made judgments of their status. These included the following:

(1) What was the evaluator's opinion of the suspect's attitude on the following dimensions: "Insincere," "Unconcerned," "Unhelpful," and "Guarded." Judgments of each of these were scored on a five-point scale, ranging from "1" to "5." A value of (1) on this scale indicated "Definitely not" and a (5) indicated "Definitely yes." Hence, lower values were associated with a lesser degree and higher values a greater degree of the "attitude," with higher scores indicating a better fit with theoretical "models" of deceptive persons' attitudes. In this scoring, evaluators were permitted to score each attitude with a zero (0) to indicate that they were unable to make a judgment. This was provided because it was recognized that some of the behaviors may not have been sufficiently distinct to permit a definitive judgment.

(2) What was the evaluator's assessment of the suspect's posture in each of the following areas: "Closed," "Uncomfortable," and "Rigid/Frozen." Judgments of each of these were scored on a five-point scale, ranging from "1" to "5." A value of (1) on this scale indicated "Definitely not" and a (5) indicated "Definitely yes." Again, lower values were associated with a lesser degree and higher values a greater degree of the postural item; higher scores indicated a better fit with "deceptiveness." As in other similar evaluations, evaluators were permitted to score each posture with a zero to indicate that they were unable to make a judgment.

(3) What was the evaluator's overall opinion as to whether or not the suspect's behavior indicated that the suspect was a "truthful" person, a "deceptive" person or that it was not possible to determine the status, that is, was "inconclusive."

(4) What was the evaluator's degree of "confidence" in his decision. This was indicated on a six-point scale, anchored at the low end with "none" (0) and "Very high" (5) at the opposite end.

## Results

Unless otherwise noted, all statistical testing used the .05 level as the criterion for statistical significance. Also, the probability levels reported are for one tailed tests unless otherwise noted.

It will be recalled that there were two different methods of establishing ground truth for the audiovisual documents included in the study, by confession or other solid evidence and factual analysis. Because these two methods differ considerably, it was important to determine whether or not this difference would affect subsequent analyses. For that reason, evaluators' scores on both the confession and the fact-analysis verified suspects were compared. This was done by separately subjecting each evaluator's scores for the various assessments of suspects' behavior to a Two-way Anova in which Status (truthful/deceptive) and Verification (confession/facts) were the two factors. These analyses did not reveal any significant effects for the Verification factor. Moreover, Chi-square tests showed no relationship between Verification status and the frequency of correct, wrong and inconclusive judgments. Therefore, the type of verification was not included as a variable in further statistical calculations.

After viewing each of the 60 BAIs, each evaluator indicated his decision of truthfulness and deception, his confidence in each decision and his rating of the suspects' attitudes and posture. Attitudinal items that were scored were: "sincerity," "concern," "helpfulness," and "guarded"; postural items included "closed posture," "comfortableness," and "rigid."

The distribution of evaluators' decisions by suspects' status is shown in Table 2. It can be seen in that table that when averaged across the four evaluators, 78% of the judgments on actually truthful suspects were "truthful" decisions, 8% were "deceptive" and 14% were "inconclusive." On deceptive suspects, the evaluators' averaged 66% "deceptive" decisions, 17% "truthful" and 17% "inconclusive." Thus, there were generally more errors made on deceptive suspects, than on truthful suspects; that is, there were more false negatives than false positives.

In actual investigations "inconclusive" decisions usually result in additional investigation of a suspect. For this reason, it is inappropriate to view these decisions as errors. Consequently, the accuracy of the evaluators' decision was calculated by excluding inconclusive outcomes. When this was done, the evaluators' accuracy on truthful suspects

TABLE 2—*Percent and number of truthful deceptive and inconclusive decisions for each evaluator by suspects' status.*

| Suspect Status/ Decision | Evaluator | | | | |
|---|---|---|---|---|---|
| | A % (n) | B % (n) | C % (n) | D* % (n) | Mean % |
| Truthful/ | | | | | |
| Truthful | 83 (25) | 80 (24) | 77 (23) | 73 (22) | 78 |
| Inconclusive | 7 (2) | 7 (2) | 23 (7) | 20 (6) | 14 |
| Deceptive | 10 (3) | 13 (4) | 0 (0) | 7 (2) | 8 |
| Deceptive/ | | | | | |
| Truthful | 20 (6) | 20 (6) | 10 (3) | 17 (5) | 17 |
| Inconclusive | 23 (7) | 3 (1) | 23 (7) | 20 (6) | 17 |
| Deceptive | 57 (17) | 77 (23) | 67 (20) | 63 (19) | 66 |

*Percentages shown in each cell were calculated separately for decisions on Truthful and Deceptive suspects for each evaluator. Chi-square tests, corrected for continuity, calculated on each evaluators' decisions, excluding inconclusives, and suspects' actual status were, for evaluators A through D, respectively: $\chi^2(1) = 18.6$, Phi = .64; 21.6, Phi = .65; 31.9, Phi = .88; 21.7, Phi = .71.

TABLE 3—*Correlations between pairings of evaluators on decisions of truthfulness and deception.*

|              | Evaluator |       |       |       |
| ------------ | --------- | ----- | ----- | ----- |
| Evaluator    | A         | B     | C     | D     |
| A            | ...       | .71   | .87   | .58   |
| B            | ...       | ...   | .60   | .63   |
| C            | ...       | ...   | ...   | .72   |

ranged between 89% and 100%, with a mean accuracy for the four evaluators of 91%. On deceptive suspects the evaluators' accuracy ranged between 74% and 87% with a mean of 80%. The mean accuracy across all evaluators and all suspects was 86%.

Further statistical analysis was performed to examine the relationship between evaluators' decisions and suspects' actual status (when inconclusive judgments were excluded). These analyses showed statistically significant relationships for all four evaluators. The strength of these relationships, determined with the Phi coefficient, was calculated for each evaluator; as shown in Table 2, Phi was .64, .65, .88 and .71, for evaluators A, B, C, and D, in order.

To determine evaluators' agreement in judgments of truthfulness and deception, each of the six possible pairs of evaluators' decisions were compared. The percentage of instances in each pair when the two evaluators reached a common decision (not counting inconclusive judgments) ranged between 86% and 98% with a mean of 89%. In addition, each evaluator's decisions across all 60 subjects were correlated with those made by each of the other evaluators. These correlations, calculated, of course, with inconclusive decisions included, are shown in Table 3. As indicated, they ranged between .58 and .87 for the six pairings of evaluators.

It will be recalled that evaluators indicated their confidence in their decisions and also scored each suspect with respect to certain attitudinal and postural characteristics. The mean scores calculated across all four evaluators for each of these characteristics, separately indicated for truthful and deceptive suspects, are shown in Table 4. (Scores of "0" on the behavioral measures, indicating an inability to make a judgment, were excluded from the calculations.) Here it can be seen that evaluators' confidence was not

TABLE 4—*Means and standard deviations for evaluators' scorings of confidence and of suspects' behavior and attitudes.*

|                       | Truthful ($n = 30$) |      | Deceptive ($n = 30$) |      |           |
| --------------------- | ------------------- | ---- | -------------------- | ---- | --------- |
| Measurement           | Mean                | SD   | Mean                 | SD   | $t(58)=$  |
| Evaluator             |                     |      |                      |      |           |
| Confidence            | 3.28                | .70  | 3.35                 | .85  | −0.3 n.s. |
| Suspects' Attitudes:  |                     |      |                      |      |           |
| Sincerity             | 1.95                | .44  | 3.17                 | .81  | −7.3*     |
| Concern               | 1.90                | .46  | 2.92                 | .83  | −5.9*     |
| Helpfulness           | 1.94                | .57  | 3.32                 | .80  | −7.7*     |
| Guarded               | 2.28                | .68  | 3.63                 | .78  | −7.2*     |
| Suspects' Posture:    |                     |      |                      |      |           |
| Closed                | 2.73                | .94  | 3.48                 | .97  | −3.0*     |
| Comfortableness       | 2.43                | .53  | 3.38                 | .73  | −5.6*     |
| Rigid                 | 2.69                | .58  | 3.33                 | .72  | −3.8*     |

*Significant difference between truthful and deceptive suspects, 1 tailed tests, $P < .001$.

*significantly* different for decisions made on truthful (*M* = 3.3) and deceptive suspects (*M* = 3.3) [t(58) = −.33, *P* > .10]. That is, they were equally confident in their decisions regardless of suspects' actual status. Additional analysis of confidence scores showed that the mean confidence score on correct decisions was significantly higher than on incorrect decisions, excluding inconclusives, for three of the four evaluators. For evaluators A through D, in order, the mean scores on correct and incorrect decisions were: 3.6 and 2.8 [*t*(49) = 2.0, *P* < .01]; 3.9 and 2.5[*t*(55) = 3.6, *P* < .01]; 3.3 and 2.3[*t*(44) = 1.7, n.s.]; 3.3 and 2.0 [*t*(46) = 2.7, *P* < .01]. Hence, evaluators' were generally more confident when they judged suspects' status correctly than when they were wrong.

Also shown in Table 4 are the mean scores for the attitudinal and postural characteristics on both groups of suspects. Here, it can be seen that deceptive suspects' mean score on each of the items was significantly greater than that for truthful suspects. For example, deceptive suspects' average score on "sincerity" was 3.17 (*S* = .81) whereas truthful suspects averaged 1.95 (*S* = .44); this difference was statistically significant and indicated that deceptive suspects were seen to display the (lack of) "sincerity" believed to be characteristic of actually deceptive persons to a greater degree than did the truthful suspects. Similarly, deceptive suspects were found to be significantly more apt to show a "closed posture," more characteristic of those who are concealing the "truth" than those who are not; the mean scores here were 3.48 (*S* = .97) and 2.73 (*S* = .94) for deceptive and truthful suspects, respectively. In other words, for all of the measures of suspects' attitudes and posture deceptive suspects were seen to show more characteristic "deceptive" behaviors than truthful suspects.

Because the behavioral items produced similar effects, inter-item correlation coefficients were calculated on the (four evaluators' average) scores for each item across all 60 suspects; these are shown in Table 5. In that table the items have been grouped according to whether they reflected an "attitudinal" behavior or one that showed a dimension of the suspects' posture. The former category included concern, guarded, helpful and sincerity; the latter, closed, comfort and rigid. It can be seen in Table 5 that the attitude items were strongly inter-correlated, with coefficients ranging between .85 and .90. The items in the posture category were less highly correlated with each other, with *r* ranging between .37 and .67. The *r* values between the posture items and those in the attitude category ranged between .39 and .81.

Given the strong inter-correlations of the behavioral items, it was decided to merge all "attitudinal" items into one measure; this was done by calculating the mean value for all evaluators across all four of the attitude items to produce a single "attitude" score. A similar measure, a "posture" score was calculated on the three "posture" items. These attitude and posture scores were then separately subjected to statistical analysis.

The result of this analysis showed that the mean attitude score on truthful suspects, 2.0 (*s* = .50), was significantly smaller than that on deceptive suspects, 3.3 (*s* = .73),

TABLE 5—*Inter-item correlations for seven behaviors of suspects rated by evaluators.*

| Item | Attitudes | | | | Posture | | |
|---|---|---|---|---|---|---|---|
| | C | G | H | S | Cd | Ct | R |
| Attitudes | | | | | | | |
| Concerned (C) | ... | .85 | .87 | .88 | .57 | .70 | .45 |
| Guarded (G) | | ... | .90 | .90 | .67 | .81 | .54 |
| Helpful (H) | | | ... | .89 | .54 | .69 | .49 |
| Sincerity (S) | | | | ... | .53 | .73 | .39 |
| Posture | | | | | | | |
| Closed (Cd) | | | | | ... | .67 | .37 |
| Comfort (Ct) | | | | | | ... | .39 |
| Rigid (R) | | | | | | | ... |

804   JOURNAL OF FORENSIC SCIENCES

[$t$(58) = 7.6, $P$ < .001]. Analysis of the posture score also revealed a statistically significant effect, with a mean score of 2.6 ($s$ = .52) on truthful suspects and 3.4 ($s$ = .62) on deceptives [$t$(58) = 5.3, $P$ < .001]. Thus, the attitudes and postures of the suspects were consistently in the direction predicted by the empirically developed model on which the BAI is based.

**Discussion**

These findings suggest that when questioned in a structured Behavior Analysis Interview the behaviors of suspects who attempt to conceal their involvement in serious acts of wrongdoing vary in many respects from those who do not. The behaviors of deceptive suspects, in other words, differ from those of truthful suspects. These behavioral differences are detectable in the "attitudes" displayed toward the issue under investigation and the interview process, and in postural as well as possibly other behaviors. However, it is important that we point out here that to be meaningfully evaluated, behaviors such as those considered here must be evaluated in the context of the setting in which they occur. This implies, of course, that behavior analysis as it is practiced in the BAI, involves the evaluation of substantially more behavioral information, and more types of information, than those which are commonly the subject of research on the relationship between deception and behavior [*10,12*].

It is also important to point out that in actual Behavior Analysis Interviews the interviewer has access to not only all of the behavioral data considered in this study, but other information as well. That is, in an actual interview, the suspect, in addition to being asked behavior-provoking questions, would also be asked investigative questions to ascertain motivation, propensity, and opportunity to commit the offense. During the BAI, the interviewer also has control over the selection, sequence, and timing of questions, as well as the ability to ask follow-up questions to clarify ambiguous responses. Moreover, the interviewer often has access to information about the suspect's background, as well as the suspect's role in the investigation. This information, of course, may assist in evaluation of behavior and allow the interviewer to estimate independently the probability of the suspects' involvement in the crime. While the contribution of these additional sources of information to an interviewer's decision-making is unknown, it can be seen that the range of data, behavioral and otherwise, that is available in an actual BAI may contribute differently in real-life from what has been shown here.

There are three other important points to be kept in mind when considering these findings. First, all of the expert evaluators in this study were well trained and highly experienced in interpreting the kind of behavioral information submitted to them. Whether or not others with lesser or different qualifications would do as well is simply not known. In fact, recent research of Ekman and O'Sullivan [*21*] suggests that even among those with a professional interest in the detection of liars from behavioral differences, such as police detectives, there may be considerable variation.

A second point is that the clarity of behavioral responses exhibited by a suspect during an interview may be influenced by the interviewer's ability to evoke such behaviors. That is, it is possible that important features in the interaction between an interviewer and the interviewee are determinative of at least some of the behavioral data studied here. Other interviewers who are less able to elicit meaningful behavior from suspects might not produce similar kinds or amounts of behavioral information.

Finally, although these results show that there are observable behavioral differences between those who tell the truth and those who do not the specific behavioral features that contribute to those differences are not certain. Further research is necessary to reveal the nature and source of these cues.

In spite of these limitations, it is true, nevertheless, that the behavioral data evaluated here were derived from actual suspects involved in investigations of serious wrongdoing. This feature alone, as indicated at the outset of this report, distinguishes these findings from most other research. When considered in that light, the Behavior Analysis Interview appears to be empirically well grounded. Although other research has reported only a moderate discrimination between truthful and deceptive persons based on behavioral observations [10,12,29], almost all of this research has been carried out in a laboratory environment, usually in conditions in which the subjects had little to gain by telling the truth and little to lose by lying. In contrast, in this study the subjects were involved in real-life investigations; they knew that there were serious consequences for failing to be identified as truthful. Moreover, here the behaviors that were assessed were those occurring in interviews specifically designed to elicit behaviors and attitudes believed to discriminate between truthful and lying suspects. Judging from these results such interviews are quite effective and yield a relatively high overall accuracy of about 85%. Because these data were real-life based, however, there is an important qualification to be made.

Unlike laboratory studies, in field settings it is extremely difficult to develop an adequate measure of "ground truth," that is, a criterion that establishes with certainty the "innocence" or "guilt" of a suspect that is truly independent of the process being evaluated. This problem complicates the interpretation of field, or real-life, based research such as the present study. In this study, for example, two primary measures of ground truth were used: confessions, which implicated a "guilty" suspect and at the same time exonerated an "innocent" suspect in the same case, and factual analysis, a method to determine the probability of involvement (or the lack of it) in an offense based on information compiled about a suspect's activities related to the offense but without any direct observation of the suspect or his/her behavior mannerisms.

In this study, the interviewers, who administered the actual BAIs in the confession-verified cases, no doubt considered information that was not available to the evaluators, such as investigative data, when rendering their field opinions. The evaluators, however, did not have access to such data and were forced to rely only on their assessment of responses to the behavior-provoking questions asked during a BAI. Because both the interviewers and the evaluators had access to the same behavioral information, however, it could be suggested that the congruence between the outcome of the original BAI and evaluators' assessment of the suspects' truthfulness, reveals only a measure of the consistency between the original and subsequent evaluations.

This problem of criterion contamination in confession-based cases is an important one. However, the study also included cases that used factual analysis to establish ground truth. In these cases the criterion that led to their inclusion did not make use of evaluation of the behaviors that were assessed by the evaluators. It is possible, however, that the suspects' behaviors that were evaluated (by the four evaluators) may have been related to the activities that were incorporated in the factual analysis review and therefore were contaminated in that indirect way. For that reason, there was some, albeit small, possibility of contamination. Thus, while there may have been contamination of both of the major criteria used in the study, it is important to note that the two quite different criteria did not produce significant differences in evaluators' outcomes.

Ground truth for two of the suspects included in this study was established not by confession or factual analysis but rather by incontrovertible evidence that was developed. In both instances, the suspects were found to have been "truthful" in their BAI. The decision in each instance was confirmed by the fact that the money the suspects were believed to have stolen from their employer, whose documentation erroneously indicated receipt, had actually been misdirected by the sending company to another location. If it were possible to develop ground truth criteria in a large number of cases such as occurred in these two instances, the interpretation of findings would be less problematic.

806   JOURNAL OF FORENSIC SCIENCES

Unfortunately, such cases do not occur frequently. Hence, while confessions—and perhaps factual analysis—are the most practical and dependable criteria for field-based research of the kind reported here, their limitations must be carefully considered. For this reason, these findings shoul( be cautiously generalized to real-life settings.

In spite of the caveats to be considered, these findings support the observations of field practitioners with respect to the Behavior Analysis Interview. The BAI appears to be a procedure in which persons with a professional interest in sorting truth-tellers from liars, including, of course, almost all police investigators, would benefit from training. Further research is necessary to determine the effect of such training on the ability to elicit and to judge behavior and on the contribution that it may make to investigator's performance.

### References

[1] Eck, J., *Solving Crimes: The Investigation of Burglary and Robbery*, Washington, D. C., Police Executive Research Forum, 1983.

[2] Ericson, R., *Making Crime: A Study of Detective Work*, Toronto, Canada, Butterworth and Company, 1981.

[3] Greenwood, P., Chaiken, J., and Petersilia, J., *The Criminal Investigation Proce.s*, Lexington, MA, D. C. Heath and Company, 1977.

[4] Miyazawa, S., *Policing in Japan: A Study on Making Crime*. Albany, New York, State University of New York, 1992.

[5] Wilson, J., *The Investigators*, New York, Basic Books, Inc., 1978.

[6] Horvath, F., "Verbal and Nonverbal Clues to Truthfulness and Deception During Polygraph Examinations," *Journal of Police Science and Administration*, Vol. 1, 1973, pp. 138–152.

[7] Trovillo, P., "A History of Lie Detection," *Journal of Criminal Law, Criminology, and Police Science*, Vol. 29, 1939, 1/p. 848–881.

[8] Morris, D., *Manwatching—A Field Guide to Human Behavior*, New York, Harry Abrams Inc. Publishers, 1977.

[9] Nierenberg, G. and Calero, H., *How to Read a Person Like a Book*, New York, Pocket Books Publishers, 1971.

[10] Burgoon, J., Buller, D., and Woodall, W., *Nonverbal Communication: The Unspoken Dialogue*, New York, Harper & Row, 1989.

[11] Carpenter, R., "The Statistical Profile of Language Behavior with Machiavellian Intent or While Experiencing Caution and Avoiding Self-Incrimination," *Annals of the New York Academy of Sciences*, Vol. 606, 1990, pp. 5–17.

[12] Ekman, P., *Telling Lies*, New York, W. W. Norton and Co., 1985.

[13] Ekman, P. and Friesen, W., "Nonverbal Leakage and Cues to Deception," *Psychiatry*, Vol. 32, 1969, pp. 88–106.

[14] Ekman, P., Friesen, W., and Scherer, K., "Body Movement and Voice Pitch in Deceptive Interactions," *Semiotica*, Vol. 16, 1976, pp. 23–27.

[15] Feldman, R., Devin-Sheehan, L., and Allen, V., "Nonverbal Cues as Indicators of Verbal Dissembling," *American Educational Research Journal*, Vol. 15, 1978, pp. 217–231.

[16] Knapp, M., Hart, R., and Dennis, H., "An Exploration of Deception As a Communication Construct," *Human Communication Research*, Vol. 5, 1974, pp. 270–285.

[17] Kraut, R., "Verbal and Nonverbal Cues in the Perception of Lying," *Journal of Personality and Social Psychology*, Vol. 36, 1978, pp. 380–391.

[18] Mehrabian, A., *Nonverbal Communication*, Chicago, Aldine Atherton, 1972.

[19] Streeter L., Krauss, R., Geller, V., Olson, C., and Apple, W., "Pitch Changes During Attempted Deception," *Journal of Personality and Social Psychology*, Vol. 35, 1977, pp. 345–350.

[20] Knapp, M. and Comandena, M., "Telling It Like It Isn't: A Review of Theory and Research on Deceptive Communication," *Human Communication Research*, Vol. 5, 1979, pp. 270–285.

[21] Ekman, P. and O'Sullivan, M., "Who Can Catch a Liar?," *American Psychologist.*, Sept. 1991, pp. 913–919.

[22] Reid, J. and Arther, R., "Behavior Symptoms of Lie Detector Subjects," *Journal of Criminal Law, Criminology and Police Science*, Vol. 44, 1953, pp. 104–108.

[23] Barland, G., "Detection of Deception in Criminal Suspects: A Field Validation Study, Unpublished dissertation, University of Utah, 1975.

[24] Horvath, F. and Jayne, B., "A Pilot Study of the Verbal and Nonverbal Behaviors of Criminal Suspects During Structure Interviews," Unpublished paper, U. S. Dept. of Defense Grant # 89-R-2323, 1990.

[25] Horvath, F., "The Effect of Selected Variables on the Interpretation of Polygraph Records," *Journal of Applied Psychology*, Vol. 62, 1977, pp. 127–136.

[26] Inbau, F., Reid, J., and Buckley, J., *Criminal Interrogation and Confessions*, 3rd ed., Baltimore, Williams and Wilkins, 1986.

[27] Reid, J. and Inbau, F., *Truth and Deception: The Polygraph (Lie Detector) Technique*, Baltimore, Williams and Wilkins, 1977.

[28] Jayne, B., "Factual Analysis in Employee Theft Investigations," unpublished manuscript prepared for *The Investigator Anthology*, Chicago, J. Reid & Associates, 1990.

[29] Kraut, R. and Poe, D., "On the Line: The Deception Judgments of Customs Inspectors and Laymen," *Journal of Personality and Social Psychology*, Vol. 39, 1980, pp. 784–798.

Address requests for reprints or additional information to
Frank Horvath, Ph.D.
School of Criminal Justice
512 Baker Hall
Michigan State University
East Lansing, MI 48824
(517) 355-2197
(517) 336-1787 (FAX)

# [14]

Social Behaviour, Vol. 2, 1–17 (1987)

# Training Police Officers to Detect Deceptive Eyewitness Statements: Does it Work?

GÜNTER KÖHNKEN

*Department of Psychology, University of Kiel, Olshausenstr. 40, 2300 Kiel 1, Fed. Rep. Germany*

## ABSTRACT

The present experiment examined the ability of police officers to discriminate between truthful and deceptive eyewitness statements and the effectiveness of training to enhance detection accuracy. A modified lie detection procedure was used to achieve more similarity of the stimulus material with eyewitness statements. In particular, factual statements instead of private feelings or attitudes, longer and complete statements instead of the middle 20 to 30 seconds of a message, and only one judgement per sender instead of a series of within-sender judgements were used. The results under these modified conditions were strikingly similar to previous findings for standard lie detection procedures. Police officers did not perform better than chance expectations and training did not increase the accuracy level compared to a no-training control group. Additional analysis revealed that lie detection accuracy was positively correlated with age, but negatively associated with length of on-the-job experience.

## INTRODUCTION

One of the major tasks in police investigations and court trials is the evaluation of eyewitness testimonies. This evaluation has to take into account two basically different sources of unreliability: witnesses may be susceptible to unconscious and unintended errors, caused for example by forgetting, post-event information, biased instructions, etc. These types of errors occur although the witnesses are motivated and try hard to give correct and complete statements. Contemporary eyewitness testimony research has examined numerous variables that could produce increases or (perhaps more often) decreases in the *accuracy* of eyewitness performance (for reviews of this line of research see e.g. Clifford and Bull, 1978; Loftus, 1979; Yarmey, 1979; Lloyd-Bostock and Clifford, 1983; Wells and Loftus, 1984). Another important factor determining the correctness of a statement is the willingness of a person to tell the truth. A witness may intentionally and consciously

0885–6249/87/010001–17$08.50
© 1987 by John Wiley & Sons, Ltd.

*Received 22 August 1986*
*Accepted 2 October 1986*

2      *Günter Köhnken*

try to deceive the police or the jury. This raises the question of the *credibility* of a given witness statement, compared to the accuracy, which is affected by unintended errors.

Two major research strategies have been applied to the field of credibility research. One strategy examines the objectively measurable behavioural correlates of truth and deceit such as, for example, head and body movements, gesture, gaze, speech disturbances, skin resistance, etc., i.e. the *encoding* or *expression* of truth and deception. Another approach is primarily concerned with the *decoder's* perspective or *impression* side of credibility. From this perspective it has been investigated whether judges are able to detect deceptive messages, which behavioural cues they utilize for their judgement, etc. The differentiation of truth and deceit by means of exact analyses of various behaviours (verbal, non-verbal, extralinguistic, and psychophysiological) or based on impression judgements will be referred to as *lie detection* or detection of deception. This general term thus includes the traditional psychophysiological detection of deception or polygraph method. However, the polygraph method has primarily been applied to the examination of suspects, and it is unclear whether this technique may be generalized to the analysis of witness statements (Köhnken, 1987). The scope of this article will therefore be limited to the evaluation of extralinguistic and non-verbal behaviour and the message content. The accuracy at detecting deception, i.e. the proportion of correct assignments or the hit rate, will be referred to as *detection accuracy*.[1]

The basic prerequisite of any reliable assessment of credibility is the assumption that truth or deception can be inferred from some kind of overt indicators which are consistently related to credibility. Several recent meta-analyses on more than 40 experimental studies (Zuckerman, DePaulo and Rosenthal, 1981; Zuckerman and Driver, 1984; DePaulo, Stone and Lassiter, 1985) provide empirical evidence that there are in fact substantial associations between the credibility of a message and overt behaviours. DePaulo *et al.* (1985) have demonstrated that of 24 different verbal, non-verbal, and extralinguistic behaviours, 14 were significantly related to credibility. According to these results liars are, in general, engaged in more and/or longer speech hesitations, they produce more speech errors, speak with higher voice pitch, and show longer response latencies. The non-verbal behaviour of the average deceiver is characterized by increased frequencies of eyeblinks, dilated pupils, and more adaptors (i.e. self-manipulating gestures). In addition, there is some experimental evidence that truthful and deceptive statements differ in content-related characteristics such as the amount of details (Köhnken and Wegener, 1982). Thus it may be concluded that a systematic evaluation of these behavioural cues should allow the assessment of message credibility with better than chance accuracy. However, the assessment of most of these behavioural correlates of credibility requires sophisticated observational skills and sometimes the use of technical equipment like a polygraph or a computer. Since jury members and police officers generally cannot be expected to have these skills, this diagnostic approach is limited to trained psychological experts.

Research on the decoding side of credibility has shown that the ability of untrained raters to discriminate between true and deceptive statements is generally not very impressive. In two recent reviews of more than 30 decoding studies, Zuckerman *et al.* (1981) and DePaulo *et al.* (1985) report that the average accuracy of lie detection in studies with a chance expectation of 50 per cent varies within a range of 45–60 per cent. Although disappointingly low, the accuracy of detecting deception is significantly above chance except if facial cues only are available. However, even hit rates in the upper part of this range are by far insufficient for the judgement of eyewitness statements in real court cases or criminal investigations. They would simply mean that at best four out of ten classifications are wrong; i.e. actually true statements are judged as lies or actually deceptive statements are rated true. The meta-analysis by Zuckerman *et al.* (1981) has also shown that the error frequencies are not distributed equally across these two categories. In general, results indicate a truthfulness bias, i.e. judging a deceptive statement as true is more likely than erroneously taking a true statement as deception (Zuckerman *et al.*, 1981). Thus there is some probability that more than half of the 40 per cent errors occurring in credibility judgements might be false truth ratings.

Two questions emerge from this situation: First, are the results of the previous laboratory studies generalizable to real-life settings, and second, is it possible to improve the detection accuracy of raters? To assess the potential ecological validity of previous laboratory research with regard to witness statements, the basic characteristics of the experimental procedures must be examined. In a typical lie detection study, senders are instructed to describe persons they like, dislike, dominate, and submit (or feel indifferent or ambivalent about). Each of these target persons is described in two modes – truth and deception. In the truthful mode senders are instructed to describe their true feelings toward the target. In the deceptive mode they are asked to convince the interviewer that their feelings were opposite to what they actually felt (see e.g. Zuckerman, Koestner and Alton, 1984). The messages of the senders are videorecorded and displayed to untrained lay raters, usually introductory psychology students, who have to judge the credibility of each description. A closer look at this procedure reveals that it differs at least in three important aspects from the task of judging the veracity of real eyewitness statements.

First, it is rather uncommon that the major task of witnesses is to report their feelings. Instead, they give statements about social situations, events, physical environments, etc. (see Stone, 1984, for an extensive discussion of circumstances which might raise the question of statement credibility in daily court practice). It has been argued elsewhere (Miller and Burgoon, 1981; Köhnken, 1987) that the deceptive construction of a factual statement differs in fundamental task characteristics from the confabulation of a private feeling. For example, a social event has to be fitted into a physical environment, the basic sequence of a social situation, time schedules, etc. Some of these facts may be known to the police. Thus the witness has to take care that he does not report details which are discrepant with these known facts. Control processes like these are usually not necessary for the description of private feelings since senders rarely run the risk that the raters know their true feelings. The construction of deceptive factual statements should therefore be a cognitively more difficult task than lying about internal emotions. Hence, with regard to a cognitive approach to lie detection, better detection accuracies for factual statements may be expected. In addition, Miller, Bauchner, Hocking, Fontes, Kaminski, and Brandt (1981) have reported that factual and emotional deceptions may be associated with different behavioural patterns.

Second, in previous studies raters have usually judged the credibility of eight

4      *Günter Köhnken*

rather short different messages of each sender. In practice, however, police officers or juries conduct lengthy and often repeated interrogations with witnesses, particularly if the credibility of the statement is at question. In many cases some of the facts are already known from other pieces of evidence. This provides the opportunity to compare the witness's demeanour during those parts of the statement which are in agreement with other facts and those which are at question. This extended interaction increases the familiarity with the witness's behaviour. There is some evidence that this kind of familiarity enhances the subjects' ability to detect deception (Brandt, Miller and Hocking, 1980). In addition, a study by Zuckerman *et al.* (1984) has demonstrated that even subjects who received no feedback concerning the accuracy of their judgements achieved considerable gains in accuracy from the first four to the second four messages of the same sender. It may therefore be speculated that detection accuracy in real-life cases is higher than the accuracy scores which were obtained with the standard procedures of previous experiments.

Third, almost all of the lie detectors in previous studies were untrained and (with regard to their lie detection task) inexperienced introductory psychology students. Contrary to this, police officers, attorneys, prosecutors, etc. usually have at least some amount of on-the-job experience in judging the statements of witnesses and perpetrators. This experience might result in higher accuracy rates than those of inexperienced students. In addition, detecting deceptive statements is a rather important aspect of their job, and they might therefore be more highly motivated to perform successfully than undergraduate students. However, DePaulo and Pfeifer (1986) have demonstrated that on-the-job experience *per se* has little or no facilitating effect on lie detection success. In a comparison of the hit rates of undergraduate students, new police recruits, and advanced police officers in a standard lie detection test no significant differences were found. The actual mean accuracy scores were 54 per cent for students, 53 per cent for new police recruits, and 52 per cent for advanced officers.

To summarize, it is still unclear whether the results of previous laboratory studies do generalize to real-life settings concerning witness statements. There are some arguments in favour of higher accuracy rates in real investigations, but there are also arguments against this. To get more insight into the dynamics of evaluating eyewitness statements, different procedures, deception tasks, and subjects have to be used which are more similar to the situation of court trials and/or police investigations. One purpose of the present study was to examine whether accuracy rates observed under these conditions would be different from the results of previous studies using the standard lie detection procedure.

A second question of considerable practical importance deals with the trainability of lie detection skills. Low accuracy rates of untrained and inexperienced students should not be worrying if it were possible to enhance detection accuracy by training professionals to detect deception. Only a few experiments have examined this question. Again, there is some evidence for an optimistic view, as well as evidence for a more pessimistic expectation. In two recent studies, Zuckerman and his co-workers investigated the effects of feedback on learning to detect deception. Zuckerman *et al.* (1984) used the standard lie detection procedure with four truthful and four deceptive person descriptions of each sender. In five experimental conditions subjects had to judge the credibility of each description and received different amounts of feedback informing them whether the message was in fact truthful or deceptive (e.g. for the first four descriptions before or after the message, for all eight descriptions, etc.). In general, the results showed that the amount of feedback given was positively related to the accuracy of detecting lies enacted by the same sender. Detection accuracy was increased from chance level (0.5) up to 0.70 as a result of practice and feedback. There was, however, no transfer of this learning effect to other senders. In a follow-up study, Zuckerman, Koestner and Colella (1985) investigated whether this result would be modified by the availability of different communication channels (i.e. face only, speech only, and face plus speech). The results showed that feedback improved subjects' ability to detect deception when they had access to senders' speech behaviour, but not if facial information only was available. Contrary to the Zuckerman *et al.* (1984) study, this time there was also some improvement across senders. In absolute terms, however, the gains in detection accuracy were rather small.

Another training approach was used in a study by DePaulo, Lassiter and Stone (1982). Previous research had shown that deception is most successfully detected if verbal, particularly extralinguistic, information is available for the raters. Therefore it was hypothesized that decoders should perform better if they attend to these particularly revealing communication channels. To investigate this prediction, subjects were instructed to pay particular attention to extralinguistic behaviour, nonverbal behaviour, or content-related characteristics. For subjects in a control condition no special attentional instructions were given. Credibility ratings were made in a traditional lie detection test with person descriptions as deception tasks. However, contrary to almost all other relevant studies, communication channels were not presented in isolation. Instead, subjects had fully audiovisual access to the senders, which constitutes a more realistic setting regarding the evaluation of witness statements. Deceptiveness ratings were made on a nine-point scale. The results show that even a rather simple intervention like directing subjects' attention to the more revealing communication channels increased their ability to discriminate truth from deceit. A computation of the *d* statistic (Cohen, 1977) showed, for example, that subjects' detection accuracy in the control group was 0.74 standard deviations worse than chance, compared to 1.06 standard deviations better than chance in the attend-to-tone condition. This effect was, however, limited to the ratings of truthful messages while the detection accuracy for deceptive descriptions was not significantly altered.

To summarize, the few available results suggest that there might be some potential for improvement in raters' ability to detect deception. It is not absolutely clear, however, whether the observed learning effects generalize across senders and if so, under what conditions transfer occurs. Also, it still remains to be clarified whether the results of previous studies using the standard lie detection procedure could be replicated under different conditions. The present experiment was designed to examine the hypothesis that different training conditions (i.e. information and directing attention to different communication channels) should improve subjects' ability to discriminate between true and deceptive eyewitness statements. In contrast to the DePaulo *et al.* (1982) study, subjects were not only instructed where to direct their attention, they were also informed about the particular behaviours within the different communication channels. To enhance

6     *Günter Köhnken*

ecological validity, police officers with various amounts of on-the-job experience were used as subjects, and the description of social events instead of private feelings was used as deception task.

## METHOD

### Subjects

Eighty male police officers of three different ranks participated as subjects on a volunteer basis. Their mean age was 28.7 years (SD = 7.1) with a range of 19 to 47 years. The average on-the-job experience was 10.9 years (SD = 6.3) with a range of 3 to 26 years. All subjects were recruited from training courses for police officers. They were informed that their task would be to rate the credibility of videotaped eyewitness statements. The results of this investigation would be used to develop a training package for police officers to discriminate true and deceptive eyewitness testimonies. Since no reason was given for any misleading information, all questions concerning the experiment were answered correctly. However, subjects were informed only that they would receive some kind of training, but no information was given concerning the differential types of training. It was emphasized that all personal information would be treated as strictly confidential. Their names would only be used to create the groups, and would later be deleted from the material. Also, it was promised that they would receive information about the results of the study.

### Material

The stimulus material used to assess the ability of subjects to detect deception had to be constructed with particular regard to the characteristics of eyewitness statements. Instead of the commonly used lie detection test (cf. Zuckerman, Amidon, Bishop and Pomerantz, 1982; DePaulo, Lanier and Davis, 1983), where senders are instructed to describe their feelings (e.g. like or dislike) towards various persons, the description of social events was used as deception task. Stimulus materials for these descriptions were two video films of about 10 minutes length each. Film 1 showed a group of six male and female adolescents. One of the boys stole money out of one of the girls' handbags. When the boy was suspected of being the thief he escaped through a window. Film 2 depicted the conflict of a recently divorced couple concerning the custody for a child. The last sequence of the film showed the father violently pulling the child into his car and driving away.

Psychology students were used as senders. To simulate the situation of a witness, senders had to be sufficiently motivated to be successful with their lies. In addition, the reports had to be planned. To motivate senders in the deception condition, psychology students were selected who wanted to become clinical psychologists. They were told that empirical research had shown that an important skill of successful counsellors and clinical psychologists is the ability to deceive effectively. Since counsellors sometimes might be affected personally by their clients' reports, it would be absolutely necessary to hide their thoughts and emotions in order to maintain a neutral interview atmosphere and not to influence their client in any way. Particularly in marital counselling this kind of deception would be extremely important since negative statements of one spouse may not affect the therapist's feelings concerning the other. Senders were told that the aim of the experiment was to evaluate a test to select potentially successful counsellors, and that thereafter they would receive feedback about their prospective success as clinical psychologists. To allow for planning and rehearsal, senders were informed after viewing the film that they had about 5 minutes to plan their report. Pilot research had shown that this period was sufficient for the stimulus material used.

Twenty senders were processed on an individual basis. At the beginning of the session they received the instruction that their face would be videotaped while viewing a film in order to investigate their facial reactions on various film sequences. The reasons for this manipulation were: (1) to create a situation of incidental learning similar to the perceiving conditions of eyewitnesses who usually do not know while perceiving an event that they have to give a report about it later; (2) the bogus pipeline video-recording was introduced to habituate the senders to the video-recording prior to the actual experimental part of the session. After viewing one of the films, senders were placed on another chair in the same room in front of a neutral grey background where they were recorded by another video camera. The video-recordings were performed with a ¾ inch JVC video-cassette recorder (system U-matic) and a Philips colour camera. Senders were informed that it would be necessary to get some distance from the film contents. Therefore they were instructed to report the course of their previous day as correctly and completely as possible, including for example the time they arose, their clothing, exact meals, etc. These reports were later used as baseline for the credibility judgements. After completing this report, senders received their randomly assigned instruction to lie or to tell the truth. Senders in the truth condition were told that the actual aim of the experiment was the investigation of their perceptual accuracy and memory capacity. Therefore it would be their task to recall what they saw in the film as completely and correctly as possible. Senders in the deception condition received the misleading 'counsellor skill' information described above. Deception senders were instructed to change the event that they observed in the film in one particular detail. Senders who saw film 1 (theft) where instructed to tell this story as if another girl in the group and not the actual thief had stolen the money. In the deception instruction for film 2 (kidnapping) senders were instructed to conceal the actual kidnapping and tell the story as if the child had spontaneously accompanied his father. They were told that their videotaped reports would be shown to trained observers. It would be their task to convince the observers that their version of the story was the true one. After completing their reports senders were thoroughly debriefed.

Of these twenty messages four had to be selected as stimulus material for the main experiment. Since the average duration of one statement was approximately 4 minutes, and the time the police officers were available for the experiment was limited, only a maximum of four statements plus the respective baseline messages could be used as stimulus material. The selection of four statements was performed in two steps. In the first step all technically suboptimal recordings were discarded. Also all deceptive reports which were easily identified in a pilot screening test (for example because senders made statements regarding their deception task) were excluded. From the remaining material one true and one deceptive report for each

8     *Günter Köhnken*

of the two films were selected at random. The length of these reports were 6 minutes (film 1, true), 4'31" minutes (film 1, deceptive), 3'4" minutes (film 2, true), and 3'18" minutes (film 2, deceptive), respectively. The video-recordings of these selected reports, together with the respective baseline interviews, were copied on to a VHS cassette with the baseline interview always first, followed by the critical report of the same sender. To standardize the baseline reports in length, only the first 2 minutes of each report were copied.

## Training conditions

All subject raters first received some general information in written and oral form about eyewitness testimony, accuracy, and credibility to make sure that all had a common basic understanding of the issue and their task. This general introduction was followed by one of four different types of information. In the *general introduction* subjects were informed that two primary sources of unreliability might distort eyewitness reports. First, a report may be influenced by unintended and unconscious errors. This source of unreliability would be referred to as *accuracy* of a report. On the other hand a witness might intentionally and consciously tell a lie, i.e. he knows the actual details of an event and conceals or falsifies the whole event or some aspects of it. This source of unreliability would be referred to as the *credibility* of a report. Subjects were instructed that a positive judgement of credibility does not necessarily imply the absence of any error. Their task would only be to judge the credibility without regarding any potential sources of unintentional errors. They were also instructed that the credibility of a statement would not be determined by a trait such as general trustworthiness. Instead, credibility should be conceived as a state-dependent and particularly motivation-dependent behaviour. Following this general instruction, subjects received the special information according to their experimental condition, again in a written and oral form.

## No-information control group

Subjects in the no-information control group only received the general introduction with no further information regarding the way in which to judge the credibility of a statement.

## Non-verbal behaviour

Subjects in the non-verbal behaviour training group were told that it had been shown that lies can best be detected in the non-verbal behaviour of a witness. Since it would be impossible for a witness to concentrate on the content of his statement and simultaneously control all his non-verbal behaviour, clues to deceit should appear in the non-verbal behaviour as the less controllable area. Therefore the judges should devote all their attention to the non-verbal behaviour channel, and look for possible clues to deceit. Following this general information the major aspects of non-verbal behaviour were defined and demonstrated. These behaviours were head movements, eyeblink, gaze, illustrators, adaptors, body movements, and leg and foot movements. Since the empirical results regarding non-verbal correlates of deception are not very consistent as to which particular behavioural changes are caused by deception (e.g. Zuckerman *et al.*, 1981), subjects were informed that deceivers show some changes in their non-verbal behaviour compared to true statements of the same senders, but it would be impossible to predict where exactly these changes would appear. Subjects were also instructed that it would be of crucial importance to compare thoroughly the non-verbal behaviour during the certainly true and the critical statement. High or low frequencies of particular non-verbal behaviours would be of little or no dianostic value if they appear during both statements. Only then, if differences between the true and the critical statement were observed, could they be interpreted as clues to deception.

*Speech behaviour*

Subjects in the speech behaviour training group were told that it had been shown that lies can best be detected in the speech behaviour of a witness. Since it would be impossible for a witness to concentrate on the content of his statement and simultaneously control all his speech behaviour, clues to deceit should appear in the speech behaviour as the less controllable area. Therefore the judges should pay all their attention to the extralinguistic behaviour channel and look for possible clues to deceit. Extralinguistic behaviour was defined as all utterances that were not relevant to the content of the statement (i.e. speech rate, filled pauses, word fragments, stuttering, repetitions, self-reflections, parenthetic remarks, corrections, false starts, diversity of vocabulary, and syntactic complexity; see Köhnken, 1985, for more detailed descriptions of these categories). A previous experiment (Köhnken, 1985) had demonstrated that these behaviours differed significantly between truthful and deceptive reports. The categories were defined and demonstrated with examples. As in the non-verbal behaviour training group, subjects were informed that no consistent lie syndrome could be expected. Thus they had to monitor the senders' speech behaviour in a true and the critical statement, and look for general differences. Only if differences in speech behaviour occurred between the certainly true and the critical statement could these be interpreted as indicators of deception.

*Content of the statement*

Subjects in this group were trained according to the statement analysis approach (Köhnken and Steller, 1986; Steller and Köhnken, 1987). They were instructed to pay particular attention to the content of the statement, since deceptive reports could best be detected from special characteristics of their content. Witnesses would not be able to create a falsified statement with the same content qualities that true statements usually have. Therefore the raters should direct all their attention to the content of the message. Particular emphasis was laid on the statement reality criteria, such as logical consistency, amount of details, space–time interrelationships, accounts of unusual details, and spontaneous corrections (See Köhnken and Steller, 1986; Steller and Köhnken, 1987), for a more detailed description of these criteria). The criteria were defined and demonstrated with several examples. The subjects were instructed that deceptive statements would be characterized by fewer of these criteria, or that they would be less pronounced, compared to true statements of the same sender. Therefore it would be of crucial importance to compare the certainly true and the critical statement of each sender and look for any differences in these criteria.

10     *Günter Köhnken*

*Procedure*

Subjects were run in randomly compiled groups of four to six judges. The subjects of each group were sent from their classes to the training room in a previously determined random order. After arriving in the training room they received additional information about the general procedure of the experiment, followed by the introduction to their judgement task. Subjects in the no-information control group were then sent to an adjacent room where they judged the credibility of the recorded statements, while the three training groups worked through their proper training packages. After this step they were sent to the adjacent judgement room. The training sessions had an average length of approximately 60 minutes in all three groups. For the no-information control group the session lasted approximately 15 minutes. No attempt was made to fill the remaining 45 minutes in this group with any placebo activity. Variations of some minutes occurred as a result of the number of questions that were asked by the subjects. The experimenter who conducted the training sessions was unfamiliar with the video-recordings and therefore did not know the behavioural and content cues the senders actually exhibited.

After completing the training session, subjects were sent to an adjacent room where the stimulus material was presented to them by two of the experimenter's assistants. They were blind with regard to the respective training condition of each group. One of them operated the video equipment while the other one gave the instructions, handed out the material, etc. The following procedures and instructions were identical for all four groups. Subjects first received their response sheets and were asked to answer the general questions concerning age, on-the-job experience, rank, etc. They were then informed about the further procedure. They were told that they would see four pairs of statements with a true statement (the baseline interview) always first, followed by the critical statement of the same sender. It was further explained that several versions of the same basic events were recorded for this research programme. This had enabled a module-wise combination of the various versions. Hence, the fact that some statements about the same event might differ in some aspects would be no valid indicator that one of these reports had to be deceptive, since senders may have observed different versions of the same basic film. Also, the videotaped statements had been selected randomly. Therefore it might be the case that all statements were true, all were deceptive, or that they might occur in any other combination.[2] Each group would be presented with a different video-tape with different senders in different combinations of truth and deception. In fact the tape was identical for all groups; however, the sequence of the statements was counterbalanced on a group-to-group basis. Prior to each baseline interview subjects were informed that the following statement would be the truthful one. After the critical statement the tape was stopped and subjects indicated on their response sheet whether the statement was true or deceptive, as well as their confidence in the correctness of that judgement on a five-point scale ranging from 'not at all certain' (1) to 'absolutely certain' (5). After completing the ratings, subjects were finally debriefed and urged not to tell any other participant in the experiment about their training package since that might lead to confusions and uninterpretable results. Subjects were later informed about the results of the study.

## RESULTS

*Accuracy scores*

The accuracy at detecting deceptive and true statements was defined as the proportion of correct judgements. The mean overall accuracy score was 0.45 (SD = 0.24). This value is not significantly different from chance expectations ($t(79)$ = 1.86, *n.s.*). The mean accuracy score across training conditions for true statements was 0.58 ($SD$ = 0.32), which is significantly above chance ($t(79)$ = 2.24, $p$ < 0.03 two-tailed, $d$ = 0.50). For deceptive statements the mean accuracy level was 0.31 ($SD$ = 0.32), a value significantly lower than chance expectations ($t(79)$ = − 5.42, $p$ < 0.001, $d$ = 1.19). This discrepancy indicates that subjects performed considerably better at judging truthful compared to deceptive statements.

*Confidence*

Subjects indicated their confidence in the correctness of their judgements on a five-point scale with higher values indicating greater confidence. The mean overall confidence score across training conditions and senders was 3.66 ($SD$ = 0.65). Separated for true and deceptive statements, the mean confidence scores were 3.64 ($SD$ = 0.83), and 3.66 ($SD$ = 0.84), respectively. Similar to previous studies, subjects located the average confidence in the upper half of the scale, indicating a relatively high amount of confidence in the accuracy of their ratings.

*Confidence–accuracy relationship*

The overall correlation between accuracy and confidence across senders and training conditions was 0.06, which is not significantly different from zero. Obviously, subjectively experienced confidence is not a valid indicator of the actual correctness of a decision. This result is identical with the median accuracy–confidence correlation across six different studies, reported by Zuckerman *et al.* (1981) and very similar to the correlation of 0.02 reported by DePaulo and Pfeifer (1986). For true statements the correlation was 0.10 ($p$ > 0.10). There was, however, a significant negative correlation between confidence and detection accuracy for deceptive statements ($r$ = −0.24, $p$ < 0.02), indicating that lower accuracy rates were associated with greater subjectively experienced confidence when the credibility of deceptive statements was judged. The correlations across all statements for the control group, non-verbal behaviour group, content group, and speech behaviour group were −0.04, −0.10, 0.26, and 0.06. The overall accuracy–confidence – correlations for the three ranks were 0.03, 0.01, and 0.18. None of these correlations were significantly different from zero, or from each other.

*Age and experience*

Age was not substantially associated with the overall accuracy rate ($r$ = 0.07, n.s.) and with the accuracy rate for deceptive statements ($r$ = −0.12, n.s.). However, the correlation between age and detection ability for truthful reports was significant ($r$ = 0.23, $p$ < 0.03). The difference is reliable ($z$ for the difference of dependent correlations = 2.46, $p$ = 0.013). The fact that age was significantly correlated with accuracy scores for truthful, but not for deceptive, statements indicates that older subjects did not simply have a higher truthfulness bias. Instead, they were selectively more accurate in judging the truthful compared to the false

12    *Günter Köhnken*

Table 1. Detection accuracy[a] for true, deceptive, and all statements combined

|                 | Control group | Non-verbal behaviour | Content characteristics | Speech behaviour |
|-----------------|---------------|----------------------|-------------------------|------------------|
| True statements | 0.63          | 0.53                 | 0.69                    | 0.48             |
| False statements| 0.32          | 0.32                 | 0.26                    | 0.33             |
| All statements  | 0.47          | 0.42                 | 0.48                    | 0.40             |

[a] Proportion of correct identifications of truths and lies.

statements than their younger colleagues. Since age and amount of on-the-job experience are interrelated, the question arises if this age–accuracy correlation is primarily a function of age, of experience, or both. For further examination of this question, partial correlations between age and accuracy were computed, controlling for the experience variable. This increased the age–accuracy correlation across all statements from 0.07 to 0.21 ($p = 0.032$) and for deceptive statements from −0.12 to 0.10 (n.s.), while the correlation for truthful statements remained unchanged ($r = 0.22$, $p = 0.025$). Consequently, the partial experience–accuracy correlation controlling for age was negative ($-0.20$, $p = 0.041$ for all statements, $-0.16$, $p = 0.084$ for truthful statements, and $-0.15$, $p = 0.10$ for deceptive statements). The correlations between age and overall confidence, as well as the confidence for the judgement of true and of deceptive statements, did not approach significance. The experience variable, operationalized as the time spent in police service, did not substantially correlate with any of these variables.

*Training effects*

Table 1 shows the mean accuracy scores in the three training conditions and the no-information control group for all statements combined and for true and deceptive reports separated. A 4 (training conditions as between subject factor) × 2 (true vs. deceptive statements as within-subject factor) analysis of variance revealed no significant training effects as the main experimental factor ($F(3,76) < 1$). Therefore the hypotheses that trained subjects would perform better in judging the credibility of statements than subjects in the no-information control group and that the accuracy rates would be different among training groups, was not confirmed. Consistent with previous studies, the type of statement (truth vs. deceit) yielded a significant difference in accuracy scores ($F(1,76) = 35.20$, $p < 0.001$, $d = 1.36$). The size of this effect is almost identical with that reported by DePaulo and Pfeifer (1986) for a similar sample but different stimulus material ($d = 1.28$). The interaction between experimental group and type of statement was not significant, indicating that the better performance on truthful statements was not changed by training conditions. Also, the subjective confidence ratings for all statements and for true and deceptive statements separated were not affected by training conditions.

**DISCUSSION**

The present experiment investigated the lie detection accuracy of police officers. To adjust the task characteristics to the evaluation of witness statements a modified testing procedure was constructed. In particular, factual statements instead of the description of private emotions or attitudes, longer statements with an average length of 4 minutes instead of only the middle 20 to 30 seconds of person descriptions, and only two statements of each sender (one truthful statement as baseline and one critical statement) instead of eight consecutive messages were used as stimulus material.

In general the results obtained under these modified conditions were strikingly similar to the findings of other relevant studies that used the standard lie detection test. Police officers did not perform better than chance expectations. The mean overall hit rate was 45 per cent which is – although at the lower limits – within the range of 45–60 per cent average accuracy scores observed in previous studies (see Zuckerman *et al.*, 1981). Furthermore, the overall mean confidence of subjects in the correctness of their decisions ($M = 3.66$ on a five-point scale with higher values indicating greater confidence) is also comparable to confidence ratings reported in previous studies. Together they demonstrate that subjects feel considerably certain about the correctness of their ratings. Police officers do not differ in this aspect from introductory psychology students, neither in the modified testing procedure used in this study nor in a standard lie detection test applied by DePaulo and Pfeifer (1986). As in almost all other studies, amount of confidence was, however, not a valid indicator of the actual correctness of decisions (mean accuracy–confidence correlation = 0.06). Finally, subjects were much more successful at identifying truths ($M = 58$ per cent) than lies ($M = 31$ per cent). Again, this difference is in accordance with consistent findings of 11 out of 15 studies reviewed by Zuckerman *et al.* (1981) and of a recent experiment by DePaulo and Pfeifer (1986). To summarize, the results of this experiment give some evidence that findings from previous studies using the standard lie detection test and inexperienced subjects may be generalized to a sample of police officers and a lie detection procedure with more similarity to the evaluation of eyewitness statements.

There was, however, an interesting difference to the DePaulo and Pfeifer (1986) results concerning the impact of the age variable. While DePaulo and Pfeifer found a negative correlation between age and accuracy (older subjects were less accurate), the overall correlation in this study was not significant ($r = 0.07$). However, the age–accuracy correlation was significant for the judgement of truthful statements ($r = 0.23$), indicating that older subjects performed better than their younger colleagues when judging truth, but not when judging deceit. Partialling out the effect of the on-the-job experience variable revealed that the overall age–accuracy relation became more positive ($r = 0.20$) while the partial correlation of experience and accuracy controlling for age was significantly negative. Hence, subjects obviously learned contradicting lessons from life and job experiences. Life experience increasingly helped them to successfully discriminate truth from deceit, while on-the-job experience supported a truthfulness bias, thus decreasing accuracy particularly for deceptive statements.

The main initial hypotheses of the experiment were not supported by the data. That is, subjects who had received some kind of training and information about how to discriminate truth from deceit were no more accurate than subjects in a no-information control group. Also, directing attention to and giving information about, extralinguistic characteristics did not produce higher hit rates than emphasizing the importance of non-verbal behaviour or than providing no information at all. Furthermore, contrary to expectation, the modified materials and procedures did not lead to higher detection accuracies than the standard lie detection test.

Several factors may account for this discrepancy. First, the low overall detection accuracy at about chance level might indicate that in fact no consistent clues to deception exist which are strong enough to allow a reliable judgement of credibility. However, the meta-analytical studies of Zuckerman *et al.* (1981), Zuckerman and Driver (1984), and DePaulo *et al.* (1985), do not support this hypothesis. These reviews provide evidence that there are indeed significant associations between various behaviours and the actual credibility of a message. In addition, the quantitative reviews of more than 30 experimental studies on the judgement of deception have demonstrated that the overall detection accuracy significantly exceeds chance level. These findings would be difficult to explain without the assumption of substantial relations between credibility and overt behaviours.

Second, the lack of any training effect could be a consequence of the judgement procedure. This would, for example, explain the discrepancies with the findings of DePaulo *et al.* (1982), who had reported substantial gains in accuracy simply by directing subjects' attention to the senders' speech behaviour. For example, subjects in the DePaulo *et al.* study rated each statement on a nine-point scale of deception, while the stimulus material was basically dichotomous in nature. It is therefore unclear by which factors the ratings were determined in addition to the global truth/deceit dichotomy. Perhaps the subjects' responses reflect a mixture of credibility and confidence ratings. More important, however, seems to be the fact that the gains in detection accuracy in the DePaulo *et al.* study are not reported differentially for messages of the same and of different senders. Thus we do not know if subjects achieved increased hit rates only for consecutive messages of the same stimulus persons, or if the effect also generalized across senders. There is some evidence that training effects may be limited to the judgement of messages of the same senders (Zuckerman *et al.*, 1984). Since only one critical statement of each sender was used in the present study, no within-sender learning, and consequently no improvement in detection accuracy, could occur. Furthermore, the instructions used in this experiment and in the DePaulo *et al.* study differed markedly in complexity. In our procedure, subjects had to learn an extensive set of behavioural descriptions that were at least in part new to them. In addition, they were informed that it would be necessary to compare these behaviours between two relatively long statements. This required the careful observation of rather subtle behaviours like, for example, pupil dilation or syntactical complexity and the storage of their impressions, while simultaneously attending to the next statement and the accompanying behaviour. In summary, what had been expected to enhance subjects' accuracy to detect deception might have produced the opposite result because it exceeded their information-processing capacity.

Learning to detect deception across different senders is probably a much more difficult task than to judge statements of the same senders. As Zuckerman *et al.* (1984) have argued, subjects probably learn a person-specific deception code when they observe a series of statements of the same sender with varying credibility. This does not help them to judge other deceivers, since they have different deception codes. Consequently, if subjects are to be trained to judge various senders, training should not focus on single behaviours as cues to truth and deceit. Instead, subjects have to learn how to detect the *idiosyncratic* deception patterns of each sender, i.e. they have to learn a diagnostic procedure rather than a fixed set of diagnostically relevant cues. Obviously the training procedure applied in this study was not sufficient to teach subjects such complex skills. This conclusion, however, does not imply that it is impossible to learn how to detect deceptions of different senders. It means that a training package has to be developed that takes into account the information-processing capacities of subjects as well as the requirements of the highly complex task characteristics. On the other hand, if we conceive the credibility judgement in part as a cognitive task, success might also be enhanced by reducing the task difficulty. For example, if raters have knowledge about the content of the statements in advance, it would be unnecessary for them to attend to this source of information simultaneous to the monitoring of non-verbal or extralinguistic behaviour. In the same way the use of simple rating scales may release cognitive capacity otherwise occupied by storage tasks. Also, very little is known about the process of judging eyewitness statements. The investigation of the basic mechanisms which determine this process (e.g. cognitive heuristics, decision-making and impression-formation strategies) may reveal fruitful information for the design of training packages.

Finally, it should be mentioned that the generalization from the present results to on-the-job lie detection abilities of police officers might be premature. The low overall detection accuracies may simply indicate that the modified judgement procedures and materials, particularly the stimulus statements, may still not be sufficiently similar to the judgement of the credibility of real witness statements. Although factual statements were used which were almost eight to ten times longer than the common 20 – 30 second descriptions of private feelings, there were still considerable differences to real witness statements. Stone (1984) has given a comprehensive description of the circumstances under which the issue of credibility may arise in real criminal cases. We are currently developing more elaborate material which takes into account some of these specified conditions (e.g. longer and repeated statements, higher personal involvement of the senders, different types of lies, the manipulation of context factors such as motivation to lie, prior information of the judges on the basic event, other types of evidence, etc.).

## REFERENCES

Brandt, D.R., Miller, G.R. and Hocking, J.E. (1980). The truth–deception attribution: effects of familiarity on the ability of observers to detect deception. *Human Communication Research*, **6**, 99–110.
Cifford, B. and Bull, R. (1978). *The Psychology of Person Identification*, Routledge & Kegan Paul, London.
Cohen, J. (1977) *Statistical Power Analysis for the Behavioral Sciences* (rev. ed.). Academic Press, New York.
DePaulo, B.M. and Pfeifer, R.L. (1986). On-the-job experience and skill at detecting deception. *Journal of Applied Social Psychology*, **16**, 249–267.
DePaulo, B.M., Lanier, K. and Davis, T. (1983). Detecting the deceit of the motivated liar. *Journal of Personality and Social Psychology*, **45**, 1096–1103.
DePaulo, B.M., Lassiter, G.D. and Stone, J.I. (1982). Attentional determinants of success at detecting deception and truth. *Personality and Social Psychology Bulletin*, **8**, 273–279.

16    *Günter Köhnken*

DePaulo, B.M., Stone, J.I. and Lassiter, G.D. (1985). Deceiving and detecting deceit. In B.R. Schlenker (ed.), *The Self and Social Life*. McGraw-Hill, New York.

Köhnken, G. (1985). Speech and deception of eyewitnesses: an information processing approach. *Proceedings of the XXIII International Congress of Psychology, Acapulco, 1984,* Vol. 7. North-Holland, Amsterdam.

Köhnken, G. (1986). Verhaltenskorrelate von Täuschung und Wahrheit: Neue Perspektiven in der Glaubwürdigkeitsdiagnostik. *Psychologische Rundschau,* 37, 177–194.

Köhnken, G. (1987). Behavioral correlates of statement credibility: theories, paradigms, and results. In F. Lösel, J. Haisch and H. Wegener (eds), *Advances in Legal Psychology: psychological research in the criminal justice system.* Springer, Berlin. (In press.)

Köhnken, G. and Wegener, H. (1982). Zur Glaubwürdigkeit von Zeugenaussagen. Experimetelle Überprüfung ausgewählter Glaubwürdigkeitskriterien. *Zeitschrift für Experimentelle und Angewandte Psychologie,* 29: 92–111.

Köhnken, G. and Steller, M. (1986). *Assessment of the credibility of children's witness statements within the German procedural system.* Paper presented at the Conference 'Child Witnesses: do the courts abuse children?', Oxford, December.

Lloyd-Bostock, S.M.A. and Clifford, B.R. (eds) (1983). *Evaluating Witness Evidence: recent psychological research and new perspectives.* Wiley, Chichester.

Loftus, E.F. (1979). *Eyewitness Testimony.* Harvard University Press, Cambridge, MA.

Miller, G.R. and Burgoon, J.K. (1981). Factors affecting assessment of witness credibility. In R. Bray and N. Kerr (eds), *The Psychology of the Courtroom.* Academic Press, New York.

Miller, G.R., Bauchner, J.E., Hocking, J.E., Fontes, N.E., Kaminski, E.P. and Brandt, D.R. (1981). '. . . And nothing but the truth': how well can observers detect deceptive testimony. In B.D. Sales (ed.), *Perspectives in Law and Psychology,* vol. II: *The Trial Process.* Plenum Press, New York.

Steller, M. and Köhnken, G. (1987). Statement analysis: credibility assessment of children's testimonies in sexual abuse cases. In D.C. Raskin (ed.), *Psychological Techniques in Law Enforcement.* (In preparation.)

Stone, M. (1984). *Proof of Fact in Criminal Trials.* Green & Son, Edinburgh.

Wells, G.L. and Loftus, E.F. (eds), (1984). *Eyewitness Testimony: psychological perspectives.* Cambridge University Press, New York.

Yarmey, A.D. (1979). *The Psychology of Eyewitness Testimony.* Macmillan, London.

Zuckerman, M. and Driver, R.E. (1984). Telling lies: verbal and nonverbal correlates of deception. In A.W. Siegman and S. Feldstein (eds), *Nonverbal Communication: an integrated perspective.* Erlbaum, Hillsdale, N.J.

Zuckerman, M., Amidon, M.D., Bishop, S.E. and Pomerantz, S.D. (1982). Face and tone of voice in the communication of deception. *Journal of Personality and Social Psychology,* 43, 347–357.

Zuckerman, M., DePaulo, B.M. and Rosenthal, R. (1981). Verbal and nonverbal communication of deception. In L. Berkowitz (ed.), *Advances in Experimental Social Psychology,* vol. 14. Academic Press, New York.

Zuckerman, M., Koestner, R. and Alton, A.O. (1984). Learning to detect deception. *Journal of Personality and Social Psychology,* 46, 519–528.

Zuckerman, M., Koestner, R. and Colella, M.J. (1985). Learning to detect deception from three communication channels. *Journal of Nonverbal Behavior,* 9, 188–194.

## ACKNOWLEDGEMENTS

I thank the police officers for their participation in this experiment. Also, I am indebted to Silke Foelser and Gerhard Stein for their assistance in conducting the study. Requests for reprints should be sent to Günter Köhnken, Department of Psychology, University of Kiel, Olshausenstr. 40, 2300 Kiel, Fed. Rep. of Germany.

**NOTES**

1. There is some inconsistency regarding the use of this term in the literature. In some publications the discrimination between truthful and deceptive messages has been designated as 'deception accuracy' (e.g. Zuckerman, DePaulo and Rosenthal, 1981; DePaulo, Stone and Lassiter, 1985) while in other articles the terms 'detection accuracy' was used (e.g. Zuckerman, Koestner and Colella, 1985; Zuckerman, Koestner and Alton, 1984; DePaulo, Lassiter and Stone, 1982).
2. It cannot be excluded that the fact that two different versions of the same basic event were reported by the senders had any influence on the subjects' credibility judgements. However, none of the subjects mentioned any suspicion with regard to this point during the final debriefing.

# Part V
# Evaluating Testimony

# [15]

Med. Sci. Law (1988) Vol. 28, No. 3 Printed in Great Britain

# Retracted confessions: legal, psychological and psychiatric aspects

GISLI H. GUDJONSSON

*Senior Lecturer, Institute of Psychiatry, De Crespigny Park, London, SE5 8AF*

JAMES A. C. MacKEITH

*Consultant Psychiatrist, Bethlem Royal Hospital, Monks Orchard Road, Beckenham, Kent*

## ABSTRACT

This brief review paper is concerned with the phenomenon of retracted confession statements from legal, psychological and psychiatric viewpoints. The importance of distinguishing between three psychologically different types of 'false confession' is emphasized. The paper provides the clinician with a conceptual framework and ways of assessing alleged false confession cases.

## INTRODUCTION

The purpose of this paper is to review the legal, psychological and psychiatric aspects of retracted confessions in order to assist clinicians in the assessment of cases where defendants have retracted self-incriminating statements made to the police during interrogation. Psychologists and psychiatrists are nowadays increasingly asked to provide expert evidence in these cases. Knowledge of the subject matter and the application of recently developed assessment techniques is growing.

During the past five years we have assessed a large number of cases where defendants have retracted confessions previously made to the police and where it was the principal evidence against them. In this paper we draw upon the literature and our experience with these cases and provide the reader with a conceptual framework for carrying out assessments. We describe recently developed assessment methods which may assist clinicians in their evaluations and when preparing court reports, and emphasize the complementary skills of psychologists and psychiatrists.

There is an important distinction to be made between retracted or disputed confessions and 'false' confessions. It is common in criminal proceedings for defendants to retract confessions made during police interviews, but how many of them are true 'false' confessions is not known. It would be naive to believe that all, or even most, retracted confessions are true 'false' confessions. However, a sufficient number of false confession cases have been identified to warrant concern and a systematic account of the phenomenon.

## RETRACTED STATEMENTS

There is a general tendency among the judiciary to be sceptical about retracted confessions. According to Price (1985), this scepticism was widespread among the judiciary in the well-publicized Confait case. Such scepticism is not surprising when one considers the frequency with which suspects retract confession statements made during police interviews and the potentially damaging effect of a confession on the defence, especially when it is presented as a written and signed statement. Where alternative evidence is lacking or limited when the case goes to court, the incentive to retract a previously made confession may be strong in some cases.

The work of Baldwin and McConville (1980) and Mitchell (1983) highlights the importance of confession evidence in the committal papers. In the former study, there was a confession rate of about 50 per cent in London and Birmingham (the two samples studied). In the Mitchell study, carried out on 394 defendants who came before the Worcester Crown Court in 1978, about 70 per cent had confessed to the police. The two studies show that

188     Med. Sci. Law (1988) Vol. 28, No. 3

over 90 per cent of those who had made a written confession were convicted; and that 25 and 28 per cent respectively of those pleading not guilty at the trial had made oral and/or written confessions during police interviewing. Thus, even if confession statements are retracted and a 'not guilty' plea entered during the trial, the great majority are convicted. However, it is important to remember that a confession in the committal papers is not invariably fatal to the defence as some contested confessions are regarded as unreliable by the jury.

Vennard (1984) looked at disputes within trials over the admissibility and accuracy of self-incriminating statements in the London area. 'Trials within trials', or disputes in the trial proper over the reliability of incriminating statements, occurred in 13 per cent of contested cases in the Crown Court and 6 per cent in cases tried summarily in the Magistrates' Court. 'Trials within trials' took place in 7 per cent of contested Crown Court charges. In only 3 out of 22 'trials within trials' cases were the challenged statements made inadmissible by the judge. This study shows that only in a very small minority of cases do challenges to confession admissibility bring about exclusion of such evidence. The work of Vennard (1984, 1985) indicates that, not suprisingly, written confessions are much less easily challenged by the defence than oral confessions.

Suspects retract previously made confessions for a variety of reasons. What proportion of such cases are genuine 'false' confessions is unknown. The reasons defendants give for having made the alleged false confession usually concern the conduct and circumstances of the police interviews. It is often claimed that the statements were involuntary as the result of police pressure, or it is alleged that the Judges' Rules were not followed. In the Vennard (1984) study the three most common reasons given for having made the alleged false confession were: (i) a promise by the police of an early release from custody if the defendant confessed; (ii) prolonged detention in police cells; and (iii) actual or threatened violence on the part of the police.

## LEGAL ASPECTS

The two central legal issues regarding confessions are the 'confession issue' and the 'exclusion issue' (Mirfield, 1985). The former arises when the defence denies that the confession alleged by the

prosecution was made by the accused. The issue is whether or not the accused made the confession he or she is alleged to have made. The 'exclusion issue' is more commonly raised in court and refers to the defence alleging that the confession was made under pressure or by hope of advantages. If believed by the trial judge or magistrate they may use their discretion to exclude the confession (i.e. make it inadmissible during the trial). Prior to the Police and Criminal Evidence Act 1984, the legal significance of incriminating statements made by suspects during police interrogation was guided by the Judges' Rules and Home Office Administrative Directions (Home Office, 1978). The Judges' Rules emphasized that the fundamental condition of admissibility in evidence is that the statement 'shall have been voluntary, in the sense that it has not been obtained from him by fear of prejudice or hope of advantage, exercised or held out by a person in authority, or by oppression'. The Administrative Directions supplemented the Judges' Rules and specified the conditions under which a suspect was to be questioned. Administrative Direction Four dealt with police officers being advised to 'apply special care' when interviewing mentally handicapped people. If police officers failed to comply with the Judges' Rules and Administrative Directions a judge could elect to exclude the confession as not being 'voluntary' or being the product of oppressive questioning.

The Police and Criminal Evidence Act 1984 (Home Office, 1985a) represents a major change in police practice and the judicial process. The Act is supplemented for practical implementation by Codes of Practice (Home Office, 1985b). The four Codes (A, B, C and D) came into force on 1 January 1986 and supersede the provisions made in the Judges' Rules. They reflect some of the views of the Royal Commission on Criminal Procedures and provide guidelines for the police as required under section 66 of the Police and Criminal Evidence Act. Code C deals with the 'detention, treatment and questioning of persons by police officers'. As far as confessions are concerned, the new Act adopts two tests for the admissibility of confessions, which are contained in section 76(2). This requires the prosecution to prove statutory voluntariness beyond reasonable doubt. The two specific elements to the exclusionary rule are 'oppression' and 'reliability', expressed by sections 76(2) a and b respectively. These are:

(a) The confession must not have been obtained by 'oppression'. The word oppression is defined in section 76(8) to *include* 'torture, inhuman or degrading treatment and the use or threat of violence (whether or not amounting to torture)'. The Code of Practice (C) provides the police with an indication about the kind of things which may amount to oppression (e.g. deprivation of sleep or refreshments, prolonged questioning).

(b) The confession must not have been obtained 'in consequence of anything said or done which was likely, in the circumstances at the time, to render unreliable any confession which might be made by him in consequence thereof'.

The Code of Practice (C) has provisions for the interviewing of mentally ill and mentally handicapped persons. The most important provisions are:

1. A mentally ill or mentally handicapped person must not be interviewed or required to sign a statement in the absence of an 'appropriate adult' (e.g. a relative, a guardian or a mental health professional) unless a police officer of the rank of a superintendent or above considers that the delay will involve an immediate risk of harm to persons or serious loss or damage to property.

2. If a police officer suspects or is told in good faith that the suspect is mentally ill or handicapped he should treat the person as such within the provisions of the Code.

3. The Code states 'It is important to bear in mind that although persons who are mentally ill or mentally handicapped are often capable of providing reliable evidence, they may, without knowing or wishing to do so, be particularly prone in certain circumstances to provide information which is unreliable, misleading or self-incriminating'.

Breaches of the Codes lend support to arguments favouring unreliability under section 76(2)b. The important legal arguments and consequences of breaches have recently been highlighted by Beaumont (1987). He describes two cases where expert psychological evidence about educational deficits and the inability of the defendants to understand the caution were critical to the defence case.

The relevance and admissibility of a confession are a matter of law and are dealt with by the judge, whereas the question of the *weight* of the admissible confession is a matter for the jury. In a magistrates' court the bench deals with both the admissibility and weight issues.

## FALSE CONFESSION

It is at present impossible to estimate the frequency with which individuals confess to crimes they have not committed. One major problem is that the 'ground truth' (i.e. what actually happened) often remains unknown even after the trial (Gudjonsson and MacKeith, 1982). In practice cases of false confession may not readily be accepted as such by the courts. Only when some 'new' evidence becomes available is the original confession likely to be seen as unreliable.

However, a number of cases have been documented in the literature of genuine false confession (for reviews see Borchard, 1970; Brandon and Davies, 1972; Kassin and Wrightsman, 1985). Such confessions often consist of written and signed statements that are subsequently proven to be falsely self-incriminating.

The most publicized and legally influential case of false confessions in England is that of the Confait Case (Price, 1985). The case involved three youths who falsely confessed in some detail to murder and arson in 1972. After being convicted they spent three years in custody before being released. All three were exonerated in 1979 after the real murderer was apprehended.

After the convictions were quashed by the Court of Appeal, a special enquiry was set up under the chairmanship of Sir Henry Fisher and a report was published in 1977. As the written confessions made by the youths had been quite detailed, and made in the presence of their parents, Sir Henry Fisher wrongly concluded that 'the confessions could not have been made as they were unless at least one of the three boys had been involved in the killing of Confait and in the arson at 27 Doggett Road' (The Fisher Report, 1977). Furthermore, he concluded that two of the boys *could* have been present and taken part in the killing of Confait. Sir Henry Fisher's conclusions are important from a psychological perspective because they illustrate the point that information about the killing was subtly communicated by the police to the boys during ques-

190      Med. Sci. Law (1988) Vol. 28, No. 3

tioning. This made their confessions look credible to Sir Henry Fisher and perhaps to others.

Brandon and Davies (1972) looked at cases where defendants had been convicted mainly on the basis of their own confession, and subsequently the conviction had been quashed or the defendant pardoned. They found that many of the defendants appeared to possess certain idiosyncratic vulnerabilities. These fell into three groups: (i) cognitive deficits (e.g. low intelligence and illiteracy); (ii) low chronological age; and (iii) mental disturbance (e.g. depression). It is important to remember that this work is based on anecdotal case histories and not on a systematic study. Anecdotes do provide an important insight into the phenomenon of false confessions, but unfortunately no systematic study has ever been carried out which provides a method to distinguish reliably between genuine false confessions and genuine true confessions. Gudjonsson and Clark (1986) have provided a detailed theoretical model for understanding the process and outcome of police interrogations. The model integrates the 'leading questions' and 'negative feedback' aspects of suggestibility described by Gudjonsson (1984) and provides a conceptual framework as well as assessment strategies for evaluating retracted confessions. The two basic enduring psychological characteristics relevant to erroneous testimony are considered to be *interrogative suggestibility* and *compliance*. Suggestibility refers to the tendency of the individual to *accept* uncritically information communicated during questioning. It can be reliably measured by a standardized test (Gudjonsson, 1984, 1987a). Compliance, on the other hand, is the tendency of the individual to go along with requests or demands made by people perceived to be in authority, even though the person does not necessarily agree with them (Gudjonsson, 1987b). The main difference between suggestibility and compliance is that the former implies personal acceptance of a proposition. No such personal acceptance of the proposition or request is required in relation to compliance; that is, the person does as requested in order to avoid conflict or confrontation, *not* because of personal acceptance of the request.

## Psychological types of false confession

Kassin and Wrightsman (1985) have suggested three psychological types of false confession. These are:

### 1. *The voluntary confession*

These are offered by people in the absence of any form of external pressure. The common pattern is for these people to go voluntarily to the police station and confess to crimes they have not committed. For example, over 200 people voluntarily confessed in the United States to the Lindbergh kidnapping. In our view, there appear to be at least four different motives for voluntary confessions: (i) a morbid desire for publicity or notoriety; (ii) a desire to aid or protect the real criminal; (iii) the guilt-ridden individual who believes that confessing to the crime will relieve him or her of guilt about some real or imagined previous transgression; and (iv) the mentally disordered person who cannot adequately distinguish between reality and fantasy.

### 2. *The coerced-compliant confession*

This type of false confession is elicited by the nature of the police interview process and the individual is fully aware that he or she did not commit the crime they confess to. That is, the individual does not freely confess but does so because of his or her perception of some immediate instrumental gain. The person may be aware of the potentially long-term consequences of the confession, but the perceived immediate gain (e.g. no more pressure by police officers, being allowed to go home) may be far more powerful in the short term. The individual may believe that somehow the truth will come out later and their innocence will then be established.

### 3. *The coerced-internalized confession*

This type of confession most commonly results from a 'memory distrust syndrome' described by Gudjonsson and MacKeith (1982). Here the person becomes at least temporarily persuaded during police interviewing that he or she might have or did commit the crime they are accused of because they do not trust their own memory and begin to accept suggestions offered by the police.

The case of Peter Reilly (Barthel, 1976) gives a good illustration of how a coerced-internalized confession can occur. When returning home one night Peter Reilly discovered the body of his murdered mother. He notified the police who subsequently gave him a polygraph test, which he failed (i.e. he had a 'deceptive outcome'). The police then used the outcome from the polygraph test to persuade Mr Reilly that he had murdered his mother. He initially denied the murder but gradually became confused and began to distrust his memory, stating 'Well it really looks like I did it', resulting in his signing a written confession. Two years later independent evidence became available which showed that Mr Reilly could not have committed the murder.

It seems on the basis of the available evidence that most cases of false confession that come before the courts are of the compliant-coerced type. These confessions are best explained by the person's desire to escape from a highly stressful and aversive situation. The perceived immediate instrumental gains for confessing become a much more powerful influence on the individual's behaviour than the uncertain long-term effects of the confession, even when the alleged offence is serious.

Whether police pressure and coercion result in a coerced-compliant or a coerced-internalized confession depends on two sets of factors. The first are the idiosyncratic vulnerabilities of the individual. A tendency to become easily confused when placed under pressure, lack of confidence in one's memory and reconstruction of events, and marked susceptibility to suggestion, are probably the most prominent characteristics that make individuals prone to internalizing erroneous information communicated during police questioning. Secondly, there are the nature and circumstances of the police interviews. Coerced-compliant confessions are most easily elicited through aggressive interviewing techniques, whereas coerced-internalized confessions are produced by a more gentle, subtle and trusting form of interviewing. This is because the latter type of confession is dependent upon the individual actually coming to accept the police officers' account of events. Coerced-compliant confessions do not require any such private acceptance and the individual falsely confesses only in order to escape from an intolerable situation.

Another difference between the coerced-internalized and coerced-compliant types of confession has to do with the nature and duration of the confession. The coerced-compliant individual will stick to the false confession only while it has some instrumental value (e.g. until he or she is released from custody or when a solicitor arrives). The coerced-internalized individuals may not retract the confession for quite a while, because they continue

to believe that they must have or might have committed the offence. In fact, the original memory of events may even become permanently distorted and the individual is unable for ever to recall what actually happened at the material time. More commonly, however, once the pressures of the police interview and detention are over and the person's confusional state is settled, the original memory comes back and the individual realizes with certainty that he or she is innocent.

## POLICE INTERVIEWING TECHNIQUES

The nature of the interviewing techniques used by the police are important in several respects. First, they may determine whether or not the accused confesses to the crime in connection with which he or she is being questioned. Second, certain police interviewing techniques may increase the likelihood of a false confession occurring. Third, as discussed above, the type of false confession may be associated with the specific nature of the police interviewing (e.g. subtle v. aggressive). Fourth, it is evident from the Police and Criminal Evidence Act and the Codes of Practice that there is now more emphasis on police behaviour when considering the admissibility and reliability of self-incriminating statements.

Police officers in England and Wales receive little training in interviewing and commonly develop the necessary skills through experience. Various strategies for obtaining a confession from resistant suspects have been reported in the literature (e.g. Inbau and Reid, 1967; Irving and Hilgendorf, 1980). These include confronting suspects with damaging evidence, employing 'information-bluff tricks', minimizing the seriousness of the offence, persuading suspects that it is in their best interest to confess, manipulating self-esteem, 'befriending' the suspect and showing a great deal of understanding and sympathy, and employing the 'Mr Nice and Mr Nasty routine'. The extent to which manipulative tactics are used by police officers can be seen from direct observational studies. For example, Wald et al. (1967) found that the tactics recommended by Inbau and Reid (1967) were frequently employed by police officers in Connecticut. Similarly, Irving (1980) found that police officers in Brighton, England, were using interviewing techniques described in American textbooks on interrogation.

192    Med. Sci. Law (1988) Vol. 28, No. 3

## PSYCHOLOGICAL AND PSYCHIATRIC ASSESSMENT

Retracted confessions involve varied and complicated processes which usually require a detailed assessment of the following:

### Depositions

This involves studying the relevant statements which provide background to the case and the content of the alleged erroneous statements. Sometimes the statements themselves provide important information about the duration, nature and type of interrogation techniques utilized. With the new Codes of Practice a separate 'custody record' must be kept by the police which provides certain information about the arrested person's behaviour while in custody and things offered by the police (e.g. replacement of clothing, meals, visitors).

Gudjonsson and Haward (1983) show how 'forensic stylistic' techniques can be used to identify the true authorship of written confession statements, when the authenticity of these is being challenged.

### Idiosyncratic psychological variables

A range of variables may be relevant depending on the individual case, including intellectual and neuropsychological status, and those of personality. A detailed psychological and psychiatric assessment of the individual may reveal specific vulnerabilities. Persistent personality characteristics such as the presence of phobic symptoms, proneness towards anxiety, memory problems, suggestibility and compliance, give a good indication of ways in which the individual is likely to have coped and reacted to the demand characteristics of the police interview. These qualities may be usefully assessed many years after the alleged false confession was made.

Psychological and psychiatric contributions complement each other and often both are required. In addition to the psychological treatment of mental disorders, the clinical psychologist is trained to administer standardized tests and to study both normal and abnormal behaviour in an objective way. Important indications about certain behavioural characteristics can be compared with those of other groups of subjects (e.g. people of similar age and background to the defendant). The psychiatrist, on the other hand, is a medically trained person who has specialized in mental disorders. These are often relevant to understanding the physical and mental state of the defendant at the time of the police custody and interviews.

### The suspect's mental state

This involves carrying out a careful retrospective analysis of the suspect's behaviour prior to, during and after the police interviews. This may provide important information about the relevant stress-related reactions of the individual concerned and his or her ability to cope with their predicament. The suspect's concerns and state of mind while in police custody may be significant. Did he or she suffer from any physical condition of relevance, for example, peptic ulcer causing pain in the absence of food? Was the person withdrawing from the effects of illicit drugs, alcohol or medication? Had the person slept and eaten normally before the interview? Is there any evidence that the person was disorientated and confused at the time of the interviews, or was suffering from a psychiatric disorder such as an anxiety state or depression? Special care should be taken in examining cases where the suspect is likely to have been experiencing a bereavement reaction while in police custody. This condition may make people exceptionally vulnerable to perceived pressure, especially when they are accused of harming the person they are mourning. Often mental disorder can augment vulnerable qualities and distort the suspect's perceptions of police intentions and behaviour. A psychiatric disorder may also be precipitated by the stressful circumstances of being in police custody and interviewed as a suspect. Suspects who are unfamiliar with police procedures are likely to experience the greatest stress and uncertainty. If the stress is of short duration, the probability is that only if it is of extreme intensity will there be psychiatric sequelae. If, however, the stress is prolonged suspects are more likely to succumb and develop symptoms. Clearly some can cope with these stressors better than others.

Post-traumatic Stress Disorder is a defined condition which has been identified in some people after being interrogated while in custody. If the person suffers from this condition afterwards then this will support the suggestion that the individual was overwhelmed by stress at the time of the police interview and custody, which may have impaired his or her capacity to give a reliable statement. A full medical, psychiatric and developmental history should be obtained when this is considered relevant to the legal issues and the person's welfare. Significant findings may require further enquiries and investigations. Obtaining corroboration and information from independent informants may be very important, especially if defendants are examined a long time after the police interview and the alleged false confession.

In addition to the interrogation techniques themselves there are a number of conditions that can act as a stressor and on occasions these may be more important than the interrogation in producing a false confession. Some of these are: (i) Being kept in custody for a long time; (ii) not being allowed access to a solicitor, family or friends; (iii) having no control over the physical environment; (iv) being in an unfamiliar environment; (v) being subordinate to a powerful legitimate authority; (vi) not being able to eat, sleep and rest properly; (vii) feeling intimidated by the police officers; and (viii) being fearful for personal safety and for mental and physical health.

## CONCLUSIONS

We have in this paper given a brief résumé of the current state of knowledge concerning retracted statements and the identification of false confessions. It is not known how often people confess to serious crimes that they did not commit. However, it is firmly established that false confessions *do* occur on occasions. Why and how false confessions happen depends primarily on three broad factors. First, the particular experiences and needs of the individual. Second, the degree of pressure the suspect is placed under while in police custody and during interviewing. Third, the idiosyncratic vulnerabilities of the suspect which influence how he or she copes with the pressure and demand characteristics of the police interviews. This does not mean that those who falsely confess are invariably mentally handicapped or mentally ill. Normal people are likely to confess to crimes they have not committed if they are placed under sufficient, or the right type of, pressure. Indeed, if the pressures are extreme then it is the characteristics of those who do not confess which are likely to be most unusual.

## REFERENCES

Baldwin J. and McConville M. (1980) Confessions in Crown Court Trials. Royal Commission on Criminal Procedure, Research Study No. 5. London, HMSO.

Barthel J. (1976) *A Death in Canaan.* Thomas Congdon Books.

Beaumont M. (1987) Confessions, Cautions, Experts and the Subnormal after R. v. Silcott and others. *New Law Journal*, August 28, 807–14.

Borchard E. M. (1970) *Convicting the Innocent. Errors of Criminal Justice.* New York, Da Capo Press.

Brandon R. and Davies C. (1972) *Wrongful Imprisonment. Mistaken Convictions and their Consequences.* London, George Allen and Unwin Ltd.

Fisher Report (1977) Report of an Inquiry by the Hon. Sir Henry Fisher into the circumstances leading to the trial of three persons on charges arising out of the death of Maxwell Confait and the fire at 27 Doggett Road, London SE6. London, HMSO.

Gudjonsson G. H. (1984) A new scale of interrogative suggestibility. *Personality and Individual Differences*, 5, 303–14.

Gudjonsson G. H. (1987a) A parallel form to the Gudjonsson Suggestibility Scale. *British Journal of Clinical Psychology*, 26, 215–21.

Gudjonsson G. H. (1987b) Compliance in an interrogative situation: A new scale. In preparation.

Gudjonsson G. H. and Clark N. (1986) Suggestibility in Police Interrogation: A Social Psychological Model. *Social Behaviour*, 1, 83–104.

Gudjonsson G. H. and Haward L. R. C. (1983) Psychological analysis of confession statements. *Journal of the Forensic Science Society*, 23, 113–20.

Gudjonsson G. H. and MacKeith J. (1982) False Confessions. Psychological Effects of Interrogation: A Discussion Paper. In A. Trankell (Ed.) *Reconstructing the Past: The Role of the Psychologist in Criminal Trials.* Stockholm, P. A. Norstedt and Soners Forlag.

Home Office (1978) Judges' Rules and Administrative Directions to the Police. Circular No. 89/1978.

Home Office (1985a) Police and Criminal Evidence Act 1984. London, HMSO.

Home Office (1985b) Police and Criminal Evidence Act 1984 (s. 66). Codes of Practice. London, HMSO.

Inbau F. E. and Reid J. (1967) *Criminal Interrogations and Confessions.* Baltimore. Williams and Wilkins.

Irving B. (1980) Police Interrogation. A Case Study of Current practice. Research Study No. 2. London, HMSO.

Irving B. and Hilgendorf L. (1980) Police Interrogation. The Psychological Approach. Research Study No. 1. London, HMSO.

Kassin S. M. and Wrightsman L. S. (1985) Confession Evidence. In S. M. Kassin and L. S. Wrightman (Eds) *The Psychology of Evidence and Trial Procedure.* Sage Publications.

Mirfield, P. (1985) *Confessions.* London, Sweet & Maxwell.

Mitchell B. (1983) Confessions and Police Interrogation of Suspects. *Criminal Law Review*, September, 596–604.

Price C. (1985) Confession Evidence, the Police and Criminal Evidence Act and the Confait Case. In J. Baxter and L. Koffman. London, Professional Books Ltd.

194      Med. Sci. Law (1988) Vol. 28, No. 3

Vennard J. (1984) Disputes Within Trials Over the Admissibility and Accuracy of Incriminating Statements: Some Research Evidence. *Criminal Law Review*, January, 15–24.

Vennard J. (1985) The Outcome of Contested Trials.

In D. Moxton (Ed.) *Managing Criminal Justice*. A Collection of Papers. London, HMSO.

Wald M., Ayers R., Hess D. W., Schantz M. and Whitebread C. H. (1967) Interrogations in New Haven: The impact of Miranda. *Yale Law Journal*, 76, 1519–1648.

# ANNOUNCEMENT

## Meeting

**Uses of the Forensic Sciences — Forensic Science on Trial** an international conference to be held in Glasgow from 12–15 April 1989. This will follow the pattern of the last such conference with mornings devoted to plenary lectures and afternoons to short 30 minute papers in parallel sessions. You are invited to submit short papers in the areas of Forensic Science, Forensic Medicine, Law, Crime Investigation, Odontology and any other field related to the Forensic Sciences, to Windsor Conferences and Exhibitions, 26 Windsor Crescent, Elderslie, Johnstone, PA5 9QU, U.K.

*Behavioral Assessment*, Vol. 13, pp. 265–291, 1991
Printed in the USA. All rights reserved.

# Statement Validity Assessment:
# Interview Procedures and Content Analysis of
# Children's Statements of Sexual Abuse

DAVID C. RASKIN

*University of Utah*

PHILLIP W. ESPLIN

*Phoenix, Arizona*

This article describes Statement Validity Assessment (SVA), which is a set of
techniques and procedures for obtaining and evaluating statements by children
who have allegedly been sexually abused. SVA consists of a structured interview of the child witness, a system for analyzing in detail the content of the
child's recorded statement (Criteria-Based Content Analysis), and an overall
method (Validity Checklist) for analyzing the validity of the allegations contained in the statement. The need for SVA in sexual abuse cases is described,
together with the history and rationale of its development and details of the
interview and assessment procedures. Some of the research on SVA is
described, but the reader is referred to a companion article (Horowitz, this
issue) for a detailed presentation of the research literature.

Key Words: statement validity assessment; child sexual abuse; content analysis;
interview techniques.

There is a long history of interest and psychological research concerning
children's abilities as witnesses, techniques for interviewing children, and
their susceptibility to suggestion (see Ceci & Bruck, 1991; Ceci, Ross, &
Toglia, 1989; Ceci, Toglia, & Ross, 1987). However, only recently has
attention been paid to differences between accounts provided by typical
bystander witnesses and accounts provided by participants in the events
under investigation (e.g., Raskin & Esplin, 1991). A number of researchers
(Ceci, 1991; Ceci & Bruck, 1991; Pettit, Fegan, & Howie, 1990; Raskin &
Esplin, 1991; Steller, 1991; Yuille & Wells, 1991) have pointed out serious
problems with much of the research concerned with potential impacts of

Requests for reprints should be sent to David C. Raskin, Department of Psychology, University of
Utah, Salt Lake City, UT 84112.

interview techniques on the accuracy of children's statements in sexual abuse cases and the related effects of children's susceptibility to leading and suggestive questioning (e.g., Goodman & Helgeson, 1988; Saywitz, Goodman, Nicholas, & Moan, 1989).

With some notable exceptions (Ceci, DeSimone, Putnick, & Nightingale, in press; Clarke-Stewart, Thompson, & Lepore, 1989; Pettit, Fegan, & Howie, 1990; Steller, Wellershaus, & Wolf, 1988), research has failed to consider motivational differences between bystander witnesses who lack direct involvement in an incident and children who may be motivated to misrepresent incidents of sexual abuse. Bystander witnesses are motivated simply to assist investigations of various crimes, but in sexual abuse cases direct participation and relationships to the accused and other parties at interest may affect the accuracy of reports provided by children who have allegedly been abused.

Research in this area has typically followed the traditional approach of evaluating the relationship of perceptual and memorial abilities of the child witness to the accuracy of the description of the events, rather than being concerned about the potential impacts of the child's motives to report on the validity of the statement. Children are often capable of providing substantially accurate accounts of complex events (valid statements), but under some circumstances they may provide descriptions of events they did not experience (invalid statements). Unlike some approaches (e.g., Faller, 1984), the techniques described in this paper assume that children sometimes provide invalid statements, and interview procedures and assessments of the obtained statement explicitly consider factors that may give rise to invalid statements.

In our system, the term validity refers to accounts that are based on personal experience, even though some details of the statement may be inaccurate, as distinguished from invalid accounts that are invented by the child or are the consequence of influence by others. We use the term validity not in the technical sense of the validity of a psychological test but according to the more general definition of validity as "well-grounded; sound... based on truth or fact... legally sound and effective... qualities that give inner strength and capacity to resist challenge and attack" (Morris, 1969, p. 1414). It is this latter definition that is most relevant to children's statements concerning sexual abuse as they are considered within our legal system. It is crucial to recognize that children's descriptions of personal experiences often contain some inaccuracies, especially concerning peripheral or minor details, but they may still be valid. From a forensic point of view, it is more appropriate to describe this type of statement as valid than to describe it as accurate, since the latter would be incorrect, misleading, and subject to attack in court.

Forensic assessment requires interview techniques designed to elicit relatively complete information from a child in the form of a tape-recorded statement and systematic evaluation procedures to determine the likelihood that this statement about sexual abuse is a basically accurate account of events actually experienced by the child (a valid statement). Statement Validity Assessment (SVA) represents such an approach. It is not a psychological test in the technical sense, but an assessment procedure designed to provide guidance to investigators and evidence that is often useful in administrative and court proceedings. SVA has developed from 40 years of clinical experience based on general psychological and investigative principles, as is the case with most other methods in current practice. Some, but not all parts of the SVA procedures have been subjected to laboratory and field research (for a detailed presentation of the research, see Horowitz, this issue).

## STATEMENT VALIDITY ASSESSMENT

The precursors of SVA, known as Statement Reality Analysis, were developed in Germany in the 1950s (see Undeutsch, 1989, for a brief history). The underlying hypothesis is that a statement derived from memory of an actual experience differs in content and quality from statements based on invention or fantasy. This has been referred to as the Undeutsch hypothesis (Steller, 1989). Based on the early work of Undeutsch, a 1955 ruling by the Supreme Court of Germany required the use of psychological interviews and assessments of credibility in most child sexual abuse cases. This led to the development in Germany and Sweden of various interview procedures and content criteria to assess the credibility of statements made by alleged victims of sexual abuse (Steller & Koehnken, 1989; Undeutsch, 1982).

In spite of 35 years of such applications in more than 30,000 cases (Arntzen, 1982), only recently have there been major efforts to develop a relatively standardized and scientifically based method for interviewing children and systematically evaluating the content of their statements to assess the validity of allegations of sexual abuse (Raskin & Esplin, 1991; Raskin & Steller, 1989; Raskin & Yuille, 1989). To meet investigative objectives and the need to protect children and society in sexual abuse cases in the United States, Raskin and Steller began the development of SVA in 1985. Since then, it has been modified and extended to satisfy the requirements of American justice systems (Raskin, Esplin, & Horowitz, 1991).

The current version of SVA, as described in this paper, represents a partial shift from the traditional German emphasis on the application of content criteria to analyze and interpret the child's statement to a broader analysis that focuses somewhat more on the interview procedures and potential sources of influence on the contents of the child's statement. It is heavily influenced by recent research on the memorial capacities of children and the suggestibility of child witnesses (Doris, 1991; Fivush & Hudson, 1990; for a comprehensive review, see Ceci & Bruck, 1991).

SVA is designed to generate a set of alternative hypotheses about the nature of a reported event, the validity of the accounts, and the identities and roles of the participants. The primary aim is to quickly obtain information that can aid in determining whether a crime has occurred and how best to protect the child and apprehend the responsible person(s). During this investigative process, information may be developed that can serve as the basis for filing formal charges and possibly be presented as evidence in a civil and/or criminal proceeding. In many instances, a compelling video-taped interview of the child may be used to confront the accused and settle the case, often by confession. In the small, but significant proportion of cases where the allegations are false (Brigham, 1991; Raskin & Yuille, 1989), it is important to make a determination as early as possible in order to minimize the problems created both for the falsely accused person and the child who has invented or been coached to make a false accusation. It must be emphasized that the main value of SVA lies in its utility for gathering information, guiding investigations, making administrative decisions, and exercising prosecutorial discretion. In some cases, the results of SVA are presented as evidence through expert testimony in court.

SVA consists of three major components: (a) a structured interview of the child witness, (b) a criteria-based content analysis (CBCA) that systematically assesses the contents and qualities of the obtained statement according to the Undeutsch hypothesis, and (c) integration of the CBCA with information derived from a set of questions (Validity Checklist) that combine the results of the content analysis with other relevant information and factors derived from an analysis of the interview(s). This process yields an overall assessment of the probable validity of the statement that is based on all of the foregoing and any other available information that may assist in interpreting the obtained results. It is important to note that the purpose of SVA is to provide an assessment of the *validity of the recorded statement, not of the general credibility of the child witness.*

The interview procedure had its origins in the work of Undeutsch (1982) and was modified by Steller (1986). Following several years of research and experience with Steller's methods, the version described here was developed jointly by Esplin, Raskin, and Horowitz (Raskin, Esplin, & Horowitz, 1991). The content analysis (CBCA) also had its origins in the work of Undeutsch (1982, 1989), with additional material drawn from Arntzen, Szewczyk, and Trankell (Steller, 1989; Steller & Koehnken, 1989). Based on recent research (see Horowitz, this issue), we have modified the list of content criteria and their definitions (Raskin, Esplin, & Horowitz, 1991). The Validity Checklist also evolved from Undeutsch's Statement Reality Analysis (Undeutsch, 1982, 1989) and was reorganized by Steller and Raskin (1986). Subsequent research and experience in many sexual abuse investigations and court cases produced further revisions that resulted in the current version of the Validity Checklist (Raskin, Esplin, & Horowitz, 1991).

It should be noted that many aspects of the interview and validity assessment procedures are not based on research that directly compares specific procedures, which would be very difficult to conduct, but are derived from the general psychological and developmental literature (for overviews, see Ceci & Bruck, 1991, and Garbarino, Stott, & Faculty of the Erikson Institute, 1989) combined with extensive experience in conducting interviews and performing assessments in actual cases. Although other approaches may utilize similar procedures, they may also differ in major ways (e.g., American Academy of Child and Adolescent Psychiatry, 1988; Jones & McQuiston, 1988; MacFarlane & Waterman, 1986; Sgroi, Porter, & Blick, 1982; Slicner & Hanson, 1989; Walker, 1988; White, Strom, Santilli, & Quinn, 1987). Since adherence to our recommended interview techniques and procedures is necessary to maintain the integrity of CBCA and SVA, it is necessary to provide a rather detailed description of the recommended interview process.

## STATEMENT ANALYSIS INTERVIEW

### General Principles

A structured interview of the child witness (alleged victim) must precede the CBCA, and the interviewer must be familiar with the content criteria in order to understand the specific requirements and procedures of the interview. This technique is designed for the situation in which someone has reported that the child has made an allegation of sexual abuse. Therefore, the SVA interviewer is not confronted with the common situation where someone suspects that the child has been sexually abused but no disclosure has been made. The latter situation is frequently reported by parents, school counselors, social workers, and therapists, but it does not provide an adequate basis for proceeding with an investigative interview.

Since there is no accepted set of diagnostic indicators nor any recognized child sexual abuse syndrome (Corwin, 1988; Levy, 1989), mere suspicions of sexual abuse should be carefully explored by other, nonsuggestive means and evaluated along with other reasonable explanations for the observed behaviors. If the child does make an allegation during the course of such explorations, then it is appropriate and imperative that the child be interviewed as soon as possible by a trained and skilled investigative interviewer who is not the person that elicited the allegations and who has no preexisting relationship with the child. This interview is not therapy, and having the same person perform both tasks, which employ different methods for different purposes, may create a dual-role conflict. These potential problems have been recognized by professional associations, and such dual-role conflicts are discouraged (e.g., American Academy of Child and Adolescent Psychiatry, 1988; Committee on Ethical Guidelines for Forensic Psychologists, 1991).

These procedures can be utilized with child witnesses from approximately 2-1/2 to 17 years of age. However, children below age 4 may present special problems of limited verbal and cognitive abilities and social skills, discomfort, short attention span, and poor control during the interview. Adolescent witnesses may present other problems in terms of considerably more sexual knowledge, skills at manipulating the interview situation, and control issues. The interviewer must be sensitive to these problems and should recognize that some child witnesses cannot be productively interviewed.

This type of interview normally lasts between 20 and 45 minutes, sometimes longer when special problems require resolution of alternative hypotheses (see below). Certain guidelines should be followed to maximize the information obtained and minimize ambiguities, disruptions, and distress experienced by the child. In our experience, anatomical dolls, puppets, drawings, good touch/bad touch games, and toys are generally unnecessary and should be avoided whenever possible. They frequently distract the child from the task of providing complete and accurate descriptions, and they can be suggestive, provoke fantasy, and lack a scientific basis (Everson & Boat, 1990; Levy, 1989; Raskin & Yuille, 1989). For example, Everson and Boat reported that in a sample of 223 children between 3 and almost 6 years old who were not suspected of having been abused, more than 15% demonstrated clear or suggestive intercourse positioning when the interviewer provided them with anatomical dolls (for a summary of this literature, see Ceci & Bruck, 1991). The most convincing evidence is an unambiguous and detailed statement in the child's own words.

The interviewer should take great care to use language and concepts that are appropriate for the age and cognitive development of the child. Questions or comments that create an unreasonable expectation or performance burden for the child or that imply criticism or praise should be totally avoided. Questions should be asked one at a time, obtaining an answer prior to asking the next question. Multiple questions are confusing to adults as well as children and create ambiguities as to the meaning of the answer, or nonanswer. If the child does not answer immediately, the interviewer should be patient and wait, repeating or rephrasing the question if necessary. The interviewer who does not wait for answers may never find out what the child might have said.

Sometimes the interviewer is more uncomfortable than the child, which can lead to problems. Children are often less inhibited or ashamed than adults, especially since young children do not have the same understanding of sexual events as do adults. If the interviewer suggests that it is difficult or embarrassing to discuss the sexual matters, the child may become as inhibited as the interviewer. If the child expresses shame or embarrassment, the interviewer can reassure the child that the interviewer is accustomed to talking with children about such matters and it will be easy for them to talk about it without embarrassment. This is usually all that is needed to get the child started. Crying and other forms of disruptive behavior should not be addressed directly, as this can magnify the problems by shifting the child's attention from the cognitive task of recalling and describing the events to a focus on emotional factors and distress. Instead, the topic or focus should be immediately shifted to something less threatening or emotional, such as "I can't see those pretty eyes" or "I can't see how many teeth you have. Let's count them." Once the emotion has subsided, the interviewer can return to the cognitive focus of the interview.

The interviewer must be prepared to persevere in asking questions in order to obtain a complete and accurate statement, even if it may become somewhat difficult or unpleasant for the child. This is critical in order to resolve the issues, to protect an abused child from further harm, to apprehend the perpetrator, or to help a child as soon as possible to acknowledge a false allegation made against an innocent person. These are the primary purposes and goals of an investigative interview. However, the interviewer should be sensitive at all times to the emotional state and well-being of the child and should never be aggressive or engage in pressure tactics, which can be counterproductive.

*Preliminary Preparation*

Prior to beginning the interview, the interviewer should become familiar with as much case material as possible. This should include investigative and medical reports; all statements and reports made by others; the reported contents and contexts of the original and subsequent disclosures by the child; all previous interviews by investigators, professionals, and adults; available information about the child's cognitive and social development and any medical or psychological problems; living arrangements and any history of drug or alcohol abuse or violence in the family; significant adults and their relationships to the child witness and among each other; information that may indicate prior exposure of the child to sexually explicit materials or activities; and any prior history of confirmed or alleged sexual abuse of the child, family members, or close acquaintances.

Prior to interviewing the alleged victim (child witness), interviews of other family members (parents, grandparents, siblings) may be helpful. It is usually advisable to interview the child's parent or custodian in order to obtain information that may be useful in the interview, such as their knowledge of the allegations, the terms the child uses for the relevant body parts, the child's family members, friends, pets, interests and typical activities, and any other information that may help the interviewer to establish rapport, especially with young children and adolescents.

## Alternative Hypotheses

The interviewer should develop a set of hypotheses that may be explored, modified, or rejected during the course of the interview. In most cases, the primary hypothesis is that the allegations against the accused are valid. Alternative hypotheses often include, but are not limited to, the following:

1. The allegations are basically valid but the child has substituted a different person for the perpetrator,
2. The fundamental allegations are valid, but the child has invented or been influenced to make additional allegations that are false,
3. The child has been influenced or pressured to make a completely false allegation to serve the needs of someone else,
4. The child has made a false allegation for personal motives of revenge, gain, or to help someone else, and
5. The child has fantasized the allegations, possibly because of psychological problems.

The major purpose of the interview is to gather as much information as possible in order to evaluate the alternative hypotheses. Therefore, the interviewer must prepare a plan for the interview, which may require adjustments as the interview progresses. It is helpful to make a brief list of topics and questions that must be covered during the interview, make very brief notes during the interview as reminders to cover additional questions that arise, and review the list before terminating the interview. The latter may be accomplished during a short break when the interviewer may leave the room and possibly confer with investigators or other professionals who are observing. The specific approach to exploring and comparing the alternative hypotheses will vary as a function of the case information, the material elicited from the child during the interview, and application of the Validity Checklist to the material available at the conclusion of all interviews and CBCA analyses.

Some experts (e.g., White, this issue; White, Strom, Santilli, & Quinn, 1987) have advocated that the interviewer be blind with regard to the specific allegations, so as not to bias the outcome of the interview. However, to begin the interview totally ignorant of the allegations and the important surrounding information would make it virtually impossible to develop alternative hypotheses, conduct a complete interview, and obtain the information necessary to confirm the validity of the allegations or to reject them in favor of the most reasonable alternative hypotheses. This blind approach is analogous to asking a detective to interview a witness to a crime without knowing anything about the initial report, the details of the crime, the identities of the suspect and other witnesses, or any other evidence that might be helpful in solving the crime. Some may believe that a blind approach is a means to prevent bias and undue influence by the interviewer, but recent research with preschool children (Pettit et al., 1990) indicates that blind interviewers tend to ask leading questions and that they obtain the least amount of information from children. Carefully structured interviews conducted by well-prepared interviewers can overcome problems of potential bias and influence and can also obtain more useful information.

## The Interview Setting

The setting of the interview is important. It should be a supportive but neutral atmosphere designed to maximize the performance level of the child witness. This begins with a friendly introduction to the child outside of the interview room. With young children, a playroom may be useful for the initial introduction, but the interview should always be conducted in a pleasant and simply furnished room that is as free as possible from distracters, such as toys and games. The child should be seated in a comfortable chair that brings the child near the level of the interviewer. This facilitates communication, helps the child to perform at a relatively high cognitive level, and assists in controlling very young children by setting physical boundaries. No other person should be present during the interview, especially significant adults such as parents or caretakers. It may sometimes be necessary to have other professionals observe from outside the room by video monitor, but they should never be allowed to interrupt the interview. The interview must be recorded in its entirety, preferably on videotape with equipment located unobtrusively.

In order to apply CBCA and SVA effectively, the interviewer must attempt to obtain as complete a statement as possible using a structured interview designed to maximize the amount of information provided by the child witness and to minimize contamination of its contents by the interviewer and other adults and previous interviewers. At the same time, the main goal is to obtain extensive free narrative without imposing unnecessary structure. The resulting statement should reflect the child's memory and knowledge of the events, as described by the child.

Since it is well known that accuracy is usually highest when free recall procedures are used (Dent, 1991; Garbarino et al., 1989, p. 53; Goodman & Reed, 1986; Poole & White, 1991), direct questions are asked only after completion of the free narrative phase and only when necessary. Direct questions must be followed by open questions that attempt to elicit a free narrative concerning any allegations or affirmative responses elicited by direct questions. Suggestive questions are inappropriate, except when appropriately employed toward the end of the interview to assess the child's susceptibility to suggestion (see below). The overriding principle is that material the child provides spontaneously or in a free narrative is always superior to brief, simple responses elicited by direct questions.

### Establishing Rapport and Context

The interviewer should escort the child to the interview room, in the presence of the accompanying adult, when necessary. After separation and starting the tape, the interviewer should engage the child in conversation, drawing on the information previously obtained about the child. It is useful to ask the child about something interesting or pleasant that the interviewer knows the child has recently experienced. This builds rapport and encourages a narrative performance style. It also provides a free narrative sample and baseline assessment of the child's verbal, cognitive, expressive, and memorial capacities that can be used to adjust the interviewer's language and questions during the interview. This sample is also used for comparison purposes when performing the CBCA. If no suitable topic is readily available, this can be accomplished by asking the child to describe chronologically all activities since getting up that morning, including the trip to the site of the interview.

The child should be motivated to be completely truthful during the interview. The interviewer should establish a pleasant but serious atmosphere that conveys the expectation that only the truth will be related about events that really happened. It may be useful to discuss the difference between truth and lies and to emphasize the importance of telling the truth in the interview, keeping in mind that children under age 9 usually do not understand how deceit breaks trust and that many preschoolers do not consider it wrong to exaggerate or add fantasized material (Pettit et al., 1990). The interviewer should not pressure the child or create performance expectations that may interfere with a productive interview, such as conveying an unwillingness to accept the child's responses. The interviewer should maintain control at all times to keep the child focused on the purpose of the interview and to prevent the child from physically or psychologically avoiding the task at hand, without causing the child to experience physical discomfort or unnecessary distress.

### Eliciting a Free Narrative

If the child spontaneously mentions the situation or allegations under investigation, the interviewer should encourage a free narrative immediately.

Otherwise, the interviewer must introduce the topic in a general, non-leading manner. Possible lead-in questions might take the form, "I understand there is a problem in your family and I need you to tell me about it so that I can help" or "I understand that something may have happened to you and I need you to tell me all about it as best you can." If the child does not begin right away, be patient. If the child appears confused, it may be necessary to give a minimal hint to get the child started, such as "I understand that you told your mom something about what happened to you and now you're here to tell me about it" or "I heard that someone did something to you, who was that? [child indicates] Okay, now tell me all about that as best you can." Never ask questions in a form that permits the child to avoid or not cooperate, such as "Would you like to tell me about what happened?"

Once the child begins to describe the events, the interviewer must be patient, must never interrupt the child, and must try to encourage and maintain the free narrative as long as possible until the child seems to have finished. The interviewer must concentrate on obtaining the child's statement in the child's words, not the interviewer's version of what the child should say. When the child pauses, maintain the narrative by simple devices, such as "uh huh," "and then," restating the child's last few words, or briefly summarizing by saying "so you told me ___ , and then what happened?" When the child appears to have finished describing the events, the interviewer should ask open-ended questions such as, "Did anything else happen? [Yes] Tell me about that."

If the child does not initially provide complete descriptions of one or more incidents, the child should be allowed to complete the narrative. Only then should the interviewer attempt to elicit more detailed descriptions about each of these incidents. Allowing the child to recall and relate whatever comes to mind maximizes the likelihood of obtaining all of the important information. Imposing specific structure too early in the interview may preclude obtaining valuable information. Sometimes the allegations involve a series of events over a period of time, resulting in a script memory. Under these circumstances, the child may have difficulty focusing on only one event, and the interviewer should assist the child by asking, "Tell me about the time you remember best" or "Tell me about the last time [the first time] it happened." This often produces a more detailed description without any specific suggestion as to content.

## Cue Questioning

These open-ended questions are used to elicit additional detail that seems necessary to complete descriptions of events already described or to elicit information about events that previous statements or other sources indicate may have happened. The child might be asked, "You said that something also happened in the car, tell me about that," or "I heard that something may have happened at the swimming pool, tell me about that." Sometimes a more specific cue drawn from information provided prior to the interview may be used, such as "I heard that there may have been something that made a buzzing sound, tell me about that." Note that these questions contain a specific reference or cue, but they always end with an open question designed to elicit a more detailed description without suggesting the content.

## Direct Questioning

Direct questioning should be used only if the previously elicited material has inadequate detail or requires clarifications of ambiguities, apparent inconsistencies, or implausibilities. For example, the child described a sexual act of penetration but did not mention anything about the removal of clothing. The interviewer might say, "I am a little confused. You said he put his pee-pee in your bottom but everyone had their clothes on. Tell me how that happened?" or "So, you said he was sitting next to you and then he put his thing inside you. How did that happen?" Direct questions are used to elicit additional information without suggesting what the answer should be, and they should always end or be followed right away with an open question to ensure an opportunity for the child to provide detail that goes beyond anything that might be specifically implied by the question. For example, it may be necessary to ask a young child, "Did she take your clothes off?" If the answer is "Yes," the next question is "Tell me about that."

## Probing Questions

Specific, probing questions may be needed, depending on the hypotheses to be explored and the content and quality of the material obtained up to this point in the interview. If the child's statement appears to strongly support the allegations against the accused and the alternative hypotheses seem very unlikely, it may be unnecessary to pursue other possibilities. However, some cases require further exploration at this point in order to obtain information to evaluate alternative hypotheses. One type of problem arises when a child describes something that seems unlikely, such as having been abused at an early age and not being able to remember much about it. The question might be, "You told me he did that when you were only two, but you said you don't remember it. How do you know what happened?"

Another problem arises when there are contradictions within or between statements by the child or others. In order to avoid creating a confrontational atmosphere, the interviewer can express confusion and request the child's assistance. For example, the child stated that the event occurred in the evening when the mother was away, his sister was at home, and the accused (baby-sitter) locked the sister in her room prior to the alleged sexual acts; however, the sister denied any such events. The interviewer might say, "I am a little confused. You told me that he locked Annie in her room, but I thought Annie said she wasn't even there. I need you to help me understand that."

If there is a suspicion that the child has been influenced by others, questions may be asked for evaluating that possibility, such as "Did anyone talk to you about what you should say to me?" or "Has your mom told you what to say today?" Affirmative answers to these probing questions should always be followed with an open question if the child does not volunteer additional information. The answers to these questions may either clarify the ambiguity or provide information that confirms an alternative hypothesis and disconfirms the primary hypothesis. This can be difficult and risky with young children who have not yet developed metamemory (Nelson, 1986) or who do not clearly understand the meaning of this question.

It must be emphasized that even if the primary hypothesis is that the allegations are invalid for one reason or another, the interviewer must begin by attempting to elicit a free narrative concerning the allegations. If the child fails to provide content and quality that support the allegation, the interviewer can be more confident in exploring the alternative hypotheses using probing questions and follow-up open-ended questions to elicit free narrative concerning the possible invalidity of the allegations. However, during the free narrative portion, the child may actually provide convincing content and descriptions that can form the basis for rejecting alternative hypotheses and reinforcing the hypothesis that the original allegations are valid.

The free narrative is crucial in finding out what the child is able to report, independent of what the interviewer or others believe that the child will report. If the interviewer does not provide such an opportunity but influences and contaminates the contents of the child's statement, then we may never know what happened. Influence and contamination have occurred in many celebrated problem cases, such as the McMartin Preschool case (Blumfield, 1990; Hagedorn, 1991; Roark, 1990) and the Kelly Michaels and Robert Fijnje cases (Ceci & Bruck, 1991). In the Jordan, Minnesota, cases (Humphrey, 1985), one of the children recanted and then admitted that he invented detailed descriptions of abuse because he "could tell what they wanted me to say by the way they asked the questions" (Benedek & Schetky, 1989, p. 915).

## Suggestive Questions

If the child shows indications of suggestibility during the interview or possible effects of inappropriate influence inferred from other information, it may be useful to further explore this toward the end of the interview, after other purposes have been accomplished. This is especially important when the interview has failed to produce convincing support for the validity of the allegations and/or the child has made statements that are very unrealistic or unlikely to be valid. In these circumstances, the interviewer may ask questions designed to elicit additional unrealistic descriptions, such as "Did anything like this ever happen when your mom was at home?" or "when your teacher was in the room?" or "when you were riding your bicycle?" Such questions must be used with caution and only when there is good reason to do so. Inappropriate or unnecessary suggestive questioning might cause a child to acquiesce and weaken an otherwise valid statement. Therefore, if the child accepts a suggestion, an open question (e.g., "Tell me about that") should always follow. If the child rejects suggestions, it may reduce the likelihood that the allegations are the result of influence or suggestibility or it may simply mean that the child recognizes the implausibility of the suggested events. Since it is possible that a child may demonstrate suggestibility even though the allegations are valid or reject suggestions when providing an invalid account, the mere presence or absence of suggestibility is not definitive for assessing the validity of the allegations (see Validity Checklist below).

*Ending the Interview*

When the interviewer has attempted to obtain and clarify all of the information in accord with the interview plan, it is time to end the interview. It should always end on a positive tone that leaves the child feeling good, even when the child has discussed matters that are emotionally distressing or has admitted making an invalid accusation. In either case, the child will be relieved at having told the truth. The interviewer should introduce a topic that will be pleasant for the child to discuss, such as plans for the upcoming holiday, a birthday, an outing with friends or family, or school activities. Finally, the child should be thanked for coming and then returned to the custodian.

## CRITERIA-BASED CONTENT ANALYSIS

The basic purpose of CBCA is to determine if the qualities and specific contents of the child's recorded statement obtained during the structured interview are indicative of a report produced by attempts to recall actual memories or if they appear to be the result of invention, fantasy, or influence by another person. The verbal content of the statement is analyzed by applying a set of criteria to the verbatim transcript obtained from the tape recording of the entire interview. When applying the content criteria,

## TABLE 1
### Content Criteria for Statement Analysis[a]

**General Characteristics**

1. Logical Structure — Is the statement coherent? Is the content logical? Do the different segments fit together? (Note: Peculiar or unique details or unexpected complications do not diminish logical structure.)
2. Unstructured Production — Are the descriptions unconstrained? Is the report somewhat unorganized? Are there digressions or spontaneous shifts of focus? Are some elements distributed throughout? (Note: This criterion requires that the account be logically consistent.)
3. Quantity of Details — Are there specific descriptions of place or time? Are persons, objects, and events specifically described? (Note: Repetitions do not count.)

**Specific Contents**

4. Contextual Embedding - Are events placed in spatial and temporal context? Is the action connected to other incidental events, such as routine daily occurrences?
5. Interactions — Are there reports of actions and reactions or conversation composed of a minimum of three elements involving at least the accused and the witness?
6. Reproduction of Speech — Is speech or conversation during the incident reported in its original form? (Note: Unfamiliar terms or quotes are especially strong indicators, even when attributed to only one participant.)
7. Unexpected Complications — Was there an unplanned interruption or an unexpected complication or difficulty during the sexual incident?
8. Unusual Details — Are there details of persons, objects, or events that are unusual, yet meaningful in this context? (Note: Unusual details must be realistic.)
9. Superfluous Details — Are peripheral details described in connection with the alleged sexual events that are not essential and do not contribute directly to the specific allegations? (Note: If a passage satisfies any of the specific criteria 4-18, it probably is not superfluous.)
10. Accurately Reported Details Misunderstood — Did the child correctly describe an object or event but interpret it incorrectly?
11. Related External Associations - Is there reference to a sexually-toned event or conversation of a sexual nature that is related in some way to the incident but is not part of the alleged sexual offenses?
12. Subjective Experience — Did the child describe feelings or thoughts experienced at the time of the incident? (Note: This criterion is not satisfied when the witness responds to a direct question, unless the answer goes beyond the question.)
13. Attribution of Accused's Mental State — Is there reference to the alleged perpetrator's feelings or thoughts during the incident? (Note: Descriptions of overt behavior do not qualify.)

**Motivation-Related Contents**

14. Spontaneous Corrections or Additions — Were corrections offered or information added to material previously provided in the statement? (Note: Responses to direct questions do not qualify.)
15. Admitting Lack of Memory or Knowledge — Did the child indicate lack of memory or knowledge of an aspect of the incident? (Note: In response to a direct question, the answer must go beyond "I don't know" or "I can't remember.")
16. Raising Doubts About One's Own Testimony — Did the child express concern that some part of the statement seems incorrect or unbelievable? (Note: Merely asserting that one is telling the truth does not qualify.)
17. Self-Deprecation — Did the child describe some aspect of his/her behavior related to the sexual incident as wrong or inappropriate?
18. Pardoning the Accused — Did the child make excuses for or fail to blame the alleged perpetrator, or minimize the seriousness of the acts, or fail to add to the allegations when an opportunity occurred?

[a] Adapted from Raskin & Esplin (1991).

shown in Table 1, it is necessary to consider the age, experience, and cognitive skill level of the witness.

Implicit in the Undeutsch hypothesis is the assumption that only a person who actually experienced an event is likely to incorporate certain types of contents into a statement that describes the experience. For example, it is assumed that persons who invent an account are unlikely to speak as if they are reexperiencing the episode, such as describing actual speech by one or more participants, or to indicate how they or the accused person felt or what they were thinking at the time of the incident, or to relate an unexpected intrusion of another person who disrupted the event, or to accurately describe objects or acts with which they were not familiar and whose purpose or meaning they did not understand.

The Undeutsch hypothesis also assumes that persons who fabricate accounts are also unlikely to say things that could be interpreted as indicating that they are making up a story. For example, dissembling witnesses may take risks in drawing attention to the fact that their accounts are not believable, and they might not spontaneously make corrections in their accounts. Furthermore, witnesses who invent stories to cause problems for someone else are not likely to state that it was at least partly their fault that the sexual abuse incident occurred or that the alleged offenses were really not very serious. According to the Undeutsch hypothesis, these elements reinforce the validity of a statement by a witness, indicating that it is likely to have been produced from actual memory, as opposed to fabrication, fantasy, or some other source of information or influence.

Although the assumptions underlying the use of the content criteria were originally derived from clinical experience in more than 30,000 actual cases in Germany (Arntzen, 1982; Steller & Koehnken, 1989; Undeutsch, 1989), recent research has provided general support for the utility of CBCA in differentiating between valid and invented statements obtained from children (Boychuk, 1991; Raskin & Esplin, 1991; Steller, 1989; Yuille, 1988) and even statements made by adults (Landry & Brigham, in press). The three criteria based on the general characteristics of the statement as a whole and most of the 10 criteria that refer to the specific contents of the statement have been shown to differentiate between valid and invalid statements. However, the five content criteria that are based on assumptions concerning motivations of the reporting witness have received only mixed support (Boychuk, 1991; Steller, 1989). A detailed description of the current status of research on CBCA is provided by Horowitz (this issue).

A major limitation of CBCA is the difficulty in applying it to situations where the witness has other sources of information from which to invent an accusation that incorporates some or many of the content criteria. Thus, a child witness who had prior sexual experience, such as a sexually active adolescent or preadolescent or a child who has been sexually abused by someone other than the accused, might provide a convincing but false statement by drawing on memories derived from other experiences. Therefore, such possibilities must be considered when conducting the interview and especially when applying the Validity Checklist after the CBCA has been completed.

Three major categories of content criteria are used in CBCA. The analysis of the transcript of the recorded statement begins with an evaluation of the general characteristics of the statement. It then proceeds to identify specific contents that may be present, and it concludes with attempts to locate specific passages that are based on assumptions concerning the motives of a truthfully reporting witness. Each of these 18 criteria is defined in Table 1, and we shall attempt to illustrate the latter two categories with examples of passages that satisfy each of the criteria. A complete exposition is not possible in this article, and more extensive descriptions and examples are available in Raskin et al., (1991). In order to learn to use this method effectively, it is advisable to receive the type of training offered in 2- or 3-day workshops. However, research indicates that 45 to 90 minutes of training is sufficient to enable college students to significantly improve their accuracy in differentiating between valid and invalid statements given by children (Steller, 1989) and by adults (Landry & Brigham, in press).

The first category requires an examination of the statement as a whole to assess the presence or absence of **General Characteristics** (Criteria 1–3). For the statement to be considered realistic, it must have a *logical structure* and contain a *quantity of details* that meaningfully describe and illustrate the alleged sexual events. These characteristics are expected in all valid statements. Obviously, a statement that is fundamentally without logic and lacking in basic details cannot be accepted as valid. Even an invalid account must have some details, but a valid account should give enough detailed information to provide a basis for knowing the specific nature of the acts and some of the surrounding circumstances (see Table 1). For example, if the alleged abuse occurred in a place or circumstances familiar to the child (a day care or home setting), then additional details must be provided to demonstrate that sexual acts occurred there. However, in assessing the presence of these criteria, it must be recognized that a relatively simple sexual incident described by a young and inexperienced child tends to have simpler structure and fewer details than an account of complex and repeated sexual acts provided by an older, more experienced child. Therefore, the evaluator must adjust the criterion to consider those factors along with the child's cognitive and expressive skills as demonstrated during the interview.

*Unstructured production* is also very important because it refers to the style and sequence of descriptions that are characteristic of accounts generated from actual memory of an experience. However, an overly structured account may lack a free narrative description because of the child's limited cognitive or expressive skills or excessive structure imposed by the interviewer. Therefore, unstructured production is important but not an absolute requirement for a valid statement, and this issue is specifically addressed in the Validity Checklist.

The remaining two categories are comprised of Criteria 4–18 that refer to particular passages in the statement, rather than the statement as a whole. In evaluating the presence or absence of these criteria, the underlying question for each criterion is whether a witness who may be misrepresenting the events would be likely and is capable of inventing a statement with these contents and qualities. This is especially useful when analyzing a statement obtained from a child who has limited knowledge and experience in sexual matters. Such a witness would have great difficulty relating a fabricated account that would satisfy even a few of these content criteria.

**Specific Contents** refers to particular passages in the statement. Such contents provide the concreteness and vividness characteristic of actually experienced events. The first two specific criteria are especially important. *Contextual embedding* is expected in valid accounts, but it may also be present to a lesser extent in fabricated accounts. Since a sexual event must occur at *some* time and at *some* location, only obviously unconvincing accounts would be totally lacking in context. Therefore, the presence of this criterion requires more than a minimal description of context of the type "He did it to me at home when my parents were out." For example, a 7-year-old boy related, "Mr. S. would ask me to come over and play after school 'cause Mrs. S. had to go clean people's houses then. We would go in his garage and play with the electric train. We had to take off our clothes and put on bathrobes 'cause our clothes might get dirty and my mom would be mad at me. Then he would put his hand inside and touch my thing."

Similarly, even an invalid description of a sexual event must incorporate at least some actions on the part of the accused person. Simply describing events in the form "He did X, and then he did Y, and then he did Z" is not sufficient. The criterion of *interactions* requires a a minimum of three elements in the form of actions and reactions involving at least the accused and the witness, hence the term interactions. For example, a 13-year-old girl stated, "and then he hit me, and then he took my shirt off [actions by the accused], and then I was struggling from him [reaction by the witness], and then he unbuttoned my pants [action by the accused], and then I tried to kick him away from me [reaction by the witness]."

Other specific contents are expected to occur relatively less frequently, even in valid accounts. Therefore, the validity of a statement is strongly supported by the presence of some criteria, but their absence does not necessarily invalidate the statement. This is especially true for many of the remaining criteria. *Reproduction of speech* may be absent in a substantial proportion of statements, but its presence can be very compelling. A child who was not abused is unlikely to provide what appears to be a verbatim reproduction of an utterance that is expressed in terms of the different speakers. For example, a 9-year-old girl who was assisting her mother in a prostitution business stated, "She asked me if I could just answer the phone, and I said 'Yeh,' and she told me, 'Just say that someone will call you back and it's a hundred dollars per hour.'" When the speech incorporates adult expressions that are obviously appropriate to a situation that would normally be unfamiliar to children (as in this example), it reinforces the inference that it was recalled from memory of the experience.

*Unexpected complications* refers to contents that are unlikely to be incorporated into fictitious accounts, even by adult deceivers and most especially not by children. For example, a child would be unlikely to invent the unexpected arrival of another person, especially if it has rather novel elements, such as "We were on the bed and he was rubbing my thing. He stopped when they knocked on the door to bring us our pizza." Even an adult would be unlikely to tell the child to fabricate an unanticipated event such as, "I fell off the couch and hit my head on the coffee table, so he had to stop."

The criterion of *unusual details* speaks for itself. For example, it is highly unlikely that a 4-year-old boy could obtain information to invent a description of a pedophile who molested children at preschool. He related, "Dr. T. would take us in the bathroom to check for sand in our pants and see if sand was in our butts. He put on one white glove when he checked our butts." Since *superfluous details* are not essential to the allegations, they support the inference that the child is recalling the event from memory of the experience. For example, a 9-year-old girl described, "I was in my room taking my afternoon nap and he was outside. Then he came in and put the cat outside like he always does 'cause he gots allergies, and then he came in my room."

*Accurately reported details misunderstood* is a criterion that is even less frequently encountered, but its presence can be very compelling. It is extremely unlikely for children to invent something that is generally unfamiliar to them, describe it correctly, and also demonstrate a misunderstanding of their own inventions. For example, an 8-year-old girl described, "It's like his privates, but it's his snake. It's like a white stick with a brown, round ball on the top and it makes noises." *Related external associations* provide information that indirectly indicates a sexual relationship with the child, making it unlikely to be invented. It would be expected in relating an alleged incident only when a sexual relationship with the child has actually occurred, because such relationships are the only ones likely to provide the context for this type of sexually-toned material. For example, a 14-year-old girl stated, "He talked about the women he had done it with and the differences in them."

Descriptions of *subjective experience* may occur when the witness recalls thoughts or feelings experienced during the incident. A witness who did not have this subjective experience is unlikely to invent this type of detail, whereas such descriptions are often spontaneously offered when people attempt to recall an emotionally laden event that they experienced. For example, a 12-year-old boy related, "He took me out in the desert and that was when I thought he was gonna kill me." Similar considerations underlie the importance of *attributions of accused's mental state*. Since information about another's subjective state is not directly observable and must be inferred from other information and behavior, such contents may be even less likely to be invented, especially by children who are relatively unsophisticated and generally unable to assume the psychological perspectives of adults. Such attributions strengthen the validity of the account. An example was provided by an 8-year-old girl who reported, "I told him to stop and he wouldn't, 'cause he didn't hear me 'cause he was dreaming."

The final category of content criteria, **Motivation-Related Contents**, refers to motives of the witness in the sense that a fabricating witness is not expected to incorporate such contents into the account. Thus, a lying or coached witness is expected to attempt to maintain the basic story without modification, to try to answer all questions even if that requires additional fabrication, and not to raise doubts about the believability of the story, blame oneself for the events, or minimize the negative characterizations of the accused. However, this category includes some criteria that one could argue might be provided by a witness who has fabricated an allegation and is experiencing some ambivalence about having done so. This could be expressed in the form of concerns about actual untruthfulness and lack of knowledge, or blaming oneself and pardoning the accused because the allegations are not true. Furthermore, these criteria may be different from the other criteria in that they require inferences about witnesses' motivations, which is not the same as making inferences about the characteristics of reports derived from the memory of an experience. Based on these considerations and the questions raised by some research (Steller, 1989), it is advisable to be cautious with these criteria until more research data are available.

Attempts to recall an actual experience, especially a complex set of events, do not typically result in complete and strictly chronological descriptions. It is quite common to observe *spontaneous corrections or additions* to the statement, even when it has been told more than once. However, witnesses who have fabricated an account cannot rely on directly recalling and then describing the contents of memory of an actual experience. Instead, they usually create a relatively simple script that is followed carefully, so as not to make errors of omission or commission that would draw attention to possible inconsistencies. When additions or corrections are *spontaneously* offered, these are likely to represent reports from actual memory. For example, a 13-year-old girl stated, "Then he pulled the dining room table chair out and, no, actually then he talked about sexual things again, about if I had ever masturbated myself." If the addition or correction is not spontaneous but is a response to a direct question by the interviewer, the answer cannot satisfy this criterion.

Most child witnesses may assume that they should remember and know all of the details about an experience that adults seem to indicate are important. Therefore, *admitting lack of memory or knowledge* by a child who has fabricated an incident is much less likely to be spontaneously offered than when the child is sincerely reporting an experience but does not know or remember certain aspects of the incident. If the interviewer makes a request for specific information, such an admission must go beyond a simple statement of "I don't remember" or "I don't know." For example, a 9-year-old girl said in response to a question about remembering, "Uh-uh. I forgot all about this except for the part when we were in the car."

*Raising doubts about one's own testimony* implies the possibility that the witness is insincere. Therefore, a witness who has invented an allegation may wish to avoid drawing the interviewer's attention to that fact, whereas a truthfully reporting witness may recognize the implausibility of accusing a respected adult or relating what they think adults will view as an unlikely event. For example, a 15-year-old girl stated, "You know, this thing is so weird and Mr. L. is so nice that I thought nobody would ever believe me. That's why I didn't want to tell my mom."

A witness who is acting out of revenge or a motive for personal gain is unlikely to engage in *self-deprecation* or to minimize the damage to the falsely accused by *pardoning the accused*. However, children who have been sexually abused often blame themselves for what happened. For example, an 8-year-old girl said, "I know I shouldn't have gone in that there bathroom 'cause maybe I should have waited for G." Frequently children have ambivalent or generally positive feelings or affections for the perpetrator and wish to minimize the problems created by the disclosure, especially when the accused is a family member. Under such circumstances, they may excuse the unacceptable behavior or attempt to minimize the extent or seriousness of the sexual acts. For example, a 10-year-old girl said, "I know he didn't want to hurt me. He was just really drunk and he looked really sad the next day, and is he going to jail?"

A thorough evaluation of the statement usually requires several passes through the transcript. The CBCA provides an assessment of the quality of the statement and useful information regarding the likelihood that the statement was produced from actual memory of the described events, as opposed to invention or fantasy. Presently, there are no specific rules for the number of criteria that must be satisfied in order to support a tentative conclusion that the statement was derived from actual memory of the events. As stated earlier, the criteria of logical consistency and quantity of details must be present, taking into account the age and developmental level of the child and the nature and complexity of the alleged events. However, the number of additional criteria that should be present has not been determined. Raskin and Esplin (1991) determined the frequency of occurrence of the various criteria in a sample of 20 confirmed and 20 doubtful statements made by children in sexual abuse cases, and Yuille and Joffe used a laboratory simulation involving a staged event to make preliminary determinations about how many criteria are required to conclude that a statement is valid. Additional research is in progress (see Horowitz, this issue).

CBCA is not a sufficient basis to form a definite conclusion concerning the validity of the allegations. A child may have provided a statement lacking most content criteria for a number of reasons, fabrication being only one, and in some instances a statement containing several criteria may be a fabrication. Therefore, additional factors must be analyzed to select the most plausible explanation from the various alternatives that may be developed. This is done by means of the Validity Checklist.

## VALIDITY CHECKLIST

Regardless of the number of criteria present in the statement, the results of the CBCA must be evaluated in the context of all available information. Some information is derived from the interview itself, and other information may be obtained from other sources available to the evaluator. The Validity Checklist (Table 2) is employed to test the plausibility of various alternative hypotheses by examining particular aspects of the information.

The checklist procedure has been developed from extensive experience in sexual abuse cases in Germany and the authors' 35 years of collective experience in sexual abuse cases and other investigations. Although SVA does not provide the total answer, it is extremely useful. It forces the evaluator to explore and consider all of the available information and many possible explanations prior to, during, and after completion of the interview. Through this process, hypotheses are generated, gaps in the information may be discovered, additional information may be sought, and potentially important data or sources of information are not likely to be overlooked or ignored. This prevents premature conclusions caused by bias or preconceived notions and fosters a systematic consideration of all necessary and available information that may contribute to a fully informed and reasonable conclusion. SVA is an investigative and evaluative procedure that may provide extremely useful information and insights to those who must make decisions concerning the investigation and final disposition of sexual abuse cases. However, it is a professional investigative tool, not a formal instrument that was developed by empirical research and subjected to psychometric evaluation, as is typical of psychological tests. It can be a very useful tool for those who are skilled and experienced in the investigation of child sexual abuse allegations.

If the statement obtained from the interview is high in quality (as demonstrated by CBCA) and supports the validity of the allegations, the checklist is used to determine if other competing hypotheses can be rejected. Similarly, if a low quality statement is obtained, the checklist is used to see if there is additional support for one of the competing hypotheses or if a poor interview and/or a cognitively limited or unwilling witness may explain the low quality of the obtained statement. Regardless of the outcome of this analysis, the results provide important evidence to be considered and weighed with all other evidence before arriving at a final determination about the validity of the accusations.

The Validity Checklist presented in Table 2 consists of four general categories of information to be evaluated. They include psychological characteristics of the child as observed during the interview, characteristics of the interview that may have influenced the content obtained, information that the child may have been motivated or influenced to make a false allegation, and investigative questions and other evidence that may raise doubts about the validity of the allegations.

The checklist is used to examine a variety of possibilities in light of the various hypotheses that have been generated during the investigation and interview process. The specific items and the accompanying questions describe the type of information to be evaluated. For each of these items, a negative response by the evaluator is consistent with the hypothesis tentatively adopted on the basis of the CBCA. However, each affirmative response by the evaluator raises a question about the viability of the tentatively adopted hypothesis. Enough questions may be raised by this procedure to require entertaining alternative hypotheses. These must then be evaluated to determine if the available information provides an adequate basis to conclude that an alternative hypothesis is at least as likely to be correct. Sometimes the resolution of this question requires further interviews or additional information. Unfortunately, a detailed discussion of this procedure is not appropriate here, and a more complete account of this process with actual case illustrations can be found in Raskin et al. (1991).

## SUMMARY

We have presented a framework and procedures that have been developed to assist in the investigation of reports of child sexual abuse. The basic theme is that the interests of children and society are well served when such investigations are conducted with the best available techniques. Carefully constructed interview techniques combined with a systematic analysis of

TABLE 2
Validity Checklist[a]

### Psychological Characteristics

1. Cognitive–Emotional Limitations — Are there indications that limited cognitive abilities, unwillingness to discuss the events, or discomfort during the interview interfered with obtaining adequate information from the interview process?

2. Language and Knowledge — Was the child's use of language and display of knowledge beyond the normal capacity for a child of that age and experience and beyond what the child may have learned from the incident?

3. Affect During the Interview — Did the child display inappropriate affect during the interview or was there an absence of affect that would be expected to accompany such a report by this child?

4. Suggestibility — Did the child demonstrate susceptibility to suggestion or ask questions during the interview to attempt to obtain clues as to what to say to the interviewer?

### Interview Characteristics

5. Interview Procedures — Was this interview inadequate according to principles and procedures of statement validity assessment? Did the interviewer introduce distractions, fail to establish rapport, inadequately attempt to elicit a free narrative, fail to use open questions and appropriate follow-up questions, or fail to attempt to resolve ambiguities and apparent inconsistencies? Were reasonable alternative hypotheses ignored?

6. Influence on Statement Contents — Was there leading or suggestive questioning, pressure, or coercion in any analyzed interview of the child? Were suggestive techniques or props employed in any interview?

### Motivational Factors

7. Motives for Reporting — Does the child's relationship to the accused or other contextual variables (e.g., living arrangements or relationships among significant others) suggest possible motives for the child to make a false allegation?

8. Context of Disclosures — Are there questionable elements in the context of the original disclosure or report of the accusations? Are there important inconsistencies in the reports?

9. Influence by Others — Are there indications that others suggested, coached, pressured, or coerced the child to make a false report?

### Investigative Questions

10. Lack of Realism — Are the described events unrealistic? Are there major elements in the statement that are contrary to the laws of nature?

11. Inconsistent Statements — Are there major elements in the statement (not peripheral details) that are inconsistent or contradicted by another statement made by this child or another witness?

12. Contradictory Evidence — Are there major elements in the statement that are contradicted by reliable physical evidence or other concrete evidence?

13. Characteristics of the Offense — Is the description of the alleged sexual offense lacking in the normal details and general characteristics of this type of offense against a child? Does the description contain important elements or general characteristics that are contrary to what has been established in the professional and investigative literature concerning such offenses?

[a]Adapted from Raskin, Esplin, & Horowitz (1991).

the contents of statements (CBCA) and other available information (Validity Checklist) can provide a very effective approach for investigating and assessing the validity of sexual abuse allegations made by children.

In a small proportion of cases, problems may arise concerning developmental issues with young children, undue influence by significant adults, personality traits and other psychological factors, developmental disabilities, and psychopathology. Dealing with these problems usually requires special skills and qualifications for conducting further interviews and administering psychological tests and other assessment procedures. In such instances, it may be necessary to refer the child for further evaluation, testing, and interviews by professionals who are specifically qualified to perform these procedures.

It is our opinion that the techniques we have described are based on sound principles and scientific data in the fields of memory, developmental psychology, and interview techniques. In addition, they have been supported by considerable experience and successful application in hundreds of actual cases of child sexual abuse. Although the existing research has supported this approach, additional research is needed to further refine these methods (see Horowitz, this issue). We are confident that these techniques will continue to provide critical assistance in efforts to protect children and society.

## REFERENCES

American Academy of Child and Adolescent Psychiatry. (1988). Guidelines for the clinical evaluation of child and adolescent sexual abuse. *Journal of the American Academy of Child and Adolescent Psychiatry, 25,* 655–657.

Arntzen, F. (1982). Die Situation der forensischen Aussagepsychologie in der Bundesrepublik Deutschland. In A. Trankell (Ed.), *Reconstructing the past: The role of psychologists in criminal trials* (pp. 107–120). Deventer, The Netherlands: Kluwer.

Benedek, E. P., & Schetky, D. H. (1989). Problems in validating allegations of sexual abuse: Part 1. Factors affecting perception and recall of events. *Journal of the American Academy of Child and Adolescent Psychiatry, 26,* 912–915.

Blumfield, M. (1990, January 21). Experts blame McMartin verdict on botched interviews. *The Orlando Sentinel,* p. 14.

Boychuk, T. D. (1991). *Criteria-Based Content Analysis of children's statements about sexual abuse: A field based validation study.* Unpublished doctoral dissertation, Arizona State University, Tempe.

Brigham, J. C. (1991). Commentary: Issues in the empirical study of the sexual abuse of children. In J. L. Doris (Ed.), *The suggestibility of children's recollections: Implications for eyewitness testimony* (pp. 110–114). Washington, DC: American Psychological Association.

Ceci, S. J. (1991). Some overarching issues in the child suggestibility debate. In J. L. Doris (Ed.), *The suggestibility of children's recollections: Implications for eyewitness testimony* (pp. 1–9). Washington, DC: American Psychological Association.

Ceci, S. J., & Bruck, M. (1991). *The suggestibility of the child witness: An historical review and synthesis.* Manuscript submitted for publication.

Ceci, S. J., DeSimone, M., Putnick, M., & Nightingale, N. (in press). Age differences in suggestibility. In D. Cicchetti & S. Toth (Eds.), *Child witnesses, child abuse, and public policy.* Norwood, NJ: Ablex.

Ceci, S. J., Ross, D. F., & Toglia, M. P. (Eds.). (1989). *Perspectives on children's testimony*. New York: Springer-Verlag.

Ceci, S. J, Toglia, M. P., & Ross, D. F. (Eds.). (1987). *Children's eyewitness memory*. New York: Springer-Verlag.

Clarke-Stewart, A., Thompson, W., & Lepore, S. (1989, April). *Manipulating children's interpretations through interrogation*. Paper presented at the meeting of the Society for Research on Child Development, Kansas City, MO.

Committee on Ethical Guidelines for Forensic Psychologists. (1991). Specialty guidelines for forensic psychologists. *Law and Human Behavior*, 15, 655–665.

Corwin, D. L. (1988). Early diagnosis of child sexual abuse: Diminishing the lasting effects. In G. E. Wyatt & G. J. Powell (Eds.), *Lasting effects of child sexual abuse* (pp. 251–269). Newbury Park, CA: Sage.

Dent, H. R. (1991). Experimental studies of interviewing child witnesses. In J. L. Doris (Ed.), *The suggestibility of children's recollections: Implications for eyewitness testimony* (pp. 138–146). Washington, DC: American Psychological Association.

Doris, J. L. (Ed.) (1991). *The suggestibility of children's recollections: Implications for eyewitness testimony*. Washington, DC: American Psychological Association.

Everson, M. D., & Boat, B, W, (1990). Sexualized doll play among young children: Implications for the use of anatomical dolls in sexual abuse evaluations. *Journal of the American Academy of Child and Adolescent Psychiatry*, 29, 736–742.

Faller, K. C. (1984). Is the child victim of sexual abuse telling the truth? *Child Abuse & Neglect*, 8, 471–481.

Fivush, R., & Hudson, J. A. (Eds.). (1990). *Knowing and remembering in young children*. New York: Cambridge University Press.

Garbarino, J., Stott, F. M., & Faculty of the Erikson Institute. (1989). *What children can tell us*. San Francisco: Jossey-Bass.

Goodman, G. S., & Helgeson, V. S. (1988). Children as witnesses: What do they remember? In L. E. A. Walker (Ed.), *Handbook on sexual abuse of children* (pp. 109–136). New York: Springer.

Goodman, G. S., & Reed, R. S. (1986). Age differences in eyewitness testimony. *Law and Human Behavior*, 10, 317–332.

Hagedorn, A. (1991, April 15). Prosecution of child-molestation cases is more cautious in wake of failed cases. *The Wall Street Journal*, p. B1, B10.

Humphrey, H. H. (1985). *Report on Scott County investigations*. Office of the Attorney General of Minnesota.

Jones, D. P. H., & McQuiston, M. G. (1988). *Interviewing the sexually abused child*. London: Gaskell.

Landry, K. L., & Brigham, J. C. (in press). The effect of training in Criteria-Based Content Analysis on the ability to detect deception in adults. *Law and Human Behavior*.

Levy, R. J. (1989). Using "scientific testimony" to prove child abuse. *Family Law Quarterly*, 23, 383–409.

MacFarlane, K., & Waterman, J. (Eds.). (1986). *Sexual abuse of young children*. New York: Guilford.

Morris, W. (Ed.). (1969). *American heritage dictionary of the English language*. New York: American Heritage.

Nelson, K. (1986). *Event knowledge: Structure and function in development*. Hillsdale, NJ: Erlbaum.

Pettit, F., Fegan, M., & Howie, P. (1990, September). *Interviewer effects on children's testimony*. Paper presented at the 8th International Congress on Child Abuse and Neglect, Hamburg, Germany.

Poole, D. A., & White, L. T. (1991). Effects of question repetition on the eyewitness testimony of children and adults. *Developmental Psychology*, 27, 975–986.

Raskin, D. C., & Esplin, P. W. (1991). Assessment of children's statements of sexual abuse. In J. L. Doris (Ed.), *The suggestibility of children's recollections: Implications for eyewitness testimony* (pp. 153–164). Washington, DC: American Psychological Association.

Raskin, D. C., Esplin, P. W., & Horowitz, S. W. (1991). *Investigative interviews and assessments of children in sexual abuse cases.* Unpublished manuscript.

Raskin, D. C., & Steller, M. (1989). Assessing the credibility of allegations of child sexual abuse: Polygraph examinations and statement analysis. In H. Wegener, F. Loesel, & J. Haisch (Eds.), *Criminal behavior and the justice system: Psychological perspectives* (pp. 290–302). New York: Springer-Verlag.

Raskin, D. C., & Yuille, J. C. (1989). Problems in evaluating interviews of children in sexual abuse cases. In S. J. Ceci, D. F. Ross, & M. P. Toglia (Eds.), *Perspectives on children's testimony* (pp. 184–207). New York: Springer-Verlag.

Roark, A. C. (1990, January 25). Experts fault McMartin child interview methods. *Los Angeles Times*, A1, A26.

Saywitz, K., Goodman, G. S., Nicholas, E., & Moan, S. (1989, April). *Children's memories of genital examinations: Implications for cases of child sexual assault.* Paper presented at the meeting of the Society for Research on Child Development, Kansas City, MO.

Sgroi, S. M., Porter, F., & Blick, L. C. (1982). Validation of child sexual abuse. In S. M. Sgroi (Ed.), *Handbook of clinical intervention in child sexual abuse* (pp. 9–38). Lexington, MA: Lexington Books.

Slicner, N. A., & Hanson, S. R. (1989). Guidelines for videotape interviews in child sexual abuse cases. *American Journal of Forensic Psychology*, 7, 61–74.

Steller, M. (1986, April). *Interviewing the child witness.* Paper presented at seminar on Interviewing and Assessing Credibility of Alleged Victims and Perpetrators in Sexual Abuse Cases, St. Luke's Hospital, Phoenix, Arizona.

Steller, M. (1989). Recent developments in statement analysis. In J. C. Yuille (Ed.), *Credibility assessment* (pp. 135–154). Dordrecht, The Netherlands: Kluwer.

Steller, M. (1991). Rehabilitation of the child witness. In J. L. Doris (Ed.), *The suggestibility of children's recollections: Implications for eyewitness testimony* (pp. 106–109). Washington, DC: American Psychological Association.

Steller, M., & Koehnken, G. (1989). Criteria-based statement analysis. In D. C. Raskin (Ed.), *Psychological methods in criminal investigation and evidence* (pp. 217–245). New York: Springer.

Steller, M., & Raskin, D. C. (1986, April). *The Validity Checklist.* Paper presented at seminar on Interviewing and Assessing Credibility of Alleged Victims and Perpetrators in Sexual Abuse Cases, St. Luke's Hospital, Phoenix, Arizona.

Steller, M., Wellershaus, P., & Wolf, T. (1988, June). *Empirical validation of criteria-based content analysis.* Paper presented at the NATO Advanced Study Institute on Credibility Assessment, Maratea, Italy.

Undeutsch, U. (1982). Statement reality analysis. In A. Trankell (Ed.), *Reconstructing the past: The role of psychologists in criminal trials.* Deventer, The Netherlands: Kluwer.

Undeutsch, U. (1989). The development of statement reality analysis. In J. C. Yuille (Ed.), *Credibility assessment* (pp. 101–120). Dordrecht, The Netherlands: Kluwer.

Walker, L. E. A. (1988). New techniques for assessment and evaluation of child sexual abuse victims: Using anatomically "correct" dolls and videotape procedures. In L. E. A. Walker (Ed.), *Handbook on sexual abuse of children* (pp. 175–197). New York: Springer.

White, S., Strom, G. A., Santilli, G., & Quinn, K. M. (1987). *Guidelines for interviewing preschoolers with sexually anatomically detailed dolls.* Unpublished manuscript, Case Western Reserve University, Cleveland Metropolitan General Hospital.

Yuille, J. C. (1988, June). *A simulation study of criterion-based content analysis.* Paper presented at the NATO Advanced Study Institute on Credibility Assessment, Maratea, Italy.

Yuille, J. C., & Wells, G. L. (1991). Concerns about the application of research findings: The issue of ecological validity. In J. L. Doris (Ed.), *The suggestibility of children's recollections: Implications for eyewitness testimony* (pp. 118–128). Washington, DC: American Psychological Association.

INVITED: 3 DECEMBER 1990  FINAL ACCEPTANCE: 3 NOVEMBER 1991

# [17]

# An Evaluation of the "Cusum" Stylistic Analysis of Confessions

**Professor David Canter, C.Psychol, PhD., FBPsS, FAPA, FBIM,**
Department of Psychology, University of Surrey, Guildford, Surrey, GU2 5XH, United Kingdom.

*Abstract: In a number of notable appeal cases expert testimony, based upon Cusum analysis of written statements, has supported claims by appellants that their confessions were modified by police officers. To test the validity of this approach a number of studies have been carried out. They reveal that Cusum analysis is just as likely to indicate that material has been inserted into text when none has been inserted as when it has. There therefore must be serious doubt as to whether the Cusum testimony should have been accepted by the courts. The difficulty the courts have in evaluating evidence from scientific experts, especially from the behavioural sciences, is highlighted by the acceptance of Cusum charts. This raises important questions about the weakness of the essentially lay understanding of science that even appeal court judges may have.*

In recent cases, including the appeal in London of Tommy McCrossen in July 1991, the trial in November 1991 of Frank Beck in Leicester Crown Court and in December 1991 the trial of Vincent Connell in Dublin, evidence has been presented on behalf of the defence that draws upon the analysis of statements made by the defendant which the defence claims are not the sole production of the defendant. This evidence consists of the "stylistic" analysis of the statements using a technique which consists of the interpretation of "Cusum Charts" (Morton, 1991).

The analyses of the statements purport to determine whether they are all the utterances of one person. In most of the cases in which the technique has been used the courts have been informed that the Cusum Charts reveal that material has been inserted into the statement that was not in the verbal style of the appellant. These findings have usually been accepted by the courts in support of the case that police officers have modified confessions to make them more clearly incriminating of the defendant. The interpretation of Cusum Charts has thus been admitted as expert evidence and, in such cases as those listed above, this testimony has been upheld by the judge as of substantive relevance to the verdict.

A detailed account of the approach to interpreting Cusum Charts has been provided in three internally published reports (Morton, 1991; Morton and Michaelson, 1990; Farringdon and Morton, 1990). Given the significance assigned to this approach by the courts, and indeed the potential contribution the method would appear to have for the understanding of language production, it is clearly essential that further independent tests of this approach are carried out. The following report describes the results of such studies.

## The Cusum Charts

Central to the preparation and interpretation of Cusum Charts is the argument that each person has a unique "habit" in his speech or writing. This "habit" is proposed as a consistency, characteristic of each person, in the proportion of particular components of that person's sentences. Usually, the component used is the proportion of two and three letter words in any sentence (although the number of words starting with a vowel has also been used). It is proposed that this proportion is so consistent for each individual that any distinct variation in that proportion is *prima facie* evidence that the sentences are the utterance of more than one person.

The existence of similarity or difference in the proportions of the specific component is revealed by producing what are termed "charts". These charts are derived from counts of the number of words per sentence and the number of component words per sentence. The argument is that the "habit" is best revealed for the piece of text at issue, by calculating for each sentence two values. One is the difference between the number of words in a sentence and the average number of words per sentence. The second value is the difference between the actual number of component words per sentence and the average number of component words per sentence in that piece of text. These differences are each cumulated (hence "Cusum") to provide the basic numerical values for the analysis.

In other words, in a typical Cusum analysis as used in court, the disputed text is divided into sentences. The number of words is calculated for each sentence as are the number of two and three letter words. The average values are calculated for the sentence length and for the two and three letter words. The differences from the average are then calculated for each sentence. These differences from the average are then added sequentially for each sentence to produce two sets of cumulative values, one for the total number of words per sentence the other for the number of two and three letter words per sentence.

The central premise for interpreting these charts is that these two values should parallel each other in the utterances of any person. If they do not parallel each other then the text where they do not is the production of a different person. However, advocates of this approach maintain that numerical analysis of the correlation between these two sets of values would be difficult for the courts to understand. They therefore propose that the two sets of cumulative summation values are plotted on Cusum (or Qsum) charts and that visual inspection of the charts is sufficient to decide whether there is intruded material or not. Reports by Cusum analysts as well as their comments recorded in court transcripts, state that any text longer than 25 sentences is amenable to such analysis and that intruded material even a few sentences long can be identified to within a sentence or two.

In order to be able compare the two Cusum values directly by visual inspection the values for the two and three letter words are re-scaled so that they have the same range as the total sentence length. This is done by calculating the ranges and multiplying the two and three letter word Cusum values by the ratio of the ranges. A variety of other methods are possible for re-scaling the values in order to facilitate visual comparison of the two lines on the chart. They will each lead to different interpretations. However, because the procedures used in court have always used this particular re-scaling method it was used in all that follows. Figures 1 and 2 show typical Cusum charts produced by this means.

### FIGURE 1

Q-Sum Chart Illustrating "Similarity" in Writing "Habit"
for 2 and 3 Letter Words compared with Sentence Length

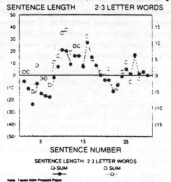

SENTENCE NUMBER

SENTENCE LENGTH  2-3 LETTER WORDS
Q-SUM        O SUM

## Interpretation of the Cusum Charts

It is claimed by Cusum analysts that visual examination of the charts is sufficient to establish whether a "habit" is consistent enough to indicate whether the text is the work of more than one author. If the two lines diverge from one

### FIGURE 2

Q-Sum Chart Illustrating "Dissimilarity" in Writing "Habit"
for 2 and 3 Letter Words compared with Sentence Length

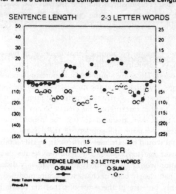

SENTENCE NUMBER

SENTENCE LENGTH  2-3 LETTER WORDS
Q-SUM        O-SUM

another to any marked degree then it is assumed that this is evidence for different authors being involved.

Both explicit and implicit rules can be gleaned from available reports and examples of material discussed in court for determining whether the lines diverge. Explicitly Morton states that if the "...variations within the charts are as large as the variations between them this may taken as evidence of a consistent habit" (1991, page 20). In other words, the charts are examined visually to see if the difference between the sentence length Cusum lines and the 2 and 3 letter words Cusum lines is greater, for a number of points along the lines, than the largest difference between any two points on one line. If they are greater then this divergence is taken be of a magnitude that implies that more than one author is involved. However, examination of examples which are described as divergent by Morton and his colleagues suggests that implicitly any consistent difference between the lines, especially if the lines cross each other, are taken as an indication of the sort of significant variation that would imply multiple authorship.

Morton and Michaelson (1990) argue that sometimes especially long sentences may distort the charts. To deal with this they propose that a transparent overlay of one of the lines be used. This can then be visually adjusted to see if a better match can be achieved. If this is not possible then the material that does not match is claimed to be by a different author. On the basis of these interpretations the material in Figure 1 would appear to be consistent and therefore the writing of one author. However, Figure 2 illustrates the sort of divergence that would indicate another author being involved. Cusum analysis would lead to the conclusion that from sentence 12 to sentence 22 in Figure 2 there is an author that is different from the remainder of the text. In fact, as indicated in detail in the notes to Figures 1 and 2, all the text is taken from the current paper, all being the definitive writing of one author. (The Cusum Charts in

Expert Evidence, 1992, pp. 93-99

Figures 1 and 2 were derived from an early draft of this paper before editorial and reviewers' comments had been incorporated. This ensured that the analysis was based on the unique writing of one person. However, these illustrations are only intended as examples of the Cusum procedure not to be a stringent test of it.)

Of course, it might be assumed that in order to make my point I have carefully modified my writing to produce the results I want. There are a number of important responses to this charge. The first is that the great strength of the Cusum approach is that it is overtly systematic and numeric, at least up to the point of interpreting the charts. So any readers can examine their own material to test the probabilities for themselves. Secondly, the subtlety of the Cusum charts is such that it would be extremely difficult to modify a piece of writing *post hoc* to produce the required results. Such a modification would also be likely to generate very distorted text that had clearly been uncharacteristically modified. It is presumably because of these reasons that the courts have been so ready to accept Cusum testimony.

A further point is that Cusum analysts do emphasise that it is virtually impossible for people to modify those aspects of their utterances that are demonstrated in Cusum charts. An illustration is taken of the novel by Simon Brett *The Booker Book*, in which a deliberate attempt is made to write different chapters in the styles of other novelists. The Cusum charts analysis of this is taken to show that the novelist's own 'habit' is nonetheless consistent throughout all these attempts at pastiche (Morton and Michaelson, 1990). Figures 1 and 2 are therefore a relevant first step in challenging the value of Cusum charts. They may be a rare, unusual example of single authorship being shown to be "divergent". Studies to be reported later suggest that they are not.

It is claimed in internal reports (Morton, 1991, Morton and Michaelson, 1990) and in oral evidence in court that the "habit" being revealed is remarkably consistent for each person. Examples are cited from the works of a single authors written over twenty years apart claiming that they reveal consistencies. Some Cusum analysts even claim that the "habit" is consistent for the same person no matter whether that person is speaking or writing (Morton and Michaelson, 1990).

## Lack of any explanation for the phenomena

No published accounts can be found to indicate what the psychological or linguistic processes are that generate the "habit" that Cusum analysts claim to be so consistent. There is therefore serious question as to whether it is anything other than a random property of the arithmetic of language. As such it would not be expected to have any inherent qualities linking it to a particular person.

Unlike finger prints or blood types, the way a person writes or speaks is created by structured thought processes.

Therefore, in order to demonstrate that an aspect of a person's utterances are unique to that person it is important to explain why such special characteristics are likely to exist. Otherwise it will be difficult to know what potentially contaminating factors need to be considered. If such controls are not taken it is possible that any results are a coincidental artefact produced by processes independent of the person who is speaking or writing.

No aspect of human behaviour that has been studied to date reveals such high levels of consistencies that are claimed for the Cusum technique. Psychologists explore the consistencies of the measuring instruments they use, such as psychometric tests or the analysis of statements, by correlating two measurements made with the same instrument on the same person, or material, at two points in time. This is known as the "reliability" of the measuring instrument (see Runkel and McGrath, 1972, especially chapter 6). With very long tests one form of reliability is to correlate one part of the test with another part, or say even numbered questions with odd numbered questions. This is known as "split-half" reliability. The general levels of reliability indicated by these measurements can be compared with the consistencies claimed for the Cusum technique.

For example, measurements of intelligence from one time to the next, using highly developed and consistent tests, would not claim reliabilities above 0.9, indicating that only 81% of the variance is common from one situation to the next. Many well established measures are deemed valuable with reliabilities below 0.7, indicating that only 49% of the variance is common from one time to the next. Therefore if the "habit" revealed in the Cusum charts really is even more stable than these established measures having close to 100% reliability as claimed by its protagonists, for both practical and theoretical reasons it is essential to establish the developmental process that leads to such stability. If no developmental process is implied this leads to the challenging suggestion that a young child would reveal the same "habits" when grown to adulthood.

Central to the judgement of Cusum charts that leads to the inference of single or multiple authorship is the comparison of the number of two and three letter words with the number of words in the sentence as a whole. Two and three letter words are chosen by Cusum analysts both because they are regarded as having little significance in the sentence and because they occur reasonably frequently. In other words, they are seen as a component of the sentence that will vary only randomly.

In so far as this is true it must mean that longer sentences will have more of such words and shorter sentences fewer of them. In general, to the extent that two and three letter words are random constituents of any language, there will be a consistent relationship between their frequency and the number of words in the sentence as a whole.

It will therefore be an arithmetic inevitability that any text, randomly generated or otherwise will demonstrate broad consistency in the proportion of two and three letter words that exist in any sections of that text. Existence of such consistency is evidence for the basic assumptions that two and three letter words are a random component of the language. If that assumption is correct then the consistency is arithmetically inevitable.

However, the visual demonstration of consistency in the charts may appear to indicate something of psycho-linguistic significance just because the two lines parallel each other. It does not necessarily. If most text shows the consistency then variations from that consistency could be random artifacts of no substantive significance.

The lack of a strong theoretical basis to the claims for Cusum charts strengthens the need for very thorough empirical exploration of this method and the validity of any conclusions drawn from using it.

## Lack of clear empirical support for the procedure

In neither of the reports cited (Morton, 1991, Morton and Michaelson, 1990) nor in testimony to court has a full account been presented of the empirical basis for the assertion that Cusum charts demonstrate habits unique to a person. The reports provide many illustrations of revealing consistency in the Cusum plots for the same author, when that is known to be the case, and a number of examples illustrating the patterns revealed for different authors involved in the same text. The statement was also made that in over 800 cases the procedure has been successful (*R. v. Beck, Haynes and Lincoln*, Crown court, Leicester, November 9, 1991), but the witness did not clarify or summarise the comparisons made in these cases.

In particular Cusum analysts do not present evidence to indicate the proportion of situations in which text by one author is wrongly attributed to more than one author and compare this with tests of multiple authorship being mistakenly considered to be by one person. They simply claim that the technique is extremely robust; a claim which a number of British courts have accepted.

## A statistical measure for comparing Cusum lines

A long and widely recognised methodological principle (Huff, 1955) states that reliance on visual comparisons of any chart to make definitive statements is inherently unreliable. The same material presented in two different visual forms can lead to quite different conclusions. The apparent size of a component of a picture can be modified by the context in which it is put. Two people looking at the same visual representation may come to quite different conclusions. This is why mathematically based inferential statistics have been developed to give precise arithmetic cut-off points. The various modifications to the

interpretation of Cusum charts through the use of transparencies, adds further subjectivity to this interpretation process. Someone chooses the scale, the starting and finishing points and suggests differences or similarities for people to see. This leads to the possibility that there can be considerable doubt as to when a Cusum chart actually shows similarity or difference.

A thorough empirical test of the Cusum procedure therefore requires a statistical calculation of the similarities between the two sets of Cusum values. For such a test to be a valid assessment it should reflect the similarities in the profiles of the two lines on the chart. In other words, a measure is required that reflects the correlation between the relative Cusum values within the two sets of numbers. Spearman's rank order correlation (often known as Rho) is an appropriate statistic to do this (see Siegel, 1956).

This correlation coefficient is calculated by putting each set of values in rank order. In this case the cumulative sum of the differences of each sentence from the average sentence length and the number of two or three letter words could be ranked. Then the square of the differences between the ranks for each sentence is summed and applied to a standard formula in order to give a value that varies between +1.00, if the two lines parallel each other exactly, and -1.00 if they are the mirror image of each other. If the relationship is random then the correlation will be 0.00. Clearly, if there is a section of the chart that appears divergent, then the value of Rho will be less than +1.00. For illustrative purposes it can be noted that the Rho value for Figure 1 is 0.93 and for Figure 2 is 0.74, showing that the relationship between the lines has more randomness in it for Figure 2 than for Figure 1.

One further advantage of using a correlation coefficient is that it does not require any scaling factor, as do the charts. It can be calculated directly on the original Cusum values.

The central proposition of the Cusum technique can therefore be turned into a precise, testable hypothesis. This is that text which is the product of more than one author will generate distinctly lower Rho values between the two sets of Cusum figures than text that is known to be the work of one author.

If a simple bench mark level for Rho is introduced, then the comparisons of Rho values can be carried out very directly by seeing whether the Rho values are above or below that predetermined level. The exact value of the criterion is of no substantive significance to test the theory, because the central Cusum proposition would lead to the hypothesis that more single authored text would be above the bench mark level than multiple authored text, whatever the level chosen.

A comparison level of 0.9 is proposed. This is the informal criterion that is often used in the development of psychological measuring instrument below which they are not regarded as acceptably "reliable" (Runkel and McGrath, 1980). Texts that generate Rho values below this could be

Expert Evidence, 1992, pp. 93-99

taken as indicating "multiple authorship" and texts above this value could be taken as from one author. The hypothesis is therefore that known single authored texts will produce substantially more Rho values above 0.9 than texts known to be the product of more than one person.

This application of Rho is especially appropriate if all the material consists of the same number of sentences. In the studies that follow all examples consisted of 30 sentences. The Rho value for Figure 1 is above the comparison level of 0.90 at 0.93. For Figure 2 it is below the level indicating a lack of consistency in the text. As already mentioned, both figures are based upon sentences drawn from the present paper, all written by the author. This one example, does not support the central Cusum hypothesis.

## Comparison of single and multiple authored texts

To carry out further empirical tests to see if the examples of Figures 1 and 2 were typical of Cusum analysis the writings of ten different authors were collected together. Each example of text was known to have been written entirely by only one person. Of course, it is never possible to be absolutely sure that an utterance is the product of one person. Even if they are observed writing or saying something they may have memorised it. However, if material is used that was not prepared for any specific test, and it is obtained directly from that author's own personal records, then it is unlikely that deliberate falsification has taken place. Furthermore, if ten different individuals who are not in contact with each other are each used as originating authors this further reduces the risk of all the material being presented as single authored when it was in fact the work of more than one person. The material included letters, extracts from novels, papers to conferences, proposals submitted to university committees, dissertations, court transcripts and conference papers. In all 107 examples of text were obtained. These samples were drawn *ad hoc* from what was available and cannot therefore be taken as representative of English utterances. Nonetheless, the definitive claims for the Cusum procedure would be refuted by any counter-examples. Some degree of support for a weaker, probabilistic hypothesis is also a possible outcome for a coherent series of tests such as those carried out.

Rho values were calculated between the two and three letter word Cusums and the sentence length Cusums for the 107 examples of text. In 51 cases the Rho value was less than 0.90, i.e. 48% were inconsistent with the hypothesis of single authorship. This means that in virtually half the cases Cusum analysts would have mistakenly reached the conclusion of multiple authorship, because they claim that the habit has close to 100% reliability. As mentioned, use of a criterion different from than 0.90 would have given a different proportion of cases below that value. The really critical comparison is of the proportion of multiple and single authored texts above the criterion.

To make this comparison random combinations of the original material were prepared. This consisted of taking sections from one author and randomly combining it with a section from another author. The sentence sequence was maintained in each section so that there was only one point of change from one author to another. The cumulative summations would thus be predicted to diverge after this point. If the Cusum approach is not supported by this simple combination then it is unlikely to survive more complex admixtures of material. One hundred and thirty examples of text known to combine material from different authors were produced. Only 45 of the 130 had Rho values lower than 0.9, that is only 35 per cent. of the sample was below this threshold for consistency. In other words, the Cusum comparisons would have mistakenly supported the claim for single authorship in two out of three cases.

These tests suggest that the Cusum technique may actually be less likely to show multiple authorship for combined authors than for single authors. Certainly these results indicate that the Cusum technique is just as likely to identify two authors when there is one as when there are two.

## A further test of cusum hypothesis for confessions

It is just possible that the complex transactions that characterise a confession draw on processes for which the Cusum analysis is more appropriate than the earlier examples. To test this possibility, further examples were obtained of uncontested confessions each made by one person and also an account of a victim's experience of being in the King's Cross Underground Station fire (Donald and Canter, 1990). An additional examination was made of a monologue, written and performed by an actor confessing to a number of crimes.

By breaking these uncontested, single authored accounts into sections each of 30 sentences for study, 52 examples of text were generated. Rho values were calculated as before and the same criterion of 0.90 was used. It was found that 15 out of the 52 examples had values below the criterion, i.e 29 per cent.. For these examples, then, nearly a third of the cases could have mistakenly led to the assumption of intruded material if Cusum charts had been the main basis for forming the judgement.

In order to test further whether the procedure might nonetheless indicate a trend in the direction of the Cusum hypothesis the material from the personal accounts was combined into mixed authorship texts as had been done for the earlier examples. Of the 87 examples studied 25 had Rho values below 0.90, once again 29 pre cent.. Confessions therefore appear to operate in much the same way as other examples of text. The Cusum technique does not distinguish reliably between single and multiple authored text.

## Further testing using visual inspection

The results using Rho, and even the somewhat conservative criterion of 0.90, produce such a strong challenge to the validity of the Cusum approach to the determination of authorship that it was thought appropriate to attempt to use the visual inspection of the charts as Morton and his colleagues advocate (Morton, 1991; Morton and Michaelson, 1990; Farringdon and Morton, 1990). They say that anyone who understands the technique and is sensitive to the mode of interpretation can make a judgement on Cusum charts, and they provide a systematic list of the stages the interpretation should go through (see Morton and Michaelson, 1990 at page 68). A research assistant was therefore trained to make the judgement of intruded material by visual inspection of the Cusum charts as described in the published material and reports submitted to the courts. It was established that in general she was sympathetic to the Cusum approach and expected the tests would provide some vindication of the Cusum technique. However, she was not told the origins of the material or allowed to study the actual written text. She was asked to make her judgement solely by looking at the Cusum charts.

The research assistant was given all the material used in the tests described above. Table 1 summarises the results of her judgements

**Results of Visual Inspection of Cusum Charts to Determine Authorship**

| WRITTEN TEXTS | | |
|---|---|---|
| Single author | 107 | 71 (66) |
| Combined authors | 130 | 89 (68) |
| PERSONAL ACCOUNTS | | |
| One person | 52 | 32 (62) |
| Combined people | 87 | 52 (60) |

Table 1.

The figures in Table 1 once again show that the trained research assistant was not able to use the Cusum charts to distinguish between mixed authorship any more reliably than the Rho calculations. The percentages judged to be of mixed authorship are virtually identical for each set of material. They also show that the use of the Cusum charts, by one research assistant at least, was almost twice more likely to indicate mixed authorship in any verbal material than the Rho calculations were.

There, therefore, does not appear to be any increase in the validity of the Cusum approach as a result of visual inspection of the charts. There does, however, appear to be an increased risk of mistakenly assuming mixed authorship when visual inspection is the sole mode of determination.

## What Is happening in Cusum charts?

Undoubtedly Cusum analyses reveal variations within texts. Variations, that is, in the proportions of two and three letter words per sentence, and of other components of the sentence. An important question is the source of these

variations. The studies that have been reported here do not support the hypothesis that the variations are a consequence of mixed authorship. They indicate that in many cases the discrepancies to which Cusum charts draw attention may suggest mixed authorship when only a single author is involved. There is therefore the question of whether these variations are of substantive psychological significance at all. Are they a product of the individual psychology of the person making the utterances or the social processes within which the utterances are made?

Because language has evolved to facilitate social interaction it is not surprising to find that it varies enormously depending on the particular situation in which it is elicited. Research has demonstrated that the way a person writes or speaks varies between social groups and different activities and settings (Herrmann, 1982). There are also a number of studies that demonstrate that the length of an utterance and the frequencies of pauses is a function of the amount of cognitive processing that is involved in making the utterance (Goldman-Eisler, 1968). Therefore when a person is talking about something that they find difficult or complex, or with which they are not very familiar, they are likely to have frequent pauses and consequently short utterances. It is possible that the conversion of speech into sentences tends to equate an utterance bounded by long pauses into a sentence. If this were the case then the variations in sentence length that are at the heart of a Cusum comparison would be a reflection of differing levels of familiarity or complexity of the material at that point in the material.

Some combination of variations in the situation and in the cognitive demands of the material, rather than the personality characteristics of the author, are therefore possible hypotheses for what produces the variations in the Cusum charts. It is also possible that Cusum charts do reflect something genuinely random in human utterances. Yet, because there is the possibility of interpreting some of these random patterns to mean multiple authorship, the adversary process of the law has encouraged people to see something substantive when they wish to support defendants' claims of modified confessions. Future research must determine whether the Cusum technique does characterise anything important about writing or speech.

Of course, there is the possibility that the advocates of the Cusum approach have a special way of interpreting their charts that is particularly sensitive to mixed authorship and does not lead to the misattributions illustrated above. Given the results above, they would either need to demonstrate that ability, under the types of controlled conditions that would be appropriate to psychology experiments, or they would need to specify more precisely how they interpret the Cusum charts so that others could replicate their findings. If the skill is a demonstrable ability only of very few individuals then its status as an objective scientific procedure, rather than as an art, would still be in grave doubt.

Expert Evidence, 1992, pp. 93-99

Clearly it would be exceptionally valuable if the courts could be provided with a technique that would allow explicit statements to be made about the authorships of statements to within a couple of sentences. It is a valiant goal. But earlier theories and approaches along these lines have been vigorously criticised for the quality of the methodology (Krippendorf, 1980; Smith, 1985).

The studies reported in the present paper suggest that a similar criticisms may be appropriate for the Cusum approach. Yet that approach has been accepted by a number of British and Irish courts as important evidence suggesting that material had been inserted into written confessions.

There, therefore, appear to be some weaknesses in the criteria used by the courts for determining the validity of expert testimony. A number of proposals may be made that could be used as guidelines for the evaluation of proposed expert testimony.

1. Is there evidence that the technique has been evaluated by other experts in the field? By far the most direct test of this is that studies using the technique have been published in reputable, refereed journals.

2. Is there evidence that other experts would come to similar conclusions using the procedures? This is established by published replications by different authorities.

3. Have appropriate attempts been made to challenge the hypotheses central to the techniques? The published literature will indicate this.

4. Have appropriate statistical probabilities been calculated? It is curious that in the use of DNA the courts require very high levels of probability before they accept DNA linking, but in the case of Cusum visual inspection of the charts was deemed admissible.

The rapid developments in science, particularly the social sciences, are generating many findings of potential significance to the courts. Their potential utility may mean that they are brought in as evidence before their scientific credibility has been established. Judges and juries do not evaluate scientific findings in the same way as expert scientists do. It is not appropriate for scientific debate to be conducted in court. It may therefore be suggested that the courts should seek overtly, in all cases where new scientific approaches are being proposed, to establish the scientific standing of the technique and the theory underlying it, before evidence using those procedures is admissible. The law of the United States of America emphasises peer support for expert evidence that can be directly demonstrated (Kassin *et al.*, 1989). British courts do not do so as emphatically. One of the major contributions of Cusum analysts may therefore transpire to be the improvement of British legal practice with regard to the evaluation of the scientific status of behavioural techniques used in expert evidence.

## Bibliography

Donald, I, and Canter, D, 1990, Behavioural aspects of the King's Cross disaster (in) *Fires and human behaviour*, Canter, D. (ed) London: David Fulton.

Farringdon, M.G, and Morton, A.Q, 1990, *Fielding and the Federalist*, Glasgow: University of Glasgow Department of Computing Science Research Report, R6.

Goldman-Eisler, F, 1968, *Psycholinguistics; Experiments in spontaneous speech*, London: Academic Press.

Herrmann, T, 1982, *Speech and situation: A psychological conception of situational speaking*, Berlin: Springer-Verlag.

Huff, D, 1955, *How to lie with statistics*, London: Gollancz.

Kassim, S.M, Ellsworth, P.C, and Smith, V.L, 1989, The 'general acceptance' of psychological research on eyewitness testimony: A survey of the experts, *American Psychologist*, 44(8): 1089-1098.

Kriffendorff, K, 1980, *Content analysis: An introduction to its methodology*, California: Sage Publications Inc.

Morton, A.Q, 1991, *Proper words in proper places*, Glasgow: University of Glasgow Department of Computing Science Research Report, R18.

Morton, A.Q, and Michaelson, S, 1990, *The qsum plot*, Edinburgh: University of Edinburgh Department of Computer Science.

Runkel, P.J, and McGrath, J.E, 1972, *Research on human behavior*, New York: Holt, Rinehart and Winston.

Siegel, S, 1956, *Non-parametric statistics for the behavioral sciences*, New York: McGraw-Hill.

Smith, M.W.A, 1985, An investigation of the basis of Morton's method for the determination of authorship, *Style*, 19(3): 341-367.

# Part VI
# Delinquents' Characteristics

# [18]

## SIR CYRIL BURT

### CONCLUSION

*Manfred.*        I would spare thyself
    All further colloquy.  And so—farewell.
                  *[Exit Manfred.*
*Abbot.*  This should have been a noble creature : he
    Hath all the energy which would have made
    A goodly frame of glorious elements,
    Had they been wisely mingled ; as it is,
    It is an awful chaos—light and darkness—
    And mind and dust—and passions and pure thoughts,
    Mix'd, and contending without end or order,
    All dormant or destructive : he will perish,
    And yet he must not ; I will try once more :
    For such are worth redemption ; and my duty
    Is to dare all things for a righteous end.
    I'll follow him—but cautiously, though surely.
                  *[Exit Abbot.*
            BYRON, *Manfred*, **III. i.** *ad fin.*

I HAVE now worked through the whole list of characteristics discovered or discoverable in delinquents such as those we have been studying. I have taken each point in order, noting its frequency, describing its effects, and indicating how best it may be treated and eased. Nothing remains except briefly to summarize the whole review.

Is there, we may ask in conclusion, any all-pervading principle, whether of causation or of treatment, deducible from our detailed discussions ?

*Causation : (a) Multiplicity of Contributory Factors.*—When we glance back through page after page, and turn in succession to table after table, one striking fact leaps out in bold relief—the fact of multiple determination. Crime is assignable to no single universal source, nor yet to two or three : it springs from a wide variety, and usually from a multiplicity, of alternative and converging influences. So violent a reaction, as may easily be con-

600        THE YOUNG DELINQUENT

ceived, is almost everywhere the outcome of a concurrence of subversive factors : it needs many coats of pitch to paint a thing thoroughly black. The nature of these factors, and of their varying combinations, differs greatly from one individual to another : and juvenile offenders, as is amply clear, are far from constituting a homogeneous class.

Hitherto, the fund of possible explanations invoked by the criminologist has been much too narrow. Ordinarily he is content to trace delinquency in the young to but four or five all-powerful causes—sometimes, indeed, to no more than one. Drink, epilepsy, a defective moral sense, some outstanding feature of heredity, or some common characteristic of a city life, is seized upon in isolation, and made accountable for all. With the same exclusive emphasis, some solitary panacea has been correspondingly put forward. It is as if one should explain the Amazon in its flood by pointing to a rivulet in the distant Andes, which, as the tributary that is farthest from the final outflow, has the honour of being called the source. Dry up the rill, and the river still flows on. Its tributaries are countless, though all stream into one sea.

Crime, no less, is the outcome of many confluents. How wide a variety of adverse causes may contribute to youthful delinquency is graphically shown by the figures I have already given. In all, more than 170 distinct conditions have been encountered, every one of them conducive to childish misconduct.

*Causation : (b) Variety of Major Factors.*—Yet, in any given case, amid all the tangle of accessory factors, some single circumstance not infrequently stands out as the most prominent or the most influential.[1] Often, as we

---

[1] This seems to have been the experience of other investigators; see, *e.g.*, Healy, *The Individual Delinquent*, p. 162. We ourselves started with a fourfold classification of factors : (1) the principal or most conspicuous influence (if any) ; (2) the chief co-operating factor or factors ; (3) minor predisposing or aggravating conditions ; (4) conditions present but apparently inoperative. This subdivision, however, proved too elaborate for so small an array of cases ; and, for the present preliminary account, it has seemed advisable to reduce the classification to the simpler twofold distinction as above described.

## CONCLUSION 601

have seen, it can be definitely established that the child in question showed no delinquent tendencies until the year of some unfortunate event. An illness, a new demoralizing friendship, the death or the remarriage of a parent, the emergence within the growing child himself of some fresh interest or instinct—some dated crisis of this kind has often ascertainably preceded, and perhaps has plainly precipitated, his first violation of the law. At times, and with the same abruptness, so soon as the untoward condition has been removed, his perversity has diminished and his outbreaks have ceased. In other instances, some salient quality of the child's own mind, existing from birth or inherited from his parents, goes far to explain his misconduct—a strong sex instinct, a weak and suggestible temper, or a general deficiency of common sense. In many cases, however, to look for one paramount influence is a more doubtful and precarious business; and to sift causative conditions into major and minor may be little more than an arbitrary assortment, based, it is true, on long inquiries and on many consultations, but of value only for a rough and summary review. If we restrict our reckoning to the main, predominating factors, thus singled out wherever possible, we are still confronted with a long catalogue of causes, each making straight for lawless conduct : and we may still count up as many as seventy different conditions, each forming, in one instance or another, the principal reason for some child's offence.

Table XXII gives my final summary.[1] Major factors seemed discernible in about 96 per cent. of the cases, leaving only 4 per cent. (fewer still among the girls) with the major factor undetected or unassigned. In addition, subordinate factors [2] were recorded about 850

---

[1] The figures are shown in the form of percentages, and indicate the number of times the item specified was observed per hundred cases.

[2] Many of these are, of course, but aspects or consequences of other factors ; thus, the death of the father may lead to poverty, weak discipline, remarriage of the mother, and a ' step-father complex ' (itself with two or three distinguishable components)—all separately enumerated in the tables.

602          THE YOUNG DELINQUENT

times per hundred cases—rather more with the girls, rather less with the boys. On an average, therefore, each delinquent child is the product of nine or ten subversive circumstances, one as a rule preponderating, and all conspiring to draw him into crime.

The types of condition noted, however, are far from peculiar to delinquent families. The same circumstances were observed in the non-delinquent cases nearly 330 times per cent.—that is, about three per case instead of nine or ten. Thus, with children of the same social class, identical conditions may coexist without plunging them into a criminal career. It must, therefore, as a rule, be either the number of factors or the particular combination of them, that renders delinquency a probable result.

I have, partly for purposes of exposition, grouped this multitude of causal influences under a dozen or more main heads. These headings are set out in the table that follows. The number of individual cases showing influences of each type or class have already been given in Table III.[1] If we mark down the dominant factor in each instance, then, in accordance with this grouping, it becomes possible to classify delinquent individuals into corresponding causal categories. Such a classification—crude and approximate, as it must be, like all attempts to pigeonhole unique individual souls under a few psychological patterns—is, as I have tried to show, of great suggestiveness for treatment.

*The Relative Importance of Congenital and Non-congenital Factors.* — Among the many problems of causation, one is fundamental. What, in the production of juvenile crime, is the relative importance of heredity and of environment, or, more precisely, of inborn or congenital factors, on the one hand, and post-natal influences, on the other ? The issue is an old one. It is of far more than purely speculative interest. Hereditary factors are, from their very nature, irremediable. Apart from measures of eugenics—measures which will not be adopted in this generation, and, when they are

[1] Chapter II, page 53.

# CONCLUSION 603

## TABLE XXII

### SUMMARY OF CONDITIONS

| | DELINQUENT. | | | | | NON-DELINQUENT. | | |
|---|---|---|---|---|---|---|---|---|
| | Boys. | | Girls. | | Average | Boys. | Girls. | Average. |
| | Major Factor. | Minor Factor. | Major Factor. | Minor Factor. | | | | |
| **I. Hereditary Conditions:** | | | | | | | | |
| A. Physical . . . | 2·4 | 48·9 | 4·2 | 51·5 | 53·1 | 30·5 | 33·2 | 31·8 |
| B. Intellectual . . | 4·0 | 34·2 | 1·4 | 30·1 | 35·6 | 8·5 | 8·0 | 8·2 |
| C. Temperamental (with pathological symptoms) | 11·3 | 26·1 | 15·0 | 35·4 | 42·2 | 24·0 | 15·5 | 19·7 |
| D. Temperamental (with moral symptoms) . | 8·8 | 117·1 | 12·4 | 168·0 | 145·9 | 32·5 | 41·5 | 37·0 |
| Total . . . . | 26·5 | 226·3 | 33·0 | 285·0 | 276·8 | 95·5 | 98·2 | 96·7 |
| **II. Environmental Conditions:** | | | | | | | | |
| A. Within the Home. | | | | | | | | |
| 1. Poverty . . | 3·2 | 84·6 | — | 82·4 | 85·5 | 80·5 | 76·0 | 53·9 |
| 2. Defective family relationships . . | 5·7 | 111·4 | 12·3 | 143·5 | 131·3 | 38·0 | 32·5 | 35·2 |
| 3 Defective discipline | 8·9 | 82·9 | 8·2 | 51·7 | 79·5 | 12·0 | 11·0 | 11·5 |
| 4. Vicious home . | 1·6 | 37·4 | 7·0 | 66·3 | 51·5 | 10·0 | 9·5 | 9·7 |
| B. Outside the Home . | 10·5 | 57·0 | 5·5 | 50·2 | 63·7 | 22·0 | 19·5 | 20·7 |
| Total . . . . | 29·9 | 373·3 | 33·0 | 394·1 | 411·5 | 162·5 | 148·5 | 131·0 |
| **III. Physical Conditions :** | | | | | | | | |
| A. Developmental . . | 1·6 | 18·8 | 2·7 | 32·5 | 25·8 | 3·5 | 8·5 | 6·0 |
| B. Pathological . . | 9·6 | 104·1 | 6·9 | 123·4 | 119·3 | 73·5 | 83·5 | 78·5 |
| Total . . . . | 11·2 | 122·9 | 9·6 | 155·9 | 145·1 | 77·0 | 92·0 | 84·5 |
| **IV. Psychological Conditions .** | | | | | | | | |
| A. Intellectual . . | 11·4 | 82·9 | 6·8 | 78·5 | 90·9 | 35·5 | 38·5 | 37·0 |
| B. Emotional | | | | | | | | |
| 1. Inborn | | | | | | | | |
| a. Specific . . | 10·5 | 95·4 | 12·3 | 80·0 | 100·6 | 24·5 | 14·0 | 19·2 |
| b. General . . | 13·0 | 34·3 | 16·2 | 33·9 | 48·1 | 10·0 | 13·5 | 11·7 |
| 2. Acquired | | | | | | | | |
| a. Interests . | 7·3 | 56·9 | 4·2 | 38·2 | 55·7 | 18·0 | 16·5 | 17·2 |
| b. Complexes . . | 13·0 | 56·1 | 16·5 | 96·1 | 85·1 | 17·5 | 35·0 | 26·2 |
| Total . . . . | 55·2 | 325·6 | 56·0 | 326·7 | 380·4 | 105·5 | 117·5 | 111·3 |
| No major factor assignable . | 3·7 | — | 1·4 | — | — | — | — | — |
| Grand Total (II, III, & IV only ²) . . . | 100·0 | 821·8 | 100·0 | 876·7 | 937·0 | 345·0 | 358·0 | 326·8 |

¹ See foot-note (1) to Table IV.

² Hereditary conditions, enumerated under I as occurring in the family history, have not been included in the grand totals, since presumably they have already been reckoned, as occurring in the children themselves in headings II, III, and IV.

adopted, can but affect generations still unborn—
nothing can root out an inherited tendency. Its operation, indeed, may be modified ; its effects may be forestalled ; its evil possibilities may be converted into
good ; and its deficiencies may be eked out or supplemented by positive training and teaching. But the
inborn tendency itself. just because it is inborn, can never
be uprooted. Influences, on the other hand, that reside
in the environment, are in their essence not immutable :
in theory, at any rate, they can be altered, if they cannot
be removed. The distinction, therefore, should it be
valid scientifically, is one of great practical moment.

It is proper, however, to realize that the antithesis is
in some ways an abstraction. The alternatives implied
are not wholly exclusive. Between what is instinctive
and what is acquired, there is no sharp, clean-cut division.
Even were the mind an edifice of two entirely separate
storeys—an innate foundation, and a superstructure of
learning, piled up after birth—nevertheless, in actual
fact, what we test and examine is, not the architecture
of the mind, but its processes ; not detachable segments,
but composite functions. No test measures pure native
capacity, quite apart from all knowledge ; no test
measures inborn temperament, quite apart from developed
habits and interests.

Let us, however, so far as our inexact methods will
permit, endeavour to disengage the two, and weigh
the influence of all that is pre-natal against the influence
of all that is post-natal.

To gain light upon this problem, I have tried to sort
out every case in which the factors, whether principal
or accessory, were of a congenital type. Under this
rubric I have included all such physical conditions as
appeared to be directly inherited or at least constitutional, all intellectual conditions that are now generally
assumed to be inborn (as mental deficiency and general
dullness), all states of general emotionality not due to
adolescence, and all examples of a natural over-development of some primary instinctive disposition. Instances
of mere educational disability, of repressed complexes

## CONCLUSION          605

and harmful habits, and of defective or undesirable interests, I have placed on the other side. We have thus a division of cases and causes into those predominantly congenital and those predominantly acquired.

Altogether, congenital factors, whether major or minor, are found some 249 times per cent. among the delinquents, but only 72 times per cent. among the non-delinquents. Non-congenital factors are entered 688 times per cent. among the delinquents, and 254 times among the non-delinquents. Thus congenital factors have been recorded among delinquents rather more than three times as often as among non-delinquents; and non-congenital factors rather less than three times as often. If we consider in each case the major factor alone, we find it to belong to the congenital group among 36 per cent. of the boys and among 41 per cent. of the girls : so that, in well over one-third of all the cases, but in rather less than one-half, some deep constitutional failing proves the primary source of misconduct.

Hence, the share of innate conditions in the productions of juvenile delinquency is beyond doubt considerable. These, indeed, are the cases that are likely to prove the most obdurate, and to stand mainly in need of palliative rather than punitive measures. But it would be a gross distortion—a mistake too commonly deduced from current fatalistic theories—to paint every criminal as the helpless victim of his inborn nature. At the same time, it will be perceived, there still remains a large balance of offenders—between 60 and 65 per cent. of the total—whose lawless actions have been precipitated primarily by the difficulties of their environment or by the events of their own past life. Thus the part played by heredity or endowment is, in a majority of cases, that of a minor or predisposing cause.[1]

---

[1] The distribution of principal causes into congenital and non-congenital reveals a proportion, at first sight, decidedly dissimilar in my own cases to that announced by previous investigators. The disagreement, however, is not beyond all hope of reconciliation. Differences in material, and differences of classification, often seem capable of explaining it away. Healy, for example, whose thorough case-studies are often

606          THE YOUNG DELINQUENT

The outcome of my whole analysis has been reduced
to its simplest form in the last column of Table III.[1]
The figures measure the degree of association between
juvenile delinquency, on the one hand, and the various
types of condition observed, on the other. With the
loose data inevitable in sociological inquiries, statistical
coefficients must not be too zealously pressed. Broadly
speaking, however, the averages suggest the following
deductions. All the conditions enumerated in the table
—hereditary, environmental, physical, and psychological
—are positively correlated with delinquency; but no
one of them singly to a very high degree. To attribute
crime in general either to a predominantly hereditary
or to a predominantly environmental origin appears
accordingly impossible; in one individual the one
type of factor may be pre-eminent; in another, the
second; while, with a large assortment of cases, both
seem, on an average and in the long run, to be of almost
equal weight.

Judged by the coefficients, the following proves to be
the order of importance of the various conditions we
have reviewed: (1) defective discipline; (2) specific
instincts; (3) general emotional instability; (4) morbid
emotional conditions, mild rather than grave, generating
or generated by so-called complexes; (5) a family history
of vice or crime; (6) intellectual disabilities, such as
backwardness or dullness; (7) detrimental interests,
such as a passion for adventure, for the cinema, or for
some particular person, together with a lack of any

cited by hereditarians, finds environmental influences playing the decisive
part in only 25 per cent. of his examinees. He, however, has dealt
with recidivists alone—with older, more hardened, and more frequently
offending types; many of them, too, having been picked out by the
court as in special need of examination at a psychopathic institute,
comprised a number disproportionately large of gross aberrations of a
constitutional kind. My own cases, on the other hand, have been
selected, so far as possible, to form a fair representative sample of the
ordinary city delinquent; and therefore reveal external influences more
clearly (see *Brit. Journ. Med. Psych.*, 1923, III, i, pp. 1–2; and, for a
further discussion of other findings on this problem, *ibid*, pp. 17–18).

[1] See again page 53.

## CONCLUSION    607

uplifting pursuits; (8) developmental conditions, such as adolescence, or precocity in growth; (9) a family history of intellectual weakness; (10) defective family relationships—the absence of a father, the presence of a step-mother; (11) influences operating outside the home—as bad street companions, and lack or excess of facilities for amusement; (12) a family history of temperamental disorder—of insanity or the like; (13) a family history of physical weakness; (14) poverty and its concomitants; and, last of all, (15) physical infirmity or weakness in the child himself.

Heredity appears to operate, not directly through the transmission of a criminal disposition as such, but rather indirectly, through such constitutional conditions as a dull or defective intelligence, an excitable and un-balanced temperament, or an over-development of some single primitive instinct. Of environmental conditions, those obtaining outside the home are far less important than those obtaining within it; and within it, material conditions, such as poverty, are far less important than moral conditions, such as ill discipline, vice, and, most of all, the child's relations with his parents. Physical defects have barely half the weight of psychological and environmental. Psychological factors, whether due to heredity or to environment, are supreme both in number and strength over all the rest. Intellectual conditions are more serious than bodily; and emotional than intellectual; while psycho-analytic complexes everywhere provide a ready mechanism for the direction of over-powering instincts and of compressed emotional energy into open acts of crime.

If we consider major causes only, the inferences are much the same. Among personal conditions, the most significant are, first, the mental dullness which is not severe enough to be called deficiency, and, secondly, the temperamental instability which is not abnormal enough to be considered pathological. Among social conditions, by far the most potent is the family life; and, next to it, the friendships formed outside the home. These four conditions are paramount. Between them,

608     THE YOUNG DELINQUENT

as main determining factors, they account for more than 50 per cent. of juvenile delinquencies and crimes. Every cause and every influence, however, no matter what its special form may be, is found to operate, and can only operate, through its inner psychological effects. Conduct and misconduct are always, in the last analysis, the outcome of mental life.

TREATMENT.—Of the cases here examined, nearly all have been under supervision for at least three years; many, for nearly nine or ten. It is, therefore, possible to glean some preliminary notion of the efficacy of the measures advised.

Let me select those cases with which, directly or indirectly, I have been able to keep in touch over a period of twelve months or more. They may be divided into two groups : first, those in which the essential recommendations were duly carried out; secondly, those in which it was not found practicable to apply or to maintain the treatment recommended. In number the two groups are almost equal. Among the former, I find that in 62 per cent. an apparent cure resulted— that is, no delinquency has been notified for at least one year, and no fresh delinquency seems likely to ensue. In 36 per cent. progress has been, on the whole, satisfactory, though incomplete—that is, either the delinquencies more recently reported have diminished in number and gravity, or else, though no delinquencies have been reported, there still remains a suspicion that they have been or may be repeated. In only 2 per cent. have the reports proved wholly disappointing. Within the second group, those where the treatment advised was not adopted, 12 per cent. appear to have undergone a cure, spontaneous and complete ; 23 per cent. appear to be making moderate progress : the large, unsatisfactory remainder consist for the most part either of cases of some deep congenital disorder, or of cases where some hopeless home condition, from which the child cannot be permanently freed, is lurking in the background.[1]

---

[1] The children thus followed up constitute no more than a handful— but 137 in all. A more detailed survey I propose to publish later on,

## CONCLUSION 609

It is a familiar saying, that knowledge of a subject has never reached a truly scientific stage until it can be made a basis for reasonable prediction. Astronomy is a science; and we deduce the hour of an eclipse from our knowledge of the heavenly bodies. Physics is a science; and we deduce the volume of a gas from our knowledge of the effects of temperature. Has criminal psychology attained or approached, in any measure, to this deductive plane?

The groups just studied have been small, the methods of inquiry have been empirical, and the duration of the whole research has covered scarcely ten short years. The results put forward, therefore, can claim to be no more than first approximations. Any conclusion must be tentative, and any hypothesis provisional. Nevertheless, the figures quoted seem to show beyond demur that, for many cases and within a wide margin, a forecast is permissible. After an intensive study of the child and his conditions, after a reasoned assignment of his causal category, the outlook achieved over his whole situation will generally afford some warrantable guide for discreet prognostication. We can say of one that, were his home-circumstances improved and a proper occupation provided, his high intelligence would be certainly sufficient to induce a reform; of another that, after the crisis of adolescence is over, he will probably settle down to honest work; of a third that the one hope of a recovery lies in a swift removal from the old home and the old associations; and, of a fourth, that his mind is so deeply and incurably defective that there is no other safeguard but to seclude him in an institution for the remainder of his life.

Nor are our conclusions limited to individuals alone. We may extend them to the treatment of the whole problem of juvenile delinquency. We may, having learnt a little of human nature in the young, attempt to lay down certain broad and general principles for the

when it has been possible to follow up a larger number of cases for a longer period of time. The percentages given in the summary above, therefore, are to be viewed as but rough and preliminary figures.

## 610     THE YOUNG DELINQUENT

prevention of crime in general, as well as for the reclamation of the particular case. These practical deductions, the upshot of the whole inquiry, may be summarized to the following effect.

(1) All young persons who show delinquent tendencies should be dealt with at the earliest possible stage. Parents should be taught that the pre-school period is a period vitally decisive : it is then that the foundations both of moral character and of temperamental eccentricity are first laid down. Teachers should be urged to watch, and when necessary to notify, all who show anti-social inclinations ; the reports should be made in the infants' department, or, at the latest, soon after the child's promotion to the senior school. In the school itself, the training of character, as well as the instruction of the intellect, should form an integral part of education. When at last the school-period is over, after-care workers should be persuaded to extend their supervision to the social conduct, as well as the industrial efficiency, of children who have just left ; and, above all, special efforts should be made to meet the transitional phase of adolescence.

(2) The problem of delinquency in the young must be envisaged as but one inseparable portion of the larger enterprise for child welfare. Crime in children is not a unique, well-marked, or self-contained phenomenon, to be handled solely by the policeman and the children's court. It touches every side of social work. The teacher, the care committee worker, the magistrate, the probation officer, all who come into official contact with the child, should be working hand in hand, not only with each other, but with all the clubs, societies, and agencies, voluntary as well as public, that seek to better the day-to-day life of the child.

(3) The delinquent himself must be approached individually as a unique human being, with a peculiar constitution, peculiar difficulties, and peculiar problems of his own. The key-note of modern educational thought is individuality—self-realization, to be sought and attained, not by collective instruction nor by imposed

## CONCLUSION 611

uniformity and repression, but by separate adjustments and readjustments for each particular child. If this is needed for the normal, how much greater must be the need among the abnormal, the neglected, the delinquent ! The court, therefore, and whatever authority has to grapple with such cases, must at all times regard not the offence, but the offender. The aim must be not punishment, but treatment ; and the target not isolated actions, but their causes. Since these causes seldom float conspicuously upon the surface, such authorities must have access to all available information, and possess means to make for every case intensive investigations of their own. On each main aspect, they must have expert help. A social investigator must report upon home circumstances ; a medical officer must inspect the child for physical defects ; a psychologist must be at hand to apply mental tests, to assess temperamental qualities, and to analyse unconscious motives. A psychological clinic, embodying all these different workers studying the same cases scientifically, side by side, is the most pressing need of all.

(4) The remedies, in the same way, will be adapted, not to the nature of the offence, but to the nature of the factors provoking it. Already, the outworn maxim of traditional justice, that the punishment should fit the crime, though set to memorable music in an optimistic key, is now giving place to the sounder principle that the treatment must fit the delinquent. Full advantage is to be taken of the various methods of disposal sanctioned by the newer statutes. Probation should be employed with a larger freedom, and at the same time with finer discrimination ; it should include, for each separate case, not merely passive surveillance, but active and constructive efforts. Institutions for the delinquent should continue their laudable development towards a less uniform organization and a less repressive code. Special establishments, more particularly, are wanted, not only for the defective and for the supernormal, but also for the dull who cannot be certified as defective, and for the unstable and neurotic who cannot be treated

612          THE YOUNG DELINQUENT

as insane. And, with a minuter classification both of cases on the one hand, and of voluntary homes and residential schools on the other, efforts should be made to assign each ill-adjusted child to the place most suited to his special needs. After-care, in particular, calls for further extension : to lavish a hundred pounds upon the intensive training of a youth in an institution, and then suddenly to fling him loose into the old environment, sparing neither time nor trouble for further aid and following-up, is not economy but waste.

(5) Fuller knowledge is urgently wanted : it is wanted both in regard to the causation of crime, and in respect of the relative efficacy of different remedial measures. Only from the organization of research can this fuller knowledge come ; and organized research means an established criminological department. The fruits of such research should be made immediately accessible to the practical officer ; and courses of instruction should be arranged where all who have to deal with the young offender may learn the latest and best-accredited results of modern criminal psychology.

(6) Finally, society must aim at prevention as well as at cure. Housing, medical treatment, continued education, the psychological study of children in the schools, improved industrial conditions, increased facilities for recreation, the cautious adoption of practicable eugenic measures, and, above all, sustained investigation into all the problems of childhood—these are but a few of the countless needs to be supplied, if delinquency in the young is to be, not merely cured as it arises, but diverted, forestalled, and so far as possible wiped out.

Poets have extolled the innocence of infancy, the birthright of each growing boy before the shades of the prison-house close over him. The psychologist, the teacher, the harassed parent, know too well that moral perfection is no innate gift, but a hard and difficult acquirement. The perfect child has still to be born and bred. And the practical man can but echo the

## CONCLUSION 613

aspiration of Anatole France : ' Espérons dans ces êtres inconcevables qui sorteront un jour de l'homme, comme l'homme est sorti de la brute. Saluons ces génies futurs ! ' [1]

[1] *Le Jardin d'Épicure*, pp. 115–16. ' Let us hope for these inconceivable beings who shall one day develop out of man, as man has evolved from the brute. Let us salute these future prodigies ! '

# [19]

## JOHN BOWLBY

### (VII) CONCLUSION AND SUMMARY

From its earliest days psycho-analysis has emphasized the critical importance of the child's first few years. Despite this there has been relatively little systematic investigation of possible adverse factors in the young child's environment. The investigation reported here has sought to remedy this situation by enquiring into the early environment, and in particular that part of it comprised by the parents, of a number of habitual thieves. The result has been that certain specifically adverse circumstances have been identified and their significance demonstrated both statistically in the whole group and clinically in a few individual cases. The conclusion has been drawn that, had it not been for certain factors inimical to the healthy development of the capacity for object-love, certain children would not have become offenders. Conversely, and equally important, it may be concluded that the socially satisfactory behaviour of most adults is dependent on their having been brought up in circumstances, for-

tunately common, which have encouraged or at least permitted the satisfactory development of their capacity to make object-relationships. These findings thus not only confirm the general psycho-analytic thesis that it is the early years which count in character development, but demonstrate beyond doubt that the elucidation of the problem of juvenile delinquency is dependent upon psycho-analytic investigation. Nevertheless it would be foolish to suppose that psycho-analytic investigation alone, even extended to cover statistical enquiries of the kind reported here, would be sufficient. Though juvenile delinquency is to a great degree a psychological problem, it is also a problem of sociology and economics.

We must remember that the cases studied in this investigation are not a typical sample of Court cases. They are a highly selected sample, referred to a Child Guidance Clinic because they were specially difficult or because the child was obviously not emotionally normal. There are many other sorts of children charged in Court and in these cases factors of the kind inculpated in this paper may well be few or indeed absent. On the other hand, poverty, bad housing, lack of recreational facilities and other socio-economic factors, will play a large part. Juvenile delinquency as a total problem is in fact the outcome of many and complex factors and until the effects of these are studied *together* in an adequately planned and combined research the weight to be attached to each will remain unknown. In consequence, though this research has placed emphasis on the psycho-analytic factors, we have no method of ascertaining how important these factors are in the total problem which the Home Office and the Courts have to deal with. The remark of an experienced probation officer that about one-third of the cases coming into Court are of the kinds described in this paper is our only clue.

Should this estimate be accurate or even nearly accurate, the problem of providing adequate treatment would be vast, for it is evident that no treatment which leaves the basic emotional problems in these cases unsolved can be more than palliative. Moreover, even when psycho-analytic treatment can be attempted, progress is extremely slow and difficult. One outstanding reason for this is, of course, that the disorders are already of many years' duration when they first come for treatment. For instance, the average age of the Affectionless children in this series was about ten years. This means that the condition had been present and progressing for at least seven years. My conclusion therefore is that all these cases must in future be diagnosed and treated before the child is five, and preferably before three. This may appear a fantastic view. But no doubt the same might have been said of physicians who advocated the early treatment of tuberculosis in the days when only advanced conditions were seen. Since those days, we have learnt to diagnose tuberculosis, whether of bone or joint or lung, in its earliest stages, and no sacrifice is thought too great to secure its cure, even though the symptoms presented are, to the layman, trivial.

In precisely the same way we may look forward to a time when the diagnosis of delinquent character is regularly made in the child's early years. That we can learn to do this there can be not the slightest doubt. The case of Florence W., aged $3\frac{1}{2}$, demonstrates that if we are on the look-out for the diagnostic signs in early life, they can be detected. The help of infant welfare centres and nursery schools must be enlisted. Well-trained play-analysts must be provided to give treatment. Medicine must step in and cure these cases long before they are even eligible to come before a Court of Law. For in dealing with chronic delinquents the machinery of law is starting at a serious disadvantage. No child may be charged before the age of 8 years, by which time the disease is far advanced. Looked at as centres for the prevention and cure of crime, such an arrangement might be compared to a national network of cancer-clinics, pledged to take no case of less than five years' standing.

But if early diagnosis is important, how much more vital is prevention. Certain factors, it is true, cannot be prevented. Deaths, whether of mother or little brother, will occur, but even here an understanding of the child's emotions may enable timely help to be given. Anxious and nagging mothers also may always be with us, but again an understanding of their problem and the provision of play centres and nursery schools will go far to ameliorate the lot of their children. The prolonged separation of young children from their mothers may also on occasion be unavoidable. Nevertheless, if all those who had to advise on the upbringing of small children, and not least among them doctors, were aware of the appalling damage which separations of this kind have on the development of a child's character, many could be avoided and many of the most distressing cases of chronic delinquency prevented.

## SUMMARY

(1) The characters and psychiatric history of 44 juvenile thieves referred to a Child Guidance Clinic are compared with those of 44 children also referred to a Clinic who did not steal. About half the thieves had indulged in regular and serious stealing, in most cases over a long period of time. In only 12 had the stealing been relatively slight, and one of these later turned out to be a chronic thief.

(2) In sex and intelligence there was no significant difference between the groups. Only two thieves were of low intelligence.

(3) Economic status was not specially investigated, but was believed not to differ between the two groups. Few in either group were dependent on support from public funds.

(4) The thieves are classified according to their characters. Only 2 were regarded as fairly ' Normal' emotionally, 9 were Depressed, 2 Circular, 13 Hyperthymic, 14 of a character type which has been christened ' Affectionless ' and 4 Schizoid or Schizophrenic. There are no Affectionless Characters amongst the controls, a difference which is significant.

(5) The Affectionless children are significantly more delinquent than the other thieves. All but one were serious offenders, the majority truanting as well as stealing. They constitute more than half of the more serious and chronic offenders. It is argued that these Affectionless delinquents constitute a true psychiatric syndrome hitherto only partially recognized.

(6) Ætiological factors are discussed under three main headings : possible genetic factors, early home environment and contemporary en-

vironment. The difficulty of isolating the influence of genetic factors from environmental factors is discussed. Five factors are treated statistically : (i) genetic, (ii) prolonged separations of child from mother or foster-mother in the early years, (iii) ambivalent and anxious mothers, (iv) fathers who openly hate their children, and (v) recent traumatic events.

(7) Eighteen thieves had a parent or grand-parent who was mentally ill with psychosis, psychopathic character or severe neurosis, an incidence of mental illness which is almost identical to that in the control group. Though comparative figures are not available, this incidence is almost certainly higher in both groups than it would be in a control group of normal children. Both genetic and environmental factors are likely to play a part in producing this association.

(8) Seventeen of the thieves had suffered complete and prolonged separation (six months or more) from their mothers or established foster-mothers during their first five years of life. Only two controls had suffered similar separations, a statistically significant difference. 12 of the 14 thieves who were of the Affectionless Character had suffered a prolonged separation in contrast to only 5 of the remaining 30 thieves, a difference which is again significant. Clinical evidence is presented which shows that a prolonged separation is a principle cause of the Affectionless (and delinquent) Character.

(9) Of the 27 thieves who had not suffered an early separation 17 had mothers who were either extremely anxious, irritable and fussy or else rigid, domineering and oppressive, traits which in all cases mask much unconscious hostility. Five of the 27 had fathers who hated them and expressed their hatred openly. In these respects, however, the thieves do not differ from the controls, although it is extremely probable that both groups would differ substantially from a group of normal children.

(10) Five of the thieves had suffered traumatic experiences, four in connection with their mothers' illness or death and one over a brother's death. Six others had been seriously upset by a relatively recent unhappy experience. Evidence is brought to show that stealing is in some cases a symptom of a Depressive State.

(11) The incidence of the five factors enumerated does not differ significantly as between the less serious cases of stealing and the controls. The incidence both of ambivalent mothers and recent traumatic events is lower in the case of habitual thieves than it is in the other two groups. The incidence of prolonged separations of the small child from his mother or foster-mother is significantly greater in the case of the habitual offenders than in the other groups. It is concluded that whilst the other four factors may well be of considerable importance for the pathogenesis of

unstable and maladapted children in general, including some delinquents, prolonged separations are a specific and very frequent cause of chronic delinquency.

(12) The pathological effects of prolonged separations and the psychopathology of the Affectionless thief are discussed very briefly. Attention is drawn (a) to the strong libidinal and aggressive components in stealing, and (b) to the failure of super-ego development in these cases following a failure in the development of the capacity for object-love. The latter is traced to lack of opportunity for development and to inhibition resulting from rage and phantasy on the one hand and motives of emotional self-protection on the other.

(13) The relationship of stealing to truancy and sexual offences is discussed. Evidence is advanced that the Affectionless Character is prone to both, and that a substantial proportion of prostitutes are probably of this character.

(14) A plea is made for a combined research in which both psycho-analytic and socio-economic factors are investigated. Without such research the relative effect of either group of factors in explaining the total problem of juvenile delinquency will remain unknown.

(15) The treatment of delinquent character is difficult. Since it is possible to diagnose an Affectionless Character at the age of three years and possibly earlier, a strong plea is made for early diagnosis and early treatment. Above all, attention should be given to prevention ; many prolonged separations could be avoided.

BIBLIOGRAPHY

(1) ARMSTRONG, C. P. (1932). *660 Runaway Boys* (Boston, Badger).

(2) BOWLBY, J. (1940). *Personality and Mental Illness* (London, Kegan Paul).

(3) —— (1940). ' The Influence of Early Environment in the Development of Neurosis and Neurotic Character ', *Int. J. Psycho-Anal.*, **21**, 154.

(4) BURT, C. (1925). *The Young Delinquent* (University of London Press).

(5) CARR-SAUNDERS, A. M., MANNHEIM, H. and RHODES, E. C. (1943). *Young Offenders* (Cambridge University Press).

(6) GLUECK and GLUECK (1934). *One Thousand Juvenile Delinquents. Their Treatment by Court and Clinic* (Harvard University Press).

(7) GORDON. R. G. (1937). ' Delinquency in Relation to the Broken Home ', *Arch. Dis. Childh.*, **12**, 111.

(8) HEALY, W. and BRONNER, A. F. (1936). *New Light on Delinquency and its Treatment* (Yale University Press).

(9) LANDERS, J. L. (1938). ' Observations on Two Hundred Dartmoor Convicts ', *J. ment. Sci.*, **84**.

(10) NORWOOD EAST, W. and HUBERT, W. H. DE B. (1939). *The Psychological Treatment of Crime* (London, H.M. Stationery Office).

(11) PARTRIDGE. J. M. (1939). ' Truancy ', *J. ment. Sci.*. **85**.

(12) STENGEL, E. (1939). ' Studies on the Psycho-

56    FORTY-FOUR JUVENILE THIEVES: THEIR CHARACTERS AND HOME-LIFE

pathology of Compulsive Wandering ', *Brit. J. med. Psychol.*, **18**, 250.

(13) YOUNG, H. T. P. (1937). 'Temperament in Adolescent Male Offenders ', *J. ment. Sci.*, **83**.

(14) LEAGUE OF NATIONS (1938).  *Prostitutes: their Early Lives.  (Enquiry into Measures of Rehabilitation of Prostitutes*, Part I) (Geneva).

# [20]

# The Dynamics of Specialization in Juvenile Offenses*

ROBERT J. BURSIK, JR., *Institute for Juvenile Research, Chicago*

*ABSTRACT*
   *A major step forward in the statistical analysis of offense specialization was made by Wolfgang et al. through their use of stochastic modeling. However, this paper proposes that the results that were obtained are not as clear as might be hoped because they did not distinguish between offense dynamics that reflected the marginal distributions of the sample as a whole (and thus may be considered random) and dynamics that significantly deviated from this distribution. An analysis of similar longitudinal data for white and nonwhite delinquents shows statistically significant evidence of offense specialization and a random distribution of offenses if no specialization occurs (with one major exception). The implications and problems of the model are discussed.*

The importance of the idea of offense specialization to the development of juvenile delinquency theory has been long recognized in sociology and criminology. One of the first researchers to collect pertinent data, systematically, on this matter was Clifford Shaw, who used very detailed case study material to highlight the dynamics of social processes that were associated with the patterns of adolescent illegal behavior. These dynamics became a central theme in much of Shaw's work, for he felt that a "delinquent act is part of a dynamic life process, and it is artificial to view it except as an integral part of that process" (b, 8). Several of his published studies have become classics in the social sciences (a, b, c). The incredible richness of detail found in these reports often leaves the reader with the impression of being privy to an intimate view of the growth and development of the behavior patterns of these youth.

   Unfortunately, the generalizability of these studies to the population of adolescent offenders was not clear, since the selection of a youth for a case study was based on a far from random process. For example,

*The data for this paper are taken from those used in the author's dissertation while at the University of Chicago. I would like to express my gratitude to Donald J. Bogue, James S. Coleman, and Gerald Suttles of the University of Chicago, and Tony Meade of the Institute for Juvenile Research for helpful comments and criticisms.

852 / Social Forces / vol. 58:3, march 1980

"Sidney" (b) came to Shaw's attention through his involvement in a widely publicized rape case in Chicago. Expansions of Shaw's work with large-sample, longitudinal data sets appeared only sporadically for several decades (Ferguson, Wilkins). During the middle sixties, however, the amount of published research on the topic began to accelerate until, at present, the dynamic approach to delinquency has regained its status as a top research priority (cf. Elliott and Voss; Robin; Robins and Wish; Shannon; Wolfgang et al.)

Two problems have consistently plagued much of this research. One very thorny problem has been the methods used to collect the data. An often heated debate has persisted in sociology about the relative merits of using officially collected data (such as police records) as opposed to self-reported data collected directly from the youth. Although the arguments are long and involved, there are two primary issues: (1) there is much delinquency hidden from official sources since many offenses are never reported or acted on;[1] (2) official statistics reflect law enforcement activity and organization due to the discretionary factors involved in the apprehension and arrest of youth and are thus virtually useless as actual indicators of delinquent behavior (Chambliss and Nagasawa). These issues have been discussed in great detail elsewhere, but I am quite sympathetic to the view of Hindelang et al. and Reiss that the two approaches measure different aspects of delinquency and are more complementary than contradictory.

The debate is especially relevant to longitudinal approaches to delinquency. On a self-report instrument, a youth who has committed only a very few offenses might be expected to recall the nature and timing of these offenses fairly accurately. But one who has committed twenty or thirty offenses can in no way be expected to recall the nature of all of them accurately, must less their temporal ordering. Therefore, a respondent is typically asked in these instruments if s/he has committed a given offense never, once, two, or three times, or often during a given time period. Self-reported data can only give rough estimates of the sequence and level of delinquency and are more appropriate in pursuing questions about the prevalence of an offense in a population rather than the rate of incidence. Official records also cannot specify accurately the types and timing of all of a youth's offenses. But for a certain proportion of them, highly specific temporal information is available. These records therefore seem better suited to address the problem of offense specialization because the sequence of offenses is central to the nature of the problem. Official data are used in the analysis section of this paper; however, their limitations must be made clear.

A second problem is that data obtained in these longitudinal studies tend to overwhelm the statistical techniques available for their analysis. In case study approaches, one might simply use time as a unifying framework for organizing the interpretation of a youth's offense history. Translating this approach to large samples so that one may generalize to some population through statistical techniques is far from being a clean process and usually loses the rich flavor of the case study. The problem is one of effectively analyzing a group of youths who commit different numbers of offenses at different times during adolescence within different environments and who are subject to differential changes in these environments over time, while sustaining a synoptic view of the dynamics of delinquency. This problem is not limited to delinquency, of course; it arises consistently in such fields as social mobility research. The approaches to date have been far from totally satisfying, leading Carr–Hill and MacDonald to conclude that there are no completely satisfactory techniques available.

Criminological approaches to the solution of this problem have met with varying degrees of success, but usually at the expense of compromising the full extent of the data. Shannon, for example, attempted to construct typologies of delinquent histories through geometric and Guttman scaling techniques, but in doing so, was not able to save the temporal structure of the offenses. Robins developed an actuarial method that was used to assess the effect that the commission of one offense had on the probability of the future commission of another offense (Robins and Taibleson) but it is very inefficient for the analysis of long strings of events. These approaches have been able to investigate one dimension of specialization (either the offense types committed or the temporal aspects) but at the cost of neglecting the other.

A great breakthrough in juvenile delinquency research occurred in 1972 when stochastic (probabilistic) models were first used by Wolfgang et al. to analyze data of this type. Although the approach does present some problems (discussed in the concluding section), it allows for a more efficient analysis of specialization patterns than had been achieved previously.

## The Wolfgang, Figlio and Sellin Model of Specialization

The Wolfgang et al. analysis (hereafter referred to as WFS) utilized the police, court, and school records of 9,945 Philadelphia males from the time they were 10 years of age until they reached 18. The dynamic aspects of offense specialization were modeled by a first-order Markov chain. This stochastic model assumes that the probability that a youth commits offense type $j$ at time $t$ depends solely on the offense type committed at time $t-1$. For their purposes, WFS considered the commission of the first offense as time 1, the second offense as time 2, and so forth. They therefore hypothesized that the nature of an offense is only related to the type of offense that had been committed immediately beforehand, and *not* to the offenses that the youth may have committed before that time, i.e.,

$$P(X_t = \text{offense } j / X_0, X_1, \ldots, X_{t-1}) = P(X_t = \text{offense } j / X_{t-1})$$

854 / Social Forces / vol. 58:3, march 1980

The possible offense types that are under consideration are called the "states" of the model. WFS defined six of these states: nonindex crimes, personal injury crimes, theft offenses, property crimes, offenses that combined the first four states, and desistance (no crime). Using the first nine offenses that these youth had committed (representing eight transitions from the offense at time $t - 1$ to the offense at time $t$), they computed an overall matrix of the probabilities of committing offense $j$ given that offense $i$ had just been committed. This matrix, $P_{ij}$, is assumed to be constant or stationary across all of the transitions and generates the movement between offenses. The maximum likelihood estimates of this matrix can be derived by:

$$\hat{P}_{ij} = \sum_t n_{ij}(t) / \sum_t n_i(t-1) \qquad \text{(Anderson and Goodman)}[2]$$

where the $n_{ij}(t)$ represents the number of individuals who have moved from offense $i$ at time $t - 1$ to offense $j$ at time $t$ and $n_i(t-1)$ represents the total number of individuals who had committed offense $i$ at time $t - 1$. The algorithm, then, derives the matrix of conditional probabilities that a youth will commit offense $j$ given that he has just committed offense $i$ subject to the constraint:

$$\sum_j \hat{P}_{ij} = 1.00$$

The transition matrix produced by WFS is presented in Table 1. Using the $\chi^2$ tests outlined by Goodman (a), they tested for the stationarity of the transition probabilities across the offense sequence and found that the hypothesis of a constant generating matrix could not be rejected at the $p = .05$ level of significance. The first-order model also fit the data much better than the zero-order model (which assumes that all offenses are random) and the second-order model (which assumes that an offense depends on the previous two offenses).

WFS defined specialization as the likelihood that an offense of any

**Table 1.** THE GENERATING TRANSITION PROBABILITY MATRIX OF WOLFGANG, FIGLIO, AND SELLIN

| Offense Committed at Time = T-1 | Offense Committed at Time = T | | | | | |
|---|---|---|---|---|---|---|
|  | Nonindex | Personal Injury | Theft | Damage | Combination | Desistance |
| Nonindex | .4473 | .0685 | .1054 | .0228 | .0492 | .3068 |
| Personal injury | .4090 | .0920 | .0854 | .0222 | .0600 | .3314 |
| Theft | .4051 | .0530 | .2130 | .0235 | .0928 | .2126 |
| Damage | .5013 | .0882 | .1463 | .0529 | .0343 | .1770 |
| Combination | .3922 | .0703 | .1378 | .0169 | .1350 | .2478 |
| Desistance | .0000 | .0000 | .0000 | .0000 | .0000 | 1.0000 |

Source: Wolfgang et al. (183).

type will be followed by a similar offense (180). They felt that there were some indications of specialization in Table 1 since for all of the offense types except nonindex crimes, the conditional probability of committing an offense was greatest when it was preceded by a similar offense. However, they concluded that the strength of this specialization was very hard to determine since the probabilities of a like-to-like transition were not particularly high.

It is the position of this paper that the transition probabilities *in themselves* do not constitute the proper focus for testing the specialization hypothesis. From pages 180–82 of the WFS book, it is possible to determine the marginal distribution of the offense types committed during offenses two through nine:[3] 59.3 percent of the offenses are nonindex crimes; 8.5 percent are personal injury; 18.8 percent are theft; 4 percent are damage; and 9.4 percent are combinations. If the process were purely random, with no relationship between the type of offense committed at time $t$ and that committed at time $t - 1$, the transition probabilities out of each offense type (the rows of the matrix) would be approximately of the same magnitude and reflect the marginal percentage distribution. Although the probability of committing two damage offenses consecutively is only .053, this may be much higher (or lower) than would be expected from a purely random process. To discern any tendency toward specialization, one would have to turn up evidence of more specialization than one would randomly expect.

## A Residual Analysis of Specialization

As part of another study, 750 youths who were adjudicated delinquent in the Cook County, Illinois juvenile court and who had reached their 17th birthday by the time of the data collection were randomly sampled from the files of the court. The folders in the court library are cumulative, so that all of a youth's police contacts and court appearances prior to the time of sampling may be obtained. The sample is not strictly comparable to that of WFS since it represents only youth who at some time were pronounced officially delinquent by the court. However, the data are completely suitable for the problem of determining aspects of specialization and highlighting the problems noted above.

The offenses were grouped into four categories: personal injury offenses (such as murder, rape, assault), personal property offenses (such as robbery and strong-arm robbery), impersonal property offenses (such as theft and burglary), and "other" offenses (such as disorderly conduct and drug abuse). Although WFS included desistance as a distinct category, it was not included here since including youth with very few offenses might confound patterns that are present in the more active youth for whom the specialization question is more meaningful. In order to eliminate this state,

856 / Social Forces / vol. 58:3, march 1980

only youth who had committed at least five offenses (representing four transitions) were used in the analysis (the sample was too small to raise the criterion to nine offenses as did WFS). A total of 134 whites and 335 nonwhites qualified for the analysis.

The race-specific generating matrices are presented in Tables 2a and 2b.[4] None of the $\chi^2$ tests significantly violate the assumption of stationarity, so it may be assumed that the first-order Markov chain provides a good fit to the data. The patterns of the transition probabilities resemble those of WFS in that only three of the like-to-like transitions show a conditional probability greater than .5. The columns also show that the probability of committing a specific offense is usually highest when the previous offense is similar in nature. However, the tendency to follow an offense with a similar offense is not particularly striking. For example, both racial groups are more likely to follow a personal property offense with an impersonal property offense rather than another personal property offense. In five of the eight rows, the probability is actually higher that a youth does not repeat an offense. Overall, although there is some evidence of specialization, it is not very convincing.

This is the point at which WFS left their analysis: limited support for the existence of specialization. However, as in the WFS study, the marginal distributions are highly skewed. Thus, the transition matrices reflect a combination of random movement based on the tendencies of the sample as a whole and deviations from this pattern. Were one able to show that, although some of the transition probabilities are not high, they nonetheless depart markedly from what should be expected by chance, this could be taken as evidence of nonrandomness. If these tendencies were found in the like-to-like transitions, this might be taken as evidence of some degree of specialization.

A potentially fruitful analytic approach is to view these transition matrices as contingency tables. The row totals given to the right of the matrices represent the total number of youth who ever committed the given offense at time $t - 1$, thus being in a position to make a transition to their next offense. If this total is multiplied by the individual probabilities in the row, the probabilities can be converted into the number of youth who have ever made a given transition. If this is done for each offense, the generating matrix can easily be converted into a contingency table, with each youth appearing four times.

When the transition probability matrices are approached in this way, techniques that have been developed for the analysis of contingency tables might prove especially useful in the investigation of two aspects of the dynamics of offense histories. Is there, in fact, a tendency over time for youth to specialize in certain types of delinquency more than should be expected? For example, does a youth who engages in such "other" offenses as drug abuse tend significantly to restrict him or herself to a repetition of

**Table 2a.** GENERATING TRANSITION PROBABILITY MATRIX: TRANSITIONS 1–4 NON-WHITE DELINQUENTS–COOK COUNTY, ILLINOIS

| Offense Committed at Time = T-1 | Personal Injury | Personal Property | Impersonal Property | Other | Row N |
|---|---|---|---|---|---|
| Personal injury | .1744 | .1512 | .3721 | .3023 | 172 |
| Personal property | .1420 | .2485 | .3609 | .2485 | 169 |
| Impersonal property | .0981 | .1190 | .5498 | .2331 | 622 |
| Other | .1353 | .1088 | .3873 | .3687 | 377 |
| Column N | 166 | 183 | 613 | 378 | |

Offense-Specific $\chi^2$ Test of the Stationarity of Transition Probabilities Over Time

| | | |
|---|---|---|
| Personal injury | 8.3861 | n.s. |
| Personal property | 4.1198 | n.s. |
| Impersonal property | 9.3428 | n.s. |
| Other | 2.3529 | n.s. |

Degrees of freedom for each test: 9

**Table 2b.** GENERATING TRANSITION PROBABILITY MATRIX: TRANSITIONS 1–4 WHITE DELINQUENTS–COOK COUNTY, ILLINOIS

| Offense Committed at Time = T-1 | Personal Injury | Personal Property | Impersonal Property | Other | Row N |
|---|---|---|---|---|---|
| Personal injury | .1395 | .2093 | .3721 | .2791 | 43 |
| Personal property | .1667 | .2083 | .4167 | .2083 | 24 |
| Impersonal property | .1098 | .0447 | .5447 | .3008 | 246 |
| Other | .0628 | .0359 | .3722 | .5291 | 223 |
| Column N | 51 | 33 | 243 | 209 | |

Offense-Specific $\chi^2$ Test of the Stationarity of Transition Probabilities Over Time

| | | |
|---|---|---|
| Personal injury | 9.8305 | n.s. |
| Personal property | 6.4857 | n.s. |
| Impersonal property | 6.4173 | n.s. |
| Other | 4.2601 | n.s. |

Degrees of freedom for each test: 9

858 / Social Forces / vol. 58:3, march 1980

those offenses? Or does a youth who engages in these offenses tend significantly to move into new forms of delinquency such as theft or burglary (impersonal property offenses)?

The key to this type of analysis hinges on the relationship between the observed number of youth who make a given transition and the number that would be expected to make the transition on the basis of chance alone, i.e., the traditional $\chi^2$ test of independence. Such deviations definitely occur in the generating matrices since the overall $\chi^2$ statistics for the white and nonwhite contingency tables are 60.3 and 65.4 respectively, both highly significant at $p < .001$. It would be tempting to simply compare the observed and expected scores for each cell to note the significant deviations, but Hauser has shown very clearly that this may still be confounded by the marginal distributions. However, the solution that he proposes is based on the vast body of research that has accumulated in the social mobility area. Since there is a great scarcity of comparable data for offense specialization that would allow one to make reasoned estimates of the relative ease of certain transitions, as he suggests, it does not seem warranted to use such an approach.

Rather, the analysis will proceed in two steps corresponding to the research objectives noted above. The first step examines the residual structure of the diagonals of the two matrices to see if there are signs of specialization based on the observed/expected ratio. Then, given the criterion that someone does *not* repeat an offense during the next time period, an analysis is made to search for any significant movements into other types of offenses.

The analysis of the diagonal structure of the matrices can be strengthened by computing the adjusted standardized residual as suggested by Haberman:

$$ASR_{ij} = \{(\text{observed}_{ij} - \text{expected}_{ij})/SQRT(\text{expected}_{ij})\}/$$
$$SQRT\{(1 - n_i./n..)(1 - n._j/n..)\}$$

The numerator is cell $(i,j)$'s contribution to the overall $\chi^2$ statistic prior to squaring (sometimes called the standardized residual). This retains the important information that an observed value was above or below the expected value for that cell under the independence hypothesis. The denominator represents an asymptotic maximum likelihood estimate of the standard deviation of each cell. The adjusted standardized residual for each cell can then be viewed as an approximately standardized normal deviate and interpreted as such, allowing for tests of significance for the departure of each cell from independence. Using this test in conjunction with the computed ratio of the observed values and the expected values, it is possible to determine if these ratios are significant indicators of specialization.

Table 3 shows the residual structure of the white and nonwhite diagonals. The transition from personal injury offenses to personal injury offenses for white delinquents is the only specialization transition that does not prove to be significant. For both groups, the greatest observed/expected ratio is for personal property offenses, indicating that the deviation from randomness is most marked for this offense type. Except for the personal injury offenses, the rank order of the specialization tendencies is very similar by race. However, there appears to be a much greater tendency for whites to specialize in personal property offenses than for nonwhites. This difference should be viewed with caution, since the expected value in that cell is very small (1.48) and there were only five observed transitions of that type.

Thus, there is definite evidence that some degree of specialization occurs in the offense histories of white and nonwhite delinquents. But what about the transitions that were nonspecialized? If a youth does not repeat an offense, are there pronounced tendencies to move into certain other types of behavior? To test this proposition, Goodman's (b) model of quasi-independence was used. This approach eliminates the diagonals of the contingency table and conducts a modified $\chi^2$ test of independence. It therefore checks to see if there are indications that, given a transition has been made into a different kind of offense, the offense committed at time $t$ is independent of the offense committed at time $t-1$.

For nonwhite delinquents, the analysis shows that if specialization does not occur, the type of offense committed at time $t$ is random (Table 4a). The $\chi^2$ statistic for the quasi-independence model does not reject the hypothesis of independence between the offenses committed at time $t$ and time $t-1$, and none of the adjusted standardized residuals is significant. But white delinquents do make a nonspecialized transition that is statistically significant from personal injury offenses to personal property offenses (Table 4b).

**Table 3.**  TESTS FOR OFFENSE SPECIALIZATION IN THE DIAGONALS OF THE TRANSITION MATRICES*

| Offense Type | Whites | | Nonwhites | |
|---|---|---|---|---|
| | Ratio of Observed/ Expected | Adjusted Standardized Residual | Ratio of Observed/ Expected | Adjusted Standardized Residual |
| Personal injury | 1.4677 | 1.03 | 1.4073 | 2.15* |
| Personal property | 3.3802 | 3.06† | 1.8196 | 4.53‡ |
| Impersonal property | 1.2013 | 3.91‡ | 1.2018 | 6.32‡ |
| Other | 1.3573 | 5.58‡ | 1.3072 | 4.41‡ |

*Residual significant at the .05 level.
†Residual significant at the .01 level.
‡Residual significant at the .001 level.

*Criminal Detection and the Psychology of Crime*

**Table 4a.** ADJUSTED STANDARDIZED RESIDUALS FOR QUASI-INDEPENDENCE MODEL OF OFFENSE SPECIALIZATION NONWHITE–DIAGONALS OMITTED*

| Offense Committed at Time = T-1 | Offense Committed at Time = T | | | |
|---|---|---|---|---|
| | Personal Injury | Personal Property | Impersonal Property | Other |
| Personal injury | 0.0 | 0.56 | -0.76 | 0.39 |
| Personal property | 0.80 | 0.0 | -0.07 | -0.53 |
| Impersonal property | -1.07 | 0.95 | 0.0 | 0.09 |
| Other | 0.57 | -1.45 | 0.63 | 0.0 |

$x^2$ Test of Quasi-Independence = 3.90 n.s.

Degrees of freedom = 5

*Significant at the .05 level.

    The random nature of nonrepeated offenses (excluding the one white exception) is an important finding, for it is evidence that there is not a pronounced transition from one type of offense to another (the image that comes to mind is the desperate junkie who turns to theft to support his habit). The part played by the personal injury offense in the dynamics of delinquency is also very interesting. There is a pronounced tendency for whites to become involved in these offenses only on a random basis, indicating that a white youth who makes a career of personal assaults is very rare. Once they have committed an offense of this type, they tend to move into another offense type. Nonwhites, on the other hand, do show some evidence of specialization in these offenses and, if the offense is not repeated, there are no marked patterns of entry into other offenses. Cross-sectional studies have often noted that whites and nonwhites tend to commit different types of offenses, with nonwhites being involved to a greater extent in more serious crime (Elliott and Voss). It now appears that differential aspects are also present in the dynamics of personal injury offenses, which are of a more serious nature than the other three offense types.

## Comments

Although the transition probabilities indicate that specialization in most offense types is not typically a dominant feature of a youth's offense history, the residual structure of the matrices shows definite evidence of some specialization tendencies for the white and nonwhite samples. However, it still leaves the dynamic study of delinquency in a very rudimentary position. Stochastic models, as enlightening as they may be, are still not completely satisfying. Using the finite Markov chain model has arbitrarily restricted our sample to those youths who have committed five or more

**Table 4b.** ADJUSTED STANDARDIZED RESIDUALS FOR QUASI-INDEPENDENCE MODEL OF OFFENSE SPECIALIZATION WHITES–DIAGONALS OMITTED*

| Offense Committed at Time = T-1 | Offense Committed at Time = T | | | |
|---|---|---|---|---|
| | Personal Injury | Personal Property | Impersonal Property | Other |
| Personal injury | 0.0 | 4.08† | -1.66 | -0.40 |
| Personal property | 1.23 | 0.0 | -0.14 | -0.69 |
| Impersonal property | 0.45 | -1.55 | 0.0 | 0.52 |
| Other | -1.02 | -0.87 | 1.08 | 0.0 |

$\chi^2$ Test of quasi-independence = 19.70.‡

  Degrees of freedom = 5.

    *Significant at the .05 level.

    †Significant at the .01 level.

    ‡Significant at the .001 level.

offenses, and has only analyzed the first five offenses. Therefore, a great deal of data has been lost. Even if those youth who had committed fewer than five offenses were included in the analysis (with a desistance state added for them to move into at the appropriate time), as the sequence number of the transition increases, the active portion of the sample becomes smaller so that the high-order transitions of the most active delinquents would be unanalyzable. There are, of course, other stochastic models that use calendar time as the frame of reference and thus avoid this problem (Coleman, a; Cox and Lewis; Tuma et al.), but these models have been primarily developed for the analysis of a series of binary responses (commit a crime/do not commit a crime). The models could be fit to the longitudinal patterns of each offense category separately, but it would then be impossible to study the patterns of switching between offense types.

More importantly, the Markov model represents specialization in the aggregate, assuming that everyone in the sample is characterized by identical transition probabilities. Coleman (b) has observed that no matter what behavior is measured, this assumption of homogeneous transition rates is highly unrealistic. The division of the sample into more homogeneous groupings on the basis of variables consistently shown by cross-sectional studies to be related to delinquency (such as the family, the school, and the peer group) would not only make the models very cumbersome, but also would require very large samples if even rudimentary interactions were to be investigated.

Finally, specialization in terms of a Markov model has a very limited sense: the consecutive commission of like offenses. It might be very reasonably argued that even though a youth rarely commits the same offense two times in a row, most of that youth's offenses might be of the same

862 / Social Forces / vol. 58:3, march 1980

type, especially if there is a high level of delinquent activity. For example, if specialization were redefined to be the fact that over 50% of one's offenses are of the same type, very different information might be obtained. Table 5 shows the distribution of specialization in the Cook County sample under this new definition. Immediately apparent is the fact that a large percentage of both racial groups may be said to specialize; nonwhites, however, are significantly more likely to be nonspecialized offenders. If a white youth specializes, it is most likely to be in impersonal property or "other" offenses; nonwhite youths are most likely to specialize in impersonal property offenses. Not very many of either racial group commits more than 50 percent of their offenses within the more serious categories of personal injury or personal injury offenses.

Table 5. THE DISTRIBUTION OF YOUTH COMMITTING OVER 50% OF THEIR OFFENSES IN A GIVEN OFFENSE CATEGORY

| Offense | White | Nonwhite |
|---|---|---|
| Personal injury | 1.5 | 1.5 |
| Personal property | 1.5 | 0.9 |
| Impersonal property | 34.3 | 32.5 |
| "Other" offenses | 28.4 | 14.9 |
| No specialization | 34.3 | 50.1 |
| | 100.0 | 100.0 |
| | N = 134 | N = 335 |

$x^2 = 14.8680$          D.F. = 4                    p 1t .01

Approaching specialization in this manner presents aspects of the offense history that were not at all apparent in the Markovian approach. However, it has the same flaws as the analytic techniques of earlier investigators. A sizeable part of the sample is lost (those youths committing fewer than five offenses) because it would be meaningless to set a cutoff point of 50 percent if a youth had only committed one offense. Also lost is the temporal structure of the data; it is impossible to study patterns of offense switching over time. Yet, the information that such measures are able to impart is very enlightening and important.

The analysis of specialization can be greatly improved if the standard approaches, such as the 50 percent cutoff definition, are combined with more dynamic approaches such as the Markov model since each model is able to uncover information lost to the other. We propose that the use of residual analysis in the dynamic models may increase the sensitivity of the interpretation of the dynamics of delinquency and help to discern processes not readily apparent by a visual inspection of the transition probabilities.

## Notes

1. Erickson and Empey and Elliott and Voss estimate that more than 90 percent of all offenses go unnoticed or unacted on by the police.
2. WFS did not use maximum likelihood estimates of the generating matrix in their analysis but, rather, averaged the individual conditional probabilities for each of the separate transition matrices. This, however, does not affect the discussion or analysis to follow.
3. The marginals are restricted to offenses two through nine since these reflect the distribution of the offenses being moved into at time *t*.
4. The raw data matrices may be obtained from the author.

## References

Anderson, T. W., and Leo A. Goodman. 1957. "Statistical Inference About Markov Chains." *Annals of Mathematical Statistics* 28(1):89–110.

Carr-Hill, R. A., and K. I. MacDonald. 1973. "Problems in the Analysis of Life Histories." *Sociological Review Monograph* 19(July):57–95.

Chambliss, W. J., and R. H. Nagasawa. 1969. "On the Validity of Offical Statistics: A Comparative Study of White, Black, and Japanese High School Boys." *Journal of Research in Crime and Delinquency* 6(January):71–77.

Coleman, James S. a:1964. *Introduction to Mathematical Sociology.* Glencoe: Free Press.

———. b:1964. *Models of Change and Response Uncertainty.* Englewood Cliffs: Prentice-Hall.

Cox, D. R., and P. A. W. Lewis. 1966. *The Statistical Analysis of Series of Events.* London: Methuen & Co.

Elliott, Delbert S., and Harwin L. Voss. 1974. *Delinquency and Dropout.* Lexington, Mass.: Heath.

Erickson, M. L., and L. T. Empey. 1963. "Court Records, Undetected Delinquency and Decision-Making." *Journal of Criminal Law, Criminology, and Police Science* 54(December):456–69.

Ferguson, Thomas. 1952. *The Young Delinquent in His Social Setting.* London: Oxford University Press.

Goodman, Leo A. a:1962. "Statistical Models for Analyzing Processes of Change." *American Journal of Sociology* 68(July):57–78.

———. b:1968. "The Analysis of Cross-Classified Data: Independence, Quasi-Independence, and Interactions in Contingency Tables with or without Missing Entries." *Journal of the American Statistical Association* 63(December):1091–1131.

Haberman, Shelby J. 1973. "The Analysis of Residuals in Cross-Classified Tables." *Biometrics* 29(1):205–20.

Hauser, R. M. 1978. "A Structural Model of the Mobility Table." *Social Forces* 56 (March):919–53.

Hindelang, Michael J., Travis Hirschi, and Joseph Weis. 1978. *The Measurement of Delinquency by the Self Report Method.* Draft of an Interim Report to the Center for Studies of Crime and Delinquency, National Institute of Mental Health.

Reiss, A. J., Jr. 1976. "Settling the Frontiers of a Pioneer in American Criminology: Henry McKay." In James F. Short, Jr. (ed). *Delinquency, Crime, and Society.* Chicago: University of Chicago Press.

Robin, G. D. 1964. "Gang Member Delinquency: Its Extent, Sequence and Typology." *Journal of Criminal Law, Criminology, and Police Science* 55(March):59–69.

Robins, L. N., and E. Wish. 1977. "Childhood Deviance as a Developmental Process: A Study of 223 Urban Black Men from Birth to 18." *Social Forces* 56(December):445–73.

Robins, L. N., and M. Taibleson. 1972. "An Actuarial Model for Assessing the

**864 / Social Forces / vol. 58:3, march 1980**

Direction of Influence Between Two Datable Life Events." *Sociological Methods and Research* 1(November):243–70.

Shannon, L. W. 1968. "Scaling Juvenile Delinquency." *Journal of Research in Crime and Delinquency* 5(January):52–65.

Shaw, Clifford R. a:1930. *The Jackroller.* Chicago: University of Chicago Press.

———. b:1931. *The Natural History of a Delinquent Career.* Chicago: University of Chicago Press.

———. c:1938. *Brothers in Crime.* Chicago: University of Chicago Press.

Tuma, N. B., M. T. Hannan, and L. P. Groeneveld. 1979. "Dynamic Analysis of Event Histories." *American Journal of Sociology* 84(January):820–54.

Wilkins, Leslie T. 1960. *Delinquent Generations.* Home Office Studies in the Causes of Delinquency and the Treatment of Offenders. London: H. M. Stationery Office.

Wolfgang, Marvin E., Robert M. Figlio, and Thorsten Sellin. 1972. *Delinquency in a Birth Cohort.* Chicago: University of Chicago Press.

# Part VII
# Typologies of Criminal

# [21]

## SCALING DELINQUENT BEHAVIOR *

F. IVAN NYE AND JAMES F. SHORT, JR.

*State College of Washington*

IDENTIFICATION and measurement of the basic variable has long been a problem for researchers in juvenile delinquency. Delinquency has, in fact, generally been treated not as a variable, but as an attribute. Groups and individuals are treated as delinquent or non-delinquent according to official judgment. The socio-economic and other biases inherent in the dichotomy are well known.

A further weakness of the dichotomy for etiological purposes is that it involves the unknown but important effect of the institutionalization process itself on the relationship of the adolescent to his parents, siblings, school, and other significant groups. Are these relationships the same after arrests, probation, supervision and incarceration?

Occasionally, the simple institutionalized-non-institutionalized dichotomy has been altered by taking into consideration the frequency and seriousness of offenses for which delinquents have been arrested and/or committed, but this is the exception rather than

the rule. Depth interview material from the clinical literature has shown some of the weaknesses of this dichotomy, but such data are rarely amenable to statistical interpretation.

The pioneer work of Robison and Schwartz, together with the studies of Porterfield, Wallerstein and Wyle, and Murphy, Shirley, and Witmer,[1] have further pointed up the futility of basing etiological research and theory solely on the institutionalized-non-institutionalized dichotomy. More recent research has added to the findings of these earlier studies and indicates the feasibility of extensive research on reported delinquent behavior in non-institutionalized as well as institutionalized populations.

### THE DATA

The data reported in this paper were gathered during the winter and spring of 1955

* The writers wish to thank their colleagues, Vernon Davies and John Lillywhite, for valued suggestions, and Matilda White Riley and Jackson Toby for consultation concerning certain aspects of image analysis. Responsibility for errors or omission remains entirely with the authors.

This paper is part of a larger study investigating the extent and nature of delinquent behavior. It is financed in part by grants from the Social Science Research Council and the College Committee on Research of the State College of Washington.

[1] Sophia Robison, *Can Delinquency Be Measured?* New York: Columbia University Press, 1936; Edward E. Schwartz, "A Community Experiment in the Measurement of Juvenile Delinquency," reprinted from *National Association Yearbook 1945*, Washington: U.S.G.P.O., 1947; Austin L. Porterfield, "Delinquency and its Outcome in Court and College," *American Journal of Sociology*, 49 (November, 1943), pp. 199–208; James S. Wallerstein and Clement Wyle, "Our Law-Abiding Lawbreakers," *Probation*, 11 (April, 1947), pp. 107–112; Fred J. Murphy, Mary M. Shirley, and Helen L. Witmer, "The Incidence of Hidden Delinquency," *American Journal of Orthopsychiatry*, 16 (October, 1946), pp. 686–696.

## SCALING DELINQUENT BEHAVIOR

from three sources: (1) a sample (N= 2350); of the public high school students in three contiguous cities (population 10,000–40,000) in a far-western state [2] (2) the state training schools [3] for boys and girls in this western state (N=320); (3) the public high school students in one rural district, a rural-urban fringe district, and a suburban town in a mid-western state (Ns=171, 158, and 267, respectively, for a total "mid-western" N of 596).

Data were collected from students in these schools who were in school at the time of our visits, by means of questionnaires developed by the writers. Certain background items and a delinquency check list were common to all questionnaires. Only data from the boys in these schools are reported in this paper. The questionnaires were administered to the western sample simultaneously in all regular classrooms without advance notice so as to eliminate rumor and speculation. In all cases, it was stressed that questions asked were for research purposes only. Anonymity was emphasized, and a sealed "ballot box" was placed in each room so that each student could deposit his own questionnaire.

Several reliability checks were employed. Items were included in the questionnaires to detect the overconformer. These were behavior items considered by the general public to be undesirable but considered by the writers to be universal. A response of "no" to three or more of these was considered sufficient reason for elimination of the respondent.[4]

In an opposite group were a few individuals who pretended to have committed every

crime in the book. If a public school respondent indicated, as a few did, that he or she had committed all 21 delinquencies a maximum number of times, it was considered that he would be housed in the state training school rather than being at large, and his data were eliminated.

A third small group of non-cooperators was found among individuals who completed questionnaires in an inconsistent or haphazard manner. A sufficient number of interlocking questions were present to eliminate this type.

A fourth type of response problem was posed by the extremely poor reader. A few students whose reading ability was still sixth grade or lower had been passed into high school. This problem was acute with a few training school boys. In some of these cases a portion of the questionnaire was completed satisfactorily and the responses retained for purposes of the study.

For one or more of the above reasons approximately 1 per cent of the public school student questionnaires were considered invalid and eliminated. The rate of loss was higher for the training school respondents, amounting to some 10 per cent of the boys' and 4 per cent of the girls' questionnaires. It is felt that these losses were not excessive. For the respondents retained, two further indications of reliability are available. Scaling of the data provides one of these.[5] Similarity of scale patterns obtained from the far west and mid-west samples provides the other (see below).

Two indications of validity are presented. First, all items are violations of laws or are offenses on the basis of which adolescents are adjudicated. This is an indication of face validity.[6] Second, the scale scores differentiate between groups "known to be different" on the delinquent behavior dimension. These

---

[2] In the western schools, data were gathered employing four questionnaires, each administered to a 25 per cent sample. Three of the four included the delinquent behavior items.

[3] Training schools are, in part, successors to the state reformatories. They are intended (in this state) to house persistently or seriously delinquent children aged 18 or under.

[4] These admittedly contain an element of the arbitrary. They were utilized in conjunction with other indications of non-co-operation on the part of the respondent. It was felt that the gain in reliability due to the use of these techniques outweighed the small loss in numbers occasioned by their use. These techniques were employed during the initial coding of the data, without reference to problems of measurement or particular hypotheses.

[5] ". . . If scalogram analysis shows that essentially only a single factor is operating, in the responses, this must mean that there cannot be many additional factors, including unreliability." Louis Guttman, "Problems of Reliability" in Samuel A. Stouffer, Louis Guttman, Edward A. Suchman, Paul F. Lazarsfeld, Shirley A. Star, and John A. Clausen, *Measurement and Prediction*, Princeton: Princeton University Press, 1950, p. 305.

[6] William J. Goode and Paul K. Hatt, *Methods in Social Research*, New York: McGraw-Hill, 1952, p. 237.

characteristics of the scale are discussed in more detail below.

### SCALE CONSTRUCTION

An initial list of 21 items of criminal and anti-social behavior was constructed.[7] Three criteria were employed in their selection: items were desired which would (1) provide a range from trivial to serious crimes, (2) be committed by an appreciable segment of the population, and (3) be admitted under favorable circumstances. To this list were added "trap" questions.

From the initial 21-item delinquency check list nine items were selected for scaling on the criteria that (1) the items might measure a common dimension and (2) the offenses were committed by an appreciable proportion of the respondents. These were:

1. Driven a car without a driver's license or permit? (Do not include driver training courses) (1) very often..., (2) several times..., (3) once or twice..., (4) no....
2. Taken little things (worth less than $2) that did not belong to you? (1) no..., (2) once or twice..., (3) several times..., (4) very often....
3. Bought or drank beer, wine, or liquor? (Include drinking at home) (1) no..., (2) once or twice..., (3) several times..., (4) very often....
4. Purposely damaged or destroyed public or private property that did not belong to you? (1) very often..., (2) once or twice..., (3) several times..., (4) no....
5. Skipped school without a legitimate excuse? (1) no..., (2) once or twice..., (3) several times..., (4) very often....
6. Had sex relations with a person of the opposite sex? (1) no..., (2) once or twice ..., (3) 3 or 4 times..., (4) 5 or 6 times..., (5) 7 or 8 times..., (6) nine times or more....
7. Defied your parents' authority (to their face)? (1) no..., (2) once or twice..., (3) several times..., (4) very often....
8. "Run away" from home? (1) no..., (2) once..., (3) twice..., (4) three times...,

(5) four times..., (6) five times..., (7) over five times....
9. Taken things of medium value (between $2 and $50)? (1) very often..., (2) several times..., (3) once or twice..., (4) no....

These items were scaled by employing a sub-sample from the western sample of boys aged 14 and 15. Trichotomizing these items and employing the Cornell technique, a reproducibility coefficient of .78 was obtained. This was improved to .97 by employing the Israel Gamma image analysis.[8] Image analysis, a refinement of scale analysis, is designed to remove "idiosyncratic" elements from the data. Although the nine items scale satisfactorily, two items were committed by less than 10 per cent of the western high school samples. Since such items are of marginal value to a scale, a shorter scale was developed for the measurement of delinquent behavior in the non-institutional population.

*A Seven-Item Scale.* For the above reasons, "runaway from home" and "taken things of medium value (between $2 and $50)" were dropped. Images were scaled and a reproducibility coefficient of .98 was obtained for all the boys aged 14 and 15 years in the western samples. Two additional samples—all boys aged 16 and over from the western and mid-western high schools, and boys aged 14 and 15 from the mid-western schools—were subsequently image-scored and scaled. Reproducibility coefficients for these image scales ranged from .97 to .99.

The image scale pattern for the western and mid-western high school boys is illustrated in Table 1. Data used in this table are a random sub-sample of 40 boys aged 16 or older from each group. An examination of Table 1 shows a number of deviations in detail, but the over-all scale pattern appears similar for the two samples.[9] Two hundred fifty-four, or 90.7 per cent, of the 280 re-

---

[7] The writers accept Tappan's argument for legal definition of crimes and delinquencies, but take exception to his insistence that only those adjudicated as criminals or delinquents are properly the subject of sociological inquiry. See Paul W. Tappan, "Who is the Criminal?" *American Sociological Review*, 12 (February, 1947), pp. 96–102.

[8] This procedure, developed by Louis Guttman to minimize "idiosyncratic" elements, is described in M. W. Riley, J. W. Riley, and J. Toby, *Sociological Studies in Scale Analysis*, New Brunswick: Rutgers University Press, 1954, Chapter 18.

[9] It was felt that Table 1 was complex without adding dual sets of errors and frequencies; however, there were for the western responses 5 errors, for mid-western 9, for reproducibility coefficients of .981 and .968 respectively.

## SCALING DELINQUENT BEHAVIOR      329

TABLE 1. SCALOGRAM OF DELINQUENT BEHAVIOR RESPONSES OF BOYS, AGES SIXTEEN AND OVER

| | 1* | 2 | 3 | 4 | 5 | 6 | 7 | 1 | 2 | 3 | 4 | 5 | 6 | 3 | 7 | 5 | 4 | 7 | 1 | 2 | 6 |
|---|---|---|---|---|---|---|---|---|---|---|---|---|---|---|---|---|---|---|---|---|---|
| | A | A | A | A | A | A | A | A | B | B | B | B | B | C | B | C | C | C | C | C | C |
| 1 | ⊠ | ⊠ | ⊠ | ⊠ | ⊠ | ⊠ | ⊠ | | | | | | | | | | | | | | |
| 2 | ⊠ | ⊠ | ⊠ | ⊠ | ⊠ | ⊠ | ⊠ | | | | | | | | | | | | | | |
| 3 | X | ⊠ | ⊠ | ⊠ | ⊠ | ⊠ | ⊠ | ⊠ | O | | | | | | | | | | | | |
| 4 | X | ⊠ | ⊠ | ⊠ | ⊠ | ⊠ | ⊠ | ⊠ | O | | | | | | | | | | | | |
| 5 | X | X | ⊠ | ⊠ | ⊠ | ⊠ | ⊠ | ⊠ | O | O | | | | | | | | | | | |
| 6 | X | X | ⊠ | ⊠ | ⊠ | ⊠ | ⊠ | ⊠ | O | O | | | | | | | | | | | |
| 7 | X | X | ⊠ | ⊠ | ⊠ | ⊠ | ⊠ | ⊠ | O | O | | | | | | | | | | | |
| 8 | X | X | ⊠ | ⊠ | ⊠ | ⊠ | ⊠ | ⊠ | O | O | | | | | | | | | | | |
| 9 | X | X | ⊠ | ⊠ | ⊠ | ⊠ | ⊠ | ⊠ | O | O | | | | | | | | | | | |
| 10 | X | ⊠ | ⊠ | ⊠ | ⊠ | ⊠ | ⊠ | ⊠ | O | | | | | | | | | | | | |
| 11 | X | ⊠ | ⊠ | ⊠ | ⊠ | ⊠ | ⊠ | ⊠ | O | | | | | | | | | | | | |
| 12 | X | ⊠ | ⊠ | X | ⊠ | ⊠ | ⊠ | ⊠ | O | | | | | O | | | | | | | |
| 13 | | ⊠ | ⊠ | X | ⊠ | ⊠ | ⊠ | ⊠ | ⊠ | | | | | O | | | | | | | |
| 14 | | ⊠ | ⊠ | X | ⊠ | ⊠ | ⊠ | ⊠ | ⊠ | | | | | O | | | | | | | |
| 15 | | O | ⊠ | X | ⊠ | ⊠ | ⊠ | ⊠ | ⊠ | | X | | | O | | | | | | | |
| 16 | | O | ⊠ | X | ⊠ | ⊠ | ⊠ | ⊠ | ⊠ | | X | | | O | | | | | | | |
| 17 | | | ⊠ | X | ⊠ | ⊠ | ⊠ | ⊠ | ⊠ | ⊠ | | | | O | | | | | | | |
| 18 | | | O | X | ⊠ | ⊠ | ⊠ | ⊠ | ⊠ | ⊠ | X | | | O | | | | | | | |
| 19 | | | O | X | ⊠ | ⊠ | ⊠ | ⊠ | ⊠ | ⊠ | X | | | O | | | | | | | |
| 20 | | | O | X | ⊠ | ⊠ | ⊠ | ⊠ | ⊠ | ⊠ | X | | | O | | | | | | | |
| 21 | | | | X | ⊠ | ⊠ | ⊠ | ⊠ | ⊠ | ⊠ | | | | O | | | | | | | |
| 22 | | ⊠ | | X | ⊠ | ⊠ | ⊠ | ⊠ | ⊠ | | | | | O | ⊠ | | | | | | |
| 23 | | O | | | ⊠ | ⊠ | ⊠ | ⊠ | X | ⊠ | X | ⊠ | | O | | | | | | | |
| 24 | | O | | | ⊠ | ⊠ | ⊠ | ⊠ | X | ⊠ | X | ⊠ | | O | | | | | | | |
| 25 | | O | | | ⊠ | ⊠ | ⊠ | ⊠ | X | ⊠ | X | ⊠ | | O | | | | | | | |
| 26 | | | | | O | ⊠ | ⊠ | ⊠ | X | ⊠ | ⊠ | ⊠ | ⊠ | O | X | | | | | | |
| 27 | | | | | | ⊠ | ⊠ | ⊠ | ⊠ | ⊠ | ⊠ | ⊠ | ⊠ | | | | | | | | |
| 28 | | | | | | O | ⊠ | ⊠ | ⊠ | ⊠ | ⊠ | ⊠ | ⊠ | | X | | | | | | |
| 29 | | | | | | O | ⊠ | ⊠ | | X | ⊠ | ⊠ | ⊠ | | X | | O | | | | |
| 30 | | | | | | O | ⊠ | ⊠ | | X | ⊠ | ⊠ | ⊠ | | X | | O | | | | |
| 31 | | | | | | O | ⊠ | ⊠ | | X | ⊠ | ⊠ | ⊠ | | X | | O | | | | |
| 32 | | | | | | O | ⊠ | ⊠ | | X | O | ⊠ | ⊠ | | X | X | O | | | | |
| 33 | | | | | | O | ⊠ | ⊠ | | ⊠ | | ⊠ | ⊠ | | X | ⊠ | | | | | |
| 34 | | | | | | O | ⊠ | ⊠ | O | | | ⊠ | ⊠ | | X | ⊠ | X | | | | |
| 35 | | | | | | O | ⊠ | X | | | O | ⊠ | ⊠ | | X | ⊠ | ⊠ | | O | | |
| 36 | | | | | | O | ⊠ | ⊠ | | | | ⊠ | ⊠ | | X | ⊠ | | | | | |
| 37 | | | | | | | ⊠ | X | | | O | ⊠ | ⊠ | | X | ⊠ | | | O | | |
| 38 | | | | | | | ⊠ | ⊠ | | | | X | ⊠ | | ⊠ | ⊠ | | | | | O |
| 39 | | | | | | | ⊠ | ⊠ | X | X | | X | O | O | ⊠ | ⊠ | | X | | O | O |
| 40 | | | | | | | O | | | | | | | ⊠ | | ⊠ | ⊠ | X | X | ⊠ | ⊠ |

* 1 = Driving without a license.
  2 = Taking little things.
  3 = Bought or drank beer, wine, or liquor.
  4 = Skipped school without an excuse.
  5 = Had sex relations with opposite sex.
  6 = Destroyed property.
  7 = Defied parents' authority.

X = Response of western boy.
O = Response of mid-western boy.
⊠ = Response from each group.
A = Do not admit to delinquent act.
B = Admit once or twice.
C = Admit act several times or very often.

In the above scale, driving without a permit "once or twice" and "several times" were combined. While this is satisfactory for the boys 14 and 15 years of age, it does not discriminate well for those 16 and over. For trichotomous treatment of older boys' behavior it is preferable to combine several times with very often.

sponses in Table 1 are identical for the two groups.

While the populations comprising the western and mid-western scales differ in some respects, e.g., city-size and section of the country, they are alike in other important respects. Ethnic composition is stable, both populations being overwhelmingly native caucasian, and age and sex are standardized. Furthermore, both represent non-institutional populations. Close comparabil-ity between scales constructed on the basis of data from both groups may be taken as a further indication of reliability. Similar scale patterns likewise suggest similarity of populations in the two geographic areas with respect to this dimension.

Similar scales for 14 and 15 year old boys resulted again in close comparability between the western and mid-western groups. We conclude that a moderated degree of unidimensionality has been found between these items

TABLE 2. DISTRIBUTION OF DELINQUENCY SCALE TYPES FOR BOYS, AGES SIXTEEN AND SEVENTEEN *

| Scale Type | Offense Number † | | | | | | | | | | | Public School | | Training School | |
|---|---|---|---|---|---|---|---|---|---|---|---|---|---|---|---|
| | 1 | 2 | 3 | 4 | 5 | 6 | 7 | 8 | 9 | 10 | 11 | Number | Cumulative Per Cent | Number | Cumulative Per Cent |
| 00 | 0 | 0 | 0 | 0 | 0 | 0 | 0 | 0 | 0 | 0 | 0‡ | 0 | 0 | 0 | 0 |
| 01 | 1 | 0 | 0 | 0 | 0 | 0 | 0 | 0 | 0 | 0 | 0 | 128 | 22.5 | 0 | 0 |
| 02 | 1 | 1 | 0 | 0 | 0 | 0 | 0 | 0 | 0 | 0 | 0 | 53 | 31.8 | 0 | 0 |
| 03 | 1 | 1 | 1 | 0 | 0 | 0 | 0 | 0 | 0 | 0 | 0 | 32 | 37.4 | 0 | 0 |
| 04 | 1 | 1 | 1 | 1 | 0 | 0 | 0 | 0 | 0 | 0 | 0 | 133 | 60.7 | 3 | 2.4 |
| 05 | 2 | 1 | 1 | 1 | 0 | 0 | 0 | 0 | 0 | 0 | 0 | 15 | 63.3 | 2 | 4.0 |
| 06 | 2 | 1 | 1 | 1 | 1 | 0 | 0 | 0 | 0 | 0 | 0 | 4 | 64.0 | 0 | 4.0 |
| 07 | 2 | 1 | 1 | 1 | 1 | 1 | 0 | 0 | 0 | 0 | 0 | 46 | 72.1 | 3 | 6.4 |
| 08 | 2 | 1 | 2 | 1 | 1 | 1 | 0 | 0 | 0 | 0 | 0 | 97 | 89.1 | 20 | 22.4 |
| 09 | 2 | 1 | 2 | 2 | 1 | 1 | 0 | 0 | 0 | 0 | 0 | 2 | 89.5 | 0 | 22.4 |
| 10 | 2 | 1 | 2 | 2 | 1 | 1 | 1 | 0 | 0 | 0 | 0 | 34 | 95.4 | 20 | 38.4 |
| 11 | 2 | 1 | 2 | 2 | 1 | 1 | 1 | 1 | 0 | 0 | 0 | 1 | 95.6 | 0 | 38.4 |
| 12 | 2 | 2 | 2 | 2 | 1 | 1 | 1 | 1 | 0 | 0 | 0 | 2 | 96.0 | 0 | 38.4 |
| 13 | 2 | 2 | 2 | 2 | 1 | 1 | 1 | 1 | 1 | 0 | 0 | 4 | 96.7 | 3 | 40.8 |
| 14 | 2 | 2 | 2 | 2 | 1 | 1 | 2 | 1 | 1 | 0 | 0 | 4 | 97.4 | 1 | 41.6 |
| 15 | 2 | 2 | 2 | 2 | 2 | 1 | 2 | 1 | 1 | 0 | 0 | 2 | 97.7 | 8 | 48.0 |
| 16 | 2 | 2 | 2 | 2 | 2 | 2 | 2 | 1 | 1 | 0 | 0 | 9 | 99.3 | 26 | 68.8 |
| 17 | 2 | 2 | 2 | 2 | 2 | 2 | 2 | 1 | 1 | 1 | 1 | 1 | 99.5 | 5 | 72.8 |
| 18 | 2 | 2 | 2 | 2 | 2 | 2 | 2 | 1 | 2 | 1 | 1 | 3 | 100.0 | 34 | 100.0 |
| Total § | | | | | | | | | | | | 570 | | 125 | |

* The coefficient of reproducibility of this scale is .975.

† Offense numbers refer to the following delinquent acts: (1) Driving a car without a driver's license or permit. (2) Taking little things (worth less than $2) that did not belong to you. (3) Buying or drinking beer, wine, or liquor (include drinking at home). (4) Skipping school without a legitimate excuse. (5) Purposely damaging or destroying public or private property. (6) Sex relations with a person of the opposite sex. (7) Taking things of medium value ($2 to $50). (8) Taking things of large value (worth more than $50). (9) "Running away" from home. (10) Defying parents' authority to their faces. (11) Narcotics violations.

‡ In all cases "0" indicates that the offense has not been committed by boys in this scale type. In the case of all trichotomized items except heterosexual relations the score "1" indicates commission of the offense once or twice and a score of "2" indicates commission of the offense more than once or twice. A score of "1" for heterosexual relations indicates commissions of the offense from one to four times, while a score of "2" indicates commission more than four times. In the case of dichotomized items a score of "1" indicates commission of the offense one or more times.

§ Eight public school boys and one training school boy were lost to the scale due to excessive non-responses to the delinquency questions. The procedure followed in handling non-responses was to assign them to the modal category, 0, 1, or 2. This was done, however, only when at least six of the eleven delinquency items had been answered.

of delinquent behavior and that the dimension is scalable for the two populations when the same items are employed.

The seven-item scale satisfactorily ordered the non-institutional population. It was felt that for populations of "official delinquents" or combined institutional and non-institutional populations, a scale including *more serious* offenses would better isolate the most serious offenders in both groups. For this reason an eleven-item scale was developed.

*An Eleven Item Scale.* Combining data from public and training school boys makes possible utilization of data regarding more

serious delinquencies. To the seven-item scale were added four of these more serious delinquencies. These were "running away from home," "taking things of medium value (worth $2 to $50)," "taking things of large value (worth more than $50)," and "used or sold narcotic drugs." Delinquency scale types isolated for 16 or 17 year old western state public and training school boys are presented in Table 2.

The amount of "overlapping" between the official and the non-official delinquents is here specified more closely than has been done in previous research. This is an important consideration in estimating the validity of the scale. In order to insure maximizing the differences in delinquent conduct between the two groups studied, the cutting point between scale types 09 and 10 in Table 2 should be selected. This cutting point maximizes the differences between the two groups of boys in involvement in delinquent behavior, as measured by this scale, at 67.1 per cent (the difference between 89.5 per cent of the public school boys at scale type 09 and 22.4 per cent of the training school boys at this point on the scale). This percentage measures the extent to which the scale discriminates between the training school and public school boys. According to this scale, 22 per cent of the training school boys are less delinquent than are the most delinquent 10 per cent of the public school boys.

Initially, it was thought that the eleven-item scale, embracing as it does a more serious range of delinquent behavior, would more clearly differentiate training school boys from public school boys. When these two groups are compared on the basis of the seven-item scale previously discussed, however, it is found this scale differentiates between them even more effectively than does the eleven-item scale. A maximum difference between training school and public school boys, as measured by the seven-item scale, is found at scale type 08, this difference being 71 per cent (the difference between 85 per cent of the public school boys and only 14 per cent of the training school boys).

### CONCLUSION

These delinquency scales are in no case presented as final or definitive. They are experimental, methodologically and substantively. They represent an application of a familiar scaling technique and a new scoring technique. They have been tested on four samples with similar results.

The discovery of unidimensionality among these delinquency items and the ranking of individuals in terms of this dimension constitutes an etiological advantage in the sense that the incidence of certain types of behavior in terms of configuration of the offenses is an important aspect of etiology. Further, the scales as measures of reported behavior eliminate socio-economic biases related to differential punishment procedures by police and courts, and minimize the effect of the criterion variable on the independent variables. The question of motivation (for the delinquent act), and thus the isolation of behaviorally more meaningful patterns of delinquency, must be further developed in terms of correlations of delinquency items.

It is not the suggestion of this paper that the study of delinquency by scales of reported behavior should replace the collection of official data. No other system of data collection seems practicable on a continuing basis. Some etiological research must remain in the manipulation of officially defined problems and statistics, particularly of the study of murder, treason, and other very serious offenses. Furthermore, reported behavior requires favorable public relations with parents and school and the protection of the anonymity of the respondent. Despite these problems, if research is to be extended appreciably beyond the institutionalized-noninstitutionalized dichotomy, some such measure of delinquent behavior must be employed. Research into further methodological problems and substantive implications of these data is continuing.[10]

---

[10] The writers have employed these scales in studies relating delinquent behavior to psychosomatic symptoms, differential association, socio-economic status, rejection of parents, broken and unhappy unbroken homes, and spatial mobility. A bibliography is available from the writers.

# RESEARCH REPORTS AND NOTES

## TWO DIMENSIONS OF DELINQUENT BEHAVIOR *

JOHN FINLEY SCOTT
*University of California, Berkeley*

In the published form of delinquency research, participation in delinquent activity is usually treated as an attribute. The question has been raised, however, as to whether or not delinquency can instead be treated as a variable. Nye and Short show that some delinquent acts are scalable.[1] Since the discovery of a scale means that an ordinal relation between otherwise unconnected items has been found, Nye and Short have shown that delinquent behavior can be considered to have at least one of the properties of a variable. Although the ultimate utility of scale analysis for the demonstration of behavioral variables remains very largely an unsettled question, studies of this type represent an advance over the classical investigations which compare such categories as delinquents and non-delinquents, and recidivists and non-recidivists. Often implicit in the design of such studies is the premise that all delinquent acts are homogeneous and that they do not need to be distinguished, either as to degree of delinquency or as to kind, in inquiry into the conditions under which they occur.

But there may be different kinds of delinquency, as well as varying magnitudes of the same kind. Nye and Short find an area of delinquent behavior which is unidimensional according to the criteria of the Guttman scale. This paper, however, reports a scaling study in which two distinct dimensions of delinquent behavior are indicated. This suggests that it may be useful to consider delinquency as a multidimensional phenomenon.

* This paper is the result of work undertaken while at Stanford University. I wish especially to acknowledge the valuable advice and editing provided by Paul Wallin, who also made the data available for their present use. Louis Guttman offered the important suggestion to attempt to obtain two scales. Also consulted were Miss Jennifer Hanke and Hanan C. Selvin of the University of California. Responsibility for the present form of the manuscript, of course, is entirely my own.
[1] F. Ivan Nye and James F. Short, Jr., "Scaling Delinquent Behavior," *American Sociological Review*, 22 (June, 1957) pp. 327–331.

In an attempt to form a delinquency scale, many items on the original roster failed to scale. But when these items were considered separately, they formed a separate scale. The difference in the manifest content of the items of these scales suggests that there may be an important difference betwen delinquents whose activity is directed against anonymous individuals or corporate property and those whose behavior bears on their own "primary group." Since the population studied and the items used both differ markedly from those of the study by Nye and Short, it is not possible directly to compare the two sets of scales.

The question of whether youthful criminal behavior, or any form of deviant behavior, is unidimensional or multidimensional is an important one. For if several dimensions emerge from a class of actions previously regarded as homogeneous, more regular correlation between these new classifications and antecedent conditions may obtain, from which more accurate predictions can then be made. The categories of deviant behavior usually derive from considerations other than empirical analysis and prediction.[2] The Guttman scale represents one method which can be used in the study of deviance to indicate whether a traditional classification of actions is homogeneous or heterogeneous.

### THE DATA OF THE STUDY

This paper reports two scales: the first consists of eight items; the second, of four items, indicating within the population studied two dimensions of delinquent activity. The data for the scales were questionnaire responses of male college students enrolled in undergraduate courses in criminology, collected over a period of three years. As a part of the course assignment, all students answered anonymous questionnaires concerned with the frequency with which they had been involved in a wide range of delinquent behavior. Instructions to the students prior to the administration of the questionnaire emphasized the complete anonym-

[2] For example, the overall category of "juvenile delinquency" refers to conduct which, if carried out by adults, would be subject to provisions of law, usually the criminal law: the concept has a historico-legal, rather than sociological, point of departure.

ity of the responses; it was also stressed that the research value of the data depended in large part on the students' candor in reporting their behavior.

The scales are based on a section of the questionnaire covering offenses of stealing, taking, borrowing without permission, and evading payment. Fifteen such acts were tested for unidimensionality, and are listed below in the order in which they appear in the questionnaire. The respondents were asked to indicate the frequency with which they had committed each type of offense—"never," "once," "sometimes," or "often."

1. Stealing from orchards or gardens
2. Stealing from food stores
3. Stealing from other stores
4. Stealing from hotels or restaurants
5. Stealing from parents
6. Stealing from friends or acquaintances
7. Shortchanging parents or others
8. Bicycle theft
9. Accepting stolen goods
10. Stealing public signs, highway equipment, etc.
11. Evading payment in buses, movies, telephones, soda fountains, etc.
12. Failure to return stolen goods when owner known
13. Stealing auto parts or gasoline
14. Stealing from vacant buildings or buildings under construction
15. Entering illegally or breaking into home or building

## SCALOGRAM ANALYSIS OF ITEMS

The original plan for the study of these data did not include scalogram analysis; thus the fifteen items listed above were not included in the questionnaire for the purpose of testing their undimensionality. In order to undertake such analysis, the questionnaire responses of 100 male respondents were randomly selected from the population of several hundred students to whom the questionnaire had been administered. Using the "Cornell Technique" of scale analysis, each student's response to each of the fifteen items was scored for frequency of commission. The respondent was then ranked according to his total score, and the items were tested for unidimensionality. In this first operation, which considered all fifteen items in calculating a respondent's rank position, seven of the items failed to scale, while the remaining eight formed a scale (the first of the two noted above), with a coefficient of reproducibility of .90 using dichotomized response patterns throughout, meeting as well the other formal criteria of scalability. The rank order of the eight scaled items, with the least common offense listed first, is given below. Numbers in paren-

these indicate the frequency (of the total of one hundred) in each scale type.

8. Bicycle theft (5)
11. Evading payment in buses, movies, soda fountains, etc. (6)
9. Accepting stolen goods (3)
13. Stealing auto parts or gasoline (8)
14. Stealing from vacant buildings or buildings under construction (15)
2. Stealing from food stores (19)
3. Stealing from other stores (11)
1. Stealing from orchards or gardens (15)

In addition there were twenty-two respondents who either reported no offenses or whose incidence of any offense was too infrequent to place them in a scale type. These items have in common the characteristic of suggesting injury to anonymous persons or to impersonal property, and are not associated with the more intimate interpersonal relations of the offender.

Analysis of the seven remaining items show that they can be classified into two types: first, three items which, in relation to the first sclae, form a quasi-scale; and second, the remaining four items which decisively fail to scale, using the ranking procedure by which the first scale was obtained. The quasi-scale items (again in order of increasing frequency) are:

15. Entering illegally or breaking into home or building
10. Stealing public signs, highway equipment, etc.
4. Stealing from hotels or restaurants

These three items rank near the middle of the scale. Their manifest content is comparable to that of the first scale in referring to action against anonymous persons or impersonal property. The content of the non-scale items, however, suggests that their commission would affect known individuals relevant to the actor's personal affairs, reducing thereby the cohesiveness of his primary-group relations in the event that they were practiced with any great frequency.

The four items listed below were then scaled, ranking respondents on a total score for these items only. For these "interpersonal" items, the order of increasing cumulative frequency is as follows:

12. Failure to return stolen goods when owner known (3)
6. Stealing from friends or acquaintances (8)
5. Stealing from parents (20)
7. Shortchanging parents or others (12)

The remainder of the one hundred selected respondents reported little or no incidence of these four offenses. For this second scale the coefficient of reproducibility is .94, using dichotomized responses. The significance of this statistic is markedly reduced, first, by the relative infrequency of these offenses in relation to the respondents' total incidence of delinquent acts, and second, by the relatively few items used to establish the scale dimension. But considered together the two scales suggest that there may be two dimensions of delinquent behavior composed of actions which respectively do and do not affect the actor's interpersonal relations. Since the scale analysis involves a secondary use of materials designed for other purposes, no claim is intended that the questions are cast in the form best suited to illustrate the different modes of delinquency outlined here. Because the discovery in this respect was unanticipated, however, it may seem to some sociologists to be all the more interesting; and in any case the findings suggest that research (not necessarily scale analysis) explicitly designed to analyze delinquent behavior in such terms as the degree to which it affects interpersonal relations, specifiable individuals, and anonymous, impersonal, or corporate property, may find more substantial evidence in the areas to which these two dimensions point.

In scale analysis it is possible to obtain many dimensions by mistake where one dimension describes the data equally well, as an artifact of the complex labor and occasional confusion involved in the mechanics of scaling. A plurality of scales may be only selective components of a larger scale. A test of the non-homogeneity, or classificatory distinctiveness, of two or more scale dimensions is afforded by a correlation of each respondent's rank-position (or scale-type) on each of the scales. Two or more scales with a given coefficient of reproducibility and the same number of items which correlate perfectly with each other will form a single gross scale with the same coefficient of reproducibility as that of the component scales. A similar but more involved relation obtains for two such scales which show a perfect negative correlation; and generally for positive correlations, the coefficient of reproducibility of a gross scale formed of component scales of given constant coefficients of reproducibility is a function of the degree of correlation between each respondent's rank-position on each of the component scales.[3] The test of correlation, then, shows that two scales constitute two dimensions as the value of the correlation approaches zero; they constitute one dimension, and are components of a larger scale,

as the value of the correlation approaches plus or minus one.[4]

This correlation was calculated for the two scales described here, yielding a Pearsonian $r$ of .16. Especially with regard to the "inflationary" effect (from a zero correlation) on the value of $r$ for given data, which results from the use of relatively few categories (eight and four scale types for the first and second scales respectively), this low value argues strongly that the two scales describe (for the sample population) separate and distinct dimensions of delinquent acts, and are not merely components of a larger scale.

### IMPLICATIONS OF THE DATA

In addition to the limitations of the formal coefficients discussed above, the results of this study are subject to at least three principal qualifications. The first is the unknown variance between respondents' reports of their behavior and the actual incidence of that behavior, especially when the actions in question are often violations of standards widely held. This problem is not, of course, unique to this study. Second, no substantial claim can be made that these data are representative of any population other than that from which the scaling sample was drawn. Third, the interpretation of the manifest content of the delinquent acts reported here as having distinctively personal and impersonal consequences is in no way conclusive. This last limitation results directly from the use of data in secondary analysis; it could easily be overcome in a study in which the first concern is the establishment of the two dimensions discussed here. Consequently it should be stressed that these results are offered strictly in a heuristic capacity and not a confirmatory one.

Perhaps the basic notion provided by these two scales is that delinquent acts affecting anonymous persons or impersonal property occur together in a distinctive pattern which should not be confused with one made up of acts that introduce conflict and injury into interpersonal relations. This in turn suggests differences in the antecedent conditions that give rise to each type of delinquency. Data are not available in this study on the conditions antecedent to the delinquent behavior itself. But the speculation that "normal" socialization to deviant subcultures is antecedent to "impersonal" delin-

---

[3] This follows from Samuel Stouffer's discussion in "An Overview of the Contributions to Scaling and Scale Theory," in *Measurement and Prediction, Studies in Social Psychology in World War II*, Vol. IV, Princeton: Princeton University Press, 1950, p. 18.

[4] Correlations of this sort are carried out, but not discussed, in Erik Allardt, "Drinking Norms and Drinking Habits," in *Drinking and Drinkers*, Helsinki: The Finnish Foundation for Alcohol Studies, 1956, p. 67.

## RESEARCH REPORTS AND NOTES                     243

quency and that "abnormal" socialization in disorganized family situations is antecedent to "personal" delinquency may be warranted.[5]

### CONCLUSION

The Guttman scales presented here are intended as an example of the application of scale analysis in the study of delinquent behavior. Because of the formal characteristics of the scales, together with the characteristics of the population studied and the means whereby the data were collected, the dimensions reported above should be regarded as a plausible point of departure for more thoroughgoing research rather than evidence of the patterns of delinquent behavior in populations of general interest. More firmly, however, the scales do suggest the utility of viewing delinquency as multidimensional, whatever the content of the dimensions. Scale analysis, the orthodox role of which has been the classification of attitudes, is one useful method for delimiting various categories of behavior. Delinquency provides only one example.

# [23]

*The Journal of Social Psychology*, 1963, **61**, 273-277.

## DIMENSIONS OF DELINQUENT BEHAVIOR*[1,2]

*Department of Psychology, Vanderbilt University*

HERBERT C. QUAY AND LAWRENCE BLUMEN

### A. INTRODUCTION

Research studies have generally considered all delinquent acts as belonging to a single general class. Recently, however, at least two studies have indicated that there may be different kinds of delinquency.

Nye and Short (3) have found a number of delinquent acts which were unidimensional according to the criteria of a Guttman type scale. These investigators isolated a seven-item unidimensional scale from a longer delinquency checklist which had been administered to large samples of high school boys. The offenses comprising the scale were: 1) driving without a license, 2) taking little things, 3) buying or drinking alcoholic beverages, 4) skipping school, 5) having sex relations with the opposite sex, 6) destroying property, and 7) defying parental authority. While these items have demonstrated statistical unity, an examination of item content fails to reveal what might be called psychological unity; the items seem quite divergent when considered from the point of view of possible psychological meaning or underlying motivation.

In a somewhat similar study Scott (6) administered a number of items regarding delinquent acts to a group of college students. Using scalogram analysis he was able to identify two dimensions for the items comprising his original scale. The first was composed of six items relating to thefts of various kinds, one item in regard to the possession of stolen goods, and one item having to do with evading payment in busses, movies, etc. Conceptually, all of these items had to do with offenses of an impersonal nature; all were directed against corporate entities or unknown individuals. Scott's second dimension was composed of four items: 1) failure to return stolen goods when the owner was known, 2) stealing from friends or acquaintances,

* Received in the Editorial Office on February 16, 1962. Copyright, 1963, by The Journal Press.
1 This study was facilitated by a grant to the junior author from the National Science Foundation undergraduate research participation program.
2 The use of the IBM 650 electronic computor was made possible by National Science Foundation grant number NSF-G1008 to the Computer Center of Vanderbilt University.

3) stealing from parents, and 4) shortchanging parents or others. Scott noted that this dimension has the psychological unity that the person affected by the delinquent act is in the interpersonal realm of the actor. As Scott cogently points out, the motivation for offenses comprising the two dimensions may be quite different. He hypothesizes that the antecedents of impersonal delinquency may be the assimilation of delinquent mores while the antecedents of interpersonal delinquency may be abnormal socialization in a pathological family environment.

These studies seem to suggest the following conclusions: (*a*) there may be different dimensions of delinquency; (*b*) these dimensions may well be related to different social and psychological antecedents; and (*c*) dimensionality of delinquency is extremely important in terms of its implication for research into the etiology of what has heretofore been considered to be a unitary phenomenon.

The purpose of this study was to explore further the dimensionality of delinquent behavior using institutionalized delinquents as $Ss$ and using factor analysis as a method of deriving the dimensions.

## B. METHOD

### 1. *Subjects*

$Ss$ were 191 white male juvenile delinquents who had had repeated court contact and at least one commitment to a correctional institution. This selection procedure attempted to maximize both the opportunity of $Ss$ to be guilty of a wide variety of delinquencies and the probability that official juvenile court records would reflect as much of this activity as possible.

### 2. *Procedure*

A checklist of delinquent acts was prepared on the basis of studies of the incidence of juvenile offenses. This checklist contained more than 50 delinquent acts, but the elimination of 37 of these was necessary as will be noted below.

Case records gathered and maintained by juvenile-court personnel were then studied in order to determine which of the offenses each $S$ had apparently committed. These determinations were made by the junior author.

After the original checklist had been completed for each $S$ it was found that many offenses had occurred too infrequently to be included in the statistical analysis; only those 13 delinquent acts which were judged to have been committed by at least 10 per cent of the $Ss$ were retained for analysis.

To determine rater reliability for the judgment of the presence or absence of the offenses retained for analysis, a sample of 34 records was reanalyzed after a lapse of approximately five weeks. As a measure of reliability, phi coefficients were calculated for each offense separately. These coefficients ranged from 1.00 (assault) to .38 (property theft), with a median of .88. Only three fell below a value of .80 while seven were above .85. It should be noted that the upper limit of the phi coefficient is frequently less than 1.00 when marginal totals are unequal; thus coefficients obtained here generally tend to be underestimated. A further analysis indicated that unreliability was present in less than 10 per cent of all judgments made. While the reliability of the ratings made from the records is quite satisfactory, no claim whatsoever can be made about the reliability of the "raw" data contained in these records, except that these data were collected by probation workers with considerable experience.

The next procedure involved the intercorrelation of the 13 delinquent acts by use of phi coefficients. The resulting matrix was subjected to a centroid factor analysis. Five factors were extracted after which the residual matrix contained no element larger than .10. These factors were then rotated by the quartimax routine of Neuhaus and Wrigley (2), a procedure which results in orthogonal factors and provides a mathematical approximation to simple structure.

## C. Results

The rotated factors may be found in Table 1. Factor I can be seen to load primarily on truancy with theft of property negatively loaded and no other variable with a loading greater than .14. This factor seems to represent truant behavior which is not systematically accompanied by any other delinquency and is inversely related to theft.

Factor II has its largest loadings on driving without a license, reckless driving and liquor violations, with smaller loadings on auto theft and larceny. This factor seems most representative of delinquencies pertaining to the use of automobiles in an irresponsible manner and may well reflect an impulsivity and a thrill-seeking reaction.

Factor III is loaded primarily on assault, disorderly conduct and liquor violations. This factor seems to be a clear representation of hostility and aggression directed toward others which may be most apt to be manifest under the influence of alcohol.

Factor IV has loadings of greater than .20 only on runaway and vandalism. This suggests a dimension of escape coupled with aggression against the impersonal environment.

TABLE 1
ROTATED FACTOR MATRIX

|                        | I     | II    | III   | IV    | V     | $h^2$ |
|------------------------|-------|-------|-------|-------|-------|-------|
| Assault                | .06   | .18   | .40   | —.10  | .16   | .23   |
| Larceny                | —.05  | —.25  | .16   | .12   | .02   | .11   |
| Disorderly             | .08   | .06   | .42   | .10   | —.05  | .20   |
| Vandalism              | —.02  | .04   | .13   | .28   | —.05  | .10   |
| Runaway                | .06   | .11   | —.05  | .26   | .29   | .17   |
| Truancy                | .62   | .07   | .10   | .08   | —.05  | .41   |
| Possessing stolen      |       |       |       |       |       |       |
| goods                  | .10   | .12   | —.09  | —.03  | —.29  | .12   |
| Liquor violations      | .08   | —.38  | .36   | —.04  | —.11  | .29   |
| Auto theft             | .00   | —.20  | .02   | .44   | .04   | .24   |
| Bicycle theft          | .14   | .12   | —.10  | .04   | .26   | .11   |
| Property theft         | —.45  | .04   | .18   | .15   | —.16  | .28   |
| Driving without        |       |       |       |       |       |       |
| license                | —.07  | —.74  | .00   | .02   | —.03  | .55   |
| Reckless driving       | .05   | —.64  | —.09  | .02   | .00   | .42   |

Factor V has its largest positive loadings on runaway and bicycle theft and a negative loading on the possession of stolen goods. This factor is quite probably associated with age; the younger delinquent would probably be most apt to commit these two offenses and least apt to be guilty of possession of stolen goods.

As can be observed in Table 1, the communalities for most of the variables are quite low. This, of course, indicates that much of the variance of this group of delinquencies cannot be accounted for by the group factors extracted in this analysis.

## D. DISCUSSION

The results of this exploratory research suggest the presence of five independent dimensions of delinquent acts all of which seem fairly easily interpretable. There appear to be certain similarities between the factors isolated here and the dimensions found previously. Factor III, representing aggression and hostility may well be a manifestation of similar motivations as may underlie Scott's (6) interpersonal delinquency dimension. Further, Scott's impersonal dimension may be reflected in both Factors II (impulsive thrill-seeking and IV (impersonal aggression).

Of interest is the fact that no clear "delinquency for profit" factor emerged. The variance of larceny, property theft, and possessing stolen goods was distributed rather randomly across all factors and the communalities for these variables were particularly low. The absence of this factor, which one might associate with participation in a delinquent or criminal subculture, may reflect the lack of such participation by the majority of our Ss.

It is intriguing to speculate about the relationships of the dimensions of delinquent behaviors found here and the dimensions of delinquent personality which have been identified in previous researches. Factor II (impulsive thrill-seeking) and Factor III (interpersonal aggression) might well be related to Hewitt and Jenkins' (1) Unsocialized Aggressive; Reiss' (5) Weak Ego; and Peterson, Quay, and Cameron's (4) Psychopathic Dimensions. Factor IV (escape and impersonal aggression) might well be related to the dimension of neurotic delinquency identified by Peterson, Quay, and Cameron (4). It is for further research to establish relationships between the dimensions of delinquent behavior on the one hand and the dimensions of personality and social background on the other. The use of this type of approach does appear to offer much more promise than the more traditional study of delinquency as a unitary phenomenon.

## E. Summary

The court records of a sample of 191 white male delinquents were analyzed for the presence or absence of 13 delinquent acts. Correlations between the separate offenses were obtained and factor analyzed. After rotation, four factors emerged which were interpreted as reflecting uncomplicated truancy, impulsivity and thrill-seeking delinquency, interpersonal aggression, and impersonal aggression. A fifth factor appeared to be related to age. The results were discussed in terms of dimensions of delinquent behavior obtained by different methods in two previous studies, and possible relationships with previously defined personality correlates of delinquency were suggested.

## References

1. Hewitt, L. E., & Jenkins, R. L. Fundamental Patterns of Maladjustment: The Dynamics of Their Origin. Springfield, Ill.: Green, 1946.
2. Neuhaus, J. O., & Wrigley, C. F. The quartimax method: An analytic approach to orthogonal simple structure. *Brit. J. Statist. Psychol.*, 1954, **7**, 81-91.
3. Nye, F. I., & Short, J. F., Jr. Scaling delinquent behavior. *Amer. Sociol. Rev.*, 1957, **22**, 327-331.
4. Peterson, D. R., Quay, H. C., & Cameron, G. R. Personality and background factors in juvenile delinquency as inferred from questionnaire responses. *J. Consult. Psychol.*, 1959, **23**, 395-399.
5. Reiss, A. J., Jr. Social correlates of psychological types of delinquency. *Amer. Sociol. Rev.*, 1952, **17**, 710-718.
6. Scott, J. F. Two dimensions of delinquent behavior. *Amer. Sociol. Rev.*, 1959, **24**, 240-243.

*Department of Psychology*
*Northwestern University*
*Evanston, Illinois*

# [24]

BRIT. J. CRIMINOL. Vol. 15 No. 2 APRIL 1975

## OFFENDER TYPOLOGIES—TWO DECADES LATER

DON C. GIBBONS (*Portland, Oregon*)*

IN the period immediately following the second world war, a major criminological interest, particularly among sociologists, grew up around offender typologies. A number of persons offered arguments holding that adult and juvenile lawbreaking involves a heterogeneous collection of activities which must be broken down for study into more homogeneous units. According to this view, typologies or categorisations of offender patterns, types, syndromes, or role-careers are required in order that (a) progress can be made on the etiological task, and (b) efficacious treatment of offenders can be developed.

The causal contention is that no single theory can be uncovered to account for such diverse types of lawbreaking (or for the persons who engage in them) as embezzlement, forcible rape, arson, gang delinquency, aggressive delinquency, female delinquency, and so forth. Instead, separate but perhaps inter-related etiological hypotheses must be developed for each distinct offender type. The closeness of this perspective to the medical model of separate syndromes or disorders, each arising out of a different disease pattern or other set of causal factors, is readily apparent.

The case for typologies and diagnostic classifications in correctional therapy closely parallels the etiological view. The basic argument is that differential treatment must be developed in which various tactics such as psychotherapy, group counselling, reality therapy, behaviour modification, or other strategems would be matched with particular offender types. The treatment would be fitted to the offender, thereby bringing about more effective rehabilitation than is now being achieved.

An early and important articulation of the typological view regarding juvenile delinquents was made by Hewitt and Jenkins (1944), based on research data from a study of referrals to a child guidance clinic. These investigators asserted that there are two major, distinct kinds of delinquents encountered in guidance clinic settings. In another typological statement, Cohen and Short (1958) argued that the population of juvenile delinquents is made up of a number of different types of misbehaving adolescents. Unlike Hewitt and Jenkins, these theorists drew upon a variety of impressionistic evidence to support their claims about types of offenders. Among the patterns hypothesised by Cohen and Short was a " parent male delinquent subculture ", along with a number of other variants of working-class gang delinquency.

A third, well-known description of delinquent types is found in the work of Cloward and Ohlin (1960), who contended that lower-class, subcultural delinquents fall into several quite distinct types. Still another statement on these matters was made by Kinch (1962), who summarised a large number of essays in the criminological literature that had offered some contentions

*Ph.D. Department of Sociology, Portland State University.

OFFENDER TYPOLOGIES—TWO DECADES LATER

about delinquent types. Kinch reported considerable agreement among different theorists and researchers, so that three main types of delinquents turned up in many of the essays he reviewed. But it should also be pointed out that most of the reports on delinquent types collated by Kinch were speculative in character, rather than the result of careful research investigations. In another speculative statement, Fisher (1962) argued that there are three basic kinds of delinquents encountered in correctional settings. Finally, recent reviews of typological contentions have been made by Ferdinand (1966) and the National Clearinghouse for Mental Health Information (1967).

Turning to typologies of adult offenders, one essay calling for the development of such classifications was presented by Garrity and myself (1959). We also reviewed a sizeable body of research data that we felt lent support to typological claims. Somewhat later, we offered a tentative criminal typology (1962), spelling out some of the dimensions along which offenders might be classified. I have presented further arguments about offender typologies in causal analysis and in correctional therapy in a book (Gibbons, 1965) designed to serve as a primer on differential treatment for neophyte correctional workers. A number of criminology textbooks have also centred about a typological perspective, including Bloch and Geis (1970), Clinard and Quinney (1973), and Gibbons (1970a, 1973).

Much hope has been held out for typologies as major devices for bringing about marked growth in etiological understanding and improvement in the effectiveness of correctional intervention directed at lawbreakers. But, what has been the yield from typological ventures during the past several decades? How much progress has been made on the discovery of valid offender classifications? After several decades of typological endeavour, perhaps the time has come for a critical assessment of this work, with an eye towards answering these kinds of questions.

This article offers a general review and critique of typological efforts in criminology. In the pages to follow, some attention is given to distinctions among different kinds of typologies. Additionally, some of the criteria for evaluating offender taxonomies are enumerated. The major portion of the article is centred on the examination of a number of classificatory schemes in terms of these criteria, including the role-career typologies I have developed. We shall see that typological efforts have not entirely lived up to the early expectations voiced for them. Finally, this article will attempt to indicate some of the obstacles that confront classificatory ventures in criminology and corrections.

### Kinds of Typologies [1]

#### Causal and diagnostic typologies

There are two basic kinds of typologies which can be developed, classified in terms of the purposes they are to serve. *Causal* or etiological typologies identify patterns of crime or criminal behaviour that are hypothesised to

---

[1] An excellent brief discussion of different kinds of typologies and criteria for good typologies can be found in Hood and Sparks (1970).

DON C. GIBBONS

develop from specific etiological backgrounds. Thus some observers have singled out such types as " naive cheque forgers ", on the assumption that persons who engage in certain forgery activities are also the product of an identifiable developmental process such as " isolation and closure " (Lemert, 1953). In a similar fashion, patterns of crime have been identified, with the end in mind of discovering social-structural correlates that produce the different kinds of lawbreaking.

A second kind of typology is the diagnostic one, designed to provide the basis for treatment intervention. Some of the classificatory schemes that have been advanced in the literature have been offered as useful both for diagnostic and causal purposes. For example, I have argued that the role-career types which I have identified are etiologically significant and that, in addition, they have utility in correctional treatment. But other taxonomic devices that have been put forth have been characterised either as diagnostic or etiological schemes, but not as both.

The I-Levels formulation currently being employed in delinquency treatment in California is a prominent example of a typology which has been offered as a diagnostic tool (Gibbons, 1970b). However, the I-Levels theory also contains a relatively explicit and controversial perspective on delinquency causation. That is, the argument strongly implies that delinquents are to be found predominantly at low levels of interpersonal maturity and that they are involved in misbehaviour as a consequence of their socialisation deficiencies. Non-offenders, on the other hand, are assumed to be more interpersonally mature on the average, and thereby insulated from juvenile lawbreaking.[2] However, these hypotheses about delinquents and non-offenders have not been subjected to research scrutiny. Furthermore, there is considerable evidence from other research studies which points in a direction different from the I-Levels argument (Gibbons, 1970a). That is, there is a relatively large quantity of data that appears to show that delinquents are not markedly less well-adjusted, emotionally healthy, or interpersonally mature than non-offenders.

There are several points to be noted concerning causal and diagnostic typologies. First, it may well be that valid classificatory schemes that provide the basis for significant etiological discoveries may be exceedingly difficult, if not impossible, to construct. Second, it may be possible to devise diagnostic instruments having treatment utility which are independent of causal typologies (Hood and Sparks, 1970, pp. 124–25). Third, development of the latter may be less difficult than is articulation of the former.

### Typologies of crime, criminals, and personalities

Typologies in the criminological and correctional literature can be classified in another way, namely, in terms of their content or behavioural dimensions. Some classificatory schemes have identified *patterns of crime*, such as

---

[2] Rita Grant Warren, one of the developers of the I-Levels formulation, has argued in a personal communication that the theory does not content that offenders are generally at lower levels of interpersonal maturity. Nonetheless, the interpretation placed upon the argument by many persons parallels the remarks here. Also, the reader ought to examine the original formulation of the theory (Sullivan, Grant and Grant, 1957).

OFFENDER TYPOLOGIES—TWO DECADES LATER

homicide, political crime, organised crime, and so forth. Here, emphasis is upon the ingredients of criminal *acts* rather than characteristics of criminal *persons*. A second group of typologies has dealt with types or *patterns of offenders*, in which the focus is upon describing the characteristics of individuals. A third collection of schemes involves *categorisations of personality types*, rather than typologies of offenders. The I-Levels system falls into this third category, in that there presumably are many non-delinquent youths who would be found in one or another low-maturity level in that scheme. Typologies of personality patterns differ from taxonomies of offenders, for the latter sort lawbreakers into categories from which law-abiding citizens are absent.

Relatively little attention has been paid in criminology to the development of typologies of crime, with most of the attention centring instead upon explication of classifications of offenders. Even so, it is likely that efforts to develop taxonomies of criminality may be more profitable or easier to accomplish than endeavours to evolve career-oriented offender typologies. Classifications of forms of crime involve the identification of commonalities to be found in single criminal *incidents*, such as offender-victim relationships, while the development of offender career classifications requires that we pay attention to the patterning of multiple instances of conduct of individuals over time. Behavioural stability in lawbreaking may be more uncommon than implied in offender typologies.

## Criteria for Judging Typologies

There are a number of criteria for typologies which could be listed, depending upon the purposes which the schemes are designed to serve. However, the major requirements of taxonomic systems are easily stated.

First, a typology which is to have some utility in etiological analysis or correctional treatment must possess *clarity* and *objectivity*. That is, the characteristics or dimensions which are employed for purposes of identifying types must be clearly specified. Different observers must be able to apply the scheme to actual offenders and must be able to make reliable assignments of specific persons to the categories of the typology.

A second requirement of a good typology is that the types or categories in the scheme should be *mutually exclusive*. Actual lawbreakers ought to fit into one and only one category within the typology. Although some offenders may show some movement from one pattern to another over time, they ought to be classified into only one type at any particular point in time. That is, it should not be the case that a person would be assigned simultaneously to both category A and category B within a typology.

A third requirement of an adequate taxonomy, whether it is to be used in etiological analysis or in correctional treatment, is that it must be *comprehensive*. In other words, all or most of the population of actual offenders ought to be placed within one or another type within the scheme. Finally, *parsimony* is a requirement of a good typology. Diagnostic or etiological schemes ought to have relatively few categories within them, although it is difficult to identify *a priori* the numerical limits of a useful, parsimonious typology.

DON C. GIBBONS

Nonetheless, a typological system with several hundred types within it would appear to be too unwieldy to be of much value.

These criteria for typologies are obvious enough. The point to be noted about them is that they are often violated in practice. In the review of typologies to follow, we shall see that many of them are defective in terms of one or another criterion.

## Some Existing Typologies

### Typologies of crime

Let us first examine some of the typologies of crime which have been advanced. One of these, by Clinard and Quinney (1973), lists nine categories of crime, defined in terms of the dimensions of criminal career of the offender, group support of criminal behaviour, correspondence between criminal behaviour and legitimate behaviour patterns, and societal reaction. These authors identify such types as occasional property crime, conventional crime, and political crime. Several points should be noted regarding their taxonomy. First, the categories within it are very broad ones, including forms of criminality within them which do not seem very similar, as, for example, political crime which includes everything from political protest behaviour to espionage. Second, the Clinard and Quinney classification is somewhat ambiguous, for it is not entirely clear as to whether they have in mind a taxonomy of crime or of criminal persons. Schemes such as the Clinard and Quinney one seem most useful for textbook purposes and have little or no applicability to correctional endeavours.

Other crime typologies include the mathematically-complex scheme by Shoham, Guttman, and Rahav (1970). A more well-known taxonomy is contained in the Kinsey research on sex offenders, in which sexual offences were classified in terms of the age of the victim or co-participant, and also in terms of whether the acts were forced or consensual in nature, as well as whether the victims or co-participants were children, minors, or adults (Gebhard, Gagnon, Pomeroy, Christenson, 1965). Combinations of these dimensions yielded 12 possible types of behaviour. This is not a taxonomy of criminal offenders, for in all likelihood individual lawbreakers often engage in two or more of these patterns of activity and in other forms of criminality as well, over time.

### Typologies of delinquents

The main focus of this article is upon typologies of crime and criminals, rather than upon taxonomies of delinquents and delinquency. However, it ought to be noted that typologies of delinquents have been put forth in great number, so that there are considerably more of these in the criminological literature than there are classifications of adult offenders (Ferdinand, 1966). Then, too, the most widely-used and well-known diagnostic typology currently in use in correctional practice is the I-Levels scheme in California (Gibbons, 1970b).

Typologies of delinquents are not without flaws, for many of them are defective in terms of the criteria we have noted previously, particularly with

OFFENDER TYPOLOGIES—TWO DECADES LATER

regard to clarity and objectivity. A good many delinquent typologies which have been advanced are relatively anecdotal or vague in character, so that considerable difficulty would be encountered in reliably placing actual offenders within the categories of the scheme. It might be noted that the I-Levels system is not entirely satisfactory in this regard, for difficulties have been reported in the utilisation of it in correctional practice (Gibbons, 1970b; Hood and Sparks, 1970, pp. 193–214). In particular, delinquent wards are classified by means of information derived from clinical interviews with them, rather than on the basis of more objective data. No very specific defining characteristics are enumerated for the types; hence the interviews involve a heavy measure of subjective judgment on the part of the interviewers. Finally, some researchers have noted difficulties in placing delinquent wards within the typology categories, even with the looseness of classificatory techniques that are involved.

Efforts to test out a typology by sorting out actual offenders into the categories within it have been quite rare, both with regard to juvenile and to adult offenders. The I-Levels system is exceptional in this regard, for here attempts have actually been made to employ the system in correctional practice, by classifying delinquent wards into the types in the system.

In the few cases at hand of research efforts to employ a delinquent typology, the results have been fairly discouraging. For example, take the contentions of Cloward and Ohlin (1960) regarding varieties of subcultural delinquency. Researchers who have examined the behaviour patterns of gang delinquents have reported that *versatility* in delinquent activities rather than behavioural specialisation best describes these lawbreakers (Gibbons, 1970). Thus empirical investigations have failed to confirm these claims about types of delinquents. The criminalistic, conflict, and retreatist subcultures hypothesised by Cloward and Ohlin have not been found to exist in the real world.

Even though research studies have failed to verify any of the delinquent typologies that have been put forth to date, one might well argue that the prospects for development of an etiologically or diagnostically useful delinquency typology are greater than for the articulation of an adequate criminal typology. Although there is a good deal of variability of delinquent behaviour, it is exceeded by the wide range of lawbreaking patterns encountered among adult offenders.

*Typologies of criminals*

There is a fairly sizeable collection of criminal typologies which have been offered in the criminological literature, as well as an even larger number of descriptions of specific, single forms of criminal conduct such as " naïve cheque forgers ". Let us examine a sample of these categorisations.

One typological scheme dealing with adult offenders is that of Schrag (1944, 1961a, 1961b). His classification dealt with inmate types in the prison community. According to Schrag, prisoners exhibit patterns of social role behaviour which the inmate argot identifies by the labels, " square John ", " right guy ", " ding ", " outlaw ", and " politician ". In general, these

DON C. GIBBONS

roles are centred about loyalty attachments to other prisoners, thus the " right guy " is a loyal member of the inmate subculture while the " square John " is an alien in that system. Schrag's observations regarding inmate social types were relatively impressionistic ones, drawn from his experiences while employed in a state penitentiary.

Another set of claims about inmate social types, closely parallel to those of Schrag, has been made by Sykes (1958, pp. 84–108). He indicated that prisoners in the New Jersey State Prison employ convict argot in which roles such as " ball buster ", " gorilla ", " merchant ", and " center man " are identified. But Sykes' observations were also quite impressionistic, thus the specific identifying characteristics of these inmate types are far from clear. Furthermore, there is considerable ambiguity regarding the portion of the inmate population that would fall into these prisoner types.

One indication of the relationship between typological descriptions and the real world can be found in the work of Garabedian (1964). In an attempt to replicate the observations of Schrag, Garabedian studied a sample of prisoners in the same prison from which Schrag's report emanated. He identified incumbents of prisoner social roles through inmate responses to a series of attitude items on a questionnaire. On the one hand, about two-thirds of the subjects did fall into the Schrag types but, on the other, about one-third were unclassifiable. Moreover, although the social correlates, such as prior offence records, participation in prison programmes, and attitudes towards the penitentiary, that are said to accompany the role types were observed, many of the associations were much less striking than implied in some of the writings on prisoner types. The conclusions of this study were two-fold, for it demonstrated that social types exist and also indicated that the Schrag typological scheme implies considerably more regularity of inmate behaviour than is actually observed.

The major implication for typological efforts to be drawn from the Schrag-Garabedian case is that pessimism is probably in order as far as expectations for developing a comprehensive adult offender typology are concerned. That is, given the fact that a number of inmates fell outside the types in the inmate taxonomy, we might expect to find an even larger proportion of unclassifiable offenders when our attention turns to the larger, more heterogeneous mixture of lawbreakers outside penal institutions.

Another typology generated inductively in an institutional setting was that of Roebuck (1966), dealing with 1,155 inmates in the District of Columbia Reformatory. His typology was based on legal categories of offence behaviour studied within the framework of criminal careers. Prison inmates were sorted into classes on the basis of their total crime record as indicated in official records. Types such as " negro armed robbers " and " negro jack-of-all-trades offenders " were identified, with 13 types being specified in all. Note that this scheme was based on prison inmates and probably fails on the comprehensiveness criterion.

A different approach to typology development is represented in the recent essay of Daniel Glaser (1972), in which he identified 10 criminal patterns, including such types as " adolescent recapitulators ", " subcultural as-

OFFENDER TYPOLOGIES—TWO DECADES LATER

saulters ", " vocational predators ", " crisis-vacillation predators ", and " addicted performers." Although Glaser drew upon research findings, his typological scheme is relatively speculative in character. More importantly, while it may be of some heuristic value in providing some structure to speculation about differential social policies for different offenders, Glaser's typology does not specify the characteristics of criminals in sufficient detail for the scheme to be reliably applied to actual lawbreakers with much precision. In short, there is little reason to suppose that different observers would be able to sort offenders reliably into categories such as " adolescent recapitulator ".

One common occurrence when persons begin to examine some specific " type " of offender in detail is the proliferation of sub-types, in order to capture the variability of behaviour within the type. For example, consider McCaghy's (1967) research on child molesters, offenders who might be expected to appear as relatively homogeneous. He reports that he found six separate types of child molesters, including the " high interaction molester ", the " incestuous molester ", the " career molester ", and the " spontaneousaggressive molester ".

This proliferation of sub-types of criminals can also be seen in the essays on murder by Guttmacher (1960), and Neustatter (1967). Both argued that murders come in a variety of types; thus Guttmacher claimed that there are nine kinds of murderers, while Neustatter listed 10 types. Both of these persons advanced anecdotal schemes lacking in clarity and objectivity. Another and more recent listing of sub-types of offenders, which is also impressionistic and relatively crude in definition, is Conklin's (1972) four types of robbery offenders (professional, opportunist, addict, and alcoholic robbers).

The preceding material indicates that general and abstract typologies which identify a relatively small number of criminal types thought to include most actual offenders can be formulated. But, at the same time, these abstract typologies are not so useful in actual research or correctional practice. When we begin to try to evolve typologies that are sufficiently explicit and detailed as to be consistent with the facts of criminal behaviour, we soon discover that a markedly increased number of categories is required in order to capture the variability among actual offenders. The criterion of parsimony is quickly violated.

On this point, I am reminded of the efforts of the pioneering nineteenth century taxonomist, Henry Mayhew (Tobias, 1966, pp. 62–64). He produced a table of the different types of criminal, with 5 major headings, 20 minor headings, and over 100 different categories! Mayhew's typology included such types as " thimble-screwers ", " mudlarks ", " snoozers ", " snow gatherers ", and " sawney hunters ". A contemporary parallel to Mayhew's large list of types can be seen in the inductively developed scheme used in the San Francisco Project (Adams, Chandler, and Neithercutt, 1971). In that study, the present offences of probationers, along with their ages, prior record of offences, and their scores on the California Personality Inventory So

DON C. GIBBONS

(Socialisation) Scale were trichotomised, yielding 54 possible types of probationers.

The point to be made here is that in the search for a typology which does justice to the richness and variability of offender behaviour, we may run the danger of developing a scheme of such elegance, with so many specific types in it, that the typology frustrates efforts at causal analysis or differential treatment, rather than serving as an aid.

### Gibbons' role-career typologies

Although a number of sociologists have offered offender typologies, it seems fair to say that the role-career efforts in which I have been involved over several decades represent the most ambitious of all these ventures. That is, my endeavours have included the detailed explication of the theoretical underpinnings of role-career taxonomies. Also, the schemes I have developed spell out the characteristics which identify particular offender types; hence these schemes are amenable to research confirmation or otherwise.

The key feature of the typological work which which I have been identified is the stress on *role-careers*, involving the attempt to specify criminal behaviour patterns which describe the lawbreaking life career of individual persons. This interest grew out of the common-sense observation that an individual who steals a car today, for example, may be implicated in quite a different kind of misbehaviour tomorrow. Accordingly, criminal typologies which centre about specific forms of illegal activity are not adequate. At the same time, although it may not make sense to speak of " receivers of stolen property ", " second degree burglars ", or " larceny by bailee-offenders " as role types, it may be possible to identify patterns such as " semi-professional property offenders " as distinct types, made up of individuals who specialise in a variety of identifiable predatory acts.

The basic model involved in role-career analysis is one of *sequential stages* through which deviants are presumed to proceed. Probably the clearest prototype of a stable career in deviance is the chronic alcoholic pattern identified by Jellenik (1962), in which individuals get caught up in a sequence of increasingly more deviant drinking activities, one stage following the other. At any one point in time it is possible to identify specific individuals who are involved in the chronic alcoholic career but who are at different points in the career.

Some of the existing criminological research material suggests that some criminal careers made up of related episodes of behaviour which unfold over time do exist. We have already taken note of research on " naïve cheque forgers " (Lemert, 1953). Some other studies which lend at least some general support to the view that there are careers or stabilities in criminal deviance are those by Peterson, Pittman, and O'Neal (1962), and by Frum (1958).

The typologies of delinquents and of criminals revolve around five defining dimensions or definitional variables. Types have been identified in terms of various combinations of characteristics exhibited by offenders within the categories of *offence behaviour, interactional setting, self-concept, attitudes,* and *role-career*. The last category is one in which the overall career *pattern* of

OFFENDER TYPOLOGIES—TWO DECADES LATER

lawbreaking activity is described. The typologies which have been developed around these dimensions offer descriptions of such types as " naïve cheque forger ", in which the forgery behaviour of the individual is described, along with the social circumstances (interactional setting) in which it occurs. The naïve cheque forger is also identified in terms of a self-concept pattern centring about notions of dependency and a non-criminal self-image, along with attitudes of the sort: " You can't kill anyone with a fountain pen."

The typologies also include statements about the social backgrounds of the various types which have previously been identified in terms of the definitional dimensions. These background characteristics are enumerated within the rubrics, *social class, family background, peer group relations,* and *contact with defining agencies.* The latter category identifies some of the hypothesised effects upon offenders of various correctional experiences which they undergo. The involvement of the offender with agencies of social control may operate as a *career contingency* which influences the subsequent course of his deviant career.

The typologies which I have articulated involve nine delinquency role-careers (Gibbons, 1965) and 21 adult offender types (Gibbons, 1973). The two typologies involve the following categories:

*Delinquent typology*

1. Predatory gang delinquent
2. Conflict-gang delinquent
3. Casual gang delinquent
4. Casual delinquent, non-gang member
5. Automobile thief—" joyrider "
6. Drug user—heroin
7. Overly aggressive delinquent
8. Female delinquent
9. Behaviour problem delinquent

*Criminal typology*

| | |
|---|---|
| 1. Professional thief | 11. Personal offender, " one-time loser " |
| 2. Professional " heavy " criminal | |
| 3. Semi-professional property offender | 12. " Psychopathic " assaultist |
| | 13. Statutory rapist |
| 4. Amateur shoplifter | 14. Aggressive rapist |
| 5. Naïve cheque forger | 15. Violent sex offender |
| 6. Automobile thief—"joyrider" | 16. Non-violent sex offender |
| 7. Property offender, " one-time loser " | 17. Incest offender |
| | 18. Male homosexual |
| 8. White-collar criminal | 19. Organised crime offender |
| 9. Embezzler | 20. Opiate addict |
| 10. Professional " fringe " violator | 21. " Skid Row " alcoholic |

Now, how valid are these typologies? How closely do actual offenders fit within the types? How comprehensive are the typologies? Attempts to sort actual offenders according to some typological scheme have been quite rare,

DON C. GIBBONS

but several attempts have been made to do so with the role-career scheme.

The Gibbons' classifications have been employed in a limited way in two experimental projects within corrections. One of these was conducted at the Stonewall Jackson Training School in Concord, North Carolina, and dealt with delinquent offenders (1970). A second project involved a community-based probation treatment programme for semi-professional property offenders, carried on in Utah under the joint auspices of a private corporation and the state correctional agency (1971). In these two projects, quite crude procedures were used to pick out offenders who were thought to be members of certain types identified in the typologies. Also, these two projects made no attempt to sort a large, diversified group of lawbreakers into a number of the categories of the typologies. Hence these two projects cannot be offered as convincing evidence of the utility of the typological schemes.

A third correctional project utilising the typologies took place in the San Mateo County Probation Department in California (Hartjen and Gibbons, 1969). That study was a much more comprehensive one and is of more significance for the general issue of the validity of typologies.

In the San Mateo County study, a small group of probation officers attempted to classify probationers, sorting them into the types of adult criminals and juvenile offenders identified in *Changing the Lawbreaker*. The officers added two types of their own, " alcoholic delinquents " and " marijuana hippies ", which they claimed were fairly commonly encountered in probation caseloads.[3]

The methodological procedures employed by the probation offenders included the development of abridged profiles or typological descriptions of offenders, with both background and definitional dimensions being included. Then, groups of three probation officers acting as " judges " read case records of actual probationers, comparing the data in case files against the profiles. Each judge evaluated cases independently without consultation with the other researchers. A probationer was designated as an incumbent of a type if at least two of the three judges assigned him to that type.

Approximately 650 probation cases were examined by the probation officers. In brief, the results of the diagnostic effort were that 312 of the 655 probationers were categorised as falling within a type in the typologies. Of these, the largest share (60·8 per cent.) were classified as alcoholic delinquents; non-violent sex offender, " rapos "; marijuana offender, " hippies "; or naïve cheque forgers. Of the 343 persons not assigned to a type, 312 were judged by at least two officers as not falling into any type within the typology. Stated differently, there was a relatively high degree of rater-agreement in the research, for officer-judges either agreed that a person was a particular type or that he was not any of the types under study.

What of the remaining probationers who were not initially classified? Are

---

[3] It ought to be noted in passing that the study was not officially sponsored by the agency and that this project was conducted by the workers in their free time. Accordingly, the large investment of time which the officers made in the study was quite remarkable. These remarks should condition any observation about the crudeness of the classificatory procedures employed in the project. Also, while the classification methods were relatively simple, the tactic of employing judges and profile descriptions is not an uncommon one, and it was particularly appropriate for the task in this instance.

### OFFENDER TYPOLOGIES—TWO DECADES LATER

there perhaps some types within which they fall, but which have not yet been identified in any existing typology? Using a parallel technique of independent judges, Hartjen sifted through the probationers who had not been assigned to the typology, in order to see whether there were similarities among them that had escaped the attention of typology developers. Using offence records, he managed to place most of these individuals (330 of the 343) into seven " types ", with 26·5 per cent. of them being classified as " non-support offenders " and 22·1 per cent. as property offenders. Even so, these *ad hoc* types did not appear to differ from each other in terms of commitment to deviance, social background characteristics, or other variables.

This study does offer some encouragement for those who would endeavour to develop differential treatment programmes centred about diagnostic types, in that a fairly large number of offenders were classified into types. On the other hand, the research lacked the precision that one would hope to achieve in taxonomic endeavours. In particular, the judges were restricted to data contained in probation reports. As a consequence, offenders were classified largely in terms of offence behaviour and social background characteristics. The classificatory activities did not involve self-concept and attitudinal items, at least not in a systematic way. It seems likely that if the probationers had been subjected to a battery of personality tests such as the California Personality Inventory So Scale, and had their test scores been included in their files, the officer-judges would have encountered considerably more difficulty in assigning them to typology categories. Also, it is probable that larger numbers of probationers who do not fit into a type would have been found had more precise rules for classifying them been employed.

Regarding the approximate half of the probationers who were not initially placed in the typologies but who were eventually assigned to some other " types ", most of these offenders were involved in " folk crime ". " Folk crime " is Ross's (1960–61) term for forms of lawbreaking arising out of laws introduced to solve problems related to the increased complexity of modern society. These offences usually draw little public attention, they involve little social stigma, persons of relatively high status are often involved in them, and they are frequently dealt with in a variety of administrative ways. Probation caseloads apparently include a number of novices in criminality who do not move on to more complex forms of lawbreaking and who do not become committed to careers in deviance (Gibbons, 1972).

One other observation about these results has to do with the matter of parsimony and comprehensiveness. Although the offender typologies utilised here include a relatively large number of types, additional categories had to be constructed *ad hoc* to encompass the probationers. Quite probably, even more types would have to be evolved if we were to extend our attention to offenders in other settings outside probation.

The final typological effort involving the role-career framework is currently going on at the Diagnostic Depot of the Illinois state corrections system at Joliet, Illinois. There, efforts are being made to sort incoming prisoners into a set of types modified from the Gibbons' role-career scheme. Unfortunately, no results are yet at hand from this project, thus it cannot be utilised in the

DON C. GIBBONS

present review and critique. However, the eventual findings from that effort ought to represent a kind of crucial test of the utility of typological formulations, in that the research is being conducted with a large and relatively heterogeneous collection of lawbreakers. The best guess at this point is that the typological scheme that results from this Illinois project will not be universally applicable to offenders outside that state or that correctional system.

### Career Typologies: An Assessment

Although it is perhaps too early for unequivocal assertions about the long-term prospects for career-oriented typologies, the evidence to date does not seem encouraging. To begin with, the research surveyed here indicates that no fully comprehensive offender typology which subsumes most criminality within it yet exists. Then, too, some criminologists have suggested that new forms of lawbreaking are emerging, additional to traditional ones (Sykes, 1972). If so, these emergent types of criminal behaviour will have to be accommodated in typologies.

Additionally, it is by no means clear that existing typologies of criminals are empirically precise. It has yet to be shown that the degree of patterning or regularity of offence behaviour which typologies assume truly does exist in most cases of criminality. For example, the San Mateo study examined probationers at one point in time and did not gather data on the patterning of offence career behaviour over time. On this same point, there has been almost no research dealing with hypothesised social-psychological correlates of offence behaviour, so that it remains to be demonstrated that cheque forgers are dependent personalities, that semi-professional property criminals exhibit common attitudinal patterns, and so on.

These remarks come down to one central conclusion: the notion of identifiable careers in criminality may be an hypothesis about behaviour which is too clinical (Taylor, Walton, and Young, 1973, pp. 150–166). The language of " types ", " syndromes ", " behavioural roles ", and the like may be inappropriate for many criminals. Instead, it may be that many lawbreakers exhibit relatively unique combinations of criminal conduct and attitudinal patterns, or at least we may only be able to group them with considerable difficulty into some very general categories or types.

A good deal of criminological attention in recent years has been drawn to the contemporary theorising in the sociological field of deviance, particularly to the writings of " labelling " theorists. Sociologists such as Lemert (1972) have argued that many deviants, including criminals and delinquents, " drift " into misbehaviour or that their conduct is a risk-taking response to value-conflicts in society. The conventional image of the deviant whose conduct is the consequence of internalised motives which differentiate him from non-lawbreakers is relatively absent in the writing of labelling theorists. They assert the importance of societal reactions, turning points, career contingencies, and the like, arguing that individual careers in deviance do not usually follow some kind of straight line progression of behavioural deviation. Instead, variability rather than regularity may be most characteristic of

OFFENDER TYPOLOGIES—TWO DECADES LATER

offenders; lawbreakers engage in flirtations with criminality; individuals get drawn into misconduct for a variety of reasons and many of them manage to withdraw from deviance. In all of this, labelling theorists suggest that deviant careers do not unfold from " within the skin " of actors, so to speak, so much as they develop in response to various contingent events that occur to them along the way, including experiences with correctional organisations.

If we follow deviance arguments very far, we would be led to turn away entirely from the search for *types of criminal persons*, investing our energy instead in the development of descriptions of interactional processes or patterns. That is, we might search for generalisations which would describe the ways in which norm-violators, social audiences, and agents of organisations such as prisons or probation agencies are all bound together in interactional patterns which result in various outcomes on the part of the deviant. John Irwin's (1970) account of the career of the felon is a case-in-point of analysis of this kind.

In conclusion, I have become increasingly sceptical about the prospects for uncovering a relatively parsimonious set of criminal role-careers. Let me also note in passing that the typological assumption that clear-cut causal processes can be identified for role-careers, involving some specific set of earlier life experiences out of which criminal motivation developed, is also open to serious question. I have commented on an alternative view of criminal etiology in detail in another essay (Gibbons, 1971) where I drew attention to " risk-taking " processes in criminality, involving persons who are not specifically motivated to engage in lawbreaking. The essay placed much heavier emphasis upon situational pressures and factors in criminal etiology than has been customary in criminological theorising in the past. If those observations are on the mark, they would serve to de-emphasise the importance of typologies in causal analysis.

My guess is that in so far as the search for typologies turns out to be profitable in corrections, it will be as a consequence of the further development of statistical classifications such as the base expectancy system of analysis (Gottfredson, 1970) or predictive attribute analysis (Wilkins and Smith, 1970). These techniques of inductive analysis involve relatively modest goals, centring about the development of classificatory devices based on specific groups of offenders within certain limited correctional settings. They in no way involve the grand ambitions of theoretically-derived typologies. But the latter may be an illusory goal, in that the regularity and patterning assumed to characterise lawbreaking may not exist. The real world may stubbornly resist our efforts to simplify it by means of offender typologies. After two decades of work in this tradition, relatively little progress in typological directions can be discerned.

REFERENCES

ADAMS, W. P., CHANDLER, P. M. AND NEITHERCUTT, M. G. (1971). "The San Francisco project: a critique." *Federal Probation*, December, 45–53.

BLOCH, H. A. AND GEIS, G. (1970). *Man, Crime, and Society*. 2nd ed. New York: Random House.

DON C. GIBBONS

CLINARD, M. B. AND QUINNEY, R. (1973). *Criminal Behavior Systems.* 2nd ed. New York: Holt, Rinehart and Winston.

CLOWARD, R. A. AND OHLIN, L. E. (1960). *Delinquency and Opportunity.* New York: The Free Press.

COHEN, A. K. AND SHORT, J. F., Jr. (1958). " Research on delinquent subcultures." *Journal of Social Issues,* **3,** 20–37.

CONKLIN, J. E. (1972). *Robbery and the Criminal Justice System.* Philadelphia: J. B. Lippincott.

FERDINAND, T. N. (1966). *Typologies of Delinquency.* New York: Random House.

FISHER, S. (1962). " Varieties of juvenile delinquency." *Brit. J. Criminol.* **2,** 251–261.

FRUM, H. S. (1958). " Adult criminal offense trends following juvenile delinquency." *Journal of Criminal Law, Criminology and Police Science,* May–June, 29–49.

GEBHARD, P. H., GAGNON, J. H., POMEROY, W. B. AND CHRISTENSON, C. V. (1965). *Sex Offenders.* New York: Harper and Row.

GIBBONS, D. C. (1965). *Changing the Lawbreaker.* Englewood Cliffs, N.J.: Prentice-Hall.

GIBBONS, D. C. (1970a). *Delinquent Behavior.* Englewood Cliffs, N.J.: Prentice-Hall.

GIBBONS, D. C. (1970b). " Differential treatment of delinquents and interpersonal maturity levels theory: a critique." *Social Service Review,* March, 22–33.

GIBBONS, D. C. (1971). " Observations on the study of crime causation." *American Journal of Sociology,* September, 262–278.

GIBBONS, D. C. (1972). " Crime in the hinterland." *Criminology,* August, 177–191.

GIBBONS, D. C. (1973). *Society, Crime, and Criminal Careers.* 2nd ed. Englewood Cliffs, N.J.: Prentice-Hall.

GIBBONS, D. C. AND GARRITY, D. L. (1959). " Some suggestions for the development of etiological and treatment theory in criminology." *Social Forces,* October, 51–58.

GIBBONS, D. C. AND GARRITY, D. L. (1962). " Definition and analysis of certain criminal types." *Journal of Criminal Law, Criminology and Police Science,* March, 27–35.

GLASER, D. (1972). *Adult Crime and Social Policy.* Englewood Cliffs, N.J.: Prentice-Hall.

GOTTFREDSON, D. M. (1970). " The base expectancy approach," in Johnston, N., Savitz, L. and Wolfgang, M. (eds.) *The Sociology of Punishment and Correction.* 2nd ed. New York: John Wiley and Sons.

GUTTMACHER, M. S. (1960). *The Mind of the Murderer.* New York: Farrar, Straus and Giroux.

HARTJEN, C. A. AND GIBBONS, D. C. (1969). " An empirical investigation of a criminal typology." *Sociology and Social Research,* October, 56–62.

HOOD, R. AND SPARKS, R. (1970). *Key Issues in Criminology.* New York: McGraw-Hill.

OFFENDER TYPOLOGIES—TWO DECADES LATER

IRWIN, J. (1970). *The Felon*. Englewood Cliffs, N.J.: Prentice-Hall.

JELLENIK, E. M. (1962). " Phases of alcohol addiction," in Pittman, D. J. and Synder, C. R. (eds.) *Society, Culture, and Drinking Patterns*. New York: John Wiley and Sons.

JENKINS, R. L. AND HEWITT, L. E. (1944). " Types of personality structure encountered in child guidance clinics." *American Journal of Orthopsychiatry*, January, 84–94.

KINCH, J. W. (1962). " Continuities in the study of delinquent types." *Journal of Criminal Law, Criminology and Police Science*, September, 323–328.

LEMERT, E. M. (1953). " An isolation and closure theory of naive check forgery." *Journal of Criminal Law, Criminology and Police Science*, September–October, 296–307.

LEMERT, E. M. (1972). *Human Deviance, Social Problems, and Social Control*. 2nd ed. Englewood Cliffs, N.J.: Prentice-Hall.

McCAGHY, C. H. (1967). " Child molesters: a study of their careers as deviants," in Clinard, M. B. and Quinney, R. (eds.) *Criminal Behavior Systems*. New York: Holt, Rinehart and Winston.

NATIONAL CLEARINGHOUSE FOR MENTAL HEALTH INFORMATION (1967). *Typological Approaches and Delinquency Control: A Status Report*. Washington, D.C.: U.S. Department of Health, Education, and Welfare.

NEUSTATTER, W. L. (1957). *The Mind of the Murderer*. New York: Philosophical Library.

PETERSON, R. A., PITTMAN, D. J. AND O'NEAL, P. (1962). " Stabilities in deviance: a study of assaultive and non-assaultive offenders." *Journal of Criminal Law, Criminology and Police Science*, March, 44–48.

ROEBUCK, J. B. (1966). *Criminal Typology*. Springfield, Ill.: Charles C. Thomas.

ROSS, H. L. (1960–61). " Traffic law violation: a folk crime." *Social Problems*, Winter, 231–241.

SCHRAG, C. C. (1944). *Social Types in a Prison Community*. M.A. thesis. Seattle: University of Washington.

SCHRAG, C. C. (1961a). " Some foundations for a theory of correction," in Cressey, D. R. (ed.) *The Prison*. New York: Holt, Rinehart and Winston.

SCHRAG, C. C. (1961b). " A preliminary criminal typology." *Pacific Sociological Review*, Spring, 11–16.

SHOHAM, S., GUTTMAN, L. AND RAHAV, G. (1970). " A two-dimensional space for classification of legal offenses." *Journal of Research in Crime and Delinquency*, July, 219–243.

STONEWALL JACKSON SCHOOL. *Project Report: An Empirical Evaluation of Delinquency Typologies*. Raleigh: North Carolina Department of Corrections.

SULLIVAN, C. E., GRANT, D. J. AND GRANT, M. A. (1957). " The development of interpersonal maturity: applications to delinquency." *Psychiatry*, 378–385.

SYKES, G. M. (1958). *The Society of Captives*. Princeton, N.J.: Princeton University Press.

SYKES, G. M. (1972). " The future of criminality." *American Behavioral Scientist*, February, 403–419.

DON C. GIBBONS

TAYLOR, I., WALTON, P. AND YOUNG, J. (1973). *The New Criminology*. London: Routledge and Kegan Paul.

TOBIAS, J. J. (1967). *Crime and Industrial Society in the 19th Century*. London: B. T. Batsford.

UTAH STATE DIVISION OF CORRECTIONS (1971). *Quarterly Narrative Report: Utah Community Based Treatment Program*. Salt Lake City: Utah State Division of Corrections.

WILKINS, L. T. AND SMITH, P. M. (1970). " Predictive attribute analysis," in Johnston, N., Savitz, L. and Wolfgang, M. (eds.) *The Sociology of Punishment and Correction*. 2nd ed. New York: John Wiley and Sons.

# Part VIII
# Property Crime

# [25]

Journal of Police Science and Administration
Copyright © 1976 by Northwestern University School of Law

Volume 4, No. 4
Printed in U.S.A.

## CLUSTER ANALYSIS OF BURGLARY M/Os*

### EDWARD J. GREEN, CARL E. BOOTH and MICHAEL D. BIDERMAN

Edward J. Green, Ph.D., is presently professor and head of the department of psychology at the University of Tennessee at Chattanooga. He is a consultant with Police Research Consultants and is the author of *Psychology for Law Enforcement.*

Carl E. Booth holds a B.S. degree in psychology from the University of Tennessee at Chattanooga and is presently a detective with the Chattanooga Police Department, with which he has been affiliated since 1968. Detective Booth is also a consultant with Police Research Consultants.

Michael D. Biderman, Ph.D., is presently assistant professor in the department of psychology at the University of Tennessee at Chattanooga. He has special interests in the fields of computer analysis, mathematical models and multivariate scaling techniques.

Excessive case loads are the "normal" condition for detective divisions in most metropolitan police departments. It is not at all unusual for a plainclothes officer to be assigned as many as 15 separate cases for follow-up investigation within a one-week period. Obviously, every effort is made to assign cases that appear to be related to those already being investigated by the particular police officer, but there is little, apart from intuition on the part of the supervisor, that assists him in the selection of cases for such assignment.

To the degree that a detective is working on a group of related cases, presumably arising from the criminal activities of a single individual or group of individuals, then his effectiveness is enhanced. His efforts are not scattered over a series of unrelated incidents, and the very concentration of cases provides additional information and leads that can augment his investigatory efforts. Conversely, the random assignment of unrelated cases for follow-up work dilutes the effectiveness of investigation and leads all too often to perfunctory efforts of little, if any, value. A low rate of clearance can be the result of a variety of factors, but casual case assignments must rank among the most significant reasons for a poor showing in clearances.

Intuition or experience can and does go a long way toward effective detective work, as it assists in defining the probable grouping of criminal activities by individuals. Intuition is, fortunately, susceptible to improvement. A hunch is usually based upon real information, although the person having the hunch may be unable to verbalize the basis for his hunch. The hunch is an example of clinical judgment, provided that judgment has validity based upon years of practical experience in the field. To the degree that the judgment is based upon real discriminations, the information that makes possible those discriminations may be clarified and made more explicit.

## SIGNIFICANCE OF THE TECHNOLOGY

House burglaries are perpetrated by persons who have preferred targets and specific M/Os. A police officer may have little difficulty in recognizing the work of a particular criminal where that person has established a record of operations in his district. The recognition of an individual criminal is based upon certain signatures of M/O. In one city, such a burglar habitually broke through the rear walls of buildings, circumventing burglar alarms. Another group of teenagers developed a method of breaking into residences through windows of homes, taking only loose cash. A drug addict, with an $80-a-day habit who was working the

*The authors gratefully acknowledge the cooperation of Sherrif Jerry Pitts and Sergeant William Cox of the Chattanooga Police Department for making available the actual crime statistics used in this report.

same residential area, only lifted major appliances such as color TVs. He fenced these goods for the money he required for drugs. The characteristics and conditions of the residence burglaries reflected the criminals' behavior with a high degree of reliability.

If these characteristics can systematically be identified, it should be possible to employ techniques of statistical analysis that objectify the bases of the educated guess, hunch, intuition, or whatever else the experienced officer calls his discriminatory abilities. Such a statistical analysis will not provide better information than good judgment, but it can systematically process more information than any single police officer can possibly handle. Cases are reported daily that may never come to the attention of the particular police officer who could readily recognize the M/O. Detectives, lacking complete knowledge of everything that comes into the department, cannot possibly coordinate their efforts in the most efficient manner. It is obviously true that five detectives working on assignments tracking down, say, five individual burglars who have committed eight break-ins within one week will do better than they will if each is tackling eight random cases where each investigator is crossing the tracks of the others, needlessly duplicating their efforts. Lacking the big picture, each investigator is handicapped by being unable to see the emerging outlines of the characteristics of the criminals' styles.

## DESCRIPTION OF INNOVATION

To study the possibility that statistical analysis might assist in identifying such patterns of criminal activity, a series of 38 break-ins were simulated in which differing M/Os were incorporated into the incident reports. The analytic procedures were as follows. First, a measure of similarity of pairs of crimes was defined. This measure was proportional to the number of characteristics of a pair of crimes had in common within seven categories. The categories were location of entry, side of entry, location on block, method of opening, day of week, value of property, and type of material taken. The "type of material" category was divided into eight subcategories. The measure of similarity was simply the number of identical characteristics within the first six categories and the eight subcategories of type of material taken. Thus, a pair

of crimes could have a similarity value ranging from 0 (no characteristics in common) to 14 (all characteristics in common). For example, consider cases 1 and 2. Table I illustrates how the measure of similarity between these two cases was computed.

Note that this measure of similarity treats the characteristics within the type of material category differently than it does the rest of the categories. For the subcategories within the type of material category, similarity between two cases was increased if a particular type of material was either taken or ignored in both cases (for example the failure to take small appliances in both cases 1 and 2 in the table). It should also be noted that this measure of similarity gives more weight to the type of material taken than to the rest of the categories. Obviously, many other measures of similarity could be considered. Other possibilities are currently being investigated.

After similarity values between each pair of crimes were obtained, these values were input to a nonmetric multidimensional scaling program.[1] This program was designed to represent the cases by points in a two-dimensional space such that distances between pairs of points corresponded to the similarity between corresponding pairs of cases. Specifically, if a pair of crimes was highly similar, the program positioned the points representing the cases close together. If a pair of crimes was dissimilar, the program positioned the points representing the two cases far apart in the space. In this case, distance between any pair of points varied inversely with the similarity between the corresponding pair of cases.

The clusters outlined in Figure 1 were drawn by one of the present authors without prior knowledge of which cases were actually created to cluster together. Other, more objective measures of clustering, based on interpoint distances in a multidimensional space and on the original similarity values themselves, have been investigated.[2]

In the selection of cases for simulation, it was determined in advance that the break-ins should

[1] R. M. Johnson, "Pairwise Nonmetric Multidimensional Scaling," *Psychometrika, 38* (1973), 11-18.

[2] S. C. Johnson, "Hierarchial Clustering Schemes," *Psychometrika, 32* (1967), 241-254; J. C. Lingoes, *The Guttman-Lingoes Nonmetric Program Series* (1973).

TABLE I

*Comparison of Two Cases as Analyzed For Similarity*

| Category | Case 1 | Case 2 | Similarity |
|---|---|---|---|
| Location of entry | Window | Roof | 0 |
| Side of entry | Back | Garage | 0 |
| Location on block | Middle | Middle | 1 |
| Method of opening | Forced | Broken | 0 |
| Day of week | Tuesday | Thursday | 0 |
| Value of property | 30-50,000 | Less than 30,000 | 0 |
| Type of material taken | | | |
| Small appliance? | No | No | 1 |
| Major appliance? | Yes | No | 0 |
| Money? | No | No | 1 |
| Credit cards? | No | Yes | 0 |
| Checks? | No | Yes | 0 |
| Jewelry? | No | Yes | 0 |
| Tools? | No | No | 1 |
| Gems? | No | Yes | 0 |
| | | Final measure of similarity | 4 |

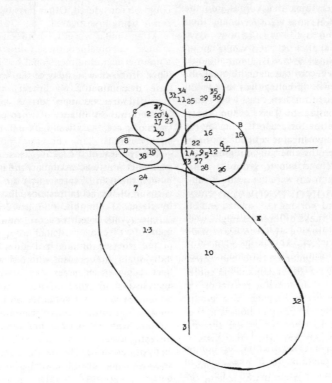

FIGURE 1

*Two Dimensional Representation of 38 Simulated Crimes. Each Number Represents a Crime. Contours Outline Subjectively Determined Clusters and Were Drawn Without Prior Knowledge of Which Crimes Represented Similar M/Os.*

represent five different foci of criminal activity. The M/Os were chosen to simulate the actual patterns of burglars functioning in the city of Chattanooga. One group was constructed where the burglar normally forces entry through a door and takes any small object that can be readily transported, with a preference for tools, guns, jewelry, credit cards and cash. Another group represented an individual with a preference for middle-income housing, who normally forced entry through windows, and who had a preference for large appliances. A third group represented the M/O described earlier, where entry was effected through a wall in lower-income housing, from which the thief took TV sets. A fourth group had to do with cases involving expensive homes, isolated at the end of a block, from which a variety of materials might be stolen, but which always involved the theft of jewelry. The fifth group again showed a preference for targets that were physically isolated, but where the materials taken were most commonly small appliances, and where entry was most often forced in lower-income homes.

The match achieved by the statistical analysis and the predetermined groupings was very good. The program grouped all the cases of entry through the wall together. Two random cases were also ascribed to this group. Of the seven jewel thefts from high-income residences, three (see Figure 1) were ascribed to one group, E, three to group B, and two to group D. The differences in assignment were the result of substantial departures from the pattern of entry through a door, and working the isolated end of the block. Both of these differences might well be significant indicators of M/Os to distinguish among criminals. Consequently, although this classification was fragmented into the three groups by the analysis, the fragmentation could very reasonably be a meaningful separation in practice. Six cases were assigned to a group characterized by window entry of houses in the middle of the block, where entry was forced, major appliances taken, and where there was a preference for middle-income dwellings. Six of the eight cases in group C make up that group. Nine of the 11 cases of group B are made up of the juvenile simulation where the residences were not selected in advance, but were targets of opportunity; where small appliances were the materials taken in most instances; and where the houses were usually isolated at the end of a

### TABLE II

*Correspondence Between Predetermined Simulated Grouping and Statistically Derived Clusters*

| Group | | | | | | | | | |
|---|---|---|---|---|---|---|---|---|---|
| A | | B | | C | | D | | E | |
| Sim | Stat | Sim | Stat | Sim | Stat | Sim | Stat | Sim | Stat |
| 21 | 21 | 5 | 5 | 1 | 1 | 2 | — | 3 | 3 |
| 29 | 29 | 11 | — | 4 | 4 | 8 | 8 | 6 | — |
| 31 | 31 | 12 | 12 | 17 | 17 | 19 | 19 | 7 | 7 |
| 34 | 34 | 14 | 14 | 23 | 23 | 20 | — | 9 | — |
| 35 | 35 | 15 | 15 | 27 | 27 | 22 | — | 10 | 10 |
| 36 | 36 | 16 | 16 | 30 | 30 | 38 | 38 | 13 | 13 |
| — | 11 | 18 | 18 | — | 2 | | | 24 | 24 |
| — | 25 | 25 | — | — | 20 | | | 32 | 32 |
| | | 26 | 26 | | | | | | |
| | | 28 | 28 | | | | | | |
| | | 33 | 33 | | | | | | |
| | | 37 | 37 | | | | | | |
| | | — | 9 | | | | | | |
| | | — | 22 | | | | | | |

block. In no case was day of the week a significant discriminator. In short, the analysis achieved what was hoped for. As shown in Table II, there was an 80 percent correspondence between the pre-analysis groups and those derived statistically.

The real test of the technique is, of course, in its application to actual data. Validation depends upon clearances of cases where a determination is made of the actual responsibility for specific burglaries. From this, one can determine the certainty with which one can view the assignment of a case to a particular group as indicative of the working of one individual or group of individuals. Actual cases where clearances have been achieved provides this validation if the analysis is done blind and if the analysis groups crimes together in accordance with cleared data on who was responsible for committing specific crimes. Such an analysis has been completed. Fifteen actual cases were subjected to the analysis described. These cases were cleared and known to have been the work of three different burglars or groups of burglars working in the city of Chattanooga. The clusters derived from computer analysis are shown in Figure 2. The correspondences between cases for which the three criminal groups were responsible and the statistically derived clusters is presented in Table

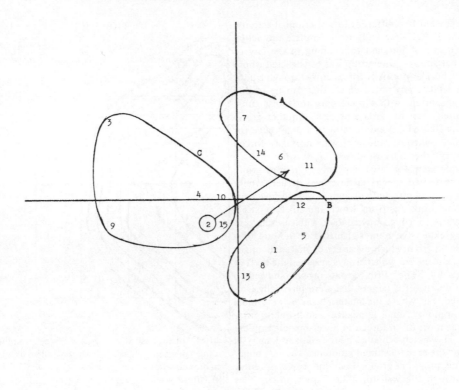

FIGURE 2

*Two Dimensional Representation of 15 Solved Crimes. Each Number Represents a Crime. Contours Out-line Subjectively Determined Clusters and Were Drawn Without Prior Knowledge of Which Crimes Were the Work of the Three Separate Burglars Whose Crimes Were Studied. One Case (Case 2) Was Assigned to An Inappropriate Group.*

III. The correspondence between actual and analytic groups is 93 percent.

The clusters around which the contours are drawn in Figures 1 and 2 are subjectively determined. Groups of crimes do emerge to naive scrutiny of the data when they are so presented. Obviously, a more objective means of defining clusters is desirable. Such an objective procedure has been employed for the 15 actual cases. Figure 3 shows clusters generated by PEP-I, a computer program for nonmetric probability clustering.[3] This program sequentially parti-

[3] J. C. Lingoes and T. Cooper, "PEP-I: A FORTRAN IV (G) Program for Guttman-Lingoes Nonmetric Probability Clustering," *Behavioral Science,* *16* (1971), 259-261.

tioned the points until all partitions and sub-partitions were identified.

TABLE III

*Correspondence Between Actual Criminal Patterns and Statistically Defined Groups*

| Burglar A | | Burglar B | | Burglar C | |
|---|---|---|---|---|---|
| Actual Cases | Stat Groups | Actual Cases | Stat Groups | Actual Cases | Stat Groups |
| 2 | — | 1 | 1 | 3 | 3 |
| 6 | 6 | 5 | 5 | 4 | 4 |
| 7 | 7 | 8 | *8 | 9 | 9 |
| 11 | 11 | 12 | 12 | 10 | 10 |
| 14 | 14 | 13 | 13 | 15 | 15 |
| | | | | | 2 |

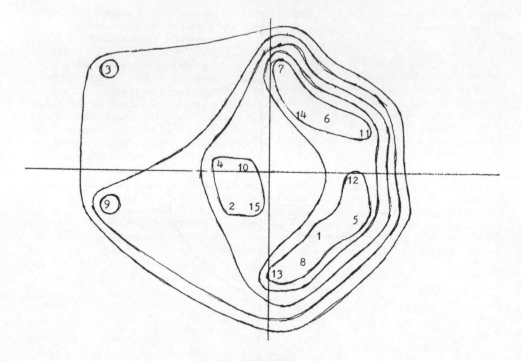

FIGURE 3

*Two Dimensional Representation of 15 Solved Crimes*
*With Contours Drawn Around Computer-Identified Clusters.*

In this analysis essentially the same groupings appear as in Figure 2. The data upon which this analysis is based are the same as before. The difference is that the computer program identified the clusters. It is seen that groups A and B are grouped as before. Group C is, of course, a more loosely structured group of crimes, one of whose primary characteristics is the very fact of greater heterogeneity in technique. Case 2 is erroneously assigned to group C rather than to A as before. In short, the objectified analysis confirms the subjective clusters.

The phenomenal success of this technique in grouping the crimes of the three burglars must be noted with some caution, however. We deliberately chose three criminals with clearly defined M/Os. Moreover, no data were included from the casual, target-of-opportunity type of burglary whose perpetrator may not soon repeat his crime. Such data would blur the precision with which this analysis assigns cases. Never-

theless the basic groupings would remain. Error would be introduced by the occasional assignment of random cases to specific groups. This, however, is an error that also occurs when assignments are based upon human intuition.

## GENERAL APPLICATIONS

The results of this validation study provide strong encouragement to the belief that this type of data processing can yield benefits of enormous significance in facilitating police operations. Specifically, the analysis described here can be applied to the data of daily incidence reports with the following advantages:

1. An up-to-date running record could be achieved against which new cases could routinely be compared for assignment to investigative teams. A comprehensive assessment of current M/Os could thereby maximize

efficient use of the detective division in follow-up investigations.

2. Where current statistics are available, a new incident report could well provide hot leads on the activity of suspects who are already reasonably well identified. The progressive pattern could be determined over time, and anticipation of moves to fence stolen merchandise could lead to more effective surveillance and eventual apprehension.

3. Criminals often work their own neighborhoods, so a geographical separation of sets of burglaries will usually indicate the work of different groups of people. Where crimes are all committed in one general area, however, other discriminators are needed to identify the work of different parties. Statistical analysis provides the means of making those discriminations.

4. Comprehensive summaries of the M/Os characteristic of particular groups could be built up, against which an evaluation could be made of the probable characteristics of the perpetrator of a new incident. For example, the general profile of, thefts by juveniles can be expected to differ from that of the adult addict, or the specialist in the theft of jewels, coins, furs, or silver plate. Once those profiles are determined, a specific case can be compared and a probability statement generated to indicate the type of criminal who should be sought. In short, crime statistics could be used to draw the profile of the criminal. The individual's operation is, in general, as characteristic as his fingerprints. The class of criminal can be expected to show similar consistencies.

# [26]

## Dermot Walsh

There are no age restrictions for burglary, but as Reppetto[19] found in Boston, the typical burglar is a young male. Both he and Chappell[20] use three-part classifications for grouping burglars by age. Over 31 per cent of Chappell's group were under fourteen and 24 per cent were aged between fourteen and seventeen, the rest being eighteen and over. Over 60 per cent of the juveniles were first offenders. The ages of burglars involved in the 100 detected cases in Exeter are shown in Appendix 2 Table 4. (However, double counting is involved, since the same man may have committed several offences and be recorded several times as a result, and frequently there are several burglars involved in the same break-in, which is why the total of Table 4 is greater than the number of detected cases.) With these reservations in mind, 81 per cent of the burglars are aged thirty or under, and over half (52 per cent) are aged twenty and under. These figures suggest that the majority, as they mature, graduate from burglary to normal work or to more prestigious crime.

58                              *Break-Ins*

In the sample of burglars drawn from localities all over England, only one was twenty-one years old and most of them (21) were between twenty-one and forty, the oldest being sixty-four. The official Exeter figures on ages of detected burglars show that the burglars interviewed are slightly older than average.

Fourteen of the burglars interviewed expressed a preference for burgling alone and nine of them preferred to operate with a friend, in pairs. One man had in the 1930s burgled as one of a group of eleven![21] (Preferences for operating alone or working in groups are given for the detected offenders in Exeter 1976 in Appendix 2, Table 5.) Most burglars apparently prefer to operate alone, and this trend seems more marked with ageing. Perhaps the older they grow, the less burglars trust companions. There was a slight tendency for the young to go in groups or gangs,[22] and for the old to go alone. There were no gangs of three, but there was one each of a gang of four, five and six people. The ages in the gang of six were two of fifteen, two of fourteen, thirteen and nine. The most disturbing feature is the very large number of young burglars.

Specific factual evidence from interviewing the victims sheds more light on the number of burglars involved per incident in the undetected cases. Taking all the cases of victims together, in 46 per cent of them, only one man had been involved per incident, and in only 15 per cent of cases were two or three people known to have been involved, as evidenced by material traces or accounts from witnesses. But 37 per cent of householders did not know and could not tell how many burglars had been involved in their break-ins. Put together this seems to suggest in general burglars prefer to go alone or in pairs, with large gangs being confined to youngsters.

Insofar as the sample of burglars interviewed could be divided into 'types' on the basis of age, skill, method or outlook, the presumption was that each 'type' would have different targets in view and a different target logic. One main division was in terms of age and maturity. The older burglars were more cautious, nervous and cynical than the ones under thirty who

## Burglars 59

exhibited more carefree, happy-go-lucky, unrestrained attitudes and less personal discipline when actually engaged in burglary.

For example, in talking about his choice of a house to break into, one youngster said '. . . no choosing. I was out drinking . . . (it was) spur of the moment. I did not need the money . . . (it was) something to do.' Or again, 'I didn't care much if I got caught.' Describing his behaviour before coming to prison another said, 'I was a lunatic . . . I was a very petty housebreaker, not a professional,' and another young burglar told how he broke into one particular house, 'I leant something [a ladder] against the house to climb up to get in to the open bathroom window . . . it accidentally broke the ground floor window in the process . . . I went in that way.'

The younger burglars could again be divided fairly easily into those with dedication and high job involvement, who by their twenties are on the way to being careerists, and those who would be quite prepared to switch their type of crime rapidly, depending on expediency (and who perhaps are equally prepared to be violent should this be thought to be necessary or inevitable).

The most obvious career burglars were in the thirty to forty age group: competent, physically very strong, anxious and wary, determinedly non-violent and very selective in their choice of house. Such men once inside the victim's house place a premium on being tidy, disciplined and ultra-calm. They are also much given to pseudo-logic about their behaviour. Sometimes this was very well and convincingly developed, for example, about lines of sight or particular courses of action, but often it was illogical, and could be countered by another apparently equally logical foolproof scheme suggesting the exact opposite. The easiest way to view this 'logic' is as an attempt to legitimate idiosyncratic, security-giving choices, based largely on habit and designed to reduce uncertainty. These men also displayed many rituals on the job (which can frequently lead to their being caught), such as wedging open doors with cushions, removing light bulbs and greasing doorsteps. In prison they are model prisoners, quiet, well-adjusted men, but well-adjusted to a life of crime.

Older burglars had been chastened by experience and, lacking the anarchic amorality of the youngsters they demonstrated much more caution, alertness and greater adherence to arbitrary ethical codes. These men of between fifty and sixty were very, very cautious, non-violent and exceedingly fearful (given the task, almost incapacitatingly so), of any human contact whilst burgling. The ones seen showed a detectable shift away from houses as targets towards locations without people, such as warehouses and factories at night. There were two old failed burglars who had fatalistically switched to easier crime, such as shoplifting and cheque fraud, one of whom said ruefully, partly in jest, when he had difficulty opening the door to the room, 'I'm not much of a burglar am I?' There were, too, burglars who drank a great deal when not in prison, and who financed their drinking through burglary.

Few men bothered to try to justify their actions at all. One of those who did said about his activities, 'I don't scream if I get caught. I know the difference between right and wrong. I take my chances. . . I go for the rich [people] . . . they are covered by insurance.' Another argued, '. . . after a burglary [that is one of his], I look at the reports in the papers . . . the majority of people claim an extra third on the insurance . . . I feel that I am doing them a favour.'

Most of these burglars readily saw themselves as predatory, but predatory with courage and initiative, and they were generally prepared to categorize themselves as 'masters' or 'failures'. The most obvious, widely shared feature which they had in common was generalized high anxiety.

Most had been to secondary school. Two had been to grammar school and two, because of their age, had only been to elementary school. The majority were employed at the time of their last offence,[23] eleven of them in skilled trades, particularly the building and construction industry. Reppetto[24] who found a similar number suggests that the explanation for such a finding is that there are significant parallels between such work and burglary, particularly that both involve job freedom, ready wages and physical prowess, skill and risk. He makes the point that rehabilitation programmes could well bear this in mind. The other major occupational concentration was in the hotel business which provided six of these burglars. (A factor of possible importance here is that this occupational experience would accustom them to dealing with strangers in intimate surroundings such as bedrooms.) The most noticeable occupational gaps were that there were no men with backgrounds of shop or office work, and only one professional (a teacher). Seven of the group had worked in jobs which accustomed them to heights and involved the use of ladders, such as miners, tree surgeons, builders' labourers and house painters. Staff had indicated that usually many of the sentenced burglars they held had been window-cleaners, an occupation which involves knowledge of house layout, techniques of opening windows from the outside, and familiarity with ladders, but only one man in this group was a professional window-cleaner. In short, nearly all of these men had been manual workers. In Chappell's sample of 54 offenders[25] most were also manual workers or semi-skilled labourers, but a difference was that 35 of them were unemployed at the time of their last offence.

As far as the *reason* for burgling, some knew exactly what they wanted and were breaking in for particular sorts of antiques, jewellery or silver, but most were interested in money rather than goods. One pointed out that stealing goods involved a buyer, and using a buyer involved trust. As he said, 'I don't trust my own shadow and that goes everywhere I go.' Of the sixteen burglars who had specifically stated that their object was money, two went in just for money from gas, electricity or television meters. One of these said, of this, 'Three flats equals three meters equals £200.' Since most were chiefly interested in money only, the disposal problem was slight, since the money would just be spent, '. . . waste it, spend it. I have no respect for money,' or, 'spend it on clothing, accommodation and feeding,' or 'buy drugs'. Eleven of the burglars said that they would sell any goods obtained, and some would use a buyer whom they had contacted in advance. (A point on which there is no information is the amount of income through burglary which a burglar forgoes whilst in prison.)

The selection of the house and gaining access to it calls for initiative, resolution and daring (albeit misplaced), and the burglars were clearly aware that this was so, and many were quietly proud of their skill and 'bottle' (courage). Of the several who said that they were now no longer interested in burglary, one explained it by saying '. . . the thrill has gone'. Burglary for these men seemed to combine the excitement of the (well-fed) hunter, and a means of expressing independence (in an anonymous urban setting of conformity), as well as satisfying various self-conceptions of masculinity. So far from being in it for what they can get out of it (which is usually not very much, as the police themselves say, other types of crime have higher monetary rewards), many of these men seem to enjoy the activity itself, and the excitement, the sense of liberty and predatory freedom which they get from burglary as much as the gains.

However this sample included only older burglars, and young burglars (under twenty) will almost certainly be different in many important respects. Burglary by youths and children is important because the proportion of such crimes is increasing. The local Probation Department was contacted with a view to interviewing some burglars, including youngsters on Probation. Permission was given to do so, but unfortunately at the time no burglars at all were on probation in this area.

In the absence of any interviews with young burglars – a rather serious weakness – it becomes important to reconstruct what is known about them from talking to older burglars, the police, and of course their victims. Certain facts emerge with a startling clarity. Young burglars are generally less discriminating than older ones in their choice of houses to break into, and in what is taken from them. Reppetto[20] established that whereas burglars over the age of twenty-five are more likely to choose single family houses, younger ones are more likely

## Burglars 63

to choose multi-family ones. It appears that frequently young burglars break into a house, not because they think that rationally it contains a good deal of money or cashable property, but because they know the owner to be vulnerable (perhaps an old person, or a woman living on her own). Older burglars are more likely to break into such houses only coincidentally, rather than deliberately.

Young burglars tend to steal less of value per burglary, and to steal odder and more unusual things, often items of low cash value which happen to catch their fancy – more of a form of looting than systematic theft. Their lack of rationality is perhaps also reflected in the amount of pointless, destructive damage that they frequently commit in a house, such as defecating in beds, tying the sheets in knots, slashing furniture, splashing fluids over materials and defacing pictures. Very often too, a special signature may be left such as a threat, slogan or initials written up prominently on a wall or mirror.

There is a tendency for them not to operate alone, but to share responsibility for breaking in by working in pairs or groups, and they display less technical skill in breaking into the house, frequently making several ineffectual attempts before succeeding. Being younger, when caught, they receive lighter punishments (for possibly more disruptive crime) and subsequently they may graduate to different crime forms without showing strong loyalty to any particular type of offence.

Turning now to information about burglars provided by the sample of victims, understandably most householders (69 per cent) had no notion how long the burglars had spent in their house. Fifteen per cent knew for certain that the burglars had spent a quarter of an hour or less in the house and there was only one case where the burglars had slept in the house. There were several instances where the burglar was interrupted or disturbed in his crime. For this particular sample of houses, about a quarter of the burglars were caught and about three-quarters were not. The greater the time lag between the burglary and police involvement, the harder the task of detection is of course, but the more often the burglar burgles, the more likely he is to get caught. Most householders (60 per cent) had no idea if their burglar had used a car to travel to their house, but in 23 per cent of cases it was clear that no car or van had been used.

Since the majority of burglars were not caught, few householders could tell if they had seen the burglar in the neighbourhood for any length of time beforehand, 10 per cent at least certainly had. Householders were then asked if they felt that the burglars knew them as people or knew *of* them. Several people appeared to credit burglars with omniscience, saying 'they know' (about movements or domestic details), and one woman living on her own and feeling that she had been victimized because of this said, 'Near here, there's another woman living on her own . . . burglars know who these people are.' In as much as 36 per cent of cases (at a very conservative estimate), the burglar was someone who was known to the householder (such as a work-mate, neighbour or a local) and not a stranger. Only 11 per cent of householders felt that the burglars had been watching their house in advance of the burglary, and of these none knew for how long. In 63 per cent of cases the householders felt that the burglary had been totally impersonal and that the burglars had known little or nothing about them. In three cases the burglar was someone who had done work for the householder (laying turf, tree-felling, decorating), where, for example, the householder had asked a man to hurry the job because they would be 'away on holiday next week'). In six cases the burglar was just vaguely 'someone we knew'. For example a babysitter ('I used to do his washing for him'), a son's friend or a lodger who had stolen a tin of cash from his landlord containing £400 and was caught when he went to a garage and asked them to force it open for him. (In two of these cases victims had earlier had relatives stealing sizeable amounts of money from them.) In thirteen cases the burglar was a neighbour, for example the son of a neighbour living in the flat below climbed up the drainpipe and in through the open kitchen window of the flat above and stole two weeks' rent and a hundred teabags, and, in another case, a neighbour's son came in to steal a cigarette-lighter and the baby's christening presents.

During the interviews with the victims it emerged that the jobs that the known burglars had were cook (2), gardener (2), painter and roadmender. There were several groups of schoolboys and a number of individuals from community homes or on bail. Sometimes there were 'family gangs' where everyone was in the 'business' (father stealing, mother preparing the goods for sale, daughters selling), and there was one instance of a soldier from the nearby barracks who broke into a house and just quietly sat down and took two cameras to pieces. When caught, he said he was 'bored stiff'.

Obviously a great many of these burglars were children. In one case neighbours had seen a group of twelve- to thirteen-year-old boys walk past the house before the burglary and say, 'We could have a go in there.' Equally obviously the level of expertise and craft was mainly low, as Chappell[27] also found. Many of the adults were people engaged in itinerant, semi-legal, semi-illegal activities, part-time crime in fact, whereby they would for example re-turf lawns and do a fair day's work for a fair day's pay, or perhaps clean windows, but if the opportunity arose for a break-in, or a 'window catch' (theft from a window) they would also do that too. And then in recollecting the circumstances of their burglary, householders said such things as 'A window-cleaner called just before the burglary,' or again, 'Just before the burglary I had had the windows cleaned, ... for the first time in ten years.'

188            *Notes and references*

19. Reppetto, *op.cit.*
20. Chappell (1965b).
21. Most burglars' slang dates from an era when large gangs were common and needed to have a secret argot to communicate. Large gangs were most common in the 19th century but continued up to the 1940s in London (Beveridge, 1947, p. 71). Examples of this slang are as follows: *getter* (letterbox thief), *creeper* (walk-in thief), *linesman* (go-between to the thief and the receiver), *fence* (receiver), *mosker* (professional pawner), *screwsman* or *carries the iron* (shop or housebreaker), *bent gear* (stolen property), *bogey bell* (burglar alarm), *drum* or *gaff* (house or building), *stick* or *cane* (jemmy), *talkered* (premises fitted with silent burglar alarm system), *screwing* (housebreaking), *take sights* (looking out for a suitable house to break into), *turn over* (to search premises). Cf. Jackson (1962).
22. Chappell (1965b), p. 264, found that the typical juvenile incident involved two or more people.
23. Perhaps the most coveted job for a burglar, of course, is to work as a burglar alarm installer or maintenance man if only he can get it. Through this work he obtains detailed knowledge which can be exploited (usually after a suitable interval has elapsed) and all access difficulties are removed. Infrequently, crime prevention firms and commercial security organizations inadvertently employ burglars, with disastrous

Notes and references   189

consequences. For example, Mr Pace was an engineer employed by a London security firm to reset defective burglar alarms. In this capacity on seven occasions he also engaged in burglary at the same time. (*The Sun*, 18 February 1977.)

24. Reppetto, *op.cit.*
25. Chappell (1965b).
26. Reppetto, *op.cit.*
27. Chappell (1965b).

# Bibliography

BEVERIDGE, P. (1947) *Inside the CID* (London: Evans Bros Ltd.)

CHAPPELL, D. (1965b) 'The development and administration of the English law relating to breaking and entering' (Ph.D. thesis, University of Cambridge).

JACKSON, R. L. (1962) *Criminal investigation* (London: Sweet & Maxwell).

REPPETTO, T. A. (1974) *Residential crime* (Cambridge, Massachusetts: Ballinger).

# Motive-Based Offender Profiles of Arson and Fire-Related Crimes

By
DAVID J. ICOVE, Ph.D, P.E.
*Senior Systems Analyst*
*Behavioral Science Investigative Support Unit*
*National Center for the Analysis of Violent Crime*
*FBI Academy*
*Quantico, VA*
and
M. H. (JIM) ESTEPP
*Fire Chief*
*Prince George's County Fire Department*
*Upper Marlboro, MD*

In the Washington, DC, metropolitan area, investigators from the Prince George's County, MD, Fire Department (PGFD) periodically meet with specialists from the FBI's National Center for the Analysis of Violent Crime (NCAVC). The subject of these conferences concerns a timely research project into the motivation of persons involved in fire-related crimes.

The study is based on the analysis of data from 1,016 interviews of juveniles and adults arrested for arson and fire-related crimes, primarily during the years 1980 through 1984, by the PGFD's Fire Investigations Division. The offenses include 504 arrests for arson, 303 for malicious false alarms, 159 for violations in bombing/explosives/ fireworks laws, and 50 for mis-

cellaneous fire-related offenses. NCAVC researchers consider this the largest-existing comprehensive data base of interviews for arson and related offenses.

The overall purpose of this computer-assisted analysis was to create and promote the use of motive-based offender profiles of individuals who commit incendiary and fire-related crimes. Specifically, the study identifies and develops a statistically significant offender profile based on the motive for the crime as determined by experienced PGFD fire investigators.

Historically, the earliest large-scale scientific study detailing the motives of arsonists, published in 1951, used 1,145 subjects,[1] while the most recent, in 1984, studied 225 adults.[2] Prior re-

search on arsonists and fire-related criminal offenders, including that conducted by the FBI, failed to address completely the broad issues confronting modern law enforcement. Of primary concern are the efforts to provide logical, motive-based investigative leads for incendiary crimes. Furthermore, even though several common motives for arson exist, recent criminal justice literature taken from FBI studies repeatedly cites the profiles of the pyromaniac and professional arsonist.[3]

For purposes of this and previous FBI studies on firesetters and fire-related offenders, a motive is cited as an inner drive or impulse that is the cause, reason, or incentive that induces or prompts a specific behavior.[4] For legal purposes, the motive is often helpful in

*"The overall purpose of this computer-assisted analysis was to create and promote the use of motive-based offender profiles of individuals who commit incendiary and fire-related crimes."*

Dr. Icove

Chief Estepp

explaining why an offender committed his or her crime.

To compound the problem, scientific literature and research on arsonists have been conducted largely from the forensic psychiatry viewpoint.[5] Many researchers do not necessarily assess the crime from the law enforcement perspective. They may have limited access to full adult and juvenile criminal data bases and case files, and they rely on the interviews of the offenders as being correct. They do this without the capabilities and time to validate the information through followup investigations. Other researchers have cited that methodological difficulties, with small sample sizes of interviews and skewed data bases, may also bias the previous studies.[6]

Therefore, fire and law enforcement communities have taken upon themselves the task of conducting their own independent research into violent incendiary crimes. One of the primary missions of the NCAVC is to participate in and perform such independent research, as well as to provide various academic and technical assistance otherwise unavailable to these agencies.[7]

**Research Methods**

Since 1977, the PGFD Fire Prevention Bureau's investigators have conducted their own research into the backgrounds of violent offenders by interviewing juveniles and adults arrested for arson and related offenses. These offenses include malicious false alarms, bomb threats, bombings, and even cross burnings. A PGFD fire investigator designed and implemented a code-for-computer interview research instrument to aid in the motivation study.

In 1985, the FBI's Technical Services Division keypunched the PGFD arrest interviews, which allowed NCAVC researchers in Quantico, VA, to then analyze the data.[8] This analysis approach safeguarded the confidentiality of the offender data.

**Findings**

The 1,016 offenders interviewed most frequently targeted five types of properties—residential properties (44%), educational properties (31%), fields/forests (10%), other structures (10%), and vehicles (6%). Revenge and excitement-motivated offenders predominantly targeted residential properties (26%), while vandals selected educational facilities (29%).

Table 1 lists the characteristic profile variables studied in this analysis, arranged by their logical categories of victimology, demographics, socioeconomics, alcohol/drug abuse and criminal history, and behavioral characteristics. Table 2 displays six categories of reported motives for these incidents, which include specific subcategories, with their relative percentages.

In the order of their occurrence, this study reports these arson and related crime motives as vandalism (49%), excitement (25%), revenge (14%), other (8%), crime concealment (2%), and profit (1%). Tables 3 depicts the cross-tabulations of the profile characteristics versus the six categories of reported motives.

After cross-tabulating the data and performing a chi-square analysis, the researchers of this study observed a statistical significance in these categories of reported motives. Their analyses indicate that relationships exist between the various profile characteristics and the reported motives. Table 3 shows the summary statistical analysis,

TABLE 1—Categories of Data Variables Studied

| Category | Variable |
|---|---|
| Victimology | Targeted Property |
|  | Time of Day |
|  | Day of Week |
|  | Season of Year |
|  | Method of Operation |
| Demographic | Age in Years |
|  | Sex |
|  | Race |
|  | Formal Education |
|  | Occupational Status |
| Socioeconomic | Marital Status |
|  | Type of Housing Resides |
|  | Living with Whom |
|  | Socioeconomic Status |
| Alcohol/Drug Usage | Alcohol/Drug Usage |
| and Criminal History | Prior Police/Fire Record |
|  | Case Disposition |
| Behavioral | Presence at Fire Scene |
|  | Distance from Residence |
|  | Accompanied at Offense |
|  | Post-Offense Presence at Scene |
|  | Social Attitudes Professed |

including the number of degrees of freedom and probability of the results being more than a chance occurrence.

**Offender Profiles**

As previously mentioned, the researchers aggregated the reported motives according to their local categories of victimology, demographics, socioeconomics, alcohol/drug abuse and criminal history, and behavioral characteristics. Based on these groupings, they have made the following observations on the motive-based offender profiles.

**Vandalism**

Juveniles (96%) most often committed vandalism-motivated crimes. Individuals in this category lived primarily in lower middle class homes (47%) with both parents (63%). Their crimes occurred during the morning (34%) and afternoon (56%) hours on the weekdays (89%) of the school year, with minimal activity reported during the summer months (14%). These young criminals most frequently ignited fires with materials on hand (46%), followed by causing malicious false alarms (25%) and violating various bombing/explosive/fireworks laws (19%).

The offenders interviewed did not report using alcohol or drugs; yet, some already had contact or were arrested by fire or police officials (29%). Many lived within 1 mile of the crime scene (51%), and a majority reported being accompanied by one or more individuals (73%) at the time of the offense. A large minority remained at the crime scene (41%).

**Excitement**

Mostly juveniles (69%) committed arson and fire-related crimes merely for the excitement. Offenders in this category no longer lived with both parents (55%). These offenders caused false alarms (50%) and ignited fires with materials on hand (32%) during the afternoon (42%) and evening (33%) hours. A majority denied using alcohol or drugs (69%); yet, a large minority had prior contact or arrests by fire or police officials (47%). These offenders often lived within 1 mile from the crime scene (72%) and most often committed the crime while alone (53%). The post-offense behavior of many excitement-motivated offenders showed that they remained at the crime scene (62%).

**Revenge**

Adults made up a large majority (81%) of the revenge-motivated offenders, with approximately one-half of them single (53%). Females also formed a significant part of this offender group (28%). Most of the offenders, who did not live with both their natural parents (75%), planned their revenge, targeting residential properties (72%). The revenge-motivated offender chose afternoon, evening, and early morning hours (91%) during the weekends (50%—Friday, Saturday, and Sunday) in the fall and winter months (61%). They most frequently ignited fires with materials on hand (50%) or flammable liquids (17%) and caused or reported malicious false alarms (20%).

*"[The] FBI/PGFD research study ... provides new insights into the motive-based profile approach."*

Slightly over one-half of these offenders (55%) used alcohol, drugs, or both prior to or during the offense. Most offenders had prior contact or arrests by the fire or police authorities (69%) and lived within 1 mile of the crime scene (63%). Most of these revenge-motivated offenders acted alone (64%), and many offenders left the crime scene, never to return (42%).

**Other Motives**

This study contains only limited interview data on the arrest of offenders motivated by crime concealment and profit. However, we included the results

here since the overall analysis demonstrated statistical significance when these motives were grouped together. Also, casual observations can also be made from this limited data.

The 18 offenders motivated by crime concealment were predominantly single (78%), adult (72%) males (72%) of marginal or less income (56%) who used arson and related crimes to conceal other offenses. A large number of them started fires with materials on hand (67%). Most of these events occurred during the evening or early morning hours (94%) during the summer or fall season of the year (78%).

While concealing crimes, a majority of the offenders were under the influ-

ence of alcohol and/or drugs when committing the arson or fire-related offense (78%). All of the crime concealers had prior contact or arrests by fire or police officials (100%), and most lived more than 1 mile from the crime scene (67%). One or more persons accompanied half of the offenders at the time of the offense, and a majority stayed away from the crime scene (67%).

The 11 offenders concerned with profit motives were predominantly juveniles (64%), all of whom committed their offenses during the evening or morning hours, on weekdays, and in the winter, spring, or summer months.

TABLE 2—Categories of Motives Studied

| Motive | Specific Category | Subtotal N (Pct.) | Total N (Pct.) |
|---|---|---|---|
| Vandalism | Vandalism—General | 364 (73) | |
| | Children Playing with Fire | 89 (18) | |
| | Peer Pressure | 44 ( 9) | |
| | Harassment of Fire Dept. | 5 ( 1) | |
| | | | 502 (49) |
| Excitement | Thrill Seeker | 122 (47) | |
| | Attention Seeker | 110 (43) | |
| | Fire Fighter Wanting Action | 18 ( 7) | |
| | Sexual Perversion | 4 ( 2) | |
| | Pyromania | 2 ( 1) | |
| | Heroic Fire Fighter | 2 ( 1) | |
| | | | 258 (25) |
| Revenge | Revenge—General | 56 (39) | |
| | Revenge—Relationship Problem | 54 (37) | |
| | Harassment of Victim | 28 (19) | |
| | Jealousy | 6 ( 4) | |
| | Terrorism | 1 ( 1) | |
| | | | 145 (14) |
| Crime Concealment | Coverup—Breaking and Entering | 13 (72) | |
| | Coverup—Murder | 4 (22) | |
| | Coverup—Other Crime | 1 ( 6) | |
| | | | 18 ( 2) |
| Profit | Monetary Gain—For Hire | 6 (55) | |
| | Monetary Gain—Insurance Fraud | 5 (45) | |
| | | | 11 ( 1) |
| Other | All Other Motives | 27 (33) | |
| | Undetermined Motives | 55 (67) | |
| | | | 82 ( 8) |
| | | | 1016 |

They almost always (91%) used either flammable liquids, bombs, fireworks, or explosives in their incendiary crimes. A majority lived with both natural parents (55%) in marginal to upper income households (91%). A majority of these profit-motivated offenders had past contact or arrest by the authorities (55%), and a minority used drugs or alcohol prior to or while committing the crime (27%). Many lived more than 1 mile from the scene of the crime (73%)

and acted with someone else (73%). As for post-offense behavior, a little over one-half of the offenders left the crime scene and never returned (55%).

**Discussion**

In 1980, researchers from the FBI's Behavioral Science Services (formerly the Behavioral Science Unit) published a study of the common characteristics of offenders to aid in profiling arsonists.[9] Our FBI/PGFD research study not only highlights these common characteristics but also provides new insights into the motive-based profile approach.

While past FBI studies have consistently shown that arson and related-crime offenders tend to be young, the PGFD data base further discriminates the age of offenders according to their motives for committing these various types of crimes. For example, they found generally that juveniles commit excitement crimes and vandalism, while adults tend to commit revenge and crime concealment offenses.

Some firesetters also report false alarms or bomb threats. In the PGFD data base, false alarms constitute the primary method of operation for excitement (50%) and the secondary cause of vandalism (25%) offenses. The study found that arson is a compulsive crime. For all motives, except profit, the offenders frequently used materials on hand to set their fires.

Males make up the majority of arson and fire-related offenders; however, the NCAVC researchers are beginning to study female offenders.[10] They are particularly interested in the frequency of female offenders (28%) that emerged from the PGFD data base in revenge-motivated crimes.

Race does not appear to be a correlate with arson and fire-related motives. However, the researchers intend to conduct additional research to determine what specific correlations occur in victim-offender relationships.

General research conducted by the FBI indicates that the use of alcohol and/or drugs appears to loosen an offender's inhibitions at the crime scene. The PGFD data base provides some support to this observation, with particular note to the revenge-motivated

## "... generally ... juveniles commit excitement crimes and vandalism, while adults tend to commit revenge and crime concealment offenses."

crimes. Furthermore, previous studies may not have reflected the recent influx of drugs into our society.

The PGFD data base documents the offenders' prior contact with fire or police authorities. This observation underscores the importance of automated and complete records systems, as well as the desirability of joint cooperation among agencies.

Researchers raised the important issue of the distance an offender resides from the crime scene. The PGFD data base demonstrates that the offender often lives close to the crime scene, sometimes less than a mile away.

In the past, police and fire officials believed the majority of arson and related offenses to be solitary crimes—that most offenders committed these crimes alone. However, the PGFD data base disproves this broad assumption. Often, one or more participants or observers accompanied the offenders to the crime scene. This observation may explain the peer pressures associated with juveniles. It may also provide the incentive to look for other witnesses or defendants in what authorities initially consider a solitary crime.

This study also demonstrates the importance of documenting and photographing crowds at crime scenes. A large minority of the offenders admitted to either remaining at the crime scene or returning to it later. These actions may depict the conscious effort of the offenders to critique the fire suppression or investigation or to return to destroy or remove crucial physical evidence from the scene.

### Future Research Plans

The FBI/PGFD team plans future joint research to address questions on the demographics of fire-related crimes. A study of the demographics

TABLE 3—Results of the Chi Square Analysis Grouped by Vandalism, Excitement, Revenge, and All Other Motives

| Observed Category Variable | Vandalism | Excitement | Revenge | Conceal Crime | Profit | Others | Chi Square | Degrees of Freedom | Probability of Chance |
|---|---|---|---|---|---|---|---|---|---|
| *Targeted Property* | | | | | | | 401.9 | 12 | 0.0000 |
| Residential | 141 | 159 | 104 | 5 | 2 | 41 | | | |
| Educational | 293 | 15 | | | 7 | 3 | | | |
| Other Structural | 15 | 38 | 16 | 5 | | 11 | | | |
| Fields and Forests | 37 | 37 | 5 | 3 | 1 | 18 | | | |
| Mobile and Vehicles | 16 | 9 | 20 | 5 | 1 | 9 | | | |
| *Time of Day* | | | | | | | 286.7 | 9 | 0.0000 |
| 0000–0559 | 18 | 28 | 44 | 12 | 2 | 22 | | | |
| 0600–1159 | 168 | 35 | 13 | | 7 | 7 | | | |
| 1200–1759 | 282 | 109 | 35 | 1 | | 27 | | | |
| 1800–2359 | 34 | 86 | 53 | 5 | 2 | 26 | | | |
| *Day of Week* | | | | | | | 94.0 | 18 | 0.0000 |
| Sunday | 25 | 45 | 36 | 1 | | 10 | | | |
| Monday | 72 | 34 | 12 | 4 | 2 | 21 | | | |
| Tuesday | 81 | 40 | 22 | 3 | 3 | 8 | | | |
| Wednesday | 115 | 33 | 21 | 6 | 1 | 7 | | | |
| Thursday | 92 | 42 | 15 | | 4 | 13 | | | |
| Friday | 87 | 30 | 23 | 2 | 1 | 13 | | | |
| Saturday | 30 | 34 | 14 | 2 | | 10 | | | |
| Undetermined | | | 2 | | | | | | |
| *Season of Year* | | | | | | | 35.3 | 9 | 0.0002 |
| Spring (Mar-May) | 170 | 61 | 29 | 2 | 4 | 16 | | | |
| Summer (Jun-Aug) | 72 | 54 | 27 | 8 | 2 | 23 | | | |
| Fall (Sep-Nov) | 149 | 66 | 46 | 6 | | 28 | | | |
| Winter (Dec-Feb) | 111 | 77 | 43 | 2 | 5 | 15 | | | |
| *Method of Operation* | | | | | | | 116.3 | 12 | 0.0000 |
| Material on Hand | 233 | 82 | 72 | 12 | 1 | 41 | | | |
| Flammable Liquid | 15 | 10 | 24 | 5 | 3 | 6 | | | |
| Bomb/Explsve/Fireworks | 95 | 30 | 16 | 1 | 7 | 10 | | | |
| Malicious False Alarm | 125 | 128 | 29 | | | 21 | | | |
| Other | 34 | 8 | 4 | | | 4 | | | |
| *Age in Years* | | | | | | | 404.7 | 3 | 0.0000 |
| Juvenile | 484 | 178 | 27 | 5 | 7 | 36 | | | |
| Adult | 18 | 80 | 118 | 13 | 4 | 46 | | | |
| *Sex* | | | | | | | 392.9 | 6 | 0.0000 |
| Male | 136 | 200 | 91 | 13 | 4 | 60 | | | |
| Female | 21 | 14 | 40 | | | 9 | | | |
| Not Reported | 345 | 44 | 14 | 5 | 7 | 13 | | | |
| *Race* | | | | | | | 318.2 | 6 | 0.0000 |
| White | 63 | 126 | 63 | 11 | 3 | 45 | | | |
| Black | 89 | 87 | 67 | 4 | 4 | 22 | | | |
| Other & Not Reported | 350 | 45 | 15 | 3 | 4 | 15 | | | |
| *Formal Education* | | | | | | | 217.1 | 9 | 0.0000 |
| 0-6 Years | 156 | 78 | 6 | 3 | | 18 | | | |
| 7-9 Years | 235 | 71 | 22 | 6 | 6 | 14 | | | |
| 10+ Years | 98 | 89 | 78 | 3 | 4 | 35 | | | |
| Not Reported | 13 | 20 | 39 | 6 | 1 | 15 | | | |
| *Occupational Status* | | | | | | | 368.5 | 6 | 0.0000 |
| Unemployed | 16 | 30 | 45 | 10 | 2 | 26 | | | |
| Employed | 11 | 46 | 67 | 3 | 2 | 19 | | | |
| Not Working & Undet. | 475 | 182 | 33 | 5 | 7 | 37 | | | |

Notes: 1. Based upon the alpha calculated for a Type I error rate, the probability of one false rejection of the null out of the 21 Chi Square tests performed in 66 percent.

| Observed Category Variable | Vandalism | Excitement | Revenge | Conceal Crime | Profit | Others | Chi Square | Degrees of Freedom | Probability of Chance |
|---|---|---|---|---|---|---|---|---|---|
| **Marital Status** | | | | | | | 235.3 | 6 | 0.0000 |
| Single | 489 | 243 | 77 | 14 | 8 | 67 | | | |
| Married | | 4 | 22 | 1 | 2 | 5 | | | |
| Separated, Divorced, Other, and Undet. | 13 | 11 | 46 | 3 | 1 | 10 | | | |
| **Type of Housing Resides** | | | | | | | 26.8 | 6 | 0.0004 |
| Single Family | 324 | 154 | 85 | 10 | 11 | 47 | | | |
| Multi-Family | 172 | 83 | 48 | 5 | | 30 | | | |
| Other or None | 6 | 21 | 12 | 3 | | 5 | | | |
| **Living with Whom** | | | | | | | 241.5 | 9 | 0.0000 |
| Father and Mother | 317 | 117 | 36 | 5 | 6 | 38 | | | |
| Father or Mother | 148 | 85 | 19 | | 2 | 13 | | | |
| Relatives | 14 | 19 | 16 | 5 | 1 | 5 | | | |
| Spouse/Alone/Other | 23 | 37 | 74 | 8 | 2 | 26 | | | |
| **Socioeconomic Status** | | | | | | | 81.7 | 12 | 0.0000 |
| Poverty/Marginal | 140 | 71 | 62 | 10 | 5 | 35 | | | |
| Lower Middle | 234 | 86 | 34 | 2 | 4 | 16 | | | |
| Middle | 99 | 74 | 35 | 2 | | 21 | | | |
| Upper Middle/High | 13 | 23 | 6 | | 1 | 4 | | | |
| Undetermined | 16 | 4 | 8 | 4 | 1 | 6 | | | |
| **Alcohol/Drug Usage** | | | | | | | 402.6 | 6 | 0.0000 |
| Not Used | 155 | 179 | 30 | | | 27 | | | |
| Alcohol and/or Drugs | 22 | 46 | 79 | 14 | 3 | 32 | | | |
| Undetermined | 325 | 33 | 36 | 4 | 8 | 23 | | | |
| **Prior Police/Fire Record** | | | | | | | 107.3 | 6 | 0.0000 |
| Police or Fire Contact | 87 | 89 | 78 | 12 | 3 | 31 | | | |
| Police or Fire Arrest | 60 | 32 | 22 | 6 | 3 | 13 | | | |
| None or Undetermined | 355 | 137 | 45 | | 5 | 38 | | | |
| **Disposition** | | | | | | | 287.3 | 9 | 0.0000 |
| Intake Closure | 226 | 41 | 6 | 2 | 4 | 10 | | | |
| Conviction | 7 | 36 | 37 | 6 | 2 | 9 | | | |
| Closed or Exceptional | 139 | 53 | 4 | | | 22 | | | |
| Other or Undetermined | 130 | 128 | 98 | 10 | 5 | 41 | | | |
| **Distance from Residence** | | | | | | | 32.7 | 3 | 0.0000 |
| Less than 1 Mile | 258 | 187 | 92 | 6 | 3 | 55 | | | |
| Greater than 1 Mile | 244 | 71 | 53 | 12 | 8 | 27 | | | |
| **Accompanied at Offense** | | | | | | | 145.5 | 6 | 0.0000 |
| Alone | 129 | 136 | 93 | 9 | 3 | 47 | | | |
| With Others | 365 | 115 | 46 | 9 | 8 | 31 | | | |
| Undetermined | 8 | 7 | 6 | | | 4 | | | |
| **Post-Offense Presence at Scene** | | | | | | | 167.9 | 9 | 0.0000 |
| Did Not Leave | 204 | 159 | 55 | 5 | 4 | 63 | | | |
| Returned Later | 3 | 6 | 13 | 1 | 1 | 1 | | | |
| Did Not Return | 285 | 52 | 61 | 12 | 6 | 12 | | | |
| Undetermined | 10 | 41 | 16 | | | 6 | | | |
| **Social Attitudes Professed** Self: / Others: | | | | | | | 236.4 | 12 | 0.0000 |
| Likes / Likes | 112 | 112 | 49 | 7 | | 34 | | | |
| Likes / Dislikes | 7 | 19 | 25 | 1 | | 4 | | | |
| Dislikes / Likes | | 19 | 2 | 1 | 1 | 2 | | | |
| Dislikes / Dislikes | 3 | 19 | 12 | 3 | 2 | 12 | | | |
| Undetermined | 380 | 89 | 57 | 6 | 8 | 30 | | | |

2. For purposes of calculation, the above tables were collapsed to four motive categories of vandalism, excitement, revenge, and all others.

could compare urban growth, housing, and land use patterns. For example, studies on the geography of violent crimes cite the micro-and macro-level analyses of arson as it relates to theories on urban morphology.[11] Previous research into the geographic patterns of arson fires in Prince George's County has demonstrated temporal (time-of-day, day-of-week, etc.) relationships within their fire incident data.[12]

Both the FBI and PGFD plan to continue updating and refining this study because, as with other research endeavors, new knowledge generates even more unanswered questions. They plan to address these and other questions in future joint FBI/PGFD research efforts.

FBI

**Footnotes**

1 N.D. Lewis and H. Yarnell, "Pathological Firesetting (Pyromania)," Nervous and Mental Diseases Monograph 82, Coolidge Foundation, New York, 1951.

2 G. Molnar, L. Ketiner, and B.T. Harwood, "A Comparison of Partner and Solo Arsonists," *Journal of Forensic Sciences*, JFSCA, vol. 29, No. 2, April 1984, pp. 574–583.

3 A.O. Rider, "The Firesetter: A Psychological Profile," *FBI Law Enforcement Bulletin*, vol. 49, Nos. 6–8, June–August 1980.

4 Ibid.

5 R.G. Vreeland and M.B. Waller, "The Psychology of Firesetting: A Review and Appraisal," National Bureau of Standards, Grant No. 7-9021, December 1978; supra notes 1–3.

6 R.B. Harmon, R. Rosner, and M. Wiederlight, "Women and Arson: A Demographic Study," *Journal of Forensic Sciences*, JFSCA, vol. 30, No. 2, April 1985, pp. 467–477; supra note 2.

7 R.L. Ault, Jr., "NCAVC's Research and Development Program," *FBI Law Enforcement Bulletin*, vol. 55, No. 12, December 1986, pp. 6–8.

8 Computer analysis used the Statistical Analysis System (SAS) program: A.J. Barr, et al, *A User's Guide to SAS76*, SAS Institute, Raleigh, NC, 1976.

9 Supra note 3.

10 Vreeland and Waller, supra note 5.

11 D.E. Georges, "The Geography of Crime and Violence: A Spatial and Ecological Perspective," Resource Papers for College Geography, No. 78-1, Association of American Geographers, Washington, DC, 1978.

12 D.J. Icove and M.O. Soliman, "Arson Information Management System: Users Guide and Documentation," International Association of Arson Investigators, U.S. Fire Administration Agreement EMW-K-0812, Marlboro, MA, 1983; D.J. Icove, *Principles of Incendiary Fire Analysis*, Ph.D. dissertation, College of Engineering, University of Tennessee-Knoxville, 1979.

# [28]

SOCIAL SCIENCE RESEARCH **24**, 63–95 (1995)

## Getting into Street Crime: The Structure and Process of Criminal Embeddedness

BILL McCARTHY

*University of Victoria, Victoria, Canada*

AND

JOHN HAGAN

*University of North Carolina, Chapel Hill, and University of Toronto, Toronto, Canada*

Combining insights from Granovetter's research on embeddedness, Coleman's work on social capital and Sutherland's theory of differential association, we suggest that embeddedness in networks of deviant associations provides access to tutelage relationships that facilitate the acquisition of criminal skills and attitudes, assets that we call "criminal capital." We test our hypotheses with structural equation models of drug-selling, theft and prostitution among a sample of homeless youth (N = 390). Our results reveal that embeddedness in criminal networks enhances exposure to tutelage relationships and that crime increases with such exposure. These results remain when controls are introduced for home and school experiences, time at risk, situational adversity, and previous criminal experiences. Our analysis raises doubts about assertions that crimes are crudely impulsive acts that require little learning or skill and reflect a general imperviousness to others. Instead, a sensitivity to others, particularly potential tutors, appears to enhance crime by allowing for the acquisition of criminal capital in a tutelage relationship. © 1995 Academic Press. Inc.

In his work on the social structure of economic action, Granovetter (1973, 1974, 1985, 1992) exposes several shortcomings of employment and occupational mobility theory, particularly the neglect of social relations. He notes that sociological explanations emphasize norms and values, psychological perspectives accent early predispositions and propensities, and economic accounts concentrate on self-interested calculations of rewards and costs, all without adequately considering the role of proximate social relations in finding and changing jobs. These approaches overlook the

Address reprint requests to Bill McCarthy, Dept. of Sociology, University of Victoria, P.O. Box 3050, Victoria, BC V8W 3P5, Canada.

*Criminal Detection and the Psychology of Crime*

MCCARTHY AND HAGAN

social networks in which individuals are embedded and through which they share information, bargain, and negotiate with one another in their occupational movements. Coleman (1988,1990) extends these insights, observing that embeddedness is an important source of "social capital" involved in the formation of human capital.

Granovetter's analysis has broader relevance, for example, to explanations of less conventional and putatively anti-social behaviors such as crime. Among the most important of these is Gottfredson and Hirschi's (1990) recent blending of sociological and psychological perspectives that focuses on self-control. This theory explains crime as the failure of familial socialization to establish self-control early in the life course. From this perspective, criminal behaviors reflect inadequate self-control and a general insensitivity or imperviousness to others (see also Herrnstein and Wilson, 1985). Moreover, they are crudely impulsive, poorly planned activities that require little learning or skill.

The notion of indifference to others is implicit also in economic accounts that treat crime as the result of cost-benefit analyses in which actors weigh the rewards of crime against the projected likelihood or costs of punishment (Becker, 1968; Becker and Landes, 1974; Block and Heineke, 1975; Ehrlich, 1973; Sah, 1991; Schmidt and Witte, 1984). These explanations assume that actors choose criminal activities in the same autonomous fashion that they presumably select more conventional economic behavior. From this perspective, explaining "criminal behavior . . . does not require ad hoc concepts of differential association, anomie and the like" (Becker 1968, p. 176) nor a "resort to hypotheses regarding . . . social conditions . . ." (Ehrlich, 1973, p. 521).

The above approaches are similar in their emphasis on asocial, impersonal, and autonomous features of criminal behavior and their underestimation of the significance of embeddedness in social relations. Thus, they are reflective of a growing tendency to ignore that getting into crime, like getting a job, is a social phenomenon.

In contrast, we suggest that extending Granovetter's perspective can refocus attention on the role of associations in accounting for involvements in crime; in so doing, this perspective recalls neglected insights of one of America's foremost sociological criminologists, Edwin Sutherland.[1] Specifically, we argue that our understanding of criminal activities, especially those that can yield economic gains, is enhanced by uniting Sutherland's ideas about learning crime with Granovetter's notion of social embeddedness and Coleman's concept of social capital. We test this combined

[1] Although Sutherland regarded his theory of differential association as his central contribution (see Cohen, Lindesmith and Schuessler 1956) it is severely criticized (Hirschi and Gottfredson 1980; Kornhauser 1978) and often ignored (see Matsueda, 1988; Stitt and Giacopassi, 1992).

theoretical approach with data gathered from a sample of homeless youths, many of whom commit instrumental crimes of selling drugs, theft, and prostitution.

## CRIMINAL EMBEDDEDNESS, CAPITAL, AND THE SOCIAL LEARNING OF CRIME

According to Granovetter (1985, p. 487), purposive economic actions are embedded when formed in interaction with others in networks of social relations. These behaviors are influenced by the composition of such networks and the acquisition of information from network members. Granovetter's work on "getting a job" (1974), "the strength of weak ties" (1973), and job mobility (1992) supports his thesis that contacts facilitate entry and advancement in employment. Although he recognizes that background factors (e.g., class, family, and school experiences) influence economic action, Granovetter maintains that the foreground structural relations in which individuals are embedded exert more telling effects.

Granovetter's approach has several parallels with Sutherland's differential association theory of criminal behavior. According to Sutherland (1947), criminal behavior is learned through connections with people who violate the law. These "criminal" contacts provide a forum to learn techniques as well as motives, drives, rationalizations, and attitudes that facilitate crime. Individuals adopt criminal definitions and engage in crime when this exposure exceeds contact with non-criminal attitudes and behaviors.

Sutherland's theory originated in his interviews with professional thieves (Sutherland 1942). From these, he (1937, p. 212) concluded that careers in theft follow from ". . . contact with professional thieves, reciprocal confidence and appreciation, a crisis situation, and tutelage." In focusing on contacts and tutelage, Sutherland accentuates learning from mentors who introduce criminal skills. His further emphasis on crisis situations adds another structural component to his approach, a dimension reflected in Sutherland's early research on homeless adults and probably related to his formative research during the Great Depression (Sutherland and Locke, 1936).

Sutherland returned to his ideas about associations and tutelage throughout his career, including in his last major work, *White Collar Crime* (1949). In this study, Sutherland provides biographical sketches of white-collar employees who received on-the-job instruction in crime as part of their employment (240–250). The result of Sutherland's investigations is an explanation of crime that crosses class boundaries with its attention to four elements: affiliation with criminals in intimate personal groups, communication with these individuals about deviant attitudes, tutelage in techniques for specific criminal endeavors, and the adoption of definitions that legitimate law-violation. The generalizability of this approach is reflected in Sutherland's assertion that, although some crimes arise independently of contacts with others (1942,1944) and do not require specific skills or involve skills that can be learned in non-criminal environments, "most . . . require training" (1947, p. 213).

Although the theory of differential association has been reformulated several times and served as a point of origin for other explanations, Sutherland's ideas about tutelage have not been rejected. For example, Glaser's (1956) differential identification and Burgess and Akers' (1966; see also Akers et al., 1979) differential reinforcement theories both recognize the centrality of learning deviant behaviors from accomplished lawbreakers. This assumption is also central to the works of several subcultural theorists, including Cohen (1955,1966) and particularly Cloward and Ohlin (1960), as well as those from the labeling tradition (e.g., Becker, 1963). This recognition contrasts with more contemporary views of crime as asocial, unskilled, impulsive events and encourages our attempt to revive interest in how the skills for specific crimes are acquired.

Like Sutherland, Granovetter (1985,1992) also highlights social structure as facilitating action; yet, he also underscores that social structure alone is not determinative. Instead, Granovetter maintains that embeddedness in a social structure acquires further influence as it generates trust, establishes expectations, and reinforces social beliefs and norms. Coleman (1988,1990) elaborates, noting that social embeddedness is a resource that constitutes a valuable form of "social capital." According to Coleman, social capital resembles other types of capital in that it is a resource that facilitates productive action. For example, social capital generates obligations, expectations, and trustworthiness, as well as information channels and norms and sanctions. Moreover, these all contribute to an individual's or a group's capacity to engage in social action. Yet, as Coleman (1988, p. 598) argues, social capital is unique: "Unlike other forms of capital, social capital inheres in the structure of relations between actors and among actors." We submit that this is true across classes and contexts, and in criminal as well as in more conventional careers.

The process that Sutherland calls tutelage forms a bridge between Granovetter's notion of social embeddedness and Coleman's conception of social capital. Embeddedness in tutelage relationships with those already proficient in crime is a source of social capital, for example, as a channel for information. This flow of information provides access to skills and knowledge about crime in the same way that contacts, associations, or ties in more conventional lines of work supply actors with leads to jobs and other business-related knowledge. Thus, embeddedness in ongoing criminal networks may establish the foundation for the development of a type of human capital (Schultz, 1961; Becker, 1964) we call "criminal capital." This criminal capital includes knowledge and technical skills that can facilitate successful criminal activity. Conversely, embeddedness in non-criminal networks, particularly those involving family members and educational personnel, provides exposure to more conventional types of non-criminal social capital.

Embeddedness and criminal capital have further significance in that they resonate with Sutherland's concerns about the origins of differential association. Although differential association occupies the cornerstone of Sutherland's work, he emphasized also the structural determinants of these associations, specifically normative conflict and differential social organization. According to Sutherland (1947), normative conflicts arises in heterogeneous societies where groups conflict over norms, values, and interests. Differential social organization translates this conflict into crime by influencing the probability that individuals are exposed to competing definitions. The important elements of social organization are those that influence the probability of exposure to criminal behavior patterns as a source of criminal capital (e.g., unemployment, living in a high-crime area, or lack of formal and informal sources of social control). As we argue below, homelessness reflects the type of differential social organization that Sutherland envisioned as contributing to the emergence of crime.

Our approach to crime synthesizes the insights of Granovetter, Coleman, and Sutherland and in so doing differs from sociological, psychological, and economic explanations reviewed earlier. Although we accept that crime can be characterized by anti-social lapses in self-control and rational-choice calculations, we maintain that it is more immediately influenced by the criminal embeddedness and criminal capital that salient social contacts and connections engender. In underemphasizing these possibilities, rational choice and self-control theories encourage a more utilitarian approach to crime, rather than the more sociological one suggested here. In our view, even street crimes tend not to be the asocial, unplanned, unskilled activities that recent sociological, psychological, and economic theories imply.

We also maintain that attention to other foreground factors such as the "crisis situation" suggested by Sutherland (see also McCarthy and Hagan, 1992) add to our understanding of crime. Our recognition of both background and foreground factors reflects our support for Becker's (1963) distinction between simultaneous and sequential models. Although we differ in methodological preferences, we agree with Becker (1963, p. 24) that participation in crime is best understood by models that incorporate changes that occur across time, particularly the "career contingencies" of individuals as they move from one social world to another and leave behind old networks to become embedded in new ones.

## ETHNOGRAPHIES AND EMBEDDEDNESS

Classic, as well as more recent ethnographies provide evidence of the importance of embeddedness and criminal capital for particular illegal behaviors among adolescents. In *The Gang*, Thrasher (1927) notes that associations with gang-members (e.g., pp. 252–266, 369–408) and criminally inclined adults (e.g., pp. 149, 154) provide a forum for the observation and transmission of the skills of thievery:

> How to . . . fleece a storekeeper, empty slot machines, pick a pocket, go shoplifting, 'roll' a drunken man, get skeleton keys, steal an automobile, sell stolen goods to "fences," purchase guns, engineer a holdup, operate stills, burglarize a store, trick the police, and so on-this is the type of technical knowledge for which the gang acts as a clearing house. (p. 390)

More than half a century later, Sullivan (1989) documents the communication of skills and values in the social organization of adolescent crime in three inner city New York neighborhoods. Although Sullivan notes that relatively unskilled youths also commit crimes, he reports that the most successful individuals attribute their prosperity to the acquisition of skills learned from other, more experienced youths and adults. Even car theft, which can serve as a prelude to more advanced criminal activities, often involves some initiation and instruction. Sullivan (1989, p. 142) offers as an example the following excerpt from one of his interviews:

> *Mike Concepcion:* I learned in one day. This friend of mine. Cisco, you could say he recruited me. We went up to a car that was already stripped but it still had the ignition. He showed me how to take off the door cylinder with pliers. Then there's this tool called a butterfly, it's a bad tool, you stick it in the key and just slap it out in one shot and pull the starter and turn it with a screwdriver.
>
> *Interviewer:* But you say the car was already stripped?
>
> *Mike Concepcion:* It was, like practice, just practice. This was in the afternoon. The same night, I went out and did it myself.

Sullivan notes that instruction in drug selling is also common and is often facilitated by associations with dealers, consignments from those already working in the drug-trade, and from associations formed in "reefer stores."

Padilla (1992) reaches comparable conclusions from his study of theft and drug dealing among the "Diamonds," a pseudonym for a gang of Puerto Rican youths in Chicago. Padilla (1992, p. 121) reports that new recruits often achieve competence in theft by "working together with another gang member who has experience, whose role is that of mentor and leader." After demonstrating expertise in stealing, new members progress to running, dealing, and occasionally distributing drugs. For most youths this is a "gradual process of learning skills and establishing a network of relationships with significant members of the organization in order to become dealers" (p. 151). Padilla (p. 151) emphasizes that:

> to be sure, drug dealing represents far more than simply a spontaneous activity carried out by youngsters who are given an amount of drugs to sell. Drug dealing

is a job, and, like other jobs, it must be learned over time. It requires a considerable investment of time to acquire skills, plan, and operate systematically.

Research on adolescents who sell sex for money provides similar findings. In a study of male hustlers in Toronto, Visano (1987) describes the apprenticeship, sponsoring, emotional support, and sharing of trade secrets and legitimating devices that are centerpieces of adolescent prostitution. According to Visano, "the requirements of hustling are learned by direct assistance, imitation, and repetition" (p. 130) in which "on-the-job instructions are anchored in friendship associations" (p. 131). This process is exemplified in Luckenbill's (1985, p. 137) recording of a young male's description of his entry into prostitution in Chicago:

> An older friend of mine took me to a park . . . a hustling spot . . . He took me down there, and we were walking around there. And he was explaining about drag queens and gay life, and tricks, and this and that, and money and all of this. And a friend of his, a guy that he had tricked with before, came around. And he set the whole thing up . . . He did all the talking about the money and everything.

Other studies of adolescent male (e.g., Reiss 1961) and female prostitution (see Weisberg 1985) document similar patterns, although for young women, instruction from a pimp, or older hustlers working for a pimp, may be more common (Weisberg, 1985).

Although these ethnographies support our thesis that embeddedness in criminal associations provide the criminal capital that facilitates entry and advancement into certain crime, our ability to generalize from these studies is limited by two factors. First, most ethnographies use small samples: Sullivan's research involved 38 youths; Padilla studied intensively, at most, a few dozen gang members; Visano spoke with 33 males; and Luckenbill interviewed 28 hustlers. Second, these studies include respondents sampled on the basis of their criminal activities or in juvenile gangs. Given the connection of gang membership to crime, these samples provide little variation in crime (i.e., there are few non-participants or youths who infrequently offend) and thus restrict the possibilities for testing explanations of crime.

## STREET YOUTH AND CRIME

Our study involves a sample of adolescents ($N = 390$) who left or were ejected from their familial or institutional home (e.g., group home) and were "living on the streets" (i.e., with a series of friends, in shelters and hostels, or on the street) in Toronto, Canada in 1987–1988.

We use these data for a number of reasons. Compared with adolescents sampled in most high school surveys, those who live on the street occupy structural locations that capture the differential social organization that Sutherland envisioned: they are economically marginalized; they have more extensive exposure to people involved in crime, particularly the economic crimes of the street; and they experience little of the social control normally encountered by youths (e.g., parental and teacher supervision). Nonetheless, unlike youths studied in most ethnographies, many street youth report little or no involvement in crime (see McCarthy and Hagan, 1991). In addition, the adversity often involved in life on the street (e.g., lack of food, shelter, or employment) makes homelessness an appropriate context to test Sutherland's view that tutelage in crime often follows an emergency or crisis that places a person in a precarious position.

We recognize that homeless adolescents differ significantly from other teenagers in terms of their backgrounds (e.g., extent of familial neglect and abuse, school experiences, and exposure to and involvement in crime); however, recent research suggests that such differences have weak effects on street crime compared to those of street experiences (McCarthy and Hagan, 1992). Furthermore, the effects of these different backgrounds can be effectively controlled through conventional statistical analysis of variation in these experiences and involvement in crime within street samples (see Hagan and McCarthy, 1992; McCarthy and Hagan, 1992). However, to enhance confidence in our data and to reduce concerns about effects of sample selection bias, we test our results with data collected from a sample of high school youths. We elaborate on these data and the relevant findings under Results.

In our analysis we concentrate on three common street crimes that have an economic element: drug selling, theft, and prostitution. Moreover, because success in these activities may involve specific knowledge and skills, they allow us to examine the saliency of criminal embeddedness and the acquisition of criminal capital through tutelage. Although we do not assume that these crimes mirror the level of sophistication of professional theft analyzed in Sutherland's work, we do suggest that they require some skill. Serious theft demands some proficiency in the operation of specific tools and knowledge about where and how to sell stolen merchandise (Sullivan, 1989; Padilla, 1992), drug dealing requires that one know something about materials used to "cut" particular drugs so that customers will not notice the adulteration (see Hunt, 1990; Johnson et al., 1990; Padilla, 1992; Jacobs, 1993), and success in prostitution requires that one know where to work and how to recognize "bad dates" (Visano 1987). Moreover, all require the skills of how to deal with legitimate customers and how to distinguish them from undercover police, as well as knowledge of how much to charge for particular products and services.

## DATA, VARIABLES, AND METHODS

In 1987–1988, social service workers estimated that between 10,000 and 15,000 thousand homeless adolescents lived on the streets and in shelters of Toronto (see Janus et al., 1987). We used a purposive sampling design to study these youths in social service agencies that provided services for street youths and public "street" locations frequented by homeless adolescents. The former included six public shelters/hostels and three counseling agencies, while the latter consisted of street corners popular for panhandling, city parks, bus stations, and other sites commonly used for spending the night on the street.

Potential respondents answered several screening questions (e.g., about age and current living status) and a reading assessment test before completing our anonymous self-report questionnaire; in addition, they received information on their rights as respondents. Of the 475 adolescents approached, 12% refused to participate and another 6% did not finish the survey. All respondents received $10 worth of restaurant coupons.

Approximately 66% of our sample are male and 34% are female. At the time of the survey, 20% of respondents were 16 years of age or younger, 21% were 17, 23% were 18, and 36% were 19 years old. About 62% were sleeping in a shelter, 12% were residing temporarily with friends or relatives, 23% were "living on the street," and 3% were housed in hotels or an unspecified location (see McCarthy and Hagan, 1992, for additional information).

*Crime measures.* Following Sutherland (1947), we treat each type of crime as conceptually distinct rather than collapsing crime categories to form an omnibus scale (see Table 1 for variable labels, descriptions, and summary statistics and Appendix A for coding details). Specifically, we use LISREL VII (Jöreskog and Sörbom, 1989) to estimate separate covariance structural models for drug selling, theft, and prostitution (see Matsueda, 1982; Matsueda and Heimer, 1987).

We measure drug selling with responses to two questions about selling marijuana (or other cannabis products) and other illegal drugs (hallucinogenics, cocaine, and heroin). We observe theft with four items: theft of, or stealing from a vehicle, and stealing or shoplifting goods worth $50 or more. To minimize the number of paths in our model of theft, we group these items in pairs and create two summed scales. Measurement of prostitution is limited to one indicator: selling sex for money. To control for time "at risk," we divide each indicator of crime by the number of weeks since the respondent last lived at home. Furthermore, because of the skewness and kurtosis of our indicators, we use the natural log of each criminal activity.

*Explanatory constructs.* We capture criminal embeddedness with respondent reports of criminal friendships established before leaving home and after arriving on the street. We measure these associations through respondents' reports of the proportion of their friends at home and on the street who had been arrested or sold drugs; for the period on the street, we also add the proportion of friends who worked in prostitution.

TABLE 1
Descriptive Statistics ($N = 390$)

| | | $x$ | SD |
|---|---|---|---|
| $\xi_1$ | Gender | | |
| $X_1$ | "What is your sex?" | .667 | .472 |
| $\xi_2$ | Age | | |
| | "How old are you?" | 17.597 | 1.457 |
| $\xi_3$ | Parental attachment | | |
| $X_3$ | "Did your mother know who you were with/where you were when you were out?" | 2.413 | 1.543 |
| $X_4$ | "Did your father know who you were with/where you were when you were out?" | 1.941 | 1.499 |
| $X_5$ | "Did you talk with your mother about your thoughts and feelings?" and "Would you like to be the kind of person your mother is?" | 1.564 | 1.430 |
| $X_6$ | "Did you talk with your father about your thoughts and feelings?" and "Would you like to be the kind of person your father is?" | 1.364 | 1.387 |
| $\xi_4$ | School experiences | | |
| $X_7$ | "How often did you do homework, projects, etc. after school?" | 1.703 | 1.329 |
| $X_8$ | "What was your average grade in your last year at school?" | 3.215 | 1.524 |
| $X_9$ | "How often did you have trouble with your teachers?" | 1.903 | 1.267 |
| $\eta_1$ | Criminal networks at home | | |
| $Y_1$ | "Of all of your friends, approximately how many had ever been arrested?" | 3.633 | 3.278 |
| $Y_2$ | "Of all of your friends, approximately how many were selling drugs?" | 2.033 | 2.667 |
| $\eta_2$ | Criminal activity at home | | |
| $Y_3$ | Natural logs of the frequency of selling marijuana, selling other drugs and prostitution. | 1.583 | 2.753 |
| $Y_4$ | Natural logs of the frequency of shoplifting or taking goods worth $50 or more; and of theft from, or of a vehicle. | 2.082 | 3.408 |
| $\eta_3$ | Street adversity | | |
| $Y_5$ | "Since leaving home, how often have you gone a whole day without eating?" | 1.405 | .951 |
| $Y_6$ | "Where have you spent the nights since leaving home?" | 1.644 | .942 |
| $Y_7$ | Employment experience | 1.028 | 1.433 |
| $\eta_4$ | Criminal networks on the street | | |
| $Y_8$ | "Of all of your friends, approximately how many have ever been arrested?" | 5.138 | 3.723 |
| $Y_9$ | "Of all of your friends, approximately how many sell drugs?" | 2.431 | 2.907 |

TABLE 1 — *Continued*

|  |  | $x$ | SD |
|---|---|---|---|
| $Y_{10}$ | "Of all of your friends, approximately how many hook?" | 1.669 | 2.700 |
| $\eta_5$ | Tutelage on the street |  |  |
| $Y_{11}$ | "Has anyone offered to help you sell drugs?" | .854 | 1.164 |
|  | "Has anyone offered to help you steal?" | .841 | 1.061 |
|  | "Has anyone offered to help you hook?" | .736 | 1.104 |
| $Y_{12}$ | "Did anyone help you sell drugs?" | .505 | .995 |
|  | "Did anyone help you steal?" | .738 | 1.077 |
|  | "Did anyone help you hook?" | .556 | .989 |
| $Y_{13}$ | "How did you find out that you could make money selling drugs?" | .564 | 1.154 |
|  | "How did you find out that you could make money stealing?" | .787 | 1.358 |
|  | "How did you find out that you could make money hooking?" | .508 | 1.031 |
| $\eta_6$ | Deviant attitudes |  |  |
| $Y_{14}$ | "It is right to break the law." | 2.054 | 1.031 |
| $Y_{15}$ | "It is always wrong to damage, destroy or take other's property." | 2.274 | 1.156 |
| $Y_{16}$ | "People should have the legal right to take the drugs they want." | 3.105 | 1.371 |
| $\eta_7$ | Street crime |  |  |
|  | Drug selling |  |  |
| $Y_{17}$ | Natural log of the frequency of selling marijuana | .175 (1.342)[a] | .389 (1.757) |
| $Y_{18}$ | Natural log of the frequency of selling other drugs | .102 (.884) | .301 (1.529) |
|  | Theft |  |  |
| $Y_{17}$ | Natural logs of the frequency of shoplifting and taking goods worth $50 or more | .091 (.905) | .325 (1.735) |
| $Y_{18}$ | Natural logs of the frequency of theft of, and from a car | .171 (1.691) | .405 (2.588) |
|  | Prostitution |  |  |
| $Y_{17}$ | Natural log of the frequency of having sex for money | .144 (.970) | .408 (1.656) |

[a] The first scores are natural logs divided by number of weeks since leaving home; the natural logs are in parentheses.

Ideally, we would have included measures of the proportion of friends who participated in prostitution at home and in theft both at home and on the street, but these data were not collected. We estimate separately the connections in these two living situations and emphasize street more than home friendships because of our interest in street crime. Home networks are treated more as control variables to remove background effects emphasized in dominant theories.

To measure the criminal capital that accumulates through embeddedness in tutelage relationships, we focus on crime-specific instruction offered by tutors. For example, we measure tutelage in drug selling since leaving home with respondents' accounts of offers to help sell drugs, actual assistance in selling drugs, and reported sources of information about selling drugs as a means of making money. For each item we created an ordinal scale of responses to reflect the degree of exposure to tutelage from adolescent street friends and adults. For example, our question about offers to help sell drugs has five response categories: (1) no offers, (2) offers from street friends whom the respondent believed were not actively involved in selling drugs, (3) offers from street friends or adults assumed to be actively involved in selling drugs, (4) offers from both nonselling and selling street friends, and (5) offers from drug-selling street friends as well as adults. Parallel constructions and codings were used for tutelage in theft and prostitution (see Appendix A for items and response categories).

Our analysis also adds a measure that reflect Sutherland's concern with attitudes that justify law violations. This item combines a global question that measures the respondent's opinion about when it is legitimate to break the law, with two questions that ask specifically whether it should be legal to damage, destroy, or take other's property, or take drugs. Thus, although the data do not contain items that mirror exactly the crimes we study, we have included measures concerning property and drug crimes. Nevertheless, to the extent that non-normative beliefs are crime specific, our measure of attitudes may be conservative, particularly for prostitution and perhaps drug selling.

To assess net relationships between crime and criminal embeddedness, we also control for six additional variables: age, gender, parental attachment, school experiences, criminal activity at home, and adversity on the street. We measure gender and age respectively as the respondents' reported sex and age. We calculate parental attachment with eight items used by control theorists to measure relational and instrumental dimensions of parental control or bonding (see Hirschi, 1969; Hagan, Gillis, and Simpson 1988): four involve maternal and paternal knowledge of respondents' activities when they lived at home (i.e., who they were with and where they were when they were out at night) and the remainder focus on affective relationships with each parent (i.e., how frequently they talked with their mother and father and their reported preferences to be like them). Our measures of educational experiences include three aspects of schooling emphasized in research on delinquency (see Hirschi, 1969; Elliott et al., 1985): involvement (i.e., frequency of homework), commitment (i.e., average grades), and conflict in school (i.e., trouble with teachers).

Criminal activity prior to leaving home is measured through the natural logs of two additive scales. Our first indicator uses the sum of the natural logs of the frequency of selling marijuana, selling other illegal drugs, and prostitution before leaving home. Because prostitution is a rare event at home (less than 2% of the sample had participated in it), we do not treat it as a distinct item, but combine it with drug selling. Our second measure is the sum of the natural logs of the reported frequency of four kinds of theft that parallel those used to measure stealing on the street.

The final variable we consider involves the adversity of street life and reflects the concern with personal and social crises emphasized in Sutherland's work. We measure this situational adversity in three ways: the frequency with which respondents have gone without food, the instability of their arrangements for shelter, and the frequency of employment (see McCarthy and Hagan 1992).

We estimate two models for each dependent variable.[2] The first models estimate effects of criminal embeddedness in street associations, the acquisition of criminal capital through tutelage, and the acquisition of attitudes favorable to crime. In these "reduced" models, remaining constructs are constrained to influence street crime indirectly through these three variables.

We follow LISREL's modification indices and make minor revisions to these models to include measurement error correlations. These correlations involve several variables measured at two points in time (i.e., at home and on the street): friends arrested, selling "other" drugs, and shoplifting and theft of goods worth $50 or more. Ignoring LISREL's suggestions results in models that fit the data less adequately; moreover, although there are differences in the size of slopes and standard errors, the results of these models do not differ markedly from models that do not allow these correlations.[3]

We then estimate three "full" models which allow all variables to in-

---

[2] Prior to conducting our analysis we examined possible sources of multicollinearity. In multivariate tests which regress each independent variable on those that precede it, the amount of variance explained is always less than 30%. So, effects of collinearity appear to be minor.

[3] All effects significant in the corrected drug selling and prostitution models are also significant in the uncorrected models (as are those that are nonsignificant). However, if we fail to correct for correlations between the errors associated with measures of criminal associations in the theft model, the effect of street criminal associations on tutelage is significant only at the .10 level; failure to correct for correlations between the errors associated with measures of home and street crime has a similar effect on the relationship between tutelage and street theft.

fluence street crime both directly and indirectly (measurement coefficients and standard errors for each model (Model II) are reported in Appendix B). We subsequently reestimate our models to explore an issue that arises with regard to prostitution. We conclude our analysis with three additional tests of logical implications drawn from the theoretical perspective advanced in this paper.

## RESULTS

The results of our structural models provide support for our expectations that criminal embeddedness and criminal capital increase involvement in several types of street crime. For example, in the reduced model of drug selling (see Table 2), both tutelage ($\beta = .438$) and deviant attitudes ($\beta = .378$) have strong effects on drug selling. In addition, criminal associations on the street have a sizeable influence on tutelage ($\beta = .378$) and thus operate indirectly on drug selling through this influence. In the full model (see Table 2), the effects of tutelage and criminal associations remain significant ($\beta = .269$ and $\beta = .348$ respectively), despite controlling for the effects of additional variables, including criminal networks and involvement in crime at home. Moreover, although the effect of attitudes changes direction and loses significance, its original effect remains in other models which include all background variables except criminal activity at home.

In addition to the above, a number of other findings (which in most cases appear in both the reduced and full models) warrant comment. First, criminal networks at home have a strong and direct effect on similar associations on the street (as well as on criminal activity at home). So, the process of criminal embeddedness may well begin while at home and extend into the street, where it is more fully developed. Second, in contrast to significant bivariate effects, the multivariate relationship between criminal street networks and deviant attitudes is positive but nonsignificant, whereas the association between the latter and tutelage is not only nonsignificant but negative. However, attitudes are positively associated with criminal activity at home and indirectly to criminal networks at home. These findings suggest that the development of deviant attitudes is enhanced by longer periods of exposure and that the more immediate effects of associations with criminals involve tutelage and involvement in criminal activities.[4] Third, although adversity on the street has only a weak direct relationship with drug selling, its direct effects on street associations and attitudes are significant. Thus, deviant contacts and attitudes (and subsequently tutelage and involvement in crime) appear to be encouraged

---

[4] However, our results may also reflect our use of attitude measures that do not exactly mirror the crimes we study (see Tittle et al., 1986, for evidence of the effect of using matching items).

TABLE 2
Regression Coefficients[a] for MLE Models of Drug Selling ($N = 390$)

A. Reduced model

| | $\xi_1$ Gender | $\xi_2$ Age | $\xi_3$ Parental attachment | $\xi_4$ School experiences | $\eta_1$ Criminal netwk.s at home | $\eta_2$ Criminal activity at home | $\eta_3$ Street adversity | $\eta_4$ Criminal netwk.s on street | $\eta_5$ Tutelage on the street | $\eta_6$ Deviant attitudes | $\eta_7$ Drug selling |
|---|---|---|---|---|---|---|---|---|---|---|---|
| $\xi_1$ | — | — | — | — | .010(.036) | .161(.041) | −.054(.050) | .014(.014) | −.074(.044) | .102(.036) | — |
| $\xi_2$ | — | — | — | — | .072(.037) | .004(.041) | −.066(.046) | .003(.038) | .002(.041) | −.087(.033) | — |
| $\xi_3$ | — | — | — | — | −.092(.072) | −.173(.081) | −.286(.098) | .028(.085) | .060(.089) | −.028(.072) | — |
| $\xi_4$ | — | — | — | — | −.349(.101) | −.238(.110) | −.240(.129) | .016(.106) | .160(.116) | −.115(.093) | — |
| $\eta_1$ | .016 | .115* | −.088 | −.318** | — | .626(.099) | .209(.134) | .490(.122) | .131(.141) | .064(.110) | — |
| $\eta_2$ | .220** | .005 | −.140* | −.185* | .534** | — | .023(.128) | −.043(.105) | .320(.117) | .449(.110) | — |
| $\eta_3$ | −.081 | −.099 | −.256** | −.206 | .197 | .025 | — | .403(.129) | .127(.130) | .270(.121) | — |
| $\eta_4$ | .022 | .005 | .025 | .014 | .475** | −.049 | .415** | — | .456(.137) | .146(.115) | −.204(.132) |
| $\eta_5$ | −.096 | .003 | .046 | .117 | .106 | .302** | .108 | .378** | — | −.141(.074) | .527(.099) |
| $\eta_6$ | .180** | −.154** | −.030 | −.116 | .071 | .585** | .318* | .167 | .195 | — | .627(.129) |
| $\eta_7$ | — | — | — | — | — | — | — | −.141 | .438** | .378*ᵇ | — |

$\chi^2 = 650.47$, $df = 284$, $p = .000$, $\chi^2/df = 2.290$, $gfi = .892$

*continued*

TABLE 2—*Continued*

B. Full model

| | $\xi_1$ Gender | $\xi_2$ Age | $\xi_3$ Parental attachment | $\xi_4$ School experiences | $\eta_1$ Criminal netwk.s at home | $\eta_2$ Criminal activity at home | $\eta_3$ Street adversity | $\eta_4$ Criminal netwk.s on street | $\eta_5$ Tutelage on the street | $\eta_6$ Deviant attitudes | $\eta_7$ Drug selling |
|---|---|---|---|---|---|---|---|---|---|---|---|
| $\xi_1$ | — | — | — | — | .003(.034) | .164(.041) | −.055(.050) | −.001(.040) | −.051(.044) | .140(.040) | .049(.057) |
| $\xi_2$ | — | — | — | — | .071(.035) | .008(.042) | −.062(.046) | .013(.037) | .001(.042) | −.087(.037) | −.140(.050) |
| $\xi_3$ | — | — | — | — | −.089(.066) | −.177(.081) | −.295(.096) | .053(.083) | .006(.090) | −.091(.081) | .111(.103) |
| $\xi_4$ | — | — | — | — | −.301(.090) | −.228(.106) | −.202(.121) | .041(.098) | .134(.110) | −.152(.098) | −.204(.131) |
| $\eta_1$ | .006 | .118* | −.091 | −.296** | — | .673(.102) | .218(.133) | .388(.113) | .241(.131) | .131(.113) | −.089(.152) |
| $\eta_2$ | .216** | .010 | −.143* | −.178* | .532** | — | .033(.119) | .022(.094) | .211(.108) | .296(.101) | .799(.179) |
| $\eta_3$ | −.083 | −.094 | −.273** | −.180 | .197 | .038 | — | .442(.136) | .135(.135) | .310(.141) | .105(.176) |
| $\eta_4$ | −.001 | .021 | .051 | .037 | .360** | .026 | .453** | — | .425(.125) | .041(.114) | .049(.142) |
| $\eta_5$ | −.065 | .001 | .005 | .100 | .183 | .206* | .114 | .348** | — | −.032(.075) | .326(.101) |
| $\eta_6$ | .222** | −.138** | −.088 | −.142 | .124 | .356** | .325* | .042 | −.040 | — | −.421(.216) |
| $\eta_7$ | .052 | −.147** | .071 | −.126 | −.056 | .635** | .073 | .033 | .269** | −.278 | — |

$\chi^2 = 554.47$, $df = 275$, $p = .000$, $\chi^2/df = 2.017$, $gfi = .908$

[a] Standardized regression coefficients below the diagonal, unstandardized above; standard errors in parentheses.

* $p < .05$, ** $p < .01$.

by the type of crises suggested by Sutherland. Fourth, criminal activity at home operates both directly on drug selling, as well as indirectly through its influence on attitudes and to a lesser degree, through tutelage. And fifth, the effects of gender, age, parental control, and school experiences on drug selling are primarily indirect through relationships with criminal associations and participation in crime at home, street adversity, and attitudes. Thus, it appears that the effects of more traditional types of social capital (embeddedness in family and school) have their greatest effects on pre-street crime experiences and attitudes. The latter effects suggest that attitudes toward crime originate early in the life course; however, as noted above, these attitudes are also strongly influenced by later experiences in the life course, particularly exposure to crime and street experiences.

For the most part, our models of theft strongly resemble those for drug selling. For example, both tutelage ($\beta = .378$) and attitudes ($\beta = .290$) significantly influence theft in the reduced model (see Table 3) and the effect of criminal associations operates through tutelage in stealing ($\beta = .285$). As well, tutelage retains its significant direct effect on crime in the full model ($\beta = .276$), as does associations on tutelage ($\beta = .222$), whereas the direct relationship between attitudes and crime is neutralized. Again, the disappearance of the latter effect is contingent on controlling for criminal activity at home; in models that exclude home crime, this effect remains sizeable and significant. One notable difference between the models of theft and drug selling involves the relationship between criminal street networks and crime. This association is close to zero in the full model of drug selling but sizeable and significant in the parallel model for theft ($\beta = .214$).

The effects of other variables in our models of theft also resemble those for drug selling. The only notable differences between these activities involve stronger effects of adversity and criminal activity at home on tutelage in theft. Although the consequences of adversity reinforce Sutherland's point about the role of crisis, the influence of criminal activity at home suggests that previous experiences also influence subsequent tutelage.

Our analysis of prostitution in Table 4 further suggests the saliency of tutelage. In both reduced and full models, the effect of tutelage on prostitution is strong and significant ($\beta = .560$ and $\beta = .598$, respectively). However, in contrast to theft and drug selling, attitudes do not substantially influence prostitution, nor do street associations greatly affect tutelage.[5] The distinctiveness of prostitution is further reinforced by the absence of a sizable relationship between prostitution and criminal activity

_____

[5] Note, however, that our deviant attitudes scale does not contain a measure of attitudes toward prostitution.

TABLE 3

Regression Coefficients[a] for MLE Models of Theft (N = 391)

A. Reduced model

| | $\xi_1$ Gender | $\xi_2$ Age | $\xi_3$ Parental attachment | $\xi_4$ School experiences | $\eta_1$ Criminal netwk.s at home | $\eta_2$ Criminal activity at home | $\eta_3$ Street adversity | $\eta_4$ Criminal netwk.s on street | $\eta_5$ Tutelage on the street | $\eta_6$ Deviant attitudes | $\eta_7$ Theft |
|---|---|---|---|---|---|---|---|---|---|---|---|
| $\xi_1$ | — | — | — | — | .015(.039) | .162(.038) | .051(.050) | .021(.046) | -.052(.046) | .097(.043) | — |
| $\xi_2$ | — | — | — | — | .069(.039) | .001(.037) | -.064(.046) | .007(.042) | .034(.041) | -.079(.038) | — |
| $\xi_3$ | — | — | — | — | -.110(.077) | -.158(.075) | -.280(.096) | .030(.092) | .175(.094) | -.004(.091) | — |
| $\xi_4$ | — | — | — | — | -.370(.105) | -.181(.098) | -.226(.123) | .022(.113) | .084(.112) | -.085(.103) | — |
| $\eta_1$ | .023 | .105 | -.101 | -.329** | — | .526(.090) | .181(.126) | .548(.127) | -.135(.146) | .028(.133) | — |
| $\eta_2$ | .244** | .002 | -.143* | -.159 | .521** | — | .015(.136) | -.062(.125) | .594(.138) | .596(.167) | — |
| $\eta_3$ | -.080 | -.100 | -.262** | -.206 | .185 | .015 | — | .453(.140) | .408(.163) | .396(.176) | — |
| $\eta_4$ | .029 | .010 | .025 | .019 | .514** | -.059 | .414** | — | .304(.135) | .107(.123) | — |
| $\eta_5$ | -.070 | .045 | .141 | .065 | -.119 | .528** | .350** | .285* | — | -.233(.128) | -.084(.111) |
| $\eta_6$ | .159* | -.129* | -.004 | -.082 | .030 | .650** | .417* | .124 | -.286 | — | .450(.102) |
| $\eta_7$ | — | — | — | — | — | — | — | -.066 | .378** | .290** | .424(.117) |

$\chi^2 = 718.29$, $df = 284$, $p = .000$, $\chi^2/df = 2.529$, $gfi = .885$

CRIMINAL EMBEDDEDNESS  81

B. Full model

| | $\xi_1$ Gender | $\xi_2$ Age | $\xi_3$ Parental attachment | $\xi_4$ School experiences | $\eta_1$ Criminal netwk.s at home | $\eta_2$ Criminal activity at home | $\eta_3$ Street adversity | $\eta_4$ Criminal netwk.s on street | $\eta_5$ Tutelage on the street | $\eta_6$ Deviant attitudes | $\eta_7$ Theft |
|---|---|---|---|---|---|---|---|---|---|---|---|
| $\xi_1$ | | — | — | — | .007(.035) | .169(.038) | -.043(.050) | .001(.043) | -.026(.045) | .127(.041) | -.031(.051) |
| $\xi_2$ | — | | — | — | .071(.035) | -.003(.037) | -.065(.046) | .022(.040) | .035(.042) | -.075(.039) | .098(.044) |
| $\xi_3$ | — | — | | — | -.087(.068) | -.181(.074) | -.287(.096) | .057(.090) | .155(.097) | -.045(.091) | .052(.098) |
| $\xi_4$ | — | — | -.087 | | -.307(.093) | -.211(.096) | -.228(.121) | .021(.107) | .077(.113) | -.112(.103) | -.073(.114) |
| $\eta_1$ | .012 | .117* | -.164* | -.296** | | .531(.091) | .237(.121) | .404(.112) | .003(.120) | .137(.108) | -.129(.124) |
| $\eta_2$ | .250** | -.005 | -.272** | -.183* | .478** | | -.019(.124) | .044(.108) | .459(.120) | .410(.129) | .444(.199) |
| $\eta_3$ | -.067 | -.101 | .051 | -.208 | .224 | -.020 | | .476(.139) | .473(.173) | .418(.184) | -.223(.220) |
| $\eta_4$ | .002 | .032 | .124 | .018 | .357 | .043 | .444** | | .246(.122) | .038(.106) | .235(.117) |
| $\eta_5$ | -.034 | .046 | -.044 | .059 | .002 | .407** | .399** | .222** | | -.131(.113) | .274(.134) |
| $\eta_6$ | .202** | -.119 | .042 | -.104 | .132 | .440** | .426* | .042 | -.159 | | .079(.207) |
| $\eta_7$ | -.041 | -.130* | | -.056 | -.104 | .397* | -.190 | .214* | .276* | .066 | — |

$\chi^2 = 615.73$, $df = 275$, $p = .000$, $\chi^2/df = 2.239$, $gfi = .900$

a Standardized regression coefficients below the diagonal, unstandardized above; standard errors in parentheses.

* $p < .05$, ** $p < .01$.

     MCCARTHY AND HAGAN

TABLE 4

Regression Coefficients[a] for MLE Models of Prostitution ($N = 300$)

A. Reduced model

| | $\xi_1$ Gender | $\xi_2$ Age | $\xi_3$ Parental attachment | $\xi_4$ School experiences | $\eta_1$ Criminal netwk.s at home | $\eta_2$ Criminal activity at home | $\eta_3$ Street adversity | $\eta_4$ Criminal netwk.s on street | $\eta_5$ Tutelage on the street | $\eta_6$ Deviant attitudes | $\eta_7$ Prostitution |
|---|---|---|---|---|---|---|---|---|---|---|---|
| $\xi_1$ | — | — | — | — | .017(.040) | .162(.041) | -.052(.043) | .036(.048) | -.082(.061) | .131(.043) | — |
| $\xi_2$ | — | — | — | — | .068(.040) | .004(.040) | -.081(.040) | .030(.046) | .100(.057) | -.057(.042) | — |
| $\xi_3$ | — | — | — | — | -.117(.078) | -.162(.079) | -.221(.083) | .030(.097) | .101(.123) | -.051(.087) | — |
| $\xi_4$ | — | — | — | — | .361(.103) | .172(.101) | .186(.102) | .042(.116) | .256(.150) | .077(.106) | — |
| $\eta_1$ | .026 | .101 | -.107 | -.326** | — | .590(.095) | .102(.112) | .583(.137) | -.150(.200) | .138(.141) | — |
| $\eta_2$ | .227** | .005 | -.138* | -.146 | .553** | — | .021(.113) | -.085(.129) | .009(.157) | .344(.117) | — |
| $\eta_3$ | -.101 | -.157* | -.261** | -.219 | .133 | .029 | — | .629(.187) | .987(.319) | .552(.250) | — |
| $\eta_4$ | .050 | .042 | .025 | .035 | .541** | .084 | .449** | — | .127(.189) | -.029(.128) | .003(.089) |
| $\eta_5$ | -.086 | .106 | .065 | .163 | -.106 | .006 | .536** | .097 | — | -.080(.066) | .588(.056) |
| $\eta_6$ | .208** | -.090* | -.050 | -.073 | .146 | .389** | .450* | -.033 | -.120 | — | -.033(.096) |
| $\eta_7$ | — | — | — | — | — | — | — | .003 | .560** | .021 | — |

$\chi^2 = 712.63$, $df = 260$, $p = .000$, $\chi^2/df = 2.741$, $gfi = .879$

B. Full model

| | $\xi_1$ Gender | $\xi_2$ Age | $\xi_3$ Parental attachment | $\xi_4$ School experiences | $\eta_1$ Criminal netwks at home | $\eta_2$ Criminal activity at home | $\eta_3$ Street adversity | $\eta_4$ Criminal netwks on street | $\eta_5$ Tutelage on the street | $\eta_6$ Deviant attitudes | $\eta_7$ Prostitution |
|---|---|---|---|---|---|---|---|---|---|---|---|
| $\xi_1$ | — | — | — | — | .008(.034) | .167(.040) | -.051(.044) | .017(.046) | -.080(.060) | .131(.042) | -.030(.057) |
| $\xi_2$ | — | — | — | — | .071(.035) | .001(.040) | -.082(.041) | .045(.044) | .103(.058) | -.061(.042) | -.107(.049) |
| $\xi_3$ | — | — | — | — | -.084(.068) | .179(.080) | -.237(.086) | .056(.095) | .104(.127) | -.052(.089) | -.040(.102) |
| $\xi_4$ | — | — | — | — | -.292(.090) | .209(.100) | -.194(.104) | .035(.110) | .254(.149) | -.085(.105) | .017(.122) |
| $\eta_1$ | .013 | .117* | -.083 | -.291** | — | .621(.098) | .155(.114) | .422(.123) | -.100(.165) | .121(.116) | -.336(.143) |
| $\eta_2$ | .232** | .001 | -.149* | -.176* | .524** | — | .013(.111) | .021(.113) | -.022(.146) | .347(.109) | .091(.152) |
| $\eta_3$ | -.094 | -.153* | -.264** | -.218 | .175 | .018 | — | .627(.178) | .963(.310) | .517(.238) | -.309(.315) |
| $\eta_4$ | .024 | .064 | .048 | .031 | .367** | .022 | .483** | — | .073(.172) | -.006(.114) | .201(.134) |
| $\eta_5$ | -.085 | .109 | .066 | .163 | -.064 | -.017 | .548** | .054 | — | -.081(.066) | .628(.087) |
| $\eta_6$ | .207** | -.097 | -.049 | -.081 | .116 | .395** | .440* | -.006 | -.121 | — | .117(.222) |
| $\eta_7$ | -.030 | -.108* | -.024 | -.010 | -.206* | .066 | -.167 | .141 | .598** | .074 | — |

$\chi^2 = 669.91$, $df = 252$, $p = .000$, $\chi^2/df = 2.658$, $gfi = .887$

[a] Standardized regression coefficients below the diagonal, unstandardized above; standard errors in parentheses.
* $p < .05$, ** $p < .01$.

84                          MCCARTHY AND HAGAN

at home, and by the significant negative effect of criminal associations at home on the former.

Intrigued by the results for prostitution, we reexamined the measurement coefficients (see Appendix B). We found that the loading for friends who sell drugs was considerably smaller in the prostitution model (compared to drug selling and theft models), whereas the loading for friends who hook was weakest in models of drug selling and theft. These findings encouraged us to explore the effect of eliminating the item with the lowest loading from our street networks construct. Dropping friends who hook does not substantially change our models of drug selling or theft. However, dropping drug-selling friends from the full model of prostitution produces several important changes (see Table 5): the effects of criminal street associations on both tutelage in prostitution and prostitution itself becomes strong and significant ($\beta = .374$ and $\beta = 238$, respectively); the relationship between our measures of home and street associations became nonsignificant; and a chi-square test of differences revealed that the fit of our second model is a significant improvement over our original model ($\chi^2 = 73.7$, $df = 24$, $p = .001$).[6]

We estimated three sets of additional models to further test the logical implications of our theoretical perspective. First, to test whether the effect of a particular type of tutelage (e.g., in theft) is specific to crime in that field (i.e., property crime), we replaced the crime-specific measures of tutelage with measures of tutelage in other criminal activities (e.g., we supplanted tutelage in theft in the theft model, first with tutelage in drug selling and second with tutelage in prostitution). In eight of these nine models, the effect of tutelage on crime is *nonsignificant;* the only "anomaly" is that tutelage in drug selling is significantly related to theft ($\beta = .199$).

We further explored the saliency of tutelage in a second set of models of other types of crime for which training is likely to be less or even of no importance. Specifically we estimated models of violence (individual and group assault), drug use (marijuana, solvents, hallucinogenics, and cocaine), vandalism, and possession of stolen property. Again, with one exception, each of our indicators of tutelage has *nonsignificant* effects on these crimes. The only "deviation" is perhaps understandable in that it involves tutelage in drug selling and drug use ($\beta = .198$). These two sets of tests encourage our position that tutelage is crime-specific and an integral part of learning the skills suitable to distinctive criminal activities.

As noted earlier, we also examined the possibility that our findings

---

[6] We also estimated a model of prostitution that used only home prostitution as a single indicator of crime at home. This substitution does not change the relationship between crime at home and street prostitution (it remains nonsignificant) and the effect of home crime on attitudes is reduced to nonsignificance.

## CRIMINAL EMBEDDEDNESS

85

### TABLE 5
Regression Coefficients[a] for MLE Revised Models of Prostitution ($N = 390$)

A. Model 1

| | $\xi_1$ Gender | $\xi_2$ Age | $\xi_3$ Parental attachment | $\xi_4$ School experiences | $\eta_1$ Criminal netwk.s at home | $\eta_2$ Criminal activity at home | $\eta_3$ Street adversity | $\eta_4$ Criminal netwk.s on street | $\eta_5$ Tutelage on the street | $\eta_6$ Deviant attitudes | $\eta_7$ Prostitution |
|---|---|---|---|---|---|---|---|---|---|---|---|
| $\xi_1$ | — | — | — | — | .009(.037) | .169(.041) | -.050(.042) | .031(.026) | -.109(.055) | .126(.043) | — |
| $\xi_2$ | — | — | — | — | .107(.038) | .004(.040) | -.078(.037) | .035(.025) | .073(.052) | -.060(.041) | — |
| $\xi_3$ | — | — | — | — | -.110(.073) | -.167(.079) | -.217(.081) | -.048(.052) | .133(.109) | -.063(.085) | — |
| $\xi_4$ | — | — | — | — | -.316(.093) | -.159(.095) | -.156(.093) | .046(.057) | .207(.125) | .097(.097) | — |
| $\eta_1$ | .014 | .111** | -.105 | -.311** | — | .608(.098) | .101(.110) | .080(.068) | -.135(.142) | .130(.111) | — |
| $\eta_2$ | .237** | .005 | -.143* | -.141 | .548** | — | .025(.110) | -.041(.066) | .026(.139) | .353(.115) | — |
| $\eta_3$ | -.100 | -.157* | -.264** | -.197 | .129 | .036 | .381** | .301(.115) | .830(.255) | .529(.214) | — |
| $\eta_4$ | .079 | .088 | -.074 | .074 | .131 | -.074 | .381** | — | .897(.211) | -.007(.133) | — |
| $\eta_5$ | -.115* | .077 | .086 | .138 | -.091 | .019 | .437** | .373** | — | -.076(.070) | .471(.165) |
| $\eta_6$ | .201* | -.095 | -.061 | -.097 | .132 | .399* | .420* | -.005 | -.115 | — | .487(.165) |
| $\eta_7$ | — | — | — | — | — | — | — | .186** | .464** | -.054 | -.086(.083) |

$\chi^2 = 646.35$, $df = 236$, $p = .000$, $\chi^2/df = 2.739$, $gfi = .895$

*continued*

TABLE 5 — *Continued*

B. Model II

| | $\xi_1$ Gender | $\xi_2$ Age | $\xi_3$ Parental attachment | $\xi_4$ School experiences | $\eta_1$ Criminal netwk.s at home | $\eta_2$ Criminal activity at home | $\eta_3$ Street adversity | $\eta_4$ Criminal netwk.s on street | $\eta_5$ Tutelage on the street | $\eta_6$ Deviant attitudes | $\eta_7$ Prositution |
|---|---|---|---|---|---|---|---|---|---|---|---|
| $\xi_1$ | — | — | — | — | .005(.031) | .170(.041) | -.051(.043) | .030(.026) | -.106(.054) | .126(.043) | -.050(.056) |
| $\xi_2$ | — | — | — | — | .065(.032) | .001(.040) | -.078(.040) | .038(.025) | .071(.052) | -.065(.041) | -.107(.047) |
| $\xi_3$ | — | — | — | — | -.079(.060) | -.177(.079) | -.226(.083) | -.045(.052) | .132(.109) | -.061(.086) | .011(.097) |
| $\xi_4$ | — | — | — | — | -.244(.077) | -.181(.095) | -.162(.095) | .045(.057) | .207(.125) | -.100(.098) | .023(.111) |
| $\eta_1$ | .010 | .122 | -.090 | -.288** | — | .707(.117) | .126(.128) | .089(.077) | -.113(.159) | .140(.127) | -.340(.048) |
| $\eta_2$ | .239** | .001 | -.151* | -.160 | .529** | — | .031(.109) | -.039(.064) | .003(.134) | .360(.113) | .109(.153) |
| $\eta_3$ | -.100 | -.153* | -.268** | -.198 | .131 | .043 | — | .302(.112) | .788(.248) | .524(.211) | -.223(.274) |
| $\eta_4$ | .077 | .099 | -.070 | .073 | .122 | -.071 | .398** | — | .908(.215) | -.005(.040) | .608(.186) |
| $\eta_5$ | -.013 | .075 | .085 | .138 | -.064 | .002 | .428** | .374** | — | -.080(.070) | .509(.091) |
| $\eta_6$ | .199** | -.103 | -.059 | -.099 | .118 | .404** | .424* | -.003 | .120 | — | .104(.217) |
| $\eta_7$ | -.050 | -.108* | .007 | .015 | -.183* | .078 | .115 | .238** | .485** | .066 | — |

$\chi^2 = 596.22$, $df = 228$, $p = .000$, $\chi^2/df = 2.615$, $gfi = .900$

[a] Standardized regression coefficients below the diagonal, unstandardized above; standard errors in parentheses.

\* $p < .05$, \*\* $p < .01$.

were influenced by sample selection biases resulting from our exclusive use of data from homeless youths. In this test, we combined our Toronto street data with comparable information from a sample of adolescents who lived at home and attended school ($N = 562$; response rate = 68%). These data were collected in the same year as the data on homeless youths and were obtained from randomly chosen students attending Grades 9 through 12 in three randomly chosen Toronto high schools (see Hagan and McCarthy. 1992). These youths completed a 30-min self-report questionnaire that paralleled the one used for the street sample. Previous analyses reveals that although these groups differ markedly in their background experiences (particularly with regard to familial abuse and neglect and exposure to crime), these differences have little effect on street crimes, particularly in comparison to those that arise from street experiences; moreover, these effects remain when the data are corrected for possible sample selection bias (see McCarthy and Hagan, 1992).

To explore the effect of sample selection bias in the present analysis, we transformed our indicators into additive scales and weighted the two data sets (i.e., the homeless and at home samples) to reflect the larger youth population of Toronto. Using the combined samples we estimated probit models of homelessness and used the resulting hazard rates in ordinary least-squares models of drug selling, theft, and prostitution (see McCarthy and Hagan, 1992, for further details of this procedure). The results of these models that correct for sample selection bias are consistent with the findings reported above: participation in crime increases significantly with tutelage in each type of offense; moreover, criminal associations on the street are nonspuriously associated with tutelage, while attitudes are more strongly influenced by criminal associations and involvement in crime at home.

## DISCUSSION

It is a widely perpetrated fiction, according to Coleman (1990, Chapter 12), that society is simply a set of independent individuals who act to achieve goals that are determined autonomously. Coleman traces this fiction to two sources: that individuals are the most immediately tangible actors in society and the extraordinary impact on our thinking of political philosophers of the seventeenth and eighteenth centuries who emphasized self-determination and the rights and responsibilities of individuals. Sociological, as well as psychological and economic explanations of crime, increasingly embrace derivations of these ideas in their portrayals of crime as the product of utilitarian calculations, individual failings, and resistance to social and self-control. These perspectives see such deficiencies as leading individuals to selfishly choose crime as a source of short-term gains. Advocates of these accounts dismiss as unnecessary the argument that one learns criminal behaviors through associations with criminals and instruction in specific behaviors (e.g., see, Becker, 1968; Ehrlich, 1973; Kornhauser, 1978; Hirschi and Gottfredson, 1980; Gottfredson and Hirschi, 1990). Furthermore, writers in these approaches maintain that the majority of criminal acts are unsophisticated behaviors that do not require special expertise; they assume guidance in crime is unnecessary.

Sutherland's work provides a sharp contrast. From his early study (1936) of *Twenty Thousand Homeless Men* with Harvey Locke, Sutherland displayed a continuing concern with exogenous structural conditions of differential social organization that stimulate the learning processes that lead to crime; moreover, he consistently focused on contexts he thought most likely to provoke these processes. The homeless were of recurring concern, for example, reappearing in Sutherland's (1937, pp. 223–224) discussion of the history of theft in *The Professional Thief*.

Nonetheless, Sutherland emphasized that structural conditions such as homelessness do not by themselves cause crime. He made the same point with regard to other correlates of crime, including age and gender, and noted that the key is to identify and document processes through which such factors operate. According to Sutherland, these processes involve affiliation with deviants, tutelage in and mastery of criminal skills, and exposure to and adoption of definitions favorable to crime. These insights have remained central to reformulations of Sutherland's theory and have been integrated into several alternative explanations. Moreover, Sutherland's concept of tutelage anticipates the attention more broadly given by Granovetter and Coleman to the significance of embeddedness in specialized social networks and the accumulation of social capital through contacts and communication.

Our findings are consistent with this more social conception of crime. They suggest that adverse experiences such as life on the street and homelessness lead to an embeddedness in criminal street networks and exposure to mentors or tutors who transmit skills that constitute forms of criminal capital and facilitate involvement in crime. Instead of being indifferent and impervious to others, youths in our study appear sensitive to the capacities of others to relay information and skills relevant to participation in types of economic crime. The effects of these experiences are related to but also independent of background variables often treated as measuring predispositions or propensities to crime.

Our analysis also reveals that a number of factors, including age and gender, effect crime through criminal associations, tutelage, and attitudes. Thus, our research suggests that embeddedness in criminal networks and the subsequent acquisition of criminal capital are important aspects of getting into crime, in much the same way that similar processes are involved in getting a job and achieving occupational mobility in the conventional world of work.

It is important to emphasize that the theoretical approach we advocate does not discount the role of background factors that may include a propensity to crime formed early in the life course; for example, in the at-home experiences of the youths in our study. A reflection of this possibility is that in all of our models, criminal associations at home have significant and substantial net effects on those on the street, and in our models of drug selling and theft, criminal activity at home has substantial effects on tutelage on the street. The goal of our theoretical approach is to articulate a more elaborate and comprehensive causal understanding of street crime that includes links among prior criminal activity, networks at home and on the street, and tutelage. We have demonstrated the effects of the latter while taking into account effects of the former.

Our extension of analysis to transitional street experiences focuses attention on the process of criminal embeddedness and the formation of criminal capital in a manner that is encouraged by the work of Sutherland, Granovetter, and Coleman. Granovetter (1992, p. 238) notes that to focus more exclusively on the modeling of propensity risks ". . . mistaking a starting point for the end of the theoretical road." This mistake was identified in Hirschi and Selvin's (1967, p. 128) classic critique of delinquency research, when they observed that "intervening variables of this type are no less important than variables further removed from the dependent variable . . . ." Granovetter (1992) also notes that there is a "thinness" to theoretical accounts that dwell on propensity and neglect intervening transitional processes in the causation of social and economic behavior. Recent ethnographic accounts of crime have filled this void with "thick descriptions" of life course transitions in and out of crime during adolescence and adulthood. Quantitative attention to the structure and process of criminal embeddedness and the formation of criminal capital can help to reestablish a balance between these modes of criminological research by providing better articulated and more elaborate accounts of transitions into street crime.

Future research might build upon our findings by further refining the measurement of criminal embeddedness, capital, and attitudes. In this paper we focus on selection into a tutelage relationship; additional explanatory power may follow from measures of the characteristics of mentors (e.g., their attitudes, values and extent of criminal experience), and the explicit teaching, mastery and adoption of specific criminal skills and attitudes.

Subsequent research should explore the relationship between the accumulation of criminal capital and various measures of criminal success. Our measures of the frequency of criminal activity are to some extent proxies of such success. That is, although a continuation of criminal activity does not always denote prosperity in it, prolonged involvement in crime may reflect this outcome. Youths may become frequent offenders because of past training and skill or because of success in escaping the law (i.e., incarceration or police contact). However, success probably can be measured more directly. Measurement of financial returns and profits obtained through crime are an important possibility. Other indicators may include the ability to avoid detection or apprehension, career duration, specialization, and prestige within criminal hierarchies (see Matsueda et al., 1992).

In closing, we note that our attention to street youths constitutes a telling test of the effects of social embeddedness in that such youths are customarily assumed to be disorganized and unsophisticated participants in crimes that in turn are thought to involve little skill or learning. Moreover, although our findings contrast with those predicted by recent sociological explanations of crime, they are consistent with a number of classic and contemporary ethnographies of urban youths. Our results highlight oversights associated with assuming that crime results solely from predetermined characteristics and remind us that ignoring the effects of life situations on adolescents seriously underestimates the importance of social embeddedness in criminogenic environments.

## APPENDIX A

### Coding Information for Variable Indicators

$\varepsilon_1$  Gender
   (0) female (1) male
$\varepsilon_2$  Age
   13 through 19
$\varepsilon_3$  Parental attachment
   "Would you like to be the kind of person your mother/father is?"
   (0) Not at all (1) In some ways (2) In most ways
   (3) In every way
   All other items
   (0) never (1) sometimes (2) usually (3) always
$\varepsilon_4$  School experiences
   "How often did you do homework, projects after school?"
   (0) never (1) rarely (2) sometimes (3) often (4) always
   "What was average grade in your last year of school"
   (0) 0 to 40 (1) 41 to 50 (2) 51 to 60 . . . (6) 91 to 100
   "How often did you have trouble with your teachers?"
   (0) always (1) often (2) sometimes (3) rarely (4) never
$\eta_1$  Criminal networks at home
   All items
   0–10:  (0) 0 (1) 1% to 10% . . . (10) 90% to 100%
$\eta_2$  Criminal activity at home
   Natural log of responses to questions asking how frequently the

### APPENDIX A — *Continued*

respondent committed the act in question *before* leaving home (originally coded from 0 to 90)

$\eta_3$ Adversity on the street

"Since leaving home how often have you gone a whole day without eating?"

(0) never (1) once or twice (2) a number of times (3) most of the time

"Where have you spend the nights since leaving home"

(0) with friends or relatives (1) hostels and shelters (2) on the street and in hostels (3) on the street in hostels and private hotels

Employment experience since leaving home

(0) Employed (1) Once employed, now unemployed (2) Never employed

$\eta_4$ Criminal networks on the street

All items

0–10: (1) 1% to 10% . . . (10) 90% to 100%

$\eta_5$ Tutelage on the street

> We used nine questions to measure tutelage; three for each type of criminal activity (i.e., drug selling, theft, and prostitution). Respondents could choose more than one response category for each question and they could add additional answers. The following categories were created from these responses

"Has anyone offered to help you sell drugs/steal/hook (get started–show you the ropes)?"

(0) No one offered (1) Street friends not known to be involved in activity offered (2) Street friends assumed to be involved or an adult offered (3) Both groups of street friends (uninvolved and involved) offered (4) Involved street friends and adults offered

"Did anyone help you sell drugs/steal/hook?"

(0) Did not do the activity in question or no one helped

(1) Street friends not known to be involved in activity helped

(2) Street friends assumed to be involved or an adult helped

(3) Both groups of street friends (uninvolved and involved) helped (4) Involved street friends and adults helped

"How did you find out that you could make money selling drugs/stealing/hooking?"

(0) Did not do the activity or new from non-street sources (e.g., own volition, home experiences) (1) Talked with street friends not known to be involved in activity (2) Talked with (a) street friends known to be involved, (b) an adult who said money

92                     MCCARTHY AND HAGAN

## APPENDIX A — *Continued*

could be made this way, or (c) an adult who said s/he would
sell the drugs to you/buy the stolen goods/help you hustle
(3) Talked with two of either a, b, c in (2) (4) Talked with a,
b, *and* c in (2)

$\eta_6$  Deviant attitudes
"It is right to break the law."
(1) never (2) in a few cases (3) sometimes (4) often (5) in
most cases
"It is always wrong to damage destroy or take other's property."
"People should have the legal right to take the drugs they
want."
(1) strongly disagree (2) disagree (3) uncertain (4) agree
(5) strongly agree

$\eta_7$  Street crime
Natural log of responses to questions asking how frequently the
respondent committed the act in question *since* leaving home
(originally coded from 0 to 90)

## APPENDIX B

### Measurement Coefficients for MLE Models of Drug Selling, Theft, and Prostitution (Full Models)

|  |  | Drug Selling | | | Theft | | | Prostitution | | |
|---|---|---|---|---|---|---|---|---|---|---|
| $\xi_1$ | Gender[a,b,c] | | | | | | | | | |
|  | $X_1$ | 1.000 | — | .997 | 1.000 | — | .997 | 1.000 | — | .997 |
| $\xi_2$ | Age | | | | | | | | | |
|  | $X_2$ | 1.000 | — | .997 | 1.000 | — | .997 | 1.000 | — | .997 |
| $\xi_3$ | Parental attachment | | | | | | | | | |
|  | $X_3$ | 1.000 | — | .612 | 1.000 | — | .609 | 1.000 | — | .597 |
|  | $X_4$ | 1.279 | .179 | .783 | 1.287 | .185 | .783 | 1.335 | .196 | .797 |
|  | $X_5$ | .485 | .103 | .297 | .466 | .104 | .284 | .459 | .105 | .274 |
|  | $X_6$ | .697 | .109 | .426 | .684 | .110 | .417 | .704 | .111 | .421 |
| $\xi_4$ | School experiences | | | | | | | | | |
|  | $X_7$ | 1.000 | — | .589 | 1.000 | — | .586 | 1.000 | — | .604 |
|  | $X_8$ | .744 | .144 | .431 | .741 | .148 | .434 | .734 | .145 | .443 |
|  | $X_9$ | 1.037 | .177 | .565 | .955 | .181 | .559 | .893 | .169 | .534 |
| $\eta_1$ | Criminal networks at home | | | | | | | | | |
|  | $Y_1$ | 1.000 | — | .598 | 1.000 | — | .608 | 1.000 | — | .606 |
|  | $Y_2$ | 1.430 | .164 | .856 | 1.400 | .170 | .850 | 1.405 | .168 | .851 |
| $\eta_2$ | Criminal activity at home | | | | | | | | | |
|  | $Y_3$ | 1.000 | — | .757 | 1.000 | — | .674 | 1.000 | — | .718 |
|  | $Y_4$ | 1.814 | .083 | .616 | 1.100 | .111 | .741 | .936 | .104 | .672 |

CRIMINAL EMBEDDEDNESS 93

## APPENDIX B — *Continued*

| | | Drug Selling | | | Theft | | | Prostitution | |
|---|---|---|---|---|---|---|---|---|---|
| $\eta_3$ | Street adversity | | | | | | | | |
| | $Y_5$ | 1.000 | — | .661 | 1.000 | — | .641 | 1.000 | — | .536 |
| | $Y_6$ | .604 | .128 | .399 | .672 | .123 | .431 | .894 | .152 | .479 |
| | $Y_7$ | .227 | .103 | .150 | .221 | .102 | .142 | .454 | .127 | .243 |
| $\eta_4$ | Criminal networks on the street | | | | | | | | |
| | $Y_8$ | 1.000 | — | .644 | 1.000 | — | .687 | 1.000 | — | .696 |
| | $Y_9$ | 1.199 | .130 | .772 | 1.040 | .113 | .715 | .971 | .111 | .676 |
| | $Y_{10}$ | .646 | .098 | .416 | .625 | .092 | .429 | .684 | .095 | .476 |
| $\eta_5$ | Tutelage on the street | | | | | | | | |
| | $Y_{11}$ | 1.000 | — | .786 | 1.000 | — | .761 | 1.000 | — | .942 |
| | $Y_{12}$ | .819 | .076 | .644 | .604 | .077 | .460 | .357 | .055 | .337 |
| | $Y_{13}$ | .864 | .077 | .679 | .990 | .088 | .753 | .881 | .051 | .830 |
| $\eta_6$ | Deviant attitudes | | | | | | | | |
| | $Y_{14}$ | 1.000 | — | .629 | 1.000 | — | .628 | 1.000 | — | .631 |
| | $Y_{15}$ | .886 | .111 | .558 | .902 | .112 | .567 | .886 | .111 | .559 |
| | $Y_{16}$ | .932 | .113 | .587 | .923 | .113 | .580 | .934 | .113 | .589 |
| $\eta_7$ | Street crime | | | | | | | | |
| | $Y_{17}$ | 1.000 | — | .952 | 1.000 | — | .754 | 1.000 | — | .989 |
| | $Y_{18}$ | .793 | .068 | .755 | .794 | .117 | .599 | — | — | |

[a] See Table 1 and Appendix A for descriptions and coding details.

[b] For each variable, the path from the first indicator to the latent variable was set to 1: unstandardized regression coefficients are reported first; standardized errors second, and standardized coefficients third.

[c] $p < .01$ for all coefficients except between work and adversity in the theft and drug-selling models ($p < .05$).

## REFERENCES

Akers, R., Krohn, M., Lanza-Kaduce, L., and Radosevich, M. (1979), "Social learning and deviant behavior: A specific test of a general theory," *American Sociological Review* **44**, 636–655.

Becker, G. (1968), "Crime and punishment: An economic approach," Journal of Political Economy **76**, 169–217.

Becker, G. (1964), Human Capital, National Bureau of Economic Research, New York.

Becker, G., and Landes, W. (1974), Essays in the Economics of Crime and Punishment, Columbia University, New York.

Becker, H. (1963/1973), Outsiders: Studies in the Sociology of Deviance, Free Press, New York.

Block, M. K., and Heineke, J. M. (1975), "A labor theoretic analysis of the criminal choice," American Economic Review **65**, 314–325.

Burgess, R., and Akers, R. (1966), "A differential association–reinforcement theory of criminal behavior," Social Problems **14**, 128–147.

Cloward, R., and Ohlin, L. (1960), Delinquency and Opportunity: A Theory of Delinquent Gangs, Free Press, New York.

Cohen, A. (1955), Delinquent Boys: The Culture of the Gang. Glencoe, Free Press.

Cohen, A. (1965), "The sociology of the deviant act: Anomie theory and beyond," American Sociological Review **30**, 5–14.

Cohen. A., Lindesmith. A., and Schuessler. K. (1956), The Sutherland Papers, Indiana University, Bloomington.

Coleman, J. (1990). Foundations of Social Theory. Harvard University, Cambridge, MA.

Coleman, J. (1988), "Social capital in the creation of human capital," American Journal of Sociology **94**, S95–S120.

Elliott, D., Huizinga, D., and Ageton, S. (1985). Explaining Delinquency and Drug Use, Newbury Park, Sage.

Ehrlich, I. (1973). "Participation in illegitimate activities: A theoretical and empirical investigation." Journal of Political Economy **81**, 521–565.

Glaser. D. (1956). "Criminality theories and behavioral images," American Journal of Sociology **61**, 433–444.

Gottfredson. M.. and Hirschi. T. (1990), A General Theory of Crime, Stanford University Press. Stanford.

Granovetter. M. (1973), "The strength of weak ties," American Journal of Sociology **78**, 1360–1380.

Granovetter. M. (1974), Getting A Job: A Study of Contacts and Careers, Harvard University, Cambridge, MA.

Granovetter. M. (1985). "Economic action and social structure: The problem of embeddedness," American Journal of Sociology **91**, 481–510.

Granovetter, M. (1992), "The sociological and economic approaches to labor market analysis: A social structural view," in The Sociology of Economic Life (M. Granovetter and R. Swedberg, Eds.), Westview, Boulder.

Hagan. J., Gillis. A. R.. and Simpson. J. (1988), "Feminist scholarship, relational and instrumental control, and a power–control theory of gender and delinquency," British Journal of Sociology **39**, 301–336.

Hagan. J.. and McCarthy. B. (1992), "Streetlife and delinquency," British Journal of Sociology **43**, 533–561.

Hirschi. T.. and Selvin. H. (1967), Delinquency Research, Free Press, New York.

Hirschi. T. (1969). Causes of Delinquency, University of California, Berkeley.

Hirschi. T., and Gottfredson. M. (1980). "Introduction: The Sutherland tradition." in Understanding Crime—Current Theory and Research (T. Hirschi and M. Gottfredson. Eds.), Sage, Beverly Hills.

Hunt. D. (1990), "Drugs and consensual crimes: Drug dealing and prostitution," in Crime and Justice—A Review of Research (M. Tonry and J. Wilson, Eds.), Vol. 13, pp. 159–202 University of Chicago, IL.

Jacobs. B. (1993). "Undercover deception clues: A case of restrictive deterrence." Criminology **31**, 281–299.

Janus. M.-D., McCormack. A., Burgess. A., and Hartman. C. (1987). Adolescent Runaways—Causes and Consequences. Lexington, Toronto.

Johnson. B.. Williams. T.. Dei. K.. and Sanabria. H. (1990), "Drug abuse in the inner city: Impact on hard-drug users and the community," in Crime and Justice—A Review of Research (M. Tonry and J. Wilson. Eds.), Vol. 13. pp. 9–67, University of Chicago, IL.

Jöreskog, K.. and Sörbom. D. (1989), LISREL VII, User's Reference Guide. Scientific Software, Mooresville, IN.

Luckenbill. D. (1985). "Entering male prostitution." Urban Life **14**, 131–153.

Kornhauser. R. (1978). Social Sources of Delinquency, University of Chicago, IL.

Matsueda. R. (1982). "Testing control theory and differential association: A causal modelling approach." American Sociological Review **47**, 489–504.

Matsueda. R. (1988). "The current state of differential association theory," Crime and Delinquency **34**, 277–306.

Matsueda, R., and Heimer, K. (1987), "Race, family structure, and delinquency: A test of differential association and social control theories," American Sociological Review **52,** 826–840.

Matsueda, R., Gartner, R., Piliavin, I., and Polakowski, M. (1992), "The prestige of criminal and conventional occupations: A subcultural model of criminal activity," American Sociological Review **57,** 752–770.

McCarthy, B., and Hagan, J. (1991), "Homelessness: A criminogenic situation?" British Journal of Criminology **31,** 393–410.

McCarthy, B., and Hagan, J. (1992), "Mean streets: The theoretical significance of situational delinquency among homeless youths," American Journal of Sociology **98,** 597–627.

Padilla, F. (1992), The Gang as an American Enterprise, Rutgers University, New Brunswick, NJ.

Reiss, A. (1961), "The social integration of queers and peers," Social Problems **9,** 102–120.

Sah, R. (1991), "Social osmosis and patterns of crime." Journal of Political Economy **99,** 1271–1295.

Schmidt, P., and Witte, A. (1984), An Economic Analysis of Crime and Justice, Academic Press, Orlando.

Schultz, T. (1961), "Investment in human capital." American Economic Review **51,** 1–17.

Stitt, B. G., and Giacopassi, D. (1992), "Trends in the connectivity of theory and research in criminology," The Criminologist (Official Newsletter of the American Society of Criminology) **17,** 1–6.

Sullivan, M. (1989), "Getting Paid"—Youth Crime and Work in the Inner City, Cornell University, Ithaca.

Sutherland, E. (1937), The Professional Thief—By a Professional Thief: Annotated and Interpreted by Edwin Sutherland, University of Chicago, IL.

Sutherland, E. (1942/1956), "Development of the theory," in The Sutherland Papers (A. Cohen, A. Lindesmith, and K. Schuessler, Eds.), pp. 13–29, Indiana University, Bloomington.

Sutherland, E. (1944/1956), "Critique of the theory," in The Sutherland Papers (A. Cohen, A. Lindesmith, and K. Schuessler, Eds.), pp. 13–29, Indiana University, Bloomington.

Sutherland, E. (1947), Principles of Criminology, 4th ed., Lippincott, Philadelphia.

Sutherland, E. (1949/1983), White Collar Crime—The Uncut Version, Yale University, New Haven.

Sutherland, E., and Locke, J. (1936), Twenty Thousand Homeless Men: A Study of Unemployed Men in the Chicago Shelters, Lippincott, Philadelphia.

Thrasher, F. (1927), The Gang—A Study of 1,313 Gangs in Chicago, 2nd ed., University of Chicago, IL.

Tittle, C., Burke, M. J., and Jackson, E. (1986), "Modelling Sutherland's theory of Differential Association: Toward an Empirical Clarification." Social Forces 405–433.

Visano, L. (1987), This Idle Trade: The Occupational Patterns of Male Prostitution, VitaSana, Concord, Ontario.

Wilson, J., and Herrnstein, R. (1985), Crime and Human Nature, Simon and Schuster, New York.

Weisberg, D. K. (1985), Children of the Night; A Study of Adolescent Prostitution, D.C. Heath, Lexington, MA.

# [29]

# THE BRITISH JOURNAL

## OF

# CRIMINOLOGY

| Vol. 29 | Winter 1989 | No. 1 |

## INSURANCE FRAUD

MICHAEL CLARKE (*Birmingham*)*

*A limited inquiry into how the British retail insurance industry manages fraudulent claims reveals a concentration of frauds in the travel, motor, and home and business contents sectors, with fire an increased hazard, especially in the latter case, where large sums are at risk. The structure of British insurance in respect of fraud control is described, including the important role of loss adjusters, and a number of recent initiatives at industry level are discussed. These appear to indicate increasing recognition of the damage being done by insurance fraud but, for a variety of reasons, many companies are reluctant to take bold and public steps to combat fraud. Fears are widely expressed that public goodwill, and the relationship based on utmost good faith, would be eroded by a more aggressive stance.*

### The Nature of the Inquiry

This inquiry is confined to frauds by insureds upon insurers in the mass retail sector in Britain.[1] Informants agreed that the problem was effectively restricted to travel, motor, household and commercial contents and fire policies;[2] life assurance was excluded because it has traditionally been a risk that attracted very few frauds.[3]

* Department of Social Administration, University of Birmingham. A version of this paper was presented to the International Conference on Fraud and Corruption at the University of Liverpool, July 1987. I am grateful to the organisers and participants for their comments and also to the editor and reviewers of the *British Journal of Criminology*. My thanks to all those who co-operated in my investigations, and also to the Faculty of Commerce and Social Science and the former Department of Sociology of the University of Birmingham, the latter for assistance with research expenses.

[1] It is hence not concerned with frauds by insurers and their agents of the kind that has recently troubled Lloyds of London (on this see Hodgson, 1984; Clarke, 1986, ch. 3); nor is it concerned with maritime or aviation insurance, even though fraud in the former has recently given rise to considerable concern (Ellen and Campbell, 1981); nor is it concerned with insurance frauds outside Britain.

[2] In insurance terms, household and commercial contents policies do of course usually include fire cover. The reason for my categorization of fire separately is that the fraud problems posed by it are distinctive.

[3] This is partly because of the care of insurers when long-term assurance with high sums payable is involved, and partly because of the efficiency of death certification in the UK. In recent years, however, fraud has become a problem, though not, so far, such as to compare with the other risks associated with fraud. One area where model efforts have been made to eliminate such frauds is foreign deaths, because of laxness in death certification in certain Third World countries. Mercantile and General Re-insurance has taken the lead in developing a profile of the likely fraudster and producing a well-researched guidebook on handling unusual death claims. Between 1982 and 1987 M & G recorded 80

MICHAEL CLARKE

The inquiry was limited to matters of general policy and experience as regards the incidence and management of fraud. Hence, although individual cases were often mentioned for the purposes of illustration, a detailed review of a representative series of cases was not attempted. Rather, the objective was to obtain the views of those directly involved in the management of insurance fraud in order to identify the perceived extent of the problem and the apparent effectiveness of its management. To this end, senior members of major insurance companies, loss adjusting practices, the police, and fire services were interviewed at length.[4]

What can be expected from such an investigation? The academic literature revealed no previous research on insurance fraud in Britain and very little in the United States. Efforts were made to identify useful sources in the insurance industry literature, but again it appears that with the exception of law and legal cases, little exists. This leaves the academic investigator very dependent upon his informants. Although in most cases interviews were preceded by a fairly lengthy letter explaining the objectives of the research, discussion was unstructured and informants were encouraged to raise issues which they considered important.

The benefit of such an exercise depends significantly upon whether at least elements of an agreed view of the situation emerge from the informants, and whether, where there are differences of view, the reasons for them also emerge. If there is an enormous diversity of experience and opinion, it may fairly be said that further detailed work is essential. When the subject of investigation is as professionalised, as comparatively integrated, and as long-established as insurance, and where informants are senior personnel with long experience, the likelihood of this happening is of course less and so it proved to be. The report that follows identifies the considerable areas of agreement about insurance fraud; most informants had their idiosyncracies which have not been

cases with £18·3 million at risk investigated, of which 56, involving £15·4 million, proved fraudulent; 19, involving £1·8 million, genuine; and 5, involving £1·1 million, ongoing. The warning signs are precise and numerous enough to enable all cases falling under the combination of factors to be investigated. They are (a) foreign deaths (India and Pakistan account for 57 of the cases investigated, Ghana and Nigeria for 16); (b) protection cover, i.e. term assurance which expires without endowment benefit, and is therefore cheap for large sums insured; (c) policies with several companies; (d) lives below age 35; (e) claims in the first two or three years of the policy; (f) unusual causes of death, e.g. snake-bite, cholera, road accident; (g) female murders (a number of females have been murdered abroad for insurance monies); (h) policies sought deliberately by the insured rather than actively sold by a broker, as is usually the case with life assurance. With fraudulent claims running constantly at about £3 million per annum, M & G are confident that the situation is now under control.

The issue which gives rise to greater disquiet, particularly with the advent of AIDS, is non-disclosure. Many lives already insured will end prematurely from this hitherto unknown cause, and as a 'moral' disease whose medical features are not yet well or widely understood, diagnosis may be late and death certificates may not identify AIDS as the cause. AIDS has interacted with the problem of non-disclosure of health risks on life assurance proposals that has in large part been encouraged by the industry itself. Thus, company medical examinations are now not required below quite high sums assured; the wording of questions on medical history is often vague, allowing proposers to err; and proposal forms are often filled in rapidly and in public by brokers, in circumstances where full and honest answers about intimate medical problems are scarcely encouraged. Finally, the industry has been encouraged to use a shortened proposal form, especially where life assurance is linked to house purchase. Initially, no medical information at all was asked for, which precipitated a flood of substandard lives. As in other areas of insurance, a desire to simplify access to insurance and to speed acceptance of the risk has resulted in a considerable weakening of the steps traditionally taken by insurers to protect themselves and of course the interests of sound lives. See M & G (1987), Leigh (1987), Cooper (1987), and Gaselee (1986).

[4] Specifically, 11 major insurance companies were approached and interviews held with senior staff in the claims departments of 5. Senior staff in 6 adjusting practices were interviewed at length. Four of these were amongst the largest in Britain, the remaining two being smaller. The police are involved in a limited number of insurance fraud cases, and a representative of one of the Fraud Squads was interviewed at length. The fire service is necessarily involved in cases of fraudulent arson, and senior staff of the fire investigation unit in a large fire service were interviewed at length.

2

included. The questions of whether the views taken by the industry are justifiable and how this may be evaluated, and whether present fraud management practices are appropriate, are addressed briefly at the end of the paper.

The insurance industry is characterised by a considerable caution about airing its concerns in public, to the point of secretiveness on many issues.[5] In part this derives from competition between companies, in part the private and confidential nature of the insurance contract; in a larger part, however, it arises from an extreme sensitivity to negative publicity, enhanced in recent years by the spread of consumerism and consumer journalism which, in the industry's view, delights in portraying insurers as grudging payers of claims or, even worse, as making unfounded allegations of fraud to avoid payment. The insurers' difficulties, as will become clear, are that it is often possible to be sure that a claim is fraudulent, but much less easy to prove it.

An elaboration of these points and of the distinctive problems posed by fraud to insurers is presented in the following section. This is followed by an outline of the measures to control fraud. In this light it is possible to review the evidence, which is far from definitive, on the incidence of fraud in respect of various kinds of risk. A section on the detection and management of fraud draws together the evidence of the preceding sections, and the paper concludes with an overall appraisal of the nature and control of retail insurance fraud.

## The Nature of Insurance Fraud and the Attitude of the Industry

Insurance is a civil contract whereby the insurer undertakes to cover specified risks incurred by the insured and to pay out on agreed terms to compensate for losses incurred under those risks. Despite the long history of insurance, running back in Britain in more or less its present form as far as the eighteenth century, and the consequent experience in underwriting, dealing with claims, and adopting appropriate policy conditions, it is still difficult to apply an abstract schedule of terms and conditions to reality: the unexpected always happens to a greater or lesser degree. For this reason, the relationship between insurer and insured is said to be characterised by the utmost good faith. This implies that both parties will abide by the spirit of the contract rather than exploit its terms. In practice it implies that the insured will disclose all matters relevant to the policy and the insured risks, whether or not specifically asked to do so, and that the insurer will not take refuge in the policy terms and conditions to resist a claim which in essence is obviously legitimate. It should not be forgotten that insurance arises out of the need for protection against catastrophe: death, serious injury, major property loss; in the past, and even today, it may stand between the insured and personal ruin. The good faith of the companies is hence vital to the confidence of the insured. Equally, however, the large sums involved are an obvious target for fraud, and not only for reasons of sheer greed. The insured's business may be on the point of failure or be under pressure from creditors; the insured may have suffered a burglary and lost items, the major value of which is sentimental and therefore not recoverable from insurance; he

---

[5] Because of this reticence, all informants requested absolute anonymity for themselves and their organisations, which I undertook to provide. In the case of adjusters, the police and the fire service, access was not unduly difficult. Insurance companies were less accessible; claims managers were on the whole more difficult to interview than others, more measured in their responses, more likely to deflect and even refuse questions, and better prepared with a statement of their own.

MICHAEL CLARKE

may not have included an item lost under the policy or may have failed to renew cover; the insured may have suffered illness or injury; all of these circumstances and many others provide incentive enough for the insured to attempt to claim what he is not entitled to by fabricating or elaborating a claim.

There are at least nine sources of difficulty from the point of view of the insurer in coping with fraud whilst adhering to the principle of utmost good faith.

1. As a result of a series of legal cases in the latter part of the nineteenth century, it has become accepted, contrary to the industry's previously strong view and practice, that exaggerated claims do not constitute fraud.[6] The courts have held that the process of settling a claim is a business one, subject to negotiation and judgement of values on both sides, and that wide differences of opinion and the adoption of positions for bargaining purposes are normal. This means that a claim grossly exaggerated in value cannot be repudiated as a try-on, and even if the quantum is exaggerated it is best to be cautious. Only if items are claimed for which clearly did not exist, nor form part of the loss, can the claim be contested with confidence as fraudulent. The importance of this is not that companies and their adjusters are without resources to negotiate exaggerated claims, but that this takes time, effort, and money, and that in the end a payment may have to be made even though the intent of the exaggeration was fraudulent. The standard policy clause voiding the policy in the case of fraud cannot be applied to cut this process short.

2. Actual fraud, i.e. fabricated loss, is also difficult to prove legally. While a company may reach informed judgement, on the basis of its inquiry, that a claim is fraudulent, it risks civil suit if it dismisses it on these grounds. Companies are fearful of becoming involved in such cases and losing (see below); hence even those instances involving claimants unlikely to press the claim are usually judged by legal criteria. Proof required in civil cases is normally that of balance of probabilities, rather than beyond reasonable doubt as in criminal cases; and civil cases are almost all heard before a judge alone, without the risks of emotive appeals to a jury. Recent cases, however, have established that where the defence is fraud, a substantial preponderance of probabilities has to be demonstrated because of the seriousness of the allegation.[7] It follows from what has been said so far that recourse to avoiding the policy by allegations of fraud is an extreme step for a company to take in the face of a claim. How extreme is further indicated by the points that follow.

3. Because of the emotive nature of their business, insurance companies have a relatively strong service ethic. In the words of one company's current advertising campaign, they 'don't make a drama out of a crisis'. The industry demonstrates utmost good faith in settling what appear to be reasonable claims on generous terms and not carping unduly. It is a view held by adjusters and claims officers equally that their objective is to co-operate with the claimant to give him compensation under the policy. Such a service ethic obviously militates against the cautious approach necessary to detect and pin down frauds.

[6] The most frequently cited are Cann v. The Imperial (1875), and Norton v. Royal (1885). The view was succinctly put by Goddard in London Assurance v. Clare, 57, *Lloyds List Reports*, 254 'Mere exaggeration is not conclusive evidence of fraud, for a man might honestly have an exaggerated idea of the value of his stock or suggest a high figure as a bargaining price.' On legal aspects of fraud and arson, see Entwhistle (1970), 191 ff.

[7] One of the leading cases is S & M Carpets (London) v. Cornhill Insurance Company (1982), CLY 1659, which was followed in a recent case, Broughton Park Textiles v. Commercial Union Assurance Company; see *Current Law*, Sept. 1986, item 163.

4

INSURANCE FRAUD

4. More generally, attitudes and practices appropriate to processing claims submitted in good faith cannot coexist with those necessary for fraud detection. There is a fundamental difference of stance to the insured: one involves taking most of what he says on trust as fact, and only clarifying details where necessary; the other accepts nothing and seeks evidence and corroboration at all stages, taking statements and photographs, inquiring of others associated with the insured, checking with industry sources, employing specialist advisers. This latter process is complex, slow, and hostile, where the former is straightforward, rapid, and co-operative. Quite different skills and recording practices are needed, but perhaps more importantly in the industry's view, a suspicious mind is required. Suspicion of claimants has been a recognised occupational hazard among insurers and adjusters at least since the nineteenth century,[8] the danger being that an experience of gross deception on a few dramatic occasions will sour attitudes to the multitude of honest claimants, antagonise them unfairly, and so in turn ruin the company's reputation. This incompatibility between a hostile and a co-operative mode of processing a claim poses a fundamental dilemma for insurers in managing fraud.

5. This is exacerbated by the demand for promptness in dealing with claims. If the insured has suffered a severe loss he needs rapid remedy, and cash is usually the quickest means. If, however, his claim subsequently appears doubtful, even a partial prompt payment may be used to undermine the company's will to resist, and once money is paid out it is of course difficult to recover.

6. There are also direct costs in adopting a cautious policy and, even more so, resisting a claim. Resistance implies at least that the insured has not made out a claim which, if he is honest, will be of considerable importance to him; if fraud is the grounds of resistance, it implies calling the insured a liar and a cheat: this requires more time and consultation by more senior and qualified personnel, which is costly. The principal means of recovering such costs is premium income. While money saved on bad claims is to the honest policyholders' benefit, the costs of investigating doubtful claims exhaustively can easily exceed the value of the claim,[9] given the nature of modern mass retail insurance—travel, burglary, and motor claims are often less than £2,000, and many are less than £500.

7. Perhaps more important for the company, however, are the potential indirect costs of vigorous resistance to doubtful claims. There is lively competition between the insurance companies, and even the long-established majors with current non-life annual premium incomes in the one to two billion pounds range are not immune from competition. An aggressive policy on doubtful claims is in due course communicated to the public, not least by brokers, who may advise customers to insure elsewhere if they wish to avoid delay, irritation, and embarrassment if they have a claim. The history of insurance indicates that survival rather than high profitability is the name of the game, with cycles of rises and falls in premiums taking place. In good times additional players are attracted to the business and they cut rates to gain market share. Rate cutting leads to losses and to the retreat of the less established and less well capitalised, but it may well affect the profitability of the established in the process.

[8] See, e.g. Cato-Carter (1972), 95, 'The evidence does not show that he [a leading assessor in the latter 19th century] was afflicted by that rare phobia of incurable suspicion that has occasionally been known so to permeate an assessor that he becomes almost incapable of believing that any fire is accidental, or any claim innocent of fraudulent intent.' A similar point is made in Cato-Carter (1984).

[9] That is, from the insurer's point of view, exceed the proportion of the claim which they would normally feel justified in paying.

MICHAEL CLARKE

8. An additional difficulty in recent years has been the enhanced awareness of insured's rights through consumerism, with a particularly influential role being played by regular press features and broadcast programmes. Whatever the truth of the matter, there is a conviction in the industry that the publicity involved is almost invariably negative. An image is portrayed of the unfortunate claimant who is ignored, browbeaten, and maligned by the vast bureaucratic, slipshod, and, worst of all, uncaring insurance company. Even though it is recognised that some consumer advice and publicity organisations are now aware of the problem of fraud and of their facilities being abused, it is nevertheless pointed out that the result is that doubtful cases do not always get an airing, and perhaps that the companies' view is sought more carefully and frequently, but not that companies ever feature as the exploited party. Fear of this kind of bad publicity, which continues in many quarters to be considerable, is founded upon the conviction that one or two cases where the company can be shown to have behaved poorly can receive such wide publicity and provoke such strong identification on the part of the public as actual or potential insureds as to undo the work of years of patient claims work and millions of pounds of advertising.[10]

9. Mass retail insurance has benefited from sustained expansion since the 1950s. The spread of car and home ownership and the rise in package holidays have vastly increased the number of insureds.[11] Businesses, even small ones, are today generally covered against at least burglary and fire. This has meant that many people now hold insurance who in the past would not have contemplated it. From the companies' point of view, this widening of the social catchment of insureds—they are no longer exclusively middle or upper class—interacts crucially with the rise of consumerism, which has involved a much greater assertiveness on the part of insureds and a general decline in public morality. Not to put too fine a point on it, insurers are fair game, much like the Inland Revenue and VAT: large, wealthy, bureaucratic organisations whose main preoccupation is collecting their annual premiums. The net outcome of these changes, it is asserted, is that the attitude of insureds to claims has changed. So far from being deferential to company procedures and experience, they are now assertive, if not aggressive, and in cases of doubtful claims, often truculent if not brazen. Insurers are made forcibly aware that claimants will make trouble if claims are not settled promptly and in full; and aggressive encounters, even picketing claims managers' homes, leave a lasting impression. Some managers go as far as to say that an aggressive pursuit of a claim by

[10] One case in particular is worth mentioning because of its very considerable impact: it seemed to confirm all the fears of how badly things can go wrong. Bernard Saltman ran a furniture retail business in Aylesbury (Wilson, 1983, pp.195–203). In 1979 it caught fire shortly after staff had left the premises. Saltman claimed £160,000, and the insurers sent in a forensic expert to establish the cause of the fire; £50,000 was paid out after the insurers admitted liability, but then Saltman was charged with arson. At the trial the judge in his summing-up to the jury was evidently satisfied that the fire was accidental, and doubtful of the insurer's expert's judgements. Nonetheless, the jury convicted, and there were no legal grounds to appeal. Saltman was jailed for two years. The case was widely featured in the press following the initial BBC Radio 4 'Checkpoint' report and gave rise to a campaign in Parliament. Two additional experts were engaged and concluded that the cause of the fire was accidental. After some resistence the case was referred by the Home Secretary to the Court of Appeal which quashed the conviction on 27 July 1982, including in its judgement trenchant criticism of the insurer's forensic expert. Such a miscarriage of justice is wholly exceptional: forensic experts' judgements can occasionally be seriously at fault, but insurance companies do not habitually set out to destroy blameless, hard-working businessmen who have the misfortune to suffer a fire loss. Yet it has been in the latter terms that the insurance industry has perceived the effects of the publicity.

[11] Department of Employment Family Expenditure Statistics reveal, for example, that the percentage of households with contents cover rose from 67·6 per cent in 1965 to 76·4 per cent in 1985. Regrettably, insurers will not release any useful statistics on the number, value, and type of policies issued over the years for reasons of commercial competition.

6

an insured, and in particular threats of publicity, is evidence of a doubtful claim. If the insurer is to resist or doubt a claim, he must hence be sure of his ground, for he may have to justify all his actions to company management, to the public, or to a court.

## The Organisation of Fraud Control

How then do insurers manage their defences? The major companies have a staff of claims inspectors who check and if necessary investigate claims up to a value of around £2,000. Smaller companies tend to have fewer such staff, and in consequence may only deal internally with claims up to about £500. Some companies will send out claims as small as £100. Claims which appear doubtful, or for other reasons complex, whatever their value, are also likely to be sent out for investigation and report to loss adjusters.

Britain is distinctive in making such extensive use of loss adjusters to appraise and report on claims. Adjusting developed as a separate profession in Britain in the course of the nineteenth century (see Cato-Carter, 1984). Up to the 1860s it was the practice of many insurers to require insureds to have their claim attested by a parish churchwarden as a check on its honesty and accuracy. In the latter half of this century the competition created by the foundation of new companies who did not insist on this, together with an on increasing recognition that it made claimants unduly dependent on the whim of churchwardens and was inevitably unfair to Catholics, Jews, and dissenters, increased the role of assessors (as they were then called). Their position was further aided by the lack of branch offices of insurance companies until the end of the century. Assessors frequently also worked as auctioneers, valuers, and surveyors, which experience conferred the benefits of familiarity with prices and business practice in a variety of fields. Assessors, and later adjusters, thus came to substitute a rational and technical system of claims investigation for the character test on the claimant enshrined in the churchwarden system.

As insurance expanded in the numbers and value of policies written, in the number of companies in business, and in the variety of risks insured, the technical complexity of adjusting grew, so that by the inter-war period it had established itself as a small but increasingly essential profession servicing the insurance industry. Individually, however, adjusting was and perhaps remains by no means secure. Adjusters have always been dependent upon building up relations with insurers by giving good service; personal relations between individual adjusters and claims staff are probably still important and in the past were decisive. Insurers have found it useful to retain adjusters in large part because of the concentration of expertise in adjusting. Modern practices include staff with backgrounds in accountancy, quantity surveying, various branches of engineering, and in the police, as well as insurance. It is also convenient, when dealing with claimants, for insurers to be able to refer to the independence of adjusters; and adjusters, for their part, stress the impartiality of their work, although retained and paid for entirely by insures.[12] It is up to the insurer not only which practice of adjusters he picks to deal with a claim, but which individual adjuster he asks to deal with it.[13] If

---

[12] Thus, for example, the President of the CILA: 'It is the impartiality of the chartered loss adjuster that picks out our profession from almost any other that I can think of. The adjuster preserves his impartiality at all times, favouring the interests of neither the insured nor the insurer.' *Post Magazine and Insurance Monitor*, 3 Sept. 1981, p. 2174.

[13] The point is not that claims invariably go to a trusted individual, rather than the practice in general, but that they may if the claims manager so decides.

MICHAEL CLARKE

the insurer is dissatisfied with an adjuster he can easily go elsewhere, whereas if he were reliant on internal claims staff this would be much less easy.[14]

With the 1939–45 war and the post-war expansion of business and commerce, both insurance and adjusters prospered mightily. The Chartered Institute of Loss Adjusters was granted Royal Incorporation in 1961, when it had perhaps 200 members. Membership grew to 402 in 1975 and 764 by 1986. It is still not necessary to be an Associate or Fellow of the Institute in order to practice as an adjuster, and most partnerships have many staff who are not fully qualified as adjusters but are either in the process of becoming so or are valued for their other professional qualifications.

On the whole, therefore, it falls to adjusters to detect and pursue fraud. They are hence beset with the same fundamental dilemma as insurers as regards their stance to the claimant, whether hostile or co-operative (see point 4 above).[15] On this score, adjusters have certain advantages. They deal only with larger and more complex claims, and much of the bureaucratic routine is shouldered by insurance claims departments. They accumulate considerable experience and can call on a range of professional in-house skills in investigating a claim. In cases of doubtful claims, they may circularise their colleagues elsewhere to solicit information about the claimant's insurance history. The problems of the style of investigation may be partially overcome by the specialisation of the practice, or of individuals in it, in fraud, although only one large practice has a specialist fraud unit staffed by ex-policemen. This means in turn that cases registered as doubtful by claims departments can be referred to adjusters with experience in fraud.

There are, on the other hand, drawbacks. Adjusters are remote from claims departments and have to ask them for information from their records. While this will normally be readily forthcoming it has to be sought out, and adjusters have no direct access to insurance company records or direct influence on how they are kept or organised. Further, adjusters have to be instructed, and this causes delay, especially with smaller claims. Thus, a large fire may see adjusters on the scene within hours, while in a small commercial burglary it may be several days, in the course of which evidence may be lost, tampered with, or destroyed. Speed and accurate recording are vital to success in

---

[14] Just how sensitive relations with adjusters can be is attested by two well-known cases. One of the largest practices of adjusters, Robins, Davies and Little, was founded by one Arthur Thwaites, who took the business to considerable heights in the latter part of the nineteenth century, when he was unfortunate enough to make an error of judgement in assessing a fire claim at a private boarding school (see Cato-Carter, 1972, chs. 17–18). He recommended resistance on the grounds of arson by the principal and owner. The claim went to arbitration and the insured not only won his claim and costs but began a campaign against Thwaites, publishing a pamphlet denouncing the insurers. The effect was to destroy Thwaites' reputation and very nearly destroy the business, which was only saved by the energies of his junior partners and the substitution of their names for his. Ironically, he was not wrong in his suspicion of arson: he later obtained judgment against a former pupil of the school. In the second case, a group of arsonists in the 1930s led by Leopold Harris set a long series of fires and were successful in claiming insurance in many cases. Their distinctive characteristic was the ability of Harris to gain the co-operation, active or passive, of people in the fire service, the salvage corps, and adjusters, as well as various front men, stooges, and rogues. Twenty-two people were eventually convicted as a result of the deft investigation not of the police, but of a solicitor experienced in the insurance world, Sir William Crocker, later President of the Law Society. The affair soured relations between adjusters and insurers for some time. See Crocker (1967) and Dearden (1986).

[15] Adjusters accept an explicit responsibility to be alert to the signs of a fraudulent claim. Accountants, by comparison, maintain that their concern with an overall evaluation of the company means that compliance work cannot be undertaken simultaneously since quite different methods of evaluation are required. It is recognized, however, that there is increasing political pressure for accountants to accept a role in fraud detection, and the same dilemmas will arise as to whether their attitude to the client is hostile and questioning or co-operative and accepting. See Allan and Forde (1986).

8

fraud inquiries. The two-tier system inevitably incurs delay and may also lead to inadequate recording: initial statements, photographs, samples, and vital material evidence must be taken as soon as possible after the loss (or 'loss'); if the claim is passed in the routine manner to adjusters and not flagged as doubtful, these procedures may not be as prompt, accurate, rigorous, and comprehensive as necessary. The outcome is that adjusters frequently complain that insurers pay out on claims which their inquiries have shown to be bad, while insurers say that although they accept the adjuster's view, they have been given inadequate hard evidence to resist the claim, especially if the claimant is persistent and employs a solicitor.

This difficulty interacts with that of money. Adjusters are paid by insurers by negotiation, but they would usually expect there to be a relation between the size of the adjusted loss and the fee. Doubtful and fraudulent cases require much more time and consultation, including on occasion the hiring of outside experts such as forensic scientists and private detectives. This adds greatly to expense, for which the adjuster must obtain prior clearance, though most say that insurers will normally back them. However, unless insurers expect a fraud investigation,[16] such inquiries are an unanticipated extra expense which, if a claim is not successfully resisted, require the company to recover the money in premium income. There is thus no incentive for adjusters to be over-zealous in detecting fraud, and history demonstrates that it is dangerous to be overly suspicious. Whilst adjusters are universally emphatic that they pursue fraud when they find it, and that they develop a nose for it with experience, there is evidently no material incentive to find it, and some disadvantages in the structure of their situation to its detection and effective pursuit. Also there is nothing in their professional training examinations which prepares them specifically in fraud detection and control.

The obvious remedy is enhanced fraud control by insurers, either by flagging claims as doubtful or, even better, avoiding giving cover to those termed bad moral risks, i.e. fraudsters. In practice, the two are often interlinked, since improved checks on insurance proposals and improved record-keeping by insurers to allow a review of the proposer's insurance history before he is taken on risk would not encroach on the remit of adjusters. This would, however, involve additional time and personnel, and hence cost. Insurers certainly do undertake checks at the underwriting stage in a limited number of cases, but they are secretive about their nature. The only identifiable source of such checks, apart from the new Motor Loss Register (see below) is the Fire Loss Bureau (FLB). This shadowy organisation is funded by a number of the major insurance companies. It was developed at least as early as 1975 to attempt to control fire losses, which were then, as now, mounting, including losses through fraudulent arson.[17] Its records, which include all claims of £50,000 and above, are kept on manual files to avoid problems with the Data Protection Act. Its subscribers are sensitive about its existence, though there are moves afoot to give it a more routine, extensive, and public role. On the whole, however, the industry's attitude to it reflects that to record-keeping to control fraud in general: it is timid, fearful of public outcry about blacklists and highly

---

[16] One adjuster arranged to accept claims from a Lloyds syndicate which specialised in underwriting bad risks at high rates, expecting 75 per cent of claims to be doubtful. The CILA used to issue a fee scale for settlements up to £500,000, but has not done so recently because of concern by the Office of Fair Trading about its implications for competition. The scale assumed cases to be of a routine, i.e. non-fraudulent, character.

[17] According to one informant, the FLB now deals with all large property losses, whether from fire or otherwise. As is evident from my cautious remarks on it, the main weakness of the FLB in fraud control is that many insurers and adjusters know little or nothing about its existence and are hence unable to refer cases to it.

MICHAEL CLARKE

cost-conscious. For this reason, the FLB's very existence is only reluctantly acknow-ledged. Also, its remit is with fire loss in general, not with fraud in particular, and though characterised as helpful by some adjusters, it is not fully geared to fraud control. Most of the inquiries it deals with are concerned with claims, and it would appear that checks at the proposal stage, where they occur, are largely in-house.

## The Incidence of Insurance Fraud

It is difficult to reach an informed judgement here. While many in the insurance world maintain that fraud has not increased disproportionately to the increase in insurance in recent years, others suggest that there has been a significant increase at least in some areas. There is general agreement, however, that fraud is not out of control. Given the problems of detection already referred to, and companies' reluctance to make allega-tions of fraud without clear, usually documentary, proof, the number of recorded in-stances is very small; most cases do not get further than being classified as doubtful, even if they are resisted (see below). Record-keeping on fraudulent and doubtful claims, is poor, although some companies have very recently begun to keep fuller records. Fraud has also, as discussed above, to be distinguished from exaggeration, some of which is deliberate. Estimates for exaggerated claims range up to 50 per cent. There is broad agreement that real fraud, i.e. claims partially or wholly fictitious, are between 1 and 5 per cent. Whilst this indicates a relatively low incidence, it leaves the absolute numbers open to a range of variation of a factor of five, which is clearly un-satisfactory. More will be said below on the undetected or dark figure.

Three other generalisations appear possible about the incidence of fraud. First, most cases occur in the first year of the policy, and frequently in the first few months. Secondly, frauds can for the most part be grouped into three categories: the opportun-ist, or one-off instances, usually as part of a genuine loss; the amateurs who started as opportunists and, having been successful once, decide to try again; and the profes-sionals, who are better organised, dedicated to making significant amounts of money from insurance fraud, and may well involve a range of accomplices. The latter are much the smallest group, but because of the large size and numbers of claims involved they may pose a serious problem. Finally, as mentioned above, the areas of insurance in which, by common agreement, fraud is concentrated, are travel, motor, household and commercial contents, and fire. The problems created vary and they are therefore con-sidered separately below, but it is worth adding at this juncture that characteristic claims vary in size from less than £1,000 for travel to £10,000–£1,000,000 for commer-cial fires.

## Travel

This is accepted as the area in which fraud is hardest to control. The numbers of foreign holidaymakers, let alone business travellers, run into millions. The number of policies is almost equally vast. The risks are also unusual from the insured's point of view. He is no longer in control of, or even familiar with his surroundings, as he is in his home, and the combination of crowds and foreign cultures and languages has its effect: people do fool-ish things when abroad that they would not contemplate at home. It is hard to dis-entangle bad luck, naïvety, recklessness, and fraud. Claims, especially for property loss, are relatively small; medical claims are larger, though better secured through evidence of treatment. The difficulty with property claims is official recording of the loss: the nearest police station may be distant and may in fact provide no copy of the report of a loss, or even, indeed, refuse to record it.

Spotting bad claims and resisting them is hence difficult. Experience of the behaviour of travellers when subjected to property loss or illness abroad provides some assistance. Most policies contain conditions insisting on reasonable care of property, but cost is an obvious difficulty in resisting small claims, even by the reckless. Nor is this area of insurance immune from the attentions of professionals. In one case, an estimated 120 to 150 claims were made against five companies using a variety of names and addresses.[18]

The best that insurance companies seem able to do at present is to contemplate restricting their activity in the field if they fear excessive bad claims; to channel business through reliable brokers who will partially screen out fraudulent clients; to impose more restrictive policy conditions to reduce recklessness; and to require more extensive disclosure at proposal to identify repeaters.

*Motor*

Motor insurance is an area in which, despite successive large increases in rates in recent years, it has proved very hard for insurers to show consistent profits. The motor trade is notorious for its sharks and its participation in the hidden economy, and every motorist must be familiar with the question, on presenting a car for estimate with body damage, 'Is this an insurance job?' The implication is that if it is, VAT will be added to the bill and other defects of long standing may well be included in the work. About these areas of malpractice insurers seem unable to take effective action. They are usually more concerned to ensure that the repairs are completed competently. The 'little bit extra' that the insured and the garage make is reflected in higher premiums the following year.

The garage may in some cases suggest that the vehicle is not worth the insured's repairing, in which case comprehensive cover will provide the owner with its written-off value. For those who reply that they only have third party, fire, and theft cover, the suggestion may be that they 'lose' the car, preferably in the nearest crusher, and report it stolen. Insurers confirm that cars reduced to small metal blocks are indeed hard to identify. One police raid on a crusher recently produced 114 log books, of which over 100 had been reported as stolen vehicles.[19]

Various estimates have been made of the incidence of such fraudulent losses in Britain in recent years. Such cases are said to have been mounting for seven to ten years, but particularly rapidly over 1983–6, and they are a well-recognised problem in other countries. In the United States, in certain areas, they reached epidemic proportions, and insurers have established and publicised special investigation units, staffed

---

[18] The claimant had obtained the company stationery of a travel agency and had obtained or forged a doctor's stamp. The claims were for cancellation of long-distance holidays because of illness. The claimant was detected by a claims inspector when he failed to add up his claim accurately and a phone call to the travel agent produced no record.

[19] One informant said that wrecked cars can be insured as good ones, there being no inspection of vehicles by insurers before accepting the risk. The car can then be reported stolen; MOT certificates can be obtained by those with the right connections, and 'the attitude of the DVLC at Swansea to insurers varies from the disinterested to the downright uncooperative.'

11

MICHAEL CLARKE

with trained investigators. This seems to have been effective,[20] the publicity about special investigations being coupled with that about prosecution. British insurers also decided to tackle this problem recently, partly as a result of increased losses and partly because of the clear and deliberate nature of the fraud and the danger of its becoming fashionable if unchecked. Some companies had already gone to the extent of refusing fire or theft cover in areas of the country where doubtful total losses have been largest. In 1987 all motor insurers combined to establish the Motor Insurance Anti-Fraud and Theft Register (MIAFTR), which centralises records of all total losses on a computer. It is expected that 300,000 claims a year will be recorded, at an annual cost of £150,000. The register is capable of sophisticated matching of cases, with the object of detecting both theft and fraud cases, though it is likely to be most effective against repeat offenders: the value of insurance records generally lies not in the individual claim but in making connections with previous and associated claims. MIAFTR is thus a first modest step in a direction which may be pursued in other areas of insurance in the future.

*Household and commercial contents*

Although items included in the all-risks section of household policies are subject to many of the difficulties that characterise travel insurance, most household losses concern burglary or accidental damage, and most doubtful claims involve the former. A significant number of bad claims arise, but this is held by many practitioners to be scarcely surprising, given that three-quarters of households now have contents cover, and this includes many who do not understand much about the nature of insurance.[21] Because the insured has control over his home and contents and may be expected to be familiar with them, careful questioning in doubtful cases can yield significant results, though apparently wealthy claimants with larger sums insured pose a greater problem. Once again, however, the difficulty is the very large number of policies and claims, many of which are not great. Most doubtful claims do not arise as a result of completely bogus burglaries, but rather from genuine losses which are then added to. Once successful, a fraudulent claimant may go on to become a dedicated amateur, insuring with different companies. Until the claims history is revealed, usually by adjusters who act for several companies or whose suspicions are aroused, detection is not especially likely. As in most insurance fraud, detection on the first occasion is much less likely, provided the claimant is modest and especially if it is a fraudulent addition to a genuine claim. Not only are mistakes more likely over time, but insurers' resistance will be aroused by multiple claims, and it should not be forgotten that cover can be declined as a bad risk by insurers without any detailed justification. Insurance is a voluntary annual contract by both parties.

---

[20] See Ghezzi (1983). On the Californian refinements of auto fraud, see Kelson (1975). Organised motor fraud has also been a serious problem in Europe. 'In North Rhine-Westphalia, for example, a special commission of the Landeskriminalamt conducted investigations of 50 gangs consisting of more than 1,000 drivers engaged in professionally causing wilful accidents. Some of the cars used were involved in up to 18 accidents within two years. The German Association of Third-Party Insurers estimated the damages caused by this type of crime at about DM 500 million, representing 4·2 per cent of the whole premium earned in a year' (Tiedemann, 1977, p. 33).

[21] For example, claims may be lodged in respect of more than one policy for the same loss. In some instances, this may of course be deliberate fraud, but gross naïvety (two premiums therefore two claims) is recognised as a problem in some cases.

Householders are also vulnerable in being easily accessible and identifiable and usually not protected by professional advisers. Further, most proposal forms contain questions as to previous claims and insurance history, including whether cover has ever been declined. A false declaration in any particular voids the entire policy. Given that the objective of the household policy is security against burglary, fraudulent habits constitute a considerable risk for the householder, and it is a field in which opportunists probably predominate. Some amateurs persist, but professionals are largely absent.

*Fire*

Fire is one of the oldest forms of insurance, and many of the great modern companies began as fire offices. It ranks as a major hazard, and most houses (if only at the insistence of building societies), and most businesses (including these days many small businesses), are insured against it. The sums at risk are very large, ranging up to £10 million and more. In recent years, awareness of fire prevention and techniques to achieve it have improved greatly, and the insurance industry has for the past twenty years sponsored the Fire Protection Association to promote fire safety and train people in its techniques. While the technical side of fire safety—building materials and design, installation of fire control equipment, and recognition of the hazards of particular processes and materials—has advanced, the human side is presently an area of considerable effort. Many fires are started as a result of poor security and lack of adequate safety practices—accumulations of rubbish, lack of enforcement of safety routines, lack of staff awareness of fire hazards. Fires have thus continued to constitute a very great problem, exacerbated on the one hand by the continuing increase in size of commercial premises and of the stock contained in them, and on the other by a marked growth of arson.

Arson has undergone sustained expansion, not only in Britain but also in the United States and the rest of Europe, over the last fifteen years or so, and now contitutes a major, if not the major, fire hazard.[22] Insurers seem to be convinced, however, that this increase is only in small part accounted for by insurance fraud. There are some grounds for accepting this. In the case of well-established, large companies, the directors and the company probably have more to lose from a fire than to gain. Insurers are clear that fraudulent arson is not a problem in large companies. Arson by vandalism on all types of premises has shown a marked increase (according to a Home Office working party on this subject established in 1978), and doubts about the connection between the arsonist and the owner in commercial cases may be allayed, at least in part, by the extent of arson in schools; of 1,992 fires at schools in 1984, 1,108 were deliberate. Arson can also sometimes be shown by police inquiries to be clearly connected with some cause other than fraud, e.g. a disgruntled employee, or not infrequently a means of covering up another crime, such as burglary or even murder.

Arguably, the insurer is in a stronger position in relation to arson than other insurance frauds. The fire service will attend and obtain useful evidence of the time, seat, and extent of the fire, the use of accelerants, and evidence of break-in. In recent years, brigades have set up fire investigation units (FIUs) to deal with arson, and have been

[22] A recent well-researched study by the giant Munich Reinsurance Co. indicated that 30 per cent of fires in West European countries were arson. The number of deliberate and doubtful fires in the UK has risen from 15,300 in 1979 to 34,000 in 1984; the number of cases of arson recorded by the police from 11,640 in 1979 to 18,889 in 1984 and the number of convictions from 1,907 in 1979 to 2,491 in 1984 a low clearup rate (Home Office S3 Division, 1986).

13

MICHAEL CLARKE

successful in reducing greatly the number of fires attributed to unknown causes. Although their input is inevitably less, the police now take a significant interest in arson, and co-operation with fire services is in some areas better than in the past. Because of the size of claims, adjusters will probably be instructed promptly, and should be able to begin their inquiries, including the hiring of forensic experts if appropriate, in time to secure evidence. Time is critical here: in the immediate aftermath of a major fire, witnesses are still shocked and easily interrogated. Even if the principal is safely distant, frontmen may be caught out. Further, as the debris is normally disturbed and cleared and unsafe structures frequently brought down shortly after a fire, it is essential to sift it and take samples and photographs. If this is done, vital evidence of what was destroyed in the fire and how it started and spread may be obtained. To this can be added the vital question, *cui bono*, and at least the area of investigation for fraud mapped out.

None the less, the Chief Fire Officer of the West Midlands felt constrained to say in public recently that the FIU investigations showed that thirty-three out of thirty-nine fires at industrial premises in the first ten months of 1985 were deliberate, and that 'I formed a clear impression (two years ago) that there were people in the business of arson for profit. I was, and I remain, convinced.'[23] It is one thing to identify arson, however, quite another to prove it. Experience indicates that certain areas of business—the garment and fabric trade, for example–are particularly vulnerable, as are certain types of premises, such as unattended warehouses. Where such a fire occurs, and where subsequent inquiries show a history of business problems or fire claims (or both), or current financial difficulties, suspicion of arson must be great. The difficulty lies in successful resistance to the claim, since if it is large enough for the insurers to spend some time investigating it, it is also large enough for the claimant to employ professional advisers too—accountants, lawyers, and insurance assessors, who do the same job as adjusters but act for claimants. The insurers may thus be forced into a position of either paying a claim, or denying it with a clear expectation of having to fight a civil action in consequence. Because of the difficulty of winning and the odium of losing, many insurers admit to paying out against their better judgement.

It is against this background that the distribution of perceived fraudulent arson should be seen. The cases in which insurers succeed most easily are the small ones perpetrated by the small businessman or householder who is in financial or emotional difficulties (divorce can be a basis for fraudulent arson). Such a person will be largely unadvised and inexperienced and is already concerned at his financial position: arson is an act of desperation. The larger-scale arsonist, by contrast, is well advised, pays a professional arsonist through an intermediary, organises the circumstances most carefully to get times and personnel right, has his accounts in order (albeit a false one), and uses an assessor and a lawyer to press for prompt payment. The stakes at risk are large, and the arsonist does not have to commit a fraud more than once every couple of years. The main chance of detecting him, if he does not make mistakes in the individual instance, is via his insurance history, and that may be difficult because of changes in location, aliases, the use of frontmen, the use of the company form, and the use of offshore bases. Great care and patience are necessary on the part of adjusters to trace the trail of the professional arsonist, and even when identified he may be impossible to deal with other

[23] *Birmingham Post*, 15 Oct. 1985.

INSURANCE FRAUD

than by refusing further insurance cover. However, insurers seem on the whole reasonably sanguine about the problem of professional arson for profit, rating its incidence way below that of the opportunist/amateur group.

Of all the areas of insurance fraud, fire seems to offer the greatest opportunities to the professional, and provided he is cautious, learns by experience, and is not too greedy, has the smallest chances of detection (it was greed and recklessness—hubris—that undid Leopold Harris). So far as I am aware, no systematic attempt has yet been undertaken by insurers to identify the real extent of fraud in this area (as in others), yet the rise of arson in general (for most of which, of course, insurers have to pay), is none the less causing considerable concern in the insurance world.[24] This has led to moves to establish better co-operation between the relevant public services—police, Home Office, forensic, fire brigade, and insurers—and perhaps to promote the Fire Loss Bureau into a more public role as an effective clearing house.

## *The Detection and Management of Fraud*

So far, an account has been given of the balance of advantage between insurers and fraudsters and the outlook of insurers. In so doing a certain amount has been said about what might be called the natural history of a fraudulent claim. Some emphasis has been laid upon the constraints of insurers, and especially adjusters, in checking every claim fully for fraud. How, then, are suspicions first aroused?

Adjusters almost universally attest to developing a nose for bad claims, a sense of something out of place. Such a hunch will prompt factual enquiries which, if any of them give grounds for more concrete suspicions, will precipitate more exhaustive efforts. One warning sign generally accepted is a claim submitted not long after cover begins—most detected frauds take place in the first year of the policy and many of them in the first six months. There may then be anomalies or peculiarities in the way that the claim is submitted, or in the nature of the explanation offered for the loss, which alerts the claims inspector or adjuster—experience will provide stereotypes of normal claims of various types. One would expect that the inexperienced fraudster, unfamiliar with events in a real loss, might make errors and that s/he[25] would not know much about claims-handling procedure. Considerable weight, however, is given in addition to the fact that fraudsters are foolish:[26] they make silly mistakes in their stories, contradict themselves at interview, produce palpably false or altered documentation, protest violently if not paid promptly, threaten insurers with publicity through consumer organisations, and generally betray a lack of confidence in their supposedly rightful expectations of being paid. The picture of the fraudster presented so far is hence hardly that of the smooth conman: lack of knowledge and preparation, unnecessary errors, and a tendency to flap. One wonders whether it is only the incompetent fraudsters who are detected.

Once suspicions are aroused, adjusters will obtain the insurer's clearance to run a full

---

[24] See, e.g. CILA (1985) and the publications of the Fire Protection Association, particularly its journal, *Fire Protection*. Working parties are now established with the European Conference of Fire Protection Associations and on various UK topics, e.g. schools and historic buildings.

[25] Women were quite frequently cited as fraudsters, especially on house contents burglary claims, but no estimates of prevalence were given. Suspicious fire and motor claims were by implication almost universally taken to be by men.

[26] A view evidently of some long standing. Crocker's account of the Leopold Harris case contains similar remarks, by no means confined to the Harris fires.

MICHAEL CLARKE

inquiry and ask for checks on the claimant's history from insurers and other adjusters. Written statements will be taken from the claimant and other relevant parties—witnesses and potential witnesses, for example—approached and questioned. The police and fire service will be approached, though relations in the former case are not close. In the past, burglary claims were routinely circularised to the police, but in the 1970s the Association of Chief Police Officers decided to refuse to respond to such circulars any more because of pressure of work. Inquiries how have to go to the officers directly involved, and their co-operation varies widely from force to force according to policy, and from officer to officer according to personal relations with adjusters, pressure of work, and the officer's views on insurance and fraud. There is no formal basis for liaison between insurers and the public services, despite their common interests in certain cases.

The interests of the public services also differ from those of insurers. The responsibilities of the fire service are the safety of persons and property and the establishment of the causes of fires, whether accidental or deliberate. Those of the police include fraud, but fraud has a low priority compared to the pressures to solve crimes of violence, maintain public order, and promote public welfare (attending at accidents, etc.). Individual officers not uncommonly take the view that organisations as large and wealthy as insurers should be responsible for sorting out their own problems.[27] The police are also not organised to detect fraud. Recording of crimes takes place at division level; if a culprit for burglaries and simple arsons cannot be identified in about 48 hours the search is abandoned, leaving the pattern of offences in a locality to produce the answer over time. The clear-up rates for both arson and burglary are low in comparison to offences of violence against the person. Scenes-of-crime officers are trained to deal with arson and do attend, but they are relatively few in number and have other crimes to deal with. Insurers and adjusters are not, on the whole, impressed by police performance or co-operation in relation to fraud. That of the fire service is regarded as better and improving with the development of FIUs, but is still limited.

Insurers, moreover, are not especially interested in persuading the police, in particular, to take an active interest. Insurance is regarded as a private contract between insurers and insured; even if criminal fraud is committed, the tendency of insurers is to deal with the matter themselves unless there is clear evidence for prosecution, in which case it is passed to the police with the expectation of effective action. As stated above, insurers are very wary of losing court cases and incurring adverse publicity. More fundamentally, however, claims are regarded by insurers as matters to be settled between them and the insured privately. Adjusters, who are in the front line in this respect, are specifically instructed that, if evidence of a criminal offence is uncovered in their inquiries, they have an obligation to disclose it to their principals but not to act as an informant to the public authorities (police, customs and excise, etc.).[28] The strategy of

---

[27] A view which seems to be gaining official support. The Metropolitan Police recently announced (Leppard, 1988) that the work of its cheque and credit card fraud squad and art and antiques squad was to be passed to a subsidiary of the Post Office. Senior police sources were cited as maintaining that banks, building societies, auctioneers, and airlines should use their profits to police themselves, and private security companies should be encouraged to participate in this work. The implications of this policy, if further developed, are in my view substantial.

[28] The following is the opinion of the Honorary Solicitor to the CILA as circulated to members: 'There is no legal obligation, at least in the circumstances of fraud, evasion and irregularities indicated above, in respect of which you seek advice or generally in other cases upon adjusters or his principals to report such facts to the relevant authority. There is a

INSURANCE FRAUD

managing claims is hence geared towards avoiding payment of bad ones rather than towards the exercise of civic obligation in denouncing crimes.[29]

Once this principle has been understood, the strategy adopted to manage bad claims becomes more intelligible. Few are finally categorised as fraud, because of the difficulties of proof and risks of publicity, but also because the objective is to advise the insurer of bad claims and to resist payment. If payment is successfully denied and the insured does not sue, and he is also denied further cover, the insurer's interests are protected. The object of inquiries is hence to accumulate enough evidence to put pressure on the claimant to reduce or drop his claim, or at the very least to deter him from making a fraudulent claim again. The stronger the doubts in the mind of the adjuster, the greater will be his efforts to obtain evidence against the claimant. Interviews may hence be repeated, stories checked, the proposal by the insured checked, and the policy conditions insisted upon. At the very least, this is likely to give the insurer grounds for reducing a claim—most insureds will fail to produce adequate evidence that they owned all the items claimed and that they had the value claimed. Evidence that items were purchased can be checked with suppliers, and falsified receipts exposed, since most large suppliers keep sales documents for some years for VAT purposes. Once this methodical inquiry produces evidence of misrepresentation, the claimant is under pressure and frequently withdraws or modifies his claim.[30] When the adjuster is satisfied that the claim as modified is roughly the loss actually and reasonably sustained, he may recommend payment, along with a refusal to provide further cover. In doing so, he has, of course, to be most judicious. He must not provoke the claimant into going to law unless he has solid grounds to offer the insurer for repudiating the claim. The important point for present purposes is that the adjuster's role is that of an intermediary in a private, semiformal negotiation between insurer and insured, which is intended to protect the insurer's interest in avoiding a public and formal confrontation. Adjusters hence become used to quite extraordinary and implausible changes of story by the insured. No matter what they may think about the claimant deserving to be behind bars, or made a crim-

legal obligation upon the adjuster to report such facts to his principals. It is appropriate for the adjuster, having reported the facts to his principals, to leave it to them to consider whether they have a moral obligation to report the facts to the relevant authority. In judging that, insurers will no doubt have regard to the context in which they have received the particular information and their commercial interests.'

[29] Work on the regulatory agencies (e.g. Hawkins and Thomas, 1984; Baldwin and McCrudden, 1987), suggests a tempting parallel as regards the adoption of compliance or deterrent strategies of control. But regulatory agencies' raison d'etre is intervention to control wrongdoing on behalf of the victims and society, whereas insurers exist to indemnify policyholders and to make a profit. It is therefore an open question whether they intervene to identify and pursue fraud. Some informants were emphatic that they were reluctant to do so and would sooner ignore fraud and raise premiums to cover the losses.

Rock's (1973) account of debtors is closer to that of insureds. The relation between the parties is a civil one and remains private unless the creditor/insurer wishes to make it public. The difference lies in the fact that bad debts are self-disclosing, whereas fraudulent insurance claims are not. Creditors hence have to take a decision to ignore bad debt, whereas insurers have to take a decision to find out if there is any insurance fraud. Detected insurance fraudsters also potentially have a similar status to the bankrupt they cannot obtain further insurance cover. Although widely mentioned as a sanction, most insurers recognise that lack of communication among them at present means that only the most persistent and incompetent offenders are likely to suffer this penalty.

[30] Such evidence does not have to amount to conclusive proof. Once the adjuster has made clear, at least by implication, his doubts as to the good faith of the insured and his reluctance to recommend payment of the claim, the insured is offered the opportunity, frequently accepted, of not pressing the claim further, while no doubt denouncing the insurance company for its abuse of the 'small print' of the policy.

MICHAEL CLARKE

inal bankrupt, their restraint is maintained. The option of criminal denunciation is left to insurers, who are disinclined to exercise it without secure evidence.[31]

## Conclusions

From this perspective, fraud appears as something of an embarrassment to the insurance industry. It is a violation of the values of service, fair dealing, and utmost good faith on which it is proud to act. There are considerable difficulties and, not least, costs, in its control. The industry's interest in the private settlement of claims by negotiation favours the management of claims that are erroneous or dishonest, rather than their denunciation as criminal. Not a few of its practitioners admit that claims are and have been paid that are fraudulent, to the detriment of honest insureds and to the public interest. The major internal difficulty in adopting a more vigorous approach to fraud lies in cost. Insurance companies are in a number of cases very large and have modern, computerised record-keeping systems. The adjusting profession is now well-established, experienced, and well distributed in the country. The resources exist to resist fraud, and more particularly, to identify it more effectively, but the deployment of additional resources to that end has to be justified in terms of the money saved. The conventional means of doing so in the industry is in terms of claims not paid or reduced, but the real value of an effective fraud control system would lie in its capacity to deter the abuse of insurance.

As things stand at present, the industry has relied on experience to estimate the incidence and damage done by fraud. On the evidence it has itself provided, there are surely grounds at least for the deployment of limited resources to establish as far as possible the true extent of fraud in different areas.

There are signs of change in the industry's attitude to fraud, of which the creation of MIAFTR and its deliberately public launch is the most prominent. There is also considerable sentiment expressed privately to bring the FLB into a similarly public and more effective role. There is better co-operation with the fire service, following the establishment of specialist fire investigation units, and, to a lesser extent, with some police. At least one major insurer has shifted deliberately to a more aggressive policy on fraud because of concern at past lenience; government concern about the problem of fraud in general; resentment at the increasingly brazen nature of some attempts at fraud; and a perception that the fever of consumerism may have abated, and consumer lobbies now be prepared to acknowledge that they are abused by fraudsters on occasion. There is also evidence of increasing co-operation with insurers in Europe, which will include a concern with improved fraud control measures. These are but straws in the wind, however, whether it be a wind of change or not.

At root, there is a fundamental incompatibility between the profit-oriented objective of the insurance industry, in getting business and generating premium income, and vigorous fraud control. Competition for new business has involved appealing to sectors of the population which have not in the past sought insurance, and the strategy seen to be essential to achieving a competitive edge in this expanding market has been held to

---

[31] Thus, there was a discernible tendency by insurers to say that they had always pursued fraud and refused to pay out while other companies were more willing to compromise, but at the same time to say that if there was inadequate evidence to prosecute there was inadequate evidence to refuse to pay, having already admitted that the company's involvement in prosecutions was infrequent.

18

be an emphasis upon easy access, informality, and lack of complex form-filling and delay in accepting proposals. The simplification of insurance proposals and lack of checks on proposers also reduces insurers' costs. Yet lack of detailed enquiries at proposal stage makes it harder to detect persistent fraudsters and to resist an exaggerated or fraudulent claim. And the nemesis of the informal strategy lies in the danger that insurance will come to be seen as so easy a target for fraud that most self-respecting policy holders will attempt to exploit their insurers at some time or other, on the grounds that only the naïve pay out premiums indefinitely without making a claim.[32]

More vigorous and public fraud control measures by insurers would signal to the public that fraud will not be tolerated, and that attempts stand a reasonable chance of detection and denunciation. Such measures would include (*a*) much greater public recognition by insurers of the fraud problem; (*b*) careful evaluation of information required on proposal and claims forms to ensure that questions essential to fraud control are included, and the storage of this information in a manner which makes retrieval straightforward; (*c*) training of claims and underwriting staff in fraud detection and awareness; (*d*) development by specialist personnel, on a co-operative basis between insurers, of information exchanges not only about individual persistent fraudsters but also the collation of information on attempted frauds and the construction of sophisticated profiles of warning signs of doubtful claims (as has been achieved most notably by life assurers in respect of foreign deaths (see n. 3). However, despite the increasing pressures on insurers to improve the system of fraud control, they seem reluctant to take the bold, collective and public steps necessary (see Buckingham, 1986).

## REFERENCES

ALLAN, R. and FORDE, W. (1986). *The Auditor of Fraud*. London: Auditing Practices Committee.

BALDWIN, R. and MCCRUDDEN, C., eds. (1987). *Regulation and Public Law*. London: Weidenfeld & Nicolson.

BUCKINGHAM, L. (1986). 'Data Pool Urged to Cut Insurance Fraud'. *Lloyds List* (London), 7 Nov.

CATO-CARTER, E. F. (1972). *The Real Business*. London: Robins, Davies & Little (adjusters).

CATO-CARTER, E. F. (1984). *Order Out of Chaos: A History of the Loss Adjusting Profession*, vol. 1. London: Chartered Institute of Loss Adjusters.

CILA—CHARTERED INSTITUTE OF LOSS ADJUSTERS (1985). *Arson and Fraud: 7th Annual Congress Report*. London: CILA.

CLARKE, M. J. (1986). *Regulating the City*. Milton Keynes: Open University Press.

COOPER, B. (1987). 'The Claims Manager's Problem' (mimeo). M & G Claims Symposium, Cheltenham.

CROCKER, W. (1967). *Far from Humdrum*. London: Hutchinson.

---

[32] A reinforcement of this point was nicely put by Sir Dennis Marshall (CILA, 1985, p. 26): 'If I am right in my belief that insurers are incurring increasing criticism from the media and the public when they are forced to resort to policy avoidances to avoid payment of claims which they believe to be dishonest and fraudulent, then it does seem to me that, unattractive from the point of view of competition it may be, there is a case for making those inquiries which lead to the refusal to insure undesirable and uninsurable risks, rather than accept the proposal and wait until the loss has occurred before relying upon a repudiation of the policy itself as a defence.'

One source said that in the early 1980s a company refused to pay claims on the basis of documentary evidence alone and required a personal interview on the basis of a questionnaire, with the consequence of an immediate withdrawal of 10 per cent of claims and a subsequent further decline in their number.

MICHAEL CLARKE

DEARDEN, H. (1986). *The Fire Raisers*. London: Ellis & Buckle (adjusters).

DULWICH, R. H. (1984). 'Fraudulent Claims'. *Chartered Insurance Institute Journal*, 3 Aug.

ELLEN, E. and CAMPBELL, D. (1981). *International Maritime Fraud*. London: Sweet & Maxwell.

ENTWHISTLE, T. B. (1970). 'Fraud and Arson': *Post Magazine and Insurance Monitor* (London), 29 Jan.

GASELEE, J. (1985). 'Fiddling the Motor Insurance'. *Insurance Age* (London), Dec.

GASELEE, J. (1986). 'Life and PHI Swindles: How to Curb Them'. *Post Magazine and Insurance Monitor* (London), 3 July.

GHEZZI, S. (1983). 'A Private Network of Social Control: Insurance Investigation Units'. *Social Problems* (Chicago), 3/5.

HAWKINS, K. and THOMAS, J. M., eds. (1984). *Enforcing Regulation*. Dordrecht: Kluwer-Nijhoff.

HODGSON, G. (1984). *Lloyds of London: As Reputation at Risk*. London: Allen Lane.

KELSON, C. (1975). 'Insurance Fraud Investigations', *Police Chief* (Los Angeles), May.

LEIGH, S. (1987). 'Non-disclosure: A Rising Tide?' (mimeo). M & G Death Claims Symposium, Cheltenham.

LEPPARD, D. (1988). 'Yard Will "Privatise" Fraud Investigations'. *Sunday Times*, 14 Feb., p. A4.

LEVI, M. (1987). *Regulating Fraud*. London: Tavistock.

LITTON, R. A. (1987). 'Crime and Insurance'. *Geneva Papers on Risk and Insurance*, 12 (July), 217 ff.

M & G—MERCANTILE AND GENERAL RE-INSURANCE (1987). *Unusual Death Claims*. Cheltenham: M & G Re.

ROCK, P. (1973). *Making People Pay*. London: Routledge & Kegan Paul.

SHARP, C. T. H. (1988). *A Profession Emerges: A History of Loss Adjusting*, Vol. 11. London: CILA.

TIEDEMANN, K. (1977). 'Phenomenology of Economic Crime'. In *Council of Europe Collected Studies in Criminological Research*, Vol. 15, *Criminological Aspects of Economic Crime*, p. 33. Strasbourg: Council of Europe.

WILSON, J. (1983). *Roger Cook's Checkpoint*. London: Ariel Books.

20

# Part IX
# Violent Crime

# [30]

# Psychological Frustration—
# A Comparison of
# Murderers and Their Brothers

### STUART PALMER

THE FIFTY-ONE men convicted of murder [in a study sample] apparently experienced psychological frustrations which were significantly greater in number and intensity than those experienced by their control brothers. These psychological frustrations arose largely from the following: physical defects which were, in effect, social stigmas; overly rigid, inconsistent, and emotional behavior by the parents, especially the mothers; severely frightening experiences of a definitely traumatic nature; and lack of acceptance, approval, and prestige in school and community. Battered by physical frustrations, the murderers were further beset by psychological frustrations which swelled their reservoirs of aggression to a point where that aggression eventually would, and finally did, burst its confines violently.

Ten of the murderers and two of the brothers were reported by the mothers to have been born with some extreme, severe, visible physical defect. None was born with more than one such defect. These defects were of the type that would be likely to cause others to react negatively, that might well cause the individual social embarrassment in childhood, adolescence, and adulthood.

The preponderance of such defects in the murderer group

*A Comparison of Murderers and Their Brothers*     135

as compared to the brothers is statistically significant at the five percent level (using a two-by-two table, $X^2 = 6.046$). One murderer was born with an abnormally large head; a second with a club foot; several with eyes which were, and appeared to other individuals to be, abnormal. Still another was born with a badly twisted neck, and so on.

The mother of a boy who at nineteen had killed a near stranger after an argument said to me, "I don't know that it had anything to do with the trouble he got in, but he was always so sensitive like about that neck. He thought people was looking at him. I used to tell him, 'Now, nobody's thinking anything about it,' but he had it in his head that they was always looking at him."

Visible physical defects of an extreme nature which occurred *after* birth were over three times as prevalent among the murderers as among the control brothers. Specifically, these defects were present in the cases of sixteen murderers and of five brothers. ($X^2 = 7.256$; $P < 0.01$; two-by-two table used.) No individual had more than one such defect.

These, too, were the kinds of defects which are likely to cause embarrassment in social situations: facial scars, crippled legs and arms, and the like. And that embarrassment can be considered a frustration factor.

Many murderers do not, of course, have any such defects. Still, it is important to note that among the fifty-one murderers there was a total of twenty-six instances of extreme visible physical defects (those which were present at birth combined with those which developed later); among the fifty-one control brothers there was a total of only seven defects. Thus, there were almost four times as many visible defects among the murderers as among the brothers, according to the mothers' statements. It may be that in the cases of the defects which occurred after birth the murderers tended, more often than the brothers, to become involved in situations, such as fights and accidents, where they were likely to be disfigured. Nevertheless, the defects, once existent, can reasonably be assumed to have led to psychological frustration.

Consider now the parents' actions toward the murderers and control brothers. To what extent did the parents cause psychological frustration in their sons? On the basis that a mother's behavior toward a newborn child is likely to be influenced by whether she wished to give birth, the mothers were asked, "How happy or unhappy were you when you found out that you were going to have the child?" The mothers' answers distributed themselves in the way shown in Table 1.

Of course, the mothers' answers may have been distorted. They may not have wanted to admit they had been unhappy about giving birth. Also, knowing now that one son was a murderer, they may have remembered their feelings prior to his birth as more negative than they were at the time. Nonetheless, fourteen of the mothers said they had been somewhat or very unhappy about the prospect of the murderers' births while only four said they had felt that way about the coming of the control brothers' births.

TABLE 1. *Mothers' Attitudes Toward Prospective Births of Murderers and Control Brothers*

|  | NUMBER OF MURDERERS | NUMBER OF BROTHERS |
| --- | --- | --- |
| Very Happy | 19 | 23 |
| Somewhat Happy | 7 | 11 |
| Neutral | 9 | 12 |
| Somewhat Unhappy | 9 | 2 |
| Very Unhappy | 5 | 2 |
| Don't Know | 2 | 1 |
| Total | 51 | 51 |

In interviewing the mothers, I had the distinct feeling that in actuality they had resented the births of the murderers more frequently than those of the brothers. In some cases, the mother was not married when she became pregnant; in others, she had too many children to handle as it was; in still other cases, she was not well and pregnancy was an added burden. Here are statements by two mothers which bear on this point:

"Well, the truth is, me and my husband wasn't married then—when I found out I was going to have him. He did the right thing, I'll say that. We was married right away. But I was afraid somebody's find out. It was a terrible time."

A trim little woman who had had ten children, one of whom had strangled to death a young girl, said: "I tell you, I had

*A Comparison of Murderers and Their Brothers*      137

eight of them running around. I was run ragged and I come to find out I was going to have another. This is too much, I said to myself, but what could I do? He came, all right. And what happened? The worst thing that could. He went out and—and—" The mother could not bring herself to say that her son had committed murder.

The mothers were also asked whether they were "getting along" with their husbands "very well," "moderately well," or "poorly" when their sons were born. The responses indicated no real differences in cases of the murderers as compared with the control brothers. Fifteen of the mothers said they were "getting along poorly" when the murderer sons were born, and fifteen said they were "getting along poorly" when the brothers were born.

As I have mentioned previously, the parents seldom separated or divorced. But in a fair number of cases they were clearly very unhappy living together. However, even where there was a wide difference in the ages of the murderers and control brothers, the parents were on the whole probably as unhappy during the infancies and childhoods of the brothers as of the murderers. The main point here is that in about a third of the families, very likely more, the murderers developed in an atmosphere of severe parental discord which was largely kept hidden from public view.

I would characterize the mothers' approach to the murderers, during infancy and childhood, as one of doing generally what appeared to be the accepted thing and of mixing with this a great deal of disguised aggression. According to this view, the mother's aggression could have caused frustration and hence aggression in the child. There appears to me to have been an interplay of aggression and frustration between mother and son with the father somewhat indirectly involved.

The interplay seems to have proceeded frequently in this fashion: the child had been frustrated physically through illness or other factors. This made the child aggressive, especially difficult. The mother, frustrated because of her low station in life and high expectations, directed her aggression against the difficult child, the murderer-to-be. He became all the more aggressive although not necessarily in obvious, direct ways. The mother, upset and exasperated, occasionally directed her aggression toward the father as well. He retaliated toward her and sometimes toward the child. To the father, the child seemed to be the root of the trouble.

According to the mothers, they tended rather equally to be solicitous of the murderers' and control brothers' needs during infancy. When asked the question, "What did you usually do when the child cried during his first year of life?" the mothers responded in this way:

|                                    | NUMBER OF MURDERERS | NUMBER OF BROTHERS |
|------------------------------------|:---:|:---:|
| Went to Child Immediately          | 27  | 27  |
| Waited 5 or 10 Minutes, Then Went to Child | 15  | 19  |
| Let Child "Cry It Out"             | 8   | 5   |
| Other                              | 1   | 0   |
| Total                              | 51  | 51  |

There was a definite tendency for the mothers to feel that they had pampered their children during the first year of life. But the possibility that they actually did so is not borne out by answers to other questions. For example, the schedules the mothers followed when caring for the infants were rather rigid, just slightly more so for the murderers than for their brothers.

The mothers were asked, "How rigid were you in trying to keep to a definite time schedule while caring for the child during the first two years of his life?" In a majority of cases of both murderers and control brothers, the mothers said that they were very rigid or moderately rigid:

|                    | NUMBER OF MURDERERS | NUMBER OF BROTHERS |
|--------------------|:---:|:---:|
| Very Rigid         | 18  | 15  |
| Moderately Rigid   | 13  | 12  |
| Moderately Flexible | 13  | 19  |
| Very Flexible      | 7   | 5   |
| Total              | 51  | 51  |

Again, when asked the more specific question, "During the first two months of the child's life, did you feed him on a fixed schedule, on demand, or on a combination of the two?" the mothers' replies indicated that they were slightly more rigid

*A Comparison of Murderers and Their Brothers*      139

with the murderers than the control brothers. Here is the distribution of responses:

|  | NUMBER OF MURDERERS | NUMBER OF BROTHERS |
|---|---|---|
| Fixed Schedule | 28 | 20 |
| Demand Schedule | 11 | 15 |
| Combination | 11 | 14 |
| Don't Know | 1 | 2 |
| Total | 51 | 51 |

Going by the mothers' reports, thirty of the murderers and twenty-five of the control brothers were bottle-fed during the first two months of life. Conversely, seventeen of the murderers and twenty-four of the brothers were breast-fed. The remaining four murderers and two brothers were both breast- and bottle-fed. Bottle-feeding is probably less rewarding than breast-feeding. But, the differences in numbers of murderers and brothers so fed are not large enough to warrant attaching any extreme importance to them. However, I was struck by the fact that many of the mothers appeared to have guilt feelings about not having breast-fed their children—murderers and control brothers alike:

"I tried but I couldn't. I should of, I guess. But it wouldn't work and I had to give it up."

"The milk was—what you call sour. I had to use the bottle. What else could I do?"

I asked this mother, "Do you think feeding a baby from the breast is better than from the bottle?"

"That's what I'm saying. But like I told you. The milk was what you call sour. I *had* to use the bottle."

There were no real differences in the ages of the murderers and the control brothers when the mothers started weaning from the breast or bottle. Early weaning can be considered a frustrating experience, and I had thought the murderers might have been weaned relatively early but this was not the case. Six to eleven months was the most common time for weaning both murderers and brothers from the breast. And twelve to seventeen months was the most common time for weaning murderers and brothers from the bottle.

Abrupt weaning, as distinguished from early weaning, can also be considered frustrating for the child. Therefore, this matter was investigated. Here, again, there were no real differences between murderers and control brothers. Of the twenty-one murderers and twenty-six brothers weaned from the breast, a decided majority of each were weaned in a month or less. Of the forty-one murderers and thirty-five brothers weaned from the bottle, a majority of each were weaned completely in three months or less, usually less.

While no important differences were found between murderers and brothers with respect to weaning, there were significant differences as to ages at which the mothers began toilet training. On the average, the mothers said they started to toilet train the murderers at an earlier age than they did the brothers. In the cases of twenty-nine murderers and eighteen brothers, toilet training was begun before age one year. On the other hand, in the cases of twenty-one murderers and thirty-two brothers, this training was begun after age one. Information was not available for one murderer and one brother.

Why, on the average, did the mothers begin to toilet train the murderers earlier than the control brothers? I suspect that the mothers were more aggressive toward the infant murderers-to-be than toward the brothers. And the early toilet training was one indirect way in which the mothers could unconsciously vent their aggression while rationalizing their actions in the name of cleanliness. As previously mentioned, it appears that because of early illnesses the murderers were greater problems to the mothers than were the control brothers. And if the mothers unconsciously resented the potential murderers for being problems, the mothers' consequent actions only served to increase the magnitude of the frustration.

The average person finds it next to impossible to accept the idea that if toilet training is begun early and is forced, it is severely frustrating for the child. He either passes it off as of no consequence or half-jokingly says, in effect, "Sometimes you psychologists and sociologists talk as if you think everything a person does depends on toilet training."

Toilet training is neither of no consequence nor does it in itself determine completely any later behavioral form. But if a mother is not basically affectionate toward the child and if she forces him too fast in this regard, he will be greatly strained to meet her demands. He is likely in later life to be especially anxious about defecation matters and to have a vague but deep-seated feeling of deprivation.

The time required for the mothers to effect the toilet training of the murderers and brothers was also investigated. The differences between the two groups were not large. Nevertheless, the nature of the small differences found is of some importance. The time required to toilet train the murderers tended to be slightly extreme—shorter or longer than to train the brothers. Of the seventeen children trained in one month or less, ten were murderers. And of the fifteen children where training took longer than one year, ten were murderers. This is a pattern that will be evidenced with respect to certain other spheres of behavior: the training of the murderers and their actual behavior were more extreme, tended toward both ends of a given continuum to a greater degree than was the case with the control brothers.

Turning to the matter of sexual training by the mothers, it is clear that as a group the mothers were strongly repressed about sex. They attempted to strait-jacket their children, both the potential murderers and the control brothers, with respect to sex. They succeeded in making the children unduly curious about sex yet guilty when they attempted to satisfy that curiosity. And guilt feelings are frustrating.

The mothers were questioned concerning the extent to which they explained sexual matters to the murderers and brothers when they were about six years old. Forty-nine of the fifty-one mothers said they had explained nothing about sex to the children. The remaining two mothers had explained about sex to a small extent. While the mothers were usually not explicitly asked whether their husbands had explained sexual matters to the children, I gained the distinct impression that the husbands almost invariably did not do so. Discussion of sex was tabooed in the great majority of these families. Here are conversations with two mothers which bear on this point:

Interviewer: "When the boy was around six years old, did you ever explain to him about sex?"

Mother: "No. Well, maybe I should have. Or my husband, maybe he should have. But we just—we just didn't talk about things like that. Certainly not to the children. Why, my husband and me, we never talked about things like that between ourselves. We, or (brief laugh)—we had the children, of course. We were man and wife, I mean to say. But we never talked about it."

Another mother said, "No, it's not good to tell children those kinds of things. They find out enough, out on the streets, believe me, without being told at home."

"Do you think that sexual relationships outside of marriage are ever all right, under any circumstances?" I asked her.

"No, I don't. Don't believe in it. I never have."

"I don't mean as a general thing. I mean in rare cases where——"

"No cases. It's a sin before God. A sin before God."

"Do you mind my asking you these questions about sexual matters?"

"Well, no. You're supposed to be one of those psychiatrists or so-chiatrists, aren't you? Ask away. I'll say what I said, it's a sin before God."

"How did you feel about your boy getting in the trouble he did?" Her son, at eighteen, had raped and then beaten to death a middle-aged woman.

"How did I feel? I couldn't believe it. But he must of done it. He said he did."

"Do you have any idea why he did it?"

"Well, she was leading him on, from what I heard. But that wasn't all of it."

"What was the rest of it?"

"Bad blood, that was the rest of it. In spite of all I did to try to make him a good boy. It was his grandfather—his great-grandfather, his father's grandfather. He's got that blood in him. That's where it come from."

The mothers were all asked the question mentioned in the conversation above: "Do you think that sexual relationships outside of marriage are ever all right, under any circumstances?" Forty-eight of the mothers said that such relationships were never all right, were always bad. One said they were all right, not bad, under exceptional circumstances. The remaining two mothers were undecided, said they did not know. Given the fact that the forty-eight mothers who answered negatively might have been attempting to impress

*A Comparison of Murderers and Their Brothers*                143

the interviewers with their morality, their answers still have considerable importance in that they indicate a part of the face the mothers show the world with regard to sex.

The mothers were asked if they had ever made the murderers and control brothers stop sexual self-play and, if so, how old the sons were when they first stopped them. Twenty-nine of the mothers said they had never stopped the murderer sons, and thirty said they had never stopped the control brothers. Most of these mothers claimed that, to the best of their knowledge, these sons had never as children indulged in sexual self-play. Practically all children do engage in this self-play, but many of the mothers apparently had chosen to ignore the matter.

TABLE 2.    *Ages of Murderers and Control Brothers When Mothers First Stopped Sons' Sexual Self-Play*

|  | NUMBER OF MURDERERS | NUMBER OF BROTHERS |
|---|---|---|
| 3 Months or Less | 0 | 1 |
| Over 3 Months to 6 Months | 2 | 0 |
| Over 6 Months to 1 Year | 8 | 4 |
| Over 1 Year to 2 Years | 5 | 8 |
| Over 2 Years to 3 Years | 2 | 5 |
| Over 3 Years to 4 Years | 1 | 1 |
| Over 4 Years | 2 | 1 |
| Age Unknown | 2 | 1 |
| Doesn't Apply[a] | 29 | 30 |
| Total | 51 | 51 |

[a] Mothers did not stop sons' self-play.

It is interesting to note in Table 2 that of the fifteen children whom the mothers said they stopped from engaging in sexual self-play during the first year of life, ten, or two-thirds, were murderers-to-be. On the other hand, of the twenty-five children whom the mothers said they stopped after the first year, fifteen, or three-fifths, were control brothers.

The mothers were also asked to what degree, if any, they were emotionally upset the first time they observed the murderers and control brothers in sexual self-play, regardless of whether they stopped them. Again, there are no important differences when the mothers' reported reactions to the murderers and to the control brothers are compared. However, of the mothers who admitted that they had observed either the murderers or the brothers or both in sexual self-play, a great majority said that they were "very upset" rather than "somewhat upset" or "not at all upset."

With respect to their feelings about their sons' sexual self-play, here is what two fairly typical mothers had to say:

"I didn't know what to do. A little thing like that—playing with himself. Well, after all, I was afraid he might keep on doing it, when he grew up, if you understand me."

"I was so upset I had to lay down. I didn't know anything about those things, then. I came from people where those things were never mentioned. Never. I was just nineteen or twenty at the time. After I'd had the other kids I begin to see it was what they all do but I didn't know that, not then."

The mothers were questioned concerning the worst type of behavior manifested by the murderers and control brothers at age five. The answers distributed themselves as shown in the following table:

|                      | NUMBER OF MURDERERS | NUMBER OF BROTHERS |
|----------------------|:-------------------:|:------------------:|
| Sexual Self-play     | 15                  | 13                 |
| "Talking Back" to    |                     |                    |
| Mothers              | 4                   | 4                  |
| Fighting             | 2                   | 4                  |
| Stealing             | 1                   | 0                  |
| Lying                | 0                   | 1                  |
| No opinion           | 29                  | 29                 |
| Total                | 51                  | 51                 |

As is evident, in the cases of the mothers who answered the question, sexual self-play was far and away considered the worst type of act committed by either the murderers or the brothers. The mothers' most usual action when confronted by this sexual self-play was to emotionalize—cry or scream—and sometimes to hit the child as well.

The mothers were asked whether the murderers and control brothers had been sexually attacked during the first twelve years of life. The mothers said that to the best of their knowledge three of the fifty-one murderers and none of the

### A Comparison of Murderers and Their Brothers      145

brothers had been so attacked. The difference in numbers is too small to allow the drawing of any conclusions. But it is noteworthy that with respect to this and other types of situations mentioned in this chapter which might reasonably be presumed to give rise to frustration, the differences while small are almost always in such a direction that they indicate greater frustration for the murderer group than for the control group.

The question of how many murderers and brothers were as children severely frightened by other individuals, but not sexually attacked, was also investigated. The mothers said that during the first twelve years of life seven murderers and two brothers had been severely frightened once or more by some individual.

Further, the matter of whether the murderers and brothers were severely frightened by some natural event during their first twelve years was examined. According to the mothers, six of the fifty-one murderers and four of the fifty-one brothers were frightened in this way. These natural events were fires, lightning, falling rocks, and the like. Here, too, the difference is very small. But again it is in a direction which is indicative of greater frustration for the murderer group than for the control group.

We are not concerned in this chapter with the mothers' and fathers' training per se of the murderers and brothers. But we are concerned with the possible psychological frustration that the training might have caused in the children. Therefore, it will be well to consider the extents to which the mothers became angry at the children, cried, isolated themselves from the children, and were inconsistent in carrying out expected punishments and rewards. Table 3 presents this information as provided by the mothers.

With the exception of the responses for "no promised reward," the "very often" frequency occurs more among the murderers than among the control brothers. If one takes all five types of responses and summates the number of cases of murderers where the response was "very often," a total of thirty-four is obtained. And if one does the same for the control brothers, a total of eighteen is obtained. Thus, these five types of responses were directed "very often" at almost twice as many murderers as control brothers. And these

TABLE 3.  *Frequency of Selected Responses by Mothers Toward Murderers and Control Brothers During First 5 Years of Life*[a]

|  | ANGER | | CRIED | | ISOLATED SELF | |
| --- | --- | --- | --- | --- | --- | --- |
|  | M | B | M | B | M | B |
| Very Often | 12 | 9 | 10 | 3 | 5 | 1 |
| Occasionally | 18 | 25 | 8 | 18 | 9 | 7 |
| Seldom | 20 | 17 | 33 | 30 | 37 | 43 |
| Unknown | 1 | 0 | 0 | 0 | 0 | 0 |
| Total | 51 | 51 | 51 | 51 | 51 | 51 |

|  | NO THREATENED PUNISHMENT[b] | | NO PROMISED REWARD[b] | |
| --- | --- | --- | --- | --- |
|  | M | B | M | B |
| Very Often | 6 | 4 | 1 | 1 |
| Occasionally | 21 | 21 | 18 | 17 |
| Seldom | 24 | 26 | 31 | 33 |
| Unknown | 0 | 0 | 1 | 0 |
| Total | 51 | 51 | 51 | 51 |

[a] "M" designates number of cases of murderers. "B" designates number of cases of control brothers.
[b] Mothers threatened punishment, or promised reward, and then did not carry out the threat or promise.

types of responses I consider to be ones which will cause anxiety and frustration in a child.

The mothers' responses of "cried" and "isolated self" were "very often" directed at the murderers in an especially larger number of cases than they were at the brothers. Crying and self-isolation when young children do things of which the mothers disapprove are, I am convinced, very frustrating for the children. In almost any family, the mother is the symbol of the sources of life to the child. Even if she has not been a particularly attentive mother, she has nevertheless very likely supplied the children with food, warmth, clean or at least dry clothes, and some affection.

A professional thief, who had killed during a holdup but who was not a professional murderer, told me, "Whenever I did anything wrong as a kid, my mother would get very upset and cry. She'd cry and cry and she'd go to her room and lock the door but I could still hear her crying. It made me feel awful. I knew I'd done something but a lot of the time I didn't know what and she wouldn't tell me. She'd just cry."

## A Comparison of Murderers and Their Brothers          147

He was a very intelligent man with a great deal of personal insight. "When I was fifteen or sixteen, I began running around, getting in a lot of trouble. I'm not blaming mother for anything, but sometimes I honestly think I did some of those things just to hurt her for having hurt me. I knew if she found out what I was doing she'd cry, but I didn't care any more if she did."

Another man serving a life sentence for murder told me, "Anything we kids did wrong, she'd go in her room and stay there for three or four hours. Then when she'd come out she wouldn't talk to us for maybe half a day. And it happened more with me than the other kids. I always seemed to be getting in more trouble—at least doing things my mother didn't like. The thing was, she didn't seem to tell us beforehand what we shouldn't do."

Why did the mothers tend to cry and isolate themselves more with respect to the murderers than the control brothers? First, I interpret crying and isolation of this nature to have been veiled acts of aggression on the mothers' parts. Unconsciously, at least, they knew these actions would hurt the children. Second, and as hypothesized earlier, the mothers were perhaps more prone to hurt the murderers than the brothers because, generally, the murderers had been greater problems to them.

The mothers tended to be quite strict with their sons, although not in a consistent fashion. When asked the question, "Were you very strict, moderately strict, or not at all strict in training the child when he was about five years old?" the mothers replied as follows:

|                     | NUMBER OF MURDERERS | NUMBER OF BROTHERS |
|---------------------|:-------------------:|:------------------:|
| Very Strict         | 25                  | 21                 |
| Moderately Strict   | 18                  | 21                 |
| Not at All Strict   | 7                   | 9                  |
| Unknown             | 1                   | 0                  |
| Total               | 51                  | 51                 |

The mothers were also asked, "Do you think mothers of today pamper their children too much?" Thirty-one mothers said, in effect, "Yes, definitely." Seven answered, "No," and the remaining thirteen said they did not know.

At the same time, the mothers had, I felt, guilt feelings about their strictness toward their children, especially toward their murderer sons. Going on the assumption that the mothers' guilt feelings would be partially reflected by their responses, they were asked, "How often were you afraid the child would get hurt when he was about five years old?"

Regardless of how frequently the mothers *actually* were afraid their sons would be hurt when about age five, a distinctly larger number of mothers said they were frequently afraid in the cases of the murderers than in the cases of the control brothers. Twenty-four mothers responded that they were "almost always" or "usually" afraid with respect to the murderers, while only eleven said this with respect to the control brothers.

Learning the use of language is a behavioral area in which the murderers experienced a considerable amount of frustration. The mothers reported that, as a group, the murderers first spoke intelligible words at a later age than the control brothers:

| AGE IN MONTHS | NUMBER OF MURDERERS | NUMBER OF BROTHERS |
|---|---|---|
| Under 18 | 15 | 27 |
| 18–29[a] | 34 | 22 |
| 30 or Over[a] | 1 | 1 |
| Never[a] | 1 | 1 |
| Total | 51 | 51 |
| | $X^2 = 5.828$ | $P < 0.05$ |

[a] Combined for $X^2$ calculation.

There is, then, a significant difference, as reported by the mothers, in the ages at which the two groups began to speak. How does one explain this? I think the most likely explanation is that the murderers, having experienced more frustration than the control brothers during the first year of life, were somewhat blocked by anxiety. At the same time, slowness in learning to speak is, I think, frustrating in itself. The child cannot communicate his needs as well without language as with it. Therefore, his needs tend, to some extent, to go unsatisfied. Further, parents are apt to be upset with a child

*A Comparison of Murderers and Their Brothers*          149

who is slow in learning to speak and this causes him added frustration.

This phenomenon has arisen at least implicitly in preceding pages: frustration tends to beget frustration. An individual who has been severely frustrated is unduly anxious and therefore cannot learn as efficiently as he otherwise would. This makes those around him impatient, exasperated with him. They react negatively toward him, thereby increasing his frustration. He responds by some manner of aggression. In the case of slow speech learning by the murderers, I think there was this added element of aggression. The child senses that the parents want him to speak and he aggresses toward them, frustrates them, by slow learning.

This process of frustration begetting frustration seems to be an especially dominant theme in the development of the murderers. It can even grow to the point where the individual seeks frustration. He has learned to expect it and in a certain sense he feels comfortable with it.

About one-fifth of the murderers and of the control brothers, ten murderers and eleven brothers, learned some other language before they learned English. Eventually they all learned English with the exception of one murderer and one brother who were mutes. Learning one language, then learning another which is to become the major tongue, can be construed as frustrating for young children. This is not to say that learning English first, in our society, then learning at ten or eleven a foreign language, to be used as a secondary tongue, is anxiety provoking. But to learn a foreign language at home, then to enter the first grade and be forced to learn English quickly, is frustrating. And that is what most of the ten murderers and eleven brothers were forced to do. They were expected to speak English at school, the parent tongue at home. Conflict, anxiety, and frustration can be assumed to have been the result. Further, the interviews indicated that they experienced embarrassment in school because of their lack of facility with English. Of course, this embarrassment was as true for the control brothers as a group as for the murderers. Nevertheless, it is one more indication of the climate of frustration in which some of the murderers developed.

Learning to read is another important area of language

behavior. Here is the way the murderers and control brothers were distributed with respect to the general difficulty they had in learning to read, as judged by the mothers:

|  | NUMBER OF MURDERERS | NUMBER OF BROTHERS |
|---|---|---|
| Almost No Difficulty | 24 | 34 |
| Moderate Difficulty | 16 | 14 |
| Great Difficulty[a] | 9 | 2 |
| Never Learned[a] | 2 | 1 |
| Total | 51 | 51 |

$$X^2 = 6.430 \qquad P < 0.05$$

[a] Combined for $X^2$ calculation.

To a significant degree, the mothers reported that the murderer group had greater difficulty learning to read than did the control group. Here is another foundation stone for the theses that murderers have experienced more frustration than nonmurderers and that frustration begets frustration. The murderers were generally highly frustrated when they first went to school. Their resultant aggression brought more frustration upon them. Probably, their anxiety and repressed aggression tended to retard their reading. And this brought on still further frustration.

By and large, the murderers did poorly in school, did not like it, and left as soon as they could, thus virtually precluding any possibility of entering a prestigeful, satisfying occupation. Quite clearly, judging by the mothers' responses to questioning, a distinctly larger proportion of the murderers than of the control brothers disliked grammar school. Of the murderers, twenty-three were reported to have liked the first four years of grammar school, and twenty-three were said to have disliked school during that period. (Five were considered to have been neutral.) On the other hand, the mothers reported that, of the control brothers, thirty-seven liked school while only five did not. (Nine were neutral.) These differences are statistically significant at the one percent level.

A number of behavioral forms which are driven by anxiety and frustration were investigated as to whether they were manifested by the murderers and control brothers during their preadult years. They would serve, as it were, as partial indices of the degree of frustration experienced by the individuals in the two groups. Examples of the behavioral forms

*A Comparison of Murderers and Their Brothers*          151

are phobias, compulsions, stuttering, and the like. Naturally, in questioning the mothers, it was made clear in everyday terms what is, for example, the actual nature of a compulsion.

Table 4 indicates that seven of these behavioral forms— phobias, compulsions, obsessions, bedwetting, stuttering, sleep-walking, nightmares—were said by the mothers to have

TABLE 4.  *Presence or Absence of Selected Behavioral Forms Indicative of Frustration During the Preadult Years of Murderers and Control Brothers*[a]

|  | PHOBIAS | | COMPULSIONS | | OBSESSIONS | | PERSISTENT BEDWETTING | |
|---|---|---|---|---|---|---|---|---|
|  | P | A | P | A | P | A | P | A |
| Murderers | 17 | 34 | 13 | 38 | 4 | 47 | 18 | 33 |
| Brothers | 2 | 49 | 1 | 50 | 0 | 51 | 3 | 48 |
|  | $X^2 = 14.552$ | | $X^2 = 11.922$ | | | | $X^2 = 13.492$ | |
|  | $P < 0.01$ | | $P < 0.01$ | | | | $P < 0.01$ | |

|  | STUTTERING | | PERSISTENT SLEEPWALKING | | PERSISTENT NIGHTMARES | |
|---|---|---|---|---|---|---|
|  | P | A | P | A | P | A |
| Murderers | 10 | 41 | 8 | 43 | 11 | 40 |
| Brothers | 5 | 46 | 2 | 49 | 3 | 48 |
|  | $X^2 = 1.954$ | | $X^2 = 3.992$ | | $X^2 = 5.300$ | |
|  | $P > 0.05$ | | $P < 0.05$ | | $P < 0.05$ | |

[a] "P" indicates presence of behavioral form.
"A" indicates absence of behavioral form.

been manifested by a greater number of murderers than of brothers during the preadult years. With respect to presence and absence of five of these forms of behavior—all except obsessions and stuttering—the differences between the murderer and control brother groups were significant at the one or five percent levels.

Phobias, compulsions, and obsessions have much in common. Not only are they indicative of earlier frustration per se, but also there is generally a guilt component in each of the three behavioral forms. Further, they are ways of trying to handle repressed aggression. It is striking that the mothers reported thirty-four instances of phobias, compulsions, and obsessions for the murderer group and only three instances for the control brother group. It is highly unlikely that this vast difference can be accounted for on the basis that the mothers gave distorted answers to questioning.

A considerably larger number of murderers than brothers were said to have been persistent bedwetters or stutterers. These are two types of behavior that not only imply earlier frustration but that when manifested are fairly likely to beget frustration. Both bedwetting and stuttering are socially embarrassing in our society.

Most of the cases of stuttering occurred around ages six or seven and were severe for a year or two. In most instances the stuttering was almost unnoticeable as the children moved into adolescence. However, the stuttering pattern tended to return during adulthood, the mothers said, when the sons were in stress situations. And this was especially true of the murderers.

During the interviews with the mothers, questions were asked concerning how frequently the murderers and control brothers had become emotionally upset at about age five, excluding anger and temper tantrums. To a highly significant extent, the murderers as a group became upset more frequently than did the brothers. Twenty of the murderers were said to have become emotionally upset once a week or more, but none of the brothers were said to have done so this frequently. Here is another piece of evidence to bolster the view that because of early frustration the murderers were as children less emotionally stable than the control brothers.

A further point: according to the mothers, the murderers were, as a group, more solitary in childhood than were the brothers. When asked whether their sons spent a majority of their playing time alone or with other individuals at about age five, the mothers reported as follows:

| | NUMBER OF MURDERERS | NUMBER OF BROTHERS |
|---|---|---|
| Alone | 12 | 2 |
| With Other Individuals | 38 | 48 |
| Unknown[a] | 1 | 1 |
| Total | 51 | 51 |
| | $X^2 = 8.304$ | $P < 0.01$ |

[a] Not included in $X^2$ calculation.

The whole lower-class situation in which most of the murderers were immersed by circumstances of birth was a broad

## A Comparison of Murderers and Their Brothers            153

frustration factor in itself. True, it was equally so for the control brothers. But they had generally not been subjected to the extreme amounts of other frustrations that the murderers had. It is the totality of frustration we are concerned with here. To use an analogy: when you are carrying a hundred pounds on your back for a long distance, the addition of an extra ten pounds seems like a much much greater extra burden than does the same ten pounds if you have been carrying only twenty.

It is true that some individuals seem content with lower-class status and probably do not experience anxiety because of it. By and large, however, the murderers' and control brothers' parents were, in my judgment, people dissatisfied with their lot in the prestige hierarchy of the society, people with strong drives to rise in the social class system. These drives were usually frustrated but they were there. The murderers, and probably the control brothers, had similarly strong upward mobility strivings which were thwarted. The overwhelming majority of murderers with whom I have talked or whose biographies I have read have seemed to me extremely sensitive about their lack of social class prestige.

Related to this is how the murderers and control brothers felt about their occupations. The mothers were asked to judge how well the murderers liked their work just prior to the murders. In the cases of the brothers, the mothers were asked how well they liked their work when they were at ages equivalent to the murderers' ages just prior to the murders. Here are the mothers' judgments concerning how well their sons liked their work:

| | NUMBER OF MURDERERS | NUMBER OF BROTHERS |
|---|---|---|
| Very Much[a] | 10 | 21 |
| Considerably[a] | 4 | 12 |
| Somewhat[b] | 7 | 6 |
| Not at All[b] | 14 | 1 |
| Unknown[c] | 5 | 2 |
| Doesn't Apply[c] | 11 | 9 |
| Total | 51 | 51 |

$$X^2 = 19.006 \qquad P < 0.01$$

[a] Combined for $X^2$ calculation.
[b] Combined for $X^2$ calculation.
[c] Not included in $X^2$ calculation.

There was, then, a tremendous difference in how well the two groups liked their work, if one accepts the mothers' judgments as being valid. It is reasonable to assume that those who do not like their work are frustrated by it and by their general social situation. Again and again I found murderers who said they had had absolutely no interest in the occupation in which they were engaged just before they committed murder.

An Index of Psychological Frustration was constructed in much the same fashion as was the Index of Physical Frustration. One point was given the individual for the known presence in his preadult experience of each instance of fifteen selected types of psychological frustration. For example, one point was allotted for each trauma due to natural events or other individuals which occurred before the age of twelve years, physical beatings excluded. The minimum possible score on this index was zero while there was no limit as to the maximum.

The scores for the murderer group were significantly greater than for the control brother group. Ten murderers had scores of two or less while twenty-eight brothers had these scores. On the other hand, the scores of nineteen murderers were six or higher, but only three brothers had scores at that level. The mean score for murderers was 4.7; for the brothers the mean score was 2.5.

The scores were also analyzed with respect to the differences within pairs of murderers and control brothers. It was found that in thirty-four of the fifty-one pairs the murderers had higher scores than the brothers. In ten pairs, the scores were equal. And in the remaining seven pairs, the brothers had higher scores than the murderers; the difference here was usually one point.

The Index of Physical Frustration and the Index of Psychological Frustration were combined to provide an Index of General Frustration. The score for a given individual on this Index of General Frustration was found simply by totaling his scores on the physical frustration and on the psychological frustration indices. Here, seventeen murderers had scores of five or less on the Index of General Frustration as compared to thirty-six control brothers. At the other extreme, nineteen

## A Comparison of Murderers and Their Brothers          155

murderers had scores of eleven or higher while not one of the brothers had a score above ten. To the extent that the mothers' responses reflected the facts, here is great weight in favor of considering frustration as a possible major influence behind murder.

The mean score for the murderers was 9.24; for the brothers this score was 4.20. Comparing scores within pairs of murderers and control brothers, it was found that in forty-two pairs the murderer had a higher score than his brother. In five pairs the scores were equal. And in four pairs the brother's score was greater than the murderer's. That is to say, 82 per cent of the time, forty-two out of fifty-one, the scores agreed with the basic idea stated in the central hypothesis of the study: that the preadult frustration of murderers is greater than the preadult frustration of nonmurderers.

# [31]

# Robbers as Decision-Makers

FLOYD FEENEY

## Editors' Note

The interviews with 113 Californian robbers that form the basis of Floyd Feeney's chapter were undertaken in 1971 and 1972 as part of a wider study of robbery. The material has been reanalyzed here to explore the rational components of robbery, which Feeney finds to be substantial, provided that a broad definition of rationality is employed. Feeney's results, backed up by a rich store of verbatim quotes, offer a number of unanticipated insights into criminal decision making: for example, that over half the robbers claimed to do no planning, that robberies can be quite opportunistic and casual affairs (passengers waiting outside a store in the robber's car were sometimes unaware of what he was doing inside), and that some robbers were strangely reluctant to consider committing burglary. It is surprising that robbery, which is so seriously regarded by society, should frequently be embarked upon with such apparent lack of deliberation on the part of the offender, and that the more experienced the robber the less he seems to plan the offense or to worry about being caught. Although this lack of explicit planning may be more apparent than real (as Feeney remarks, experience may well provide a substitute), the lack of fear seems well founded: The sample included one individual who, in spite of having committed over 1,000 robberies by the age of 26, had been convicted only once. Such examples graphically illustrate the difficulties of deterrence or prevention, although Feeney's final paragraph contains the tantalizing suggestion that devices that make money difficult to obtain, such as no-cash systems on buses, may be more effective in preventing robberies than measures such as TV surveillance, which rely on deterrence. Finally, the fact that a number of differences were found between those who robbed commercial enterprises and those whose targets were individuals suggests, as with burglary, the importance of adopting an even more crime-specific focus in relation to types of robberies.

Because of its suddenness and its potential for serious injury or death, robbery is one of the most feared of all crimes. It is the most frequent stranger-to-stranger crime involving violence, and its rapid increase over the past several decades has been a major corrosive force in contemporary urban life in the United States and to a lesser extent in Britain and Europe. The prevention and control of robbery is consequently an important item on the social agenda on both sides of the Atlantic.

As a legal term, *robbery* covers a fairly broad spectrum of criminal activity, from the Great Train Robbery worth millions of pounds to schoolyard bullies taking lunch money from their classmates—a kind of robbery that is often not reported. As a practical matter most robberies dealt with by the police and the courts fall into a narrower range largely consisting of two categories: muggings and other attacks on individuals on the street and holdups of commercial establishments. This chapter addresses the question whether it is useful in developing policies for the control of robbery to focus on how decisions about robbery are made by the robbers themselves. The conclusion is that this is a useful perspective for addressing the robbery problem, although obviously not the only approach that may be fruitful.

This chapter is based primarily on interviews with 113 northern California offenders charged with robbery and convicted of robbery or an offense related to robbery. Although this means that the offense of conviction is in some instances not a robbery, this sample was thought to be more representative of persons doing robberies than one based wholly on persons convicted of robbery itself. The sample was stratified to include both adults and juveniles, blacks and whites, offenders involved in commercial and in individual robberies, and offenders given both long prison sentences and shorter local sentences. As robbery is largely a male enterprise, only males were interviewed. The interviews were conducted in 1971 and 1972 (Weir, 1973) and were reanalyzed for the purpose of this chapter. The discussion is based on unweighted figures. Northern California had a very high robbery rate during the period of the interviews.

Like other human beings, individuals who commit robberies make many decisions. For all but the most prolific robbers, most of these decisions concern everyday life and have nothing to do with robbery. Of those that do involve robbery, some are strategic, career-type decisions such as the decision to get involved in crime, to commit a first robbery, to continue robbing, or to desist. Others are much more tactical, such as how to choose a victim, whether to use a gun, and how to escape. It is not possible to discuss all these different kinds of decisions here, but an attempt will be made to cover some of the more important decisions and to give the flavor of the decision-making process. Some of the argument that follows is based on solid empirical evidence. Where necessary, however, this has been supplemented with impressions and fragmentary evidence.

Logically the decision to rob is a very complex matter involving the whole past of the individual considering the crime as well as that person's present situation. As robbery is generally thought of as an economic crime, it might be expected that the typical individual considering a robbery goes through some kind of mental calculus to determine whether he has a need for money and what the legitimate opportunities for getting money are—whether through work or from family or friends. If these calculations indicate a need that cannot be satisfied through legitimate means, consideration might then be given to committing a crime to acquire the money, and if so, to which crime is the most suitable. Presumably in making this calculation the individual considers the relative financial gains that might be expected from the various kinds of crimes possible and the relative risks of getting caught or otherwise harmed. Presumably also the individual considers what actions he will be required to perform in committing the crime and how he feels about undertaking these actions.

Because robbery is a serious crime with severe penalties and significant possibilities for getting hurt, individuals considering robbery might be expected to pay particular attention to these matters, and those deciding to commit the crime might be expected to give careful thought to the choice of a target and the development of a plan for reducing the chances of apprehension. It is surprising therefore to find that the northern California robbers studied do not fit this description very well. Fewer than 60% stated money as the primary aim of their robbery, over half said they did no planning at all, and over 60% said that before the robbery they had not even thought about being caught.

## The Decision to Rob

The decision to rob begins with some kind of desire. As previously indicated, fewer than 60% of the robbers said they wanted money. Twenty-four percent wanted something other than money, and 19% were involved in what might be called "accidental robberies" burglaries, fights, or other acts that were not originally intended to involve both theft and violence but which came to do so as events unfolded, as shown in Table 4.1.

Nearly a third of those seeking money wanted it for drugs, and almost as many wanted specific things such as clothes or a car. The remainder seeking money needed food or shelter or just had a general desire for money. Most of those who wanted drugs were adult heroin addicts. Some said that their habits required only a few dollars a day, whereas others said they needed $100 a day or more. Many stressed the difficulty of their situations:

But see, I would have been able to support my family if I wouldn't have had to pay for the heroin, so it didn't matter which way you split the money—whether it went

TABLE 4.1 Motivations for committing robbery (expressed in percent)[a]

| Motivation | Adults (n = 82) | Juveniles (n = 31) | All Offenders (n = 113) |
|---|---|---|---|
| Money | (64) | (35) | (57) |
| For drugs | 22 | 3 | 17 |
| For food and shelter | 11 | 0 | 8 |
| For other specific things | 18 | 10 | 16 |
| General desire for money | 13 | 23 | 16 |
| Other than money | (22) | (32) | (24) |
| For excitement, to relieve boredom or general unhappiness | 6 | 6 | 6 |
| Out of anger, upset | 5 | 10 | 6 |
| To impress or help out friends, to prove subject could do it | 4 | 13 | 6 |
| Not sure why, drunk or on drugs at time | 7 | 3 | 6 |
| Not really a robber | (13) | (32) | (19) |
| Recover money owed | 7 | 0 | 5 |
| Interrupted burglary | 0 | 13 | 4 |
| Fight turned into a robbery | 0 | 13 | 4 |
| Partner started a robbery without prior knowledge | 6 | 6 | 6 |
| Total | 100 | 100 | 100 |

[a]Percentages may not add to 100 because of rounding.

for the heroin or whether it went to the family. I mean it was still for the heroin, because if it wasn't for the heroin I wouldn't have had debts to make money for. Well, I had a family to take care of and the heroin got to the point that I didn't keep food in the refrigerator and the rent paid and bills paid, phone bill, electric bill, and it was hard to handle both things. and that's when I got into robberies.

Many of those who wanted specific things had current problems or financial needs. Several wanted money to leave the state to avoid arrest. Another was trying to pay traffic tickets to avoid being put in jail. Several juveniles had run away from a juvenile camp and wanted to leave town. Another adult had given money to his roommate for several months to pay the rent. The roommate used the money for other things, however, and suggested a robbery when the manager demanded the back rent. The offender was not earning enough at his job to cover the loss and reluctantly agreed.

Those who wanted food and shelter were generally not destitute, but their circumstances were often poor. One was in a very low-paying job:

I had a little $1.65 job working 20 hours a week, which wasn't very much, but I was still trying to make it on the legit side. but there just wasn't nothing open to me. I

4. Robbers as Decision-Makers                                        57

don't mind working, but $1.65 is kind of ridiculous.... [Robbing] was the only thing open to me at the time.

Others had no jobs but were looking for work. One adult with a good employment record was trying to find a new job. Finally he tried robbery—his first—when he ran out of other places to turn:

I needed the money for food. I tried welfare. I tried to borrow all the people that I could borrow from. Nobody else that I could borrow from. I didn't have any sources of money. I was just flat broke. I was getting it out of the savings and borrowing money from my mother, but I was getting kind of run out because she was starting to need more. I didn't even think about how much I wanted to get. I just felt that anything I got would help. It was better than nothing.

Another explained that he had a family:

There wasn't no food in the house, you know. Scrounging. And I'm forced into having to do something like this. I knew I was desperate. Besides, I was going out stealing anything I could get a hold of, get a little money to get some food.

Many in the group who said they just wanted money were not really able to explain why:

I have no idea why I did this. Well, I guess it was for money, but I didn't have no money problem, really, then. You know, everybody got a little money problem, but not big enough to go and rob somebody. I just can't get off into it. I don't really know why I did it.

The large number of juveniles who said they just wanted money were particularly vague. One apparently wanted to avoid the inconvenience of going to the bank:

For the money. I think that being involved I could use, at that time I could use the money. Yeah. I was accumulating money. Many reasons. 'Cause I got low on my pocket and I needed some pocket money. 'Cause I didn't want to go to the bank.

Over 40% of the offenders indicated that money was not the real purpose of the robbery. A quarter of these were involved in arguments or fights. One became angry at a racial slur:

I was mad at Mom. This old broad had made me mad. I seen the lady coming out of the store. I said, "Help," you know. And she said something, she mumbled something but all I know was "black." I hear that. So I got mad.

Another took a wig from a young woman who had rejected his attempt to pick her up. He did it:

Because I felt she was disrespecting me, kind of. I did it 'cause I seen fear in her. So I knew if I took this, she might start acting right ... to punish her the way she was talking.

A drunk juvenile got mad when the victim bumped into him:

It was just a sudden thing. I didn't really mean to do it. I didn't plan or nothing; it just happened. Just like that. Because he offered it to me. There's no reason. I just took it. I beat him up, you know. I was happy I beat him up. I was going to walk away and leave him there but he gave me $4. He thought I was going to cut his throat. He gave it to me. I wouldn't cut his throat. I didn't want to get busted for murder.

Some were just generally angry—one because his apartment had just been "ripped off." Another was mad at everyone:

I was mad and I had to do something to get it out of my system. I was mad at my cousins and my girlfriend. I was mad at my mom at the time.

Both also had other reasons, however:

I get a kick out of it really. Watch people's faces when they see you. They scared. I robbed because he gave me a smart answer. [Did several robberies that same evening.]

I don't know. It sounded easy and I guess we needed the money. We didn't really need it but we wanted to do something. Something to do. I don't know.

A surprising number of offenders got involved primarily because of partners. One, who had done no previous robberies, tried to help a friend and wound up in prison:

Because he asked me to help him out. He done a favor for me before. I didn't really want the money. It was an emotional thing more than anything else. Like the guy did me a hell of a favor.

Juveniles often cited the influence of friends. Several were just trying to prove they could do robberies. One had $265 in his pocket but robbed to show that he was not "scared." Another said, "People got to prove things to people. My partner didn't think I could do it."

Six percent of the offenders said their partners started something and they just went along:

Oh, in a simple sentence, I was either going to take part in the robbery then or. you know, stay there and be a part of it already as far as my mind was going then. It might have been an irrational thing because I was with the gentleman. and if the guy would have turned to me, well. I would have been caught, and blamed and made to give it up anyway. Well, we was. I felt a part of it. you know, when he [partner] committed the act, right then. I know it sounds silly, but that's the way my mind was going then.

Another sizable group of offenders simply wanted excitement or a change of some kind in their lives:

Just to cause some trouble. Well, we just wanted to try that, you know. Goof around, you know, have some fun—jack up somebody. . . . We thought we were really big and stuff like that.

I don't really have any fear of prisons or things like that. I always sort of felt like I was going back someday. [I was] disillusioned with myself . . . and with some of the compromises I was forced to make in life. And "capering" appealed to me.

I did it because I didn't care. I felt I didn't have anything to live for anyway so what the heck's the difference.

Another group did not think of themselves as trying to rob at all. They were attempting to recover money they claimed was either theirs or owed to them. Their motivation was to get what they thought belonged to them. A number had money with them or at home.

There was little difference between blacks and whites in the motivations expressed for committing their current robberies. They were about evenly divided between those saying that money was the primary reason and those saying that reasons other than money prompted the robberies.

Surprisingly, one fourth of the adult commercial robbers said that money was not their primary motivation. All of those who said they were disillusioned or depressed were commercial robbers, as were the adults who were primarily interested in excitement and a number of the adults who just went along with their partners.

## Planning

Most of the robbers appear to have taken a highly casual approach to their crimes, as Table 4.2 indicates. Over half said they did no planning at all. Another third reported only minor planning such as finding a partner, thinking about where to leave a getaway car, or whether to use a weapon. This minor, low-level planning generally took place the same day as the robbery and frequently within a few hours of it. The longest lead time was generally that needed to get a weapon if one was not already available.

Fewer than 15% or so had any kind of planned approach. The largest number of these (9%) simply followed an existing pattern for their offenses. They did little new planning for their current offenses because they already had an approach that they liked. Fewer than 5% of the robbers planned in any detail. These robbers—all adults and all involved in commercial robberies—stole getaway cars, planned escape routes, detailed each partner's actions, evaluated contingencies, and observed the layout of prospective targets. As might be expected, commercial robberies were planned more often than those of individuals (60% versus 30%).

The robbers varied greatly in the number of robberies committed. Forty percent of those seeking to commit a robbery said they were committing their first robbery, 26% said they had committed 2 to 9 robberies, 24%

TABLE 4.2 Amount of planning undertaken before committing robbery (expressed in percent)[a]

| Type of Robber | None | Minor | A Lot | Pattern Only | Number (n) |
|---|---|---|---|---|---|
| First-time robbers | 56 | 44 | 0 | 0 | ( 36) |
| Committed 2–9 robberies | 46 | 33 | 0 | 21 | ( 24) |
| Committed 10–49 robberies | 27 | 50 | 9 | 14 | ( 22) |
| Committed 50 or more robberies | 56 | 11 | 11 | 22 | ( 9) |
| Accidental robbers | 100 | 0 | 0 | 0 | ( 21) |
| Overall | 55 | 33 | 3 | 9 | (112) |
| Overall minus accidental robbers | 46 | 40 | 3 | 11 | ( 91) |
| Adults | 52 | 33 | 4 | 11 | ( 82) |
| Juveniles | 63 | 32 | 0 | 3 | ( 30) |
| Individual | 69 | 25 | 0 | 5 | ( 59) |
| Commercial | 40 | 42 | 6 | 13 | ( 53) |
| Black | 62 | 29 | 0 | 10 | ( 63) |
| White | 47 | 39 | 6 | 8 | ( 49) |

[a]Percentages may not add to 100 due to rounding.

reported 10 to 49 robberies, and 10% reported 50 or more robberies. The repeat offenders had many fewer arrests than the number of robberies mentioned, and virtually all said the police did not know about the offenses for which they had not been arrested.

Generally the amount of planning increased with the number of robberies committed. None of those not fully intending a robbery did any planning, and none of the first-time robbers did any planning other than minor planning. Twenty-one percent of those who said they had committed 2 to 9 robberies did some planning beyond the minor variety, as compared with 23% of those who reported 10 to 49 robberies and 33% of those who reported 50 or more.

The impulsive, spur-of-the-moment nature of many of these robberies is well illustrated by two adult robbers who said they had passengers in their cars who had no idea that they planned a robbery. One passenger, who thought his friend was buying root beer and cigarettes, found out the hard way what had happened. A clerk chased his robber-friend out the door and fired a shotgun blast through the windshield of the passenger's car. Other robbers, who had no transportation of their own, persuaded friends to drive them to robbery sites. In most of these incidents the friends dropped the robbers off and drove on, wholly unaware of what was about to happen.

The generally casual approach to the crime is also illustrated by the approach of many offenders to the possibility of apprehension. Over 60% of the robbers said they had not even thought about getting caught before the robbery, as Table 4.3 shows. Another 17% said that they had thought about the possibility but did not believe it to be a problem. Only 21%

4. Robbers as Decision-Makers 61

TABLE 4.3 Extent to which robbers thought about being caught (expressed in percent)[a]

| Type of Robber | Not at All | Thought Not a Problem | Thought Was a Problem | Number (n) |
|---|---|---|---|---|
| First-time robbers | 56 | 14 | 31 | ( 36) |
| Committed 2–9 robberies | 61 | 22 | 17 | ( 23) |
| Committed 10–49 robberies | 55 | 25 | 20 | ( 20) |
| Committed 50 or more robberies | 67 | 11 | 22 | ( 9) |
| Accidental robbers | 80 | 10 | 10 | ( 20) |
| Overall | 62 | 17 | 21 | (108) |
| Adults | 63 | 13 | 24 | ( 79) |
| Juveniles | 59 | 28 | 14 | ( 29) |
| Individual | 74 | 11 | 16 | ( 57) |
| Commercial | 49 | 24 | 27 | ( 51) |
| Black | 68 | 13 | 18 | ( 60) |
| White | 54 | 21 | 25 | ( 48) |

[a]Percentages may not add to 100 due to rounding.

considered the possibility a risk to be concerned about. Some, who had given no thought to getting caught before the robbery began, said that they did think about it during or immediately after, particularly when things started going wrong or they became involved in hot-pursuit chases. A few began to worry only after they had already escaped. The greatest concern was shown by the first-time robbers. A quarter of this group thought the risk of apprehension was a problem.

## Decisions Concerning Means

Only 22% of the robbers indicated that they considered doing some crime other than robbery as a means of accomplishing their ends. Of those who did consider other crimes, burglary was the crime most frequently considered and shoplifing the second. A number of robbers were also selling drugs.

Most of those who considered burglary preferred robbery. Some did so because there was more money or no need to fence the loot, some because they thought robbery was safer or because they were fearful about going into houses. Others had been caught doing burglaries. One drug user had been shoplifting to support his habit but had moved to a town where the price of the drugs was twice what he had previously been paying. He decided to rob stores because the money was better and faster:

That's the reason I went into robbing the stores. [When I came here] my habit immediately jumped to $100 a day, just the difference in dope. The dope down there and the dope up here was that different. So I said, "I can't be running around boosting and beating people on the head and doing whatever, $100 a day, man. That's crazy."

Another had been dealing drugs but quit because the police were getting suspicious. A few preferred burglaries but decided on impulse to try robbing. Three incidents began as burglaries but turned into robberies when the victim returned home unexpectedly. One shoplifting turned into a robbery in much the same way.

Fewer than 10% of those whose objective was something other than money considered any other crime. Half, however, of the highly active robbers responsible for 50 or more robberies considered some other crime. Many of those who said they did not consider any other crime had a prior arrest record for burglary or shoplifting. Although the offenders did not say so, it is possible that this prior history affected their decision to rob.

No systematic information is available as to how many offenders considered satisfying their needs through legitimate opportunities. Many of the robbers mentioned their inability to find work as a factor in their general situation, however. None of the juveniles and only 20% of the adults who robbed for money had jobs at the time of the robbery, and most of these were in low-paying or part-time jobs. White adults who robbed for money were more often working than black adults. About half of those who robbed for something other than money were working.

One of the most important tactical choices that a robber must make is whom to rob. In line with the general lack of planning, the robbers' comments as to how they chose victims were much more matter of fact than expected. Over 20% said that they chose their victims because of convenience, 15% said that the victim appeared to have money, and another 15% chose their victims because a fast getaway was possible or the risk otherwise appeared to be low. Others gave mixed reasons or did not know why they had chosen. Some typical comments as to convenience:

Just where we happened to be, I guess. Don't know.

Nothing else open at 2:00 a.m. Had been there before.

We thought it would be the quickest, you know, it's a small donut shop.

Another important tactical choice concerns the location of the robbery. A nearby site obviously is the most convenient and familiar but also carries the highest risk of recognition. Despite this risk over a third of the robbers attacked victims in their own neighborhoods and over 70% in their own towns. Moreover, only half of the 30% who robbed in another town had gone there for the purpose of committing a robbery. Fifteen percent just happened to be in the other town. Some were visiting friends or relatives; others were passing through when they decided to do a robbery.

4. Robbers as Decision-Makers 63

Even when in another town for the purpose of committing a robbery, most apparently were there for reasons other than the idea that going out of town was the best approach. One was in a town 15 miles away simply because that was the only place where he could find a gas station open after midnight. Another was driving around looking for a motel to rob, and most of the motels in the area were outside the town where he lived. His partner had suggested one closer to home, but the robber rejected it as a target because he knew one of the employees. Of the adults who went to another town to rob, only one went to a town other than one contiguous to the town in which he lived. The one exception was a fairly well-planned robbery at a major resort which involved traveling several hundred miles.

One of the juveniles who was out of town for the purpose of doing a robbery wandered around for nearly 150 miles before selecting a robbery site; another drove 100 miles from home, and a third, 50. All had decided to do the robberies on the same day and apparently were attempting to ensure success by getting a long way from home.

## Decisions Concerning Weapons and Force

Eighty percent of the offenders used some kind of weapon: 53% used guns, 19% knives, and 8% other weapons. Most said they were trying to intimidate their victims and gain control over the situation rather than to harm or dominate the victims. Most felt that showing the weapon was enough to accomplish their purpose but were prepared to use force if the victim resisted or the police came by.

A surprising percentage had qualms about the use of the weapons they carried, however, and made deliberate decisions to forego some of their advantage. Nearly 30% of those who used a "gun" used a weapon that was either not loaded or that was simulated. Sixteen percent carried guns that were not loaded, 7% simulated weapons, and another 5% toy weapons. Most wanted to be sure that no one was hurt and explained that if they had no bullets in the guns, there was no chance that they could accidentally shoot anyone:

I didn't want a real gun because I might get jittery or something. Or if I would jam somebody that got out of line. I don't know. I wouldn't shoot nobody.

It couldn't have been loaded. I made sure of that. I just didn't want it loaded. I didn't want to hurt nobody. Just wanted to more or less scare them to give me some money.

Others used a simulated weapon or kept their weapon hidden in the belief that the penalty would be less severe if they were caught:

I felt that if I got caught it'd be a lot lighter on me if I didn't have a gun than if I did.

[Gun not displayed.] Yeah, we told her we had a weapon, but we didn't show it to her. She didn't believe it because we didn't show it to her. We didn't want to hurt anyone. Man, we'd been in jail for life if we'd got caught.

For a few offenders the decision was hasty and pragmatic rather than deliberate. One explained his unloaded gun: "Probably because I didn't have any bullets handy for it." Another simulated a gun because he didn't have one but wanted the money.

Ninety percent of the commercial robbers used a weapon of some kind, and 80% used a gun. Of those who used a gun, nearly 80% used a loaded gun. Seventy percent of those who robbed individuals also carried weapons. Only a third carried guns, however, and only half of those used a loaded gun.

Eight percent of the offenders used weapons other than a gun or a knife: a screwdriver, a lug wrench, a metal bar, a pool cue, a shovel and a board, some dog spray, or a broken beer bottle. In almost every instance the weapon used was something handy when the need arose rather than an instrument carried by careful design.

Sixty percent of those who did not use weapons failed to do so because the robbery itself was an impulsive act and no weapon was readily available. Whether they would have chosen to use a weapon if they had taken more time is not known.

A few offenders deliberately chose not to use a weapon for moral or legal reasons:

I couldn't see using a weapon on a lady. I figured I could catch her off guard and grab her purse and run.

I tried to make it nonviolent. I figured if I had to go [was caught], I would go on as less as I could.

One third of the robbers or their partners hurt someone during the robbery for which they were convicted. One additional adult reported that he had shot at a victim but missed. Robbers of individuals hurt their victims more than twice as often as the commercial robbers. Juvenile offenders harmed their victims more often than did adult offenders.

Most of the offenders who hurt victims said they did so because the victims resisted. Most chose to hit their victims with their fists or a weapon rather than to shoot or cut the victim. A sixth of those encountering resistance did, however, take drastic action: shooting, cutting, or spraying liquid into the eyes of their victims.

Around 15% of the robbers used physical force right at the outset, usually to establish initial control over the situation and usually striking without warning. One said he attacked in this way because the victim "was big." Another said it was his first robbery and that he wasn't sure what to do. He got a tire jack out of the truck, and:

See, first I think, "Well, if I hit him in the head that might kill him," so I hit him on the shoulder.

A juvenile used force to flee a burglary when the house occupant unexpectedly returned.

Around 10% of the offenders hurt their victims unintentionally. In one the victim ran into another room slamming the door behind him. When the robber chased after him, the door hit the robber's gun hand, causing the gun to fire. The bullet accidentally struck the victim. Another robber deliberately pointed his gun away from the victim and sought not to fire. The gun fired accidentally, however, and the bullet struck the victim after ricocheting off a wall. In other cases one victim suffered a heart attack, and another jumped out of a moving car. The robbers were concerned because they had neither intended nor foreseen the possibility of harm to the victims.

A quarter of those who hurt somebody did so in an attempt to recover money they had some claim to. A number of these arose out of drug-selling and gambling situations. Another victim had refused to "spot" a good location for a burglary after being paid to do so. Although these victims were certainly not asking to be robbed or hurt, they were certainly not totally innocent either. In every instance in which there was an attempt to recover money someone was hurt. Whether this was because the offenders were angry or because they met resistance is not clear.

Overall, the robbers did not generally appear to use gratuitous force. In some instances the force applied was greater than necessary, but generally the robbers did not appear to take any abstract pleasure in hurting people. Only one reported the use of force for its own sake. He said that after he had hit the victim with a lug wrench, his partner then hit the victim several more times. In commenting on why his partner had done this, he said, "Knowing him, he did it for meanness. He likes to hurt people."

## Learning and Decisions to Continue

The process by which some of those committing one or two robberies become highly active offenders committing 50 or more robberies is obviously important. For some offenders this progression seems to involve an escalation from shoplifting to burglary to robbery. Several of the highly active robbers studied, however, went much more directly into robbery and at a very early age.

The information in this study is too limited to be more than suggestive. There are strong hints, however, that the key transitions take place very early. Most of the first-time robbers indicated that they felt fear and apprehension as they approached their robberies. Most also tended to be very tentative about the robberies. Many reported that they would have considered leaving the money if the victim said he would lose his job or that he needed the money for rent. The more experienced robbers, however, were much more hardened. They were much less tentative and fearful, were unmoved by any difficulties that the crime might create for the victim, and tended to view victims as objects rather than persons. This harder kind of outlook was generally present after only a few robberies.

Seventy percent of the robbers said that they did not plan to commit another offense, 14% said that they might, and 4% said that they probably would, as Table 4.4 shows. The remaining 12% said that they did not know whether they would or not. Thus a total of 30% of the offenders were willing to give some overt indication that they might commit further robberies. These indications show greater realism and honesty than might have been expected.

TABLE 4.4 Will you do more robberies? (expressed in percent)[a]

| Answer | Adults (n = 81) | Juveniles (n = 30) | All Offenders (n = 111) |
|---|---|---|---|
| No | 68 | 80 | 71 |
| Maybe | 15 | 10 | 14 |
| Probably | 2 | 7 | 4 |
| Don't know | 15 | 3 | 12 |
| Total | 100 | 100 | 100 |

[a]Percentages may not add to 100 due to rounding.

## Rationality

Many of the decisions described are clearly rational in the sense used by Clarke and Cornish (1985). The individuals making these decisions had desires and needs that they chose to satisfy by committing robberies. Whether they were generalists who also committed other crimes or specialists who concentrated on robbery, they definitely had made robbery a deliberate part of their repertoire. Although these decisions would seem more rational if they involved more planning and more concern about the possibility of apprehension, the decisions nonetheless easily meet the standards of minimum rationality. There is clearly a thinking process involved. It is not Benthamite, but it is not much different from what people do in their everyday lives. This is particularly true for the decisions made by highly experienced robbers. Although these robbers frequently say that they undertake no planning, their experience is in a sense a substitute. Many of these robbers seem to feel that they can handle any situation that arises without specific planning.

Many of the decisions involved in robberies committed for reasons other than money also seem rational in this sense. Taking property from someone you are fighting with can be instrumental in accomplishing the aims of the fight. Going along with your friends or trying to recover property can also be instrumental acts. Some of the decisions described do not meet this kind of rationality test, however. Impulse decisions to commit serious crimes while loaded on drugs or alcohol cannot easily be called rational. Even these acts can be instrumental, however, in accomplishing goals that the actor—in his stupefied state—wants. Whether it is useful to treat these as rational for the purpose of developing theories of explanation, prevention, or control is not altogether clear. It is worth noting, however, that the criminal law often does so (LaFave and Scott, 1972).

## Implications for Research

Whatever the scientific validity of the rational actor model for the purposes of developing criminological theory, the model is clearly useful for many purposes. It provides an excellent framework for analyzing and understanding the decision-making process used by offenders and puts a healthy emphasis on gaining information from offenders and on dealing with specific crime problems.

The emphasis on obtaining information directly from offenders is particularly important. Detailed discussions with offenders about their crimes and their methods of thinking and operation have already had considerable payoff in recent years, in the fine work on burglary and crime prevention that has been done in Britain (Bennett and Wright, 1984; Clarke, 1983; Maguire, 1982; Walsh, 1980), in the contribution that self-report studies have made to the study of criminal careers, and in the excellent new work in this volume. This kind of work is in its infancy, however, and there is a great deal more to be learned.

The greatest payoffs are likely to come from increased attention to the strategic decisions made by offenders and the learning process involved—the decision to rob, to continue robbing, and to desist from robbing. Studies in the past decade (Chaiken and Chaiken, 1982; Farrington, 1979; Greenwood, 1982; Wolfgang et al., 1972) have taught us a great deal about the importance of criminal careers, but we need to understand more than just the number of offenses and the sequences involved. We need to understand the thought processes and the decisions as well. In this context "decision" should not be defined too narrowly. Often there may be no single "decision" to begin robbing, to continue robbing, or even to desist from robbing. Rather, the offender has a whole thought process and belief system that ultimately lead to some kind of conclusion.

There are also likely to be substantial payoffs to further gathering of information about tactical decisions and the factual contexts as seen by the robbers. If headway is ever to be made in dealing with crime, we must access the information that offenders have and use this for purposes of prevention and control. Robbers know a lot about themselves and about robberies that no one else knows. A foreign journalist who tried to project the course of future events in Berlin in 1932 by studying only voting returns and demographics, to the exclusion of *Mein Kampf* and the Nazi platform, would today be considered very foolish.

The emphasis on particular crime problems is also timely and helpful. There are no doubt purposes for which it is useful to aggregate thinking about the Brighton hotel bombing, pilfering from the neighborhood market, and marijuana sales. For most practical purposes, however, it is much more useful to treat these as separate problems. If the solutions that emerge from separate analyses suggest some greater aggregation, that will be the appropriate time to have greater aggregation.

## Implications for Policy

The studies to date tell us some useful and important things about the decision-making process employed by robbers and help point the way toward the more sophisticated research needed to obtain a fuller picture. The extent to which this information has implications for policy in its present fragmentary state is less clear.

The robbers themselves had some ideas, as Table 4.5 shows. The most frequent suggestion they made as to ways of preventing robberies was to supply jobs or job-training programs to persons like themselves. This suggestion was made by 37% of the robbers. Fourteen percent of the robbers, however, said that it was not possible to stop people from robbing and that nothing could be done. Other suggestions made by a few offenders each included more counseling, more drug programs, target hardening, and letting offenders know the penalties in order to improve deterrence.

Some of the study findings tend to confirm the traditional police concern with apprehension. Whereas many offenders said that they did not think about being caught, some also said that they chose to rob rather than to burgle or shoplift because of prior apprehensions for those crimes. One chose to rob because he was on probation for burglary and was fearful of getting caught for that again.

There are some hints that the aversive effect of apprehension is strongest for first-time offenders who are still learning how to rob. This suggests that if apprehension could be made to take place early in the offender's career, it might be possible to interrupt the learning process and steer the offender away from robbery. This might be a gain even if the offender continued to commit some other crime such as shoplifting. The

## 4. Robbers as Decision-Makers 69

TABLE 4.5 What to do to keep guys from robbing (expressed in percent)[a]

| Answer | Adults (*n* = 82) | Juveniles (*n* = 31) | All Offenders (*n* = 113) |
|---|---|---|---|
| Can't stop people from robbing | 13 | 16 | 14 |
| Jobs, job training, social welfare programs, education | 34 | 45 | 37 |
| Improved rehabilitation programs, counseling | 5 | 3 | 4 |
| Drug programs, get rid of drugs | 2 | 3 | 3 |
| Deterrence, let them know the penalties | 1 | 6 | 3 |
| Target hardening | 1 | 3 | 2 |
| Don't know, but punishment won't stop them | 2 | 0 | 2 |
| Other, mixed comments | 21 | 13 | 19 |
| Don't know, no answer | 20 | 10 | 17 |
| Total | 100 | 100 | 100 |

[a]Percentages may not add to 100 due to rounding.

learning curve for robbery appears to be very rapid, however, and it is easier to describe the possible effects of early apprehension than to make early apprehensions. In any event, it would be useful to have more information from offenders about the effects of apprehensions and nonapprehensions at the various stages of their careers.

A more practical possibility is that of obtaining more convictions of offenders when valid arrests are made. This is particularly important in the United States where 30% to 60% of all robbery arrestees are not convicted, usually for reasons of evidence rather than innocence (Feeney et al., 1983; McDonald, 1982). This is one of the few areas in which rapid progress might be possible if the political will to address the issue existed. Its importance is indicated by the experience of one offender in the study. This offender began robbing and shooting heroin at age 13. By age 26 he had plausibly and conservatively committed over a thousand robberies without a conviction until his present sentence. He had been arrested on five occasions, but in each instance the charges were dropped. Is it any wonder that he did not worry too much about being caught?

The findings on decision making could also have implications for sentencing. If the reports that even the most active robbers do relatively little planning and rarely think about getting caught are accurate, this weakens the appeal of deterrence as a strategy for controlling robbery. Steep penalties are unlikely to deter those who do not believe they will be caught. Such penalties may, however, deter others, who then decide not to commit robberies. The fact that some offenders leave the bullets out of their guns because of the possible penalties suggests that some offenders worry about penalties more than they indicate. This may be particularly true for first offenders. The relative ineffectiveness of deterrence on those who actually rob strengthens the case for incapacitation, as incapacitation provides some measure of control over the impulsive as well as the calculating robber.

The findings suggest that, to be at all successful, prevention efforts must be very selective and highly targeted. There are some indications that robbers who plan little and act on impulse can be successfully thwarted by prevention schemes that make obtaining money more difficult and more time consuming, such as no-change bus fares and the holding of limited cash at gasoline stations (Misner & McDonald, 1970). There are also indications, however, that robbers are much less affected by prevention devices, such as bank cameras, which essentially operate on deterrence principles.

## References

Bennett, T. and R. Wright
1984 Burglars on Burglary. Aldershot, Hants, England: Gower.
Chaiken, J. and M. Chaiken
1982 Varieties of Criminal Behavior. Santa Monica, CA: Rand.
Clarke, R.
1983 "Situational crime prevention: its theoretical basis and practical scope." Pp. 225–56 in M. Tonry and N. Morris (eds.), Crime and Justice: An Annual Review of Research, Volume 4. Chicago: University of Chicago Press.
Clarke, R. and D. Cornish
1985 "Modelling offenders' decisions: a framework for research and policy." Pp. 147–85 in M. Tonry and N. Morris (eds.), Crime and Justice: An Annual Review of Research, Volume 6. Chicago: University of Chicago Press.
Farrington, D.
1979 "Longitudinal research on crime and delinquency." Pp. 289–348 in N. Morris and M. Tonry (eds.), Crime and Justice: An Annual Review of Research, Volume 1. Chicago: University of Chicago Press.
Feeney, F., F. Dill and A. Weir
1983 Arrests Without Conviction. Washington, DC: U.S. Government Printing Office.
Greenwood, P.
1982 Selective Incapacitation. Santa Monica. CA: Rand.
LaFave, W. and A. Scott
1972 Criminal Law. St. Paul. MN: West.
Maguire, M.
1982 Burglary in a Dwelling. London: Heinemann.
McDonald, W.
1982 Police-Prosecutor Relations in the United States. Washington, DC: U.S. Government Printing Office.

## 4. Robbers as Decision-Makers 71

Misner, G. and W. McDonald
  1970  The Scope of the Crime Problem and Its Resolution. Volume II of Reduction of Robberies and Assaults of Bus Drivers. Berkeley, CA: Stanford Research Institute and University of California.
Walsh, D.
  1980  Break-Ins: Burglary from Private Houses. London: Constable.
Weir, A.
  1973  "The Robbery Offender." Pp. 100–211 in F. Feeney and A. Weir (eds.), The Prevention and Control of Robbery, Volume I. Davis, CA: University of California.
Wolfgang, M., R. Figlio and T. Sellin
  1972  Delinquency in a Birth Cohort. Chicago: University of Chicago Press.

# [32]

# A multivariate model of sexual offence behaviour: developments in 'offender profiling'. I.

## DAVID CANTER AND RUPERT HERITAGE

ABSTRACT   The extrapolation of characteristics of criminals from information about their crimes, as an aid to police investigation, is the essence of 'profiling'. This paper proposes that for such extrapolations to be more than educated guesses they must be based upon knowledge of (1) coherent consistencies in criminal behaviour and (2) the relationship those behavioural consistencies have to aspects of an offender available to the police in an investigation. Hypotheses concerning behavioural consistencies are drawn from the diverse literature on sexual offences and a study is described of 66 sexual assaults committed by 27 offenders against strangers. Multivariate statistical analyses of these assaults support a five-component system of rapist behaviour, reflecting modes of interaction with the victim as a sexual object. The potential this provides for an eclectic theoretical basis to offender profiling is discussed.

## 'OFFENDER PROFILING'

Over the last decade a variety of 'profiles' have been created by behavioural scientists to assist police investigations. Although most have been produced by the FBI Behavioural Science Unit (Hazelwood, 1983), there have been some notable successes in the United Kingdom (Canter, 1988). Indeed Hazelwood (1983) claims an accuracy rate in excess of 80 per cent, and in a more detailed review Pinizzotto (1984) proposes that suspects were identified with the help of profiling in 46 per cent of the 192 cases he examined.

Holmes and DeBurger (1988) describe a psychological profile as a report on a violent crime, utilizing information and approaches from various social and behavioural sciences, intended to assist law enforcement personnel in their investigations. Other authors are even more vague, writing of a combination of brainstorming, intuition and educated guesswork (Geberth, 1983) or a collection of leads (Rossi, 1982) about an offender. Vorpogel (1982) simply describes a profile as a biographical sketch of a criminal's behavioural patterns, trends and tendencies. The question of how such profiles are produced and what the underlying psychological principles are that enable them to be created is given less emphasis in the existing publications than descriptive accounts of what profiles may contain.

No profile is all-inclusive, nor is the same information provided from one profile to another, being based on what was or was not left at the crime scene and on any other information that might be available from victim or witness statements; since the nature and amount of information varies, the profile may also vary. Ault and Reese (1980), for example, provide the following list of what may be included in a profile:

(1)  the perpetrator's race
(2)  sex
(3)  age range
(4)  marital status
(5)  general employment
(6)  reaction to questioning by police
(7)  degree of sexual maturity
(8)  whether the individual might strike again
(9)  the possibility that he has committed a similar offence previously
(10)  possible police record.

But this list omits aspects such as likely style of social interaction, general personality characteristics, possibility of associated undetected crimes and the very important matter of possible area of residential location, all of which are aspects that have been successfully included in University of Surrey profiles (Canter, 1988; Canter, 1989).

The derivation of an account of the perpetrator of a crime from knowledge of the events associated with a crime is a process open to scientific development. As pointed out by Canter (1989), it reflects the central psychological questions of how characteristics of individuals are reflected in their behaviour. In this case the characteristics are those of value to the police in identifying suspects and the behaviour is that associated with the crime.

## PRESENT FOCUS ON SEXUAL OFFENCES AGAINST STRANGERS

Profiles as an aid to criminal investigation have been produced for a variety of offences covering homicide, rape and arson (Pinizzotto, 1984). As a starting-point for empirical research, though, serious sexual offences are particularly suitable. They are crimes in which there is information about a great many of the perpetrator's actions. These actions in themselves, focusing as they do around interpersonal sexual aggression, are likely to be revealing of the individual who commits them.

The investigation of sexual assaults committed by a person unknown to the victim is also particularly difficult for criminal investigators to solve. Yet they do account for a high proportion of sexual assaults. Mulvihill *et al.* (1969) found 53 per cent of victims reported being raped by a stranger. There may well be important cultural differences in these figures, because Kocis (1982) reports for eastern Europe that 55 per cent of the victims are known to the offender and a further 40 per cent of the victims come into contact with the offender before the crime is committed; only a small minority of the victims appear to be absolute strangers. In Britain the figures available are rather closer to those for the USA. Lloyd and Walmsley (1989) report that in 1973 49 per cent of rape victims were attacked by strangers. In 1985 the figure was 40 per cent.

The studies reported here therefore focus on sexual assaults in which the victim had no prior knowledge of the offender. Some of these offenders also committed murders, usually with sexually related aspects. Sexual homicide is therefore included in the crimes examined.

## THE NEED FOR AN ECLECTIC MODEL OF OFFENDER BEHAVIOUR

The central hypotheses of profiling, open to direct empirical test, relate to the idea that offenders differ in their actions when committing a crime and that these differences reflect (and therefore correlate with) overtly available features of the offender. However, most published conceptualizations of variations in offender behaviour have tended to combine accounts of actions in an offence with explanations of the intentions, motivations and inferred offender characteristics. For example, a commonly cited approach to rapist typology, Groth's (1979), is premissed on the assumption that rape is not an expression of sexual desire but the use of sexuality to express power and anger. The typology that is derived from this perspective, as a consequence, emphasizes the various psychological functions that rape has for the offender not what varieties of action rape actually consists of.

A further example is given by the work of Prentky *et al.* (1985). Their attempts to characterize and classify rapists make little distinction between the overt behaviour as it occurs in the sexual assault and the psychodynamic processes that are taken to account for or produce that behaviour. There is little attempt to distinguish aspects of the offender's motivations and life-style from his offending

188   JOURNAL OF FORENSIC PSYCHIATRY                    Vol. 1 No. 2

behaviour. Yet any attempt to understand the actions that occur in the offence requires the classification of offence behaviour as distinct from classifications of the person in either psychological or social terms. So although each approach to classification is guided by a particular explanatory framework any composite modelling of offence behaviour for use in 'profiling' will have to draw upon all those approaches that are supported by scientific evidence.

This confusion of action and person is less problematic in the clinical context, in which earlier theoretical formulations were derived. After all, unlike a police detective, Groth had actual patients present in interviews when carrying out his research and his therapeutic mission requires him to enable the offending person to deal with his actions. Such typologies undoubtedly contribute to the understanding of the motivations of rapists and this can help to indicate why certain sorts of rapist will perform certain types of offence. Yet there remains the primary question of what variations in offence behaviour can be reliably identified without any knowledge of the person who committed them. The exploration of how any empirically validated variations relate to offender characteristics is an important issue for subsequent examination.

The focus on the perpetrator's actions is not a purely pragmatic requirement shaped by the limitations of criminal investigation, not is it naively behaviourist, assuming that it is only behaviour that is open to scientific investigation. Rather the emphasis points to the social/interpersonal nature of criminal behaviour, especially in crimes against the person. It is the variety of actions that happen in sexual attacks that indicate the different modes of relationship that offenders have with their victims. Any empirical model of offence behaviour must therefore encapsulate and explicate these variations in mode of interaction with the victim.

The literature points to a number of aspects of the relationship that a rapist has with his victim. The most obvious of these are sexuality and aggressiveness, the behaviour on which Groth (1979) bases his typology. But other writers, notably Rada (1978) and Scully and Marolla (1983), point to the fact that many rapes of strangers are carried out by men who carry out other criminal acts and for whom rape is one such mode of criminal activity. This perspective indicates that, besides the sexual acts and the violence, attention also needs to be paid to those aspects of the offence that relate to its fundamentally criminal nature.

In contrast to the issues of sexuality, aggressiveness and criminality, emphasis has also been given recently to the argument that it is the desire for social contact or intimacy that is a primary motivation in rape (Marshall, 1989). Yet it is the difficulty the offender has in achieving intimacy that leads to an assault. This perspective may be contrasted with the others, from the viewpoint of profiling research, in the attention it draws to behaviour that goes beyond physical contact to attempt some sort of personal relationship with the victim.

The contrast of Marshall's (1989) emphasis on intimacy with Groth's (1979) focus on power and aggression serves to show that, as logical as each one is, there is some potential for inherent contradictions between them. At the very least they raise questions about how a quest for intimacy and the desire for power or aggression are combined in actual behaviour in actual offences, if at all. Such possible contradictions, although not as strong, may also be seen in the difference between the emphasis on the essentially psychopathological nature of sexual assaults, as argued by those with a clinical perspective (e.g. Groth, 1979; Prentky *et al.*, 1985), compared with the views of sociologists such as Scully and Marolla (1983) who see these offenders as essentially normal males operating within criminal mores.

A further contradiction of perspective can also be seen between those such as Marshall and Groth who emphasize the fact that the attack is based upon psychological contact with a person, whether for aggressive or intimacy reasons, and those who argue that rape is fundamentally impersonal (notably Scully and Marolla, 1983). From the latter perspective the victim is an object used to satisfy a physical craving, an object with whom the offender wishes to have completely 'impersonal sex'. A view expressed strongly by Symons (1979: 284) is that 'males tend to desire no-cost, impersonal copulations'.

Broadly, then, at least five modes of interaction with the victim are suggested by these different perspectives. Each of these would be expected to have an observable counterpart in the actions that happened during an offence. Some of these actions would be hypothesized as unlikely to co-occur in the same offence, being contradictory.

In summary they refer to the following elements of sexual offence behaviour:

(1) sexuality
(2) violence and aggression
(3) impersonal, sexual gratification
(4) criminality, and
(5) interpersonal intimacy.

A number of hypotheses can be derived from this fivefold framework about the likely co-occurrences of specific behaviour in sexual assaults, given that all of these types of behaviour may potentially occur in any sexual assault.

One hypothesis is that they all occur with each other in any combination across a range of assaults. This would suggest that none of the explanations provides a basis for distinguishing between offences. A completely random combination of any behaviour with any other would also suggest that there is no consistently coherent distinction to support empirically the concepts used by each author. This is, in effect, a null hypothesis that no interpretable relationships will be found between the actions that occur in offences.

A second hypothesis is that a subset of conceptually related actions (e.g. physical and verbal aggression) will consistently happen together. Any such grouping would support the perspective related to that behaviour. If, for example, different forms of aggressive behaviour co-occurred but various attempts at intimacy were quite independent of each other, then there would be support for aggressiveness as a coherent salient aspect of sexual assault, but not for intimacy. In effect, such a result would reduce the number of explanations that are empirically distinct.

A third hypothesis is that all of these aspects of offence behaviour can be identified in details of actual events and that they therefore combine together to provide a composite model of offence behaviour. Such an eclectic model would be expected to have an interpretable structure to it. For instance, those types of behaviour that are associated in the literature, such as the sexual nature of the offence and its violence (cf. Groth, 1979), would be expected to have some empirical relationship distinct, say, from the relationship between the criminal actions and those dealing with the victim as an impersonal sex object (cf. Scully and Marolla, 1983).

Empirical evidence for either the second or third hypothesis would contribute to scientific support for the possibility of offender profiling because it would indicate that there are indeed structured variations between offenders, revealed in what they did when they committed a crime. Furthermore, such a structure, or system of behaviours, could be used as the basis for specific hypotheses about the aspects of behaviour that would be associated with differences between offenders.

This proposal, then, hypothesizes that an examination of the behaviours as they occur in actual sexual offences will reveal a structure that reflects the variety of modes of interpersonal interactions that underlie those offences. The study reported here describes an empirical test of that hypothesis.

## RELATIONSHIPS BETWEEN OFFENCE AND OFFENDER CHARACTERISTICS

The study to be reported is part of a series of studies being carried out at the University of Surrey. The central quest throughout this research is to identify associations between aspects of the offender's characteristics and offence behaviour. There are a number of ways in which such associations can be established, but whatever methods are used they will be more powerful in their application if they are part of a logical explanatory framework. The framework (or theoretical stance) adopted in the present paper (first outlined in Canter, 1989) may be characterized as a cognitive social one, in which the offender's interactions with others, on a daily basis, is seen as the key to his criminal behaviour.

This is a generalization of the hypotheses underlying the study by Silverman *et al.* (1988). They analysed the case records of 1,000 consecutive rape victims seen at a crisis centre. They found that broad differences in the approach to the victim were related to many other aspects of the offender and the offence. They showed that crimes in which an offender used a sudden attack (blitz) and those in which he used a confidence trick form of access (con) were distinct in a number of ways; the victims' characteristics, the rape settings, the victims' activities before they were raped, the assailants' characteristics, and the victims' immediate responses to the assault. The present study is the first step in elaborating a more detailed conceptualization of sexual assaults and their perpetrators.

## A STUDY OF THE STRUCTURE OF OFFENCE BEHAVIOUR

As discussed, the scientific basis to profiling requires an identification of what the main variations in the actions of offenders in relation to a given offence are. There are many possible aspects of an offence that may be considered as significant, especially if there is a victim's account to consider. The present study was an initial exploration of a range of crimes on which full information was available. It is therefore of interest as an indication whether future research following this approach is likely to be worthwhile.

## SAMPLE SELECTION AND FEATURES CONSIDERED

A total of 33 offence variables were identified through data available such as victim statements and other police reports, in order to provide a list of categorical descriptions of the behaviour across all the offences. Behavioural variables with very low frequencies across the sample were not included since little would be gained from their inclusion at this feasibility phase of the analysis. Indeed the rare characteristics may be important for linking offences to one individual, but are likely to be unique to particular individuals and therefore of less value in developing general principles. Care was taken to define variables so as to allow an easy decision to be made as to the category of behaviour. All variables were treated as dichotomous with no/yes values based on presence/absence of each behaviour in any one offence.

The full list of variables, with explanatory elaborations, used to describe offence behaviour is given in Appendix I in relation to the five modes of interpersonal interaction discussed above.

Data were collected across 66 offences, made available by a number of English police forces in response to a request for details of sexual assaults against victims unknown to the offender. These offences were committed by 27 offenders. The

33 dichotomous variables across the 66 offences provided the data matrix on which subsequent analysis was conducted.

## SMALLEST SPACE ANALYSIS (SSA) OF BEHAVIOUR MATRIX

These data were subjected to an SSA-I (Lingoes, 1973). In essence, the null hypothesis is that the variables have no comprehensible relationship to each other. In other words, it is possible that those offenders who change their actions in response to the reactions of the victim are not the same as those who talk to the victim and encourage her to indicate her reactions to the attack. It may be a common-sense assumption that these two variables will relate to each other because they both indicate a desire to initiate some relationship with the victim, but the SSA allows a test of this assumption and all the other possibilities suggested by the relationship every one of the 33 variables has to every other variable.

Although the literature, reviewed above, does suggest a fivefold way of classifying the variables and this provides a set of hypotheses for the interpretation of the SSA, the use of SSA also allows the generation of hypotheses both about the components of the behaviour under study and about the relationships between those components, the system of behaviour that exists. In other words, the analysis to be presented may best be regarded as both hypothesis testing and also of heuristic value in helping to indicate if there are any directions from the results that can be used to focus future studies aimed at developing profiling.

Smallest Space Analysis (Lingoes, 1973) is a non-metric multidimensional scaling procedure, based upon the assumption that the underlying structure, or system of behaviour, will most readily be appreciated if the relationship between every variable and every other variable is examined. However, an examination of the raw mathematical relationships between all the variables would be difficult to interpret so a geometric (visual) representation of the relationships is produced.

SSA, then, is one of a large number of procedures that represent the correlations between variables as distances in a statistically derived geometric space. Although it was first used a number of years ago (Guttman, 1954) only recently have developments in computers made it readily available for general use. As described by Guttman (1968), Smallest Space Analysis was so called because, when compared with other approaches to multidimensional scaling, it produces a solution of smallest dimensionality. This is primarily because it operates on the rank order of the original correlations rather than their absolute values.

The SSA program computes correlation coefficients between all variables, then rank orders these correlations; in this case transforming an original rectangular data matrix into a triangular matrix consisting of correlation coefficients for each variable as correlated with all other variables. It is these correlation coefficients that are used to form a spatial representation of items with points representing variables, the rank order of the distances between points being inversely related to the rank order of the correlations. Iterations are performed comparing the rank order assigned to the correlations with the rank order of the distance while adjustments are made to the geometric representation. The closer the two rank orders the better is the 'fit' between the geometric representation and the original correlation matrix, or as it is called technically the lower the 'stress'. The iterations continue until the minimal 'stress' possible is achieved, within the predesignated number of dimensions. A measure of stress called the coefficient of alienation (see Borg and Lingoes, 1987, for details) is used within the computing algorithm as the criterion to use in bringing the iterative procedure to an end. It can therefore be used as a general indication of the degree to which the variables' intercorrelations are represented by their corresponding spatial distances. The smaller the coefficient of alienation, the better is the fit, i.e. the fit of the plot to the original correlation matrix. However, as Borg and Lingoes (1987) emphasize, there is no simple answer to the question of how 'good' or 'bad' the representation is. This will depend upon a complex combination of the number of variables, the amount of error in the data and the logical strength of the interpretation framework.

In the present case the data is mainly derived from statements taken by the police from victims. As such they were not collected for research purposes, nor was the information recorded against a detailed protocol and careful training. Furthermore, the content analysis of this material was an initial exploratory attempt of the possibilities for drawing out clear, descriptive variables from this data. It would therefore be expected that the data were not error free and would contain considerable 'noise' that would reduce the possibility of interpreting the results. On the other hand, the published literature is quite rich in suggestions about the behaviour under study and, as presented above, a reasonably clear set of distinguishing concepts can be derived. A reasonable fit to the conceptual system presented would therefore be acceptable as of heuristic value for future research, even with a high 'stress' value in the SSA results.

In the SSA configuration, then, in broad terms, the more highly correlated two variables are, the closer will be the points representing those variables in the SSA space. Since the configuration is developed in respect to the relationships among variables and not from their relationship to some given 'dimension', or axis, the orientation in space of the axes of the resulting geometric representation are arbitrary, even though the relationships between the points are replicably determined. Therefore, the pattern of points (regions) can be examined directly without the need to assume underlying orthogonal dimensions.

The testing of the evidence for ways of classifying variables by examination of the regional structure of an SSA is part of an approach to research known as facet theory (Canter, 1985). The 'facets' are the overall classification of the types of variables. The spatial contiguity of the points representing them provides a test of the major underlying differences amongst these variables as revealed through their co-occurrence in actual incidents, and is therefore a test as to whether the 'facets' are empirically supported. The SSA representation therefore offers a basis for testing and developing hypotheses about the structure of relationships between offence behaviours. Contiguous behavioural variables, forming an element of an interpretable facet, provide a productive basis for future research to distinguish between offenders.

The postulation of facets goes beyond the rather arbitrary proposals of 'grouping', by using the principle of contiguity (Foa, 1958; Guttman, 1965; and Shye, 1978), which states that because elements in a facet will be functionally related their existence will be reflected in a corresponding empirical structure. In other words, variables that share the same facet elements would be more highly correlated and thus should appear closer together in the multidimensional space than variables not sharing the same element.

This idea of contiguity can be extended as a general, regional hypothesis. Items that have facet elements in common will be found in the same region of space. Likewise, variables which have very low intercorrelations will appear in different regions of the plot, indicating dissimilarity, and no membership of the same facet element. Contiguous regionality in a multidimensional space is a quite specific identification of a facet element, provided a clear statement can be made of what the variables in that region have in common. Of course, once the exploratory phase of hypothesis generation has led to the establishment of facets, or when a literature suggests facets, then the existence of contiguous regions can be used as a strong, precise test of the hypothesized facets. The usual processes of scientific replication can also be carried out.

Areas of the SSA plot which contain few or no points are also of interest. Cases such as this may indicate weak areas in the data or in fact missing facet elements. Subsequent studies may then be carried out with new data sets to test for the existence of these missing elements. In this way the interplay between the formal theory, as specified in the facets, and the empirical structure, as revealed in the regional contiguity, can lead to the identification of issues not within the original set of data.

The approach taken to hypothesis test and generation, then, is to establish whether the SSA plot, shown in Figure 1, has any interpretable regional structure to it. The general hypothesis (null) being tested here is that the variations amongst offenders as discussed above are so diffuse that no coherent interpretation of the SSA plot is possible.

## RESULTS OF SSA

The SSA-I was carried out on an association matrix of Jaccard coefficients, these

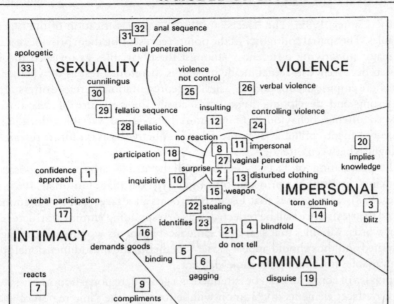

*Figure 1* SSA of behaviour in 66 sexual assaults with regional interpretations. (Numbers refer to variables in Appendix I p. 204 et seq. Labels are brief summaries of content analysis categories.)

being the most appropriate measures of association for this type of binary data. The 3-dimensional solution has a Guttman–Lingoes' coefficient of alientation = 0.22 with 22 iterations, indicating a reasonable fit for this type of data. However, the interpretation of this configuration turns out to be very close to the regional structure of the 2-dimensional solution (which has a coefficient of alienation of 0.30 in 11 iterations) so for simplicity the 2-dimensional structure will be presented. Figure 1 shows this projection of the resulting configuration.

For clarity it should be reiterated that each point is a variable describing offence behaviour. The numbers refer to the variables as listed in Appendix I, although for simplicity a brief title for the variable has also been placed on the plot. The closer any two points the more likely are the actions they represent to co-occur in offences, in comparison with points that are farther apart.

## FOCAL ASPECTS OF RAPES

A first stage in the interpretations of Figure 1, to test the hypotheses and explore the structure of offence behaviour, in the present case, is to consider the frequency of occurrence of each of the variables. Because they are all binary indications of the occurrence of actions each variable has an associated frequency in the whole sample. The SSA is derived from the associations between the

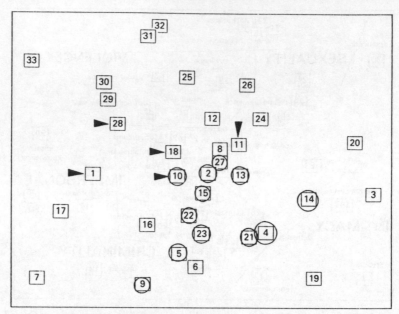

*Figure 2* SSA of 66 assaults illustrating one offence as circles, one as arrows. (Numbers refer to variables in Appendix I.) (See p. 204 et seq.)

variables and so has no inevitable link to their overall frequency. However, with dichotomous variables it is possible for those variables that are frequent to have higher associations with each other, unless there are one or more subsets of variables with lower frequencies that co-occur with high probability. The relationship, then, between the frequencies of the actions and the SSA structure is not artifactual. It is an empirical one open to some substantive meaning. Figure 3 presents the frequencies of occurrence of every offence action.

As can be seen it is possible to draw very clear contours on this diagram to cover variables that occur in more than 65 per cent of cases, in 40 per cent to 60 per cent, in 25 per cent to 35 per cent, in 20 per cent to 25 per cent, and in less than 15 per cent of cases (Figure 3). This polar sequence lends strong support to the focal (polarizing) nature of the high frequency variables. It also indicates those actions that differentiate between offences, being at the edge of the plot. As discussed later, the identification of a high frequency core and a polarizing sequence from it also opens up the possibility that the activities around this circular structure coalesce along radii, creating wedges of modes of interaction, relating directly to the decreasing frequency of those particular sets of variables.

The frequencies serve, also, as a heuristic summary of offence behaviour, showing that those behaviours further out from the core are the ones that are most distinct, giving any particular offence its specific characteristics.

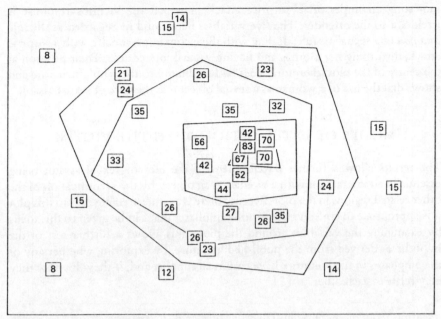

*Figure 3* Percentage frequency of assault behaviour indicated on SSA configuration with equal frequency contours.

The hierarchy of frequencies indicates that there are certain activities that are conceptually central to rape, in other words at the core of sexual assault. The activities at the outer rim reflect different aspects of the same overall phenomena, differing in their reference to some common focus.

This focus and the referents that make it up can be given a clearer meaning by considering those items at the centre of the plot. Such items share most with all the others around them and so are both literally and metaphorically central to the issues being examined. In Figures 1, 2 and 3 the following variables are central:

vaginal intercourse (27)
no reaction to the victim (8)
impersonal language (11)
surprise attack (2)
victim's clothing disturbed (13).

This core is not the overtly aggressive set of actions that Groth's (1979) typology would emphasize. It includes sexual intercourse, but not the variety of sexual activity that might have been expected if sexual desire was a totally dominating aspect of the offence. Nor are those variables central that indicate a desire to relate to the victim as might be indicated from Marshall's (1989) considerations. The discussion that best fits these variables is that of Scully and Marolla (1983), indicating an impersonal, surprise attack in which the victim's response is irrelevant to the offender. The five variables here could be regarded as the *sine qua non* of a sexual assault; dealing with the victim impersonally with a surprise attack, disturbing her clothes and having vaginal intercourse. Their position at the centre of the plot, therefore, does add credibility to the whole structure and shows that the use of a woman as a sexual object is at the core of sexual assault.

## MODES OF INTERACTION WITH THE VICTIM

The results allow a further development of the idea of sexual assault being essentially an interaction with a woman as an object, by the identification of the other related regions in the plot. Because there is an interpretable core to this plot it is appropriate to consider the various emphases that can be given to this focus by examining the variables around the plot. This allows a further test of the hypotheses derived from the published literature, by exploring whether any of the emphases in the literature have empirical support and, if they do, how they may relate to each other.

### (1) Attempted Intimacy with the Victim

As noted earlier, some discussions of rape suggest that it is the lack of ability to form intimate relationships with women that is an important aspect of the motivation to rape (Marshall, 1989). If this were ever dominant in rape then it would be expected that those actions that would indicate an attempt at intimacy, or at least some preparedness to relate to the victim as a person rather than an object, would co-occur in some rapes. Seven variables, particularly, indicate that the offender is attempting to enter, or at least not deterred from entering, into some sort of personal relationship with the victim:

the victim's reaction influences/deters the offender (variable 7)
the offender requires the victim to participate verbally during the assault (17)
the offender requires the victim to participate physically during the assault (18)
the approach is one of a confidence trick (1)
the offender is inquisitive about the victim (10)
the offender compliments the victim (9)
the offender apologizes to the victim (33).

These seven variables can be found in the lower left quadrant of figure 1.. There is therefore some support for this interpersonal aspect of the offence being a coherent and possibly significant feature of offence behaviour.

This distinct aspect of offence behaviour provides an initial heuristic basis for generating hypotheses of associations between offender and offence. Those offences in which most of these actions happen, especially those actions which are less frequent in the present sample, would be hypothesized to be correlated with significant aspects of an offender's interpersonal background. For example, following Marshall's (1989) arguments, it would be hypothesized that these offenders would have had difficulty in formulating intimate relationships with women, but that they may well have attempted this. For example, marriage to a younger woman with a very short courtship and subsequent distancing in their relationship would be predicted. Considerably more research, however, is needed both to replicate this facet element and to establish the hypothesized correlations.

## (2) Sexual Behaviour

Although it is often underemphasized in clinical accounts of rape, there can be little debate about the fact that sexual activity is a crucial component of the attack. There is therefore an important question about whether the different types of sexual behaviour are related and form distinct constituents of an attack or whether they are diffuse, related more to other aspects of the offender's behaviour.

Six variables dealt specifically with the sexual behaviour:

vaginal intercourse (27)
fellatio initially (28)
fellatio as part of the attack sequence (29)
cunnilingus (30)
initial anal intercourse (31)
anal intercourse as part of the offence sequence (32).

The top left quadrant of the plot contains all these variables.

It is interesting to note that vaginal intercourse is central to the whole plot, so that the upper left quadrant is defined by the other sexual activities.

The sexual variables, then, do form a region indicating that together they provide an aspect of offence behaviour that needs to be considered further. This accords with the arguments of Scully and Marolla (1983) that the desire for certain sorts of sexual experience is a significant facet of rape, leading to hypotheses that when a variety of sexual activities take place the offender may be found to have either considerable earlier sexual experience or a great interest in such experience as revealed through a collection of pornographic material. In general, however, the existence of a distinct region in the SSA configuration indicates that the actual sexual aspects of a sexual assault should not be undervalued, as some authorities have tended to do.

## (3) Overt Violence and Aggression

The clinical literature on sexual offences usually places most emphasis on the fact that these are aggressive violent attacks. Violence therefore seems to be a salient issue for consideration. Groth (1979), in particular, as discussed above, argues that aggression is a primary motivation in sexual assault. The following four variables dealt directly with overt violence and aggression:

violence used as a means of controlling the victim (24)
violence used, but not as a means of control (25)
aggressive verbal behaviour (26)
insulting language (12).

All four variables are to be found in the top right quadrant of figure 1. These therefore appear to be coherent aspects of the offence behaviour. For some offenders, then, this is a distinct aspect of their offending. However, it is a distinct aspect which is not overtly apparent in many offences. Their relationship to prior history of aggressiveness is worthy of exploration.

The adjacency of these aggression variables to the sexual variables is of interest, showing that they are quite likely to be linked, as the clinical literature suggests. In particular the closeness of the violence not used as control variable (25) and the anal intercourse variables (31 and 32) does indicate that this particular form of sexual act is likely to be associated with violence and may indeed be motivated by similar psychological processes.

### (4) Impersonal Interaction

The antithesis of the actions that indicate the offender is trying to relate to a person (as presented in (1) above) are the actions that treat the victim very much as an object, dealing with her as an entity entirely for the criminal's use. Six variables relate to these aspects of the offence:

'blitz' attack (3)
impersonal language (11)
no response to the victim's reactions (8)
surprise attack (2)
tearing of victim's clothing (14)
victim's clothing disturbed by offender (13).

These six variables are all to be found in the middle right segment of the plot. They therefore provide a graphic combination of quite wide-ranging behaviours indicating the offender's callous disinterest in his victim. They do, however, include a number of variables that were identified as having a high frequency and at the core of sexual assaults. The existence of a distinct region indicates that for some offenders this may be the dominant characteristic of their offending even though overall offender behaviour is somewhat biased to this aspect of assaulting, as reflected in the off-centre position of the 'core' actions.

The variable recording that the offender implies knowledge of the victim (20) is also at the edge of this region. This is difficult to interpret at this stage but possibly implies that the offender had prior knowledge of the victim, having identified her as a desirable object.

The distant, impersonal contact with the victim, indicated by this subset of variables, is hypothesized to be a reflection of a general approach to women that would be apparent in the offender's daily life. He would be predicted to be known as someone who does not regard women as experiencing the world in the same way he does, seeing them as vessels for men's desires. Clearly, such a perspective on an offender has implications for approaches to therapy as well as for assisting criminal investigations.

## (5) Criminal Behaviour and Intent

Rapists often also operate as criminals committing crimes not obviously sexually motivated. There are also a number of aspects of their sexual crimes that have non-sexual but still distinctly criminal components, such as the wearing of a mask to hide the offender's identity, or the carrying of a weapon to the crime scene. The question therefore arises as to whether these actions have some relationship and coherence.

There are seven variables that can be interpreted as reflecting criminality:

the use of bindings (5)
the use of gagging (6)
stealing from the victim (22)
the use of some form of disguise (19)
blindfolding the victim (4)
demanding goods (16)
controlling the victim with a weapon (15).

Some of these actions may be considered as more directly related to sexual sadism, notably binding and gagging, with the implication that the offender obtained some sexual gratification from these actions. That, of course, may be true in some offences, but the position of these actions in the SSA configuration near to wearing a disguise and carrying a weapon indicates that in the present sample the behaviour of binding and gagging is more readily associated with the criminality of the actions. The position of these variables on the opposite side of the plot from the sexuality and violence variables also supports the proposal that, within these offences at least, the behaviours do not indicate sexual sadism.

All seven of these criminality variables, then, are in the same regional segment of the plot at the bottom right. Interestingly two other variables are clearly within the same region; the threat to the victim not to tell anyone about the offence (21), and the informing of the victim that she is known by the offender (23). It is not difficult to conceptualize these actions as part of the criminal repertoire.

Taken together these nine variables indicate an emphasis to a criminal's behaviour that, if present to any degree, would be hypothesised to correlate with aspects of his previous criminal offences. In particular, it is hypothesized that offenders who commit many of these actions are likely to have extensive history of non-sexual crimes.

## SUMMARY AND CONCLUSIONS

In order to establish whether it is possible to derive the characteristics of a criminal from his actions when offending ('offender profiling') it was proposed that it was first necessary to demonstrate that the behaviour of offenders during a crime had some comprehensible coherence to them. Focusing on sexual assaults against strangers, theoretical accounts of variations between offenders were reviewed in order to establish the range of offence behaviours that should be examined. This review revealed that there were a variety of proposals as to the differences between sexual assaulters, some of these being contradictory.

From these considerations five aspects of a sexual assault were identified. These aspects provided a set of hypotheses about the behaviours that would co-occur during an assault. To test these hypotheses 66 offences, committed by 27 offenders, were content analysed into 33 behavioural categories. The occurrence of these categories of behaviour across all offences was examined using SSA-I.

The results of the SSA indicate that sexual assault can be understood as various ways of carrying out sexual acts in an impersonal fashion, treating the unwilling victim as an object. The results, further, lend support to all five different aspects identified from the published literature. They show that the various explanations given may be construed as different emphases of an assault, different ways of engaging in rape, any offence drawing on one or more aspect.

This set of aspects of elements that make up a rape attack forms a circular order in the SSA space. This implies that those regions which are closer together are more likely to contain actions that occur in the same offence. The sequence around the plot is therefore of some substantive, theoretical interest.

Broadly, the actions on the top half of the SSA deal with actions of interest, and are often noted by those with a psychopathological perspective on rape such as Groth (1979). They cover the variety of sexual activities and the aggressive acts. As such they cover actions that may be akin to the expressive aggression to which Prentky *et al.* (1985) draw attention. Their concept of 'instrumental aggression' may be more closely aligned with the behaviours in the lower half of the plot. These actions are also more in accord with those perspectives that take sociological or social psychological perspectives (e.g. Scully and Marolla, 1983), covering actions that are very impersonal, criminally oriented. Interestingly the social psychological view of Marshall (1989) falls between these two regions.

The closeness of the sexual activity to the violence does lend credence to the view that many sexual offences have a strongly violent aspect. The adjacency of this violence to the impersonal behaviour does reflect rather well the ways in which the one can merge into the other. The criminal behaviour is adjacent to the impersonal behaviour, reflecting the likelihood that criminality is indeed antisocial in the strong sense that it relates to an unpreparedness, or inability, to relate to other people. However, there are offences in which this inability is shown through the inappropriate attempt to form a relationship with the victim, as revealed by the adjacency of the 'intimacy' region. That such actions should be next to the sexual behaviour is also logical in that, on occasion, that implies overlapping motivations.

The sequence of types of activity shown in Figure 1, from sexual activity through criminal behaviour back to sexual activity again, is a circular sequence. No simple linear dimension running from one obvious extreme to the other can be identified. This leads to the hypothesis that all five types of activity represent different emphases of the same overall phenomena, rather than providing positions along a continuum. A further test of the validity of this hypothesis of a circular order of activities is provided by considering the frequencies of the actions, as indicated in Figure 3. As has been noted, although there is no statistical necessity for the higher or lower frequencies to be found in a specific region of the plot, it none the less turns out to be the case that the lower the frequencies the further are the actions from the centre of the configuration.

Yet quite independently of the frequencies, it is in the nature of an SSA configuration that those actions at the centre of the configuration are the ones that, empirically, have most in common with each other. Those at the periphery are the most functionally discrete. Therefore, in the present results, as action frequencies become lower so those actions became more distinctly part of the most functionally specific regions of the plot. This means that there are some actions that have a lot in common with each other, providing a core to these sexual assaults, whereas other actions reflect more specific emphases for those assaults. In other words, the distribution of the frequencies support the hypothesis of a coherent system of behaviour that has different emphases to it, adding weight to the validity of the circular order.

The overall combination of the frequencies and the radial elements (a 'radex', Guttman, 1954) all therefore reflects different aspects of the same overall phenomena, differing in their reference around the focus of the victim being treated as a sexual object by the offender, yet in a variety of different ways.

This radex model of sexual offending has a number of heuristic values. For example, examination of it indicates gaps in the empirical space where no variables are found. It can be hypothesized that the current sample does not include actions which would have gone into those locations. Future data can be used to test this hypothesis. One such instance is the occurrence of overtly sadistic aggressive behaviour in which the victim is bound as a form of humiliation which is arousing to the offender. There is no indication that any such extreme form of sexual sadism was present in the sample. If it were it is hypothesized that an SSA would place it at the extreme edge of the plot in the top region of the aggressive behaviour, but close to the boundary with the sexual behaviour. Other researchers will be able to derive many other similar hypotheses.

A further heuristic value derives from the fact that all five aspects of sexual assault contribute to all offences, but there are likely to be different combinations of constituents for different individuals. The differences in an offender's repertoire of offence behaviour can therefore be clearly established. Establishing what these combinations of major classes of behaviour are is an important objective for future research. It could be used for considering how an offender develops over a series of offences or more pragmatically for establishing whether two or more offences were committed by the same person.

Each of these five aspects also has the potential of correlating with different sets of characteristics of offenders. Study of these correlations will be a major step in the furtherance of a scientific base to offender profiling.

# Appendix I: Variables used to describe offender's behaviour during an offence as derived from content analysis of victim statements

## CODING OF VARIABLES

Thirty-three offence variables were created from a content analysis of available police records and victim statements in order to provide a list of elements common to offences. Variables with a very low frequency were not included. Care was taken to describe the definition of variables so as to eliminate discrepancies in category assignment. All variables are dichotomous with values based on the presence/absence of each category of behaviour. A description of the categorization scheme is given below.

## OFFENCE CHARACTERISTICS

### Variable 1.   Confidence Approach

1 = No     2 = Yes

The style of approach used by the offender in which any ploy or subterfuge is used in order to make contact with the victim prior to the commencement of the assault: this would include any verbal contact – questions asked, false introductions, a story told.

## Variable 2. Surprise Attack

1 = No    2 = Yes

The immediate attack on the victim, whether preceded by a confidence approach or not, where force is used to obtain control of the victim: force in respect of this variable includes threat with or without a weapon. Violence is for the physical control of the victim, i.e. exercised against the victim in order to render her available to the offender, but not the actions covered in variable 3.

## Variable 3. Blitz Attack

1 = No    2 = Yes

The sudden and immediate use of violence, whether preceded by a confidence approach or not, which incapacitates the victim: typically this is the sudden blow which leaves the victim unable to respond or react to the attack. This variable focuses on the extreme violence of the initial assault which leaves the victim incapable of reaction.

## Variable 4. Blindfold

1 = No    2 = Yes

The use at any time during the attack of any physical interference with the victim's ability to see: this only includes the use of articles and not verbal threat or the temporary use of the offender's hands.

## Variable 5. Binding

1 = No    2 = Yes

As above in respect of the use of articles to disable the victim: the categorization does not include the possible situational effect of partial stripping of the victim, nor the temporary use of manual control of the victim.

## Variable 6. Gagging

1 = No    2 = Yes

As above in respect of the prevention of noise: this does not include the manual gagging of victims commonly associated with the attack variables.

## Variable 7. Reaction (1) Deter/change

1 = No    2 = Yes

One of two reaction variables, to examine how the offender copes with, or reacts to, active victim resistance; the resistance of the victim can be verbal or physical but does not include the act of crying alone. The categorization addresses the offender and not the victim. This variable assigns a 2 to the offender who is deterred, or who changes or negotiates his intended actions upon victim reaction. The category emphasizes the change or negotiation of any act as a result of victim resistance.

### Variable 8.    Reaction (2) No difference

1 = No      2 = Yes

As above, but this variable categorizes those offenders whose action and/or intentions are not changed by victim resistance; this offender will continue the assault against an actively resisting victim. An offence in which the victim offers no resistance will be found in the categories of 1 on both variables 7 and 8.

### Variable 9.    Language (1) Compliments

1 = No      2 = Yes

The first of five variables concerned with the complexities of what is said by the offender to the victim: this is not necessarily the result of verbal interchange but is focused on the style of speech used by the offender, in the non-violent context.

This variable assigns a category of 2 to those offences in which the offender compliments the victim, usually on some aspect of her appearance.

### Variable 10.    Language (2) Inquisitive

1 = No      2 = Yes

The second language variable categorizes the offender's speech in being inquisitive of the victim. This includes any questions asked about the victim's life-style, associates, etc. There are other variables which deal with the identifying of the victim and the requirement, for example, of the victim to participate in the acts committed against her. This therefore focuses on the questions asked of the victim which are those of a non-sexual nature.

### Variable 11.    Language (3) Impersonal

1 = No      2 = Yes

This language variable categorizes those aspects of the offender's impersonal/instructive dealings with the victim. The focus is the impersonal style of the offender rather than the categorized differences between personal/impersonal. The personal style of speech will be shown in one or more of the other language variables.

### Variable 12.    Language (4) Demeaning/insulting

1 = No      2 = Yes

A non-violence language variable which categorizes offender's speech with or towards the victim that is demeaning and/or insulting: this would include profanities directed against the victim herself or women in general.

The focus of this variable is the insult and not sexually oriented comment.

### Variable 13.   Victim Clothing Disturbed

1 = No      2 = Yes

One of two clothing variables; this categorizes the offender's removal of the victim's clothing himself. The alternative category, i.e. category 1, includes the act of disrobing carried out by the victim. This act is always at the instruction of the offender and therefore the same category is used in the circumstances of a naked or semi-naked victim. The focus of this variable is on the actions of the offender and can be seen in comparison with the activities of the offender in the second clothing variable (14). It categorizes any act of removal by the offender as 2, regardless of whether the victim assisted or not.

### Variable 14.   Victim Clothing Cut/torn

1 = No      2 = Yes

This variable addresses the offender's removal of the victim's clothing by particular methods. Although there are obvious differences in the tearing or cutting of clothing, this category deals with the offender who is prepared to use an apparently more violent style in his treatment of the victim. Category 1 covers the disturbance of clothing as well as the undressed victim. The focus is on the removal of clothing and not what the offender does with it after removal.

### Variable 15.   Control Weapon

1 = Threat      2 = Weapon

The categories differentiate those offenders who are prepared to display a weapon in order to control the victim, from those who do not. Threat of the possession of a weapon and threat of physical presence are coded as '1'.

### Variable 16.   Demand Goods

1 = No      2 = Yes

This variable categorizes the offender's approach to the victim that includes a demand for goods or money. Importantly the demand categorized in this context is that which is made in the initial stages of the attack. A later variable deals generally with stealing from the victim (V22).

### Variable 17.   Victim Participation Verbal

1 = No      2 = Yes

There are two variables dealing with the requirement of the victim to participate in the offence. Both have been found to occur at the instruction of the offender. Those instructions may appear in many forms, therefore this categorization deals with the offender's requirement that the victim say words or phrases to him at his insistence. The category does not cover the occasions where an offender directs a question to the victim which does not appear to require her to answer.

## Variable 18. Victim Participation Acts

1 = No    2 = Yes

As above, but this is categorized to cover the offender's requirement that the victim physically participate. The acts demanded of the victim are those which may be in association with specific sexual demands made of her but are in addition to those sexual acts. Therefore an example may be the requirement made of the victim to kiss the offender, or to place her arms around him.

In other words, it focuses on the requirements that the victim participate in any act committed against her; in this context the expectation is to differentiate between those offenders who will commit, say, fellatio against the victim and those who commit the same act but accompanied by instructions to do specific acts associated with oral sex.

## Variable 19. Disguise

1 = No    2 = Yes

Various disguises can be and are worn by offenders; categorically the definition of them all would result in an unwieldy variable. The category of disguise in this variable, therefore, deals with those offenders who wear any form of disguise.

## Variable 20. Implied Knowledge

1 = No    2 = Yes

Instances occur within the attacks, at various times, in which the offender implies knowing the victim. This categorization records the implication that the offender knew or knew of the victim before the sexual assault.

## Variable 21. Threat . . . No Report

1 = No    2 = Yes

This is specific categorization of the verbalized threat made to a victim that she should not report the incident to the police or to any other person. This may take many forms; however, the specific threat against the victim in this context is plain when made.

## Variable 22. Stealing

1 = No    2 = Yes

The general category of stealing differentiates those offenders who do steal from those who do not.

### Variable 23.    Identifies Victim

1 = No     2 = Yes

This categorization covers offences in which the offender takes steps to obtain or attempt to obtain from the victim the details which would identify her. This may take many forms including verbal approaches, the examination of personal belongings before or after the actual sexual assault, or indeed the stealing of personal identifying documents following the assault. The act is complete if the the offender acts in any way that allows him to infer to the victim that he has identified, or can identify, her.

### Variable 24.    Violence (1) Control

1 = No     2 = Yes

This categorization of 'violence to control' identifies the use of force which is more than the physical control of the victim and which, situationally, is not the initial attack to obtain control of the victim.

The category in this variable describes the punching, kicking, etc., of the victim in order to reinforce the control the offender is seeking to exercise on the victim.

### Variable 25.    Violence (2) Not control

1 = No     2 = Yes

The categorization here deals with the offender who is prepared to use excessive violence in retaliation to perceived resistance or, in some cases, the use of violence apparently for its own sake.

### Variable 26.    Violence (3) Verbal

1 = No     2 = Yes

This variable is distinct from those dealing with the speech types directed at the victim which can be categorized as impersonal (V11), or demeaning (V12). The categorization in this variable is to address the use of intimidating language in the form of threats to maim or kill which are not necessarily associated with control or resistance. Focus is therefore on verbal violence which is *not* associated with control or resistance.

### Variable 27.    Vaginal Penetration

1 = No     2 = Yes

This variable covers whether vaginal penetration was achieved or attempted.

### Variable 28.    Fellatio (1)

1 = No     2 = Yes

This is one of two variables dealing with the forced oral penetration of the victim. The categories of this variable deal only with whether oral penetration was carried out or attempted.

### Variable 29.    Fellatio (2) In sequence

1 = No      2 = Yes

The second variable of fellatio categorizes offenders' requirements that their victims submit to oral penetration and are those whose performance of the act is part of a sequence of sexual acts. The offender who does not engage in the oral penetration of the victim will be identified as being categorized as '1' in both variables 28 and 29. Similarly the offence in which only oral sexual activity occurs will be differentiated by being categorized as '2' in variable 28, and '1' in the other sexual act variables.

### Variable 30.    Cunnilingus

1 = No      2 = Yes

This variable deals with the performance of a particular sexual act committed against the victim's genitalia by the offender's use of his mouth. In the present sample there is no sequential variable in this context as to date no cases have been seen where this act is performed alone. There is always some other sexual activity accompanying the act of cunnilingus.

### Variable 31.    Anal Penetration

1 = No      2 = Yes

This is one of two variables dealing with penetration *per* anus committed against a victim. This categorization deals only with those cases where the act was carried out. In the present sample of categorized cases the penetration is by male organ only. It includes attempts where there is clear indication of intent.

### Variable 32.    Anal Penetration In sequence

1 = No      2 = Yes

The second variable dealing with anal assault: the category addresses anal assault in sequence with other sexual acts. The offence in which anal penetration occurs or is attempted will be categorized '1' on both variables. Similarly the attacks with an anal assault only will be categorized as '2' in variable 31, and '1' in respect of the other sexual act variables.

### Variable 33.    Apologetic

1 = No      2 = Yes

This is a further language variable to deal with the specific apologetic speech used by an offender, most typically at the end of a sexual assault.

*Professor David Canter*
*and*
*Detective Constable Rupert Heritage,*
*Department of Psychology,*
*University of Surrey,*
*Guildford, Surrey GU2 5XH*

## A MODEL OF OFFENDER PROFILING    211

## NOTE

This is the first paper in an occasional series on the development of a scientific base for offender profiling to be written by Professor Canter and other members of the Profiling Research Unit at the University of Surrey. Subsequent papers will deal with variations between criminals in their offence history and personal antecedents, spatial distribution of crimes committed by an individual and the relationship this has to a criminal's cognitive representation of the area in which he commits crimes. The emerging relationships between offence behaviour and characteristics of criminals will be reviewed.

## ACKNOWLEDGEMENT

We are grateful to Milena Kovacik and Katherine King-Johannessen for their contribution to this paper. This research benefited from Home Office Contract No. SC/88/22/247/1 and support from Surrey Police Constabulary.

## REFERENCES

Ault, R. L. and Reese, J. T. (1980) 'A Psychological Assessment of Crime Profiling'. *FBI Law Enforcement Bulletin*, 49 (3): 22–5.

Borg, I. and Lingoes, J. (1987) *Multidimensional Similarity Analysis*. New York: Springer-Verlag.

Canter, D. (1985) *Facet Theory: Approaches to Social Research*. New York: Springer-Verlag.

Canter, D. (1988) 'To Catch a Rapist'. *New Society*, 4 March.

Canter, D. (1989) 'Offender Profiling'. *The Psychologist*, 2: 12–16.

Davies, G. M. (1988) 'Use of Video in Child Abuse Trials'. *The Psychologist*, 1: 20–2.

Foa, U. G. (1958) 'The Contiguity Principle in the Structure of Interpersonal Relation'. *Human Relations*, II: 229–38.

Geberth, V. J. (1983) *Practical Homicide Investigation*. New York: Elsevier.

Groth, N. A. (1979) *Men Who Rape: The Psychology of the Offender*. New York: Plenum.

Guttmacher, M. S. and Weihofen, H. (1952) *Psychiatry and Law*. New York: Norton.

Guttman, L. (1954) 'A New Approach to Factor Analysis: The Radex'. In Lazarsfield, P. F. (ed.) *Mathematical Thinking in the Social Sciences*. New York: Free Press.

Guttman, L. (1965) 'A Faceted Definition of Intelligence'. *Studies in Psychology, Scripta Hierosolymitana*, 14: 166–81 (Hebrew University, Jerusalem).

Guttman, L. (1968) 'A General Nonmetric Technique for Finding the Smallest Coordinate Space for a Configuration Point'. *Psychometrika*, 33 (3): 469–506.

Hazelwood, R. R. (1983) 'The Behaviour-Oriented Interview of Rape Victims: The Key to Profiling'. *FBI Law Enforcement Bulletin*: 1–8.

Holmes, R. M. and DeBurger, J. (1988) *Serial Murder*. London: Sage.

Kocis, L. (1982) 'Posudzovanie sexualnych delikventov'. In *Forenzne Aspekty Sexuality, Sexualita zeny*. Zbornik referatov: Kosice, September: 186–94.

212   JOURNAL OF FORENSIC PSYCHIATRY                          Vol. 1 No. 2

Lingoes, J. (1973) 'The Guttman-Lingoes Non-Metric Program Series'. MA thesis, University of Michigan.

Lloyd, Ch. and Walmsley, R. (1989) *Changes in Rape Offences and Sentencing* (Home Office research study no. 105). London: HMSO.

Marshall, W. L. (1989) 'Intimacy, Loneliness and Sexual Offenders'. *Behavioural Research in Therapy*, 27 (5): 491–503.

Mulvihill, D., Tumin, M. and Curtis, L. (1969) *Crimes of Violence. A Staff Report submitted to the National Commission on the Causes and Prevention of Violence* (Vols 11–13). Washington, DC: US Government Printing Office.

Pinizzotto, A. J. (1984) 'Forensic Psychology: Criminal Personality Profiling'. *Journal of Police Science and Administration*, 12 (1), pp. 32–40.

Prentky, R. A., Cohen, M. L. and Seghorn, T. (1985) 'Development of a Rational Taxonomy for the Classification of Sexual Offenders: Rapists'. *Bulletin of the American Academy of Psychiatry and the Law*, 13: 39–70.

Rada, R. T. (1978) 'Psychological Factors in Rapist Behaviour'. In Rada, R. T. (ed.) *Clinical Aspects of the Rapist*. New York: Grune & Stratton.

Rossi, D. (1982) 'Crime Scene Behavioral Analysis: Another Tool for the Law Enforcement Investigator'. Official Proceedings of the 88th Annual IACP Conference, *The Police Chief* (January): 156–9.

Scully, D. and Marolla, J. (1983) 'Incarcerated Rapists: Exploring a Sociological Model'. Final report for the Department of Health and Human Services Rockville, Maryland NIMH.

Shye, S. (1978) *Theory Construction and Data Analysis in the Behavioral Sciences*. San Francisco: Jossey Bass.

Silverman, D. C., Kalich, S. M., Bowie, S. I. and Edbiel, S. E. (1988) 'Blitz Rape and Confidence Rape: A Typology applied to 1,000 Consecutive Cases'. *American Journal of Psychiatry* 145: 11, 1438–41.

Symons, D. (1979) *The Evolution of Human Sexuality*. Oxford: Oxford University Press.

Vorpogel, R. E. (1982) 'Painting Psychological Profiles, Charlatism, Charisma, or a New Science?'. *The Police Chief* (January): 156–9.

# Part X
# Inferring Offender's from Offence Characteristics

# [33]

# Psychological Profiling

This investigative technique is sometimes called *offender profiling* or *psychological criminal profiling*. Reiser (1982c) dates the beginning of the development of this psychological tool to the early 1970s. He indicates that the police psychologist has a unique opportunity for direct involvement in police work and investigation by applying psychological knowledge and experience in a variety of unusual policing circumstances.

Reiser describes psychological profiling as an arcane art in which psychodiagnostic assessment and psychobiography are combined with case evidence and probabilities from similar cases to draw a picture of a likely offender. Suspected personality variables and psychodynamics are inferred from the available evidence and from victim characteristics. Reiser further points out that contrary to hopes and expectations for a scientifically derived investigative tool, psychological profiling is merely an inferential process analogous to a psychological evaluation done with an ordinary client.

Criminal personality profiling as further defined by the Behavioral Science Unit of the Federal Bureau of Investigation at Quantico, Virginia, involves the study of unsolved crimes in an attempt to provide the behavioral and personality characteristics of unidentified offenders (Horn, 1988).

The process is basically a method of helping to identify the perpetrator of a crime based on an analysis of the nature of the offense and the manner in which it was committed. The process attempts to determine aspects of a criminal's personality makeup from the criminal's choice of action before, during, and after the criminal act. The personality information is combined with other pertinent details and physical evidence and then compared with characteristics of known personality types and mental abnormalities. From this, a working description of the offender is developed.

The origins of psychological profiling are subject to conjecture. Even as early as the beginning of the 19th century, there were some descriptions in the literature of such procedures. Efforts to do similar kinds of profiling appeared in the field of criminal anthropology early in the 1800s.

262    Consultation and Operational Assistance

There is no question that criminal profilers have been influenced by the work of Arthur Conan Doyle who endowed his detective Sherlock Holmes with a tremendous capacity to understand the personality and habits of criminals from the way they smoked, walked, chose clothing, and behaved in other respects. Some of the behaviors suggested by Doyle's fiction, such as "the criminal returns to the scene of the crime," have been found to have some validity in modern application (Tetem, 1989).

## DEVELOPMENT OF PSYCHOLOGICAL PROFILING

The most concentrated efforts to standardize the technique of psychological profiling have been the work of the behavioral science unit and its staff at the FBI Academy. As an outgrowth of this unit's program of instruction in abnormal psychology for its agents, the FBI attempted to assist the law enforcement community in the preparation of psychological profiles in selected unsolved criminal cases. The FBI profilers give credit to the work of the Office of Strategic Services, which employed a psychiatrist to help develop profiles of world leaders during World War II (Ault & Reese, 1980). Criminal profiling has been productive most frequently in cases in which an offender has demonstrated repeated patterns of the same crime (Douglas, Ressler, Burgess, & Hartman, 1986).

In their original work, the FBI researchers studied serial murderers. They found certain characteristics that defined the *disorganized offender*. This individual was likely to be the first or last born child. The father usually had an unstable work history. The individual was treated with hostility as a child. The perpetrator tended to be sexually inhibited, ignorant, had sexual problems in relation to the mother, and was probably aversive to sexual behavior. Such a person would be described as frightened and confused at the time of the crime, was likely to know the victim, tended to live alone, and was likely to commit the crime in the victim's home.

The FBI research group defined the *organized offender* as an intelligent person in a skilled occupation, likely to think and plan out the crime. Such an individual is likely to be angry and depressed at the time of the murder, is likely to have a precipitating stress, and usually followed reports of the crime in the media. This individual would be likely to change jobs or leave town after committing the murder.

FBI researchers believed that one of the foundations of profiling would be that different offenders in different locations tend to commit similar crimes in similar ways because of similar personalities (Horn, 1988).

## APPLICATION

Although there are some differences of opinion, profilers in general agree that, to be appropriate for profiling, the offenses should feature some form of overt sexual activity or severe emotional disturbance on the part of the perpetrator (Tetem, 1989). The most commonly profiled cases are assaults and homicides.

In homicide cases, the profiler must first determine whether the offender is an *organized* or *disorganized* individual. The end result is a composite behavioral sketch of a personality type and not a specific person (Horn, 1988). The work of Ressler and Burgess suggests that a small percentage of criminals may be responsible for a large number of homicides (1985). Such perpetrators are now defined as "serial killers." In homicide cases, the victim is not able to give direct verbal reports of the perpetrator, and the crime scene analysis must speak for the victim.

In sexual assaults such as forcible rape, sexual molestation, and repetitive indecent exposure, the victims are valuable resources in criminal profiling because they have had close contact with the perpetrator. The profiler is able to obtain information about the offender's verbal, physical, and sexual behavior that can be helpful in deducing motive and personality (Horn, 1988).

After developing profiles of serial murderers, the FBI researchers concentrated their attention on the serial rapist. They found that half of rapes are premeditated, and the remainder are impulsive or opportunistic. Their research suggested that the commonest approaches by a rapist have been "the con," "the blitz," or "the surprise." Minimal or no force is used in the majority of instances. About half the victims resisted. The most common reaction by perpetrators to resistance was verbal threat (Hazelwood & Warren, 1990). Hazelwood and Warren (1989) carefully studied 41 serial rapists who had been tried, convicted, and incarcerated. From their interviews, they developed details of the serial rapist's family structure, sexual history, current sexual behaviors, and types of victims chosen. Table 12.1 presents the data developed by Hazelwood and Warren (1989) on the family structure of serial rapists.

Following their work on serial murderers and serial rapists, the FBI investigators developed psychological profiles of "nuisance offenders." These were essentially serious obsessive-compulsive individuals who tended to commit such crimes as repetitive exhibitionism, pyromania (arson), kleptomania, voyeurism, obscene phone calls, "poison pen" letters, and other ritualistic crimes (Reese, 1979).

Profiling research has explored the personalities and methods of a variety of arsonists and bomb setters (Rider, 1980; Douglas et al., 1986). Rider points out the scope of this problem by reporting that a total of 125,513 arrests for arson were made between 1969 and 1978. Approximately 90% of those arrested were males.

Rider further reviews the research on the personality and lifestyle of pathological arsonists and concludes that they demonstrate the following cluster of characteristics:

264     Consultation and Operational Assistance

1. Usually are under 25 years of age.
2. Often are victims of pathological and distressed rearing environments.
3. Most frequently come from a father-absent home.
4. Are mother-dominated.
5. Tend to be academically retarded.
6. Are of slightly below-average intelligence.
7. Are emotionally and psychologically disturbed.
8. Are socially and sexually maladjusted.
9. Are usually unmarried.
10. Are notably insecure.
11. Tend to have histories showing them to be cowardly.

The purpose of profiling is to help catch a criminal. In an unusual proactive application of these procedures, Hagaman, Wells, Blau, and Wells (1987) developed a family homicide profile that could be used to predict such an occurrence, and possibly to prevent the homicide.

Analyzing a series of family homicides, using traditional profiling procedures, these researchers determined that a family homicide is more likely to occur when the following situations arise:

1. Drugs or alcohol are in use at the time of the event.
2. There are cultural pressures for the perpetrator to save face.
3. The perpetrator has made previous threats of suicide.
4. The perpetrator has shown recent deep depression.
5. There has been a recent failed love relationship.
6. The perpetrator has been recently separated from the family unit.
7. The perpetrator has made a series of vengeance threats recently against the family.

Following the study, strategies for preventing family homicide were developed including:

1. Early arrest of perpetrators of family violence or abuse.
2. Identification and recording of repeated incidents of family abuse and requests for help.
3. Court-mandated counseling for repeated offenders.
4. Public education about the danger signs, where help can be obtained, and opportunities for treatment.

A number of social agencies were enlisted in this pro-active program; police officers were trained in the danger signs; and liaison was established

TABLE 12.1 Family Structure of Serial Rapists

| | N | Percentage (%) |
|---|---|---|
| Assessment of Socioeconomic Level of Subject's Preadult Home (N = 41) | | |
| Advantaged | 7 | 17 |
| Comfortable, average | 15 | 37 |
| Marginal, self-sufficient | 11 | 27 |
| Submarginal | 8 | 20 |
| Variable | — | — |
| Dominant Parental Figures (N = 40) | | |
| Mother | 20 | 50 |
| Father | 16 | 40 |
| Other | 4 | 10 |
| Quality of Relationship to Mother or Dominant Female Caretaker (N = 39) | | |
| Warm, close | 14 | 36 |
| Variable | 12 | 31 |
| Cold, distant | 2 | 5 |
| Uncaring, indifferent | 4 | 10 |
| Hostile, aggressive | 7 | 18 |
| Quality of Relationship to Father or Dominant Male Caretaker (N = 39) | | |
| Warm, close | 7 | 18 |
| Variable | 10 | 26 |
| Cold, distant | 12 | 31 |
| Uncaring, indifferent | 3 | 8 |
| Hostile, aggressive | 7 | 18 |
| Evidence That Subject Was Physically Abused by Parents/Caretakers (N = 40) | | |
| Yes | 15 | 38 |
| No | 25 | 62 |
| Evidence That Subject Was Psychologically Abused by Parents/Caretakers (N = 41) | | |
| Yes | 30 | 73 |
| No | 11 | 27 |
| Evidence That Subject Was Sexually Abused (N = 41) | | |
| Yes | 31 | 76 |
| No | 10 | 24 |

*Note:* From "The Serial Rapist: His Characteristics and Victims," by R. Hazelwood and J. Warren, 1989, *FBI Law Enforcement Bulletin, 58,* 18–25.

**266    Consultation and Operational Assistance**

between the social agencies and the police. Crisis line workers were trained in evaluating a potential for family violence and/or homicide. Figure 12.1 presents the Family Violence Interview that was developed for use by crisis line workers from the family homicide profiling research.

This interview form is designed for use by trained crisis workers receiving telephone calls from troubled citizens who are involved in or observers of potential family violence.

After the worker has established rapport and gained the confidence of the caller, basic information such as name, address, and telephone number should be recorded. This form should be filled out as soon as the worker ascertains that the caller is reporting a violent family episode in progress or about to happen.

---

### FAMILY VIOLENCE INTERVIEW

By _____

AM

Caller's Name _____ Date _____ Time _____ PM

Telephone _____ Address _____

Relationship to Instigator _____

Instigator's Name _____

Address _____ Telephone _____

\*HIGH RISK

I. *HAS THE INSTIGATOR BEEN VIOLENT BEFORE*

Has instigator caused trouble or hurt like this before?

YES \*____ NO ____ DK ____ Details: _____

II. *INVOLVEMENT WITH LAW ENFORCEMENT*

Has instigator ever had the police or sheriff come to settle him down or arrest him before?

YES \*____ NO ____ DK ____ Details: _____

III. *PREVIOUS MENTAL HEALTH RECORD*

Has instigator been mentally ill in the past?

YES \*____ NO ____ DK ____ Details: _____

IV. *RECENT DEEP DEPRESSION*

Has instigator been recently low, discouraged, or depressed?

YES \*____ NO ____ DK ____ Details: _____

V. *BACKGROUND HISTORY*

Has instigator had a recent family breakup?

YES \*____ NO ____ DK ____ Details: _____

---

**FIGURE 12.1   Family Violence Interview**

# PSYCHOLOGICAL PROFILING PROCEDURES

Horn (1988) suggests that psychological profiling involves seven steps:

1. A careful evaluation of the criminal act.
2. A comprehensive analysis of the crime scene.
3. A comprehensive analysis of the victim.
4. An evaluation of the preliminary police reports.
5. Evaluation of the medical examiner's autopsy protocol in homicide cases.

---

VI. *SEPARATION FROM FAMILY UNIT*

Has instigator recently moved out or been separated from the family unit?

YES * ___  NO ___  DK ___  Details: _____

---

VII. *THREAT*

Has instigator made any threats that you know of (suicide or homicide)?

YES * ___  NO ___  DK ___  Details: _____

VIII. Is anyone antagonizing or hassling instigator now?

YES * ___  NO ___  DK ___  Details: _____

---

IX. *ALCOHOL OR DRUGS*

Is instigator using alcohol or drugs?

YES * ___  NO ___  DK ___  Details: _____

(SCORE)  No Threat ___　　Nonspecific Threats ___

Vengeance-Based Threat * ___

---

| Decision Checkpoints | ( ) means "use own judgment" | Action |
|---|---|---|
| 1 or 2 * checked: | NO CLEAR INDICATION | E + (C) − (D) |
| 3 * checked: | VIOLENT SITUATION MAY BE DEVELOPING | C − (D) |
| 4 * checked: | EMERGENCY—VIOLENCE PROBABLE | A − B |
| 5 * checked: | EMERGENCY—VIOLENCE PROBABLE | A − B |
| 6 or more * checked: | ACUTE EMERGENCY—IMMINENT VIOLENCE | A − B |

A—CALL POLICE OR SHERIFF TO INVESTIGATE.
B—TELL INFORMANT TO AVOID INSTIGATOR. GET CHILDREN OUT.
C—REFER TO CRISIS LINE. CALL BACK IF SITUATION INTENSIFIES.
D—MAKE APPOINTMENT FOR FAMILY COUNSELING.
E—CONTINUE WITH USUAL HELP-LINE PROCEDURES.

---

**FIGURE 12.1**　*(continued)*

## 268    Consultation and Operational Assistance

6. Development of the profile with critical offender characteristics.
7. Investigative suggestions predicated on the construction of the profile.

To do the profile properly, certain materials are required including complete photographs of the crime scene and a map depicting all significant locations. The profiler should be provided with the autopsy protocol in homicide cases. A medical examiner's report is important for rape and violent assault cases. The profiler must have the victim's occupation, residences, reputation at work, physical description, marital status, financial status, family background, medical history, fears, personal habits, social habits, ordinary use of alcohol and drugs, hobbies, friends and enemies, recent changes in lifestyle, and recent court actions.

In the case of sexual assault and rape victims, the profiler must conduct careful and extended interviews with the victim regarding the rapist's behavior. An analysis of that behavior is made in an attempt to ascertain the motivation underlying the assault. A profile is compiled for an individual likely to have committed the crime in the manner reported and having the assumed motivation. Interviewing the victim is the most important step in the process; it is recommended that this be done by the investigators (Hazelwood, 1983). Detailed questions are required as to the method of approach used by the offender, the way in which the offender controlled the victim, the offender's reaction to resistance where this occurred, any sexual peculiarities of the perpetrator, the verbal activity of the offender, any sudden changes in the offender's attitude during the attack, and items that the victim finds are missing after the attack.

In many ways, the process used by a profiler in developing the criminal profile is similar to that used by clinical psychologists to make a diagnosis and treatment plan. Data is collected and assessed, the situation is reconstructed, hypotheses are formulated, a profile is developed and tested, and the results are reported back. Expertise includes a lot of experience with other investigators; exchanging ideas, accumulating wisdom, and having familiarity with a large number of cases. The hypothesis should organize, explain, and make investigative sense out of information (Douglas et al., 1986).

Douglas and his group have suggested that there are stages of psychological profiling that should be followed to come to a final criminal profile that might lead to investigation and apprehension. Figure 12.2 shows diagramatically the profile process recommended by Douglas et al. (1986).

Those who are enthusiastic about the application of psychological profiling to serious criminal acts suggest that violent crimes require investigators to be diagnosticians who study the crime scene for the messages that it emits about the perpetrator's actions during the attack. From this analysis can come an understanding of the dynamics of human behavior that characterize the perpetrator. It is suggested that the fantasies of offenders give

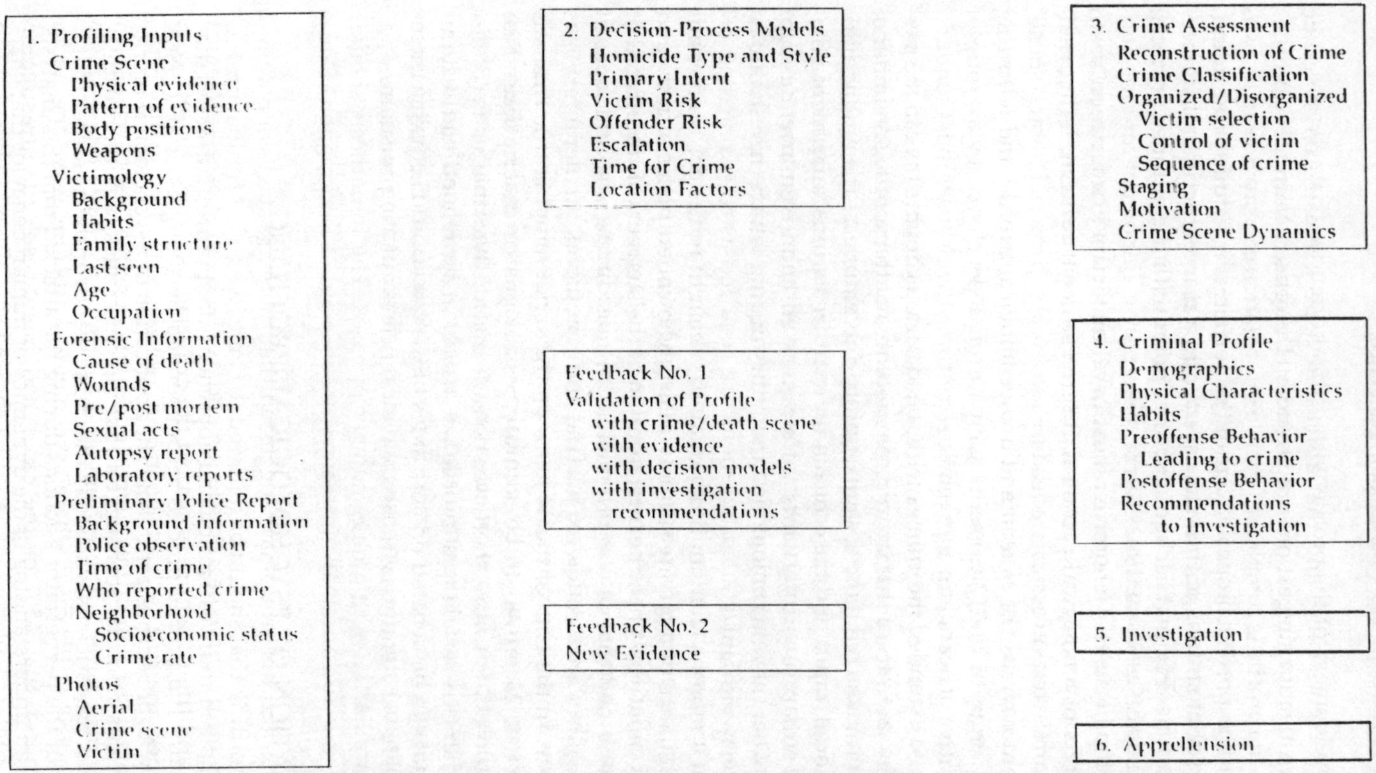

FIGURE 12.2 A Psychological Profile-Generating Process From "Criminal Profiling from Crime Scene Analysis," by J. Douglas, R. Reisler, A. Burgess, and C. Hartman, 1986, *Behavioral Sciences and the Law*, 4, 107. Copyright by John Wiley & Sons. Reprinted with permission.

270     Consultation and Operational Assistance

birth to violent crimes and that a *signature* aspect remains on the crime scene as an enduring part of each offender (Douglas & Munn, 1992).

Once the profile is completed, profile information can provide an investigator with the probable sex and age of the perpetrator, ethnic background, relative social status, marital status, educational level, occupational category, possible criminal background, and potential for continued criminal activities (Ault & Reese, 1980; Tetem, 1989).

If nothing else, the extensive review of all materials that is necessary to construct a psychological profile will often in itself bring to light previously overlooked investigative leads.

To demonstrate the outcome of a psychological profile, the following example on pp. 271–273 presents such a profile developed by a group of investigative officers and a psychologist

Although some of the police officers had serious doubts (as did the psychologist) about the accuracy and completeness of the profile, a number of stakeouts and surveillances were developed to anticipate the next activity of the serial rapist. Because of his activity in various apartment complexes, civilian security guards were canvassed and given brief descriptions of what they might look for, and hours during which they should be particularly vigilant.

About 4 months later, an individual was "caught in the act" as a result of the vigilance of a private security guard who called police officers and sheriff's deputies. When the interrogation of the suspect was completed, it was determined that he was responsible for most of the unsolved rapes in a three-county area. Following his trial and conviction, further interviews took place. In the end, of the 34 items on the serial rapist profile that was constructed, 23 proved to be accurate predictions or descriptions. Two were incorrect. For nine, there was no information available.

Whether this serial rapist profile was useful in apprehending the criminal or not can be debated on both sides of the question. The police themselves were very enthusiastic about the usefulness of the procedure.

## EVALUATION OF PSYCHOLOGICAL PROFILING

Very few efforts have been made to validate the quality of psychological profiles and their usefulness against the criteria of success. As with computer work, the rule is "garbage in and garbage out." The quality of the crime data used is of critical importance. It is possible that psychological profiling may never advance from an art form to a science (Horn, 1988).

In a review of 193 cases where psychological profiling was done, Tetem (1989) found that 45% of the cases had been resolved. Investigators claimed that 77% of the cases studied showed that the psychological profile had been of significant assistance in the investigation. In 17% of the

**PINE COUNTY SHERIFF'S OFFICE**
**BEHAVIORAL SCIENCE UNIT**
**SERIAL RAPIST PSYCHOLOGICAL PROFILE**

## INTRODUCTION

During January 1986, a series of reports of sexual battery received by this office began to demonstrate characteristics of the so-called serial rapist profile. Detective Jones, Sgt. Smith, and Lt. Brown brought preliminary crime data to the attention of Dr. Green, and initial meetings were scheduled to develop a *psychological profile* of the person who might be the perpetrator of this series of sexual assaults.

All crime reports, photos, witness statements, and other evidence were reviewed. Three victims were given psychological profile interviews. The first reported victim (January), a victim who was assaulted in April, and the latest victim (July 9, 1986) gave detailed responses to the psychological interview. Because a series of sexual assaults being investigated by the Anytown PD bore similarities to the Pine County Sheriff's Office cases, several Anytown Police Department officers met with the Pine County Sheriff's officers to share information. Detective White and Sgt. Black provided material and participated in several meetings.

It is not certain that all the cases evaluated were the work of one perpetrator. The preliminary analysis presented here is based on the evidence available and the emerging picture of the probable psychological style and motivation of the perpetrator, as he appears through the experience of victims and certain similarities in his behavior.

The man responsible for a number of sexual batteries since January 1986 is between 20 and 30 years of age. He is tall, between 6 ft and 6 ft 2 or 3 in. in height. His shoulders are quite broad, and his hips are narrow. His skin is smooth and relatively hairless. When and if he wears a mustache, it is thin and sparse. He tends to dress casually, preferring blue trousers or jeans, with checkered shirt or pullover sweatshirt, sometimes with a hood. He seems to prefer blue-colored clothes. He often wears soft or tennis shoes of a dark color. He is well-organized and self-assured. He speaks in a relatively calm voice of medium tone and resonance. He speaks with a vocabulary that suggests middle-class background and education. He is white. He wears no cologne or other noticeable scent. His shoe size is between 11 and 13. He may be bisexual or has had some homosexual experience. There is a probability that he has been arrested in the past, perhaps as a juvenile, for flashing or peeping. He sometimes wears sunglasses with mirror lenses and white frames. His hair may be brown or blond. He probably lives in an apartment. He probably has both a bicycle and a car.

## MODUS OPERENDI

The method of operation is fairly consistent. Victims are for the most part young, single apartment dwellers. They all have automobiles. The assaulter apparently prepares his plan with some care. He surveys the apartment complex where he will operate. He goes over the surrounding area

## 272     Consultation and Operational Assistance

both during the day and at night. He searches for the best place to accost his victim and where to march the victim to a secluded outdoor spot to commit the sexual assault. When he enters the victim's domicile, it is usually through a sliding glass door. He seems to prefer to get to know the victim's regular habits and to capture her as she goes about some ordinary task. Whether he takes the victim from her apartment, car, or laundry room, he seems to follow the same sequence:

1. He grabs the victim securely.
2. He is wearing a hood, a towel, or shirt around his face or dark glasses to hide his identity.
3. He tells his victim she is in danger of her life and that he is carrying a knife. He cautions her to be quiet.
4. He asks for and takes the victim's money. He shows no interest in jewelry or other valuables.
5. He walks his victim away from her apartment to a semisecluded spot nearby. He clearly knows what he is doing and where he is going. He threatens his victim if she makes any noise, cries, touches him, or resists his efforts. He seldom if ever curses. He indicates that he has been watching the victim and knows something about her routine or acquaintances in the apartment complex.
6. He commits the sexual act with a ritual where he demands a kiss, asking the victim to stick out her tongue. He performs some minimal fondling and then asks the victim to fellate him. He may attempt anal intercourse. He may enter her vaginally from the rear. He is insistent but as yet, not brutal. He does not require the victim to remove all of her clothes. He does not usually remove his clothes entirely. He may withdraw and ejaculate by having the victim masturbate him. All during these proceedings he keeps his victim blind-folded with a piece of his own clothing.
7. On completion, he has the victim dress and he heads her toward her apartment complex. He may warn her not to look or impede his escape. He leaves very quietly and disappears, either on foot or by bicycle.

About half of the incidents have occurred between Friday night and early Monday morning. He has committed these batteries between 2200 and 0600 hours. As far as can be determined, he has committed none of these acts on Thursday. He operates in fairly specific clusters of apartment complexes. He moves his locus of operation between Everytown and Anytown. The degree of force he uses is escalating. He is beginning to both threaten and abuse his victims more aggressively.

Psychologically, it would appear that this perpetrator is a fairly inward person with a limited number of close friends. He probably has sexual contacts other than in the cases where he commits sexual battery. These contacts may be bisexual. He has no regular job or has a job situation where he can control his own hours. He is both obsessional and compulsive. He is given to rituals and repetitive behavior. He needs money and his motivation may become increasingly focused on burglary and robbery. Although he may not be of high measurable intelligence, he is shrewd and can be cool and unanxious.

His personality is likely to be that of a nonconforming person. He will tend to have strong and sometimes odd ideas that he holds to strongly. He is likely to be a rebellious person with poor frustration tolerance. He will tend to be impulsive even though his crimes show an ability to plan.

This culprit is willing to take risks. He particularly enjoys teasing or frustrating authority figures. He tends to believe he is capable of being very clever. If given the chance to enhance his own image, he is likely to talk about himself more than is good for him.

When the time comes to interrogate this person, it must be done very carefully. Pressure is unlikely to be helpful. Having several clearly identifiable objects from the various crime scenes in a corner of the interrogation room will help. Flattery, sympathetic listening, and general questions are more likely to elicit his response than rigid, formal or challenging approaches. He is unlikely to respond to threats. Any appeal to his vanity (skill, glib language, style, etc.) is likely to elicit conversation from him. He is unlikely to respond to Mutt & Jeff routines by the interrogators. He will probably be more talkative with male interviewers.

## DISCLAIMER

This Profile is sketchy at best. It is a preliminary effort.

---

cases, the profile had actually identified the suspect. Ressler and Burgess (1985) report an inter-rater reliability in the classification of sexual homicide crime scenes from 76.7% to 92.6% measuring agreement between a trained FBI agent and a criteria evaluation by the authors.

Pinizzotto and Finkel (1990) compared the accuracy of professional psychological profilers with police detectives specially trained in personality profiling, police detectives who were untrained, clinical psychologists naive to both criminal profiling and criminal investigation, and undergraduate students. They found for both homicide and sex offense cases, profiles written by the professional profilers were richer than those written by the nonprofiler groups of detectives, psychologists, and students. The professional profilers had more correct answers to questions about the criminal, higher accuracy scores, and more correct lineup identifications for the sex offense cases than profilers, but the accuracy differences dissipated when they examined the homicide cases.

All in all, although psychological profiles are probably a potentially useful tool, spotting serial killers and serial rapists from those profiles is currently a difficult and unreliable procedure. As Monahan and Steadman (1984) point out, particular mental disorders do not correlate highly with specific crimes leading to some question about the point-to-point method of developing a picture of the perpetrator.

It is generally agreed that no profile can make up for a poor or incomplete crime scene investigation. To be useful, a profile's quality must be

274     Consultation and Operational Assistance

enhanced with sketches, photographs, accurate autopsy results, and thorough background investigations of the victim. In effect, psychological profiling of offenders carries the investigative process a step further than the usual crime scene investigation. The goal of criminal investigation and criminal profiling is the same and both depend on thoroughness of the crime scene investigator.

The procedure can be expected to provide usable data in only a modest number of highly specific types of crimes. Heilbrun (1992) reports the use of psychologists in the research section of the U.S. Secret Service. A form of profiling has been developed to identify, assess, and manage individuals who may pose a threat to those being protected by the Secret Service (the President, other executives, foreign dignitaries, etc.).

The most limiting factor about psychological profiling is the amount of training and preparation necessary to develop the skills necessary to accurately profile a crime. The profiler must possess an excellent knowledge of abnormal psychology, human behavior, crime scene investigative procedures, and forensic medicine. Much training and supervision are necessary before a psychologist or a police officer can function independently (Tetem, 1989).

### References

Ault ,R., Jr., & Reese, J. (1980, March). A psychological assessment of crime profiling. *FBI Enforcement Bulletin,* 49

Douglas, J., & Munn, C. (1992). Violent crime scene analysis-*modus operandi,* signature and staging. *FBI Law Enforcement Bulletin, 61* (2), 1-10.

Douglas, J., Ressler,R., Burgess,A., & Hartman, C. (1986). Criminal profiling fom crime analysis. *Behavioural Sciences and the Law, 4* (4), 401-421.

Hagaman, J., Wells, G., Blau, T., & Wells, C. (1987). Psychological profile of a family homicide. *The Police Chief, 54* (12), 19-23.

Hazelwood, R. (1983, September). The behaviour-oriented interview of rape victims: The key to profiling. *FBI Law Enforcement Bulletin,* 52.

Hazelwood, R., & Warren, J. (1989). The serial rapist: His characteristics and victims. *FBE Law Enforcement Bulletin, 58* (2), 18-25.

Hazelwood, R., & Warren, J. (1990). The criminal behaviour of the serial rapist. *FBI Law Enforcement Bulletin, 59* (2), 11-15.

Heilbrun, K. (1992). Careers. *Psychology Law Society News, 12*(3), 5.

Horn, J. (1988). Criminal personality profiling. In J. Reese & J. Horn (Eds.), *Police psychology: Operational assistance* (pp. 211-224). Washington, DC: US. Government Printing Office, Federal Bureau of Investigation .

Monahan, J., & Steadman, H. (1984, September). Crime and mental disorder. *research in brief.* U.S. Department of Justice, national Institute of Justice.

Pinizzotto, A., & Finkel, N. (1990). Criminal personality profiling-an outcome and process study. *Law and Human Behaviour, 14* (3), 215-233.

Reese, J. (1979, August). Obsessive-compulsive behaviour:The nuisance offender. *FBI Law Enforcement Bulletin,* 48.

Reiser, M. (1982c, March). Crime-specific psychological consultation. *The police chief.*

Ressler, R., & Burgess, A. (1985). The men who murder. *FBI Law Enforcement Bulletin, 54* (8), 2-6.

Rider, A. (1980, June, July, & August). Firesetter: A psychological profile. *FBI Law Enforcement Bulletin,* 49.

Tetem, H. (1989). Offender profiling. In W. Bailey (Ed.), *The encyclopedia of police science.* New York: Garland Publishing.

*The police chief.*

# [34]

Social Networks 13 (1991) 251–274
North-Holland

# The application of network analysis to criminal intelligence: An assessment of the prospects

Malcolm K. Sparrow

*Kennedy School of Government, Harvard University, 79 John F. Kennedy Street, Cambridge, MA 02138, USA*

This paper explores the opportunities for the application of network analytic techniques to the problems of criminal intelligence analysis, paying particular attention to the identification of vulnerabilities in different types of criminal organization – from terrorist groups to narcotics supply networks.

A variety of concepts from the network analysis literature are considered in terms of the promise they hold for helping law enforcement agencies extract useful information from existing collections of link data. For example, six different notions of "centrality" and the three major notions of "equivalence" are examined for their relevance in revealing the mechanics and vulnerabilities of criminal enterprises.

## 1. Introduction

The Intelligence Analysts Training Manual of the Metropolitan Police (Scotland Yard, London) bears as its frontispiece the statement:

> Analysis is the key to the successful use of information; it transforms raw data into intelligence. It is the fourth of five stages in the intelligence process: collection, evaluation, collation, analysis, dissemination. Without the ability to perform effective and useful analysis, the intelligence process is reduced to a simple storage and retrieval system for effectively unrelated data.

Intelligence agencies, despite this obvious awareness of the importance of intelligence analysis, have remained for the most part relatively unsophisticated in their use of analytic tools and concepts. They typically have plenty of data, much of it computerized, but comparatively little capability for extracting useful intelligence from it.

A great deal of that data can be presented in link form – that is, as a collection of nodes, with a pattern of connections. Graph theorists call them vertices and edges. Law enforcement agencies often call them entities and relationships. Whatever they are called they clearly lend themselves to analysis as networks. Some of the more obvious examples of such data types include contact reports (two or more people seen together at some specific time and place), telephone toll data, and financial transaction data (deposits, withdrawals, or transfer of funds between accounts).

The types of network questions to which intelligence analysts need answers are quite familiar to network analysts and graph theorists: "who is central in this organization?", "which names in this database appear to be aliases?", "which three individuals' removal or incapacitation would sever this drug-supply network?", "what role or roles does a specific individual appear to be playing within a criminal organization?", or "which communications links within an international terrorist fraternity are likely to be most worth monitoring?". All of these questions have fairly direct analogues in other fields, and most network analysts would be familiar with all the relevant network concepts.

Some other network questions, of significant interest to law enforcement agencies, are considerably beyond the state-of-the-art in network analysis techniques. They nevertheless remain network analysis questions. For example: "(from bank cash deposit records) what are the anomalies in the pattern of cash flow surrounding the Californian jewellery trade?", "(from contact reports) what significant changes have taken place in the supply operation for Columbian cocaine to New York City since this time last year?", or "(from a database of electronic fund transfers) where is there evidence of smurfing [1]?".

All these are network questions. So the concepts and tools of network analysis, and network analysts, probably have a lot to offer law enforcement. It is somewhat surprising and a little disappointing, therefore, to find almost no overlap between the literatures of network

---

[1] "Smurfing" is the breaking up of large sums of money into smaller units, and subsequent passing of each segment through multiple accounts. Used by money launderers, the practice is designed to make the money trail extremely difficult to follow.

analysis and law enforcement. The two fields have historically been quite ignorant of one another. There are just a few papers that have begun to explore the application of network analysis to intelligence analysis (for instance, Coady 1985; Howlett 1980; Davis 1981), but they have focused on relatively simple network concepts. Davis, for example, shows the importance of "liaisons", (which he calls "brokers"), in fencing operations and relates the concepts of cliques, centrality, and network density to conspiracy theory.

But in general most intelligence analysts do not have a clear idea of what the academic discipline of network analysis is. They are certainly not aware of it as an emerging discipline. Nor do they understand why it ought to be of paramount importance to their profession.

Conversely, those few network theorists who have been inclined to step outside the realm of retrospective examination of human (and occasionally animal) behavior do not appear to have stumbled into intelligence analysis. If they have, they have kept very quiet about it.

The contention of this paper is, first, that the concepts of network analysis are highly pertinent to many forms of intelligence analysis and are currently being used seldom, if at all. Second, that there is much creative and imaginative work to be done in adapting the existing concepts and tools of network analysis for direct application to intelligence databases. Third, that collaboration between the fields of network theory and intelligence analysis would benefit both a great deal. For intelligence analysis it could ultimately produce a whole new set of sophisticated tools. For network theory it will provide a new set of concrete challenges and real-world applications, not to mention some fascinating new databases (appropriately sanitized).

The purpose of this paper is to begin to deepen the dialogue between the two fields by charting some of the areas of common interest.

The sections that follow describe the state-of-the-art in law enforcement application of network analysis (Section 2); then describe the current needs of criminal intelligence analysis and the relevant properties of intelligence databases (Section 3). Section 4 examines several network analytic concepts – for instance, centrality, equivalence, strong and weak ties – and explores their application to law enforcement. Section 5, by way of conclusion, suggests what seem to be the most logical next steps in building an effective bridge between these two fields.

## 2. The state-of-the-art in law enforcement uses of network analysis

### 2.1. Anacapa charts

Use of the Anacapa charting system, as developed by Anacapa Sciences Inc., Santa Barbara, California [2], is currently the predominant form of network analysis within law enforcement. It is used particularly frequently within major fraud investigations and by Organized Crime Squads, where understanding of large and sometimes sophisticated criminal enterprises is required.

Anacapa charts constitute a two-dimensional visual representation of link data (see Harper and Harris, 1975; Howlett, 1980; Klovdahl, 1981; Coady 1985). They provide a method of making visual sense of a mass of data. They are also an extremely useful tool for communicating the results of analysis (and thus are used as briefing aids as well as aids for analysis). Anacapa charts generally depict individuals by small circles, and relationships by lines (solid or dotted according to whether the relationship is confirmed or unconfirmed). The charts may also show rectangles enclosing one or more individuals as a method of representing membership of corporations or institutions. They clearly show who is central, who is peripheral, and visually reveal chains of links connecting one individual to another. To a network analyst they look like typical network diagrams.

However, such charting systems do not actually do any analysis; they simply communicate the results. It is up to the officer preparing the chart to perform the analysis first, based upon what he knows and understands at the time. The graphical display can only communicate what the officer performing the analysis can grasp. Coady (1985) makes this quite explicit:

> Link Analysis is the graphic portrayal of investigative data, done in a manner to facilitate the understanding of large amounts of data, and particularly to allow investigators to develop possible relationships between individuals that otherwise would be hidden by the mass of data obtained.

Klovdahl (1981) explained the value of creating a visual representation of a sociogram. He says it makes things hitherto unseen become

[2] For more information contact Anacapa Sciences, Inc., P.O. Box 519, 901 Olive Street, Santa Barbara, California 93102.

painfully obvious. It is this benefit that Anacapa charts bring to intelligence analysis.

But note that the intelligent functions still take place in the minds of the analysts or investigators, and they use the chart simply as a pictorial aid. So the predominant locus for the law-enforcement community's intelligent interpretation of networks remains somewhere between the "picture on the wall" (or on the graphics display terminal) and the analyst's brain.

The analyst working to create a chart, from a set of link data, has a number of objectives in mind. First, he or she intends that the relative spatial proximity of two individuals on his or her chart will be crudely representative of their "closeness" within the criminal organization. Hence the common experience among intelligence analysts of having to keep redrawing the graph as new information, altering the apparent proximities, becomes available.

Second, the analyst aims to design the whole chart in such a way that no two connecting lines cross one other. They will often change the spatial positions of individuals, or entities, to prevent such crossings occurring.

Third, the analyst intends that "central" on the picture imply "central" within the organization. Centrality is determined at the outset by counting the total number of known associations for each individual, and picking the person with the highest number. This practice is described by Harper and Harris (1975), and is explicit within both the FBI's "Link Analysis" training manual, and in Metropolitan Police Training manuals on Intelligence Analysis. Formation of an "association matrix" (sociogram, or adjacency matrix) is described in each of these sources as a prerequisite for preparing the chart.

The individual thus designated as central is represented by a circle placed centrally on the chart. The analysts then work outwards, seeking to satisfy the first two objectives (described above) as they go. More broadly, the total number of established links (the "degree" of the node) for any one individual in the network determines whether that individual is to be treated as central or peripheral.

To a network or graph theorist these three objectives might seem a little bizarre. It is an interesting exercise to examine them against the backdrop of developed network theory. The crude representation of some notion of proximity is familiar as the objective of multidimensional scaling (see, for an introduction to the subject, Breiger *et al.*

1975; Kruskal and Wish 1978). But Anacapa charts are automatically two-dimensional. So this first objective can be translated into network theory as an attempt to find a stress-free multidimensional scaling of the network in just two dimensions. With organizations of any complexity there is no reason to believe that such a scaling will exist. There is even less reason to expect that analysts will be able to generate them manually! [3] Of course the one good reason for keeping Anacapa charts two-dimensional (whether manual or computerized), is that use of any other kind of chart as a visual aid is somewhat awkward.

The second objective – keeping the lines from crossing – is, again, sensible from a practical standpoint but theoretically perverse. It keeps the picture uncluttered and easy to follow. But it requires the network to be planar (in the graph theoretic sense)! Again, there is no reason to think that any complex criminal network will satisfy the requirements of planarity, or that it will have a representation which is even close to planar. (See any basic introduction to Graph Theory, (e.g. Wilson 1972) for a discussion of planarity, and Kuratowski's theorem (circa 1930) for a necessary and sufficient condition for planarity.)

The third objective – representing "centrality" within the organization by "centrality" on the chart – is very reasonable. But it employs a most unsophisticated concept of centrality, namely the selection of the point or points of "maximum degree" (those with the most established connections). Moreover the context in which it is applied makes the use of maximum degree potentially misleading: the determination of centrality will depend upon *who you know most about*, rather than *who is central or pivotal in any structural sense*. The danger in this practice is that it may incline an agency to pay closest attention to those it already knows most about, individuals who may not in fact be the principal characters. The practice may therefore serve to perpetuate unfortunate and misleading biases in the initial intelligence collection. Analysts are specifically warned of these dangers during Anacapa's training.

Providing a network-theoretical commentary on Anacapa charts does not, of course, diminish their usefulness in any way. They were a highly significant innovation and will remain a valuable aid to analysts for years to come. The commentary simply places this particular device within the broader landscape of network theoretic concepts, and thereby shows up some of its essential limitations as a network analytic tool.

---

[3] No Law Enforcement agency known to the author uses any of the available computerized multidimensional scaling algorithms.

## 2.2. Computerized "link analysis"

Computers are now being used to take some of the laborious manual work out of link charting. There are commercial products available (e.g. "Enhanced Computer Network Analysis Program" [ECNA] from Anacapa Sciences, California) and others under development, which incorporate the facility to lift the traditional link chart off the paper and put it on a graphics display terminal instead. It makes storage, retrieval and amendment of charts relatively speedy and efficient. It also adds the benefits of handling elastic images; images which can be enlarged, stretched, shifted and otherwise manipulated in the many and diverse ways which screens, and mice, make possible.

So computer-aided link analysis has arrived, and is clearly here to stay. It is another very valuable addition to the analyst's toolkit. But, for the most part, it is still not the computer which does much of the analysis. It is the analyst. The computer merely provides a versatile drawing board, complete with the option of burying within the picture references or sections of text (in the style of hypertext), retrievable at the click of a button.

But production of the charts from the database is far from automatic. The analyst is responsible for that, picking and choosing links from the database and asking the computer to show them to him. The analyst then shunts entities around on the screen in an attempt to produce some meaningful, planar, stress-free, centrality-preserving two-dimensional representation of the network. During this process the computer acts as a highly versatile image storage and retrieval device, but performs relatively mundane analytic tasks. Use of modern graphic user-interfaces (with windows, hypertext, and pull-down menus) have thus produced some first-class methods of *showing the results* of link analysis. But the computers are still not *doing the analysis*.

Computer-assisted link analysis significantly speeds up the generation of link charts, and makes updating or expanding them highly efficient. However, it is important for intelligence analysts to understand that use of technology in this way has not yet brought to bear on the structural analysis of criminal organizations either the computational capacity of modern computers or the sophistication of existing network analysis techniques.

## 2.3. Visual investigative analysis

Several of the more technically sophisticated law enforcement agencies also use, during major crimes enquiries, some form of "Event Flow charting" (Howlett 1980). Computerized versions of Event Flow Charts have been variously called Visual Investigative Analysis, or CAVIA (computer-aided VIA).

The basic concept, just like the Anacapa charts, looks remarkably like a network. In this case events are used as nodes, and events are connected if one either caused the other, or had to happen before it. The "Event Flow Chart" is therefore a pictorial representation of the chronology of all the relevant events surrounding the commission of the crime. Unlike Anacapa charts, it has a time line, traditionally running left to right. Preparation of such charts shows up obvious disparities in witnesses' statements or in their estimates of when things happened, and often reveals potentially fruitful avenues of enquiry.

A description of such systems by the FBI (entitled simply "Visual Investigative Analysis", FBI, US Department of Justice) explains:

> Through the use of a network (flowchart), VIA graphically displays the sequential and concurrent order of events involved in a criminal act.... Leads not ordinarily discernible through file review may become more apparent when the information is chronologically arranged.

This is not commonly considered structural network analysis by network theorists. It is mentioned here because many law enforcement officials (and analysts) think of it as network analysis. From the network theorists' point of view it is interesting mostly in that it employs the concept of "causal links", or of one event depending upon another, in much the same way that PERT (Program Evaluation and Review Technique) charts and CPM (Critical Path Method) analyses do.

## 2.4. Template matching

Some progress has also been made in the use of computers to perform "template matching", a process which helps the analyst to determine whether or not a particular type of crime is likely to have been committed, or whether a particular pattern of criminal relationships is in existence.

The FBI's "Big Floyd" prototype is an example of such a system (see Bayse and Morris 1987; and "An algorithm.." 1986). It performs the regular functions of storage and retrieval of link data, encompassing links of many different specified types. It does an excellent job of facilitating the interaction between investigator and the visually displayed network, or selected subgraphs from it. It also has first class facilities to enable the investigator to re-order and interrogate the database.

Significantly "Big Floyd" also introduces a new dimension of analysis – namely the notion of template matching. Essentially, ingredients of a criminal network are superimposed on a model template for particular kinds of deduction (example "Smith is probably guilty of embezzlement"). The template is the encapsulation of an expert investigator's accumulated experience and knowledge about a particular type of offence. If the appropriate combination of linkages exists, the deduction is probably "true". This inferential system is used as a component of an Artificial Intelligence system for investigation of organized crime activities.

## 2.5. Telephone toll analysis

Another useful, albeit extremely simple, device is pictorial presentation of telephone toll analysis as a network. Telephone numbers are used as nodes. Connecting lines are drawn wherever a call was made from one number to another. And the directed links (directed according to who initiated the call) are assigned a weight, which corresponds to the frequency of calls during some specified time period. It is a useful way to present a summary of call activity, where a criminal organization is known to be using certain telephones. The toll analysis can give some crude clues as to the command structure, and even the social cohesiveness, of the organization being monitored.

## 2.6. Structural network analysis

Despite the existence, and growing awareness, of tools such as those described above, law enforcement agencies have not pushed the frontiers of *structural* network analysis very far. Some of the available computerized link analysis packages (e.g. Anacapa Sciences' ECNA) are capable of finding connecting paths of length greater than 2 between specified entities, identifying groups and cliques, and separating large networks into their maximal connected subcomponents. But most agencies have no automated method for performing such rudimentary analyses, and remain largely unaware of the existence of such analytic capacities.

## 3. The needs of law enforcement

### 3.1. The need for strategic analysis

Traditionally law enforcement agencies, in attempting to combat the activities of sophisticated criminal organizations, have looked for some initial lead, and then have sought to exploit and develop that lead to its fullest potential. Lupsha (1980) surmised that the "lead-following" approach was not ultimately effective:

> Overall, in these [intelligence] units, there is a great deal of information collection and filing, but there is little analysis beyond the targeting and profiling of individual organized crime figures. In terms of the war against organized crime, this approach has caused some analysts to wonder if individual-oriented prosecutions merely help to open the promotion ladder within organized crime groups, moving new individuals into management positions while the group and the crime matrices they engage in continues.

Some agencies have become highly skilled at making the most of any leads they receive, frequently introducing undercover agents into an organization in order to uncover its entire workings. Some agencies quite deliberately wait, before making arrests or seizures, until they feel ready to close down the entire organization.

The problem is that such operations are difficult, dangerous, time-consuming and expensive. And many law enforcement agencies have far more leads than they have the resources to pursue. Given the fact that crime levels are not diminishing, despite countless "successes" against individual criminal enterprises, investigative agencies are discovering the need to perform strategic analysis of organized crime; that is, to try and grasp the whole picture, and to allocate investigative resources to the principal vulnerabilities of criminal enterprises and professions.

It was precisely the need to perform *strategic* analysis of the money laundering business, rather than simply follow each available lead to its natural conclusion, that gave rise to the establishment of the U.S. Treasury Department's Financial Crimes Enforcement Network in 1990 (see Kennedy 1990; Sparrow 1990). FinCEN is an intelligence operation dedicated to the analysis of the financing of criminal enterprises whatever their primary criminal activity (drugs, racketeering, vice etc.).

With that focus FinCEN has the capacity and opportunity to ask deep structural questions about trends and practices in modern money laundering techniques. Doing so should, over the long term, facilitate more effective targeting and resource allocation as well as the design of appropriate new financial regulations and controls. FinCEN, along with a few other intelligence agencies, now knows that it needs a whole new generation of sophisticated network analysis tools in order to do its job.

## 3.2. Characteristics of criminal networks

Much criminal intelligence data, as mentioned above, either appears in link form or is readily convertible to it. It would be enormously gratifying, therefore, if we could simply throw the existing network analysis toolkit at criminal intelligence databases, and come away with a set of valuable new insights. Of course it is not that easy. If it were, it would surely have been done before.

The fact is that most network analysis tools have been developed within the context of retrospective social science investigations, and they are therefore designed for use on networks which are small, static, and with very few distinct types of linkages (generally only one).

It is worth considering the properties of criminal networks, and associated intelligence databases, which present significant challenges to the science of network analysis as it now stands.

*Size*
First and foremost, criminal intelligence databases can be huge, with many thousands of nodes. The computational ramifications are obvious – mandating the use of sparse matrix techniques or extensive exploita-

tion of parallel processing should any analytical algorithm exceed $O(n^3)$. Some network analysis algorithms do claim to be able to handle very sizeable networks. For example the NEGOPY program (Richards and Rice 1981) claims to handle up to 30,000 links or so. But it contains an unfortunate reliance on a one-dimensional interim stage in the analysis of groups and cliques, which will inevitably render its results suspect when applied to networks of any complexity.

*Incompleteness*

Criminal network data is also inevitably incomplete; i.e. some existant links or nodes will be unobserved or unrecorded. Little research has been done on the effects of incomplete information on apparent structure. There is some work on the problems of statistical inference from incomplete graphs (Frank 1978), researched using random link samplings from known networks; also on the relationship between network density and structural properties (Friedkin 1981). But the relevance of such work to criminal networks is largely negated by the fact that the incompleteness in the criminal databases will be anything but random – it will be systematic, at least in part, in accordance with the biases introduced by investigative methods and assumptions. The focus of existing intelligence data is determined more by the prior subjective judgments of investigators than by objective reality.

*Fuzzy boundaries*

The boundaries of any particular criminal web are quite ambiguous. Even organized crime families are often interrelated. And many significant crime figures are significant precisely because they are connected to a number of different criminal organizations. So there is no obvious criterion by which players can be excluded or included in any one network analysis (in stark contrast to the scenarios of Sampson's monastery data or the Bank Wiring Group). Of course criminal networks, like any other, can be split unambiguously into maximal connected subcomponents, but these may still be extensive.

*Dynamic*

Criminal networks are, for all practical purposes, dynamic, not static. Each contact report, telephone call, or financial transaction has a time and date. The relationship between any two individuals is not merely present or absent (binary), nor is it simply weaker or stronger (ascribed a static analogue weighting); rather it *has a distribution over time*, waxing and waning from one period to another. Many of the most useful network questions depend heavily on this temporal dimension, begging information about which associations are becoming stronger, or weaker, or extinct.

The problematic absence of research on dynamic networks was echoed by Barnes and Harary (1983). A little work has been done on the evolution of network connections over time in dynamic networks (e.g. Hammer 1979/80), and a little on structural change within networks (Doreian 1980), but little or nothing has been done to develop algorithms for revealing significant network changes over time in the context of networks where each link has a time-dimension coordinate.

### 3.3. Effects of these properties

It could be argued that these properties are in fact quite typical of real-life networks, and that the discipline of network analysis has not as yet faced up to these broader and more general challenges. On the other hand these properties produce computational nightmares, demand algorithmic complexity, and require substantial advances in methods of statistical inference.

These properties certainly render some existing network theory concepts less useful than others. For example, the fuzzy boundaries render precise global network measures (such as radius, diameter, even density) almost meaningless. With the global measures go some, but not all, measures of centrality.

The remainder of this paper is devoted to an examination of some of the existing concepts of network theory. The intention is to provide an initial assessment of their relevance to, and promise for, criminal intelligence analysis.

## 4. Relevant concepts from social network analysis

### 4.1. Centrality

Some notion of centrality is clearly relevant. In seeking to incapacitate criminal organizations one obvious approach is to identify those players who are somehow central, vital, key, or pivotal, and target them for removal or surveillance. The network centrality, or otherwise, of individuals arrested will determine the extent to which their arrest impedes continued operation of the criminal activity. Thus centrality is an important ingredient (but by no means the only one) in considering the identification of network vulnerabilities.

The network analysis literature contains many different notions of centrality, however. Six of them seem reasonably distinct, and each will be examined briefly. The first three of these six were subject of a "Conceptual Clarification..." by Linton Freeman (Freeman 1979).

*(1) Degree.* The "degree" of any node of the network is defined as the number of other nodes to which it is directly linked. In the case of directed networks (where links have direction and may be asymmetric) the degree is usually defined as the number of paths coming *from* a node.

*(2) Betweenness.* The "betweenness" of a node is defined as the number of geodesics (shortest paths between two other nodes) which pass through it. It is a measure of how important any one node might be to effective communication within, or operation of, the network. Removing a node of high "betweenness" will, by definition, lengthen the paths connecting several other nodes, rendering communication or transactions between them less efficient. Precise measures of "betweenness" permit the counting of fractional geodesics in cases where there is a "tie" for shortest path. Also measures of betweenness in non-symmetric networks have been proposed (Gould 1987).

*(3) Closeness.* The concept of "closeness" picks as central to a network the node which minimizes the maximum of the minimal path-lengths to other nodes in the network. That is, the central node becomes the node of minimum radius, where the radius of a node is defined as the longest of its shortest connecting paths to other nodes.

*(4) Euclidean centrality after multidimensional scaling.* This idea is seldom made explicit, but is implicit in a great number of presentations. Any plot (two-or three-dimensional) of the results of multidimensional scaling makes this kind of centrality quite apparent. It is analogous-to the "center of gravity" of a network. (See Kruskal and Wish 1978 for a general introduction to MDS.)

*(5) Point strength.* A node's "point strength" is defined as the increase in the number of maximal connected network subcomponents upon removal of that node. So it is a measure of how much network

fragmentation would be caused by removal of that node. Algorithms for computing point strength have been created (Capobianco and Molluzzo 1979/80).

*(6) Business.* Finally, there is the notion of the "business" of a node – which is a measure of the local information content when the network is seen as a communications network (Stephenson and Zelen 1989). To obtain some precise numerical scale upon which to measure "business", one can imagine all nodes firing (transmitting) along each of their links once per unit time. Choose some retransmission ratio (between zero and one), whereby every received transmission is retransmitted one period later but with some loss of intensity, by each node. Keep the system firing repeatedly until the total information content of each node and each link reaches equilibrium. This will occur asymptotically and monotonically both for directed and undirected networks. Then measure each node's total transmission intensity per unit time. The equilibrium transmission intensities represent useful relative, but not absolute, indicators of "how busy" each node might be.

### 4.1.1. Applications of centrality

So, which of these six concepts are most relevant to intelligence analysis? With respect to targeting, it would appear that the second and the sixth (Betweenness and Business) would be useful measures of significance within communication networks. To apply them to large networks, however, would necessitate the addition of some severe distance limiting effects in order to avoid imponderable computational problems.

The third and the fourth (Closeness and Euclidean Centrality) become quite arbitrary if the network has arbitrary or fuzzy boundaries. But, in fact, Euclidean Centrality is probably closest to the reality of the Anacapa chart – where centrality on the chart equates with Euclidean centrality after a manual version of two-dimensional scaling – even though the practical determination of the starting (central) node was initially by its Degree.

The fifth idea, Point Strength, seems particularly important if an agency's objective is fragmentation of a criminal network. But it seems insufficiently general. The Point Strength of a node measures its fragmentation effect when regarded as a cutset of size one. But it is quite practical, and probably useful, to consider larger cutsets. So we should extend the concept of point strength to what could clumsily be called "Set Strength", being the increase in the number of disconnected components resulting from removal of a set of nodes. The notion of non-trivial cutsets is familiar to graph theorists as the subject of Menger's Theorem (Wilson 1972; Seidman and Foster 1978).

Finding minimal cutsets, or just small cutsets, that effectively sever communications channels or supply lines is a versatile and useful strategy, whether an agency is concerned to halt drug supply from one place to another or to prevent a terrorist organization from acquiring explosives. It is useful both for general network fragmentation objectives, as well as for targeted or specific disconnection objectives. It is also highly relevant to the selection of targets for communications interception, as communications between one group and another must, by definition of a cutset, pass through any cutset that would disconnect them.

In fact the practical task facing many law enforcement agencies, in seeking to rupture criminal supply operations, is to identify not just a manageable cutset, but manageable cutsets *within that agency's jurisdiction*.

Application of these various measures to asymmetric networks may have some relevance too. In drug supply networks drugs essentially flow one way and money flows the other, but the two commodities do not necessarily pass through symmetric channels. Strangling either one of those two flows is enough to put a supply operation out of business. It is therefore better to view the network as the overlay of two directed networks, even in those parts where it appears to be symmetric.

On balance it appears that the second, fifth and sixth notions of centrality (Betweenness, Point Strength, and Business) have greater relevance to the identification of network vulnerabilities than the others (Degree, Closeness, and Euclidean Centrality).

## 4.2. Equivalence

The disruptive effectiveness of removing one individual or a set of individuals from a network depends not only on their centrality, but also upon some notion of their uniqueness. The more unique, or unusual, their role the harder they will be to replace. The most valuable targets will be both central and difficult to replace.

Once again the network analysis literature offers a variety of concepts of equivalence. There are three in particular that are quite distinct and which, between them, seem to capture most of the important ideas that have been expressed on the subject. There is, in the literature, an abundance of variations on these three main themes. There has also been an abundance of confusion over the last decade between these ideas, and some rather pointless debate as to which of them is most important. Like all models, they are each important in appropriate contexts and less so in others. In the context of criminal intelligence analysis they turn out to have very different applications.

The three concepts selected for examination here are "Substitutability", "Stochastic Equivalence", and "Role Equivalence". All three types of equivalence are mathematical equivalence relations (being symmetric, transitive and reflexive) and therefore produce exhaustive partitions of any network.

*Substitutability.* This is the simplest notion of equivalence, and goes under a variety of names, including "interchangeability" and (somewhat misleadingly) "structural equivalence". A clear definition is given by Lorrain and White (1971):

> Objects $a$, $b$ of a category $C$ are structurally equivalent if, for any morphism M and any object $x$ of $C$, $aMx$ if and only if $bMx$, and $xMa$ if and only if $xMb$. In other words, $a$ is structurally equivalent to $b$ if $a$ relates to every object $x$ of $C$ in exactly the same ways as $b$ does. From the point of view of the logic of the structure, then, $a$ and $b$ are absolutely equivalent, they are substitutable.

For networks, this definition means two nodes are substitutable, or interchangeable, if they are linked to precisely the same set of nodes.

It is important to note that blockmodelling is discerning the "substitutability" of nodes as opposed to any other of the more sophisticated forms of equivalence. (See Breiger *et al.* (1975) regarding the CONCOR algorithm, a hierarchical clustering approach to blockmodelling. Panning (1982) develops goodness of fit measures for blockmodels. See Heil and White (1976) re BLOCKER, and Everett (1982) re EBLOC, a fast blocking algorithm based on a slightly extended definition of structural equivalence.)

Borgatti and Everett (1989) discuss the complete class of automorphic equivalences, and mention that substitutability (which they call structural equivalence) implies role equivalence – which it does. The converse is obviously not true. Thus substitutability is a (mathematically) stronger condition than role equivalence.

### 4.2.1. Stochastic equivalence

This is a slightly more sophisticated idea. A clear definition is given in Wasserman and Anderson (1987), definition 4:

> Given a stochastic multigraph $X$, actors $i$ and $j$ are stochastically equivalent if and only if the probability of any event concerning $X$ is unchanged by an interchanging of actors $i$ and $j$.

In other words, two network nodes are stochastically equivalent if the probabilities of them being linked to any other particular individual are the same. This notion is closer to an intuitive notion of structural equivalence than simple substitutability. Street-level drug suppliers, working for one particular distribution organization, could be seen as stochastically equivalent if they, as a group, all knew roughly 70 percent of the group, did not mix with street-level dealers from any other organizations, all received their supplies from one person, and all delivered their cash to just one, randomly selected, of three collectors.

This idea of equivalence is importantly *not* the same as substitutability, as it allows for the probabilities in the definition to be something other than zero or one (as exemplified in the hypothetical situation above). Most blockmodelling techniques could only find the equivalence classes under stochastic equivalence if all the underlying probabilities were either very low or very high (because those are the probabilities that will produce discernible zero-blocks and one-blocks in a reordered adjacency matrix).

### 4.2.2. Role equivalence

In many ways this is the most intuitive idea of equivalence, as it allows two individuals to be counted equivalent if they play the same role in different organizations, even if they have no common acquaintances at all. It has been termed "Regular Equivalence" by some. We should probably have a precise mathematical definition:

> In a network $X$, $a$ and $b$ are role equivalent if there exists an automorphism $f$ of $X$ which maps $a$ onto $b$ and $b$ onto a, and which is link-preserving. That is, $f(a) = b$ and $f(b) = a$; also $f(c)$ is linked to $f(d)$ if and only if $c$ was linked to $d$.

The important way in which this differs from substitutability is that it permits permutation of the other nodes of the network. In other words node a can be mapped onto node *b* provided you map *a*'s organization onto *b*'s organization at the same time.

Role equivalence is also intuitively quite different from stochastic equivalence. Individuals in entirely separate organizations, who are thus in disconnected subcomponents of the overall network, can still be role equivalent. They could not possibly be regarded as stochastically equivalent as each has zero probability of knowing anyone in the other's organization.

Despite the intuitive appeal of role equivalence it was not much discussed in the literature until recently. Sailer (1978) described the notion, but the confusion between role equivalence and the other forms of equivalence persisted long after. Role equivalence was mentioned by Doreian (1988) as "regular equivalence" although he did not dwell on its significance. The concept was then spelt out in great detail by Faust (1988).

Some algorithms for finding role similarities have been suggested. Everett and Borgatti (1988) present a method based on determination of a node's orbits by examining the size of successively higher order neighborhoods. Also Burt (1990) describes an approach developed by Hummell and Sodeur for detecting role equivalence by counting and classifying types of triadic relations. This method unfortunately only takes close neighborhoods into account, not any deeper structure.

### 4.2.3. Applications of equivalence

The concept of substitutability has some ramifications for the assessment of network vulnerabilities. Whether or not a target individual has a substitute has an obvious and direct bearing on the extent to which his or her removal will[1] damage the operation of the network. If another individual exists, who can take over the same role, already having the same connections, then the target individual was not well chosen. To damage the network (assuming the absence of individual capacity constraints) an agency would need to remove or incapacitate not only the target individual, but all other substitutable individuals as well. Individuals who have no available network substitutes would make more worthwhile targets.

The concept of substitutability also has relevance to detecting the use of aliases. The use of an alias by a criminal might also show up in a network analysis as the presence of two or more substitutable individuals. This is particularly likely if the analysis is performed on aggregated link data, drawn from two or more agencies or investigations. It is conceivable that the same individual could be known to different agencies by different names. In which case, the merged data would show two or more nodes for the same person. But, provided different modes of agency operation did not unduly bias the types of contacts or transactions they were likely to witness, the immediate network neighborhoods of those nodes would be similar or identical. The interchangeability of the nodes would reveal the interchangeability of the names.

There is a simple computational method of discovering such aliases within a network, should they exist. Two alias nodes would have no link joining them directly, but would have a significant number of paths of length two connecting them, one for each member of their immediate neighborhood. Existence of many paths of length two without a direct connection is, otherwise, a most unlikely phenomenon.

The concept of role equivalence is clearly applicable when considering the roles that individuals play within different criminal structures. In some ways the FBI's use of template matching can be regarded as a particular form of a search for role equivalence. The distinguishing characteristic of the template matching approach being the comparison of network individuals with a hypothetical, idealized individual (or template) rather than with another existing network node. The hypothetical individual is constructed by an investigator expert in that particular type of crime, or role.

The same concept might also be useful in performing strategic analysis of various criminal trades. Agencies might choose to focus investigative efforts on some particular, and essential, role in any criminal activity. Identification of vulnerabilities special to one role might lead to a shortage of people able to offer those services to criminal organizations. For instance, targeting courier-recruiters could help reduce cross-border currency or drug traffic, just as targeting drivers could stall armed robbery gangs. Any kind of role uniqueness represents a strategic vulnerability within a criminal profession, not least because insertion of undercover agents within criminal organizations is normally role-specific.

It is illuminating to compare the template-matching methods for role detection with the traditional approaches to blockmodelling, and to consider how each would cope with an individual who played more than one role. The issue revolves around the treatment of zeroes in the adjacency matrix, or sociogram. Blockmodelling techniques usually require two nodes not only to have a similar pattern of connections before they are deemed equivalent, but also a similar pattern of disconnections (i.e. absent links). As soon as the possibility of multiple roles is acknowledged, then the requirement to match the zeroes as well has to be dropped. Attention has to be paid only to finding the *presence* of a designated set of connections, no matter what other extraneous links are observed.

This raises the possibility of a further field of enquiry. Suppose there were a number of designated roles within a network, and a template of connections had been prepared for each role. Then a useful question might be "which set of roles best explains this individual's aggregate network connections?". The task would then be to find not just the best-fitting template, but the best-fitting set of templates.

## 4.3. Weak ties

The notion of weak ties (Granovetter 1973) may be of particular interest in finding the vulnerabilities of criminal communication networks. The "cell" structure of the Irish Republican Army fits Granovetter's model exceptionally well. IRA terrorists work together in small, well-established teams (cliques), which makes the organization particularly difficult to infiltrate. Command and control communications directing the operations of individual "cells" use channels that, within the organizational context, look exactly like Granovetter's weak ties. The most valuable communications channels to monitor, therefore, are those which are seldom used and which lie outside the relatively dense clique structures.

It is reasonable to assume more generally that weak ties are the ties which add most to the efficiency of communication within a network. They will be disproportionately represented within the network's geodesics, precisely because of their network spanning properties. Urgent or important network signals are therefore more likely to be detected on the weak ties than on the stronger ones.

Disabling communication channels which are weak ties is also likely to have the greatest effect on the completeness of network transmission, as well as upon its speed.

Note that intelligence analysts have traditionally used the terminology of "strong" and "weak" links in a very different sense – to indicate the reliability of the information rather than the links' structural importance (Harper and Harris 1975). A "strong" link has been, for analysts, one which has been "confirmed" by a second independent source.

## 5. Summary

Existing concepts from the discipline of network analysis have been shown to be relevant to the analysis of criminal intelligence. These include several different notions of centrality and of equivalence, and the concept of weak ties. There are many other network analysis concepts which might turn out to be useful also. But the object of this paper was not to be exhaustive; merely exploratory and introductory.

The law enforcement community, being largely unaware of the methods and concepts developed within the discipline of network analysis, has not yet had the opportunity to enunciate its needs for more sophisticated tools.

There are consequently two audiences for this paper; and two aims. First, for the network theorists: that it would act as a belated invitation to consider intelligence analysis as a most interesting application for their skills.

Second, for the law enforcement agencies in general and intelligence analysts in particular: that it would familiarize them with the fundamentals of network theory sufficiently to enable them to imagine what is possible, and to enable them to begin the process of specifying exactly what they need by way of additional analytic tools.

## References

Barnes, J.A. and F. Harary
    1983 "Graph-theory in network analysis." *Social Networks* 5 (2): 235–244.
Bayse, W.A. and C.G. Morris
    1987 "FBI automation strategy: Development of AI applications for national investigative programs". *Signal Magazine* May.
Borgatti, S.P. and M.G. Everett
    1989 "The class of all regular equivalences: Algebraic structure and computation". *Social Networks* 11(1): 65–90.

Breiger, R.L., S.A. Boorman and P. Arabie
    1975 "Algorithm for clustering relational data with applications to social network analysis and comparison with multidimensional-scaling". *Journal of Mathematical Psychology* 2(3): 328–383.
Burt, R.S.
    1990 "Detecting role equivalence". *Social Networks 12*: 83–97.
Capobianco, M.F. and J.C. Molluzzo
    1979/80 "The strength of a graph and its application to organizational structure". *Social Networks 2*: 275–284.
Coady, W.F.
    1985 "Automated link analysis – artificial intelligence-based tool for investigators". *Police Chief 52*(9): 22–23.
Davis R.H.
    1981 "Social network analysis – an aid in conspiracy investigations". *FBI Law Enforcement Bulletin 50*(12): 11–19.
Doreian, P.
    1980 "On the evolution of group and network structure". *Social Networks 2*: 235–252.
    1988 "Borgatti toppings on Doreian splits: Reflections on regular equivalence". *Social Networks 10*(3): 273–287.
Everett, M.G.
    1982 "A graph theoretic blocking procedure for social networks". *Social Networks 4*(2): 147–168.
Everett, M.G. and S. Borgatti
    1988 "Calculating role similarities: An algorithm that helps determine the orbits of a graph". *Social Networks 10*: 77–91.
Faust, K.
    1988 "Comparison of methods for positional analysis: Structural and general equivalences". *Social Networks 10*: 313–341.
Frank, Ove.
    1978 "Sampling and estimation in large social networks". *Social Networks 1*: 91–101.
Freeman, L.C.
    1979 "Centrality in social networks: Conceptual clarification". *Social Networks 1*: 215–240.
Friedkin, N.
    1981 "The development of structure in random networks: An analysis of the effects of increasing network density on five measures of structure". *Social Networks 3*: 41–52.
Gould, Roger V.
    1987 "Measures of betweenness in non-symmetric networks". *Social Networks 9*: 277–282.
Granovetter, Mark S.
    1973 "The strength of weak ties". *American Journal of Sociology 8*: 1360–1380.
Hammer, M.
    1979/80 "Predictability of social connections over time". *Social Networks 2*: 165–180.
Harper, W.R. and D.H. Harris
    1975 "The application of link analysis to police intelligence". *Human Factors 17*(2): 158.
Heil, G.H. and H.C. White
    1976 "An algorithm for finding simultaneous homomorphic correspondences between graphs and their image graphs". *Behavioural Science 21*: 26–45.
Howlett, J.B.
    1980 "Analytical investigative techniques: Tools for complex criminal investigations". *Police Chief 47*(12): 42–45.

Kennedy, D.M.
  1990 "On the kindness of strangers: The origins and early days of FinCEN". Teaching Case no. C16–90–1000.0 John F. Kennedy School of Government, Harvard University, Cambridge, Mass.
Klovdahl, A.S.
  1981 "A note on images of networks". *Social Networks 3*: 197–214.
Kruskal, Joseph B. and Myron Wish
  1978 *Multidimensional Scaling*. Beverley Hills, CA: Sage.
Lorrain, F.P. and H.C. White
  1971 "Structural equivalence of individuals in networks". *Journal of Mathematical Sociology 1*: 49–80.
Lupsha, P.A.
  1980 "Steps toward a strategic analysis of organized crime". *Police Chief*. International Association of Chiefs of Police, Gaithersburg, MD.
Panning, W.H.
  1982 "Fitting blockmodels to data". *Social Networks 4*(1): 81–101.
Richards, W.D. and R.E. Rice
  1981 "The NEGOPY network analysis program". *Social Networks 3*(3): 215–223.
Sailer, L.D.
  1978 "Structural equivalence: Meaning and definition, computation and application". *Social Networks 1*(1): 73–90.
Seidman, S.B. and B.L. Foster
  1978 "A note on the potential for genuine cross-fertilization between anthropology and mathematics". *Social Networks 1*: 65–72.
Sparrow, M.K.
  1990 "An evaluation of the potential of the U.S. Department of the Treasury's financial crimes enforcement network". Report prepared for U.S. Treasury and Congress.
Stephenson, K. and M. Zelen
  1989 "Rethinking centrality: Methods and examples". *Social Networks 11*(1): 1–38.
Wasserman, S. and C. Anderson
  1987 "Stochastic a posteriori blockmodels: Construction and assessment". *Social Networks 9*: 1–36.
Wilson, R.J.
  1972 *Introduction to Graph Theory*. London: Longman.
  1986 "An algorithm for finding patterns of racketeering through subgraph embedding". Informal Technical Notes, Institute for Defence Analysis. 20 August.

# Psychology of Offender Profiling

David Canter
*University of Liverpool*

## ORIGINS

The term 'offender profiling' was first regularly used by members of the FBI's Behavioral Science Unit to describe the process of drawing inferences about a suspect's characteristics from the details of his or her actions in a crime. Concerned mainly with rape and homicide (Hazelwood and Burgess, 1987; Ressler, Burgess and Douglas, 1988), they demonstrated that it was possible to draw general conclusions about the life style, criminal history and residential location of a person who had committed a number of crimes, from careful examination of where, when and how those crimes had been committed.

Although the inference processes on which the FBI agents drew were illuminated by interviews they themselves had conducted with a few dozen convicted offenders, and by their own experiences of investigating many crimes, their processes of inference derivation were broadly *deductive*, being based upon common sense as might be the basis of judicial decisions. In the tradition of the detective novel, and other less fictional accounts of the solving of crimes, the processes that the FBI agents used focused on the clues derived directly from the crime scene. They drew upon general principles, drawn from everyday experience, to deduce the implications that the internal logic of a crime might have. So, for example, a well-organised and planned crime would be hypothesised to be perpetrated by an individual who typically was well organised and planned in general (Ressler et al., 1988).

Subsequently, a number of studies—the majority of which have been conducted by the Investigative Psychology Research Group at the University of Surrey (now at the University of Liverpool)—have been able to demonstrate

*Handbook of Psychology in Legal Contexts*
Edited by R. Bull and D. Carson. © 1995 John Wiley & Sons Ltd

that the valuable insights of FBI agents can be developed by using the *inductive* processes of science. By considering empirical results from the study of the actions of a large number of criminals it has been possible to propose both theories and methodologies that elaborate the relationships between an offender's actions and his or her characteristics.

Two interrelated issues need to be distinguished here. One is the common procedure of inferring general characteristics about a person from particulars of his or her behaviour. The second issue has its roots more clearly in the traditions of scientific psychology. This is the possibility of building psychological theories that will show how and why variations in criminal behaviour occur.

The first meaning for 'offender profiling' with its origins in everyday experience, described the process whereby experienced investigators, and other people with direct knowledge of criminal activities, could give advice to detectives. As such, this procedure has roots that can be traced at least to biblical times. It is, therefore, not surprising that from the earliest years of criminal investigations, there have been attempts to draw upon similar ideas in order to give assistance to the conduct of enquiries. The senior medical officer at the time of the Jack the Ripper enquiry in 1888, provided suggestions about the characteristics of the offender in an attempt to help the police locate the killer (Rumbelow, 1988). Earlier in the nineteenth century the novelist Edgar Allan Poe had given guidance, with a similar lack of success, to police investigations in the United States. Much of what is called 'profiling' today still has its roots in this application of 'common sense'.

In what follows, I will focus on the second meaning that is developing for 'offender profiling', dealing with the psychological issues involved.

## CONSTRAINTS

There are constraints on both the information available to the police during an investigation and also on the type of information on which they can act. The constraints on the information available about the crime relate to the fact that only an account of what has happened, who the victim is, where it took place and when, is available to investigators. There is hardly ever any direct observation by the investigator, or the possibility of direct contact with the offender during the commission of the crime. This is very different from most areas of psychology, where the person of focal interest is available for close, direct observation and detailed questioning. If there is a victim who survives a crime, then that victim may be able to give the details of what occurred. But even in this case, it is unlikely that the victim can give any reliable information about the internal, cognitive processes of the perpetrator during the criminal acts. So the predictor variables are limited to those that are external to the offender.

The criteria variables (i.e. important features of the offender) are also restricted, because the information on which the police can act is limited to what is available to them in the investigative process. Details of a person's criminal history, as well as descriptions of age and appearance, occupational characteristics and domestic circumstances are all potentially available to investigating officers for any particular suspect. However, personality characteristics, detailed measures of intelligence, attitudes and fantasies are all more difficult for investigating officers to uncover. Similarly, in relation to giving guidance as to where detectives should look to find possible suspects, information about residential location, or recreational activities, for example, are more likely to be of immediate value than the issues with which psychologists are more conventionally concerned, such as locus of control or sexual predilections.

# THE CANONICAL EQUATIONS

The methodological difficulties and the need for theory in this area can be illustrated by consideration of the inferential problem at the heart of profiling as a Canonical Correlation (see Tabachnick and Fidell, 1983). Such a procedure has the objective of analysing 'the relationships between two sets of variables' (p. 146). In other words, it is an attempt to derive multiple regression equations that have a number of criterion variables as well as a number of predictor variables.

On one side of this equation are variables derived from information about the offence which would be available to investigators. On the other side, there are the characteristics of the offender that are most useful in facilitating the police enquiry. So, if $A_{1...n}$ represents $n$ actions of the offender (including, for example, time, place and victim selection) and $C_{1...m}$ represents $m$ characteristics of the offender, then the empirical question is to establish the values of the weightings ($F_{1...n}$ and $K_{1...m}$) in an equation of the following form:

$$F_1A_1 + ... + F_nA_n = K_1C_1 + ... K_mC_m$$

If such canonical equations could be established for any subset of crimes then they would provide a powerful basis for police investigations, as well as raising some fascinating psychological questions about criminal behaviour.

The first step in producing such equations is to demonstrate that there are reliable relationships between A(ction)s and C(haracteristic)s, even at the one-to-one level. Indeed, the whole possibility of an empirically based approach to offender profiling depends upon the presence of these relationships.

## A Study of the Relationship of Sexual Actions in Assaults and Offenders' Offence History

A number of studies conducted at the University of Surrey do show that this *a priori* assumption can be supported fairly readily. For example, in an unpublished study of 60 serial rapists that I carried out with Rupert Heritage, we classified the first offence of each offender in terms of the presence or absence of four sexual aspects of the assault that had a frequency that was neither very high, nor very low in the sample: i.e. (i) insistence by the offender that the victim masturbate him, (ii) oral ejaculation by the offender, (iii) aggression by the offender during the sexual activity, and (iv) aggression after it. These four A(ction) variables were each independently correlated with two variables created on the basis of whether or not the offender had a criminal record for, first, indecent exposure, and secondly indecent assault. A further two C(haracteristic)s variables were created to indicate the frequency of indecency convictions, thirdly, as a juvenile and fourthly as an adult. Each of the four A variables was then correlated with each of the four C variables.

Using conventional indicators of statistical significance, 15 out of the 16 values would be considered significant, providing definite evidence that the occurrence of certain actions during a sexual assault are more likely to be made by a man with a criminal history for indecency than not. But such results also raise many questions. For example, in this instance frequency of juvenile convictions for indecency has the highest correlation with the sexual actions, but without extensive examination of a variety of other possible C variables and the relationships they have to each other it is difficult to tell how reliable such a correlation is likely to be with other samples. This correlation may drop considerably if the sample had a lower age range, for it may just be an artefact of the age of the offenders.

## An Example of the Relationships between Rapists' Behaviour and Offender Characteristics

Carrying out a further study on the same sample of 60 rapes, a number of characteristics beyond the criminal history of the offenders were considered; these were correlated with a range of distinct offence behaviours, such as wearing gloves, binding the victim, and so on. The association coefficients in this case were not as high as for the previous analysis but the majority would pass conventional criteria for statistical significance. However, the problem that these results illustrate is that there are no uniquely strong relationships between a given A variable and a given C variable. This means that there will be a mixture of correlations within the A variables and within the C variables that will contaminate any initial attempts to establish specific relationships between these two groups of variables.

These results, thus lend some support to the possibility of establishing empirical links between the A and the C variables of the canonical correlation, for one type of crime at least. Other unpublished studies have indicated similar possibilities for burglary (Barker, 1989), workplace crime (Robertson, 1993) and child abuse (Corstorphine, 1993; Kirby, 1993). But in no case are there simple relationships between one A variable and one C variable. The central problems of canonical equations thus emerge. A variety of combinations of A weightings can just as validly give rise to a variety of combinations of C weightings. There is not one, but many possible relationships within any data set linking the As to the Cs. In concrete terms this could mean for instance that one pattern of behaviour could indicate a young man with little criminal history or just as readily an older man with a lot of criminal experience.

A second problem was identified by Tabachnick and Fidell (1983). This is the sensitivity of the solution in the A set of variables to the inclusion of variables in the C set. Minor variations in the variance or the inclusion of particular variables in the A set may radically change the weightings in the C set. So, for example, leaving out of the calculations an action because a witness or victim was not sure about it, could produce different proposals about the offender than if that action were included.

# THE OFFENDER CONSISTENCY HYPOTHESIS

One hypothesis central to profiling is that the way an offender carries out a crime on one occasion will have some characteristic similarities to the way he or she carries out crimes on other occasions. If the inherent variations between contexts, for any aspect of human behaviour, is greater than the variations between people then it is unlikely that clear differences between individuals will be found for those behaviours. This hypothesis is applicable to the situation in which a person has committed only one crime. Even in that case a 'profile' has to be based upon the assumption that the criminal is exhibiting characteristics that are typical of that person, not of the situation in which the crime was committed.

## An Examination of the Linking of Three Rapes to one Offender

This can be illustrated by an exploratory study of 17 serial rapists carried out by Hammond (1990). For each rapist three rapes were selected, representing attacks that occurred in the early, middle and late stages of their series. For each rape 16 actions were identified to cover the range of actions that occurred in the rapes. Treating the actions as all or nothing occurrences within the whole sample the probability profile for each rape was drawn up. This consisted of the expected frequency of each action for each profile of actions, derived from the frequency of each action and the frequency of each profile. Joint probability calculations were then performed for each of the 51 (3 x 17) offences by comparing their actual dichotomous profiles with the expected frequency profile. This gave an index, presented as a probability, of the specificity of the three offences for each of the 17 individuals.

The results demonstrated that in fewer than 15 per cent of the cases the probability was so low as to indicate, wrongly, that the offence was not committed by the offender convicted of it. Eleven out of the 17 rapists (65 per cent) had all their offences correctly attributed to them, showing consistency across all three offences. It is also interesting to note that in this small, exploratory study the first and third offences seemed to be more accurately identified than the middle offence. Indeed, none of the third offences were assigned a probability below 0.72.

A small study such as this, that inevitably assumes all the convictions were 'safe', cannot be taken as evidence for offender consistency, but it does serve to show that such consistency can be demonstrated by the application of conventional probability theory to a mathematical profile of criminal actions. Such procedures could be developed both as analytic tools to help establish the conditions under which consistency did occur and even have the potential for contributing directly to criminal investigations.

## An Illustration of the Comparison of a Target Offence with the Action Profiles of Other Offenders

Offender consistency has two components; the degree of variation within one offender's actions and the range of variation across a number of offenders. Although these two questions are distinguished by apparently small changes in emphasis there are potentially large differences in their implications. The actions that may be characteristic of a person across a series of offences may be quite different from those actions that help to discriminate him or her from other possible offenders in a large pool.

This can be illustrated by a study examining the actions of one rapist in relation to 45 others. This man was known to have committed 73 offences of many kinds, but for the purposes of this illustration his first known rape was examined. For this comparison ten aspects of rape were identified (drawing on the model of Canter and Heritage, 1989). Each of the 45 known rapists was assigned a characteristic profile by determining their modal behaviour across all the rapes for which they were convicted. The first rape of the target offender was then correlated with all the modal profiles of the 45 rapists, using the ten actions as the basis for the correlation.

Only 14 offenders produced correlations greater than 0.00, and only one, the target, obtained a perfect correlation. Furthermore, only two others came close in their similarity coefficients. These results illustrate that target offences can be linked to the characteristic patterns of their perpetrators, but much larger samples would be necessary to demonstrate the generality of these findings.

## The Home Range Hypothesis

One set of actions of particular significance to police investigations are those that relate to the distance that an offender travels from home in order to commit the crime. The offender consistency hypothesis would lead to the proposal that there will be some structure, (identifiable pattern) to the locations at which an offender chooses to commit crimes. A number of studies have given general support to this proposition (reviewed in Brantingham and Brantingham, 1981; Evans and Herbert, 1989).

Recent studies (Canter and Larkin, 1993) have developed this proposition to show that there are reasonably precise relationships between the distances that rapists travel between their crimes (an A variable) and the distance they are travelling from home (a C variable). Barker (1989) has also shown similar relationships for burglars. The distances that rapists travel also appears to relate to other aspects of their offence, such as whether it is committed indoors or outdoors. Therefore by combining the purely geographical information with other aspects of the offence it has been possible to produce a data base search procedure that could narrow the area of likely residence of a known offender, on average, to less than a 3 km radius (Canter and Gregory, 1994). Whatever the eventual practical benefits of these studies their theoretical import is further to support the general proposition that the way an offender commits crimes is characteristic of that individual and distinguishable from the offence 'style' of other offenders committing similar crimes.

# THE OFFENCE SPECIFICITY HYPOTHESIS

If there is the possibility that an offender will reveal some consistency in any particular crime there is the further question about how much of a criminal specialist he or she is. Much of the criminology literature suggests that especially younger offenders are quite eclectic in their forms of crime, to the extent that individuals who have committed one type of crime are likely to have committed crimes of other types. Thus even establishing distinct groups of offenders on the basis of their types of crime may prove problematic.

## A Study of the Specialisms of Juvenile Delinquents

The whole enterprise of deriving characteristics of offenders that could be reliable enough to be of utility in police investigation would be under serious threat if, as some argue, offenders are typically versatile in the types of offence that they commit. If (a) opportunity and particular circumstances are seen to determine the particular crime that is committed, and (b) social processes and aspects of individual learning give rise to a preparedness on the part of anybody to carry out a criminal act, but (c) which particular act is carried out is as much due to chance and circumstance as to the propensities of the criminal, then no criminal could be distinguished from another. Such a perspective would argue that really any criminal could commit one of a great variety of different types of offence and, therefore, it would not be possible to infer anything about the person from his or her particular crime.

Another argument, that is probably more relevant in relation to violent and obviously emotional crime, is the one that assumes these crimes are committed in states of impulsive, unplanned action. For these crimes it is postulated that people react in such an unstructured way that no aspect of their characteristics is likely to be revealed, other than possibly their characteristic impulsivity. For instance the location chosen will be a haphazard one that bears no relationship to other aspects of the individual's life. Similarly, their victims may be regarded as of no particular significance. The contrasting argument may be thought of as the *modus operandi* argument. The view that a criminal's actions are unique to that individual and therefore patterns and trends that allow the groupings of individuals are very unlikely. Any theory that is a basis for offender profiling will need to fit somewhere between the idiosyncratic perspective that is typical of *modus operandi* arguments and the generalist perspective that might be drawn from some criminological theories.

## APPROACHES TO THEORY

The challenge is to establish the themes that will help to identify and explain the links between crime-based consistencies and characteristics of the offender.

### Cause or Relationship

Conceptually there are number of different roles that a theory can play in helping to link the A and the C variables. One is to explain how it is that the C variables are the cause of the A variables. A different theoretical perspective would be to look for some common third set of intervening variables that was produced by the C variables to cause the A variables. Yet a third possibility is that some third set of variables was the cause of both the A and the C variables. A variety of theoretical perspectives that reveal greater or lesser clarity on possible relationships between A and C are available.

### *Psychodynamic Typologies*

Psychodynamic theories see the differences not so much in the crimes as in the internal emotional dynamics of the criminal, as reflected, for example, in the often quoted, rape typology of Groth and Birnbaum (1979), with its distinctions between offenders who are acting out their anger and those who are acting out desires for power. By their very nature, these theories are specific to particular types of crime. These tend to be crimes of violence and especially sexual crimes. There appear to be no attempts to apply similar psycho-dynamic consideration to, say, burglary or fraud.

What this approach usually gives rise to is the proposal of a few broad types. In effect, a small number of simple equations that link the A and C variables are proposed. Each of these equations is shaped by a trend common to the A and the C variables; the need for power, anger, control and so on. These trends may be explained in term of displacement of anger from other targets, or the feeling of lack of power and the consequent compensatory search to obtain it illegally. Stephenson (1992) has reviewed such displacement compensation theories as general explanations of criminal behaviour and found little evidence for them. Such theories are the basis of the FBI typologies of rape and murder.

## Personality Differences

An approach that emerges more directly from experimental psychology is the proposal that the A and the C variables will share underlying personality characteristics. Research conducted to explore this thesis has tended to focus on simple A variables; the crime for which a person has been convicted. Such studies compare people who have committed different crimes so, for example, robbers are compared with rapists, or burglars with child abusers. The comparison process of such studies need not have this artificial, quasi-experimental design to it, but people who have this type of hypothesis do tend to think in terms of some particular cause that has led a person to become involved in burglary or buggery and so there is a tendency to set the studies up as if a comparison of some direct causal influence were being examined.

Perhaps the most direct illustration of such an exploration is the work of Eysenck (1977), who argued that there are personality differences between different types of criminal. By comparing groups of people convicted of one particular offence on personality measurements, conclusions are drawn about the personality differences between different offenders.

The evidence for the variety of crimes in which any given individual is involved, throws some very real doubt on the possibility of explaining or predicting criminal characteristics from the particular type of crime that he or she carried out. Furthermore, any examination of the legal definition of crimes will demonstrate that there is some arbitrariness in terms of what the actual actions are that characterise a particular crime.

Despite these difficulties, however, it does seem unlikely that a person's personality is not reflected in some way in how he or she commits crimes. A person's intelligence or extroversion would be expected to have some bearing on what and how a criminal offends. The problem is identifying those 'real world' A and C variables that do have direct links to personality characteristics.

## Career Routes

A rather different approach to distinguishing between offenders can be drawn from general, criminology theory. Here the idea is that a person starts off in his or her life of crime, much as the junior office worker may start off in a large organisation. A variety of opportunities are presented and a variety of experiences are gained. Through this process, the individual learns that he or she is particularly successful or particularly attracted to certain types of activities and so a form of specialism evolves. In this framework, people become muggers, burglars or rapists as their criminal career unfolds.

There is certainly broad evidence in support of this career conceptualisation. The criminological literature shows that when aggregates of crimes are examined, serious violent crimes are typically committed by offenders who are older than those involved in minor theft. Cohort studies (notably Farrington, 1986) have also indicated the variations in crimes that cohorts are involved in at different ages. However, for such an approach to be of direct value to profiling a number of detailed studies of individuals would be necessary in order to establish just what number and variety of career routes could be found through the criminal jungle.

This perspective offers two possible forms of elaboration of the canonical correlation by adding a temporal dimension. The most complex temporal elaboration is to propose that a matrix of equations would be necessary, in essence one equation for each stage in the criminal career. This would be a daunting research task requiring considerable resources and large data sets. A simpler framework deals with the C variables as aspects of the stage a criminal is at, i.e. other personal criminal experiences.

## Socio-economic Sub-groups

A more strongly socially oriented theory of offender differences would draw attention to the sub-groups from which they are likely to come. A detailed proposal of how 'social profiles' could be drawn up for sexual mass murderers was presented by Leyton in 1983. He argued that the general social characteristics of sexual mass murderers were known, citing matters such as family breakdown and socio-economic status. Here, then, the link between the A and the C variables is postulated because they are both hypothesised to be the reflections of the same social processes of anomie and social breakdown. This perspective has potential for development if the social characteristics of sub-groups of offenders could be established. The difficulty is likely to be that most criminals are drawn from similar socio-economic circumstances so that discriminating between them in terms of these characteristics could prove very challenging. However, current studies (e.g. Robertson, 1993) do suggest that in certain types of crime, notably workplace crime and fraud, there may be quite strong differences in the types and styles of crime in relation to social sub-groups.

## *Interpersonal Narratives*

A further theoretical perspective (Canter, 1994) is emerging which attempts to build links between the strengths of all the approaches outlined above. This approach sees any crime as an interpersonal transaction that involves characteristic ways of dealing with other people. It leads to hypotheses both about the range of crimes in which an individual will be involved and his or her characteristic ways of committing those crimes. Furthermore, it leads to hypotheses about consistencies between forms of criminal activity and other aspects of a criminal's life.

In essence, it is argued that although there will be some generality of criminal activity, common across a range of offenders who have committed similar types of crime, there will none the less be a sub-set, or repertoire, of criminal activity that an individual will tend to operate within. This will be reflected both in the types of crime committed, as well as the repertoire of actions engaged in for any particular type of crime. The origin of these interpersonal themes is hypothesised to have routes in the learning of styles of interpersonal interaction. Drawing on general theories in social psychology, it can be proposed that styles of transactions will essentially be directed against other people as objects to be abused, or as vehicles that provide an opportunity for some type of interpersonal exploitation.

Two sets of hypotheses can be derived from this conceptualisation. One set of hypotheses relates to the existence of sub-sets of interrelated activities. These may be classes of crimes which offenders tend to commit, or classes of behaviour that tend to be committed within a crime. An important point here is that individuals are expected to have overlapping sets of repertoires that will have characteristic themes associated with them. It is not expected that every person will fit distinctly into one type of offender or another.

The second set of hypotheses relates to predictions about the correlations between the themes that an offender exhibits and other characteristics that he or she might have. At the most elementary level this is an hypothesis about the characteristic style of criminal transaction. So, for example, a person who goes to some trouble to control his victim during the committal of a sexual offence, binding and gagging her, for example, would be hypothesised to be someone who has thought through the exploitation of others in order to avoid capture while escaping with a criminal act. Such a person, therefore, would be hypothesised as having a range of criminal history, including the committing of offences that are not necessarily of a sexual nature.

The study by Canter and Heritage (1989) shows one approach that can help develop the narrative perspective into a set of more precise, testable hypotheses. By content analysing the actions that occurred in 63 rapes they were able to identify 57 distinct actions. A subsequent analysis of the co-occurrence of these actions demonstrated that while there were a number of actions that were common to the great majority of sexual assaults there were also interpretable trends that characterised sub-sets of the less frequent actions. These trends were interpreted in terms of the interpersonal focus of the assault: (a) the victim as an object of no concern to the offender, (b) the victim as a target to be aggressively controlled, (c) the victim as a sexual object, (d) the victim as a source for criminal activity, and (e) the victim as a person with whom a pseudo-relationship is desired. Heritage (1992) has been able to indicate that there may be important differences between the characteristics of these sub-groups, especially in terms of their previous criminal history and relationships with women.

## CONCLUSIONS

The general experience of providing 'profiles' of offenders for police investigations has been drawn upon to formulate reasonably precise research questions. It has been shown that even the elementary models that underlie these questions have an inherent complexity to them, readily encapsulated in canonical equations. The demands on theory which these complexities generate are further extended by an awareness of the practical constraints under which any theory must be applied.

It has been proposed that central to all theory building in this area is the need to demonstrate consistencies within the actions of offenders and identifiable differences between them. Examples have been presented from a range of exploratory studies to show that there are indeed likely to be differences between offenders that are based upon consistencies in the actions of individual criminals. However, it is unlikely that rigid typologies of offenders will be empirically supported; rather, there will be thematic trends to their actions that will be characteristic of both their target offence and other aspects of their personal history and life style.

Two points that emerge repeatedly from a number of studies help to give more shape to these general findings. The first is that the consistencies in a criminal's action broadly relate to whether his or her crimes involve some form of psycho-social, interpersonal contact or whether they may be described as psychologically distant exploitations of other people. The second is that the best predictor of later crime behaviour is indeed earlier criminal activity.

Taken together these two points put into high relief the central problem of recidivism; that it is rooted in psychologically entrenched ways of dealing with others. But they also point out the importance of going beyond general explanation of why people continue to offend and the need to explain why they continue to offend in a particular way.

# REFERENCES

Barker, M. (1989). Criminal activity and home range: a study of the spatial offence patterns of burglars. Unpublished Master's dissertation, University of Surrey.

Brantingham, P.J. and Brantingham, P.L. (Eds) (1981). *Environmental Criminology*. Beverley Hills, CA: Sage.

Canter, D. (1994). *Criminal Shadows*. London: HarperCollins.

Canter, D. and Gregory, A. (1994). Identifying the residential locations of rapists. *Journal of Forensic Science Society*, **34**, 169–75.

Canter, D. and Heritage, R. (1989). A multivariate model of sexual offence behaviour. *Journal of Forensic Psychiatry*, **1**, 185–212.

Canter, D. and Larkin, P. (1993). The environmental range of serial rapists. *Journal of Environmental Psychology*, **13**, 63–9.

Corstorphine, E. (1993). A comparison of sexual and physical abusers of children. Unpublished Master's dissertation, University of Surrey.

Evans, D.J. and Herbert, D.T. (1989). *The Geography of Crime*. London: Routledge.

Eysenck, H. (1977). *Crime and Personality*. London: Paladin.

Farrington, D. (1986). Stepping stones to adult criminal careers. In D.Olweus, J.Block and M. Radke-Yarrow (Eds), *Development of Antisocial and Prosocial Behaviour*. London: Academic Press.

Groth, N. and Birnbaum, H. (1979). *Men who Rape: The Psychology of the Offender*. New York: Plenum.

Hammond, S. (1990). Statistical approaches to crime linking. University of Surrey: Internal Report.

Hazelwood, R.R. and Burgess, A. (Eds) (1987). *Practical Aspects of Rape Investigation: A Multidisciplinary Approach*. Amsterdam: Elsevier.

Heritage, R. (1992). Facets of sexual assault: first steps in investigative classifications. Unpublished M.Phil. dissertation, University of Surrey.

Kirby, S. (1993). *The Child Molester: Separating Myth from Reality*. Unpublished PhD dissertation, University of Surrey.

Leyton, E. (1983). A social profile of sexual mass murderers. In T. Fleming and L.A. Visano (Eds), *Deviant Designations*. London: Butterworth.

Ressler, R.K., Burgess, A.W. and Douglas, J.E. (1988). *Sexual Homicide: Patterns and Motives*. Lexington, MA: Lexington.

Robertson, A.R.T. (1993). A psychological perspective on blue-collar workplace crime. Unpublished Master's dissertation, University of Surrey.

Rumbelow, D. (1988). *The Complete Jack the Ripper*. London: Penguin.

Stephenson, G.M. (1992). *The Psychology of Criminal Justice*. Oxford: Blackwell.

Tabachnick, B.G. and Fidell, L.S. (1983). *Using Multivariate Statistics*. London: Harper & Row.

# [36]

*Journal of Environmental Psychology* (1993) 13, 63–69
© 1993 Academic Press Ltd

0272-4944/93/010063+07$08.00/0

# THE ENVIRONMENTAL RANGE OF SERIAL RAPISTS

DAVID CANTER AND PAUL LARKIN

*University of Surrey, Guildford, Surrey GU2 5XH, U.K.*

## Abstract

A model of individual sexual offenders' spatial activity was developed based upon 45 British male sexual assaulters who had committed at least two assaults. For each offender a separate map was produced indicating the spatial locations of his offences and residence. A *Marauder* model and a *Commuter* model of offender's spatial behaviour was proposed. As an elaboration of the Marauder model, the *Circle* and *Range* hypotheses were tested against the sample of offenders. Results of the study support the Marauder model showing that most of the sample (87%) move out from their home base in a region around that base to carry out their attacks. The antithetical Commuter model was not supported within the sample. The Circle and Range hypotheses were supported demonstrating that offenders operate within a distinct offence region (in 91% of cases) and that the distance they travel to offend correlates directly with distances between offences ($r = 0.93$, $p < 0.001$). The findings clearly indicate that there is a basis for a model of offence venue choice by individuals within the sample. The present study supports the value of a theory of *domocentricity* within offenders' lives and offers potential applicability to the solving of crimes.

## Introduction

Many studies have shown that offenders usually do not travel very far from home to commit crimes (White, 1932; Pyle, 1974; Repetto, 1974; Curtis, 1974; Kind, 1987). Shaw and McKay illustrated this general trend as long ago as 1942 in their Chicago studies. They established that there is a limited area of zones in which offenders will offend and that these zones were geographically close to the zones in which the offenders lived. However, the majority of the research undertaken to date has involved case studies of, for example, classic crime series like the 'Yorkshire ripper' (Kind, 1987). Alternatively they have considered the aggregate pattern of the spatial activity of a sample of criminals (e.g. Pyle, 1974). Results from such work has provided useful case and population characteristics. In contrast to previous studies of offender movement that have emphasized the aggregate geographical behaviour of offenders, the present study explores directly the psychological question of the extent to which a general model can be developed that is applicable to any individual offender's spatial activity.

Developing a model of the sequential spatial behaviour of offenders requires tests of the validity of various conceptualisations of the psychological processes which determine where an offender chooses to commit a crime. A robust model would also be of practical value to criminal investigators because it could indicate the likely area of the offender's residence.

The starting point for any theory of an offender's selection of the venue of his[1] crime is the hypothesis that the choice of crime venues relates to some kind of home or base from which the individual operates. This hypothesis is based on the view that the offenders for whom an environmental psychology model is developed will not be random drifters of no fixed abode, but will be residing at one or more locations from which they travel to commit their crimes.

Although the environmental cognition literature is not explicit on the point, there is an implicit assumption throughout such studies that a significant determinant of the mental representations of places a person develops is the location of a person's home (as, e.g. reviewed by Golledge, 1987). The proposition is therefore that the 'domocentric' locational experiences of law-abiding citizens are a reasonable starting point for building models of criminals movements. The potential validity of such a proposition is supported by Amir's (1971) finding that even individuals who commit the impetuous crime of rape do operate from a fixed point. Amir's account of Philadelphia police file data (1958–1960) draws attention to the value of understanding more about the psychological processes underlying a criminal's spatial behaviour, raising questions about the significance of the 'fixed point' to the offender and the ways in which it might determine the location of his offences.

In contrast to the 'fixed point' having any personal significance to the offender, Shaw and McKay (1942) of the 'Chicago School' proposed that offenders who operate within city centres are reacting to processes beyond their personal experience. They state that behaviour can be explained in terms of the structure of the urban environment. For Shaw and McKay, it is the organizational geometry of cities that gives a pattern to criminal activity. They would thus suggest an arbitrary relationship between the location of offences and between offences and residence other than that the offences are enclosed by a socially recognized 'city centre'.

A somewhat different geographical emphasis is given by Rengert and Wasilchick (1985). They emphasize the importance of the journeys a criminal habitually takes around his home ground. They conducted detailed interviews with 31 burglars, and found a strong likelihood of crime being located on and around the pathways and routes that the burglar habitually used in non-criminal activities. Such journeys through familiar territory are thought to provide information around which an offender could plan his next crime, and that it is this process of information gathering that gives shape to the area in which a person chooses to commit his crimes. They go further to suggest a simple model for offenders' behaviour. The offender in this model is more likely to attack on 'his way home'. Thus the offender will operate within an area which is defined by his home and a base which he frequents; for example, his work, local bar or restaurant.

Brantingham and Brantingham (1981) have proposed more affectively based processes for crimes taking place in the area around a criminal's home. They suggest that the security offered by familiarity with the area would outweigh risks of being recognized in the commission of an offence. However, the avoidance of being recognized near a crime scene would lead to the existence of a minimum distance around the home in which the offender would tend not to offend. Brantingham and Brantingham (1981) do provide some aggregate evidence for such a 'safety zone'. Their arguments therefore lend support to the hypothesis that offenders will tend to offend not only within an area around their home but that there will be a maximum and minimum range of distances from home in which they offend.

Capone and Nicholas (1975) provide evidence that for robbery, there may indeed be some sort of criminal range. They argue that the offender's goal in crimes of this type is focused on personal gain. Thus the robber will operate within an area which yields the greatest profit and will be looking to identify those areas which have the best opportunities for success. The generality of these findings across different types of crime is an important question. It assumes that an offender in a robbery is maximizing his gain for minimum effort and will therefore travel the minimum safe distance that will offer the prospect of a successful crime. Can the same assumption of economic logic be applied to crimes that may have a more overtly emotional nature such as rape, or crimes in which there is a more considered overt risk for larger scale gain, such as armed bank robbery? Capone and Nicholas show that there is a significant difference in the lengths of armed and non-armed robbery trips, with armed trips having a greater mean distance. The present study focuses on rape, leaving robbery for future research.

There is some evidence that rapists do have similar geographical patterns to burglars. LeBeau (1987a) used centrography (originally developed by Sviatlovsky & Eells, 1937) to defend the idea of a structure to the spatial offence behaviour of the individual rapist. Centrography 'allows one to assess and measure the average location, dispersion, movements and directional change of a phenomenon through time' (LeBeau, 1987c). The sample of offenders used was 'all the lone-assistant rapes reported in the San Diego police department in 1971 to 1975'. He suggests that the offender may operate from a clear home or base, presenting evidence for a general geographical pattern of rapes around the home of the rapist.

In a further elaboration of these suggestions LeBeau (1987b) points out that although the chronic serial rapists in San Diego that he studied do vary considerably in the distance they travel from their homes, they restrict their 'attacks to within one-half of a mile from his previous attacks' (p. 325). LeBeau (1987b) supports this conclusion with year on year aggregate figures so it is difficult to establish exactly how individual offenders fit into this picture. Furthermore, there is the possibility that many offences are localized in areas that provide special types of target and opportunity. LeBeau's results therefore do raise important questions about the spatial relationships between the residential location of serial rapists and the locations in which they commit their crimes.

## Two Models: Commuter or Marauder

In general, then, it seems to be reasonable to assume the existence of a fixed base for men who carry out a number of rapes as for other offenders who commit a series of crimes. There is also some evidence that there will be an area in which the offences are committed that has some non-arbitrary relationship to that base, what might be termed a *criminal range*. The present study tests various models of the relationships there might be between an individual's criminal range and the location of their home base.

Two general models may be proposed to characterize the relationship between base and area of crime, as represented in Figure 1. The simplest assumption to make about the geometry of a criminal domain is that it is circular as this only requires the determination of a radius, no other boundary limitations are necessary. In Figure 1, therefore, the area around the home (home range) and the area in which the crimes are committed (criminal range) are represented as circles.

The first model is based on what we have called the *commuter hypothesis*. In this case the offender travels from his base into an area to carry out his crimes. This may be determined by the general geometry of the city, as would be consistent with Shaw and McKay's (1942) proposal of the use of the city centre, or it may be an area determined by regular routes that the offender takes as Rengert and Wasilchick (1985) suggest. However, whatever the particular determinants of the specific area of crime, central to this hypothesis that although there will be a domain in which the crimes are committed and this domain will have some distinct relationship to where the offender lives, there will be no clear relationship between size or location of the criminal domain and the distance it is from any given offender's home.

The commuter hypotheses, then, proposes that there is little or no overlap between these two areas and that the offender moves to a district which is outside his home range to offend. This is not to suggest that the criminal range is unfamiliar to the offender, but that it is at an appreciable distance from the area in which he habitually operates as a non-offender.

A second model may be developed on what we call the *marauder hypothesis*. In this case the base acts as a focus for each particular crime. The offender is assumed to move out from this base to commit his crimes and then return. This relates most directly to the research of Brantingham and Brantingham (1981) who see the home as a focus for the crime locations. This hypothesis implies a much closer relationship between the location of crimes and of a criminal's home, such that the further the distance between crimes the further, on average, the offender must be travelling from home.

In other words, the marauder hypothesis proposes that there is a large or total overlap of the home range and criminal range areas. The offender operates from a home/base definitely located within the boundaries of his safe area for criminal activity.

If either of these hypotheses is strongly supported it has implications for further elaboration of the related model. For simplicity of presentation the development of these implications will be left until after the first test of the two hypotheses.

*Sample and procedure*

Although the general arguments above are applicable to any offences, the present study focuses on sexual assaults. These types of crime are a particularly strong test of the essentially rational models that have been outlined. Sexual assault overtly has a profound emotional component to it and may be

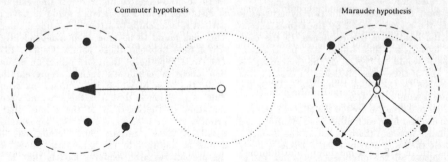

Commuter hypothesis                    Marauder hypothesis

FIGURE 1.   Hypothetical models of serial rapists' spatial behaviour. ○, Criminal range; ●, offences;  ○, home range; ○, home/base.

regarded by many as containing some strongly impulsive aspects (Amir, 1971). However, when a rapist does commit a series of assaults on women, with whom he has had no previous contact, some pattern is possible in these offences of which the offender may or may not be aware, just as for burglary or drug abuse. Sexual assaults may therefore be seen as an extreme case that tests the fundamental assumptions that an individual criminal's crime venue has some distinct relationship to his place of residence.

To carry out the study, details of 45 sexual assaulters were made available by British police forces. These included criminals who had been convicted of crimes legally regarded as 'rape', in which vaginal penetration had taken place, as well as other forms of sexual violence. All offenders had been convicted of two or more offences on women they had not known prior to the offence. A total of 251 offences had been committed by these 45 offenders. The mean rape series consisted of 5·6 offences (S.D. = 3·6) with a minimum of 2 and a maximum of 14 offences. The offenders had a mean age of 26·6 years (S.D. = 8·7) ranging from 15 to 59 years. Twenty-one offenders were broadly classified by the police as 'white' in ethnicity and the other 24 as 'black'. All the offenders operated within the Greater London area and/or the South East of England during the 1980s.

*Test of hypotheses*

The basic information available to test the hypotheses above is the geographical distribution of the offences in relation to the location of the offender's residence at the time of the offences. For each offender, a separate map was produced indicating the locations of offences and his residence. A further summary of this without the underlying base map was produced, as illustrated in Figure 2.

The most direct test of the two hypotheses is whether the region covered by the crimes encompasses the location of the residence. In the commuter hypotheses this would not be common, whereas it would be typical of the 'marauder'. A simple test of these possibilities is to examine the area covered by the offences and see whether the residence is within that area.

In order to define the area of the offences, the two offences furthest from each other were identified and the distance between them taken as the diameter of a circle that was drawn. Such a circle is likely to encompass all the offences, except for rather unusual spatial distributions. There are therefore

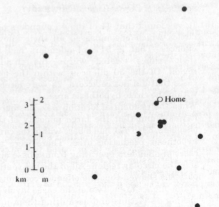

FIGURE 2. Example rape series. White, 31-year-old, inside serial rapist. ○, Home/base; ●, offences.

more precise geometrical aspects that can be derived from the marauder model, *circle hypotheses*. These hypotheses have two aspects:

(a) the offence of a single offender will be encompassed within a circle that is drawn with its diameter as the two offences that are furthest from each other;

(b) the residence of the offender at the time of the offences will be within the same circle.

Clearly such hypotheses make no allowances for variations in local topography, transport routes and so on. They relate to a generalized mental representation of the broad geographical relationships between locations. As such these hypotheses are similar to those relating to the study of distance estimation in cities (Canter & Tagg, 1975). In those studies 'crow flight' direct line estimates of distances around cities were found to have important relationships to actual direct line distances. This was found to be true even independently of travel time between those points (Canter, 1977). The circle hypotheses therefore reflect an assumption about a criminal's mental representations about the area in which he commits his crimes. This assumption is that it is the schematic representation of the location of the crimes that is primary rather than very particular topographical details of those locations. Such details may play a role in addition to the schematic 'image', but the present research explores models that do not include such details.

*Results of the tests of the circle hypotheses*

(a) It was found that 41 of the 45 offenders had circles which encompassed all their known offences. That is 91% of offenders had all their crimes located within the circular region. Of the 30 offences, within the four cases that did not co-accord, 23 were located within the circle hypothesis area.

(b) When the residential location was considered it was found that the large majority of the offenders, 39 (87%), had a base within the circle hypothesis prediction area. There were six cases of offenders operating from a base outside the circular region. All of the six spatial patterns showed that the offender commuted to the offence area. Two of the cases involved picking-up victims and assaulting them in a motor vehicle some distance from home. Two others cases involved the offenders targeting a specific street far away from their home area.

The very high proportions of offenders whose crimes are located in accordance with the circle hypotheses provides strong support for the general marauder hypothesis as being the most applicable to these sets of offenders. The commuter hypothesis therefore does not seem tenable for this sample of sexual offenders, although it may have application where very specific types of targeting, for example on prostitutes, was taking place.

*Development of the marauder hypothesis*

If offenders are operating within a circular region that also houses their base, the question arises as to the relative location of their base within their offence domain. In particular, as the size of their criminal range grows does this change the relative relationship to the domestic focus? One way of understanding and developing this argument is to make the simplifying assumption that the home is at the centre of the offence circle. If this is so then those crimes that are committed far away from each other are more likely to be further from the home than those that are nearer to each other. Such a relationship would hold true for any position that the home had in relation to the crime circle, provided the crimes were distributed around it. This more precise specification of relationships between distances is therefore an arithmetic elaboration of the geometric circle model. It can be summarized as a *Range Hypothesis*: the distance between a criminal's offences will correlate directly with the distance those offences are from his home.

A further development of this hypothesis is that if it is supported, the largest distances between offences will be greater than the largest distance between any offence and the offender's home, otherwise the home would be outside of the circle created from a diameter based on the largest distance between offences. Furthermore, if the home was at the centre of the circle then the distance from home to the furthest offence would be half of the maximum distance between offences. In other words, it is hypothesized that regression of maximum distance between offences on maximum distance from home will have a gradient that is less than 1.00 and close to 0.50. A value of less than 0.5 would only be possible if the circle hypothesis was invalid. A gradient greater than 0.5 but less than 1.00 would suggest that the home tended to be eccentrically placed within the crime circle.

The proposition by Brantingham and Brantingham (1981) that there is a safe range round the home in which crimes would not be committed would be supported in the regression equation by a constant value that was positive, but less than the average minimum distance of crimes to home.

*Test of the range hypothesis*

The scatterplot showing the relationship between the maximum distance between crimes and the maximum distance each crime is from the offender's home is given in Figure 3.

The correlation for this plot is 0.93 (highly significant at $p < 0.001$). The regression equation is $y = 0.84x + 0.61$. The gradient, at 0.84, does indicate

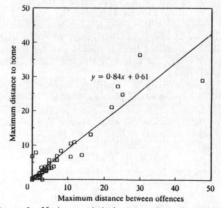

FIGURE 3. Maximum criminal range: relationship between maximum distance between crimes and maximum distance to home. $n = 45$; $r = 0.93$; $p < 0.001$.

a location within the crime circle, but suggests that it is unlikely to be close to the centre of that circle. This is a finding of some interest which will be discussed later.

The constant is also as predicted. The average minimum distance of crime to home for these offenders was 1·53 miles. The constant of 0·61 miles is well below this. There is, therefore, strong evidence for a minimum distance that the sexual offender is willing to travel from home, in accordance with the hypothesized desire to be at a safe distance away from home.

The criminal's 'safe area' for activity, as defined by this regression equation, is at least 0·61 miles from home but within an area away from all offences which is less than 84% of the maximum distance between offences.

## Discussion

The clarity of these mathematical results is little short of remarkable for what is regarded as an impetuous, emotional violent crime. They show that, whatever the rapist's experience of committing the crime, there is a basis to his choice of locations that can be modelled from relatively simple environmental psychology principles.

The relationship that a rapist's home has to the location of his crimes has been established for 45 rapists in the South East of Britain who attacked more than one woman; all of the women being unknown to the offenders before the assaults. The indications are that most offenders move out from their home base in a region around that base to carry out their attacks. However the gradient of 0·84 does suggest that there is some bias to commit a number of offences rather closer to home than would be predicted by a simple circular model. In other words, the base is not at the centre of the circle of crimes.

This eccentricity is important because it may reflect a developmental process in which offenders travel further from home at some stages of their offending career than at other stages. The present data set is not large enough to test this possibility thoroughly although there are certainly anecdotal examples of individuals that illustrate it. Such a development process could interact with the commuter and marauder models proposed. For although the marauder model was clearly the strongest candidate for describing the present sample there were a few individuals who illustrated a strong commuter process. It seems feasible that the differences

between 'commuting and 'marauding' rapists could be a function of the stages in their developments as criminals. With a larger sample this could be tested by the relationship between regression gradient and criminal experience.

The representation of the ranges as circles is, of course, a simplification. The research of both Rengert and Wasilchick (1985) and Capone and Nichols (1975) indicate the possibility that, for North America at least, the expansion of cities from a central down-town may lead to the generation of more eliptical or even sectoral patterns to the geography of serial offending. The grid-pattern of North American cities may also mean that examination of distances between offences is more appropriately carried using city-block metrics rather than the crow-flight measures that were found fruitful for British data.

There are also arguments against the use of more specific models and concrete metrics for the data examined here. The number of offences per offender was relatively small in the current sample. As a consequence very detailed models of the geographical distribution of the offences is difficult to substantiate. Furthermore, it seems very likely that the offences recorded are not all those perpetrated by the offender so models that were very restrictive in the spatial structure could be very misleading.

One further consideration is the psychological question of what exactly is being modelled in the study. If the view is taken that the model is an approximation to the internal representation of the environment that forms the basis of the criminal's actions, then there is research evidence to suggest that for large complex cities crow-flight distances do capture important aspects of a person's 'cognitive map' (Canter & Tagg, 1975). Indeed, Canter (1977, p. 90) reports that crow-flight distance estimates correlate better with both actual distance and actual time to travel around London than do time estimates, suggesting that crow-flight distances may be psychologically more primary than other forms of direct experience. This is an important issue which future research, with more data than the present, will need to explore.

The fact that rapists reveal strong democentric behaviour serves further to strengthen the general power of the location of the home in structuring people's lives. It is a process that is worthy of test in may other areas of activity, such as shopping behaviour, recreational activities, search for work, or even search for new homes. In the criminal arena it offers direct prospects for practical application in the solving of crimes.

For although the area in which an offender may be living, covered by the circle in the present model, may be very large, nonetheless where detectives are attempting to assign priorities to a long list of suspects the limitations of the circle may still be of utility. It may be possible to reduce the area of the circle by introducing further refinements into the sub-samples of offenders on which the models are based, for example more impulsive offenders may travel shorter distances, or offenders in rural areas may travel further and so on. Research exploring these possibilities has already produced some encouraging results. Investigative suggestions derived from specific studies have also been made available to police investigations with considerable success.

## Acknowledgement

We are grateful to Ellen Tsang and Helen Hughes for their assistance on the studies described.

## Note

(1) All the offenders presently being studied are male. The male personal pronoun is therefore intended only to refer to male persons throughout this paper.

## References

Amir, M. (1971). *Patterns in Forcible Rape*. Chicago: University of Chicago Press.

Brantingham, P. J. & Brantingham, P. L. (1981). Notes on the geometry of crime. In P. J. Brantingham & P. L. Brantingham, Eds., *Environmental Criminology*. Beverley Hill, CA: Sage, pp. 27–54.

Capone, D. L. & Nicholas, W. (1975). Crime and distance: an analysis of offender behaviour in space. *Proceedings of the Association of American Geographers*, pp. 45–49.

Canter, D. (1977). *The Psychology of Place*. London: Architectural Press.

Canter, D. & Tagg, S. (1975). Distance estimation in cities. *Environment and Behaviour*, 7, 58–80.

Curtis, L. A. (1974). *Criminal Violence*. Lexington, MA: Lexington Books.

Golledge, R. G. (1987). Environmental cognition. In D Stokols & I. Altman, Eds, *Handbook of Environmental Psychology*. New York, NY: John Wiley, vol. 1, 131–174.

Kind, S. S. (1987). Navigational ideas and the Yorkshire Ripper investigation. *Journal of Navigation*, 40, 385–393.

LeBeau, J. L. (1987a). The methods and measures of centrography and the spatial dynamics of rape. *Journal of Quantitative Criminology*, 3, 125–141.

LeBeau, J. L. (1987b). Patterns of stranger and serial rape offending: factors distinguishing apprehended and at large offenders. *Journal of Criminal Law and Criminology*, 78.

LeBeau, J. L. (1987c). The journey to rape: geographic distance and the rapist's method of approaching the victim. *Journal of Police Science and Administration*, 15, 129–161.

Pyle, G. F. *et al.* (1974). *The Spatial Dynamics of Crime*. Department of Geography Research Monograph No. 159. Chicago: The University of Chicago.

Repetto, T. A. (1974). *Residential Crime*. Cambridge, MA: Ballinger.

Rengert, G. & Wasilchick, J. (1985). *Suburban Burglary: A Time and Place for Everything*. Springfield, IL: C. C. Thomas Publishing.

Shaw, C. R. & McKay, H. D. (1942). *Juvenile Delinquency and Urban Areas*. Chicago: University of Chicago Press.

Sviatlovsky, E. E. & Eells, W. C. (1937). The centrographical method and regional analysis. *Geographical Review*, 27, 240–254.

White, R. C. (1932). The relation of felonies to environmental factors in Indianapolis. *Social Forces*, 10, 459–467.

# PLACE, SPACE, AND POLICE INVESTIGATIONS: HUNTING SERIAL VIOLENT CRIMINALS

by

## D. Kim Rossmo
### Simon Fraser University

**Abstract:** *Police investigations of serial murder, rape and arson can be assisted by a geographic perspective on the spatial behavior that led to the crime scene. For any crime to occur there must have been an intersection in both time and place between the offender and victim. How did this come to happen? What are the hunting patterns of predatory criminals? Environmental criminology and the routine activity approach provide a general framework for addressing these questions, and work in this area represents a practical application of theory to the real world of police investigation. By "inverting" research that has focused on relating crime places to offender residences, the locations of a series of crimes can be used to determine where an offender might reside. The probable spatial behavior of the offender can thus be derived from information contained in the known crime-site locations, their geographic connections, and the characteristics and demography of the surrounding areas. By determining the probability of the offender residing in various areas, and displaying those results through the use of isopleth or choropleth maps, police efforts to apprehend criminals can be assisted. This investigative approach is known as geographic profiling.*

## INTRODUCTION

A focus of any police investigation is the crime scene and its evidentiary contents. What is often overlooked, however, is a geographic perspective on the actions preceding the offense: the spatial behavior that led to the crime scene. For any violent crime to occur there must have been an intersection in both time and place between the victim and offender. How did this happen? What were the antecedents? What do the spatial elements of the crime tell us about the offender and his or her actions?

Address correspondence to: Kim Rossmo, School of Criminology, Simon Fraser University, Burnaby, BC Canada V5A 1S6.

What are the hunting patterns of predatory offenders? These questions are particularly relevant in cases of serial murder, rape and arson.

Environmental criminology and routine activity theory provide a general framework for addressing these questions. In addition, the model of crime-site selection developed by Brantingham and Brantingham (1981) suggests a specific approach for determining the most probable location of offender residence in cases of serial violent crimes. Research in this area represents a practical application of criminological theory to the real world of police investigation, which not only can contribute useful information to law enforcement agencies but may also open up possibilities for new and innovative investigative methodologies.

The nature of serial violent crime creates unique problems for law enforcement, requiring special police responses and investigative strategies. Klockars (1983) asserts that there are only three ways to solve a crime: (1) a confession, (2) a witness and (3) physical evidence. Traditionally, the search for witnesses, suspects and evidence has followed a path, originating from the victim and the crime scene outward. Most homicides, for example, are cleared for the simple reason that they involve people who know each other, and the process of offender identification is often only one of suspect elimination.

Such obvious connections rarely exist in cases of stranger crimes. The lack of any relationship between the victims and the offender makes these crimes difficult to solve. In conducting these types of investigations working outward from the victim is a difficult task. The alternative, then, is to work inward, trying to establish some type of link between potential suspects and the victim or crime scene. This process requires the delineation of a likely group of potential suspects; such efforts, however, can produce lists often numbering into the thousands, causing problems with information overload. In the still unsolved Seattle-area Green River Killer case, for example, 18,000 suspect names have been collected. But as of February 1992, the police have only had the time and resources to investigate some 12,000 of these (Montgomery, 1992). The Yorkshire Ripper case had, by the time it was solved, 268,000 names in the nominal index (Doney, 1990).

Clues derived from crime location and place can be of significant assistance to law enforcement in the investigation of repetitive offenses. The probable spatial behavior of the offender can be derived from information contained in the known crime site locations (e.g., encounter/apprehension sites, murder scenes, body/property dump sites), their geographic connections, and the characteristics and demography of the surrounding neighborhoods. Determining the probability of the offender residing in various areas, and displaying those results through the use of choropleth or isopleth maps, can assist police efforts to apprehend criminals. This information allows police departments to focus their investigative activities, geographically prioritize suspects and concentrate saturation or directed patrolling efforts in those zones where the criminal predator is most likely to be active. Such investigative approaches have been termed geographic profiling (Rossmo, 1995) or geoforensic analysis (Newton and Newton, 1985).

## ENVIRONMENTAL CRIMINOLOGY

Traditionally, the main interest of criminology has been the offender, and much effort has gone into studying offender backgrounds, peer influences, criminal careers and deterrence. This focus has tended to ignore the other components of crime—the victim, the criminal law and the crime. The crime setting or place, the "where and when" of the criminal act, makes up what Brantingham and Brantingham (1981) call the fourth dimension of crime—the primary concern of environmental criminology. "Environmental criminologists set out to use the geographic imagination in concert with the sociological imagination to describe, understand, and control criminal events" (Brantingham and Brantingham, 1981:21). The roots of this perspective lie in human ecology, Jeffery's bio-social learning approach and Hirschi's social control theory (Brantingham and Brantingham, 1981; Vold and Bernard, 1986).

Research in this area has taken a broad approach by including in its analyses operational, perceptual, behavioral, physical, social, psychological, legal, cultural, and geographic settings. These works range from micro to meso to macrospatial levels of analytic focus. One of environmental criminology s major interests, the study of the dimensions of crime at the microspatial level, has often led to useful findings in the area of crime prevention (see, for example, Clarke, 1992). Other projects have included the analyses of: crime trips (Rhodes and Conly, 1981); efforts to understand target and victim selections through opportunities for crime (Brantingham and Brantingham, 1981); crime prevention initiatives, notably crime prevention through environmental design (Jeffery, 1977; Wood, 1981); proposals for rapid transit security (Felson, 1989); patterns of fugitive migration (Rossmo, 1987); and other methods (see Clarke, 1992).

The spatial relationship between the offender's home and his or her crimes is an underlying theme in much of this work. Is it possible to "invert" this research and use the locations of a series of crimes to suggest where an offender might reside? By reversing the reasoning and logic of these theoretical models, it may be feasible to predict the most probable location of a criminal's residence. Such a result would allow the principles of environmental criminology and the geography of crime to be practically applied to the police investigative process.

## GEOGRAPHY AND CRIME INVESTIGATION

While police officers are intuitively aware of the influence of place on crime, they sometimes are unaware of the different ways in which geography can assist their work. In spite of this general lack of understanding, however, there are some specific examples of the use of geographic principles by the police in efforts to investigate crimes and apprehend suspects.

Some police dog handlers, for instance, have noted patterns in the escape routes and movements of offenders fleeing from the scenes of their crimes (Eden, 1985). This predictability in the movements of those under stress has been observed in both actual trackings of suspects and experimental reenactments using police dog quarries. Fleeing criminals tend to turn to the left if they are right-handed, move to the right upon encountering obstacles, discard evidentiary items to their right and stay near the outside walls when hiding in large buildings (Eden, 1985). Different patterns are found when conducting passive tracks for missing persons. Lost subjects tend to bear to the right in their wanderings, and men seem to favor downhill paths while women and children choose uphill routes (Eden, 1985).

Senior Superintendent Arvind Verma describes how the Indian Police Service in the Bihar province have used a form of geographical analysis in the investigation of certain types of crimes. *Dacoities* are robberies with violence involving gangs of five or more offenders. This type of criminal act dates back to 500 BC and usually occurs in the countryside. The lack of anonymity in a rural setting requires the *dacoity* gang to attack villages other than their own, and then only during those nights when the moon is new. There is usually little or no artificial lighting in rural India, and the lunar dark phase is a period of almost complete blackness that provides cover for such criminal activities.

Upon being notified of a *dacoity*, the police will first determine the length of time between the occurrence of the crime and first light. Knowing the average speed that a person can travel cross-country on foot then allows the police to calculate a distance radius, centered on the crime site, which determines a circle within which the home village of the *dacoity* members most probably lies. There are few vehicles and if the criminals are not home by daylight, they run the risk of being observed by farmers who begin to work the fields at dawn.

The villages located within this circle can then be narrowed down by eliminating those of the same caste as the victim village, as "brother" is not likely to harm "brother." And, if a sufficiently detailed description of the criminals can be obtained, dress, modus operandi and other details can help determine the caste of the gang, allowing the police to concentrate further on the appropriate villages. Patrols can then speed to these places and attempt to intercept the *dacoity* members, or to proceed to investigate known criminal offenders residing in the area.

In an effort to focus the Hillside Strangler investigation, the Los Angeles, CA Police Department (LAPD) attempted to determine the most likely location of the scene of the homicides. The police knew where the victims had been apprehended and where their bodies had been dumped, and the distances between these two points (Gates and Shah, 1992). The LAPD computer analysts viewed the problem in terms of Venn diagrams, with the center of each circle representing victim availability, the circumference representing offender capacity and the radius representing offender ability (Holt, 1993).

Vectors drawn from the point where the victims were abducted to the location where their bodies were found were added together to produce a common radius, which defined a circle encompassing an area of just over three square miles. The LAPD saturated this zone with 200 police officers in an attempt to find the murderers. While they were not successful, it is possible that the heavy police presence inhibited the killers, and prompted murderer Kenneth Bianchi's move from Los Angeles to Bellingham, WA. The center of this zone, the LAPD later found out, was not far from co-murderer Angelo Buono's automobile upholstery shop-cum-residence (Gates and Shah, 1992).

Geographic techniques were also used in the Yorkshire Ripper investigation. With the murders still unsolved after five and one-half years, Her Majesty's Inspector of Constabulary Lawrence Byford implemented a case review process (Kind, 1987a). Detectives had become divided over the issue of the killer's residence. One school of thought, led by the chief investigating officer, believed that the Ripper was from the Sunderland area, while other investigators thought he was a local man. After an intensive investigative review, the Byford advisory team came to the latter conclusion.

To help test this deduction, they applied two "navigational metrical tests" to the spatial and temporal data associated with the crimes (Kind, 1987a:388-390). The first test involved the calculation of the center of gravity (spatial mean) for the 17 crimes (13 murders and four assaults) believed to be linked to the Yorkshire Ripper. The second test consisted of plotting time of offense against length of day (approximated by month of year). The rationale behind this approach had its basis in the theory that the killer would not be willing to attack late at night if his return journey to home was too far.

The first navigational test resulted in the finding that the center of gravity for the Ripper attacks lay near Bradford. The second test determined that the later attacks were those located in the West Yorkshire cities of Leeds and Bradford. Both tests therefore supported the team's original hypothesis that the killer was a local man. Peter William Sutcliffe, who resided in the district of Heaton in the city of Bradford, was arrested three weeks later by a patrol constable and sergeant in Sheffield.

Newton and Newton (1985) applied what they termed geoforensic analysis to a series of unsolved female homicides that occurred in Fort Worth, TX from 1983 to 1985. They found that localized serial murder or rape tends to form place-time patterns different from those seen in "normal" criminal violence. The unsolved Fort Worth murders were analyzed by employing both quantitative (areal associations, crime site connections, centrographic analysis), and qualitative (landscape analysis) techniques.

Newton and Swoope (1987) also utilized geoforensic techniques in a retrospective analysis of the Hillside Strangler case. Different geographic centers were calculated from the coordinates of the locations of various types of crime sites. They discriminated between points of fatal encounter, body or car dump sites and victim's residences, and found that the geographic center of the body dump sites most accurately predicted the location of the residence of murderer Angelo Buono's. A search radius (circumscribing an area around the geographic center in which the killers were thought to most likely be found) was also calculated, the range of which decreased with the addition of the spatial information provided by each new murder.

## CRIMINAL GEOGRAPHIC TARGETING

The locations where crimes happen are not completely random, but instead often have a degree of underlying spatial structure. As chaotic as they may sometimes appear to be, there is often a rationality influencing the geography of their occurrence. Routine activity theory suggests that crimes tend to occur in those locations where suitable (in terms of profit and risk) victims are encountered by motivated offenders as both move through their daily activities (Clarke and Felson, 1993; Cornish and Clarke, 1986; Felson, 1986, 1987). As offenders travel among their homes, workplaces, and social activity sites, their activity space (composed of these locations and their connecting paths) describes an awareness space that forms part of a larger mental map—an "image of the city" built upon experience and knowledge.

Within a person's activity space is usually an anchor point or base, the single most important place in their spatial life. For the vast majority of people this is their residence. For others, however, the anchor point may be elsewhere, such as the work site or a close friend's home. It should be remembered that some street criminals do not have a permanent residence and may base their activities out of a bar, pool hall or some other such social activity location (Rengert, 1990). They might also be homeless, living on the street, or may be transient or mobile to such a degree that they lack any real form of anchor point.

Brantingham and Brantingham (1981) suggest that the process of criminal target selection is a dynamic one. Crimes occur in those locations where suitable targets are overlapped by the offender s awareness space. Offenders may then move outward in their search for additional targets, their interactions decreasing with distance. Search pattern probabilities can thus be modeled by a distance-decay function that show an inverse relationship between the level of interactions and the distance from the locations and routes that comprise the activity space. There may also be a "buffer zone" centered around the criminal's home, within which the offender sees targets as being too risky to victimize because of their proximity to his or her residence (cf. Newton and Swoope, 1987).

The Brantingham and Brantingham (1981) model predicts, for the simplest case, that the residence of the offender would lie at the center of the crime pattern and therefore could be approximated by the spatial mean. The intricacy of most activity spaces, however, suggests that more complex patterns may be appropriate. Rengert (1991) proposes four hypothetical spatial patterns that could be used to describe the geography of crime sites: (1) a uniform pattern with no distance-decay influence; (2) a bull's-eye pattern with spatial clustering, exhibiting distance-decay, centered around the offender's primary anchor point; (3) a bimodal pattern with crime clusters centered around two anchor points; and (4) a teardrop pattern with a directional bias oriented toward a secondary anchor point.

Situations can also be distorted by a variety of other real world factors—movement often follows street grids, traffic flows can distort mobility patterns, variations exist in zoning and land use, and crime locations may cluster depending upon the nature of the target backdrop (i.e., the spatial distribution of targets or victims). The spatial mean is therefore limited in its ability to pinpoint criminal residence.

However, combining centrographic principles and journey to crime research in a manner informed by environmental criminological theory can produce a viable method for predicting the location of offender residence from crime site coordinates. One such effort is criminal geographic targeting (CGT), a computerized geographic profiling technique used in police investigations of complex serial crimes (Rossmo, 1993). By examining the spatial data connected to a series of crime sites, the CGT model generates a three-dimensional surface, the "height" of which represents the relative probability that a given point is the residence or workplace of the offender.

Criminal geographic targeting is based on the Brantingham and Brantingham (1981) model for crime site selection and on the routine activities approach (Felson, 1986). It uses a distance-decay function $f(d)$ that simulates journey to crime behavior. A probability value $f(d_i)$ is assigned to each point $(x, y)$, located at distance $d$ from crime site $i$. The final probability value for a point $(x, y)$, representing the likelihood that the offender lives at that location, is determined by adding together the $n$ values derived at that point from the $n$ different crime sites.

The use of CGT in actual police investigations—and tests of the model on solved cases of serial murder, rape and arson—have produced promising results, usually locating the offender's residence in the top 5% or less of the total hunting area. The model is based on a four-step process:

(1) Map boundaries delineating the offender's hunting area are first established using the locations of the crimes and standard procedures for addressing edge effects.

(2) Manhattan distances (i.e., orthogonal distances measured along the street grid) from every "point" on the map, the number of which is determined by the measurement resolution of the $x$ and $y$ scales, to each crime location are then calculated.

(3) Next, these Manhattan distances are used as independent variable values in a function that produces a number that: (a) if the point lies outside the buffer zone, becomes smaller the longer the distance, following some form of distance-decay; or (b) if the point lies inside the buffer zone, becomes larger the longer the distance. Numbers are computed from this function for each of the crime locations. For example, if there are 12 crime locations, each point on the map will have 12 numbers associated with it.

(4) Finally, these multiple numbers are multiplied together to produce a single score for each map point. The higher the resultant score, the greater the probability that the point contains the offender's residence.[1]

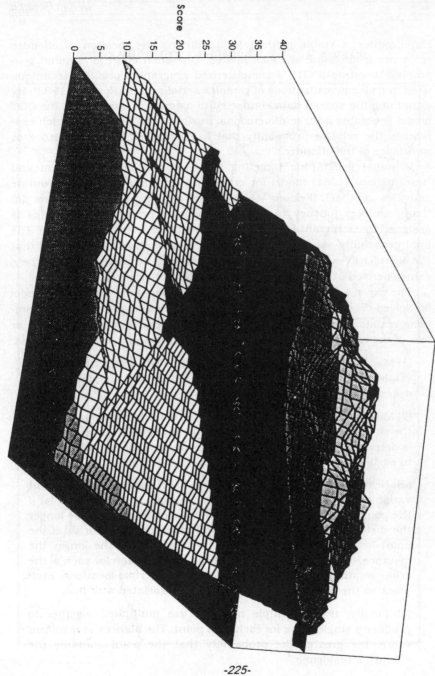

**Figure 2: CGT Choropleth Probability Map**

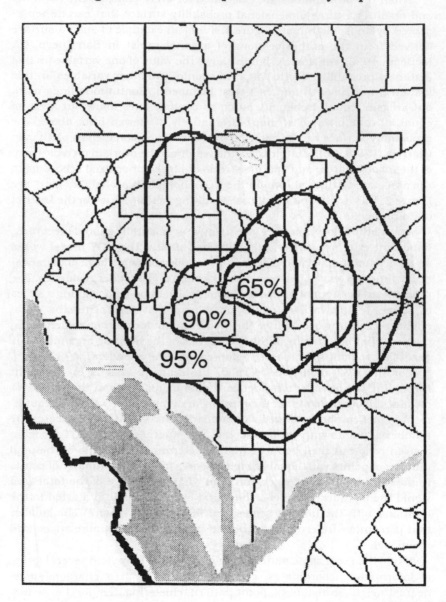

When the probabilities are calculated for every point on the map, the end result is a three-dimensional probability surface that can be represented by an isopleth map. Figure 1 shows an example of such a surface derived from the crime locations of a serial rapist in San Diego, CA (LeBeau, 1992). An isopleth graph shows the value of one variable (in this instance, probability scores) as a function of two other variables (in this instance, north-south and east-west distances). Continuous lines mark out areas of equal probability much as contour lines mark out areas of equal altitude on a relief map. Alternatively, if viewed from above, the probability surface can be depicted by a two-dimensional choropleth map (Harries, 1990). In the latter case, the result can be overlaid on a city map of the involved area, and specific streets or blocks prioritized according to the associated values shown on the CGT choropleth probability map (see Figure 2; this is a hypothetical case involving a crime series in the District of Columbia).

Any methodology, whether investigative or scientific, should meet three important criteria: validity, reliability and utility. The CGT model works on the assumption that a relationship, modeled on some form of distance-decay function, exists between crime location and offender residence. The process can be thought of as a mathematical method for assigning a series of scores to the various points on a map that represents the serial offender's hunting area. Since the model cannot locate the residence of a criminal that lies outside of the boundaries of the hunting area map, it is necessary to limit the process to non-commuting offenders.

For the CGT model to be valid, the score it assigns to the point containing the offender's residence should be higher than the scores for most of the other points on the hunting area map. How well this requirement is met can be examined with a distribution curve that indicates the number of points with various scores. The "success" of the CGT model in a given case can then be measured by determining the ratio of the total number of points with equal or higher scores to the total number of points in the hunting area. In other words, in what percentage of the total area would the offender's residence be found by a process that started in the locations with the highest scores and then worked down? The smaller that percentage (referred to as the "hit percentage"), the more successful the model.

While the geographic pattern for a crime series may yield several forms of information (coordinates, crime location type, area characteristics, nearest neighbor distances, point pattern, clustering, temporal ordering, etc.), the randomness inherent in most human behavior limits the conclusions that can be derived from a small number of crime sites. The use of more locations reduces the impact of chance. The performance of the

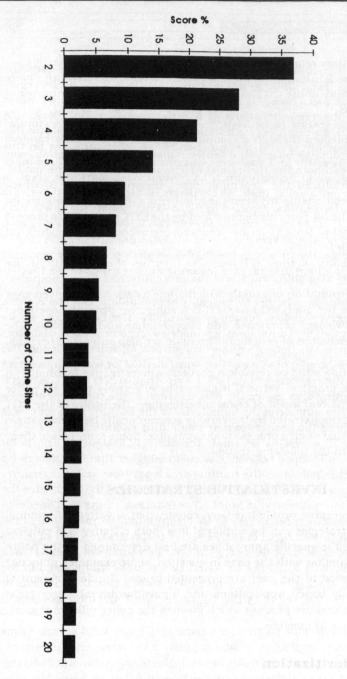

Figure 3: CGT Model Learning Curve

CGT model is thus related to the number of points available for analysis—the more crime locations, the more information and, therefore, the more precision. Validity of the CGT model is hence a function of the number of crime locations.

Monte Carlo testing (a heuristic method that uses repeated simulations), accomplished through a computer program that creates random crime site coordinates based on a buffered distance decay function, was conducted to estimate the theoretical maximum efficiency of the model. The testing produced the "learning curve" shown in Figure 3, which displays the relationship between the number of crime sites available for analysis and the hit percentage produced by the CGT model. This process established that at least six crime locations are necessary to produce hit percentages under 10%.

The reliability of the CGT model is high, as the calculations are mathematically straightforward and the procedure has been computerized. The determination of exactly which crime locations in a given case are relevant to the analysis, however, is a subjective process dependent upon the knowledge, experience and interpretation of the profiler. The qualitative dimensions of geographic profiling are also subject to personal biases.

No matter how valid or reliable a particular investigative technique, it will have little practical value if it cannot be effectively used by police detectives in the real world of crime investigation. The utility of the CGT model is best demonstrated by the various geographically based investigative strategies that such a process makes possible. Some examples of these are described in the following section.

## INVESTIGATIVE STRATEGIES

Once a geographic profile has been constructed, a variety of criminal investigative strategies can be employed in a more effective and efficient manner. While the specific approaches are best determined by the police investigators familiar with the case in question, some examples of tactics used or suggested in the past are presented below. The development of further spatially based applications and innovative investigative techniques is an interactive process which involves the police officers responsible for the case in question.

### Suspect Prioritization

If a lengthy list of suspects has been developed, the geographic profile in conjunction with the criminal offender profile can help prioritize individuals for follow-up investigative work. The problem in many serial violent crime investigations is one of too many suspects rather than too few. Profiling can help prioritize lists of sometimes hundreds if not thousands of suspects, leads and tips.

## Patrol Saturation

Areas that have been determined to most probably be associated with the offender can be used as a basis for directed or saturation police patrolling efforts. This strategy is particularly effective if the offender appears to be operating during certain time periods. Prioritized areas can also be employed for neighborhood canvassing efforts, area searches, information sign posting, and community cooperation and media campaigns. Police departments have used this approach to target areas for leaflet distribution, employing prioritized letter carrier walks for strategic household mail delivery. For example, LeBeau (1992) mentions the case of a serial rapist in San Diego who was arrested through canvassing efforts in an area determined from the locations of his crimes.

## Police Information Systems

Additional investigative leads may be obtained from the information contained in various computerized police dispatch and record systems (e.g., computer-aided dispatch systems, records management systems, the Royal Canadian Mounted Police Information Retrieval System, and the like). Offender profile details and case specifics can help focus the search at this point.

For example, the police may be investigating a series of sexual assaults that have been psychologically profiled as the crimes of an anger retaliatory rapist. Such an offender is "getting even with women for real or imagined wrongs.... the attack is an emotional outburst that is predicated on anger" (Hazelwood, 1987:178-179). His rapes are often initiated by conflicts with a significant woman in his life, and he will frequently select victims who symbolize the source of that conflict. One possible investigative strategy, then, is a search of police dispatch data for domestic disturbance calls near the dates of the rapes to see which ones originated from the area where the geographic profile suggests that the offender most likely resides.

Those police agencies that maintain computerized records detailing the descriptions, addresses and modus operandi of local offenders can also use profiling information, including probable area of residence, as the basis for developing search criteria. Many departments have such files for specific types of criminals, such as parolees or sex offenders.

## Outside Agency Databases

Data banks, which are often geographically based, as well as information from parole and probation offices, mental health outpatient clinics, social services offices and similar agencies located in the most probable areas can also prove to be of value. For example, LeBeau (1992) discusses the case of a serial rapist who emerged as a suspect after the police checked parolee records for sex offenders.

## Zip/Postal Code Prioritization

The geographic profile can also prioritize zip or postal codes in a city. If suspect offender description or vehicle information exists, prioritized zip or postal codes (representing the most probable 1 or 2% of a city's area) can be used to conduct effective off-line computer searches of registered vehicle or driver's licence files contained in provincial or state motor vehicle department records. These parameters act as a form of linear program to produce a surprisingly small set of records containing fields with all the appropriate data responses. Such a strategy can therefore produce significant results by focusing on limited areas that are of a manageable size for most serious criminal police investigations.

The following is one example of the use of this approach. The postal codes for a city neighborhood within which a violent sexual offender was attacking children were prioritized by using the criminal geographic targeting model. Planning and zoning maps were used to eliminate industrial, commercial and other non-residential areas. Socioeconomic and demographic census data were also consulted to reevaluate the priority of those neighborhoods that were inconsistent with the socioeconomic level of the offender, as suggested by a previously prepared psychological profile.

The remaining postal codes, ranked by priority of probability, were then used to conduct an off-line computer search of the provincial motor vehicle department records that contain postal codes within the addresses connected to the vehicle registered owner and driver's licence files. Suspect vehicle information and an offender description had been developed by the detectives working on the case, and this was combined with the geographic data to effectively focus the off-line search. The conjunction of such parameters can narrow down hundreds of thousands of records to a few dozen vehicles or drivers—sufficient discrimination to allow a focused follow-up by police investigators.

## Task Force Computer Systems

Task force operations that have been formed to investigate a specific series of major crimes usually collect and collate their information in some form of computerized system. Often these operations suffer from information overload and can benefit from the prioritization of data and the application of correlation analysis. Geographic profiling can assist in these tasks through the prioritization of street addresses, postal or zip codes, and telephone number areas. The details of the specific computer database software used by the task force, including information fields, search time, number of records, and correlational abilities, determine the most appropriate form that the geographic profile should take to maximize its usefulness to the police investigation.

## CONCLUSION

Geographic profiling infers spatial characteristics of the offender from target patterns. This method uses qualitative and quantitative approaches that attempt to make sense of the pattern from both subjective and objective perspectives. Criminal geographic targeting is a specific statistical method that enhances the efforts of geographic profiling by delineating the most probable areas to which the offender might be associated.

Since geographic profiling is based on an analysis of crime- site locations, a linkage analysis is a necessary prerequisite to determine which crimes are part of the same series and should be included in the development of the profile. It must also be noted that not all types of offenders or categories of crime can be geographically profiled. In appropriate cases, however, such a spatial analysis can produce very practical results from the police perspective. There are a variety of ways which geographic information about the offender can assist the investigation, including the prioritization of suspects by address or area, the direction of patrol saturation efforts and the establishment of computerized database search parameters.

Geographic profiling therefore appears to have significant investigative value in certain types of criminal cases. It is also an example of the application of criminological theory to a criminal justice problem. Through a process of "inverting" criminological and geographic research that has focused on relating crime places to offender residences, the locations of a series of crimes can be used to suggest where an offender might reside.

Environmental criminology, because of its rich context and diverse roots, has been particular fruitful in the development of practical applications and holds the promise of many future ideas for crime prevention and policing.

---

1. The function is of the form:

$$P_{ij} = \prod_{c=1}^{T} k \left[ \phi / (|x_i - x_c| + |y_j - y_c|)^f + (1 - \phi)(B^{g \cdot f}) / (2B - |x_i - x_c| - |y_j - y_c|)^g \right]$$

where:

$$|x_i - x_c| + |y_j - y_c| > B \supset \phi = 1$$
$$|x_i - x_c| + |y_j - y_c| \le B \supset \phi = 0$$

and:

| | |
|---|---|
| $P_{ij}$ | is the resultant probability for point $ij$; |
| $k$ | is an empirically determined constant; |
| $B$ | is the radius of the buffer zone; |
| $T$ | is the total number of crime sites; |
| $f$ | is an empirically determined exponent; |
| $g$ | is an empirically determined exponent; |
| $x_i, y_j$ | are the coordinates of point $ij$; and |
| $x_c, y_c$ | are the coordinates of the $c$th crime site location. |

# REFERENCES

Brantingham, P.J. and P.L. Brantingham (eds.) (1981). *Environmental Criminology.* Beverly Hills, CA: Sage.

—— (1984). *Patterns in Crime.* New York: Macmillan.

Clarke, R.V. (ed.) (1992). *Situational Crime Prevention: Successful Case Studies.* Albany, NY: Harrow and Heston.

—— and M. Felson (eds.) (1993). *Routine Activity and Rational Choice.* New Brunswick, NJ: Transaction Books.

Cornish, D.B. and R.V. Clarke (eds.) (1986). *The Reasoning Criminal: Rational Choice Perspectives on Offending*. New York, NY: Springer-Verlag.

Doney, R.H. (1990). "The Aftermath of the Yorkshire Ripper: The Response of the United Kingdom Police Service." In: S.A. Egger (ed.), *Serial Murder: An Elusive Phenomenon*. New York, NY: Praeger.

Eden, R.S. (1985). *Dog Training for Law Enforcement*. Calgary, CAN: Detselig.

Felson, M. (1986). "Linking Criminal Choices, Routine Activities, Informal Control, and Criminal Outcomes." In: D. B. Cornish and R. V. Clarke (eds.), *The Reasoning Criminal: Rational Choice Perspectives on Offending*. New York, NY: Springer-Verlag.

—— (1987). "Routine Activities and Crime Prevention in the Developing Metropolis." *Criminology* 25:911-931.

Gates, D.F. and D.K. Shah (1992). *Chief*. New York, NY: Bantam Books.

Harries, K. (1990). *Geographic Factors in Policing*. Washington, DC: Police Executive Research Forum.

Hazelwood, R.R. (1987). "Analyzing the Rape and Profiling the Offender." In: R. R. Hazelwood & A. W. Burgess (eds.), *Practical Aspects of Rape Investigation: A Multidisciplinary Approach*. New York, NY: Elsevier.

Holt, C. (1993). Personal communication to the author from a former member of the Los Angeles, CA Police Department.

Jeffery, C.R. (1977). *Crime Prevention Through Environmental Design*. 2d ed. Beverly Hills, CA: Sage.

Kind, S.S. (1987a). "Navigational Ideas and the Yorkshire Ripper Investigation." *Journal of Navigation* 40:385-393.

Klockars, C.B. (ed.) (1983). *Thinking About Police: Contemporary Readings*. New York, NY: McGraw-Hill.

LeBeau, J.L. (1992). "Four Case Studies Illustrating the Spatial-Temporal Analysis of Serial Rapists." *Police Studies* 15:124-145.

Montgomery, J.E. (1992). "Organizational Survival: Continuity or Crisis?" Paper presented at the Police Studies Series, Simon Fraser University, Vancouver, BC, February.

Newton, Jr., M.B. and D.C. Newton (1985). "Geoforensic Identification of Localized Serial Crime: Unsolved Female Homicides, Fort Worth, Texas, 1983-85." Paper presented at the meeting of the Southwest Division, Association of American Geographers, Denton, TX.

—— and E.A. Swoope (1987). "Geoforensic Analysis of Localized Serial Murder: The Hillside Stranglers Located." Unpublished manuscript.

Rengert, G.F. (1990). "Drug Purchasing as a Routine Activity of Drug Dependent Property Criminals and the Spatial Concentration of Crime." Paper presented at the annual meeting of the American Society of Criminology, Baltimore, MD.

—— (1991). "The Spatial Clustering of Residential Burglaries About Anchor Points of Routine Activities." Paper presented at the meeting of the American Society of Criminology, San Francisco, CA.

Rhodes, W.M. and C. Conly (1981). "Crime and Mobility: An Empirical Study." In: P.J. Brantingham and P.L. Brantingham (eds.), *Environmental Criminology*. Beverly Hills, CA: Sage.

Rossmo, D.K. (1987). "Fugitive Migration Patterns." Master's thesis, Simon Fraser University, Burnaby, BC, Canada.

—— (1993). "Target Patterns of Serial Murderers: A Methodological Model." *American Journal of Criminal Justice* 17:1-21.

—— (1995). "Targeting Victims: Serial Killers and the Urban Environment." In: T. O'Reilly-Fleming (ed.), *Serial and Mass Murder: Theory, Research and Policy*. Toronto, CAN: Canadian Scholars' Press.

Vold, G.B. and T.J. Bernard (1986). *Theoretical Criminology*. New York, NY: Oxford University Press.

Wood, D. (1981). "In Defense of Indefensible Space." In: P. J. Brantingham and P. L. Brantingham (eds.), *Environmental Criminology*. Beverly Hills, CA: Sage.

# [38]

# Psychic Crime Detectives:
## A New Test for Measuring Their Successes and Failures

*A controlled test of 'psychic detectives,' using a novel method, found that they were no more accurate than college students. Yet the psychics all thought they had been successful.*

RICHARD WISEMAN, DONALD WEST,
AND ROY STEMMAN

Many psychics claim to be able to help the police solve serious crime. Recent surveys suggest that approximately 35 percent of urban United States police departments and 19 percent of rural departments (Sweat and Durm 1993) admit to having used a psychic at least once in their investigations. In addition, Lyons and Truzzi (1991) report the widespread use of psychic detectives in several other countries including Britain, Holland, Germany, and France.

Most of these psychics' claims are supported only by anecdotal evidence. This is unfortunate because it is often extremely difficult to rule out nonpsychic explanations. For example, Hoebens (1985) described how some psychics have made several (often conflicting) predictions relating to an unsolved crime. Once the crime was solved, the incorrect predictions were forgotten while the correct ones were exhibited as evidence of paranormal ability. Rowe (1993) cites examples of psychics making vague and ambiguous predictions that later were interpreted to fit the facts of the crime. Lyons and Truzzi (1991) noted that it is often difficult to obtain "baseline" information for many of these predictions. For example, a psychic may state that a murder weapon will be discovered "near, or in, a large body of water." Although this may later prove to be accurate, it is difficult to know how many criminals dump incriminating objects in areas that could be seen as "large bodies of water" (e.g., streams, lakes, rivers, the ocean, etc.) and therefore establish a statistical baseline for the prediction.

Some investigators have overcome these problems by carrying out controlled tests of psychic detection abilities. One of the earliest controlled studies was conducted by a Dutch police officer, Filippus Brink. Brink carried out a one-year study using four psychics. These psychics were shown various photographs and objects and asked to describe the crimes that had taken place. Some of the photographs and objects were connected with actual crimes; others were not. In a report to INTERPOL, Brink (1960) noted that the psychics had failed to provide any information that would have been of any use to an investigating officer. However, this report is brief and, as noted by Lyons and Truzzi (1991, p. 51): "Because Brink gives us few details of his method and analysis in this report, the strength, if not the value, of his conclusions cannot really be evaluated."

Studies have been carried out by Martin Reiser of the Los Angeles Police Department. An initial study by Reiser, Ludwig, Saxe, and Wagner (1979) involved twelve psychics. Each psychic was presented with several sealed envelopes containing physical evidence from four crimes (two solved, two unsolved). The psychics were asked to describe the crimes that had taken place. They were then allowed to open the envelopes and describe any additional impressions they received from the object. The study was double-blind, as neither the psychics nor the experimenters had any prior knowledge of the details of the crimes.

The psychics' statements were then coded into several categories (e.g., crime committed, victim, suspect, etc.) and compared with the information known about the crime. For each of the psychics' predictions that matched the actual information, they were awarded one point. The psychics' performances were less than impressive. For example, the experimenters knew that 21 key facts were true of the first crime. The psychics identified an average of only 4. Similarly, of the 33 known facts concerning the second crime, the psychics correctly identified an average of only 1.8. This data caused Reiser et al. to con-

| | Individual scores (min=0, max=6) | Group scores (min=0, max=6) | Z-score | P-value (2 tailed) |
|---|---|---|---|---|
| Psychic 1 | 2.3 (1.15) | | .24 | .8 |
| Psychic 2 | 2.66 (0.57) | 2.09 (0.68) | .73 | .46 |
| Psychic 3 | 1.33 (0.57) | | -.73 | .46 |
| Student 1 | 2 (0.5) | | 0 | 1 |
| Student 2 | 2 (0.5) | 2.33 (0.57) | 0 | 1 |
| Student 3 | 3 (1.73) | | 1.21 | .22 |

**Table 1:** Individual/group means, standard deviations (in brackets), z-scores, and p-values.

clude: "The research data does not support the contention that psychics can provide significant additional information leading to the solution of major crime" (pp. 21-22).

Reiser and Klyver (1982) also carried out a follow-up study that used three groups of participants: psychic detectives, students, and police homicide detectives. Four crimes were used (two solved and two unsolved) and again physical evidence from each crime was presented to participants in sealed envelopes. Reiser and Klyver report that the data produced by the three groups was quite different in quantity and character. The psychic detectives produced descriptions that were, on average, six times the length of the student descriptions. In addition, the psychic detectives' statements sounded more confident and dramatic than those produced by either the students or the homicide detectives. Parts of the descriptions were separated into several categories (e.g., sex of criminal, age, height, etc.) and, if correct, assigned one point. A comparison between the three groups showed that although the psychics produced the greatest number of predictions, they were not any more accurate than either the students or the homicide detectives.

In August 1994 the authors of this article were contacted by a British television company involved in making a major documentary series on the paranormal (Arthur C. Clarke's "Mysterious Universe"). One of their programs was to be devoted to psychic detectives, and the producers were eager to film a well-controlled test of three British psychics. The company approached the authors and asked if we would design and carry out these tests. We agreed.

This was the first test of its type in Britain and one of only a handful carried out anywhere in the world. In addition, the methods used during previous studies have been the subject of some criticism (see Lyons and Truzzi 1991) so the authors thought it worthwhile to devise a new method for testing the claims of psychic detection.

This test compared the performance of two groups of participants: psychic detectives and a "control" group of college students. Two of the psychics were professional while the third (who will be referred to as "Psychic 1") was not, but had recently received a great deal of attention from the British media. The psychic's local police force (Hertfordshire Police Force) described him as follows:

*Richard Wiseman (to whom correspondence should be addressed) is the Perrott-Warrick Senior Research Fellow at the University of Hertfordshire, College Lane, Hatfield, Herts., AL10 9AB, U.K. Donald West is at Cambridge University. Roy Stemman is editor of Reincarnation Magazine.*

| | Accuracy rating (min=0, max=7) | Number of statements | Group scores (min=0, max=7) |
|---|---|---|---|
| Psychic 1 | 3.87 (2.57) | 15 | |
| Psychic 2 | 3.65 (1.83) | 16 | 3.83 (0.17) |
| Psychic 3 | 4.00 (1.96) | 8 | |
| Student 1 | 6.37 (0.64) | 8 | |
| Student 2 | 4.14 (2.62) | 7 | 5.63 (1.28) |
| Student 3 | 5.10 (2.13) | 5 | |

**Table 2:** Individual/group accuracy means, standard deviations (in brackets), and number of statements.

When [psychic's name] comes to the police with his dreams, he is taken seriously and the information that he passes on to his established contact, Sgt. Richard MacGregor, is acted upon immediately (*Psychic News,* November 26, 1994, p. 1)[1]

None of the students claimed to be psychic or had any special interest in criminology.

Each participant was shown three items that had been involved in one of three crimes: a bullet, a scarf, and a shoe. They were asked to handle each of the objects and speak aloud any ideas, images, or thoughts that might be related to these crimes. Participants were told that they were free to take as long as they wished and to say as little or as much as they thought necessary. During the test they were left alone in the room, but everything they said and did was filmed.

After they had finished commenting on all three objects, the participants were given three response sheets (one for each object), each containing 18 statements. Six of each of the 18 statements were true of each crime. The participants were then asked to mark the 6 statements that they believed were true about the crime in question.

Table 1 presents the individual scores for each of the six participants. None of the scores of any of the individuals was statistically significant or impressive.

It could be argued that the above method of testing might *underestimate* participants' psychic ability. For example, a participant may have made several accurate comments describing the crime in question but, nevertheless, obtained a low score if this information was not included on the list of 18 statements. For this reason, a judge not involved in the test transcribed and separated all of the comments made by the participants as the participants handled the objects. The order of these statements was then randomized within each crime and presented to two additional judges. These judges were asked to read about each crime and rate the accuracy of each statement from 1 (very inaccurate) to 7 (very accurate). Table 2 contains the average of the two judges' ratings (inter-rater reliability = .77).

Overall, the psychics made a total of 39 statements while the students made 20 statements. A paired t-test showed no significant differences for the accuracy ratings of students and psychics ($t = 2.38$, $df = 4$, $p[2$ tailed$] = .074$). This supports Reiser

and Klyver's finding that even though psychics tend to make more predictions than students, they are no more accurate.

After their predictions had been recorded, the participants were told about the crimes associated with each of the target objects. This debriefing was filmed, and it is interesting to review the way in which the participants reacted to finding out the truth about each crime:

**Crime 1. The Moat Farm murder, 1889-1903.** In 1889 an army sergeant major named Samuel Herbert Dougal wished to have an affair with his maid but first needed to dispose of his wife. On May 16, 1889, he and his wife went out for a horse-and-trap ride into the town. During the trip Dougal shot his wife in the head and buried her in a ditch. The body remained buried for four years before the police eventually discovered it. The shoes worn by the corpse were identified by a cobbler as belonging to the dead woman, and Dougal was hung for the murder in 1903.

**Crime 2. The murder of Constable Gutteride, 1927.** In 1927 a police officer (Constable George William Gutteridge from the Essex Police Force) stopped a stolen car. The driver suddenly pulled out a gun and fired two shots—one into each of Constable Gutteridge's eyes. The car was later found abandoned in Brixton, London. A six-month-long investigation resulted in two men having been caught and hanged. An important part of the incriminating evidence was the bullet removed from the scene of the crime.

**Crime 3. The killing of Margery Pattison, 1962.** Margery Pattison, a 71-year-old widow, returned to her flat and disturbed her milkman who had entered through an unlocked door and had started to look for money. An argument ensued and the man grabbed the scarf around her neck, pulled it tight, and strangled her. The man was later caught and charged with murder.

All three psychics thought that they had been successful. On hearing that Crime 2 involved the killing of a police officer, Psychic 1 noted that one of his precognitive dreams involved Police Constable Keith Blakelock (who had been killed on duty in London a few years earlier). This participant noted that he thought at the time the dream was related to Blakelock's murder, but that he now believed it related to the killing of Constable Gutteridge. The same participant remarked that he felt he had given a successful description of Crime 1, as he had said it involved a woman having been raped and murdered and that "that is the fundamental theme of the crime." Psychic 1 failed to recall that he had also said the woman was murdered by a black man and that it happened on Tottenham Court Road. Both of these statements were incorrect. This lends support to the notion that some psychic detection may appear to work, in part, because inaccurate predictions may be forgotten about later, whereas successful ones are recalled and elaborated on.

Psychic 2 remarked that he believed that the experiment showed a "good conclusion all round" and that "my colleagues and I have put the jigsaw puzzle together." He emphasized

*Psychics continued on page 58*

*Psychics from page 40*

that all three psychics believed that the scarf was involved in a suffocation, had had trouble with Crime 2, but had predicted that the shoe-related crime involved some form of burial.

Psychic 3 also thought that there had been a consensus on the scarf and shoe. Remarking on the lack of information forthcoming on Crime 2, the psychic noted that "sometimes access to information is not appropriate at certain times." Despite this, he said that he was "relatively pleased with the outcome."

In short, this study provided no evidence to support the claims of psychic detection and, as such, the results are in accordance with other controlled studies. The study utilized a novel method of evaluating psychic detection. The way in which the participants responded to being told the true nature of the crimes gives some insight into some of the

mechanisms that might cause individuals to believe erroneously that they are able to solve crimes by psychic means.

**Notes**

This research was carried out with support from the Committee for the Scientific Investigation of Claims of the Paranormal.

The authors would like to thank Granite Television, London, Melvin Harris, and Sergeant Fred Feather for helping to set up our study described in this paper. Thanks also to Matthew Smith for helping to run the experiment, and Carol Hurst for carrying out the qualitative analysis of the data. Finally, our thanks to the psychics and students who kindly gave up their time to act as subjects. Correspondence regarding this article should be addressed to Richard Wiseman.

1. Richard Wiseman contacted Sgt. Richard MacGregor of the Hertfordshire Police Force concerning this matter and received confirmation that the above statement was correct (personal communication, December 19, 1994).

**References**

Brink, F. 1960. Parapsychology and criminal investigations. *International Criminal Police Review*, 134, 3-9.

Hoebens, P. H. 1985. Reflections on psychic sleuths. Edited by Marcello Truzzi in *A Skeptic's Handbook of Parapsychology*, ed. by P. Kurtz, part 6, pp. 631-643. Amherst, N.Y.: Prometheus Books.

Lyons, A. and M. Truzzi. 1991. *The Blue Sense*. New York: Warner Books.

Herts police admit to using psychic help. 1994. *Psychic News*, Nov. 26, 3259:1.

Reiser, M., L. Ludwig, S. Saxe, and C. Wagner. 1979. An evaluation of the use of psychics in the investigation of major crimes. *Journal of Police Science and Administration*, 7(1): 1825. (Reprinted in Nickel, J. [Ed.], *Psychic Sleuths*, Prometheus Books, Amherst, N.Y., 1994).

Reiser, M., and N. Klyver. 1982. A comparison of psychics, detectives, and students in the investigation of major crimes. In *Police Psychology: Collected Papers* by M. Reiser, Los Angeles, Calif.: Lehi.

Rowe, W. F. 1993. Psychic detectives: A critical examination. SKEPTICAL INQUIRER, 17(2): 159-165.

Sweat, J. A., and M. W. Durm. 1993. Psychics: Do police departments really use them? SKEPTICAL INQUIRER, 17(2): 148-158.  □

# [39]

## RAYMOND CHANDLER

'You two characters been seeing any psychiatrists lately?'

'Hell,' Ohls said, 'hadn't you heard? We got them in our hair all the time these days. We've got two of them on the staff. This ain't police business any more. It's getting to be a branch of the medical racket. They're in and out of jail, the courts, the interrogation rooms. They write reports fifteen pages long on why some punk of a juvenile held up a

275

liquor store or raped a schoolgirl or peddled tea to the senior class. Ten years from now guys like Marty and me will be doing Rohrschach tests and word associations instead of chin-ups and target practice. When we go out on a case we'll carry little black bags with portable lie detectors and bottles of truth serum. Too bad we didn't grab the four hard monkeys that poured it on Big Willie Magoon. We might have been able to unmaladjust them and make them love their mothers.'

# Name Index